How Many Roads?
Recent America in Perspective

How Many Roads?

Recent America in Perspective

Edited by
Robert D. Marcus
State University of New York at Stony Brook

Holt, Rinehart and Winston, Inc.
New York   Chicago   San Francisco   Atlanta   Dallas   Montreal   Toronto   London   Sydney

Cover illustration by Floyd Sowell.

With Love to Betsy and Tony

Preface

In more leisurely times, Americans measured their history in generations. The era of the American Revolution stretched into the 1790s; the Age of Jackson lasted far longer than the Old Hero's presidency; the Gilded Age encompassed the last quarter of the nineteenth century. Then after World War I, events seemed to accelerate, and we began measuring our history in decades. Now the pace of change has quickened again. A generation is five years at the most, and even the early sixties seemed remote by 1968. Our sense of the present shortens, the past on which we have any perspective recedes sharply, and a gray area opens that we can comprehend neither immediately with our senses nor historically with our memory and mind.

As our ability to trace the flow of experience has diminished, our need for understanding has increased. The large achievements of the most recent decade—the sixties—allow no complacency, for they are instantly overshadowed by its towering problems. The political system responded with more spirit and generosity to the nation's concerns than it had in a generation, yet confidence in government eroded and violence not only stalked the streets, but also fractured the nation's institutions and murdered its heroes. Progress toward an end to the Cold War brought bloody and pointless slaughter instead of peace. Wealth and success at home brought a society increasingly fragmented into antagonistic groups. A rich and mature American culture that dominated the imagination of much of the world nevertheless left a nation confused at the end of the decade. It was an age of excess: too many shattering events, too many bewildering changes, too many new ideas.

This era, neither formed into history nor still before us, is the subject of these essays, in which men and women of the era tried to understand and influence their age through retrospect, reportage, prophecy, and polemic. Ideally, the material presented in this book will not only inform students but also stimulate their imaginations, but I hardly dare suggest that some single lesson will emerge. For the fruits of the 1960s are still ripening; they—and the answers to all the questions that historians can ask about the decade—are still blowing in the wind.

R.D.M.
Stony Brook, New York
November 1971

Contents

Part III: American Culture

PART I
American Politics

Introduction

The story of American politics in the 1960s is that of the rise and fall of liberalism. It begins in the late fifties, with the erosion of the brief moderate consensus constructed by Dwight Eisenhower. By 1958 that political universe was fast fading. The Right had largely kicked over the traces of Republican regularity, while the congressional campaign of that year had resulted in the election of many of the new men who would change the complexion of government in the sixties—men like Eugene McCarthy and Edmund Muskie. The election of John F. Kennedy in 1960, coinciding with a sharp rise in black activism, seemed to infuse new aspirations into American politics. The Cuban missile crisis of 1962 brought the long enduring tensions of the Cold War to unexpected resolution, and the assassination of President Kennedy, followed by the overwhelming rout of Barry Goldwater in the presidential contest of 1964, suddenly freed American politics from the major restraints under which it had labored since the late 1930s. The result, under President Lyndon Johnson, was a flowering of liberal legislation that—whatever its limits—will take a generation to digest.

Yet the limits of the liberal fruition in the mid-sixties were apparent virtually as they were taking place. Rising expectations spilled over into massive violence, while a series of blunders, some reaching back to the forties, led the nation into the longest and most demoralizing war of its history. Between conflict at home and stalemate abroad, the gains of liberal legislation were rapidly eroded, the extraordinary economic boom that endured from 1963 through 1968 finally collapsed, and the nation during 1968 —that great and terrible year of the decade—verged on chaos. The remainder of the decade represented a moving back from the brink, with caretaker administrations in virtually every major American institution—including the federal government. The nation drifted, full of ill feeling, but content to drift after a decade of hectic excitement, large achievement, and huge problems.

RICHARD H. ROVERE
Eisenhower Over the Shoulder

Richard Rovere's assessment of the Eisenhower administration, written just as it was ending, remains one of the best-balanced views of that now distant era. Rovere recognized that Eisenhower's bland and genial superintendency of national life represented a reasonable accommodation with the events of history and the national mood in the mid-fifties. But the age of Eisenhower really ended sometime in the late fifties after the Montgomery bus boycott, the Suez crisis, and, especially, the launching of the Russian sputnik in 1957.

The late fifties, which in tone anticipated the next decade, made vigorous beginnings in cultural innovation, social criticism, and more venturesome politics. Writers like John Kenneth Galbraith and C. Wright Mills wrote penetrating critiques of American institutions; the Beats presented new cultural images; young and liberal politicians entered national life in the 1958 elections; and, most important of all, black Americans voiced an impatience that promised major changes in American life. Eisenhower was generally out of step with this new emerging America, although his farewell warning against a burgeoning "military-industrial complex" remains a prophetic note. Nevertheless, the brief period of placidity that his first administration brought, which soothed old tensions and ended the Korean War, cleared the way for the new concerns that would break through the surface of American politics in the late fifties and the succeeding decade.

"The Eisenhower years," William Shannon wrote, when the period had only a few weeks to run, "have been years of flabbiness and self-satisfaction and gross materialism. . . . [The] loudest sound in the land has been the oink-and-grunt of private hoggishness. . . . It has been the age of the slob." Yes, yes— and then again no. The country did put on a lot of weight that wasn't muscle. But as for "self-satisfaction," was there ever a reasonably stable society that wasn't more pleased with itself than it had a right to be? And isn't "materialism" always "gross"? Still, Shannon has hold of what I think I would call about a two-thirds truth. There is really no denying that the fifties in the United States were years in which private hoggishness reached some spectacular heights. But "the age of the slob"—no, I don't think that will do.

There is much to be said about the Eisenhower years, a good deal in dispraise, quite a bit in

Reprinted from *The American Scholar*, Volume 31, Number 2, Spring, 1962. Copyright © 1962 by the United Chapters of Phi Beta Kappa. By permission of the publishers and the author.

praise, but one must begin, I think, by acknowledging that the period itself had a history, that it took some of its character from what had gone before, that there were important differences between the early period and the late period, and that in any case American life is never all of a piece. As one who in 1956 published a book called *The Eisenhower Years,* I am in a rather poor position to point out that historians and journalists who try to write history have a way of misleading themselves and their readers by associating epochs and pivotal events with the names of ruling or presiding figures. There is, to be sure, a sense in which an American President stamps his character on a period and a sense in which his countrymen tend to become like him. At the same time, there are powerful currents that are scarcely touched by him and, always, currents that run powerfully against him. I happen to believe that during the Eisenhower years—and in part because they *were* the Eisenhower years—many currents of great promise were running. We were a self-satisfied people, as Shannon said, yet we were terribly uneasy in our complacency and elected as Eisenhower's successor a man whose entire campaign was an assault on complacency. During the Eisenhower years, we developed—great numbers of us—an enormous dissatisfaction with our educational systems and with American intellectual life in general. Of course, it was largely the prodding of the Russians that did it. But that hardly seems to me to matter; we made, I think, some vigorous responses. It was during the Eisenhower years, too, that we became more alert than ever before to civil rights and civil liberties. It was in Eisenhower's day and Joe McCarthy's that the United States Supreme Court did more than in any preceding time to protect and secure the rights of minorities and of individuals.

And it has to be said, neither in praise nor in dispraise, that the election of Dwight Eisenhower in 1952 did not mark an abrupt transition from an elevated concern for the public interest to a base absorption with the private interest. Eisenhower's predecessor was, on balance, a good and gallant President, but not everything about his administration, or about American life in his time, was admirable. The oink-and-grunt of private hoggishness was more than audible in the Truman years; indeed, as the end drew near, it was almost deafening. There was corruption in half a dozen government agencies, and some of it was laid at the door of persons very close to the President. Much of the corruption was picayune; there was little grandeur in the larcenies. Still, hoggishness in the middle-income brackets is not much lovelier than hoggishness among the very rich. In his last year in office Truman sought to tidy things up by investigation and reorganization, but his efforts were frustrated by his subordinates, particularly in the Department of Justice where things were in the sorriest mess, and nothing of moment was done.

Corruption played a part in the retirement of the Democrats in 1952. So did the Korean War, which was as unpopular as it was just. So did Senator McCarthy's blather about Communists in the State Department, which was as popular as it was unjust. The fact is that the American people in 1952 were a confused, bitter, divided lot. We were prosperous but far from content in our prosperity. We were performing large and necessary services to freedom but not fully persuaded of the need for what we were being called upon to do, and although we had put isolationism behind us, as a simply impossible way of looking at the world, we nevertheless re-

sented a world that asked so much of us. In the preceding decade we had fought and won two overseas wars that not too many of us, at the outset, had acknowledged to be our proper concern. We had been led by Franklin Roosevelt to believe that our sacrifices (small alongside those of our major allies, but less clearly related in the minds of citizens to national security) would rid the world of its principal troublemakers. No sooner had those troublemakers—the German and Japanese militarists and the political structures that supported them—been destroyed than we were asked to arm against a new global menace, said to be even worse than the enemies so recently vanquished. In Korea we were asked to fight a particularly nasty kind of war and were told that it would be in very bad taste to seek victory of the traditional sort; having only a few years earlier absorbed the doctrine of "total war" and "unconditional surrender," we were called upon to make a quick shift to limited war and highly conditional victory.

The disagreeable turn that events had taken in the early fifties invited demagogic explanation. And a really first-rate demagogue arose to explain them with that most effective of devices for interpreting history to the masses—the conspiracy theory. McCarthy said that things were as they were because the governors had encouraged betrayal. There was a time, in late 1953 and early 1954, when, according to the polls, half the people thought he was performing a useful service.

It seems to me now that Eisenhower's election in 1952 was a good thing for the country and that the first four Eisenhower years are not to be regretted. It was a time in which a new consensus was reached and a time in which tensions were considerably eased. It would have been agree-

President Eisenhower receives model of sputnik from Premier Khrushchev, 1959. *(Elliott Erwitt, Magnum)*

able, no doubt, to have had a more imaginative and more eloquent President—a Wilkie, a Republican Adlai Stevenson, a Charles Evans Hughes. But the Republicans are our only alternative to the Democrats, and in 1952 *their* only alternative to Eisenhower was Robert A. Taft, an honorable and intelligent man but hardly a reducer of tensions. As Walter Lippmann once pointed out, it *had* to be Eisenhower in 1952 in the same sense that it *had* to be George Washington in 1789. In his first term, he did many of the things that needed doing and that could not have been done by a Democratic administration.

He had, for one thing, to end the Korean War. By 1953, when he took office, the time had come to liquidate this enterprise. By their intervention in Korea in 1950, the United States and the United Nations had made the point that they would not flinch from resisting direct aggression by international communism and that they could find the resources for resistance. This was a great turning point in the Cold War; the Communist bloc recognized it, and there were no more Koreas, and "containment" remained a feasible American policy. But by the time of Eisenhower's election, when the North Koreans and the Chinese Communists were being effectively contained north of the thirty-eighth parallel, further bloodshed was insupportable. The Truman administration had entered into negotiations with the Communists and had reached the point where the basic terms of the settlement were clear. But the Truman administration, intent on giving its domestic critics no grounds for charging it with appeasement, could not possibly have concluded the negotiations. Nor could a Stevenson administration. McCarthy and his animals would have set upon it and quite possibly have destroyed it as the effective agency of American power. There were times, indeed, when it looked as if the Republicans in Congress, ably led by Senator Knowland of California, would not let the Republican administration negotiate a settlement. The President had to use all the prestige he had, and he did just that.

Eisenhower threw only a small amount of his prestige into the destruction of McCarthy, and for this he was constantly being faulted, as doubtless he deserved to be. It is very easy for anyone to say that McCarthy should have been stopped far sooner than he was. In my judgment, those who think this might have been done at little cost by the use of presidential powers greatly underrate McCarthy's talents and the force of those currents of opinion he exploited. What seems to me remarkable is that by late 1954, less than two years after Eisenhower took office, McCarthy was done for. Eisenhower's contribution may have been slight. McCarthy did a great deal to destroy himself. But it seems to me doubtful in the extreme that the desirable end would have been reached in 1954 if the Democrats had been enjoying their sixth consecutive term in office and if the casualty lists from Korea had still been appearing every day in the papers. McCarthy had to be destroyed by his own party, and his own party out of power would not have attempted to destroy him—first, because it would have wished to use him; second, because he would not have been compelled to turn against it.

There is more to be said for the first four Eisenhower years. As James Reston once said, the President brought to NATO a valuable new member—the Republican party. For all their rhetoric about Quemoy and Matsu and Formosa and Chiang Kai-shek, he and Secretary Dulles fashioned a China policy that probably saved us from some bloody and pointless engagements in the Far East. In foreign affairs, I can see little to regret in the Eisenhower administration's stewardship during its first term.

It has never been easy for an American President to work his way out of the White House in four years. Bad luck and weak management must be combined, as they were in Herbert Hoover's day, to persuade the voters to deny a President a second term. The voters who put Eisenhower in office in 1952 made almost certain his reelection in 1956, and

one can hardly say that they did the wise thing the first time and served themselves badly the second time. Nevertheless, the second four years go a long way toward justifying William Shannon's harsh impeachments. If there is anything much to be said for them, it has escaped my notice and understanding. By 1956, the tasks that had seemed to call for the bland Eisenhower treatment had all received it, and the rest, in Washington anyway, was drift and near-slumber. The Cold War had taken on many new aspects. It had become in part a technological struggle, the kind that Americans should have relished more than any other, and Washington's response was feeble and grudging. The President, who by then had no political future to worry about, had a magnificent opportunity to take the Negro American's part in the struggle for elementary decency; he refused even to say with any vigor that he himself favored the one ideal that, historically, has been associated with this Republic as with no other. He increasingly surrounded himself with mediocrities and increasingly proclaimed as his own highest ideal the simple-minded, indeed semi-literate political economy of George Humphrey. Although he had never in his life been known as a military thinker, as distinct from a military executive, he became more and more impatient of criticism and more and more confident of his unique qualifications for deciding what we needed and what we did not need for the defense of the national interest in the mid-twentieth century.

It can be argued that he was an older soldier by several years, that he had done his work, that he had lost the men who had been closest to him in the first term, that he should not be made responsible for everything in a

time that seemed somehow destined to be squalid. On the whole, this is so. He had the same faults and virtues after 1956 that he had had before—only the faults seemed to count for more, the virtues for less. He had always been a rather irritable Dr. Pangloss, but a time came when the irritability seemed merely self-indulgent. The last half of the fifties was not made for a President who was unhurried and untroubled, disapproving only of the disapprovers. In a way, the tragedy, if that is not too large a word for it, of that period was that we did not have a President who wanted to keep abreast of the more salutary developments within American society—the intellectual ferment, the technological ferment, the struggles for equality. His growing cantankerousness and stubbornness were responses to the demands that he be more troubled, more in a hurry, more alive.

Many of the things that make us think of it as a squalid period cannot be laid at his door. He bears some responsibility for Sherman Adams and Dixon-Yates, but little for Jimmy Hoffa or Orval Faubus. The loudest of the oink-and-grunt set—the newly rich of Texas and the Southwest—were protected by Lyndon Johnson, Sam Rayburn, and Robert S. Kerr. The tide of superciliousness had begun to run before Eisenhower and is running pretty strong today. (The only youth movements that attracted much attention—the conservatives who flocked to William F. Buckley, Jr.'s banner and the beatniks—were alike in their superciliousness and in their flagrant selfishness.) But it would have helped greatly, it would have gone a long way toward redeeming the bad time, if the President of the United States had had some convictions of his own and had said what they were.

NORMAN MAILER
Kennedy—The Existential Hero

In a very close election, the vote of any constituency may be said to have determined the outcome. Norman Mailer frequently—and who knows how seriously—claimed to have elected Kennedy by delivering the hipster vote with articles like the one printed below. Mailer saw in John F. Kennedy a new kind of hero: the cool warrior, the detached fighter, the political calculator whose heart and mind were far from the madding crowd, the man to give style to the nation's raw emotions and passion to the technological and bureaucratic organizations that dominate our visions, a man who could command the processes of modern life without ever losing his disdain for every one of them.

Kennedy—with his dash, his wealth, his hard Boston speech, his beautiful wife, and his good looks—was to be America's leading man, who would fix the nation's dream life on its public institutions instead of on vacuous celebrities created by the mass media. He would bring together "the life of politics and the life of myth," for good or ill, supplying fresh energy to the public sector. Few now can doubt that Kennedy did in fact meet some of these hopes. However historians estimate the concrete achievements of his brief administration, they should not omit the intangible factors that Mailer's extravagant prose has captured.

The afternoon he arrived at the convention from the airport, there was of course a large crowd on the street outside the Biltmore, and the best way to get a view was to get up on an outdoor balcony of the Biltmore, two flights above the street, and look down on the event. One waited thirty minutes, and then a honking of horns as wild as the getaway after an Italian wedding sounded around the corner, and the Kennedy cortege came into sight, circled Pershing Square, the men in the open and leading convertibles sitting backwards to look at their leader, and finally came to a halt in a space cleared for them by the police in the crowd. The television cameras were out, and a Kennedy band was playing some circus music. One saw him immediately. He had the deep orange-brown suntan of a ski instructor, and when he smiled at the crowd his teeth were amazingly white and clearly visible at a distance of fifty yards. For one moment he saluted Pershing Square, and Pershing Square saluted him back, the prince and the beggars of glamour staring at one another across a city street, one of those very special moments in the underground history of the world, and then with a quick move he was out of the car and by choice headed into the crowd instead of the lane cleared for him into the hotel by the police, so that he

The President listens, and the Vice-President looks on, at a Cabinet meeting. *(Cornell Capa, Magnum)*

made his way inside surrounded by a mob, and one expected at any moment to see him lifted to its shoulders like a matador being carried back to the city after a triumph in the plaza. All the while the band kept playing the campaign tunes, sashaying circus music, and one had a moment of clarity, intense as a *déjà vu*, for the scene which had taken place had been glimpsed before in a dozen musical comedies; it was the scene where the hero, the matinee idol, the movie star, comes to the palace to claim the princess, or what is the same, and more to our soil, the football hero, the campus king, arrives at the dean's home surrounded by a court of open-singing students to plead with the dean for his daughter's kiss and permission to put on the big musical that night. And suddenly I saw the convention, it came into focus for me, and I understood the mood of depression which had lain over the convention, because finally it was simple: the Democrats were going to nominate a man who, no matter how serious his political

dedication might be, was indisputably and willy-nilly going to be seen as a great box-office actor, and the consequences of that were staggering and not at all easy to calculate.

Since the First World War Americans have been leading a double life, and our history has moved on two rivers, one visible, the other underground; there has been the history of politics which is concrete, factual, practical and unbelievably dull if not for the consequences of the actions of some of these men; and there is a subterranean river of untapped, ferocious, lonely and romantic desires, that concentration of ecstasy and violence which is the dream life of the nation.

The twentieth century may yet be seen as that era when civilized man and underprivileged man were melted together into mass man, the iron and steel of the nineteenth century giving way to electronic circuits which communicated their messages into men, the unmistakable tendency of the new century seeming to be the creation of men as interchangeable as commodities, their extremes of personality singed out of existence by the psychic fields of force the communicators would impose. This loss of personality was a catastrophe to the future of the imagination, but billions of people might first benefit from it by having enough to eat—one did not know—and there remained citadels of resistance in Europe where the culture was deep and roots were visible in the architecture of the past. Nowhere, as in America, however, was this fall from individual man to mass man felt so acutely, for America was at once the first and most prolific creator of mass communications, and the most rootless of countries, since almost no American could lay claim to the line of a family which had not once at least severed its roots by migrating here.

But, if rootless, it was then the most vulnerable of countries to its own homogenization. Yet America was also the country in which the dynamic myth of the Renaissance—that every man was potentially extraordinary—knew its most passionate persistence. Simply, America was the land where people still believed in heroes: George Washington; Billy the Kid; Lincoln, Jefferson; Mark Twain, Jack London, Hemingway; Joe Louis, Dempsey, Gentleman Jim; America believed in athletes, rum-runners, aviators; even lovers, by the time Valentino died. It was a country which had grown by the leap of one hero past another—is there a county in all of our ground which does not have its legendary figure? And when the West was filled, the expansion turned inward, became part of an agitated, over-excited, superheated dream life. The film studios threw up their searchlights as the frontier was finally sealed, and the romantic possibilities of the old conquest of land turned into a vertical myth, trapped within the skull, of a new kind of heroic life, each choosing his own archetype of a neo-renaissance man, be it Barrymore, Cagney, Flynn, Bogart, Brando, or Sinatra, but it was almost as if there were no peace unless one could fight well, kill well (if always with honor), love well and love many, be cool, be daring, be dashing, be wild, be wily, be resourceful, be a brave gun. And this myth, that each of us was born to be free, to wander, to have adventure and to grow on the waves of the violent, the perfumed, and the unexpected, had a force which could not be tamed no matter how the nation's regulators—politicians, medicos, policemen, professors, priests, rabbis, ministers, *idéologues*, psychoanalysts, builders, executives and endless communicators—would brick-in the modern life with hygiene upon sanity, and middle-brow homily over platitude; the myth would not die. Indeed a quarter of the nation's business must have depended upon its existence. But it stayed alive for more than that—it was as if the message in the labyrinth of the genes would insist that violence was locked with creativity, and adventure was the secret of love.

Once, in the Second World War and in the year or two which followed, the underground river returned to earth, and the life of the nation was intense, of the present, electric; as a lady said, "That was the time when we gave parties which changed people's lives." The forties was a decade when the speed with which one's own events occurred seemed as rapid as the history of the battlefields, and for the mass of people in America a forced march into a new jungle of emotion was the result. The surprises, the failures, and the dangers of that life must have terrified some nerve of awareness in the power and the mass, for, as if stricken by the orgiastic vistas the myth had carried up from underground, the retreat to a more conservative existence was disorderly, the fear of communism spread like an irrational hail of boils. To anyone who could see, the excessive hysteria of the Red wave was no preparation to face an enemy, but rather a terror of the national self: free-loving, lust-looting, atheistic implacable—absurdity beyond absurdity to label communism so, for the moral products of Stalinism had been Victorian sex and a ponderous machine of material theology.

Forced underground again, deep beneath all *Reader's Digest* hospital dressings of Mental Health in Your Community, the myth continued to flow, fed by television and the film. The fissure in the national psyche widened to the danger point. The last large appearance of the myth was the vote which tricked the polls and gave Harry Truman his victory in '48. That was the last. Came the Korean War, the shadow of the H-bomb, and we were ready for the General. Uncle Harry gave way to Father, and security, regularity, order, and the life of no imagination were the command of the day. If one had any doubt of this, there was Joe McCarthy with his built-in treason detector, furnished by God, and the damage was done. In the totalitarian wind of those days, anyone who worked in Government formed the habit of being not too original, and many a mind atrophied from disuse and private shame.

JFK calls for a New Frontier at the Democratic National Convention of 1960.   *(Cornell Capa, Magnum)*

At the summit there was benevolence without leadership, regularity without vision, security without safety, rhetoric without life. The ship drifted on, that enormous warship of the United States, led by a Secretary of State whose cells were seceding to cancer, and as the world became more fantastic—Africa turning itself upside down, while some new kind of machine man was being made in China—two events occurred which stunned the confidence of America into a new night: the Russians put up their Sputnik, and Civil Rights—that reluctant gift to the American Negro, granted for its effect on foreign affairs—spewed into real life at Little Rock. The national Ego was in shock: the Russians were now in some ways our technological superiors, and we had an internal problem of subject populations equal conceivably in its difficulty to the Soviet and its satellites. The fatherly calm of the General began to seem like the uxorious mellifluences of the undertaker.

Underneath it all was a larger problem. The life of politics and the life of myth had diverged too far, and the energies of the people one knew everywhere had slowed down. Twenty years ago a post-Depression generation had gone to war and formed a lively, grousing, by times inefficient, carousing, pleasure-seeking, not altogether inadequate army. It did part of what it was supposed to do, and many, out of combat, picked up a kind of private life on the fly, and had their good time despite the yaws of the military system. But today in America the generation which respected the code of the myth was Beat, a horde of half-begotten Christs with scraggly beards, heroes none, saints all, weak before the strong, empty conformisms of the authority. The sanction for finding one's growth was no longer one's flag, one's career, one's sex, one's

adventure, not even one's booze. Among the best in this newest of the generations, the myth had found its voice in marijuana, and the joke of the underground was that when the Russians came over they could never dare to occupy us for long because America was too Hip. Gallows humor. The poorer truth might be that America was too Beat, the instinct of the nation so separated from its public mind that apathy, schizophrenia, and private beatitudes might be the pride of the welcoming committee any underground could offer.

Yes, the life of politics and the life of the myth had diverged too far. There was nothing to return them to one another, no common danger, no cause, no desire, and, most essentially, no hero. It was a hero America needed, a hero central to his time, a man whose personality might suggest contradictions and mysteries which could reach into the alienated circuits of the underground, because only a hero can capture the secret imagination of a people, and so be good for the vitality of his nation; a hero embodies the fantasy and so allows each private mind the liberty to consider its fantasy and find a way to grow. Each mind can become more conscious of its desire and waste less strength in hiding from itself. Roosevelt was such a hero, and Churchill, Lenin and De Gaulle; even Hitler, to take the most odious example of this thesis, was a hero, the hero-as-monster, embodying what had become the monstrous fantasy of a people, but the horror upon which the radical mind and liberal temperament foundered was that he gave outlet to the energies of the Germans and so presented the twentieth century with an index of how horrible had become the secret heart of its desire. Roosevelt is of course a happier example of the hero; from his paralytic leg to the royal elegance of his

geniality he seemed to contain the country within himself; everyone from the meanest starving cripple to an ambitious young man could expand into the optimism of an improving future because the man offered an unspoken promise of a future which would be rich. The sexual and the sex-starved, the poor, the hard-working and the imaginative well-to-do could see themselves in the President, could believe him to be like themselves. So a large part of the country was able to discover its energies because not as much was wasted in feeling that the country was a poisonous nutrient which stifled the day.

Too simple? No doubt. One tries to construct a simple model. The thesis is after all not so mysterious; it would merely nudge the notion that a hero embodies his time and is not so very much better than his time, but he is larger than life and so is capable of giving direction to the time, able to encourage a nation to discover the deepest colors of its character. At bottom the concept of the hero is antagonistic to impersonal social progress, to the belief that social ills can be solved by social legislating, for it sees a country as all-but-trapped in its character until it has a hero who reveals the character of the country to itself. The implication is that without such a hero the nation turns sluggish. Truman for example was not such a hero, he was not sufficiently larger than life, he inspired familiarity without excitement, he was a character but his proportions came from soap opera: Uncle Harry, full of salty common-sense and small-minded certainty, a storekeeping uncle.

Whereas Eisenhower has been the anti-hero, the regulator. Nations do not necessarily and inevitably seek for heroes. In periods of dull anxiety, one or more is likely to look for security than a dramatic confrontation, and

Eisenhower could stand as a hero only for that large number of Americans who were most proud of their lack of imagination. In American life, the unspoken war of the century has taken place between the city and the small town: the city which is dynamic, orgiastic, unsettling, explosive and accelerating to the psyche; the small town which is rooted, narrow, cautious and planted in the life-logic of the family. The need of the city is to accelerate growth; the pride of the small town is to retard it. But since America has been passing through a period of enormous expansion since the war, the double-four years of Dwight Eisenhower could not retard the expansion, it could only denude it of color, character, and the development of novelty. The small-town mind is rooted—it is rooted in the small town—and when it attempts to direct history the results are disastrously colorless because the instrument of world power which is used by the small-town mind is the committee. Committees do not create, they merely proliferate, and the incredible dullness wreaked upon the American landscape in Eisenhower's eight years has been the triumph of the corporation. A tasteless, sexless, odorless sanctity in architecture, manners, modes, styles has been the result. Eisenhower embodied half the needs of the nation, the needs of the timid, the petrified, the sanctimonious, and the sluggish. What was even worse, he did not divide the nation as a hero might (with a dramatic dialogue as the result); he merely excluded one part of the nation from the other. The result was an alienation of the best minds and bravest impulses from the faltering history which was made. America's need in those years was to take an existential turn, to walk into the nightmare, to face into that terrible logic of history which demanded that the country and its people must become more extraordinary and more adventurous, or else perish, since the only alternative was to offer a false security in the power and panacea of organized religion, family, and the FBI, a totalitarianization of the psyche by the stultifying techniques of the mass media which would seep into everyone's most private associations and so leave the country powerless against the Russians even if the denouement were to take fifty years, for in a competition between totalitarianisms the first maxim of the prizefight manager would doubtless apply: "Hungry fighters win fights."

Some part of these thoughts must have been in one's mind at the moment there was that first glimpse of Kennedy entering the Biltmore Hotel; and in the days which followed, the first mystery —the profound air of depression which hung over the convention —gave way to a second mystery which can be answered only by history. The depression of the delegates was understandable: no one had too much doubt that Kennedy would be nominated, but if elected he would be not only the youngest President ever to be chosen by voters, he would be the most conventionally attractive young man ever to sit in the White House, and his wife— some would claim it—might be the most beautiful first lady in our history. Of necessity the myth would emerge once more, because America's politics would now be also America's favorite movie, America's first soap opera, America's best-seller. One thinks of the talents of writers like Taylor Caldwell or Frank Yerby, or is it rather *The Fountainhead* which would contain such a fleshing of the romantic prescription? Or is it indeed one's own work which is called into question? "Well, there's your first hipster," says a writer one knows at the convention, "Sergius O'Shaugnessy born rich," and the temptation is to nod, for it could be true, a war hero, and the heroism is bona fide, even exceptional, a man who has lived with death, who, crippled in the back, took on an operation which would kill him or restore him to power, who chose to marry a lady whose face might be too imaginative for the taste of a democracy which likes its first ladies to be executives of home-management, a man who courts political suicide by choosing to go all out for a nomination four, eight, or twelve years before his political elders think he is ready, a man who announces a week prior to the convention that the young are better fitted to direct history than the old. Yes, it captures the attention. This is no routine candidate calling every shot by safety's routine book. ("Yes," Nixon said, naturally but terribly tired an hour after his nomination, the TV cameras and lights and microphones bringing out a sweat of fatigue on his face, the words coming very slowly from the tired brain, somber, modest, sober, slow, slow enough so that one could touch emphatically the cautions behind each word, "Yes, I want to say," said Nixon, "that whatever abilities I have, I got from my mother." A tired pause . . . dull moment of warning, ". . . and my father." The connection now made, the rest comes easy, ". . . and my school and my church." Such men are capable of anything.)

One had the opportunity to study Kennedy a bit in the days that followed. His style in the press conferences was interesting. Not terribly popular with the reporters (too much a contemporary, and yet too difficult to understand, he received nothing like the rounds of applause given to Eleanor Roosevelt, Stevenson, Humphrey, or even Johnson), he carried himself nonetheless with a cool grace which seemed indifferent to applause, his manner somehow similar to the poise of a fine boxer, quick with his hands, neat in his timing, and two feet away from his corner when the bell ended the round. There was a good lithe wit to his responses, a dry Harvard wit, a keen sense of proportion in disposing of difficult questions—invariably he gave enough of an answer to be formally satisfactory without ever opening himself to a new question which might go further than the first. Asked by a reporter, "Are you for Adlai as vice-president?" the grin came forth and the voice turned very dry, "No, I cannot say we have considered *Adlai* as a vice-president." Yet there was an elusive detachment to everything he did. One did not have the feeling of a man present in the room with all his weight and all his mind. Johnson gave you all of himself, he was a political animal, he breathed like an animal, sweated like one, you knew his mind was entirely absorbed with the compendium of political fact and maneuver; Kennedy seemed at times like a young professor whose manner was adequate for the classroom, but whose mind was off in some intricacy of the Ph.D. thesis he was writing. Perhaps one can give a sense of the discrepancy by saying that he was like an actor who had been cast as the candidate, a good actor,

but not a great one—you were aware all the time that the role was one thing and the man another—they did not coincide, the actor seemed a touch too aloof (as, let us say, Gregory Peck is usually too aloof) to become the part. Yet one had little sense of whether to value this elusiveness, or to beware of it. One could be witnessing the fortitude of a superior sensivity or the detachment of a man who was not quite real to himself. And his voice gave no clue. When Johnson spoke, one could separate what was fraudulent from what was felt, he would have been satisfy-

ing as an actor the way Broderick Crawford or Paul Douglas are satisfying; one saw into his emotions, or at least had the illusion that one did. Kennedy's voice, however, was only a fair voice, too reedy, near to strident, it had the metallic snap of a cricket in it somewhere, it was more impersonal than the man, and so became the least-impressive quality in a face, a body, a selection of language, and a style of movement which made up a better-than-decent presentation, better than one had expected.

With all of that, it would not do to pass over the quality in

President Kennedy addressing the Conference on Physical Fitness of Youth, February 21, 1961. *(Wide World Photos)*

Kennedy which is most difficult to describe. And in fact some touches should be added to this hint of a portrait, for later (after the convention), one had a short session alone with him, and the next day, another. As one had suspected in advance the interviews were not altogether satisfactory, they hardly could have been. A man running for President is altogether different from a man elected President: the hazards of the campaign make it impossible for a candidate to be as interesting as he might like to be (assuming he has such a desire). One kept advancing the argument that this campaign would be a contest of personalities, and Kennedy kept returning the discussion to politics. After a while one recognized this was an inevitable caution for him. So there would be not too much point to reconstructing the dialogue since Kennedy is hardly inarticulate about his political attitudes and there will be a library vault of text devoted to it in the newspapers. What struck me most about the interview was a passing remark whose importance was invisible on the scale of politics, but was altogether meaningful to my particular competence. As we sat down for the first time, Kennedy smiled nicely and said that he had read my books. One muttered one's pleasure. "Yes," he said, "I've read . . ." and then there was a short pause which did not last long enough to be embarrassing in which it was yet obvious no title came instantly to his mind, an omission one was not ready to mind altogether since a man in such a position must be obliged to carry a hundred thousand facts and names in his head, but the hesitation lasted no longer than three seconds or four, and then he said, "I've read *The Deer Park* and . . . the others," which startled me for it was the first time in a hundred similar situations, talking to someone whose knowledge of my work was casual, that the sentence did not come out, "I've read *The Naked and the Dead . . .* and the others." If one is to take the worst and assume that Kennedy was briefed for this interview (which is most doubtful), it still speaks well for the striking instincts of his advisers.

What was retained later is an impression of Kennedy's manners which were excellent, even artful, better than the formal good manners of Choate and Harvard, almost as if what was creative in the man had been given to the manners. In a room with one or two people, his voice improved, became low-pitched, even pleasant—it seemed obvious that in all these years he had never become a natural public speaker and so his voice was constricted in public, the symptoms of all orators who are ambitious, throttled, and determined.

His personal quality had a subtle, not quite describable intensity, a suggestion of dry pent heat perhaps, his eyes large, the pupils grey, the whites prominent, almost shocking, his most forceful feature: he had the eyes of a mountaineer. His appearance changed with his mood, strikingly so, and this made him always more interesting than what he was saying. He would seem at one moment older than his age, forty-eight or fifty, a tall, slim, sunburned professor with a pleasant weathered face, not even particularly handsome; five minutes later, talking to a press conference on his lawn, three microphones before him, a television camera turning, his appearance would have gone through a metamorphosis, he would look again like a movie star, his coloring vivid, his manner rich, his gestures strong and quick, alive with that concentration of vitality a successful actor seems to radiate. Kennedy had a dozen faces. Although they were not at all similar as people, the quality was reminiscent of someone like Brando whose expression rarely changes, but whose appearance seems to shift from one person into another as the minutes go by, and one bothers with this comparison because, like Brando, Kennedy's most characteristic quality is the remote and private air of a man who has traversed some lonely terrain of experience, of loss and gain, of nearness to death, which leaves him isolated from the mass of others.

The next day while they waited in vain for rescuers, the wrecked half of the boat turned over in the water and they saw that it would soon sink. The group decided to swim to a small island three miles away. There were other islands bigger and nearer, but the Navy officers knew that they were occupied by the Japanese. On one island, only one mile to the south, they could see a Japanese camp. McMahon, the engineer whose legs were disabled by burns, was unable to swim. Despite his own painfully crippled back, Kennedy swam the three miles with a breast stroke, towing behind him by a life-belt strap that he held between his teeth the helpless McMahon . . . it took Kennedy and the suffering engineer five hours to reach the island.

The quotation is from a book which has for its dedicated unilateral title, *The Remarkable Kennedys,* but the prose is by one of the best of the war reporters, the former *Yank* editor, Joe McCarthy, and so presumably may be trusted in such details as this. Physical bravery does not of course guarantee a man's abilities in the White House—all too often men with physical courage are disappointing in their moral imagination—but the heroism here is remarkable for its tenacity. The above is merely one episode in a continuing saga which went on for five days in and out of the water, and left Kennedy at one point "miraculously saved from drowning (in a storm) by a group of Solomon Island natives who suddenly came up beside him in a large dugout canoe." Afterward, his back still injured (that precise back injury which was to put him on crutches eleven years later, and have him search for "spinal-fusion surgery" despite a warning that his chances of living through the operation were "extremely limited") afterward, he asked to go back on duty and became so bold in the attacks he made with his PT boat "that the crew didn't like to go out with him because he took so many chances."

It is the wisdom of a man who senses death within him and gambles that he can cure it by risking his life. It is the therapy of the instinct, and who is so wise as to call it irrational? Before he went into the Navy, Kennedy had been ailing. Washed out of freshman year at Princeton by a prolonged trough of yellow jaundice, sick for a year at Harvard, weak already in the back from an injury at football, his trials suggest the self-hatred of a man whose resentment and ambition are too large for his body. Not everyone can discharge their furies on an analyst's couch, for some angers can be relaxed only by winning power, some rages are sufficiently monumental to demand that one try to become a hero or else fall back into that death which is already within the cells. But if one succeeds, the energy aroused can be exceptional. Talking to a man who had been with Kennedy in Hyannis Port the week before the convention, I heard that he was in a state of deep fatigue.

"Well, he didn't look tired at the convention," one commented.

"Oh, he had three days of rest. Three days of rest for him is like six months for us."

One thinks of the three-mile swim with the belt in his mouth and McMahon holding it behind him. There are pestilences which sit in the mouth and rot the teeth—in those five hours how much of the psyche must have been remade, for to give vent to the bite in one's jaws and yet use that rage to save a life: it is not so very many men who have the apocalyptic sense that heroism is the First Doctor.

If one had a profound criticism of Kennedy it was that his public mind was too conventional, but that seemed to matter less than the fact of such a man in office because the law of political life had become so dreary that only a conventional mind could win an election. Indeed there could be no politics which gave warmth to one's body until the country had recovered its imagination, its pioneer lust for the unexpected and incalculable. It was the changes that might come afterward on which one could put one's hope. With such a man in office the myth of the nation would again be engaged, and the fact that he was Catholic would shiver a first existential vibration of consciousness into the mind of the White Protestant. For the first time in our history, the Protestant would have the pain and creative luxury of feeling himself in some tiny degree part of a minority, and that was an experience which might be incommensurable in its value to the best of them.

As yet we have said hardly a word about Stevenson. And his actions must remain a puzzle unless one dares a speculation about his motive, or was it his need?

So far as the people at the convention had affection for anyone, it was Stevenson, so far as they were able to generate any spontaneous enthusiasm, their cheers were again for Stevenson. Yet it was obvious he never had much chance because so soon as a chance would present itself he seemed quick to dissipate the opportunity. The day before the nominations, he entered the Sports Arena to take his seat as a delegate—the demonstration was spontaneous, noisy and prolonged; it was quieted only by Governor Collins' invitation for Stevenson to speak to the delegates. In obedience perhaps to the scruple that a candidate must not appear before the convention until nominations are done, Stevenson said no more than: "I am grateful for this tumultuous and moving welcome. After getting in and out of the Biltmore Hotel and this hall, I have decided I know whom you are going to nominate. It will be the last survivor." This dry reminder of the ruthlessness of politics broke the roar of excitement for his presence. The applause as he left the platform was like the dying fall-and-moan of a baseball crowd when a home run curves foul. The next day, a New York columnist talking about it said bitterly, "If he'd only gone through the motions, if he had just said that now he wanted to run, that he would work hard, and he hoped the delegates would vote for him. Instead he made that lame joke." One wonders. It seems almost as if he did not wish to win unless victory came despite himself, and then was overwhelming. There are men who are not heroes because they are too good for their time, and it is natural that defeats leave them bitter, tired, and doubtful of their right to make new history. If Stevenson had campaigned for a year before the convention, it is possible that he could have stopped Kennedy. At the least, the convention would have been enormously more exciting, and the nominations might have gone through half-a-dozen ballots before a winner was hammered into shape. But then Stevenson might also have shortened his life. One had the impression of a tired man who (for a politician) was sickened unduly by compromise. A year of maneuvering, broken promises, and detestable partners might have gutted him for the election campaign. If elected, it might have ruined him as a President. There is the possibility that he sensed his situation exactly this way, and knew that if he were to run for president, win and make a good one, he would first have to be restored, as one can indeed be restored, by an exceptional demonstration of love—love, in this case, meaning that the party had a profound desire to keep him as their leader. The emotional truth of a last-minute victory for Stevenson over the Kennedy machine might have given him new energy; it would certainly have given him new faith in a country and a party whose good motives he was possibly beginning to doubt. Perhaps the fault he saw with his candidacy was that he attracted only the nicest people to himself and there were not enough of them. (One of the private amusements of the convention was to divine some of the qualities of the candidates by the style of the young women who put on hats and clothing and politicked in the colors of one presidential gent or another. Of course, half of them must have been hired models, but someone did the hiring and so it was fair to look for a common denominator. The Johnson girls tended to be plump, pie-faced, dumb sexy Southern; the Symingteeners seemed a touch mulish, stubborn, good-looking pluggers; the Kennedy ladies were the handsomest; healthy, attractive, tough, a little spoiled—they looked like the kind of girls who had gotten all the dances in high school and/or worked for a year as an airline hostess before marrying well. But the Stevenson girls looked to be doing it for no money; they were good sorts, slightly horsy-faced, one had the impression they played field hockey in college.) It was indeed the pure, the saintly, the clean-living, the pacifistic, the vegetarian who seemed most for Stevenson, and the less humorous in the Kennedy camp were heard to

remark bitterly that Stevenson had nothing going for him but a bunch of Goddamn Beatniks. This might even have had its sour truth. The demonstrations outside the Sports Arena for Stevenson seemed to have more than a fair proportion of tall, emaciated young men with thin, wry beards and three-string guitars accompanied (again in undue proportion) by a contingent of ascetic, face-washed young Beat ladies in sweaters and dungarees. Not to mention all the Holden Caulfields one could see from here to the horizon. But of course it is unfair to limit it so, for the Democratic gentry were also committed half en masse for Stevenson, as well as a considerable number of movie stars, Shelley Winters for one: after the convention she remarked sweetly, "Tell me something nice about Kennedy so I can get excited about him."

What was properly astonishing was the way this horde of political half-breeds and amateurs came within distance of turning the convention from its preconceived purpose, and managed at least to bring the only hour of thoroughgoing excitement the convention could offer.

But then nominating day was the best day of the week and enough happened to suggest that a convention out of control would be a spectacle as extraordinary in the American scale of spectator values as a close seventh game in the World Series or a tied fourth quarter in a professional-football championship. A political convention is after all not a meeting of a corporation's board of directors; it is a fiesta, a carnival, a pig-rooting, horse-snorting, band-playing, voice-screaming medieval get-together of greed, practical lust, compromised idealism, career-advancement, meeting, feud, vendetta, conciliation, of rabble-rousers, fist fights (as it used to be), embraces, drunks (again as it used to be) and collective rivers of

animal sweat. It is a reminder that no matter how the country might pretend it has grown up and become tidy in its manners, bodiless in its legislative language, hygienic in its separation of high politics from private life, that the roots still come grubby from the soil, and that politics in America is still different from politics anywhere else because the politics has arisen out of the immediate needs, ambitions, and cupidities of the people, that our politics still smell of the bedroom and the kitchen, rather than having descended to us from the chill punctilio of aristocratic negotiation.

So. The Sports Arena was new, too pretty, of course, tasteless in its design—it was somehow pleasing that the acoustics were so bad for one did not wish the architects well; there had been so little imagination in their design, and this arena would have none of the harsh grandeur of Madison Square Garden when it was aged by spectators' phlegm and feet over the next twenty years. Still it had some atmosphere; seen from the streets, with the spectators moving to the ticket gates, the bands playing, the green hot-shot special editions of the Los Angeles newspapers being hawked by the newsboys, there was a touch of the air of promise that precedes a bullfight, not something so good as the approach to the Plaza Mexico, but good, let us say, like the entrance into El Toreo of Mexico City, another architectural monstrosity, also with seats painted, as I remember, in rose-pink, and dark, milky sky-blue.

Inside, it was also different this nominating day. On Monday and Tuesday the air had been desultory, no one listened to the speakers, and everybody milled from one easy chatting conversation to another—it had been like a tepid Kaffeeklatsch for fifteen thousand people. But today there was a whip of anticipation in the air, the seats on the floor were filled, the press section was working, and in the gallery people were sitting in the aisles.

Sam Rayburn had just finished nominating Johnson as one came in, and the rebel yells went up, delegates started filing out of their seats and climbing over seats, and a pullulating dance of bodies and bands began to snake through the aisles, the posters jogging and whirling in time to the music. The dun color of the floor (faces, suits, seats and floor boards), so monotonous the first two days, now lit up with life as if an iridescent caterpillar had emerged from a fold of wet leaves. It was more vivid than one had expected, it was right, it felt finally like a convention, and from up close when one got down to the floor (where your presence was illegal and so consummated by sneaking in one time as demonstrators were going out, and again by slipping a five-dollar bill to a guard) the nearness to the demonstrators took on high color, that electric vividness one feels on the side lines of a football game when it is necessary to duck back as the ballcarrier goes by, his face tortured in the concentration of the moment, the thwomp of his tackle as acute as if one had been hit oneself.

That was the way the demonstrators looked on the floor. Nearly all had the rapt, private look of a passion or a tension which would finally be worked off by one's limbs, three hundred football players, everything from seedy delegates with jowl-sweating shivers to livid models, paid for their work that day, but stomping out their beat on the floor with the hypnotic adulatory grimaces of ladies who had lived for Lyndon these last ten years.

Then from the funereal rostrum, whose color was not so rich as mahogany nor so dead as a cigar, came the last of the requests for the delegates to take their seats. The seconding speeches began, one minute each; they ran for three and four, the minor-league speakers running on the longest as if the electric antenna of television was the lure of the Sirens, leading them out. Bored cheers applauded their concluding Götterdämmerungen and the nominations were open again. A favorite son, a modest demonstration, five seconding speeches, tedium.

Next was Kennedy's occasion. Governor Freeman of Minnesota made the speech. On the second or third sentence his television prompter jammed, an accident. Few could be aware of it at the moment; the speech seemed merely flat and surprisingly void

Kennedy fans, 1960 Convention.
(*Cornell Capa, Magnum*)

of bravura. He was obviously no giant of extempore. Then the demonstration. Well-run, bigger than Johnson's, jazzier, the caliber of the costumes and decorations better chosen: the placards were broad enough, "Let's Back Jack," the floats were garish, particularly a papier-mâché or plastic balloon of Kennedy's head, six feet in diameter, which had nonetheless the slightly shrunken, over-red, rubbery look of a toy for practical jokers in one of those sleazy off-Times Square magic-and-gimmick stores; the band was suitably corny; and yet one had the impression this demonstration had been designed by some hands-to-hip interior decorator who said, "Oh, joy, let's have fun, let's make this *true* beer hall."

Besides, the personnel had something of the Kennedy *élan*, those paper hats designed to look like straw boaters with Kennedy's face on the crown, and small photographs of him on the ribbon, those hats which had come to symbolize the crack speed of Kennedy's team, that Madison Avenue cachet which one finds in bars like P. J. Clarke's, the elegance always giving its subtle echo of the twenties so that the raccoon coats seem more numerous than their real count, and the colored waistcoats are measured by the charm they would have drawn from Scott Fitzgerald's eye. But there, it occurred to one for the first time that Kennedy's middle name was just that, Fitzgerald, and the tone of his crack lieutenants, the unstated style, was true to Scott. The legend of Fitzgerald had an army at last, formed around the self-image in the mind of every superior Madison Avenue opportunist that he was hard, he was young, he was In, his conversation was lean as wit, and if the work was not always scrupulous, well the style could aspire. If there came a good day . . . he could meet the occasion.

The Kennedy snake dance ran its thirty lively minutes, cheered its seconding speeches, and sat back. They were so sure of winning, there had been so many victories before this one, and this one had been scouted and managed so well, that hysteria could hardly be the mood. Besides, everyone was waiting for the Stevenson barrage which should be at least diverting. But now came a long tedium. Favorite sons were nominated, fat mayors shook their hips, seconders told the word to constituents back in Ponderwaygot County, treacly demonstrations tried to hold the floor, and the afternoon went by; Symington's hour came and went, a good demonstration, good as Johnson's (for good cause—they had pooled their demonstrators). More favorite sons, Governor Docking of Kansas declared "a genius" by one of his lady speakers in a tense go-back-to-religion voice. The hours went by, two, three, four hours, it seemed forever before they would get to Stevenson. It was evening when Senator Eugene McCarthy of Minnesota got up to nominate him.

The gallery was ready, the floor was responsive, the demonstrators were milling like bulls in their pen waiting for the *toril* to fly open—it would have been hard not to wake the crowd up, not to make a good speech. McCarthy made a great one. Great it was by the measure of convention oratory, and he held the crowd like a matador, timing their *oles!*, building them up, easing them back, correcting any sag in attention, gathering their emotion, discharging it, creating new emotion on the wave of the last, driving his passes tighter and tighter as he readied for the kill. "Do not reject this man who made us all proud to be called Democrats, do not leave this prophet without honor in his own party." One had not heard a speech like this since 1948 when Vito Marcantonio's voice,

his harsh, shrill, bitter, street urchin's voice screeched through the loud-speakers at Yankee Stadium and lashed seventy thousand people into an uproar.

"There was only one man who said let's talk sense to the American people," McCarthy went on, his muleta furled for the *naturales*. "There was only one man who said let's talk sense to the American people," he repeated. "He said the promise of America is the promise of greatness. This was his call to greatness. . . . Do not forget this man. . . . Ladies and Gentlemen, I present to you not the favorite son of one state, but the favorite son of the fifty states, the favorite son of every country he has visited, the favorite son of every country which has not seen him but is secretly thrilled by his name." Bedlam. The kill. "Ladies and Gentlemen, I present to you Adlai Stevenson of Illinois." Ears and tail. Hooves and bull. A roar went up like the roar one heard the day Bobby Thompson hit his home run at the Polo Grounds and the Giants won the pennant from the Dodgers in the third playoff game of the 1951 season. The demonstration cascaded onto the floor, the gallery came to its feet, the Sports Arena sounded like the inside of a marching drum. A tidal pulse of hysteria, exaltation, defiance, exhilaration, anger and roaring desire flooded over the floor. The cry which had gone up on McCarthy's last sentence had not paused for breath in five minutes, and troop after troop of demonstrators jammed the floor (the Stevenson people to be scolded the next day for having collected floor passes and sent them out to bring in new demonstrators) and still the sound mounted. One felt the convention coming apart. There was a Kennedy girl in the seat in front of me, the Kennedy hat on her head, a dimpled healthy brunette; she had sat silently through McCarthy's speech, but now, like a woman paying her respects to the power of natural thrust, she took off her hat and began to clap herself. I saw a writer I knew in the next aisle; he had spent a year studying the Kennedy machine in order to write a book on how a nomination is won. If Stevenson stampeded the convention, his work was lost. Like a reporter at a mine cave-in I inquired the present view of the widow. "Who can think," was the answer, half frantic, half elated, "just watch it, that's all." I found a cool one, a New York reporter, who smiled in rueful respect. "It's the biggest demonstration I've seen since Wendell Willkie's in 1940," he said, and added, "God, if Stevenson takes it, I can wire my wife and move the family on to Hawaii."

"I don't get it."

"Well, every story I wrote said it was locked up for Kennedy."

Still it went on, twenty minutes, thirty minutes, the chairman could hardly be heard, the demonstrators refused to leave. The lights were turned out, giving a sudden theatrical shift to the sense of a crowded church at midnight, and a new roar went up, louder, more passionate than anything heard before. It was the voice, the passion, if one insisted to call it that, of everything in America which was defeated, idealistic, innocent, alienated, outside and Beat, it was the potential voice of a new third of the nation whose psyche was ill from cultural malnutrition, it was powerful, it was extraordinary, it was larger than the decent, humorous, finicky, half-noble man who had called it forth, it was a cry from the thirties when Time was simple, it was a resentment of the slick technique, the oiled gears, and the superior generals of Fitzgerald's Army; but it was also—and for this reason one could not admire it altogether, except with one's excitement—it was also the plea of the bewildered who hunger for simplicity again, it was the adolescent counterpart of the boss's depression before the unpredictable dynamic of Kennedy as President, it was the return to the sentimental dream of Roosevelt rather than the approaching nightmare of history's oncoming night, and it was inspired by a terror of the future as much as a revulsion of the present.

Fitz's army held; after the demonstration was finally down, the convention languished for ninety minutes while Meyner and others were nominated, a fatal lapse of time because Stevenson had perhaps a chance to stop Kennedy if the voting had begun on the echo of the last cry for him, but in an hour and a half depression crept in again and emotions spent, the delegates who had wavered were rounded into line. When the vote was taken, Stevenson had made no gains. The brunette who had taken off her hat was wearing it again, and she clapped and squealed when Wyoming delivered the duke and Kennedy was in. The air was sheepish, like the mood of a suburban couple who forgive each other for cutting in and out of somebody else's automobile while the country club dance is on. Again, tonight, no miracle would occur. In the morning the papers would be moderate in their description of Stevenson's last charge.

ARTHUR SCHLESINGER, JR.
The Cuban Missile Crisis of 1962

Arthur M. Schlesinger, Jr.'s portrait of John F. Kennedy during the Cuban missile crisis strikingly confirms the image that Norman Mailer posited: the cold warrior in taut control of the reins of power, perhaps more in command during a state of crisis than in the calmer activities of government, a man welcoming the ultimate challenges and meeting them with the most economical and effective means.

The missile crisis was the major event of the decade: indeed it is probable that no event could surpass it and leave behind participants to write the tale. Schlesinger was close to the decision making and his account catches the drama of those days. Since we are never to have the President's memoirs, Schlesinger's version may well take us as close to the American side of the crisis, to the feel of events at the White House, as we can get. This is the permanent value of the memoir, no matter how many questions of interpretation can be raised.

On the Russian side, we now have Nikita Khrushchev's own memoir. Yet we must still speculate about Soviet motives. The ex-Premier's account of the event repeats the reasons that he and others gave at the time: the need to defend Cuba from another American invasion. That there were deeper reasons of state behind Khrushchev's actions and that the internal politics of the Soviet Union played some important role is difficult to doubt, yet the often garrulous elder statesman says little. He makes clear how touchy Russia's relations with Cuba were and at least hints at a Russian version of the domino theory by which the loss of Cuba would undermine Russian hopes in the rest of Latin America. In short, his account offers many parallels with the American situation, suggesting that great powers—whatever their ideology—are often forced into similar modes of behavior.

1. THE GAMBLE

On July 2, 1962, Raúl Castro, the Minister of the Armed Forces of Cuba, arrived in Moscow. Either before his arrival or very soon thereafter the Soviet and Cuban governments arrived at a startling decision: that Soviet nuclear missiles were to be secretly installed in Cuba in the fall.

The Soviet Union had never before placed nuclear missiles in any other country—neither in the communist nations of Eastern Europe, nor, even in the season of their friendship, in Red China. Why should it now send nuclear missiles to a country thousands of miles away, lying within the zone of vital interest of their main adversary, a land, moreover, headed by a willful leader of, from the Russian viewpoint, somewhat less than total reliability? Castro, with characteristic loquacity, later produced a confusion of explanations. He told a Cuban audience in January 1963 that sending the missiles was a Soviet idea; he repeated this to Claude Julien of *Le Monde* in March 1963; in May he described it to Lisa Howard of the American Broadcasting Company as "simultaneous action on the part of both governments"; then in October he told Herbert Matthews of the *New York Times* that it was a Cuban idea, only to tell Jean Daniel of *L'Express* in November that it was a Soviet idea; in January 1964, when Matthews called him about the Daniel story, Castro claimed again that it was a Cuban idea; and, when Cyrus Sulzberger of the *New York Times* asked him in October 1964, Castro, pleading that the question raised security problems, said cagily, "Both Russia and Cuba participated."

As for the Russians, Khrushchev told the Supreme Soviet in December 1962, "We carried weapons there at the request of the Cuban government . . . including the stationing of a couple of score of Soviet IRBMs [intermediate-range ballistic missiles] in Cuba. These weapons were to be in the hands of Soviet military men. . . . Our aim was only to defend Cuba." The presence of the missiles, Khrushchev continued, was designed to make the imperialists understand that, if they tried to invade Cuba, "the war which they threatened to start stood at their own borders, so that they would realize more realistically the dangers of thermonuclear war." This was all very noble, and the defense of Cuba was certainly a side effect of the Soviet action. But the defense of Cuba did not really require the introduction of long-range nuclear missiles. One may be sure that Khrushchev, like any other national leader, took *that* decision not for Cuban reasons but for Soviet reasons. Pending Khrushchev's reminiscences, one can only speculate as to what these Soviet reasons were.

In a general sense, the decision obviously represented the supreme Soviet probe of American intentions. No doubt a "total victory" faction in Moscow had long been denouncing the government's "no-win" policy and arguing that the Soviet Union could safely use the utmost nuclear pressure against the United States because the Americans were too rich or soft or liberal to fight. Now Khrushchev was prepared to give this argument its crucial test. A successful nuclearization of Cuba would make about sixty-four medium-range (around 1000 miles) and intermediate-range (1500–2000 miles) nuclear missiles effective against the United States and thereby come near to doubling Soviet striking capacity against American targets. Since this would still leave the United States with at least a 2 to 1 superiority in nuclear power targeted against the Soviet Union, the shift in the military balance of power would be less crucial than that in the political balance.

Every country in the world, watching so audacious an action ninety miles from the United States, would wonder whether it could ever thereafter trust Washington's resolution and protection. More particularly, the change in the nuclear equilibrium would permit Khrushchev, who had been dragging out the Berlin negotiation all year, to reopen that question—perhaps in a personal appearance before the United Nations General Assembly in November—with half the United States lying within range of nuclear missiles poised for delivery across the small stretch of water from Florida. It was a staggering project—staggering in its recklessness, staggering in its misconception of the American response, staggering in its rejection of the ground rules for coexistence among the superpowers which Kennedy had offered in Vienna.

The decision having been made, the next problem was the development of a plan. Moscow evidently saw the operation in two stages—first, the augmentation of Cuban defensive capabilities by bringing in surface-to-air anti-aircraft (SAM) missiles and MIG-21 fighters; then, as soon as the SAMS were in place to protect the bases and deter photographic reconnaissance (a SAM had brought down the U-2 over Russia in 1960), sending in offensive weapons, both ballistic missiles and Ilyushin-28 jet aircraft able to deliver nuclear bombs. The first stage, involving only defensive weapons, required no special concealment. The second stage called for the most careful and complex program of deception. One can only imagine the provisions made in Moscow and Havana through the summer to ship the weapons, to receive them, unload them, assemble them, erect bases for them, install them on launching pads—all with a stealth and speed designed to confront the United States one day in November or December with a fully operational Soviet nuclear arsenal across the water in Cuba.

2. THE SURVEILLANCE

By late July the Soviet shipments began to arrive. Three weeks later CIA sent an urgent report to the President that "something new and different" was taking place in Soviet aid operations to Cuba. There were perhaps 5000 Soviet "specialists" now in Cuba; military construction of some sort was going on; more ships were on their way with more specialists and more electronic and construction equipment. The data suggested that the Soviet Union was refurbishing the Cuban air defense system, presumably by putting up a network of SAM sites.

The intelligence community concluded that Moscow, having resolved after a time of indeci- sion that it had a large stake in Castro's survival, had decided to insure the regime against external attack. It could thereby hope to secure the Soviet bridge- head in the western hemisphere, strengthen Castro's prestige in Latin America and show the world Washington's inability to prevent such things at its very doorstep. This all seemed logical enough. Obviously Moscow had calculated that the United States, with the Bay of Pigs still in the world's recollection, could not convincingly object to Castro's taking defensive precautions against another invasion. No one in the intelligence community (with one exception; for the thought flickered through the mind of John McCone) supposed that the Soviet Union would con- ceivably go beyond defensive weapons. The introduction of nu- clear missiles, for example, would obviously legitimatize an Amer- ican response, even possibly an invasion of Cuba. Our best Soviet experts in State and CIA con- sidered Khrushchev too wary and Soviet foreign policy too rational to court a risk of this magnitude.

Nonetheless, when a U-2 flight on August 29 showed clear evi- dence of SAM sites under con- struction, the President decided to put Moscow on notice. On September 4, the Secretary of State brought over a draft of the warning. The President showed it to the Attorney General, who recommended stiffening it with an explicit statement that we would not tolerate the import of offensive weapons. The draft as revised read that, while we had no evidence of "significant of- fensive capability either in Cuban hands or under Soviet direction," should it be otherwise, "the gravest issues would arise."

On the same day the Soviet Ambassador in Washington gave

On the beach. *(Reprinted with the permission of Farrar, Straus & Giroux, Inc., from* The John F. Kennedys *by Mark Shaw, copyright © 1961, 1964, by Mark Shaw.)*

the Attorney General an unusual personal message from Khrushchev for the President. The Soviet leader pledged in effect that he would stir up no incidents before the congressional elections in November. Then a week later, in the midst of a long and wearying disquisition on world affairs, Moscow said flatly that the "armaments and military equipment sent to Cuba are designed exclusively for defensive purposes." It added:

There is no need for the Soviet Union to shift its weapons for the repulsion of aggression, for a retaliatory blow, to any other country, for instance Cuba. Our nuclear weapons are so powerful in their explosive force and the Soviet Union has so powerful rockets to carry these nuclear warheads, that there is no need to search for sites for them beyond the boundaries of the Soviet Union.

The statement continued truculently by accusing the United States of "preparing for aggression against Cuba and other peace-loving states," concluding that "if the aggressors unleash war our armed forces must be ready to strike a crushing retaliatory blow at the aggressor." The President responded calmly two days later at his press conference that the new shipments did not constitute a serious threat but that if at any time Cuba were to "become an offensive military base of significant capacity for the Soviet Union, then this country will do whatever must be done to protect its own security and that of its allies." In the meantime, he asked Congress for stand-by authority to call up the reserves.

He had also taken the precaution of doubling the frequency of the U-2 overflights of Cuba. The evidence from flights on September 5, 17, 26, and 29 and October 5 and 7, as well as from other sources, indicated a continuing military build-up large in its proportions but still defensive in its character. The government saw no reason as yet to believe that Khrushchev intended anything beyond this; he had not, so far as we knew, lost his mind. Only John McCone had his personal presentiment that he might be planning the installation of offensive missiles. However, given the prevailing complacency on this point, McCone himself did not take this thought seriously enough to prevent his going off now for a three weeks' honeymoon in Europe. The White House staff worried about this increasingly visible Soviet presence, but it seemed to me much more a political threat to Latin America than a military threat to the United States. I found myself, as I told the President on September 13, relatively a hard-liner and felt that the State Department should tell the Soviet Ambassador in cold and tough fashion that persistence in the arming of Cuba would cause both an increase in our defense budget and a surge of national indignation which would color every other issue between our two countries. But, when I advanced this view at the Bundy staff meeting, I was confronted with the wholly proper question: "OK, but how far would you carry it if they keep on doing what you object to?"

And, across the world, ships were sliding out of Black Sea harbors with nuclear technicians in their cabins and nuclear missiles in their hatches. Khrushchev, having done his best to lull Kennedy by public statements and private messages, now in early September put the second stage of his plan into operation. He could hope that the hurricane season might interfere with the U-2 overflights and that the fall political campaign might inhibit the administration from taking drastic action. Moreover, he had an advantage unknown to us: Soviet engineering had enormously reduced the time required for the erection of nuclear missile sites. As Roberta Wohlstetter, the searching analyst of both Pearl Harbor and the Cuba crisis, later wrote, "The rapidity of the Russians' installation was in effect a logistical surprise comparable to the technological surprise at the time of Pearl Harbor."

In the meantime, Washington had been receiving a flow of tales about nuclear installations through refugee channels. Such reports had been routine for eighteen months. No one could be sure whether the sources in Cuba could tell a surface-to-air from a surface-to-surface missile; moreover, this government recalled that it had been misled by Cuban refugees before. Lacking photographic verification, the intelligence community treated the information with reserve. In the meantime, it recommended on October 4 a U-2 flight over western Cuba. The recommendation was approved on October 10, and from the eleventh to the thirteenth the pilot and plane waited for the weather to break. Sunday the fourteenth dawned beautiful and cloudless.

Senator Kenneth Keating of New York had also been receiving the refugee reports, and he treated them with no reserve at all. At the end of August he began a campaign to force the government into some unspecified form of action. In October he began to talk about offensive missile bases. If he felt the national safety involved, Keating was plainly right to make his case with all the urgency at his command. Some, however, discerned other motives, especially with the approach of the fall election. As Roger Hilsman, Director of Intelligence and Research at the State Department, later wrote, "The charge that Keating was more interested in personal publicity than in his country's welfare may be extreme. But until the Senator comes forward with a better explanation than he has

Soviet freighter carries missile launches away from Cuba, November 9, 1962. *(Wide World Photos)*

so far supplied, one of two possible conclusions is inescapable: Either Senator Keating was peddling someone's rumors for some purpose of his own, despite the highly dangerous international situation; or, alternatively, he had information the United States Government did not have that could have guided a U-2 to the missile sites before October 14, and at less risk to the pilot."

Now on the fourteenth the U-2 plane returned from its mission. The negatives went swiftly to the processing laboratories, then to the interpretation center, where specialists pored over the blown-up photographs frame by frame. Late Monday afternoon, reading the obscure and intricate markings, they identified a launching pad, a series of buildings for ballistic missiles and even one missile on the ground in San Cristóbal.

3. THE EXECUTIVE COMMITTEE

About 8:30 that evening the CIA informed Bundy of the incredible discovery. Bundy reflected on whether to inform the President immediately, but he knew that Kennedy would demand the photographs and supporting interpretation in order to be sure the report was right and knew also it would take all night to prepare the evidence in proper form. Furthermore, an immediate meeting would collect officials from dinner parties all over town, signal Washington that something was up and end any hope of secrecy. It was better, Bundy thought, to let the President have a night's sleep in preparation for the ordeal ahead.

The President was having breakfast in his dressing gown at eight forty-five on Tuesday morning when Bundy brought the news. Kennedy asked at once about the nature of the evidence. As soon as he was convinced that it was conclusive, he said that the United States must bring the threat to an end: one way or another the missiles would have to be removed. He then directed Bundy to institute low-level photographic flights and to set up a meeting of top officials. Privately he was furious: if Khrushchev could pull this after all his protestations and denials, how could he ever be trusted on anything?

The meeting, beginning at eleven forty-five that morning, went on with intermissions for the rest of the week. The group soon became known as the Executive Committee, presumably of the National Security Council; the press later dubbed it familiarly ExCom, though one never heard that phrase at the time. It carried on its work with the most exacting secrecy: nothing could be worse than to alert the Russians before the United States had decided on its own course. For this reason its members—the President, the Vice-President, Rusk, McNamara, Robert Kennedy, General Taylor, McCone, Dillon, Adlai Stevenson, Bundy, Sorenson, Ball, Gilpatric, Llewellyn Thompson, Alexis Johnson, Edwin Martin, with others brought in on occasion, among them Dean Acheson and Robert Lovett—had to attend their regular meetings, keep as many appointments as possible and preserve the normalities of life. Fortunately the press corps, absorbed in the congressional campaign, was hardly disposed or situated to notice odd comings and goings. And so the President himself went off that night to dinner at Joseph Alsop's as if nothing had happened. After dinner the talk turned to the contingencies of history, the odds for or against any particular event taking place. The President was silent for a time. Then he said, "Of course, if you simply consider mathematical chances, the odds are even on an H-bomb war within ten years." Perhaps he added to himself, "or within ten days."

In the Executive Committee consideration was free, intent and continuous. Discussion ranged widely, as it had to in a situation of such exceptional urgency, novelty and difficulty. When the presence of the President seemed by virtue of the solemnity of his office to have a constraining effect, preliminary meetings were held without him. Every alternative was laid on the table for examination, from living with the missiles to taking them out by surprise attack, from making the issue with Castro to making it with Khrushchev. In effect, the members walked around the problem, inspecting it first from

this angle, then found that, viewing it in a variety of perspectives. In the course of the long hours of thinking aloud, hearing new arguments, entertaining new considerations, they almost all found themselves moving from one position to another. "If we had to act on Wednesday in the first twenty-four hours," the President said later, "I don't think probably we would have chosen as prudently as we finally did." They had, it was estimated, about ten days before the missiles would be on pads ready for firing. The deadline defined the strategy. It meant that the response could not, for example, be confided to the United Nations, where the Soviet delegate would have ample opportunity to stall action until the nuclear weapons were in place and on target. It meant that we could not even risk the delay involved in consulting our allies. It meant that the total responsibility had to fall on the United States and its President.

On the first Tuesday morning the choice for a moment seemed to lie between an air strike or acquiescence—and the President had made it clear that acquiescence was impossible. Listening to the discussion, the Attorney General scribbled a wry note: "I now know how Tojo felt when he was planning Pearl Harbor." Then he said aloud that the group needed more alternatives: surely there was some course in between bombing and doing nothing: suppose, for example, we were to bring countervailing pressure by placing nuclear missiles in Berlin? The talk continued, and finally the group dispersed for further reflection.

The next step was military preparation for Caribbean contingencies. A Navy-Marine amphibious exercise in the area, long scheduled for this week, provided a convenient cover for the build-up of an amphibious task force, soon including 40,000 Marines;

there were 5000 more in Guantanamo. The Army's 82nd and 101st Airborne Divisions were made ready for immediate deployment; altogether the Army soon gathered more than 100,000 troops in Florida. SAC bombers left Florida airfields to make room for tactical fighter aircraft flown in from bases all over the country. Air defense facilities were stripped from places outside the range of the Cuban missiles and re-installed in the Southeast. As the days went by, 14,000 reservists were recalled to fly transport planes in the eventuality of airborne operations.

In the meantime, the Pentagon undertook a technical analysis of the requirements for a successful strike. The conclusion, as it evolved during the week, was that a "surgical" strike confined to the nuclear missile bases alone would leave the airports and IL-28s untouched; moreover, we could not be sure in advance that we had identified or could destroy all the missile sites. A limited strike therefore might expose the United States to nuclear retaliation. Military prudence called for a much larger strike to eliminate all sources of danger; this would require perhaps 500 sorties. Anything less, the military urged, would destroy our credibility before the world and leave our own nation in intolerable peril. Moreover, this was a heaven-sent opportunity to get rid of the Castro regime forever and re-establish the security of the hemisphere.

It was a strong argument, urged by strong men. But there were arguments on the other side. The Soviet experts pointed out that even a limited strike would kill the Russians manning the missile sites and might well provoke the Soviet Union into drastic and unpredictable response, perhaps nuclear war. The Latin American experts added that a massive strike would kill thousands of innocent Cubans and damage the

United States permanently in the hemisphere. The Europeanists said the world would regard a surprise attack as an excessive response. Even if it did not produce Soviet retaliation against the United States, it would invite the Russians to move against Berlin in circumstances where the blame would fall, not on them, but on us. It would thereby give Moscow a chance to shift the venue to a place where the stake was greater than Cuba and our position weaker. In the Caribbean, we had overwhelming superiority in conventional military force; the only recourse for the Soviet Union there would be to threaten the world with nuclear war. But in Berlin, where the Russians had overwhelming conventional superiority, it was the United States which would have to flourish nuclear bombs.

All these considerations encouraged the search for alternatives. When the Executive Committee met on Wednesday, Secretary McNamara advanced an idea which had been briefly mentioned the day before and from which he did not thereafter deviate—the conception of a naval blockade designed to stop the further entry of offensive weapons into Cuba and hopefully to force the removal of the missiles already there. Here was a middle course between inaction and battle, a course which exploited our superiority in local conventional power and would permit subsequent movement either toward war or toward peace.

As the discussion proceeded through Thursday, the supporters of the air strike marshaled their arguments against the blockade. They said that it would not neutralize the weapons already within Cuba, that it could not possibly bring enough pressure on Khrushchev to remove those weapons, that it would permit work to go ahead on the bases and that it would mean another Munich. The act of stopping and

searching ships would engage us with Russians instead of Cubans. The obvious retort to our blockade of Cuba would be a Soviet blockade of Berlin. Despite such arguments, however, the majority of the Executive Committee by the end of the day was tending toward a blockade.

That afternoon, in the interests of normality, the President received the Soviet Foreign Minister Andrei Gromyko. It was one of the more extraordinary moments of an extraordinary week. Kennedy knew that there were Soviet nuclear missiles in Cuba. Gromyko unquestionably knew this too, but did not know that Kennedy knew it. His emphasis was rather grimly on Berlin, almost as if to prepare the ground for demands later in the autumn. When the talk turned to Cuba, Gromyko heavily stressed the Cuban fears of an American invasion and said with due solemnity that the Soviet aid had "solely the purpose of contributing to the defense capabilities of Cuba"; "if it were otherwise," the Russian continued, "the Soviet Government would never become involved in rendering such assistance." To dispel any illusion about possible American reactions, the President read the Foreign Minister the key sentences from his statement of September 13. He went no further because he did not wish to indicate his knowledge until he had decided on his course.

In the evening the President met with the Executive Committee. Listening again to the alternatives over which he had been brooding all week, he said crisply, "Whatever you fellows are recommending today you will be sorry about a week from now." He was evidently attracted by the idea of the blockade. It avoided war, preserved flexibility and offered Khrushchev time to reconsider his actions. It could be carried out within the framework of the Organization of

American States and the Rio Treaty. Since it could be extended to non-military items as occasion required, it could become an instrument of steadily intensifying pressure. It would avoid the shock effect of a surprise attack, which would hurt us politically through the world and might provoke Moscow to an insensate response against Berlin or the United States itself. If it worked, the Russians could retreat with dignity. If it did not work, the Americans retained the option of military action. In short, the blockade, by enabling us to proceed one step at a time, gave us control over the future. Kennedy accordingly directed that preparations be made to put the weapons blockade into effect on Monday morning.

The next day the President, keeping to his schedule, left Washington for a weekend of political barnstorming in Ohio and Illinois. In Springfield, Illinois, after a speech at the State Fairgrounds, he paused to lay flowers on Lincoln's tomb.

4. THE DECISION

Kennedy left behind a curiously restless group of advisers. This became evident when they met at the State Department at eleven on Friday morning. Over Ted Sorensen's protest that a decision had been reached the night before and should not be reopened now, several began to re-argue the inadequacy of the blockade. Someone said: Why not confront the world with a *fait accompli* by taking out the bases in a clean and swift operation? It was a test of wills, another said, and the sooner there was a showdown, the better. Someone else said that it was now or never; we must hit the bases before they became operational. If we took a decision that morning, the planes could strike on Sunday. But, if we committed ourselves to a blockade, it would be hard, if not impossible, to move on thereafter to military action.

Secretary McNamara, however, firmly reaffirmed his opposition to a strike and his support for the blockade. Then Robert Kennedy, speaking with quiet intensity, said that he did not believe that, with all the memory of Pearl Harbor and all the responsibility we would have to bear in the world afterward, the President of the United States could possibly order such an operation. For 175 years we had not been that kind of country. Sunday-morning surprise blows on small nations were not in our tradition. Thousands of Cubans would be killed without warning, and hundreds of Russians too. We were fighting for something more than survival, and a sneak attack would constitute a betrayal of our heritage and our ideals. The blockade, the Attorney General concluded, would demonstrate the seriousness of our determination to get the missiles out of Cuba and at the same time allow Moscow time and room to pull back from its position of peril. It was now proposed that the committee break up into working groups to write up the alternative courses for the President—one to analyze the quarantine policy, the other to analyze the strike. Then everyone dispersed to meet again at four o'clock for a discussion of the competing scenarios.[1]

[1] The Secretary of State took little part in these discussions. John M. Hightower, who covers the State Department for the Associated Press, wrote on August 22, 1965: "Criticism over his role in the missile crisis angered Rusk to the point that he heatedly defended it in talks with newsmen on one or two occasions. He said that the responsibility of the Secretary of State was to advise the President and he did not think he should commit himself before all the facts were in. Therefore he withdrew himself from the argument for several days though Under Secretary of State George Ball, instructed by Rusk to take a free hand, presented the State Department viewpoint."

At the second meeting the balance of opinion clearly swung back to the blockade (though, since a blockade was technically an act of war, it was thought better to refer to it as a quarantine). In retrospect most participants regarded Robert Kennedy's speech as the turning point. The case was strengthened too when the military representatives conceded that a quarantine now would not exclude a strike later. There was brief discussion of a *démarche* to Castro, but it was decided to concentrate on Khrushchev. Then they turned to the problem of the missiles already in Cuba. Someone observed that the United States would have to pay a price to get them out; perhaps we should throw in our now obsolescent and vulnerable Jupiter missile bases in Italy and Turkey, whose removal the Joint Congressional Committee on Atomic Energy as well as the Secretary of Defense had recommended in 1961. After a couple of hours, Adlai Stevenson, who had had to miss the day's meetings because of UN commitments, arrived from New York. He expressed his preference for the quarantine over the strike but wondered whether it might not be better to try the diplomatic route also. We must, he said, start thinking about our negotiating position; for example, a settlement might include the neutralization of Cuba under international guarantees and UN inspection; demilitarization would, of course, include our own base at Guantanamo as well as the Soviet installations. The integrity of Cuba should be guaranteed. He also echoed the suggestion that we might want to consider giving up the Italian and Turkish bases now, since we were planning to do so eventually.

The President, still campaigning, received reports from his brother in Washington. The schedule now called for a speech to the nation on Sunday night.

By Saturday morning, however, it was evident that preparations would not be complete in time, so it was decided to hold things for another twenty-four hours. Meanwhile, the President, pleading a cold, canceled the rest of his political trip and returned to Washington. Before leaving Chicago, he called Jacqueline and suggested that she and the children come back from Glen Ora, where they had gone for the weekend.

That afternoon he presided over the Executive Committee and its final debate. McNamara impressively presented the case for the blockade. The military, with some civilian support, argued for the strike. Stevenson spoke with force about the importance of a political program, the President agreeing in principle but disagreeing with his specific proposals. A straw vote indicated eleven for the quarantine, six for the strike. The President observed that everyone should hope his plan was not adopted; there just was no clearcut answer. When someone proposed that each participant write down his recommendation, Kennedy said he did not want people, if things went wrong, claiming that their plans would have worked. Then he issued orders to get everything ready for the quarantine. On Sunday morning a final conference with the military leaders satisfied him that the strike would be a mistake. His course was now firmly set

5. THE CRISIS

I knew nothing about any of this until late Friday, October 19, when Adlai Stevenson phoned me, saying casually that he was in Washington and wondered when we could get together. He was staying at the house of his friend Dr. Paul Magnuson across the street from my own house in Georgetown, and we agreed to ride down to the State Department together the next day. When we met after breakfast on Saturday morning, he beckoned me into the Magnuson house. "I don't want to talk in front of the chauffeur," he said; and then in a moment, "Do you know what the secret discussions this week have been about?" I said I knew of no discussions; the President was out campaigning; I had presumed that everything was fine. Adlai, observing gravely that there was trouble and he had the President's permission to tell me about it, described the seesaw during the week between the diplomatic and military solutions. The quarantine, he now felt, was sure to win. He would have to make a speech early in the week at the Security Council, and he wanted me to help on it. He outlined the argument and, with due discretion, I set to work.

The secret had been superbly kept. But later in the day, when the President returned from the campaign and Rusk canceled a speech that night, a sense of premonitory excitement began to engulf Washington. Already those whose business it was to sniff things out were on the track. In the British Embassy, where a delegation of intelligence officers had come to Washington for a long-scheduled conference with the CIA, suspicions had been aroused early in the week when the meetings drew a diminishing American representation or were called off altogether. By process of elimination the 007s decided on Friday that it must be Cuba. The *New York Times*, noting the troop movements and other unusual activities, also deduced Cuba by the weekend and even speculated about nuclear missiles. James Reston wrote the story and checked it with the White House. The President himself called Orville Dryfoos, the publisher of the *Times*, to say that publication might confront him with a Moscow ultimatum before he had the chance to put his own plans into

effect; once again, the *Times* killed a story about Cuba. By Saturday night the town was alive with speculation and anticipation. A good deal of the government found itself late that evening at a dance given by the James Rowes. Here the gap between the witting and the unwitting could almost be detected by facial expressions—on the one hand, anxiety tinged with self-satisfaction; on the other, irritation and frustration. Henry Brandon, the Washington correspondent of the London *Sunday Times*, who had just returned from a trip to Cuba, began to wonder when a succession of top officials asked him elaborately off-hand questions about the mood in Havana.

On Sunday Stevenson, contemplating the problems of gathering UN backing for the quarantine, wrote down his thoughts about our UN strategy. He saw no hope of mustering enough votes in the UN to authorize action against Cuba in advance; but the OAS offered an opportunity for multilateral support, and OAS approval could provide some protection in law and a great deal in public opinion. As for the UN, he said, we must seize the initiative, bringing our case to the Security Council at the same time we imposed the quarantine. In order to avert resolutions against the quarantine, he continued, we should be ready to propose a political path out of the military crisis. His negotiating program, following his remarks to the Executive Committee, centered on the removal of Soviet military equipment and personnel—i.e., missiles, installations and the several thousand Russian specialists—under UN observation and the introduction of UN influence into Cuba in the hope of ending communist domination of the Cuban government. He would throw a non-invasion guarantee and Guantanamo into the bargain to evidence our restraint and good faith. Exercising the

prerogative freely employed that week by nearly all his colleagues, he now wrote that Turkey and Italy should not be included; this would only divert attention from the Cuban threat to the general issue of foreign bases. That problem might later be considered apart from Cuba in the context of general disarmament.

The President, however, rightly regarded any political program as premature. He wanted to concentrate on a single issue—the enormity of the introduction of the missiles and the absolute necessity for their removal. Stevenson's negotiating program was accordingly rejected. Stevenson, when I saw him that week-end, took this realistically; he felt he had done his job as the custodian of our UN interests in making the recommendation, and the decision was the President's. However, some of his colleagues on the Executive Committee felt strongly that the thought of negotiations at this point would be taken as an admission of the moral weakness of our case and the military weakness of our posture. They worried considerably over the weekend (and some of them vocally thereafter) whether, denied his political program, Stevenson would make the American argument with sufficient force in the UN debate.

I spent all day Sunday till well after midnight working at the State Department with Harlan Cleveland, Joseph Sisco and Thomas Wilson on the UN speech. At ten o'clock on Monday morning the President called me in to instruct me to go to New York and assist Stevenson on the UN presentation. He was in a calm and reflective mood. It was strange, he said, how no one in the intelligence community had anticipated the Soviet attempt to transform Cuba into a nuclear base; everyone had assumed that the Russians would not be so stupid as to offer us this pretext for intervention. I asked why

Adlai Stevenson arriving at UN during missile crisis, October 26, 1962. (Wide World Photos)

he thought Khrushchev had done such an amazing thing. He said that, first, it might draw Russia and China closer together, or at least strengthen the Soviet position in the communist world, by showing that Moscow was capable of bold action in support of a communist revolution; second, that it would radically redefine the setting in which the Berlin problem could be reopened after the election; third, that it would deal the United States a tremendous political blow. When I remarked that the Russians must have supposed we would not respond, Kennedy said, "They thought they had us either way. If we did nothing, we would be dead. If we reacted, they hoped to put us in an exposed position, whether with regard to Berlin or Turkey or the UN."

I met with him again at eleven to go over the draft of the UN speech with Rusk, Robert Kennedy and others. The President suggested a few omissions, including a passage threatening an American strike if the Soviet build-up in Cuba continued; he preferred to leave that to Moscow's imagination. The Attorney General drew me aside to say,

"We're counting on you to watch things in New York. . . . We will have to make a deal at the end, but we must stand absolutely firm now. Concessions must come at the end of negotiation, not at the beginning." Then, clutching the speech, I caught the first plane to New York.

In Washington everything awaited the President's television broadcast that night to the nation. Sorenson had been laboring over the draft since Friday. Kennedy himself was never more composed. At four o'clock he had an appointment with Prime Minister Milton Obote of Uganda. Wholly at ease, he talked for forty-five minutes about the problems of Africa and Uganda as if he had nothing on his mind and all the time in the world. Angier Biddle Duke of the State Department remarked to Obote on their way back to Blair House that a crisis of some sort was imminent; the Ugandan was incredulous and, when he heard Kennedy's speech that evening, forever impressed.

At five o'clock Kennedy saw the congressional leaders, many of whom had flown in from their home states in Air Force planes.

He showed them the U-2 photographs and told them what he proposed to do. Senator Russell of Georgia disagreed; the quarantine, he said, would be too slow and too risky—the only solution was invasion. To the President's surprise, Fulbright, who had opposed invasion so eloquently eighteen months before, now supported Russell. The President listened courteously but was in no way shaken in his decision. (Kennedy told me later, "The trouble is that, when you get a group of senators together, they are always dominated by the man who takes the boldest and strongest line. That is what happened the other day. After Russell spoke, no one wanted to take issue with him. When you can talk to them individually, they are reasonable.")

Then at seven o'clock the speech: his expression grave, his voice firm and calm, the evidence set forth without emotion, the conclusion unequivocal—"The purpose of these bases can be none other than to provide a nuclear strike capability against the Western Hemisphere." He recited the Soviet assurances, now revealed as "deliberate deception," and called the Soviet action "a deliberately provocative and unjustified change in the status quo which cannot be accepted by this country, if our courage and our commitments are ever to be trusted again by either friend or foe." Our "unswerving objective," he continued, was to end this nuclear threat to the Americans. He then laid out what he called with emphasis his *initial* steps: a quarantine on all offensive military equipment under shipment to Cuba; an intensified surveillance of Cuba itself; a declaration that any missile launched from Cuba would be regarded as an attack by the Soviet Union on the United States, requiring full retaliatory response upon the Soviet Union; an immediate convening of the Organization of American States to consider the threat to hemisphere security; an emergency meeting of the UN Security Council to consider the threat to world peace; and an appeal to Chairman Khrushchev "to abandon this course of world domination, and to join in an historic effort to end the perilous arms race and to transform the history of man."

He concluded with quiet solemnity. "My fellow citizens: let no one doubt that this is a difficult and dangerous effort. . . . No one can foresee precisely what course it will take or what costs or casualties will be incurred. . . . But the greatest danger of all would be to do nothing. . . . Our goal is not the victory of might, but the vindication of right— not peace at the expense of freedom, but both peace *and* freedom, here in this hemisphere, and, we hope, around the world. God willing, that goal will be achieved."

After the broadcast the President returned to the Mansion, sought out Caroline and told her stories until it was time for dinner. He dined alone with Jacqueline.

6. THE REACTION

We listened to the speech clustered around a television set in Stevenson's office in New York. I had found Adlai unperturbed in the midst of pandemonium. The Mission was a frenzy of activity in preparation for the Security Council. The UN had never seemed so much like a permanent political convention: so many people to be considered and cajoled, so many issues going at

once, such an inherent unpredictability about the parliamentary sequence. From the moment of the President's statement, Stevenson had to talk so much to UN delegates from other nations that he had little time left for his own speeches and strategy. Through Monday evening and Tuesday morning he snatched moments to revise and edit his remarks for the Security Council. It was reminiscent of his presidential campaigns: the last part of his address was still in the typewriter at the Mission on Tuesday afternoon when he had already begun to speak across the street at the UN.

The speech began at four o'clock. The OAS had been meeting since nine that morning. Edwin Martin had done a splendid job briefing the OAS ambassadors the night before, and Secretary Rusk, invoking the security resolution of Punta del Este, was now offering a resolution authorizing the use of force, individually or collectively, to carry out the quarantine. No one could doubt the OAS sentiment, but a number of ambassadors had not yet received instructions from their governments. As a result, the resolution establishing the legal basis for United States action was not passed until Stevenson was well into his speech.[2]

Martin, by prior arrangement, notified Harlan Cleveland the moment the OAS acted, and Cleveland instantly called Sisco in New York. Watching Stevenson on television, Cleveland could see Sisco leave the chamber to take the call, then in a moment return and place the text of the resolution on the desk in front of Stevenson. Stevenson, absorbed in his speech, talked on, apparently unaware of the sheet of paper before him. At this moment Kennedy, with characteristic at-

[2] It was passed unanimously. Uruguay, still awaiting instructions, abstained on Tuesday but changed its vote to affirmative on Wednesday.

tention to detail, called Cleveland and asked whether Stevenson knew about the OAS action. Cleveland replied that he had sent a message but feared that Adlai had not seen it. Just then on the screen Stevenson reached for the paper. Kennedy, who was also watching television, said, "I guess he has it now."

In New York Stevenson, who had been speaking with extraordinary eloquence to a hushed chamber, now read the OAS resolution. In another moment he concluded: "Since the end of the Second World War, there has been no threat to the vision of peace so profound, no challenge to the world of the Charter so fateful. The hopes of mankind are concentrated in this room. . . . Let [this day] be remembered, not as the day when the world came to the edge of nuclear war, but as the day when men resolved to let nothing thereafter stop them in their quest for peace." The President immediately dictated a telegram:

DEAR ADLAI: I WATCHED YOUR SPEECH THIS AFTERNOON WITH GREAT SATISFACTION. IT HAS GIVEN OUR CAUSE A GREAT START. . . . THE UNITED STATES IS FORTUNATE TO HAVE YOUR ADVOCACY. YOU HAVE MY WARM AND PERSONAL THANKS.

And now the tension was rising. In Cuba workmen were laboring day and night to complete the bases. Forty-two medium-range nuclear missiles were being unpacked and prepared for launching pads with desperate speed. IL-28 aircraft were being assembled. On the Atlantic at least seventy-five Soviet merchant ships, some no doubt loaded with intermediate-range missiles, were steaming toward Cuba, their courses thus far unaltered after the President's speech. Ninety ships of the American fleet, backed up by sixty-eight aircraft squadrons and eight aircraft carriers, were moving into position to intercept and search the onrushing ships. In Florida and neighboring states the largest United States invasion force since the Second World War was gathering. In Moscow, the Soviet government in a long and angry statement insisted that the weapons in Cuba were defensive, ignored the charges of nuclear missiles and savagely denounced the American quarantine.

The United Nations was only the first step in gaining world understanding of the American position. Africa now assumed vital strategic importance because Soviet flights to Cuba would have to refuel at African airports. Both Sékou Touré in Guinea and Ben Bella in Algeria sent Kennedy their assurances that they would deny Russian aircraft transit rights. (Touré later added that the problem must be kept in a Soviet-American context; if it became a Cuban-American problem, we would lose support in the uncommitted world.) Most African states, moved no doubt by their faith in the American President, indicated private sympathy.

In Western Europe support was general, though there were waverings in Britain and Italy. In Paris General de Gaulle received Dean Acheson, the President's special emissary, and, without waiting to see the aerial photographs Acheson had brought along, said, "If there is a war, I will be with you. But there will be no war." De Gaulle went on to wonder whether the quarantine would be enough, and so did Adenauer, but both strongly backed the American position. . . .

On Tuesday night Kennedy dined quietly at the White House with English friends. Cuba was hardly mentioned at the table; but after dinner he beckoned David Ormsby Gore out into the long central hall, where they quietly talked while the gaiety continued in the dining room. The British Ambassador, mentioning the dubious reaction in his own country, suggested the need for evidence: could not the aerial photographs be released? The President sent for a file, and together they went through them picking out the ones that might have the greatest impact on skeptics. In a while Robert Kennedy walked in, bleak, tired and disheveled. He had just been to see Ambassador Dobrynin in an effort to find out whether the Soviet ships had instructions to turn back if challenged on the high seas. The Soviet Ambassador, the Attorney General said, seemed very shaken, out of the picture and unaware of any instructions. This meant that the imposition of the quarantine the next day might well bring a clash.

The three old friends talked on. Ormsby Gore recalled a conversation with Defense Department officials who had declared it important to stop the Soviet ships as far out of the reach of the jets in Cuba as possible. The British Ambassador now suggested that Khrushchev had hard decisions to make and that every additional hour might make it easier for him to climb down gracefully; why not, therefore, make the interceptions much closer to Cuba and thereby give the Russians a little more time? If Cuban aircraft tried to interfere, they could be shot down. Kennedy, agreeing immediately, called McNamara and, over emotional Navy protests, issued the appropriate instruction. This decision was of vital importance in postponing the moment of irreversible action. They soon parted, looking forward with concern to the crisis of the morrow.

And so around the world emotions rose—fear, doubt, incertitude, apprehension. In the White House the President went coolly about his affairs, watching the charts with the Soviet ships steadily advancing toward Cuba, scrutinizing every item of intelligence for indications of Soviet purpose, reviewing the deployment of American forces. At one point the Air Force produced a photograph of planes lined wingtip to wingtip on a Cuban airfield, arguing that only a few bombs could wipe out the enemy air power. The President asked the Air Force to run similar reconnaissance over our own fields; to the Pentagon's chagrin, the photographs showed American planes also lined up row by row. In this manner he preserved a taut personal control over every aspect of the situation; the Bay of Pigs had not been in vain. He said to someone, "I guess this is the week I earn my salary."

He never had a more sober sense of his responsibility. It was a strange week; the flow of decision was continuous; there was no day and no night. In the intervals between meetings he sought out his wife and children as if the imminence of catastrophe had turned his mind more than ever to his family and, through them, to children everywhere in the world. This was the cruel question—the young people who, if things went wrong, would never have the chance to learn, to love, to fulfill themselves and serve their countries. One noon, swimming in the pool, he said to David Powers, "If it weren't for these people that haven't lived yet, it would be easy to make decisions of this sort."

In Buenos Aires Billy Graham preached to 10,000 people on "The End of the World."

7. WAITING ON KHRUSHCHEV

Within the Kremlin, so far as one could tell, there was confusion. The Russians had obviously anticipated neither the quick discovery of the bases nor the quick imposition of the quarantine. Their diplomats across the world were displaying all the symptoms of improvisation, as if they had been told nothing of the placement of the missiles and had received no instructions what to say about them. Ambassador Anatoly Dobrynin himself gave every indication of ignorance and confusion. As late as Wednesday a message to Robert Kennedy from Mikoyan repeated that Cuba was receiving no weapons capable of reaching the United States. Georgi Bolshakov, who transmitted the message and who had seemed to us all an honest fellow, assured the Attorney General that he believed this himself.

In New York on Wednesday Stevenson was continuing the battle for the American resolution in the United Nations. John J. McCloy, whom the President had summoned from a business trip to Germany to give the UN presentation a bipartisan flavor, was adding his weight to our councils. Then U Thant made an unexpected intervention, proposing that the Soviet Union suspend its arms shipments and the United States its quarantine to allow an interlude for negotiations. Khrushchev accepted this thought at once and with evident pleasure; but, from our viewpoint, it equated aggression and response, said nothing about the missiles already in Cuba, permitted work to go forward on the sites and contained no provisions for verification. Still, while New York and Washington agreed in rejecting U Thant's proposal, the manner of the rejection caused debate. Some in Washington appeared to fear any response which would 'entrap' us in a negotiating process; it seemed to us in New York that they must be bent to clear the road for an air strike and an invasion. Stevenson and McCloy strongly recommended a response to U Thant which would keep the diplomatic option alive.

On Wednesday night, as we were pondering these matters at the U.S. Mission in New York, I received a telephone call from Averell Harriman. Speaking with unusual urgency, he said that Khrushchev was desperately sig-

naling a desire to cooperate in moving toward a peaceful solution. Harriman set forth the evidence: Khrushchev's suggestion of a summit meeting in his reply to Bertrand Russell; his well-publicized call on the American singer Jerome Hines the night before after a Moscow concert; his amiable if menacing talk with an American businessman, William Knox of Westinghouse International; the indications that afternoon that the nearest Soviet ships were slowing down and changing course. This was not the behavior of a man who wanted war, Harriman said; it was the behavior of a man who was begging our help to get off the hook. Khrushchev had sent up similar signals after the U-2 affair in 1960, Harriman continued, and Eisenhower had made the mistake of ignoring him; we must not repeat that error now. "If we do nothing but get tougher and tougher, we will force him into countermeasures. The first incident on the high seas will engage Soviet prestige and infinitely reduce the chance of a peaceful solution." The key to it all, he went on, lay in Khrushchev's two remarks during the recent visit of Robert Frost and Stewart Udall to the Soviet Union —his observation to Frost that the democracies were too liberal to fight[3] and his observation to Udall that the Soviet Union must be treated as an equal. "We must give him an out," Harriman said again. "If we do this shrewdly, we can downgrade the tough group in the Soviet Union which persuaded him to do this. But if we deny him an out, then we will escalate this business into a nuclear war."

These words from the most experienced of all American diplomats seemed utterly convincing to me. I asked him whether he had made these points at the

[3] Actually Khrushchev never made this remark; it was Frost's interpretation in a New York press conference.

State Department. He said, "They never ask my advice about anything outside the Far East. I haven't been in on this at all." Accordingly I sent Harriman's views along to the President. Kennedy called him the next morning, and I imagine that Harriman's counsel may have strengthened his own inclination to go further along the diplomatic road. At any rate, his reply to U Thant on Thursday, while stressing that the "threat was created by the secret introduction of offensive weapons into Cuba, and the answer lies in the removal of such weapons," authorized Stevenson to continue discussions on whether satisfactory arrangements could be assured to this end. This was a second vital decision.

In Washington they had meanwhile been seeking to provide for every contingency the quarantine might create. By involving us directly with the Russians, it contained a great variety of potential risks; and the Executive Committee undertook the most intensive consideration of all possible gradations and configurations: where, when and how to stop ships, how much force to use, when to board, whether to disable the propeller and tow the ship to port. Soon they ascertained that Soviet submarines were following the ships: as quickly as possible, we put a destroyer on the tail of every submarine. It was all an amazing naval deployment, conducted with skill and efficiency. Among the destroyers to take part, apparently in the natural line of duty, was the *Joseph P. Kennedy, Jr.*

As they plotted the courses and studied the charts, Thursday seemed to confirm the encouraging signs of Wednesday and to justify Ormsby Gore's suggestion of Tuesday night that the line of interception be drawn closer to Cuba. Half the Soviet ships, the Executive Committee noted with a flood of relief, had put about and were heading home. Others were evidently waiting for further orders. Only one had entered the quarantine zone—a tanker, obviously not carrying nuclear weapons. In Washington some felt that we must react to this challenge with full military vigor; but the President decided to give Khrushchev more time and said that the tanker, once it had identified itself and thereby established the quarantine, should be permitted to proceed without boarding and search—a third vital decision.

There were other portents, and to them our intelligence community turned like Roman haruspices to the entrails of a sacrificial victim. For the first time all that long week Soviet diplomatic behavior across the world was beginning to conform to a pattern; this indicated that Moscow had at last sent out instructions. For one thing—and very odd in view of our own and the British apprehension about Soviet reprisals in Berlin—the Russians appeared to be engaged in a studied effort to dissociate Berlin from Cuba. Gromyko, who spoke at Humboldt University in East Berlin on Tuesday, instead of using the occasion for implied threats, did not even mention Cuba. By Friday V. A. Zorin, the Soviet ambassador to the United Nations, was even assuring other UN diplomats that his government would not fall into the American "trap" of retaliatory action in Berlin.

But the essence of the emerging pattern seemed to be concern for a peaceful settlement. This was what the Soviet ambassadors in London and Bonn were saying to the British and West German governments. Nor was Moscow confining its efforts to orthodox channels. In London on Wednesday, for example, Captain Ivanov of the Soviet Embassy asked a demimondain doctor named Stephen Ward to use his influence to persuade the British government to invite Khrushchev and Kennedy to a summit meeting. Ward thereupon approached Lord Arran, a peer who wrote a column in the *Evening News,* and even sent a letter to Harold Wilson, whom he did not know. Thwarted in these efforts to solve the world's problems, he soon returned to the more relaxed company of Christine Keeler.

But despite these gestures the situation was still loaded with danger. Work continued on the sites; unless this was stopped, the missiles would soon be on their launching pads. Nor had the Soviet Union yet admitted the presence of nuclear missiles in Cuba at all. On Thursday evening at the UN Stevenson returned to the debate in the Security Council. He crisply dismissed the communist argument that the United States had created the threat to the peace: "This is the first time that I have ever heard it said that the crime is not the burglary, but the discovery of the burglar." As for those who thought the quarantine too extreme a remedy: "Were we to do nothing until the knife was sharpened? Were we to stand idly by until it was at our throats? . . . The course we have chosen seems to me perfectly graduated to meet the character of the threat."

Zorin made a cocky but evasive reply. Now Stevenson took the floor again. Ironically regretting that he lacked his opponent's "talent for obfuscation, for distortion, for confusing language and for double-talk," saying sternly "those weapons must be taken out of Cuba," he turned on the Russian with magnificent scorn:

Do you, Ambassador Zorin, deny that the USSR has placed and is placing medium and intermediate-range missiles and sites in Cuba? Yes or no? Don't wait for the translation. Yes or no?

Zorin muttered something about not being in an American courtroom. Stevenson, cold and controlled:

You are in the courtroom of world opinion. You have denied they exist, and I want to know if I understood you correctly. I am prepared to wait for my answer until hell freezes over. And I am also prepared to present the evidence in this room—now!

It was a moment of tremendous excitement. At Stevenson's order, aerial photographs were wheeled on easels into the council chamber, showing the transformation of San Cristóbal from a peaceful country spot into a grim nuclear installation. Other pictures added further evidence. Zorin wanly denied the authenticity of the display. Stevenson wondered savagely why the Soviet Union did not test its denial by permitting a United Nations team to visit the sites.

Then, in a moment, Stevenson concluded: "We know the facts and so do you, sir, and we are ready to talk about them. Our job here is not to score debating points. Our job, Mr. Zorin, is to save the peace. And if you are ready to try, we are."

The Stevenson speech dealt a final blow to the Soviet case before world opinion.

8. THE LETTERS

But on Friday work still continued on the sites. In Florida the American army prepared for invasion. In Washington the pressure to attack mounted as each passing moment brought the installations closer to operation. And in Moscow there must have been deep anxiety and bitter debate.

Khrushchev had now evidently abandoned the effort to bring in more nuclear weapons. But some of the men around him—perhaps the Soviet military—were apparently determined to make the missiles already there operational as speedily as possible. Indeed, this group may have gone along with the pacific gestures of Wednesday and Thursday precisely to gain time to complete the sites. In any case, once the missiles were on launching pads, Moscow might be able to drive a better bargain.

Khrushchev himself, however, seems to have reached a different position. He knew by now that his essential gamble had failed. Whatever he had once supposed, the Americans were ready to fight. His own options were narrowing before his eyes. If he were to strike at Berlin, he would only expose the Soviet Union to nuclear attack. If he did not compose matters quickly in the Caribbean, then the great army, massing so visibly in Florida, would descend on Cuba: "on the morning of [Saturday] October 27," as he told the Supreme Soviet in December, "we received information that the invasion would be carried out in the next two or three days." If an invasion began, Khrushchev either would have to use the rockets he liked to boast about so jovially or else desert the only communist state in the Americas and condemn himself as a *fainéant* before the international communist movement. It was by now beyond the realm of tactical maneuver: all roads led to the abyss. The Soviet Chairman and the American President were the two men in the world with ultimate responsibility for nuclear war. Like Kennedy, Khrushchev had peered into the abyss before. "Immediate action," as he later told the Supreme Soviet, "was needed to prevent an invasion of Cuba and to preserve peace."

At one-thirty on Friday John Scali, the State Department correspondent for the American Broadcasting Company, received a call from Aleksander Fomin, a counselor at the Soviet Embassy, insisting on an immediate meeting. Scali, who had lunched occasionally with Fomin in the past, joined him at once at the Occidental Restaurant. The usually phlegmatic Russian, now haggard and alarmed, said, "War seems about to break out. Something must be done to save the situation." Scali replied that they should have thought of that before they put the missiles in Cuba. The Russian sat in silence for a moment. Then he said. "There might be a way out. What would you think of a proposition whereby we would promise to remove our missiles under United Nations inspection, where Mr. Khrushchev would promise never to introduce such offensive weapons into Cuba again? Would the President of the United States be willing to promise publicly not to invade Cuba?" When Scali said he did not know, Fomin begged him to find out immediately from his State Department friends. Then, reaching for a pencil, he wrote down his home telephone number: "If I'm not at the Embassy, call me here. This is of vital importance."

Scali carried the proposal to Roger Hilsman at State, and Hilsman carried it to Rusk. After discussion with the Executive Committee, Rusk asked Scali to tell the Russian that we saw "real possibilities" for a negotiation but they must understand that time was short—no more than forty-eight hours. At seven-thirty Friday evening Scali passed this word along. They met this time in the coffee shop of the Statler Hilton. Fomin, once he had satisfied himself about the authenticity of Scali's message and after a brief attempt to introduce the idea of UN inspection of Florida as well as Cuba, rose and, in his haste to get the word back, tossed down a five-dollar bill for a thirty-cent check and speeded off without waiting for the change.

Two hours later a long letter from Khrushchev to the President began to come in by cable. The Soviet leader started by insisting that the weapons shipments were complete and that their purpose was defensive. Then he declared his profound longing for peace; let us, he said with evident emotion, not permit this situation to get out of hand. The enforcement of the quarantine would only drive the Soviet Union to take necessary measures of its own. But if the United States would give assurances that it would not invade Cuba nor permit others to do so and if it would recall its fleet from the quarantine, this would immediately change everything. Then the necessity for a Soviet presence in Cuba would disappear. This crisis, Khrushchev said, was like a rope with a knot in the middle: the more each side pulled, the more the knot would tighten, until finally it could be severed only by a sword. But if each side slackened the rope, the knot could be untied.

The letter was not, as subsequently described, hysterical. Though it pulsated with a passion to avoid nuclear war and gave the impression of having been written in deep emotion, why not? In general, it displayed an entirely rational understanding of the implications of the crisis. Together with the Scali proposal, it promised light at the end of the cave. And in New York on Friday we heard that Zorin had advanced the same proposal to U Thant, and that the Cubans at the UN were beginning to hint to unaligned delegates that the bases might be dismantled and removed if the United States would guarantee the territorial integrity of Cuba. The President probably had his first good night's sleep for ten days; certainly the rest of us did.

But when the Executive Committee assembled on Saturday morning, prospects suddenly darkened. The Moscow radio began to broadcast a new Khrushchev letter containing, to everyone's consternation, an entirely different proposition from the one transmitted through Scali and embodied in Khrushchev's letter of the night before. The Soviet Union now said it would remove its missiles from Cuba and offer a non-aggression pledge to Turkey if the United States would remove its missiles from Turkey and offer a non-aggression pledge to Cuba. The notion of trading the Cuban and Turkish bases had been much discussed in England; Walter Lippmann and others had urged it in the United States. But Kennedy regarded the idea as unacceptable, and the swap was promptly rejected. This proposal was perplexing enough; but, far more alarming, word soon came that a U-2 was missing over Cuba, presumably shot down by the Russians (piloted, indeed, by the brave South Carolinian, Major Rudolph Anderson, Jr., who had first photographed the installations on October 14). American planes had thus far flown over the missile sites without interference. The Soviet action now, some felt, could only mean one thing: that the confrontation was entering its military phase. The bases were becoming operational, and the Russians were evidently determined to use force to maintain them. We had no choice, it was argued, but a military response; and our tactical analysis had already shown that strikes at the bases would be little use without strikes at the airfields, and strikes at the airfields of little use without further supporting action, so, once the process began, it could hardly stop short of invasion.

The President declined to be stampeded. Obviously, if they shot down U-2s, we would have to react—but not necessarily at once. Again he insisted that the Russians be given time to consider what they were doing before action and counteraction became irrevocable. There remained the Khrushchev letters, and the Executive Committee turned to them again with bafflement and something close to despair. It was noted that Defense Minister Rodion Malinovsky had

mentioned Cuba and Turkey together as early as Tuesday, and that *Red Star*, the army paper, had coupled them again on Friday. Could the military have taken over in Moscow? Rusk called in Scali and asked him to find out anything he could from his Soviet contact. Scali, fearful that he had been used to deceive his own country, upbraided Fomin, accusing him of a double cross. The Russian said miserably that there must have been a cable delay, that the Embassy was waiting word from Khrushchev at any moment. Scali brought this report immediately to the President and the Executive Committee at the White House (where Pierre Salinger nearly had heart failure when, in the midst of the rigorous security precautions of the week, he suddenly saw the ABC reporter sitting at the door of the President's inner office).

In the meantime a new crisis: another U-2 on a routine air-sampling mission from Alaska to the North Pole had gone off course and was over the Soviet Union; it had already attracted the attention of Soviet fighters and was radioing Alaska for help. Would the Russians view this as a final reconnaissance in preparation for nuclear attack? What if they decided to strike first? Roger Hilsman brought the frightening news to the President. There was a moment of absolute grimness. Then Kennedy, with a brief laugh, said, "There is always some so-and-so who doesn't get the word." (The plane returned safely; but perhaps Khrushchev did interpret the flight exactly as Hilsman feared; perhaps this too, along with the invasion force massing in Florida and an unauthorized statement on Friday by the State Department press officer threatening "further action" if work continued on the bases, reinforced his determination to bring the crisis to an end.)

Later that afternoon the Executive Committee met again. Rob-

ert Kennedy now came up with a thought of breathtaking simplicity and ingenuity: why not ignore the second Khrushchev message and reply to the first? forget Saturday and concentrate on Friday? This suggestion may, indeed, have been more relevant than anyone could have known. For, as Henry Pachter has argued, the so-called second letter, from internal evidence, appears to have been initiated as the immediate follow-on of Khrushchev's reply to U Thant; it began with a reference to Kennedy's reply to U Thant on Thursday and took no note of events on Friday. Moreover, its institutional tone suggested that it was written in the Foreign Office. Might it not have been drafted in Moscow on Thursday and Friday with an eye to Saturday morning release in New York? Then the so-called first letter, which reflected the movement of events well beyond the U Thant proposal and which was clearly written by Khrushchev himself, may well have been composed late Friday night (Moscow time) and transmitted immediately to Kennedy while the "second" letter was deep in the bureaucratic pipelines. Knowing heads of state and foreign office bureaucracies, one could take anything as possible.

At any rate, on October 27 Kennedy now wrote Khrushchev, "I have read your letter of October 26th with great care and welcomed the statement of your desire to seek a prompt solution." As soon as work stopped on the missile bases and the offensive weapons were rendered inoperable under UN supervision, Kennedy continued, he would be ready to negotiate a settlement along the lines Khrushchev had proposed. Then, in a sentence profoundly expressive of his desire to retrieve something out of crisis, he added: "If your letter signifies that you are prepared to discuss a detente affecting NATO and the Warsaw Pact, we are quite prepared to consider with our allies any useful proposals."

And so the message shot inscrutably into the night. Robert Kennedy carried a copy that evening to the Soviet Ambassador, saying grimly that, unless we received assurances in twenty-four hours, the United States would take military action by Tuesday. No one knew which Khrushchev letter superseded the other; no one knew whether Khrushchev was even still in power. "We all agreed in the end," Robert Kennedy said afterward, "that if the Russians were ready to go to nuclear war over Cuba, they were ready to go to nuclear war, and that was that. So we might as well have the showdown then as six months later." Saturday night was almost the blackest of all. Unless Khrushchev came through in a few hours, the meeting of the Executive Committee on Sunday night might well face the most terrible decisions.

Sunday, October 28, was a shining autumn day. At nine in the morning Khrushchev's answer began to come in. By the fifth sentence it was clear that he had thrown in his hand. Work would stop on the sites; the arms "which you described as offensive" would be crated and returned to the Soviet Union; negotiations would start at the UN. Then, no doubt to placate Castro, Khrushchev asked the United States to discontinue flights over Cuba. (As for the errant U-2 which had strayed over Russia the day before, he warned that "an intruding American plane could be easily taken for a nuclear bomber, which might push us to a fateful step.") Looking ahead, he said, "We should like to continue the exchange of views on the prohibition of atomic and thermonuclear weapons, general disarmament, and other problems relating to the relaxation of international tension."

It was all over, and barely in time. If word had not come that Sunday, if work had continued on the bases, the United States would have had no real choice but to take action against Cuba the next week. No one could discern what lay darkly beyond an air strike or invasion, what measures and countermeasures, actions and reactions, might have driven the hapless world to the ghastly consummation. The President saw more penetratingly into the mists and terrors of the future than anyone else. A few weeks later he said, "If we had invaded Cuba . . . I am sure the Soviets would have acted. They would have to, just as we would have to. I think there are certain compulsions on any major power." The compulsions opened up the appalling world of inexorability. The trick was to cut the chain in time. When Kennedy received Khrushchev's reply that golden October morning, he showed profound relief. Later he said, "This is the night to go to the theater, like Abraham Lincoln."

NIKITA KHRUSHCHEV
Khrushchev Remembers: Cuba and the Missile Crisis

At the time Fidel Castro led his revolution to victory [in 1959] we had no idea what political course he would follow. For a long time we had no diplomatic relations with the new regime. However, our people who handled Latin American affairs did know some of the Cuban leaders. They knew Raul Castro in particular. We knew that Raul was a good Communist, but it appeared that he kept his true convictions hidden from his brother Fidel. Ché Guevara was a Communist too, and so were some of the others—or so we thought. We had nothing to go on but rumors.

We decided to send Mikoyan to America to establish unofficial contacts with the leaders of the American business world. We wanted to find out what the prospects were for developing trade with America. Anastas Ivanovich had been in the U.S. before the war and still had some of his old contacts. While Mikoyan was in the U.S., Fidel invited him to visit Cuba. Mikoyan traveled around Cuba, looked things over and talked with the people.

Shortly after Mikoyan's visit we established diplomatic relations. The Americans had cut off the Cubans' supply of oil and it was urgent that we organize an oil delivery to Cuba on a massive scale. That was easier said than done. Our efforts put a heavy burden on our own shipping system and forced us to order extra tankers from Italy. When Italy agreed to sell us the tankers, it caused a sharp conflict between Italy and America. The lesson was that if a capitalist country sees a chance to make some extra money, it couldn't care less about economic solidarity.

We sent a veteran diplomat to be our ambassador in Havana. We also had [Aleksandr] Alekseyev there, a journalist who was friendly with Fidel and even more so with Raul. It was lucky we had Alekseyev there because our ambassador turned out to be unsuited for service in a country just emerging from a revolution. When the situation heated up and shooting started, he demanded that the Cubans give him a special bodyguard. The Cuban leaders were astonished and irritated. Here they were offering the enemies of the revolution far more enticing targets and going around without any bodyguards at all themselves, and now this Communist aristocrat of ours starts demanding some sort of special protection! So we recalled him and made Alekseyev ambassador in his place. He turned out to be an excellent choice.

Castro was no longer sitting on the fence; he was beginning to behave like a full-fledged Communist, even though he still didn't call himself one. All the while the Americans had been watching Castro closely. At first they thought that the capitalist underpinnings of the Cuban economy would remain intact. So by the time Castro announced that he was going to put Cuba on the road to Socialism, the Americans had missed their chance to do anything by simply exerting influence. That left only one alternative—invasion!

The Cubans asked us for arms. We gave them tanks, artillery, antiaircraft guns and some fighter planes. The Cubans had always fought with light arms only—automatic rifles, grenades and pistols. But with the help of our instructors they learned quickly how to use modern weapons.

We first heard on the radio [April 1961] that a counter-revolutionary invasion had been launched against Cuba. We didn't even know who the invaders were: were they Cuban conspirators or Americans? However, we knew that the [Bay of Pigs] invasion had to have the backing of the Americans.

Fidel's forces swung into action and made short work of the invaders. The Americans had put too much faith in the conspirators. They had assumed that with American support behind the invasion, the Cubans would topple Castro by themselves.

We welcomed Castro's victory, but we were certain that the

Americans would not let Cuba alone. Given the continued threat of American interference in the Caribbean, what should our own policy be?

While I was on an official visit to Bulgaria one thought kept hammering away at my brain: what will happen if we lose Cuba? If Cuba fell, other Latin American countries would reject us, claiming that for all our might the Soviet Union hadn't been able to do anything for Cuba except make empty protests to the United Nations. We had to think up some way of confronting America with more than words. But what exactly? The logical answer was missiles.

It was during my visit to Bulgaria [in May 1962] that I had the idea of installing missiles with nuclear warheads in Cuba without letting the United States find out until it was too late to do anything about them. I knew that first we'd have to talk to Castro and explain our strategy to get the agreement of the Cuban government. My thinking went like this: if we installed the missiles secretly and then if the United States discovered the missiles were there, after they were fixed and ready to strike, the Americans would think twice before trying to liquidate our installations by military means. I knew that the United States could knock out some of our installations, but not all of them. If a quarter or even a tenth of our missiles survived—even if only one or two big ones were left— we could still hit New York, and an awful lot of people would be wiped out. I don't know how many; that's a matter for our scientists and military personnel to work out.

The main thing was that the installation of our missiles in Cuba would restrain the United States from precipitous military action. The Americans had surrounded our own country with military bases and threatened us with nuclear weapons, and now they would learn just what it feels like. It was high time America learned what it feels like to have her own land and her own people threatened. America has never had to fight a war on her own soil—at least not in the past 50 years. America sent troops abroad to fight in two World Wars—and made a fortune as a result. America has shed a few drops of her own blood while making billions.

All these thoughts kept churning in my head the whole time I was in Bulgaria. I didn't tell anyone what I was thinking. I kept my mental agony to myself. But all the while the idea of putting missiles in Cuba was ripening inside my mind. After I returned to Moscow we convened a meeting and I said I had some thoughts to air on the subject of Cuba. I presented my idea in the context of the counterrevolutionary invasion which Castro had just resisted. I said that it would be foolish to expect the inevitable second invasion to be as badly planned and executed as the first. I warned that Fidel would be crushed and said we were the only ones who could prevent such a disaster from occurring.

We decided to install intermediate-range missiles, launching equipment and Ilyushin-28 bombers in Cuba. Soon after we began shipping our missiles, the Americans became suspicious. It was not long before they concluded on the basis of reconnaissance photographs that we were installing missiles. The Americans became frightened, and we stepped up our shipments. We had delivered almost everything by the time the crisis reached the boiling point.

There are people who argue with the benefit of hindsight that antiaircraft missiles should have been installed before the ballistic missiles to close the air space over Cuba. This doesn't make sense. How many surface-to-air missiles can you fit on a tiny sausage-shaped island?

I want to make one thing absolutely clear: when we put our

Nikita Khrushchev and other Soviet leaders attend the opera during the Cuban missile crisis, October 28, 1962. *(Wide World Photos)*

ballistic missiles in Cuba, we had no desire to start a war. Our principal aim was to deter America from starting a war. Any idiot could have started a war between America and Cuba. Cuba was 11,000 kilometers away from us. Only a fool would think that we wanted to invade the American continent from Cuba. We wanted to keep the Americans from invading Cuba, and we wanted to make them think twice by confronting them with our missiles. This goal we achieved—but not without undergoing a period of perilous tension.

One day in October President Kennedy came out with a statement warning that the United States would take whatever measures were necessary to remove what he called the "threat" of Russian missiles in Cuba. The Americans began to make a belligerent show of strength, surrounding the island with their navy. Things started churning. The Americans were trying to frighten us, but they were no less scared than we were of atomic war. We had installed enough missiles already to destroy New York, Chicago and the other industrial cities, not to mention a little village like Washington. I don't think America had ever faced such a real threat of destruction as at that moment.

Meanwhile we went about our own business. We didn't let ourselves be intimidated. Our ships headed straight through the American navy, but the Americans didn't try to stop our ships or even check them. [After the U.S. proclaimed a naval blockade, some Russian ships did idle at sea to await developments.] We kept in mind that as long as the United States limited itself to threatening gestures, we could afford to pretend to ignore the harassment. We had the same rights as the Americans. Our conduct in the international arena was governed by the same rules and limits.

The Western press began to seethe with anger and alarm. Our people were fully informed of the dangerous situation, although we took care not to cause panic by the way we presented the facts. Seeking to take the heat off the situation somehow, I suggested to the other members of the government: "Comrades, let's go to the Bolshoi Theater this evening. Our own people as well as foreign eyes will notice, and perhaps it will calm them down." We were trying to disguise our own anxiety, which was intense.

Then the exchange of notes began. I dictated the messages from our side. I spent one of the most dangerous nights at the Council of Ministers office in the Kremlin. I slept on a couch, and I kept my clothes on. I was ready for alarming news to come any moment.

President Kennedy issued an ultimatum, demanding that we remove our missiles and bombers from Cuba. I remember those days vividly. I remember the exchange with President Kennedy especially well because I initiated it and was at the center of the action on our end of the correspondence. I take complete responsibility for the fact that the President and I entered into direct contact at the most crucial and dangerous stage of the crisis.

The climax came after five or six days when our ambassador to Washington, Anatoli Dobrynin, reported that the President's brother, Robert Kennedy, had come to see him on an unofficial visit. Dobrynin's report went something like this: "Robert Kennedy looked exhausted. One could see from his eyes that he had not slept for days. He himself said that he had not been home for six days and nights.

"'The President is in a grave situation,' he said, 'and he does not know how to get out of it. We are under pressure from our military to use force against Cuba. Probably at this very mo-

ment the President is sitting down to write a message to Chairman Khrushchev. We want to ask you to pass President Kennedy's message to Chairman Khrushchev through unofficial channels. President Kennedy implores Chairman Khrushchev to take into consideration the peculiarities of the American system. Even though the President himself is very much against starting a war over Cuba, an irreversible chain of events could occur against his will. That is why the President is appealing directly to Chairman Khrushchev for his help in liquidating this conflict. If the situation continues much longer, the President is not sure that the military will not overthrow him and seize power. The American army could get out of control.'"

I hadn't overlooked this possibility. We knew that Kennedy was a young President and that the security of the United States was indeed threatened. For some time we had felt there was a danger that the President would lose control of his military. We could sense from the tone of the message that tension in the United States was indeed reaching a critical point. We wrote a reply to Kennedy in which we said that we had installed the missiles with the goal of defending Cuba and that we were not pursuing any aims except to deter an invasion of Cuba and to guarantee that Cuba would be able to follow a course determined by its own people rather than one dictated by some third party.

While we conducted this exchange through official channels, the more confidential letters were relayed to us through the President's brother. Once, when Robert Kennedy talked with Dobrynin, he was almost crying. "I haven't seen my children for days now," he said, "and the President hasn't seen his either. I don't know how much longer we can hold out against our generals."

We could see that we had to

reorient our position swiftly. "Comrades," I said, "we have to look for a dignified way out of this conflict. At the same time, of course, we must make sure that we do not compromise Cuba." We sent the Americans a note saying we agreed to remove our missiles and bombers on condition that the President give his assurance that there would be no invasion of Cuba by the forces of the U.S. or anybody else. Finally Kennedy gave in and agreed to make a statement giving us such an assurance.

As soon as we announced publicly that we were ready to remove our missiles, the Americans became arrogant and insisted on sending an inspection team to the island. We answered that they'd have to get the Cuban government's permission. Then the Chinese and American press started hooting about how Khrushchev had turned coward and backed down. I won't deny that we were obliged to make some big concessions in the interests of peace. We even consented to the inspection of our ships—but only from the air; we never let the Americans set foot on our decks. We did let them satisfy themselves that we were removing our missiles.

The situation was stabilizing. Almost immediately after the President and I had exchanged notes at the peak of the crisis, our relations with the United States started to return to normal. Our relations with Cuba, on the other hand, took a sudden turn for the worse. Castro even stopped receiving our ambassador. It seemed that by removing our missiles we had suffered a moral defeat in the eyes of the Cubans. Our shares in Cuba, instead of going up, went down.

We decided to send Mikoyan to Cuba. I said, "He will discuss the situation with the Cubans calmly." Not everyone understands what Mikoyan is saying when he talks, but he's a reasonable man.

The Americans had, on the whole, been open and candid with us, especially Robert Kennedy. The Americans knew that if Russian blood were shed in Cuba, American blood would surely be shed in Germany. It had been, to say the least, an interesting and challenging situation. The two most powerful nations in the world had been squared off, each with its finger on the button. But both sides showed that if the desire to avoid war is strong enough, even the most pressing dispute can be solved by compromise. And a compromise over Cuba was indeed found. The episode ended in a triumph of common sense.

I'll always remember the late President with deep respect because, in the final analysis, he showed himself to be sober-minded and determined to avoid war. He didn't overestimate America's might, and he didn't let himself become frightened, nor did he become reckless. He left himself a way out from the crisis. He showed real wisdom and statesmanship when he turned his back on right-wing forces in the United States who were trying to goad him into military action. It was a great victory for us, though, that we had been able to extract from Kennedy a promise that neither America nor her allies would invade Cuba.

But Castro didn't see it that way. He was angry. The Chinese were buzzing in Castro's ear, "Just remember, you can't trust the imperialists to keep any promises they make!"

After consulting with Mikoyan on his return from Havana, I decided to write a letter to Castro, candidly expressing my thoughts: "The main point about the Caribbean crisis is that it has guaranteed the existence of a Socialist Cuba . . . for at least another two years while Kennedy is in the White House. And we have reason to believe that Kennedy will be elected for a second term. To make it through six years in this day and age is no small thing. And six years from now the balance of power in the world will have probably shifted—and shifted in our favor, in favor of Socialism!"

My letter to Castro concluded an episode of world history in which, bringing the world to the brink at atomic war, we won a Socialist Cuba. The Caribbean crisis was a triumph of Soviet foreign policy and personal triumph in my own career as a statesman and as a member of the collective leadership. We achieved, I would say, a spectacular success without having to fire a single shot!

We can be gratified that the revolutionary government of Fidel Castro still lives and grows. Cuba exists as an independent Socialist country, right in front of the open jaws of predatory American imperialism. Other Latin American peoples are beginning to realize what steps they can take to liberate themselves from American imperialists and monopolists. Hopefully Cuba's example will continue to shine.

As for Kennedy, his death was a great loss. He was gifted with the ability to resolve international conflicts by negotiation, as the whole world learned during the so-called Cuban crisis. Regardless of his youth, he was a real statesman. I believe that if Kennedy had lived, relations between the Soviet Union and the United States would be much better than they are. Why do I say that? Because Kennedy would never have let his country get bogged down in Vietnam.

Kennedy's successor, Lyndon Johnson, assured us that he would keep Kennedy's promise not to invade Cuba. So far the Americans have not broken their word. If they ever do, we still have the means to make good on our commitment to Castro and defend Cuba.

GEORGE KATEB
Kennedy as Statesman

George Kateb, setting out to look behind the images of Kennedy and to assess his skill in foreign policy, is troubled by a vast gulf between assertion and action, between the rhetoric of peace and the continuing Cold War; he sees the reality of an increasingly bellicose American foreign policy under Kennedy. According to this analysis, a new direction came with the adoption of the ''McNamara strategy,'' which called for building up a broad range of military capacities to deal with threats on every level—from local insurgencies to nuclear confrontation. Under the nuclear umbrella that we had held over our allies for nearly a generation was to be added the raincoat and galoshes that would keep the ''free world'' from even a sprinkle of Communist insurgency. We became, Kateb argues, a full-fledged counterrevolutionary power under Kennedy in a way that we had not been during the Eisenhower administration.

Kateb is also interested in the personality of Kennedy that fascinated Mailer and Schlesinger. Without commenting on its significance for American culture, he considers its dangers for the conduct of foreign policy. A desire for crisis and conflict, an endless sense of testing, a desire to prove coolness under fire—all these things can lead to courting crisis, and eventually to overseas commitments beyond the nation's capacity. Just what Kennedy's legacy is in foreign policy, what his role was in the developing involvement in Vietnam, remain tantalizing questions to anyone who would attempt an evaluation of this remarkable and enigmatic man.

The dream of the political outsider is to know why men of state are doing what they do. There are, of course, some resources available to the diligent student: he can rely on the *New York Times* for an accumulation of indispensable detail, he can infer motive on the basis of a general theory of political behavior, he can immerse himself in the reading of history for the sake of plucking rough analogies from the inexhaustible record of the crimes and follies of mankind. But a nagging sense of insufficiency is always there. Detail, inference, analogy do not quite add up to the real thing. How can the student be sure that he is not catching at shadows, that he is not lost in the maze of his own imaginings, that he does not see a plot where there is only confusion or an impulse where there is in fact calculation? To be sure, his occupational hazard is

Reprinted from *Commentary* by permission of publisher and author; copyright © 1966 by the American Jewish Committee. (All footnotes but one have been omitted. —ED.)

paranoid suspicion, dirty-mindedness, motive-mongering; and his self-administered therapy is to take refuge in the epilogues to *War and Peace,* or in a desperate skepticism, or finally in an acceptance of things at face value. The lust to know what really is happening, however, cannot be checked. The voices of consolation or derision will inevitably be drowned out. The truth must be pursued. He will cling to the belief—perhaps it is a delusion—that secrecy is the one great obstacle between him and his goal, which is to perceive the time in which he lives.

So it is with enormous expectations that one opens the pages of the two recent books on John F. Kennedy by Theodore Sorensen and Arthur Schlesinger, Jr. Obviously, the whole truth will not be contained in them. Allowance must be made for tact and for national security. No single chronicler can have at his disposal more than a small amount of the raw ingredients of countless presidential and bureaucratic decisions. For all that, both Sorensen and Schlesinger were close to the center; both would want to fill in the picture; Schlesinger especially could be expected to befriend the academic inquirer by letting him in on the daily actuality of the Kennedy administration. The events covered are not yet cold: we are now locked in their ramifications. Surely the intimate truth about the years 1961–1963 will make the immediate present more intelligible?

Neither book disappoints; each deepens our understanding of the Kennedy years. It would not be correct to say that any startling revelations are made; it may even be that a few vain readers will come away from these books (especially Sorensen's) with the feeling that there is nothing at all new in them, and that what the *Times* and a few journals had not already reported and disclosed,

political shrewdness could supply. So be it. The fact remains that, at the very least, *Kennedy* and *A Thousand Days* put a great many things together, and by their very inclusiveness, permit a more definite sense of the recent past to emerge.

Truly, the sense that emerges is not the sense intended. The aim of both writers is naturally to praise—not indiscriminately, but for one main trait: newness. In the eyes of Sorensen and Schlesinger, Kennedy stood for a break with the past, and a break that was all to the good. He injected vitality into a stagnant nation, while striving to direct that vitality away from cold-war bellicosity, toward the deepest problems of the age, toward hunger, backwardness, and the craving for peace. Who can doubt that if it were only a question of Kennedy's abstract intention, this description of him would be perfectly accurate? What is so awful is that in case after case, as these two narratives (in spite of themselves) make clear, Kennedy's abstract intention gave way before pressures of one sort or another. Even more, Kennedy's initiative, in the absence of immediate pressures, was sometimes in direct contradiction to his abstract intention. To put the matter briefly: the break that Kennedy effected with the past resulted in an intensification of cold-war bellicosity, not in its lessening. Sometimes he acted deliberately; sometimes he acted as he did because he thought he could not act in any other way. The tendency of his actions, however, was to change the direction of Eisenhower's policy, and prepare the way for Johnson's activism. A good part of the story is found in these two books.

The story begins with the adoption of the so-called "McNamara strategy." This was a deliberate act of policy on the part of the Kennedy administration; a free choice, so to speak. It is certain

that if Rockefeller had been President, the same strategy would have been adopted. It is probable that if Nixon had been elected, he would have moved in the same direction as Kennedy. It is likely that only Stevenson, among the leading Democrats, would at least have tried, as President, to resist the adoption of the "McNamara strategy." Among the Republicans it had been, in fact, none other than Eisenhower who prevented its earlier acceptance, thereby causing the resignations of Ridgway, Gavin, and Maxwell Taylor. Which is to say that Kennedy's position represented no new departure in principle, but rather was faithful to widespread assumptions—assumptions shared by men wanting a more vigorous and extended American involvement in the struggle against Communism. From the very start of his administration, then, Kennedy was determined to make American capacities more powerful because more refined, even though he sincerely believed, and had believed for a long time, that the affairs of the world needed an altogether different approach.

The McNamara strategy was meant to repeal the principal military theory of the Eisenhower administration, the doctrine of massive retaliation. Under this doctrine, the Soviet Union was to be held directly responsible for any Leninist coup or insurrection anywhere in the world, and would stand to suffer an overwhelming nuclear attack as punishment for its imputed responsibility. Furthermore, the response to any Soviet conventional military move would also be an overwhelming nuclear attack. The doctrine needs only to be stated to be convicted of monstrous absurdity; but there were doubtless numerous officials who accepted it in its full absurdity. It is impossible, however, to believe that either Eisenhower or Dulles ever took their own theory literally. It may even be possible to believe that by talking about massive retaliation, Eisenhower was indirectly saying two things. First, American opposition to coups and insurrections would have to take essentially non-military forms, like bribery, good works, economic pressure, and backstage conspiracy. Second, the old cold war was over, and no overt Russian military move was foreseen. In any case, the development of American anti-guerrilla forces and, more important, the buildup of conventional forces, in the name of open American engagement, were ruled out. The costs were prohibitive; the effort provocative; the consequences treacherously uncertain. Schlesinger says half in humor, "Eisenhower could never find the use of local aggression to which nuclear warfare seemed a sensible response." But the joke is now on Schlesinger.

Kennedy initiated the abandonment of that policy. He embraced, as Schlesinger neatly puts it, ". . . the strong view taken by the service whose mission, money and traditions were most threatened by the . . . doctrine [of massive retaliation]—the Army." In his first months, he added six billion dollars to the last Eisenhower military budget. A large fraction went to the nuclear deterrent: McNamara was, and is, a firm believer in something called "flexible response": nuclear weapons must be so diverse and sophisticated as to permit selectivity and gradation in their use. This is another phantom, and I need not chase it now. The important point is that great sums were allocated to the buildup of anti-guerrilla and conventional forces. Sorensen gives the rationale: ". . . if this country was to be able to confine a limited challenge to the local and non-nuclear level, without permitting a Communist victory —then it was necessary to build our own non-nuclear forces to the point where any aggressor

would be confronted with the same poor choice Kennedy wanted to avoid: humiliation or escalation. A limited Communist conventional action, in short, could best be deterred by a capacity to respond effectively in kind." The only trouble with this rationale, in regard to Russia, is that the buildup of conventional forces was much more a provocation than a deterrence. Who could take seriously the possibility that Russia would invade Western Europe or the Near East—who except the army and its intellectuals? What was there to deter? The trouble with this rationale, in regard to revolutionary movements, is that the inability of conventional and anti-guerrilla forces to deter would soon become apparent, and America would be tempted to use its strength to destroy what it could not deter. The counterrevolutionary career would be launched in earnest, with no end in sight. A task more huge, more hopeless, could not be conceived. The view of Communism as a monolithic force was retained from the old theory of massive retaliation; but now the ambition of meeting it in all its forms became entirely serious. Containment became a universal and undiscriminating principle of foreign policy. The threats to American security were seen as infinite.

Kennedy's vision of the world comes out most clearly in his conversations with Khrushchev at Vienna in June 1961. Schlesinger's report is fuller than Sorensen's, though Sorensen's is also quite valuable. Tension over Berlin, the Laotian crisis, and the Bay of Pigs episode were the background to the conference. But the great theme was the balance of power throughout the world, and the relation of "wars of national liberation" to that balance. Delicately but insistently, Kennedy tried to get Khrushchev to see the world as he saw it.

War between the two great powers was out of the question; the use of nuclear weapons was too terrible to contemplate. But each great power had vital interests which had to be respected; let there be no miscalculation concerning the determination of either side to protect its vital interests. The effort to impose Communism by force of arms in any country would obviously imperil the balance of power in the world. The United States and the Soviet Union would compete peacefully, and allow the uncommitted world to choose freely its way of life.

Obviously, Khrushchev did not accept the responsibility that Kennedy seemed to wish to thrust on him. Sorensen paraphrases his reply: "Was the President saying that Communism should exist only in Communist countries, that its development elsewhere would be regarded by the U.S. as a hostile act by the Soviet Union? The United States wants the U.S.S.R., he said, to sit like a schoolboy with hands on the table, but there is no immunization against ideas. . . . [Khrushchev] returned time and again to the thesis that the Soviet Union could not be held responsible for every spontaneous uprising or Communist trend. . . . Castro was not a Communist but U.S. policy could make him one. . . ."

It is apparent from the reports that Khrushchev alternated between two responses. Either the Soviet Union could not be held responsible for the surge of revolutionary discontent throughout the world, or the Soviet Union could not be expected to withhold aid, when asked, to insurgent movements and new regimes. It is hard to see what else Khrushchev could have said: he was, in effect, describing the role of the Soviet Union in world affairs analogously to that of the United States. He nowhere said that the Soviet Union would export revolution in the old Trotskyist sense: not by Soviet arms, or by Soviet instigation in an otherwise tranquil situation. That there would be uncontrolled revolutionary movements could not be denied; but Soviet responsibility could not possibly extend to them.

Kennedy's words at Vienna, and the policies he followed, show that he accepted the view that all insurgencies in which Communists take part are inspired by and directed from Moscow. In turn, the triumph of any such insurgency represents a shift in the balance of power between the great power blocs, a defeat for the West, a serious impairment of its security. As Sorensen says, "The extent of U.S. commitment and of Communist power involvement differed from one to the other, but the dilemma facing John Kennedy in each one was essentially the same: how to disengage the Russians from the 'liberation' movement and prevent a Communist military conquest without precipitating a major Soviet-American military confrontation." The way out of the seeming dilemma was to increase the American anti-guerrilla and conventional capacity.

Sooner or later that capacity would be used. Political moves are determined by the means on hand as much as by anything else: men do all they can. One would like to praise Kennedy unreservedly for apparently limiting American military involvement in the Laotian crisis of 1961–1962 to dramatic but empty gestures, despite intense pressure put on him by his military advisers to land American troops in Laos. (Sorensen says his "posture . . . combined bluff with real determination in proportions he made known to *no one*. . . .") But the praise must be qualified. First, Kennedy was strongly inclined to intervene: he saw the Laotian crisis as a manifestation of the world Communist conspiracy rather than as the product of local antagonisms, in which local Communists played a part; and he thought that a Communist victory in Laos would imperil the security of the United States and its major allies. Second, the reason for staying out of Laos was, in part, the Bay of Pigs affair. " 'Thank God the Bay of Pigs happened when it did,' he would say to me [Sorensen] in September. . . . 'Otherwise we'd be in Laos by now—and that would be a hundred times worse.' " Kennedy told Schlesinger the same thing. It took one fiasco to prevent another. As it turned out, the Pathet Lao stopped short of total victory: Khrushchev, appalled at the prospect of American military intervention, managed to police an insurgency he had no part in starting and little part in sustaining. By acting as he did, Khrushchev must have lent credibility to the view that all insurgencies were his to turn on and off. The nature of his act was not seen for what it was.

The stage was set for a reversal of Eisenhower's policy in Vietnam. In May 1961, Vice-President Johnson reported to Kennedy, according to Schlesinger, ". . . the basic decision in Southeast Asia is here. We must decide whether to help these countries to the best of our ability or throw in the towel in the area and pull back our defenses to San Francisco and a 'Fortress America' concept." In October, General Maxwell Taylor made a three-week visit to Vietnam and urged positive action on Kennedy. Once again, Kennedy was induced to see a local struggle as an element in a greater struggle. Schlesinger says, ". . . given the truculence of Moscow, the Berlin crisis and the resumption of nuclear testing, the President unquestionably felt that an American retreat in Asia might upset the whole world balance." Sorensen says, "What was

The *Commander* and *Chief*. *(UPI)*

The Kennedy team. *(Cornell Capa, Magnum)*

needed, Kennedy agreed with his advisers, was a major counter-insurgency effort—the first ever mounted by this country. . . . Formally, Kennedy never made a final negative decision on troops. In typical Kennedy fashion, he made it difficult for any of the pro-intervention advocates to charge him privately with weakness." Gradually, almost insensibly, the American commitment grew and became irreversible. This is not to say that Kennedy would necessarily have permitted the expansion of American force which Johnson has permitted. It is impossible to speculate; one must simply acknowledge that by the end of 1963 "only" 15,500 American soldiers were in Vietnam. Nevertheless, it is hard to imagine Johnson's commitment having been made without Ken-

nedy's prior one, and without the wholehearted support Kennedy gave to the development of American non-nuclear capability—to the McNamara strategy. When anti-guerrilla activity fails (as it must in conditions like those in Vietnam), a next step can be taken. There will be many to say that it must be taken. Guerrilla warfare will be changed into conventional warfare, so that American technical superiority can be brought into play.

The idea that the power of the West and the Communist bloc were in a balance that required constant vigilance to be preserved drove Kennedy not only to look on insurgencies as suitable for American military involvement, but also led him to invest every direct Soviet-American problem

with a high degree of passion. The passion was of a special sort: an intense desire to avoid giving the impression of weakness. Let it be noted that this desire is not the same as the desire to give the impression of overbearing strength. No one could ever accuse Kennedy of enjoying the role of bully. The matter is more sad, more complicated. In his early book, *Why England Slept*, he expressed the belief that democracies were inherently pacific and self-absorbed, and that they had to have "shocks" to keep them alert to the dangers surrounding them. Being alert, they would not give the appearance of weakness; they would thereby dissuade aggressors from rashness. In line with this aim, Kennedy wanted to raise taxes in 1961 in order to enhance a sense of sacrifice and impress on Americans the gravity of world affairs. His ill-considered support of fall-out shelters was part of the same purpose. More than that, all one can briefly say is that Kennedy seems to have had a naturally agonistic conception of world politics. He did not look for fights; rather he thought that they were inevitable, that crisis was the normality of international relations, even in the nuclear age. (He shocked Stevenson by referring to disarmament proposals as "propaganda.") Beyond the conflict of aims that always exists between nations, Kennedy saw a contest of wills, an almost formal antagonism in which the prize was pride at least as much as any substantive outcome. In discussing Dean Acheson's advice during the Berlin crisis of 1961, Schlesinger says, "[Khrushchev's] object, as Acheson saw it, was not to rectify a local situation but to test the general American will to resist; his hope was that, by making us back down on a sacred commitment, he could shatter our world power and influence. This was a simple conflict of wills, and, until it was resolved, any effort to negotiate the Berlin issue per se would be fatal. . . . For Acheson the test of will seemed almost an end in itself rather than a means to a political end." Schlesinger and Sorensen both make it clear that the tone of Kennedy's military advisers was practically identical to Acheson's. What is so troubling is that Kennedy's reasons for policy, on numerous occasions, were similar. They prominently included the wish to appear to be accepting a challenge. He was inclined to define the world as the "realists" defined it, though possessed of a self-doubt and a magnanimity foreign to them. Fortunately, one could probably say that the United States under Kennedy never yielded in a contest of wills, was never bested. But the precedents

perhaps established, the opportunities perhaps missed, are not easily dismissed.

It would be heavy-handed to make much of the Bay of Pigs affair. Kennedy regretted the failure: he may even have regretted the effort. (The one time Sorensen raises his voice in censure of Kennedy is when he is reporting this event.) But the analysis made by Sorensen of Kennedy's mood before he allowed the expedition to get under way is fairly depressing: "He did not regard Castro as a direct threat to the United States, but neither did he see why he should 'protect' Castro from Cubans embittered by the fact that their revolution had been sold out to the Communists. Cancellation of the plan at that stage, he feared, would be interpreted as an admission that Castro ruled with popular support and would be around to harass Latin America for many years to come. His campaign pledges to aid anti-Castro rebels had not forced his hand, as some suspected, but he did feel that his disapproval of the plan would be a show of weakness inconsistent with his general stance." Anxiety was piled on anxiety, but the sharpest of them all was the fear of having himself or his country thought weak. Appearances were accorded great weight; the United States was constantly having to prove itself. But why? Who was in a position to put this country on trial, who doubted its resolve, who was ignorant of its strength, who, indeed, was not terrified of its strength (the Soviet Union and China included)?

Again, in the case of the Berlin crisis in 1961, the same anxieties are disclosed. After a while, it becomes hard to keep on worrying about Berlin; any problem loses some of its reality through continuous exposure. One does not mean to be callous; but is a mutually satisfactory settlement out of the reach of human wit? Or is the problem useful to all

parties as a source of manipulable tension? Before the U-2 incident, it seemed as if Eisenhower and Khrushchev were about to reach some accord. No accord, of course, was reached. Kennedy inherited Khrushchev's dissatisfaction, and the rigid incompetence of the imbecile East German regime. Schlesinger informs us that Kennedy "used to wonder later what had gone wrong in the spring of 1961. He thought at times that the March and May messages calling for an increased American defense effort might have sounded too threatening." The intended deterrence to crisis had helped to bring one about. What, now, to do? Kennedy's advisers, led by Acheson, as we have already seen, refused to countenance any negotiations: the possibility that Khrushchev had perhaps a troublesome situation on his hands was not granted. The exact status quo had to be maintained; some alternative to staying put on the old terms or getting out in a humiliating way was disregarded. Kennedy was determined, Sorensen says, ". . . to make [the Berlin crisis] not only a question of West Berlin's rights —on which U.S., British, French, and West German policies were not always in accord—but a question of direct Soviet-American confrontation over a shift in the balance of power." The bondage to the cold war could not be relinquished. The result was, once more, dramatic gesture: ". . . draft calls were doubled, tripled, enlistments were extended and the Congress promptly and unanimously authorized the mobilization of up to 250,000 men. . . ." The Wall was built, the crisis faded. Only the people of East Berlin had lost, securely imprisoned as they were now to become. It will not do to place, as Sorensen does, the full responsibility for the stiffness of American policy on the inertia or philo-Germanism of the State Department. Kennedy had other sources of opinion—for example, Sorensen and Schlesinger. In reflecting on the crisis, Sorensen cannot forbear from remarking, ". . . no one knew when either side, convinced that the other would back down, might precipitate a situation from which neither could back down." Only flexibility, only an avoidance of seeing one's total position implicated in every situation, only a willingness to give up the ideology of confrontation, could help to insure that intolerable situations would not emerge. The Berlin crisis uselessly impaired Soviet-American relations, and prevented (temporarily, to be sure) certain kinds of cooperation with the Soviets.

The American decision of March 1962 to resume atmospheric testing of nuclear weapons is yet another example of the politics of appearances. Russia had itself resumed testing in September 1961, and had made, Sorensen says, "important weapons progress." That is, at the time they resumed, they must have felt that the nuclear buildup implemented by McNamara had weakened their security; the arms race had taken another leap forward. As both Sorensen and Schlesinger make clear, Kennedy's decision to resume derived primarily from considerations having little to do with American military needs. Sorensen says, "Nearly all the principal advisers involved favored resuming atmospheric tests (though a few days before the tests began, McNamara startled Rusk and Bundy at lunch by suggesting that they were not really necessary)." Schlesinger says, "Jerome Wiesner maintained in December that it remained basically a political question: 'While these tests would certainly contribute to our military strength, they are not critical or even very important to our overall military posture.'" Schlesinger indicates that Kennedy

agreed more or less. Sorensen says that Kennedy ". . . still had doubts about the value of his test series (although not about the necessity of his decision). . . . Privately he speculated that fears of Soviet nuclear test progress might have been akin to previous fears of a Soviet 'bomber gap' and 'missile gap.' . . ." But still the order to resume was given. In reply to Harold Macmillan's impassioned plea to avoid resumption, Kennedy said (in Sorensen's paraphrase) that the Soviets ". . . would be more likely to attribute such a decision to weakness rather than goodwill. . . ." To Adlai Stevenson, he was equally emphatic: "What choice did we have? . . . [Khrushchev] has had a succession of apparent victories—space, Cuba, [the Berlin Wall]. . . . He wants to give out the feeling that he has us on the run. . . ." Feeling challenged, fearing to be thought fearful, Kennedy decided to do what he hated to do, and had little faith in. He could not escape the tyranny of appearances.

The Cuban missile crisis, the greatest of all crises in the Kennedy years, also contained this same obsession. Kennedy's most desperate anguish came at a moment when he felt that appearances were not to be endured; his most stunning victory came at a moment when he succeeded in altering appearances. It would be foolish to reduce the crisis to this single element of appearances; but to ignore its possibly *preponderant* role would also be foolish.

In a wonderfully lucid exposition, Sorensen describes the several theories suggested by the President's advisers to explain Khrushchev's move. (One of the most fascinating small aspects of this affair was the response of the Chinese, who accused Khrushchev of "adventurism" in trying to place missiles in Cuba—and of cowardice for removing them.) The theories mentioned by Soren-

sen are (1) that Khrushchev was testing the will of the United States, and hoped to make the United States look weak, irresolute, and faithless to its sworn commitments; (2) that Khrushchev hoped to induce us to invade Cuba in order to disgrace us in the eyes of the world; (3) that Khrushchev was genuinely concerned for Cuba's security,[1] (4) that Khrushchev was bargaining, and hoped to trade off the Cuban bases for a Berlin settlement or American bases overseas; and (5) that Khrushchev was desirous of improving his strategic nuclear position. Sorensen says that Kennedy's own analysis ". . . regarded the third and fifth theories as offering likely but insufficient motives and he leaned most strongly to the first." That is, Kennedy interpreted the move as primarily an affront to the United States, a calculated probe of weakness, a contest of wills. He increasingly insisted to his advisers that the entire matter be defined as a Soviet-American confrontation. Irrespective of interpretation, however, Kennedy insisted that the missiles "would have to be removed by the Soviets in response to direct American action." In a television interview on December 16, 1962, to which Sorensen makes only a brief allusion, Kennedy gave a splendidly candid account of his reasons for taking any risk to pre-

[1] Sorensen says, "It should be noted that the Soviet Union stuck throughout to this position. Mikoyan claimed in a conversation with the President weeks after it was all over that the weapons were purely defensive, that they had been justified by threats of invasion voiced by Richard Nixon and Pentagon generals, and that the Soviets intended to inform the United States of these weapons immediately after the elections to prevent the matter from affecting the American political campaign." Sorensen acknowledges that the administration in 1962 had been ". . . readying a plan of military action in the knowledge that an internal revolt, a Berlin grab or some other action might someday require it. . . ."

vail. He said, ". . . [the Russians] were planning in November to open to the world the fact that they had these missiles so close to the United States; not that they were intending to fire them, because if they were going to get into a nuclear struggle, they have their own missiles in the Soviet Union. But it would have politically changed the balance of power. It would have appeared to, and appearances contribute to reality."

Harold Macmillan could wonder "what all the fuss was about"; after all, Europe was used to living under the nuclear threat. He seems to have missed the point, namely that there was no military threat but instead a threat to America's reputation as a world power. Largely for the sake of great-power reputation (though other reasons, including the reputation of the Democratic party, figured), the world was brought close to a terrible event. (One assumes that this is so, but *The Penkovskiy Papers* say that Kennedy knew the Soviet nuclear capacity to be unready for action, and that Kennedy was therefore quite free to be as tough as he wanted and not incur grave risks.) Appearances do contribute to reality: reputation for power is a source of power: you are if they think you are. But was America's reputation so fragile? The irony is that America's very strength permitted Kennedy to act out of fear of being thought weak. Its very strength, however, should have permitted him to mitigate this fear. He did not carry his consciousness of American power far enough—as far as Eisenhower, before him, had carried it. And a relentless pursuit of right appearances can be catastrophic. In this instance the pursuit was not catastrophic, but what guarantee was there? Kennedy' later told Sorensen that "The odds that the Soviets would go all the way to war seemed to him then 'somewhere between

one out of three and even.'" A nuclear war to eliminate a nuclear war installation—can such thoughts be entertained?

The alternative was not mortified acceptance, but negotiation before the crisis escaped control. Stevenson, according to Schlesinger, proposed the removal of the missiles in exchange for a UN presence in Cuba, an American non-invasion guarantee, and relinquishment of the base at Guantanamo. This program struck Kennedy as premature, and some of his advisers ". . . felt strongly that the thought of negotiations at this point would be taken as an admission of the moral weakness of our case and the military weakness of our posture." The blockade was declared, unless Khrushchev backed down, ". . . the United States would have had no real choice but to take action against Cuba the next week." The implications of invasion were understood: Kennedy said that "If we had invaded Cuba . . . I am sure the Soviets would have acted. They would have to, just as we would have to. I think there are certain compulsions on any major power." Khrushchev did back down, and was freely granted a guarantee against the invasion of Cuba. But he did back down; he refused to breach the blockade; he agreed to withdraw his missiles. How is his decision to be assessed? Was it cowardice or was it sanity? Did he not also win a victory of sorts in the realm of appearances by emerging as a champion of rationality? As such, did not his reputation improve, and indirectly with it, the power of the Soviet Union?

Redefinition of radical revolution as Muscovite conspiracy, redefinition of every problem as a great-power confrontation affecting the global balance of power, the adoption of the McNamara strategy in order to have the means to act on the basis of these redefinitions—can this be all that

Kennedy bequeathed us in foreign policy? The answer is, of course, no. Who can repress nostalgia for those days in late 1962 and early 1963, when Kennedy, abetted by Pope John and Khrushchev, seemed to recapture the spirit of his inaugural address and of many of his earlier speeches? Surely this was the real Kennedy who, hitherto distracted from his mission and victimized by the foreign-policy establishment, had finally struggled free. The Cuban missile crisis may have petrified Khrushchev; it seems to have altered Kennedy. The very next morning after Khrushchev's capitulation, Kennedy told Schlesinger that ". . . he was afraid that people would conclude from this experience that all we had to do in dealing with the Russians was to be tough and they would collapse." After a shrewd analysis of the affair, he went on to say, "They were in the wrong and knew it. So, when we stood firm, they had to back down. But this doesn't mean at all that they would back down when they felt that they were in the right and had vital interests involved." But these words do not capture the full transformation. After the Cuban crisis, Schlesinger says, Kennedy's feelings ". . . underwent a qualitative change . . . a world in which nations threatened each other with nuclear weapons now seemed to him not just an irrational but an intolerable and impossible world." The proof of this sentiment came in the form of strenuous negotiation to produce the Nuclear Test Ban Treaty. The fact is that much of the strenuousness was spent on Kennedy's own military advisers. Once again, the passion for right appearances was exhibited by the Chiefs of Staff. Maxwell Taylor told the Senate Foreign Relations Committee that "the most serious reservations of the military had to do with the fear of a euphoria in the West which will eventually reduce our vigilance." Only this time Kennedy, after making some concessions to the military, rejected the logic of appearances and went ahead with the treaty.

The real victory that Kennedy won in Cuba was over his own advisers. Some would like to say that he had softened up Khrushchev: that a show of strength and determination, on such a scale and under such trying conditions, had so demoralized the Russian leader that he had no choice but to feign moderation and accept Kennedy's overtures of peace. It would be equally plausible to say that Kennedy's show of strength and determination had (for the time being) won him so much prestige and brought him so much self-confidence that he could at last prevail even over his bellicose aides, and pursue a policy that he (and Khrushchev) wanted from the beginning. Not out of a good heart, but out of cold prudence, out of dread of American power, Khrushchev had been straining to be compliant. Success in Cuba accidentally made it possible for Kennedy to take advantage of Khrushchev's wishes. Kennedy's sense of reality shone through. If he had lived, would he have imposed that sense on the men around him? One wants to believe that he would.

GEORGE N. GREEN
Texas and Dallas on the Eve

Seen from the end of the 1960s, the Kennedy administration appears anything but radical. Yet to fanatics in the early part of the decade, even its lukewarm advocacy of civil rights and a lessening of Cold War tensions appeared to be the work of dedicated members of the "Communist conspiracy." This right-wing mentality was particularly strong in the state of Texas, and especially so in the city of Dallas. It saw every manifestation of change as evidence of Communist infiltration, and every attempt at the free airing of ideas as a threat to American values. While the temptation is to dismiss such fanaticism as harmless nuttiness, to do so would be a serious mistake. The books people could read (especially in school), the ideas they heard, and the opportunities—cultural, social, and economic—open to them were heavily influenced by the intolerance of the Right. And the climate of Dallas encouraged the mistreatment of national figures, a trend which other political elements soon followed. The decline of civility and the rise of violence in recent American public life began with the Right wing of the early sixties.

The election of 1964 dealt a blow to the Right from which it spent the rest of the decade recovering. Yet in its early translating of cultural issues—such as sexual behavior, the music of the Beatles, and our view of the past—into political terms, and its organization outside the channels of conventional politics, the Right pioneered trends that were to dominate the later sixties. It would be comforting to think of these people as backward-looking fanatics whose day is past, but their forms of organization and access to money and media virtually assure that they will be heard from in the future.

I

Of the slew of extremist groups that sprang up in Texas in the 1950s and 1960s, none proved more effective in a one-shot effort than· the rancher-historian J. Evetts Haley and the outfit he spearheaded: Texans for America (many of whom were Birchers and Minute Women). Ostensibly, Texans for America was just a state branch of For America, which had been organized as a tax-exempt educational group in 1954 by Colonel Robert McCormick, owner of the *Chicago Tribune,* and by ex-congressman Hamilton Fish of New York. Since For America was openly political, it soon lost its tax-exempt status. And it soon fell under the control of different leaders—Dean Clarence Manion,

Reprinted by permission of the author (unpublished manuscript). (Footnotes have been omitted.—ED.)

formerly of the Notre Dame law school; General Bonner Fellers; and Dan Smoot, the right-wing propagandist from Dallas. Texas ranked third, behind New York and Illinois, in the number of men on For America's National Policy Committee. Notable among the Texas committeemen were Haley, multimillionaire oilman Hugh Roy Cullen, and former governor Dan Moody. The committee's main concern was foreign policy; it favored isolationism in all matters, the abolition of conscription, the build-up of air power, the abolition of immigration, and the withdrawal of diplomatic recognition of Communist nations. But other goals included the passage of "right-to-work" laws, abolition of the withholding tax, securing of total local control of education, reduction of Supreme Court authority, and impeaching of all present Supreme Court members.

Haley captured headlines and shook the academic world by turning against the school he was supposed to serve as a member of its Board of Regents, Texas Tech in Lubbock. He had been chosen for a six-year term on the board by Governor Shivers in 1952. In July 1957 the board, under Haley's prodding, fired Dr. Byron Abernathy, a government professor who had recently addressed a group of liberals who were struggling to take over the state's Democratic party. Also dismissed were Dr. Herbert Greenburg, a blind psychologist who had conducted studies in integration, and another professor whose adult education program had succeeded in direct opposition to a Haley-supported Americanism Institute on campus. None of the professors were given prior notification of their dismissal and none were granted a hearing. The entire adult education program, which was sponsored by the Ford Foundation, was abolished. At first no reasons were cited for these sudden dismissals, but the reasons were

later declared: the professors played politics. Thus Haley, who had not resigned from the board when he was a candidate for governor the year before on a ticket of virtual secession from the union, reasoned that such freedom was in poor taste for liberals and integrationists. When Haley's term expired in 1958, Governor Daniel did not see fit to reappoint him.

More than any other incident in the entire history of the school, these firings demonstrated its lack of academic freedom, a heritage that haunted the campus for years. For these abuses of academic freedom and due process, the Texas Tech Board of Directors was censured by the American Association of University Professors. The college remained on the censured list for a decade. In 1965, eight years after the firings, numerous faculty members testified that the censure hampered recruitment. They noted that the faculty had been working for administrative and board approval of meaningful commitments to the principles of academic freedom and for removal from the censured list. A tenure policy had been adopted in 1963, but it had not completely met AAUP standards. And as late as 1965 it seemed that the board was not overtly attempting to remove the censure and that the administration was not prepared to make an issue of the board's reluctance. But a new president, who was determined to get Tech off the censure list, did so in 1967.

Haley and the Texans for America next unleashed an attack on Southern Methodist University in Dallas, but this time there was opposition. In January 1960, Haley and his band mailed some eight thousand reprints of an *American Mercury* article branding SMU a seedbed of leftist internationalism. Distributed to alumni and to students' parents, the pamphlets asserted that SMU

was Dallas' principal base of operations for left-wingers. The student newspaper lashed back at the credibility of Haley's witnesses and noted that the *Mercury* was owned by Russell Maguire, a rich manufacturer who had been found by the Securities and Exchange Commission to have willfully violated the Securities Act. The Haleyites withdrew from the fray.

Public school textbooks became the foremost target of Haley's group. In the early 1960s Texas schools bought from $6,000,000 to $10,000,000 worth of textbooks a year. The state textbook committee selected five books for each public school course, from which local boards chose any one. For the benefit of the committee, Haley expounded his criteria for evaluating the texts: "The stressing of both sides of a controversy only confuses the young and encourages them to make snap judgments based on insufficient evidence. Until they are old enough to understand both sides of a question, they should be taught only the American side."

Generally, Haley proposed deleting from all textbooks any favorable mention of the income tax, Social Security, TVA, federal subsidies to farmers and schools, the United Nations, disarmament, integration, and the Supreme Court. Among those men Haley listed as subversive tools of the Communists and internationalists were Albert Schweitzer, John Gunther, Stephen Vincent Benét, Ralph Bunche, and Langston Hughes. After a publisher replied that Hughes was an internationally known Negro poet and winner of several awards, such as the Guggenheim Fellowship for Creative Writing, Haley declared that this only demonstrated the degenerate nature of the people who decided the awards. Haley accused SMU history professor Paul Boller, who had stated that the Communist party was practically defunct in this country, of being "soft on Communism, short on logic, or both." Boller's publisher, Webster Publishing Company, was labeled a Communist collaborationist for publishing a government-contracted pamphlet about Russia which was circulated among the armed forces during World War II.

Haley rallied the Daughters of the American Revolution, several American Legion posts, and various John Birchers to dominate the state textbook committee hearings in the early 1960s. He avowed that two hundred Texans were working with him and that they were assisted with propaganda from rightist groups all over the nation. Typical of Haley's group was R. A. Kilpatrick, a lawyer from Cleburne. He objected to one textbook's listing of Upton Sinclair, Jack London, Ida Tarbell, and Lincoln Steffens as novelists who wrote of the evils around them. He said this was promoting the writings of known subversives, especially since there were pictures of London and Steffens in the book. Kilpatrick also noticed that there was only one mention of Will Rogers and that at the end of the chapter the student was not asked to gather additional material on him. The lawyer concluded, "Guess he was too American for the author of this textbook!" Haleyites at various times charged that a history text picture of George Washington, done by a contemporary of the President, "looks as if George Gobel posed for the painting"; that the song "He's Got the Whole World in His Hands" smacked on one-worldism; and that Mohammed's quote "Trust in God, but tie your camel" was dangerous because Mohammed was not a true prophet.

The state textbook committee made frightening concessions to the censors. In October 1961 the committee approved fifty books for adoption, including twenty-seven the Texans for America had condemned. But the committee rejected twelve books that the group had opposed and ordered some changes in every book approved. Many other alterations were not reflected in the Texas Education Agency records because they were agreed upon orally in secret sessions between publishers and the committee. All references to, and works by, Pete Seeger and Langston Hughes were ordered deleted from Texas school books because of their connections with groups cited by the House Un-American Activities Committee. All mention of Vera Michaels Dean had to be omitted from Ginn & Company's *American History* for a similar reason. Laidlaw Brothers had to drop a reference to Dorothy Canfield Fisher. Macmillan's text, *History of a Free People,* had to take a more positive stand against Communism and had to delete the passage: "Had Wilson seen the necessity for compromise, the United States would have joined the League, although with reservations. Had that happened, there was just a chance that World War II might have been averted."

The Silver Burdett Company was forced to make numerous modifications in its geography text. Among the alterations which indicate how the character of a book can be changed by censorship were:

Original version: Today other countries help us in protecting our land against possible attack. Radar listening posts . . .
Changed to: With radar we can quickly detect the approach of enemy aircraft or missiles. But radar stations . . .

Original version: Because it needs to trade, and because it needs military help, the United States needs the friendship of countries throughout the world. But, to keep its friends, a country must help them too.
Changed to: The United States trades with countries in all parts of the world. We are also provid-ing military help to many nations. In addition, the United States helps many countries in other ways.

Even after making substantial modifications, publishers and authors discovered that many local school officials were unwilling to buy a book that had been under attack. D. C. Heath and Company estimated that their high school history book sales were $80,000 below what sales records led them to anticipate. Paul Boller contended that sales for his book were considerably reduced by the Haleyite attacks.

Moreover, Haley's crusade launched a right-wing onslaught into the Texas public schools. Superpatriots were inspired to weed out "Communism," that is, liberalism and the free exchange of ideas. In parts of West Texas the textbook battles fomented a purge of library shelves. At Amarillo's four high schools and at Amarillo College, John Birchers directed the removal from the shelves of ten novels, including four Pulitzer Prize winners. Listed as subversive or Communist and withdrawn from circulation were such works as *Andersonville, Brave New World, Marjorie Morningstar, The Big Sky, Grapes of Wrath,* and *1984.* It was ironic that *1984* should be purged since the book is usually regarded as a devastating critique of life under Communism. Some of the same volumes were purged from school libraries in Midland, where Harold Hitt, chairman of the state textbook committee, was superintendent of schools. Texans for America circulated a pamphlet declaring that forty-two books at the Midland high school library had been randomly examined and that the ten novels removed in Amarillo had been analyzed as totally unfit for consumption at any age level. Political overtones were absent from many of the censored books, but their alleged obscenity was considered part of the Communist conspiracy to undermine America's morals and conquer from within.

Elsewhere in Texas, a member of the John Birch Society condemned *Living Biographies of Great Philosophers* by Henry and Dana Thomas because of Plato's advocacy of communal living. The Bircher noted, "I can't help but believe that this is one reason we have so many sex maniacs walking around." Garth Williams' *Rabbit's Wedding* was blasted because it portrayed matrimony between a white rabbit and a black one, thus advocating miscegenation.

At Dumas, in the Panhandle, the public schools were subjected to a program of compulsory patriotism. The school board, composed of a rancher, a druggist, a lawyer, and two oil company executives, made sure the curricula included lessons in religious fundamentalism and political ultraconservatism. In Midland, Dr. William D. Kelley, an associate of Haley's in the textbook hearings, was a member of the school board. An anonymous letter was sent out to many Midland teachers asking them to evaluate their principals and administrators, with instructions to return their answers to Kelley. Kelley denied knowing anything about it. Midland was also the scene of an attempted expulsion from school of a seventeen-year-old high school senior for his "subversive" remarks in a speech —he quoted *Time* magazine's opinion of the John Birch Society.

The textbook hearings also fanned the flames of rightist extremism in Houston's schools. By 1961 Houston was probably the only place in the country where the Minute Women still functioned, at least as an action group. One of these ladies heard that Kenneth Parker, a young history teacher, had dropped a few controversial comments in class. To check for herself, she asked him to her home, played a tape recording of a superpatriot speech,

and quizzed Parker on his opinions. Still dissatisfied, she persuaded the school board president to check formally on him. She allegedly received special reports from adults who came into Parker's classes and took notes. After a long controversy, he resigned, reporting in exasperation that he was a Christian and a Kennedy Democrat. The Minute Women believed his departure was a good thing "because of his reluctance to tell us he was a Christian and the ultraliberal views he expounded in the classroom. . . ."

II

Aiding the Haleyites and Birchers in the early and middle 1960s were the religious fundamentalists of Texas. The line between the two groups is frequently obscure, of course, as exemplified by the Walter Kerr Youth Force for God and Freedom, a private, propagandistic group founded by Dr. Walter Kerr of Tyler. Dr. Kerr convinced the Texas Commissioner of Education to endorse his program aimed at molding the politics of Texas youth. The Commissioner, Dr. J. W. Edgar, wrote all 1500 public school superintendents endorsing Kerr's crusade and asking them to study it. About 150 schools took steps to adopt the program. Unnamed sponsors put up $150,000 to finance the crusade. Some decidedly nonneutral facts emerged about Kerr's organization. It could not very well treat Christians, Jews, atheists, and members of other minority faiths with equality since Kerr spoke of making conversions to Christ. Kerr also sponsored a speech by Fred Schwarz in August 1962 in which Schwarz spelled out a death struggle between Christians and Jews. Although the Youth Force director said that he was dismayed by Schwarz' speech, he went on to sponsor a Lubbock meeting of his organization which included a speech on subversion

by Robert Morris of Dallas. Morris had been counsel for Joseph McCarthy's subcommittee and was president of the very conservative University of Dallas. He was also a close political friend of Dan Smoot and General Edwin A. Walker. Also featured at the Lubbock meeting was John Noble of Illinois, a promoter and seller of John O. Beaty's anti-Semitic tract *The Iron Curtain Over America.*

Generally, however, the rhetoric of the Haleyites seemed to indicate that they drew their beliefs and their strength from the alleged individualism and lack of government paternalism in the Wild West. The religious fundamentalists drew their beliefs from the Bible Belt legacy which transformed anti-Communism into a Christian crusade; their zeal came from the Old South's "old-time religion." In political matters the zealots blended easily with the rugged individualists.

Oddly for a state with a strident extremist minority, Texas has no prominent right-wing evangelist. The most potent far-right fundamentalist influence is exuded by the Reverend Billy James Hargis of Tulsa, Oklahoma. The three-hundred-pound reverend heads the Christian Crusade, which, by 1962, had about 100,000 followers and an income of $1,000,000 a year. Hargis appeared frequently in Texas in the early 1960s, and his "Truth Broadcasts" were heard over more stations there than in any other state.

"Dr." Hargis believes that smoking and drinking are evil, that international Communism "has long subsidized pornography," that the Beatles, with their "jungle-type songs," are hypnotizing and brainwashing American youth as part of the Communist conspiracy, that political conservatives are "blood redemption militant Christians," that the assassination of President Kennedy was God's warning that

Communism must be stamped out, that Congress will collapse with the abolition of the House Un-American Activities Committee, and that our only hope is for Americans to contribute enough money to maintain such anti-Communist bulwarks as the Christian Crusade.

One of his typical speeches was delivered in Houston in June 1961, as related by Willie Morris, editor of *Harper's* magazine:

Dr. Billy James Hargis . . . arrived in a streamlined, air-conditioned bus with two bedrooms, two baths, a living room, and a radio telephone. He stayed long enough to condemn, as the *Houston Chronicle* reported, "Communism, liberalism, the National Council of Churches, federal aid to education, Jack Paar, federal medical care for the aged, Ed Sullivan, the recent Kennedy-Khrushchev meeting, Eleanor Roosevelt, disarmament, Steve Allen, and the Freedom Riders." Speaking before a phalanx of tape recorders, he dismissed the brotherhood-of-man idea as "hogwash." "I find most of those who criticize me are allied with those who follow the Communist party line," he confided.

As another observer noted, Hargis trades upon the hatreds and fears of "little old scared people," who are "delighted to find a simple answer to all the alarming changes of the Twentieth Century. . . ." The item that seemed most frightening to this observer, a young preacher, was

. . . the doglike trust his listeners have. They're nice small-town people, a little naive, confused by all that's happening. All the trends they can detect seem to be concentrating power in the big city and in big government—they have a vague suspicion and fear that everything is organized to their disadvantage. They're oriented to a willingness to believe anything bad about things they don't understand —predisposed to fear the United Nations, foreigners, to appreciate veiled hints about the colored, ready to believe they are Communists or cannibals.

Hargis' followers and colleagues in Texas include several rightist leaders. One is Wickliffe Vennard, a wealthy Houston financier and a power in the Constitution party. Vennard believes that international bankers have controlled the world for centuries. Their leading tools in this country in the early 1960s were Roger Blough, Lucius Clay, and Charles Percy, who in turn controlled the Council on Foreign Relations, which in turn put up candidates for both major parties. He defended Hitler and the Nazis as opponents of this conspiracy. Dan Smoot, he added, is "aiding and abetting" the real enemy by fighting Communists. According to one of his numerous leaflets, half a million Red Chinese are stationed just south of the Rio Grande.

At least three retired military men from Texas are prominent Christian Crusaders. Captain Kenneth Ryker of Ft. Worth, General Richard Moran of Kerrville, and General Edwin A. Walker of Dallas speak at the Crusade's annual "leadership school" and annual "youth university." Ryker is director of the Ft. Worth Freedom Center, which is the leading distributor of that city's rightist propaganda. The Captain has also published his own newsletter, *Freedom File*, since 1963 and writes for other organs such as *American Mercury*, in which he once charged that Communists run the Methodist Church. Moran, chairman of the Crusade's Advisory Board, is a self-styled expert on military history, disarmament, the "criminal international Communist conspiracy," the United States electoral system, Socialism, the Supreme Court, the Bolshevik Revolution, and Colonel House—all of which he links together. Walker, who resigned from the army after he was caught indoctrinating his troops with John Birch Society materials, is touted as the patriot who gave up his army commis-

sion to speak out against the infiltration of Communists and liberals.

Other Texas rightists supporting, and supported by, the Christian Crusade are Robert Morris, J. Evetts Haley (whose biography of Lyndon Johnson was heartily endorsed), and John R. Zengler, New Braunfels businessman, Legionnaire, and participant in the 1962 textbook purges. Texans, in fact, seem better represented in the Crusade than natives of any other state. In 1964 five of the nineteen annual Christian Crusade awards went to Texans, including "Commentator of the Year" to Dan Smoot, "Statesman of the Year" to Dallas' Republican Congressman Bruce Alger, and "Crusader Action Award" to J. W. Birkhead, retired life insurance man from Dallas. Birkhead had expended "great personal sacrifices for God and Country"—he had given thousands of dollars to the Crusade. Hargis' ten-man "faculty" for his January 1965 "Anti-Communist Leadership School" included Alger, Moran, Walker, and Ryker.

In the late 1960s the Christian Crusade seems to be a tour guide agency for Fascist lands overseas. Four times a year, in the name of "anti-Communism," Hargis leads his flocks abroad. Their purpose is to meet like-minded people in nations such as Rhodesia, Nationalist China, Spain, and Greece. On these tours Hargis seems less like a fiery Christian crusader than a mother-hen guide. The rhetoric has not changed though, as illustrated by Hargis' declaration to his tourists and Prime Minister Ian Smith that "Rhodesia is persecuted for her Christian culture."

Other than Hargis, the most influential out-of-state leader is the defrocked Presbyterian, Dr. Carl McIntire, whose "20th Century Reformation Hour" and other enterprises are centered in New Jersey. He delivers anti-United Nations, anti-Catholic, racist, and economically reactionary exhortations similar to those of Hargis, but he is more theologically oriented than the Oklahoman and thus probably more dangerous. He rarely speaks in Texas and maintains no offices in the state, but in 1962 he was heard over sixteen Texas radio stations, his fourth largest state congregation; by 1964 Texas was first with twenty-seven McIntire outlets. Since the fall of 1968, however, McIntire has been in trouble with one of his own organizations, the American Council of Christian Churches, which he founded in 1941 to counter the "Communist infiltrated" National Council of Churches. Apparently the organization is wary of his uncompromising, tyrannical leadership. With Billy James Hargis wooing the ACCC, and with McIntire's income having slipped from over $3,000,000 a year in the mid-1960s to $2,250,000 in 1968, McIntire's problems do seem to be multiplying.

Perhaps the most active and loquacious of Texas' own right-wing fundamentalists is the Reverend T. Robert Ingram, a former journalist from Colorado who came to Houston in 1954. As rector of St. Thomas' Episcopal Church in Houston, he is prominent both in the Christian Crusade and in his state's other far-rightist endeavors. In churchly matters, Ingram is in trouble with his own diocese for maintaining segregation, for failing to contribute to the missionary quota, and for characterizing the National Council of Churches as "loaded with Communists."

Among the political overtones in his sermons is his notion that the only true anti-Communists are Christians (all other religions are driven only by a "passion for death"). Since God is "on our side," and since Christians cannot deal with lying governments that violate treaties, the United States should declare war upon the USSR. Apparently Ingram

holds little hope for this eventuality, however, because the United States government is violating all Ten Commandments. Moreover, the government plans to seize all the nation's churches and to mongrelize the white Anglo-Saxon Protestants. Indeed, all governments are "inherently wicked and dark" appendages which tend to challenge the one true authority, Jesus Christ. By 1965 Ingram was concerned enough with government to become a trustee of the Americans for Constitutional Action, formed in 1958 by extremists and ordinary reactionaries to evaluate Congressional voting on the basis of "Americanism" and to support right-wing candidates.

Catering to the wealthy businessmen in his congregation, Ingram occasionally equates labor unions with the anti-Christ:

. . . labor unions have marched to virtual control of all government in the United States. For fifty years people have chorused with parrotlike stupidity, "I believe in unions, but . . ." Now we have unions and there are no buts; the union, being a frankly organized political party, has, as it did for every socialist dictator of modern times, provided a machinery of political power that is unbeatable in the old way.

The Reverend has also been highly critical of public education, urban rioters ("depraved, envy-drunk public school products"), atheists (who are "mentally ill"), mental health bills (those enacted in the late 1950s and early 1960s would "provide every state and the Federal law enforcement machinery with the mandate to imprison people for what they are thinking"), and the spread of Communistic pornography. But for all his vigorous speaking and writing for the Christian Crusade, the far-right-wing *Houston Tribune,* and his own church, Ingram is little known in Texas or even in Houston. His contribution to

rightist political causes does not seem significant.

Perhaps vying with Ingram as a fundamentalist speaker is another Houstonian, William P. Strube, Jr. Strube is president of an insurance company and vice-president of Fred C. Schwarz's Christian Anti-Communism Crusade. Schwarz, a former Australian medical doctor, began his nationwide movement in 1952 and maintains permanent offices in Houston, San Francisco, Long Beach, Philadelphia, and Sydney (Australia). He speaks often in Texas, expounding about the same theme as Hargis. Strube, a hypnotic and powerful orator, gave about 850 speeches against Communism in the 1958–1960 period alone. In 1961 he predicted complete Communist victory by 1966. In one typical performance he tapped a piece of chalk on a blackboard and declared, "Here's a Communist. There's one—here's one—there's one. Get him! Sic him! Sock him! Rock him! Have I attacked anyone? Besmirched their character or anything else?"

A host of other right-wing fundamentalists active in Texas in the 1950s and 1960s include Colonel Bob Thieme of Houston's suburban Berachah Church; Joe Jeffers, director of the Kingdom of Yahweh in Houston; Raymond R. Richey, president of the Richey Evangelistic Association of Houston and close friend of the old Kansas fundamentalist, Gerald Winrod; James A. Lovell, pastor of the First Covenant Church in Dallas, who hates "One-Worlders, Zionists, pro-Communists, Liberals, and Jews"; W. A. Crisswell of Dallas, pastor of the world's largest Baptist church; Reverend Carey Daniel, another Dallas Baptist, whose anti-Negro book, *God the Original Segregationist,* has sold over a million copies; the Reverend Ken Hutcheson of San Antonio's Lakeview Baptist Church, who supports his hatred of the public schools with the charge that 40 percent of Hitler's Gestapo had graduate degrees; and the Reverends Homer and Omer Ritchie, spiritual heirs of J. Frank Norris at the First Baptist Church in Ft. Worth, who were indicted for fraud in the sale of church bonds by a federal grand jury in 1968.

. . . No single Texas fundamentalist packs a great deal of political punch. Without Hargis, the state's right-wing fundamentalists would be virtually bereft of leadership. Even with the Oklahoman, the fundamentalists make no separate impact politically; their efforts merge with those of the rest of the far-right wing. But their efforts are pervasive. Fundamentalists dominate the extremists' airwave propaganda in Texas and the South. Scores of local preachers, mostly from the smaller, fundamentalist sects, take to the radio on Sundays to make harangues and to appeal for funds to sustain the program. In this dual use of the radio, they have been inspired in large part by such ring-wing evangelists as McIntire and Hargis.

Counting the nonfundamentalists, Texas was drenched with 150 regularly scheduled extremist messages a week in 1963 (which was an off-year compared with 1962 and 1964) from six nationally prominent organizations (these included H. L. Hunt's "Life Line," the Dan Smoot "Report," Hargis' "Christian Crusade," and McIntire's "20th Century Reformation Hour"). Texas ranked first in the nation in such broadcasts, even though the right-wing hotbed of California had seven million more people. Nationally, this off-year airwave propaganda cost about $20,000,000. Given Texas' population—one twentieth of the nation's—and the relative strength of the rightists in Texas, $1,250,000 must have been expended in the Lone Star

State alone. The right-wing programs, not including the scores of local fundamentalist broadcasts with political overtones, were clustered in the western plains cities of Amarillo, Lubbock, Midland, and Odessa, in Houston and San Antonio, and especially in the "Baptist Belt" of North Central and Northeast Texas, including Dallas and Ft. Worth. Some observers believe that these broadcasts have serious consequences only in rural areas, but this would be difficult to prove.

Certainly right-wing assaults can exert a powerful influence on a congregation. One Methodist preacher in Texas was attacked by a rightist lecturer as being "unfit to hold a pulpit" because he was a Communist fellow-traveler. After the speech the right-winger drove off to his next engagement, leaving the clergyman to grapple with the doubts newly arisen in his congregation. A Disciples of Christ preacher told of his congregation being "flooded with right-wing material" and being "drawn into that camp for lack of counterinformation." Some clergymen have taken heed of the thunder on the right. One Texas preacher, who was already in trouble for favoring ecumenicalism and civil rights for Negroes, learned that some of his deacons had called a surprise meeting of the board in an attempt to pull the church out of the National Council of Churches. The minister wrote to the NCC for materials that would answer the anticipated wild charges. The deacons read the material and rejected the move to leave the NCC, but the preacher was not sure that the extremists were beaten. When asked if the rightists might be tired of fighting, he replied, "No, they never get tired. . . ."

Dallas' political inflexibility has been bolstered by an inordinate city pride, resulting in part from the lack of a compelling

geographical reason for the city's existence. By 1960 almost 25 percent of the people employed in Dallas were in the professional-managerial category, and another 30 percent were in sales or clerical work. These people, along with the really wealthy, were the strength of the city's conservatism. Being conservative was synonymous with social acceptability. Junior executives in the insurance companies, banks, and department stores considered it useful to talk even more conservatively than the boss in order to show him and others that they had "arrived." The city had begun its slide into the grip of a conservative Establishment with the formation of the Citizens Council in the late 1930s. During and after the McCarthy period, this ultraconservatism became more strident and grew almost imperceptibly into extremism. Dallas became a city in which liberalism could not even find a respectful hearing, a denial of the tolerance essential to democracy. Widely regarded as the culprit of this situation was the withering fire of radical-right propaganda with which Dallasites were constantly besieged. The *Dallas Morning News* led the rightist drumbeat. Its publisher, Ted Dealey, even insulted President Kennedy to his face; at a 1961 news conference Dealey called for a man on horseback to lead the nation and accused the President of riding Caroline's tricycle. The *News* "fed fuel to a lot of little fires," in the words of one psychology professor. A typical example of the paper's approach occurred when President Kennedy referred to civil rights as a moral issue. "Is it moral," the *News* asked, "to follow the Communist line?" Possibly the Dallas Establishment deliberately used the right "as a means of frightening moderate and liberal dissenters into silence."

The individual who seems

best to symbolize Dallas to the rest of the world is H. L. Hunt. Having already profited from oil booms and poker in Arkansas and Texas during the 1920s, Hunt hit it really big in 1930 when he euchred seventy-year-old Dad Joiner out of oil leases worth roughly $100,000,000. He arrived in Dallas in January 1938, with several million dollars and a fifth-grade education. He did not begin his political activities until the 1950s. Texas rumors hold that Hunt has bankrolled his favorite candidates with large sums, including $150,-000 for Douglas MacArthur in 1952 and $100,000 for John F. Kennedy (and Lyndon Johnson) in 1960. There is no solid evidence to support these rumors. Hunt admits contributing up to $5000 or so to each of approximately one hundred candidates over the years, but he claims to have stopped contributing around 1958. In the early 1960s, Dallas' reactionary congressman Joe Pool went to Hunt for money and got a lecture and three rolls of Gastro-Magic, an indigestion tablet manufactured by Hunt.

The Dallas billionaire has channeled most of his political energies into propaganda outlets. In 1951 he established "Facts Forum," upon which he spent about $3,500,000 in five stormy years. As an educational enterprise, the program was tax exempt and received a great deal of free time on some 230 radio stations and 60 to 70 television stations. Supposedly presenting both sides of national issues, moderator Dan Smoot was consistently biased on the side of isolationism and ultraconservatism and discouraged honest debate. Harassed by exposés, threats of investigation, and disagreements with Smoot, Hunt closed "Facts Forum" in 1956. He replaced it with "Life Line" in 1958. By 1961 the program was aired on more than 200 radio stations, and that number

increased to 350 by 1964, to 400 by 1966, and to 480 by 1968. By the summer of 1969, "Life Line" was heard or seen on more than 560 radio and television stations, reaching an estimated five million people. The "educational," tax-free broadcasts are a mixture of Hunt's social and political notions, flag waving, and fundamentalism. Hunt's notions, as revealed in his newspaper columns, letters to the editor, and four books, include abolition of mass media criticism of the government, abolition of freedom of assembly for more than two hundred people, advocacy of dictatorship by the upper class, limitation of income taxes, to 25 percent, "limitation" of sales taxes to 100 percent, banning of guaranteed annual wages, extension of voting rights to mental patients since they have a sixth sense which gives them greater insight than normal people, and installation of the 27½ percent oil depletion allowance as part of the Constitution. Hunt credits himself with fathering the oil depletion allowance and the 22d Constitutional Amendment prohibiting third terms for presidents, with persuading Lyndon Johnson to accept the vice-presidency, and with writing much of South Vietnam's constitution.

One of the events which spread Hunt's notoriety was his pamphleteering during the 1960 campaign. He paid $10,000 for the distribution of 200,000 reprints of a sermon delivered by Reverend W. A. Crisswell, pastor of the 18,500-member First Baptist Church of Dallas. One of the Reverend's thundering remarks was: "The election of a Catholic as President would mean the end of religious liberty in America." Public indignation buried the efforts of the two superpatriots, and eventually Hunt even endorsed Kennedy for the Presidency. The billionaire came under fire again as a result

of the "Life Line" programs just before the assassination of President Kennedy. For a month before the tragedy, "Life Line" hammered at the theme that Kennedy's tyrannical regime was suppressing the right of patriots to free speech and was acting with the dishonesty of a dark dictatorship. "Extreme patriotism" was needed to remedy the situation; two days later Kennedy was shot. Critics leaped to the attack. The *New Republic* called "Life Line" "the kind of program . . . that the brooding Oswalds of the left or right wing listen to and sometimes act on." Despite his activities, or because of them, Hunt has little measurable political influence in Texas or even in Dallas. Ironically for one who symbolizes Dallas in the mind of millions, Hunt is not even a member of the city's Establishment.

One extremist protest movement which arose in Dallas in 1961 achieved national prominence; it involved the more than one hundred so-called anti-Communist groups in the city. The movement began when Harry Knickerbocker, Jr., a major in the Texas Air National Guard and a Dallas insurance man, discovered that a handful of Yugoslavian pilots were training at Perrin Air Force Base near Sherman, Texas. He wrote a letter to Senator John Tower, which was reprinted in the *Dallas Morning News,* declaring that "COMMUNISTS . . . ALL communists, regardless of nationality . . . are ENEMIES OF AMERICA. Training America's enemies constitutes giving aid and comfort to them. Giving aid and comfort to America's enemies is defined in Article 3, Section 3 of the CONSTITUTION as TREASON." He signed the letter as "an unreconstructed, unliberalized, unsocialized, uncommunized American."

Seizing upon the letter and a friendly *Dallas News* editorial,

Frank McGehee, a 220-pound Korean War fighter pilot, garage owner, and Bircher, rushed out and spent $350 of his own money to hire a hall for an "indignation" meeting. Two hundred people met on the evening of October 14, 1961; a thousand were on hand the second night, and fifteen hundred on the third. Each night McGehee and Knickerbocker harangued the crowds about the Communist pilots. And one night, McGehee recalls, "a guy came to the edge of the balcony and started floating down dollar bills. The people were throwing coins and folding money, and guys up there were writing checks and sailing them down. I sent the stagehands out with pushbrooms to sweep them up. Not counting some that got sucked into the air conditioning and some that maybe got stuck to the brooms, we got $1,509."

Within days after the first sessions of the National Indignation Convention had been held in Dallas, similar meetings were held throughout the South. McGehee invited delegates from these other meetings to journey to Dallas for a national organizing convention. He predicted ten thousand per night for November 22–24; an estimated eighteen hundred showed up. They listened to well-known extremists, and to Congressmen in Washington, who spoke via telephone and loudspeaker. Tom Anderson, publisher of *Farm and Ranch* and a member of the Birch Society's National Council, came from Nashville. Spotting J. Evetts Haley (complete with black cowboy boots and ten-gallon hat) in the audience, Anderson called him to the stage and introduced him as a man "who's been in this fight for twenty years." Haley commented: "Tom Anderson must be turning moderate. He only wants to impeach Earl Warren. I'd hang him." The hall rang with applause. Congressmen who came to the phone were more cautious. Most of them gave standard Cold War political answers to McGehee's questions regarding the deportation of Communists who were receiving military training in the United States, the cancellation of military aid to Communist countries, and the firing of people responsible for these programs. But Dallas' own congressman, Bruce Alger, did pledge: "I will be your voice in Washington."

McGehee claimed that the NIC raked in some $23,000 in Dallas alone in its first five weeks of operation. Clearly, most of the money came from individuals at the meetings, most of whom seem to have been middle class, with the upper class ranking second. The Lone Star Steel Company chipped in with an undetermined amount. Its chairman of the board was E. B. Germany, a former Texas Regular (a right-wing third party in 1944) and a close adviser to W. Lee O'Daniel. By February 1962, NIC resolutions against all aid to Communists had been introduced in the Senate by Tower and in

Secret Service agents reenact the assassination of President Kennedy, November 27, 1963. *(UPI)*

the House by Alger. About seven hundred NIC committees had been formed in two hundred congressional districts in thirty-four states. It was the fastest growing extremist group in the country.

Suddenly the training of Yugoslav pilots and the sale of planes to Yugoslavia were ended, doubtless in part because of the ruckus raised by the NIC, and Congress prohibited military aid to all Communist countries. The NIC, which had been centered around only one issue, faded fast. McGehee tried to manufacture other causes for the group and even declared his candidacy for Congress from the Austin district, but it was useless—the other causes had already been staked out by a plethora of right-wing groups. In the summer of 1964, Brigadier General Richard B. Moran, Retired, a Christian Crusader, wrote to J. C. Phillips, right-wing editor of the Borger newspaper, dunning him for money for Frank McGehee. The General wrote that McGehee was $47,500 in debt after devoting over a year to insuring the selection of "conservative constitutional delegates to political conventions."

The *Dallas Morning News* bragged that the NIC could claim a great deal of the credit for the termination of foreign aid to Communist countries, that it was the *Dallas News* that had broken the story of "Tito's airmen" training at Perrin, and that the paper was responsible for the founding of the NIC. Six years later the *Dallas Morning News*, along with virtually all United States newspapers, excoriated the USSR for its invasion of Czechoslovakia. There was considerable concern in the United States that Rumania and Yugoslavia might have been the next victims of Soviet jackpots, and if they had been, the *Dallas News* would doubtless have supported the victims in front page

stories. The paper would have provided extensive coverage . . . but possibly the editors would have neglected to mention the *News'* role in hounding Yugoslav airmen out of the country.

Besides the NIC, there were various other incidents that revealed the tone of Dallas' political atmosphere in the early 1960s. Senator and Mrs. Lyndon Johnson were hissed, roughed up slightly, and spat upon in a mob scene at the Adolphus Hotel in 1960. Far-right-wing Congressman Bruce Alger was one of the leaders of the mob. In March 1963 General Walker told reporters that the Mississippi race riots of the previous autumn were a fun-filled, amusing time. When asked if the two deaths were part of the comedy, he retorted that one was a foreign newsman who had no business there. Besides, he said, Communism was a third force in the rioting. Such fanaticism by a prominent local citizen should not have gone unchallenged, yet no reply came from the *Dallas Morning News,* the Establishment, the liberals, or anyone. On October 23 of that same year, Walker delivered a militant address protesting the visit to Dallas the next day—United Nations Day—of United Nations Ambassador Adlai Stevenson. He told his audience, which included Lee Harvey Oswald, that every street corner in Dallas was a virtual battleground against the Communists and the United Nations. The next night in the same auditorium Stevenson was conked on the head, spat upon, and heckled by some of the rightists whose passions Walker had fanned the previous evening. One man in the grip of mania kept screaming: "Kennedy will get his reward in Hell. Stevenson is going to die. His heart will stop, stop, stop. And he will burn, burn, burn." The ambassador was quoted as saying that nothing like this had ever happened to him anywhere and that he was shocked.

Also on United Nations Day, 1963, rightists distributed handbills all over town. The leaflets cast President Kennedy in the role of a wanted criminal. There were two photographs of him —the full-face and profile shots of a fugitive poster. The headline was "Wanted for Treason" and was followed by a list of seven alleged subversive activities committed by the President, such as "consistantly [*sic*] appointing anti-Christians to Federal office." The handbills were written by Robert A. Surrey, a printer and a political and business associate of General Walker's. With Kennedy's visit to Dallas less than a month away, a deep-seated uneasiness set in. On November 20, a Methodist minister attended a typical, respectable dinner party at which a young, well-educated, churchgoing couple told the other guests that they hated Kennedy and "wouldn't care one bit if somebody did take a pot shot at him." On the very day of the assassination, the *Dallas Morning News* ran a full-page advertisement identifying the President with the Communist conspiracy. The ad was signed by Bernard Weissman, an agent of a supersecret organization called CUSA, which hoped to infiltrate and eventually take over right-wing organizations, unify them, and then take control of all American politics. The $1465 advertisement was paid for by three local businessmen, including Nelson Bunker Hunt, H. L.'s son.

Immediately after the assassination it was widely assumed that a fanatical rightist had committed the deed. Many of Dallas' local extremists themselves thought so. The color completely drained from one rightist's face when the news was announced; he was convinced that one of his colleagues had committed murder. Many other Dallasites felt guilty because so many people there had hated Kennedy. It has been suggested that the aura of extremism in the city may have affected the thinking of Lee Harvey Oswald, the accused assassin. He was, in any event, psychotic, dejected over his life in the Soviet Union, greatly desirous of attention, and well aware of the popularity of the rising tide of right-wing leaders who were besieged with speaking invitations in his native Dallas–Ft. Worth area. A whole city cannot be held accountable for anything, but there was certainly nothing to be proud of on the part of a substantial number of the Dallas citizenry, including the owners of the *Dallas Morning News,* the well-educated, church-going couple at the respectable dinner party, and anyone present at the party who failed to dissent vigorously.

The assassination did not noticeably change Dallas' political climate. Both Dallas newspapers refused to accept an advertisement written by a group of theological faculty calling for a moral reassessment. A schoolteacher paying homage to the President near the assassination site gave a reporter a statement, then tearfully withdrew it when her mother said she would be fired by the Dallas public school system if she stood by it. A fourth grade teacher, Mrs. Elizabeth Cowan, was suspended by Superintendent W. T. White for writing a letter to *Time* magazine blaming the city's political atmosphere for paving the way for the assassination. Under the glare of publicity, White and the school board reinstated Mrs. Cowan. Two months after the assassination a *Dallas Morning News* editorial denounced as appeasers those who favor United States recognition of Red China, more trade with Russia, or a neutral Vietnam. Another month later an editorial cartoon in the *News* strongly implied, in reference to the United States wheat deal with Russia, that President Lyndon Johnson was helping Soviet Premier Nikita Khrushchev bury the United States. The next year, 1964, John Shea was fired from his job at Petrofina for writing an article which appeared in *Look* stating that Dallas fostered a climate of hate. An anonymous suburban housewife gave an interview in which she admitted that her liberalism was strictly private; she feared social ostracism by her neighbors, retaliation against her children at school, and loss of livelihood by her husband. . . .

HENRY FAIRLIE
Johnson & the Intellectuals
A British View

Henry Fairlie is an English journalist who sees a clear-cut division between culture and politics as the normal state of affairs, and the American penchant to mix intellectual and political activities as a categorical mistake. Whether he suffers from misconceptions about the American political system is a difficult question, for the particular kind of political conservatism that Fairlie represents scarcely exists, except as an affectation, in American life.

In retrospect it seems impossible to deny that the American intellectual community accepted the Kennedy administration with a breath-taking lack of criticism, and Fairlie's discussion of the Kennedy intellectuals and their romantic view of power at least scores a number of strong debater's points. On the other hand, his criticism of the intellectuals' attack on Johnson seems to combine an accurate diagnosis of intellectual snobbery with a general condemnation of criticism that subsequent events—especially in Vietnam—make rather hard to accept. Nevertheless, Fairlie has raised in responsible terms a question about the relationship of intellect and power that haunted the sixties: Have we the ability to profit from the vast intellectual estate that America has built in the past generation?

During the time that I have been in the United States, I have found nothing more strange or more unattractive than the way in which American intellectuals take pleasure in reviling President Johnson. It is not simply that they object to his policies in Vietnam and the Dominican Republic. It is a feeling of strong personal revulsion. "He is a slob," one of them said to me when I asked him why he disliked the President so much.

Others say much the same, if less briefly.

I have little doubt that this scorn for President Johnson as a person is one of the causes of the rather strained character of the current debate on American foreign policy. It makes the critics of his policies appear much more united than in fact they are, because they can always meet on this single point of fastidious disdain for the man. It gives their criticisms an edge which is quite incidental to their actual arguments, and lends them an excitement which titillates but is unserious. Above all, it exaggerates the barrier between them and the President, so that there is a real danger that they will cease to be able to communicate at all.

The fault, I wish to suggest, is not entirely President Johnson's. There may be much about him, as there is about any politician, which is hard to stomach. To put it delicately, he invites the severest aesthetic judgments. But that is exactly my point: I am not at all sure that such judgments have any place in political discussion.

The role of the intellectual in American political life is, of course, bewildering to an Englishman, and I find myself wondering how any sensitive intellect can bear, without damage or derangement, the solemn importance which is attached to the intellectual in the public life of this country. The real intellectual, I would have thought, must demur at such a questionable exaltation.

The professor who allows himself to become a speech writer to a presidential candidate or a special assistant to a President; the poet who allows himself to be tempted to participate in a presidential inauguration; the academic economist who leaves his university to become an ambassador: each of these (and the examples in America could be multiplied) I regard as a loss, with no adequate compensating gain. Even the amount of time given to a teach-in points, surely, to a lack of severe intellectual discipline in the intellectuals who take part.

Still, I recognize that this is a national habit, which will not be changed. The dearly bought, and even more dearly maintained, privacy of the intellectual life is something for which American intellectuals have scant regard, and on which they put a small price whenever public prominence beckons. But this is how they seem to want it, and I am concerned only to point out the obvious traps which lie in wait. For in these I see part of the

explanation of their present disillusionment with President Johnson.

Removed from his own discipline, no one is more vain than the intellectual. Precisely because his mind is able to handle ideas with ease and excitement, it is all too easily turned when he is invited to discourse outside his own field. Inside his own field, the intellectual would never lay claim to omniscience, and seldom to authority. Outside it, his claim to both is breath-taking. A man who, having devoted his life to the study of some exact historical event, would hesitate to suggest the multiple reasons why it occurred, has no hesitation in analyzing the situation in Vietnam and predicting, say, the Vietcong reaction to a hypothetical situation.

That he should do so at all is bad enough. But far worse is the

Drawing by David Levine. (Reprinted with permission from The New York Review of Books. Copyright © 1965, NYREV, Inc.)

fact that, in doing so, he cannot help resorting to an all but dishonest, and an all but contemptible, use of the methods he has learned inside his discipline. I know of few things more virtuous than the methods of the intellectual used to a fit purpose: it is all the greater prostitution, therefore, when they are employed for the purposes of largely polemical debate. Professor Michael Oakeshott has said that politics is an inappropriate activity for the young, not because of their vices, but because of their virtues. Much the same is true of the intellectual.

But his vanity leads him on; and it is his vanity which explains why, when he engages in public events, he is the most easily seduced "joiner" of them all. He will sign almost any round-robin protest. Day by day, the stereotyped literature of protest—"We, the undersigned, representing the art, humanities and sciences in the United States . . ." —falls onto his breakfast table, and he takes out his pen to make his broad-minded challenge to the forces of evil in the world, amidst the Rice Krispies. "I think you're quite right," his wife comforts him, caring for his digestion.

It has been suggested by one of the wittiest columnists in England that there is an organization called "Rent-a-Crowd," which hires out crowds that can demonstrate anywhere, against anything. I sometimes feel that there must be a similar agency on Madison Avenue, called "Rent-a-Signature," which collects and supplies, for a reasonable charge, the signatures of intellectuals. But, of course, the agency would fail: seeing what the intellectual will sign simply out of his own vanity, why bother to pay him?

The most serious consequence of the vanity of the intellectual is that he is so pathetically flattered by power. The politician is the most guileful of flatterers, the intellectual his most guileless victim. As long as the politician can be seen to be what he is—a trader for votes—the intellectual does not find it difficult to remain untouched by him. But as soon as the politician dresses himself up in fancy clothes, glamorizing his office and his power, the intellectual is a sucker for his favors; and the American intellectual, it seems to me, although one should be able to assume he is beyond the age of consent, was raped by President Kennedy.

At all times, and no matter who exercises it, power is ugly and brutalizing: President Kennedy was allowed to make it appear attractive and redeeming. Power is shoddy: President Kennedy was allowed to glamorize it. Power is for the aged: President Kennedy was allowed to cast over it the magic of youth. Power is un-intellectual: President Kennedy was allowed to give it intellectual excitement. Power is safe only if it is exercised without enchantment, without claim to reason, and without pretense to virtue: President Kennedy was allowed to endow it with all three. Power is, no doubt, necessary: President Kennedy was allowed to make it seem desirable.

I have tried to be careful in this last paragraph. I have not blamed President Kennedy for doing, or for trying to do, these things: a politician is entitled to use every trick he knows, and President Kennedy had the wit to know more than most. My complaint is that he was allowed to do them without the intellectual reacting with wariness, skepticism and, ultimately, rejection. If the intellectual is going to be fastidious about politics, he should revolt, not against a President Johnson for making politics look as beastly as it is, but against a President Kennedy for

making it look gracious, for appropriating to it virtues which it does not possess.

(I do not doubt, I should perhaps interject, that the politics of a free state does have virtue. But that virtue lies simply in the exercise of their vote by millions of ordinary, and otherwise unpowerful people: in the act itself, and not in the rightness or wrongness of what they do with it. The virtue—the grace —does not lie in any other part of the process, and certainly not in the man of power, the politician.)

If they could only see it, the intellectuals would realize that President Johnson has cleansed them or, at least, given them the opportunity to cleanse themselves. He does not make the pretense that political decision is a debate between intellectually upright ideas; and when he does, he reassuringly comes a cropper. He does not ask the arts to place a garland on his head; and when he does, it is the predictable farce of the Festival of Arts at the White House. He does not call intellectuals away from their gentle pursuits; and when he does, he gains the services of only very rum intellectuals indeed. The intellectual is on his own again, and it is to me a tragedy that he should react by pining again for political enchantment.

An English political philosopher has said that the scorn which people have for their politicians is "the rage of Caliban at seeing his face in the glass." But it is the face of Caliban which one should see reflected when one looks at a politician; and President Johnson is, by this reckoning, a most reassuring politician. How much more demeaning to be spirited away by Ariel, to gaze on politics as Ferdinand mooned over Miranda— with Mr. Theodore Sorensen, a wily and prematurely aged Prospero, always at one's elbow with his old wizard's incantations about power.

Mr. Sorensen's lectures on the Presidency (published under the title *Decision Making in the White House*) seem to me one of the most dreadful celebrations of political power that I have ever read; and I am prepared to take a bet that the objectionable feature of his forthcoming book on President Kennedy will not be the praise of the President, which is legitimate, but the praise of political power as such.

For this, of course, is another of the traps into which an American intellectual is likely to fall if he allows himself to be entangled in politics. The presidency, because it is not simply a political office, is easily exalted. In Mr. Theodore H. White's *The Making of the President, 1960,* there is one horrifying sentence. On the night of the results, he wrote, the newspaper correspondents "itched to be with the winner. Closeness to power heightens the dignity of all men." It does nothing of the sort; and newspaper correspondents, I presume and hope, "itched to be with the winner" only because it meant that they would have the better stories.

Mr. Averell Harriman, talking about President Truman's failure to dismiss petty grafters from federal positions, some of whom had access to the White House, said: "What he doesn't realize is that the American people regard the White House as a national shrine which is not to be sullied by even the appearance of misdoing." I do not believe that the American people regard the White House as anything of the kind; like all mature electorates, they have a far more sophisticated view of politics, of how Presidents are made and how they then maintain themselves in office, than intellectuals allow them. But there seems to me no doubt that President Kennedy was able to tempt intellectuals into regarding the White House as part court and part shrine; and the rediscovery that it is a profane altar after all is understandably painful.

The intellectual saw in President Kennedy, in perhaps more ways than one, a silk purse. There is, thankfully, no mistaking the sow's ear in President Johnson. (In fact, of course, some intellectuals when they touched the silk purse found, at the time, that it was a sow's ear after all—but this now tends to be forgotten.) Mr. Robert Lowell had the right idea when he refused to attend the Festival of Arts, but he gave the wrong reason. Instead of woozily muttering about Vietnam, he should have simply replied that as a poet he could not entertain such an invitation, that he had no intention of allowing his muse to pay homage to a political office. What a grotesque thought it is that, if his views on Vietnam had happened to be different, Mr. Lowell might have solemnly read "For the Union Dead" to Mrs. Lyndon Johnson. That one can recognize that it is grotesque —as it might not have seemed three years ago—is a measure of President Johnson's virtuous (if unintended) gift to the American people. By contrast, it is still hard to forgive President Kennedy for inviting the late Robert Frost to participate in his inauguration, or Frost for acquiescing in the debauch.

I do not understand what an artist like Mr. William Walton was doing, beating the drums for a politician, and a Boston politician at that—for friendship provides neither excuse nor explanation for such a bemusement with power. Nor do I understand what Mr. Arthur Schlesinger, Jr., whose *The Age of Jackson* has always seemed to me one of the most thrilling attainments of a young historian, is doing in Washington at all, away from his rigorous profession (for contemporary history is not academic history), still sniffing at the hems of power—any more than anyone seems able to explain to me what he ever did in the White House in the first place. Above all, for his is both a rare spirit and a rare intellect, I do not understand what Professor Galbraith ever thought he was up to, allowing himself to be sidetracked into becoming ambassador to India—a post not obviously calling for intellectual gifts (as Mr. Harold Wilson seems to have acknowledged by appointing the editor of the *New Statesman*)—and Professor Galbraith does not, in the end, seem to have understood either.

Intellectuals (and poets and artists) should realize that President Johnson has mercifully released them from the feeling that they owe the state a due, and one may even believe that the editor of the *New Republic* is safe from exile to New Delhi. When I read that Miss Phyllis McGinley has been dispatched as ambassador to London, I will know that the world of the intellect is again safe from the political procurer.

Mr. Harold Macmillan, himself a man of civilized and engaging intellect, has enjoyed over the years the friendship or acquaintance of many of the most considerable intellectuals in Britain. But it would never have occurred to him to debase their friendship, or their office in society *as intellectuals,* by asking them to undertake his political chores for him. The nearest he came to exacting a political function from any of them was when he permitted Professor Hugh Trevor-Roper to arrange his election as Chancellor of Oxford University, a most skillfully organized political campaign. There seems to me a fitness in this, and the American intellectual, before he disdains President Johnson, might do well to consider whether he has not neglected, in the past, this sense of fitness, whether the very personal qualities he dislikes in President Johnson are not in fact saving graces, whether it is not fortunate that political decision and the political process should again be seen clearly for what they are.

For the intellectual, of course, cannot easily apprehend politics, and anything which tempts him to believe that he can make sense either *of* the political process or *in* the political process is dangerous both to him and to the politician, but above all to the desirable communication between them. I cannot see how this communication can fruitfully take place unless both observe some fitness in their roles, acknowledge the limits of their own fields and use, with precision, their own methods and instruments without borrowing each other's. Only in this way can the exchange between them be illuminating. To put it another way, if the intellectual wishes to engage himself directly in the political process, he can only do it as Mr. McGeorge Bundy has done, by ceasing to be an intellectual, as such, and becoming a politician, as such. The difference was seen brilliantly in Mr. Bundy's annihilation of Professor Hans J. Morgenthau during the CBS teach-in.

Characteristically—for he is one of the very few Washington commentators who seem to me to write about politics at all, to recognize the political process for what it is and to write about it as it is—Mr. Joseph Kraft put his finger on the point in an article, "Kennedy and the Intellectuals," in *Harper's*, when he observed the difference between the effectiveness of those intellectuals who had properly, almost anonymously, become part of the political machine and those "who supposed they could work closely with the President, and thus shake off the bureaucratic trammels." Mr. Kraft quoted, with devastating effect, Professor Galbraith's complaint that there seemed now in politics to be no place for "the broken-field runner." In fact, of course, there never is a place for him in politics, save in exceptional circumstances, such as war, when normal political processes are in abeyance. The whole point of politics is that you cover every lap closely bunched together, and if anyone breaks away, you have a political crisis.

Unless, then, the intellectual submerges himself in politics, and in so doing ceases to be an intellectual, he will go on misapprehending the political process, expecting both too much of it and too little, imagining that it can achieve dramatic results and ignoring the quiet, usually unsung, results which it achieves in its own way.

The sternest axiom which a politician must obey is that he must not be tempted into seizing imaginary initiatives: the intellectual temperamentally believes that the opportunity for them is always there. The sternest obligation of a politician is that he must live with problems that he cannot solve, and must handle them without necessarily seeking a solution: temperamentally, the intellectual cannot bear a problem that is incapable of solution. The sternest rule which a politician must observe is that he is not acting for the future, for history, but simply for today: the intellectual temperamentally gazes into the future, forward into history. He does not as a general rule care for the untidiness—the intractability—of the present.

The raw materials with which a politician in a free state must work are usually intractable: interests which conflict, and are hard to reconcile; wills which he cannot command, but at best only persuade; resources which are limited, and on which the claims are manifold; support which must be weighed and reweighed, and may at any time wither away; problems whose nature can only be dimly, usually intuitively, perceived, but of which he must dispose, even if in ignorance. He is a painter who cannot mix his own paints; a potter who cannot choose his own clay; a composer who must score for a brass band what he had perhaps intended for a string quartet. That is the measure of his art.

That President Johnson is a great practitioner of the art is hardly denied: then why not look at him, as such; and, if one wishes, dispute with him, as such? But this is precisely the quandary in which the intellectual finds himself, for he is lost (as he should be lost) in the art of politics. "The American liberal," a Negro lawyer who works on Capitol Hill said to me, "is more interested in style than in substance"; and, again and again, American liberal intellectuals have asked me about the "style" of Mr. Harold Wilson, and complained in turn about the "style" of President Johnson. This aestheticism is not only quite irrelevant to politics; it reduces the real impact which the intellectual could, and should, have in political debate. It sharpens the edge of his criticism; it blunts the point of his attack.

Whether President Johnson is a "slob" or not is not really of interest, for he is a supreme political artist, brilliant (at least this will be conceded) in the proper political arts of flattering, cajoling, bartering, bribing, purchasing, intimidating, and (if necessary) trampling. But these are precisely the arts which the intellectual cannot employ in return and, consequently, if he engages directly in day-to-day political issues, he usually misses the target.

When I arrived in this country in March, the honeymoon between the intellectuals and the President was becoming strained, but it had not come to an end. Since then, I have been able to watch their growing doubt, disappointment, and disillusion. Doubt, disappointment, and disillusion being the proper intellectual attitude to power, I expected the intellectuals to welcome this return to a fit view of life. Instead, they have grown sour and savage—with a man who seems to me simply to be behaving as every politician does —and their reaction exposes, with a wonderful clarity, exactly why the intellectual who engages in current politics is usually lost.

First, *the intellectual is seldom able to understand the nature of a political decision.* When Mr. Attlee's Cabinet had to consider whether Turkey should be allowed to become a member of NATO, the discussion went round the table, and every possible political, economic, and strategic argument was put forward, especially by Aneurin Bevan. At last the moment came for Mr. Attlee to "collect the voices." (In the tradition of British Prime Ministers, he had until then been silent.) "Fought against the Turks at Gallipoli," he snapped. "Would rather have them on our side than the enemy's. We'll have them in."

That is, almost perfectly illustrated, political decision; and it amazes me how American intellectuals today go around shocking each other with stories about, say, how the decision to intervene in the Dominican Republic was taken. After twenty years of watching politics fairly closely, it would not in the least surprise me if I were told that it had been taken for an even more outlandish reason than Mr. Attlee gave to his Cabinet—or even that it was not, in any rational sense, "taken" at all.

"I am not sure that there is really such a thing as 'power' or 'decision,'" one of Britain's greatest Prime Ministers said to me, when I was talking to him at the end of his career. "I would certainly find it very hard to give you an example of when I have ever exercised power or taken a decision. Of course, I will try to make it all look very different in my memoirs: and, if I am lucky, part of my version will be accepted by historians, and then I will be called a great statesman. But it all happens very differently. For one thing, there is just a build-up of big and small events, of big and small factors, and they may not be brought to your notice until the issue has already been decided; and, when you eventually have to decide, it may be in response to the smallest of them all. That is not 'power' or 'decision'; you are too much in the hands of events. For another thing, the in-tray is always full. That is what politics is: trying to empty the in-tray."

But, of course, a President and a Prime Minister cannot wait until they write their memoirs to provide the justification or the rationalization of their decisions; they have to provide it immediately, and in public, to the world. A President Kennedy and a Mr. Macmillan were masters at presenting their "decisions" in great historical perspectives, and in magic vistas of intellectual enchantment. They were both men who, when they took the field, took it panoplied and accoutred, bestowing on their political decisions a quite unlikely majesty.

It is, therefore, an awful bump to come down to President Johnson's description of how he took the decision to intervene in the Dominican Republic. (Read it out of its context—and Mr. Art Buchwald could not make power look more laughable.) In one sense, I do not accept President Johnson's version any more than

I would have accepted the more self-conscious versions of President Kennedy or Mr. Macmillan; precisely because he is not used to intellectualizing his processes, President Johnson made them seem even more bizarre than they can, in fact, have been. All the same, his description of how a political decision is taken was much nearer to the truth than we care to realize.

I have listened to many descriptions of how President Johnson is supposed to take decisions —"He is ego-blocked, but not ego-distorted," was the quite solemn comment of one intellectual of renown—and I am left with the impression that he takes them for exactly the same reasons of personal and party interest, of political pressure and the pressure of events, as does any politician. If intellectuals could only forget his "style" (which, I remember saying when I first observed him in the flesh at a press conference, is really that of a Texas Macmillan), they might have more time to consider the substance of the interests and pressures to which—quite legitimately—he reacts.

The American intellectual might certainly ask himself whether much of his disdain for President Johnson's manner is not the result of a rather questionable hankering after the patrician in politics. After all, the Americans maintain a political system which gives a terrible advantage to wealth—the role which wealth played in President Kennedy's campaign for the nomination is, to an outsider, frightening—and it is, therefore, quite understandable to find the wealth and background of, say, the Roosevelts, Kennedys, and Rockefellers more bearable than the wealth and background of the Johnsons. But the motives, to say the least, are mixed, and I am not sure that it is healthy that the relationship between wealth and power in this country should be made to look congenial simply by a patrician manner. At least the "style" of President Johnson enables one to see it for what it is.

Secondly, *the intellectual imports into current political issues ideas which, although valuable in themselves, cannot be entertained in day-to-day politics.* It is part of his temperament—although this is far more true of the American than the British intellectual—that he finds power exciting, and that he is especially excited by the idea of vast and subterranean forces which are at work, implacably holding mankind in their grip. This is one reason, as has often been remarked, why he falls (usually on his face) for any "conspiracy" view of politics, or any grand theory of "historical inevitability," which happens to be going the rounds.

When Mr. Bundy referred on the CBS teach-in to Professor Morgenthau's "congenital pessimism," he was not making simply a debating point: he was making a precise and damaging intellectual one, exposing the irrelevance of Professor Morgenthau's intellectual concepts to political decision. Part of Professor Morgenthau's method is to build (and to rebuild, wherever necessary) elaborate frameworks of historical prediction and then to surrender to his guesses. That he surrenders to them is his own business. That he then asks politicians to surrender to them—to guess with him woefully at the future, and to abdicate all political choice to his presentiments— is an alarming intellectual conceit.

When the politician thinks that he hears the crack of doom —and it is the crack of doom which reverberates in Professor Morgenthau's head—he has lost the nerve for the game, and should get out.

It is an intolerable idea that any politician should abandon the present to the inscrutable future, that he should abandon present commitments to the obscure possibility that they may become insupportable, that he should abandon present opportunities to the dark fear that the situation may be worse tomorrow. You never can tell what tomorrow may bring. Winston Churchill, if he had surrendered the present to the future in 1940, would have surrendered Britain, too: the future, at the time, seemed all too clear. But he lived and acted, during those months, entirely in the present. Today, he said, is enough: and, when each new today came, we were still there.

Again, it is a common intellectual fascination to imagine that there is such a thing as the real national interest. This, certainly, is the claim made—sometimes explicitly—by Mr. Walter Lippmann in his present criticisms of the administration's policies. He claims, moreover, not only that there is such a thing as America's real national interest (which is doubtful), but that it can be discovered (which is certainly untrue), and that the politician should make it his business to discover it and obey it (which is alarming).

To concede that the politician can and should discover the real national interest, is to concede, also, that he may have discovered it, and therefore to leave no philosophical justification for questioning his actions. It is the claim made by all dictators, and there has always been, in Mr. Lippmann's political philosophy, this strong pull toward authoritarianism, toward the idea that there are some who know best what is good for the nation, the people, at large.

But this is not the immediate point. The fact is that the politician cannot be concerned with the "real" national interest, because he is bound to deal with observable facts. The idea of a real national interest is a metaphysical concept—useful to the intellectual as an instrument, but, as has been proved by several million deaths over the past hundred and fifty years, dangerous if taken literally—which has nothing to do with actuality. None of us today can *know* the real national interest of America in Southeast Asia; history will still be arguing about it a thousand years from now. The politician, therefore, must be concerned with less grand concepts: whether it is just possible to stay; whether it is just possible to meet a commitment; whether it is just possible that this risk may be more justifiable than that. For risk is the inner nature of all political decision.

"There is an important difference," Mr. Bundy said on the CBS teach-in, "between the best one can do within the framework of one's existing commitments and quitting too soon." In those deeply satisfying words there is all the qualification, all the hesitation, all the doubt, all the lack of dogma, of the real political choice. It is untidy; it leaves every end untied; it offers no clear-cut answer, since there is no answer until it happens. To the intellectual, of course, it is unsatisfactory; but that is precisely why we have politicians, so that they may cope with the untidiness of the present for us.

If Churchill had consulted Britain's "real" national interest in 1940, he would have made as fast and favorable an armistice with Germany as possible. But he did not, and it should be realized that his defiance was justified, not by Britain's heroism or Britain's strength, for the one could have been trampled on and the other was nonexistent, but by an imponderable: the fact that Hitler proceeded to miscalculate, that he thought he could leave Britain aside while he turned to conquer the East. No one could have foreseen such a frantic miscalculation by Hitler—yet, without it, Churchill's resistance would have been a lamentable misconception of Britain's real national interests.

In these and in every other concept which the intellectual uses in the discussion of current politics, he assumes a knowledge which the politician knows is not available, and argues with a certainty which the politician is bound to eschew. The charismatic leader—and President Kennedy had many of the qualities of one—will always present political decision with something of this certainty. I feel much safer with the inconclusive, even messy, arguments of the present administration.

Lastly, *the intellectual in America, by the prominence which he accepts in political life, distracts attention from the real business of politics.* Politics is, first and foremost, the eliciting, even the manufacture, of support. With all respect to the intellectuals at home, and to the qualms of some governments abroad, President Johnson is today acting with a breadth of support, and a lack of effective opposition, which strike awe in any open-eyed observer. I do not, personally, like it; I do not think it healthy that a democracy should have become so lopsided that no source of *political* opposition is easily to be found. This was the point made by a British colleague, Mr. Patrick O'Donovan, when he wrote recently in the Washington *Post* that Washington had become a one-man town.

The fault is not President Johnson's; it is the duty, as it is the right, of any political leader to seek the maximum support for his policies that he can. Where, then, does the fault lie?

It lies, first, in the stampede to President Johnson last November. America is today paying the political price for voting as if the choice were between right and wrong, between good and evil. No one assisted in presenting the choice in these terms more effectively than the intellectuals. When they should have been skulking in their lairs, using the quiet but insistent voice of the intellectual to warn that a stampede to one leader or one party is always democracy's dearest mistake, they instead helped to whip up the stampede. It was the intellectuals, as much as anyone, who created the Colossus; they, as much as anyone, who worked for the annihilation of one of the great parties of the state; they, as much as anyone, who provided the reasons why a democracy should elect a dictator.

Moreover, they still (in political terms) argue with their hands tied. President Johnson's strength rests entirely on support for his domestic program. There is only one way of damaging him, only one way of bartering with him, and that is by obstructing his domestic program. It is, quite simply, impossible to allow him a "consensus" at home, and deny it to him abroad. Politics is, in this sense, one. It is quite permissible to welcome the collapse of the Southern bloc in the Senate; but democracy will not be healthy until another—more than one— self-interested bloc emerges, ready and able to bargain with the executive, ready and able to engage the President on every front, to achieve its own selfish ends on one.

To put it quite simply, President Johnson, by his domestic program, has bribed the nation. The only way of attacking him is to refuse the bribe.

Political needs require precise political action. But this is what public opinion cannot provide today, since it is greedy for the bribes which President Johnson offers; it is what no party can provide, since the opposition party was deliberately undermined last November, by a campaign of frivolous irresponsibility; and it is what Congress cannot supply, since it dare not be seen to refuse the bribes which the President offers to their constituents. It is to this distortion of the political process that intellectuals should be paying deep attention, the urgent need for finding, *inside politics,* centers of disaffection, which can then flatter, cajole, barter, purchase, arm-twist, intimidate, and trample at least as effectively as the Chief Executive.

Beside this urgent need, a "campus revolt" is not only irrelevance but a dangerous distraction.

Nothing that I have said is intended to scoff at either political or intellectual activity. Both, in a free country, have great virtue. I have merely made a plea that the two should be kept separate, and that it is primarily the fault of the American intellectual that the two have become confused. The intellectual cannot engage in current political discussion and hope, at the same time, to think deeply or precisely. He should be using his mind now to inquire into the long-term meaning of America's huge power, into the relevance of her institutions to a situation in which this power inescapably exists, and so must inescapably confer still greater power on the executive, into the survival of powerful and independent blocs in a country which is geared more and more to federal activity and federal money. All of these, and so many more, are proper fields of intellectual inquiry, and the intellectual should be satisfied that, if he uses his instruments well, any truth which he may happen to discover will, in time, and not necessarily a long time at that, filter down into the bloodstream of the country.

ROBERT LEKACHMAN
The Age of Keynes

The most unequivocal success of the 1960s was the national economy, which sustained the longest period of expansion in its history—over six years. Much of that success was due to the "new economics," essentially a modern version of Keynesianism in which the federal government stimulates or stabilizes the economy by raising or lowering spending. This can be done by direct federal expenditures for public works or defense, or by stimulating the private sector of the economy through tax cuts. Robert Lekachman in *The Age of Keynes* puts into historical perspective the body of ideas that shaped the successful economic policies of the decade, describing how a theory first announced in the Great Depression finally came of age a generation later.

For a long time, Keynesianism was considered a liberal idea, the middle ground between a conservative concept of free enterprise and the radical idea of socialism. But, as Lekachman observes, Keynesian techniques are simply an administrative tool, which any group can use for whatever social ends it cherishes. He is particularly astute in explaining how all the Keynesian economic manipulations of the 1960s moved in the direction of expanding the private rather than the public sector of the economy. In the end, business was a major—perhaps the major—element in the broad-gauged coalition that Lyndon Johnson formed around the policy of economic expansion through cutting the rate of taxation. That fact, Lekachman is convinced, defined in advance the limits of the Great Society program.

In the United States also, postwar public policy was less than completely Keynesian until very recently. In fairness to several postwar administrations, it should be said that American officials have refused to allow continuing gold outflows caused by repeated deficits in the balance of payments to raise domestic interest rates and cause serious general recessions. However, during the Eisenhower years and the first portion of the Kennedy administration, the Presidents and their advisers, fearing adverse international repercussions, did hesitate to recommend fiscal and financial policies expansionary enough to curtail unemployment and reduce the quantity of idle resources.

Employment policy has been the glaring weakness of postwar economic management in the United States. The obvious success of the 1964 and 1965 tax abatements in reducing unemployment rates in 1965 points the moral that fiscal policy in the 1950s and even the first years of the 1960s was much too timid, far less vigorous than the American economy required in order to move from the 5 to 7 percent unemployment typical of the 1950s to the more appropriate and efficient 2.5 to 3 percent levels which in 1965 still had not been reached.

Thus, American economic policy has had its flaws until only yesterday, even according to the single criterion of economic expansion. There is little favorable to be said of the policies of the 1950s; but the 1960s deserve their fame in the record of public action as the years in which Keynesian economics became the open as well as the implicit national premise upon which two Presidents based their fiscal recommendations. This is the decade which has converted an esoteric theory into the annual exercise of distributing a fiscal surplus between tax reduction and social welfare. Possibly more startling still was business' discovery that economic expansion was assisted by the termination of the traditional civil war between Democratic national administrations and the business community. Business' recognition that prudent Keynesian fiscal policies actually promote larger markets and higher profits has had an unexpected effect. Keynesian prescriptions, the monopoly of reformers and radicals during the 1930s and 1940s, have very nearly become the favorite medicines of the established, propertied interests in the community.

This too is very recent. It is unlikely that even ten years ago any business periodical would have expended editorial space in praise of a tax slash which fur-

ther unbalanced a budget in deficit, and then gone on to give direct support to the policy's underlying principle. Yet in *Business Week*'s considered judgment, "The 1964 tax cut was not a one-shot achievement that forever more solves the nation's growth problems. On the contrary, the lesson of 1964 is that fiscal policy needs to be used actively and steadily if balanced long-term growth is to be achieved."

The institutionalization of Keynes is an indispensable element of the Great Society program as well as an aspect of President Johnson's highly successful efforts to generate national consensus on a wide range of public issues. But the beginnings of the process are located in 1961 and the short administration of President Kennedy. When John F. Kennedy entered the White House, he was still skeptical about the capacity of budget deficits to stimulate economic expansions. As a result his early approach to fiscal and monetary policy was cautious and exploratory. His initial recommendations to Congress, based largely upon the minimum proposals of the Samuelson task force report released in the interregnum between the November election and the January inauguration, included neither a tax cut nor very substantial increases in public spending. As matters turned out, the first expenditure increases to win presidential approval were military; and there was a short time during the summer of 1961, in the midst of the menacing Berlin crisis, when the President actually contemplated a tax *increase,* designed to finance larger military programs and incidentally to answer those Americans who were eager, after hearing their President's inspiring inaugural address, to find out what they could do for their country.

As his associates have recalled the change, Kennedy's conversion to a modern, Keynesian position

resulted from the disappointing failure of the economy to respond to the very limited schemes for manpower retraining, area redevelopment and the extension of unemployment compensation which Congress enacted in 1961, or even to the investment tax credit which Congress approved in the same year. During the first twelve months of that administration, the most notable economic events were controversies rather than new policies, in particular the argument between the advocates of fiscal stimulation and the counselors of caution. Led by Chairman William McChesney Martin of the Federal Reserve Board, occasionally assisted by Secretary of the Treasury C. Douglas Dillon, the prudent camp pointed to the dangers of domestic inflation and the menace of continuing gold losses to Western Europe.

The expansionists were themselves divided into two groups. The Galbraith group strongly urged a substantial expansion of public spending. As Galbraith analyzed the needs of the time, the public spending would not only stimulate the economy but would also feed the starved public services and do something to rectify the existing social imbalance between public and private spending. This was the theme of Galbraith's influential *The Affluent Society.* Theoretically, however, it is just as possible to stimulate a sluggish economy by reducing taxes as by enlarging social welfare programs or, for that matter, military spending. Hence the second expansionist school, organized by the Council of Economic Advisers, committed themselves with growing urgency to the superiority of a tax reduction over a public spending policy, partly on technical administrative grounds and partly on arguments of political feasibility. As stimulating devices, tax cuts produce their effects much more rapidly than new spending programs, which take time to get started. On the political front, Congress was believed much more receptive to tax reduction than to additional government spending, even when the budgetary impact was identical.

As this controversy within his own household proceeded, the President gave increasing public signs of his own advancing economic education. The most notable piece of evidence was that same Yale commencement address of June 1962 which has appeared before in this account. What attracted most attention was the presidential "assault" on the economic "myths" which retarded congressional action and darkened public understanding. In the course of his attack, Mr. Kennedy expressed a new personal distaste for balanced budgets. "The myth persists," he declared firmly, "that federal deficits create inflation and budget surpluses prevent it." Against this myth the President opposed recent history: "Yet sizable budget surpluses after the war did not prevent inflation and persistent deficits for the last several years have not upset our basic price stability." From the record, Mr. Kennedy inferred the sensible moral that "Obviously deficits are sometimes dangerous and so are surpluses. But honest assessment plainly requires a more sophisticated view than the old and automatic cliché that deficits automatically bring inflation."

As he administered national instruction, the President just for good measure sought to distinguish the administrative budget (upon which public comment continues to center) from two more illuminating budget concepts, the cash and the national income accounts variants, both of much more interest to economists. He had a sharp word to say as well about the real significance of the national debt: "There are myths about our public debt. It is widely supposed that this debt is

growing at a dangerously rapid rate. In fact, both the debt per person and the debt as a proportion of our Gross National Product have declined sharply since the Second World War." Strongly as the President spoke, he evidently thought it prudent to stop short of the standard textbook proposition that the size of an internally held public debt is of little importance since its handling accounts to no more than a series of income transfers among citizens of the same political jurisdiction. Certainly, there is no sense in which the public debt represents the sort of burden upon the community that a private debt does upon an individual.

The direction of Mr. Kennedy's thought was unmistakable. By December 1962, Chairman Walter Heller of the Council of Economic Advisers had succeeded in convincing him of a still more novel corollary of the fiscal stimulus doctrine. Heller's corollary was that the progressive nature of the federal tax system had the effect of moving the federal budget first into balance and then into an actual surplus well before economic expansion had engendered satisfactory levels of output and employment. As these surpluses began to pile up, they inevitably acted as a drag on further expansion, for the federal government took more and more money out of the economy and failed to increase the sums which it pushed out into the economy. Once the President accepted this analysis and applied it to the then current business expansion, he was prepared to take the bold political step of advocating a major tax reduction in the midst of a business cycle upturn, the very time when older counsels focused upon higher taxes and increased interest rates.

For the public and Congress, the argument was new and somewhat suspect. Sensibly, therefore, the President took the opportunities available to him before

Congress reconvened in January 1963 to preach it to the unconverted, of whom he had been one until so recently. In a major speech in December to the Economic Club of New York, a group of generally conservative businessmen, the President phrased his commitment to the Heller doctrine of tax drag in the assertion that "Our true choice is not between tax reduction . . . and the avoidance of large federal deficits." No, regardless of which political party governed the nation, "An economy hampered by restrictive tax rates will never produce enough revenues to balance our budget, just as it will never produce enough jobs or enough profits." The true causes of deficits were not "wild-eyed spenders" but "slow economic growth and periodic recessions." President Eisenhower's Secretary of the Treasury George Humphrey had been certain that large deficits would cause the sort of recessions that would "curl your hair." For his part Mr. Kennedy warned of the precise opposite: "Any new recession would break all deficit records." Here was something indeed to make the President's staid audience sit up and take notice. Deficits, their guest told them, came because taxes were *too high,* not because they were *too low.* In the 1960s the President of the United States was doing his distinguished best to differentiate public finance from household finance.

This speech signalized John F. Kennedy's commitment to a stimulating tax cut as the centerpiece of his 1963 legislative program. The Tax Act of 1964, which more than a year later translated a version of the President's wishes into law, has already assumed a symbolic meaning to both fiscal conservatives and fiscal modernists.

In the view of the first group, the act continues to threaten the financial moralities upon which the public reputation and the international credit of any government are founded. Only a year or so earlier, Secretary Humphrey had given pungent voice to such views when he had expressed doubt that we could "spend ourselves rich." Many congressmen quite sincerely believed that our present danger was of spending our way instead to "bankruptcy" or even "destruction." As the journalist Theodore White has put it, "Scores of Congressmen and Senators, Democrats and Republicans, are viscerally terrified that the unbalanced Budget will destroy the dollar, the life savings, insurance policies, and civilized life of Americans all together." Certainty that the fears are utterly irrational does nothing to relieve a President of the need to overcome or soften such widely dispersed emotions.

To the fiscal modernists, the tax measure was a test of the possibility that a young, magnetic, intellectually alert President could move a conservative Congress and an apprehensive public (both apparently more worried about the size of the national debt than the slow rate of economic growth and the large amount of unemployment) in the direction of twentieth-century fiscal policy. Not all the fiscal modernists had originally preferred tax cuts to spending increases. However, by now the tax cut was administration policy. As such, it was the only feasible means of economic stimulus and the chief instrument for making fiscal policy seem to the public what it really was—an important modern technique of economic management, as ideological in its implications as a dental drill.

As the bill which was the focus of these views emerged from the White House, it was a combination of tax reduction and tax reform measures, an omnibus attempt to enact simultaneously Walter Heller's release of the tax brake and the reform objectives of Secretary Dillon, Assistant Sec-

retary Stanley Surrey, Commissioner Mortimer Caplin of the Internal Revenue Service, and far from last in significance, Chairman Wilbur Mills of the House Ways and Means Committee. Upon the good will, personal influence, and legislative artisanship of Mr. Mills depended the shape and the future of the administration measure. Since Congressman Mills had conducted lengthy hearings on tax reform in past congressional sessions and had publicly avowed his attachment to overhauling the entire tax system, it was inevitable that the President's original bill would defer to Congressman Mills's known preferences. Thus, initially the prominence of the reform features impaired somewhat the clarity of the political argument as a match between the economic Neanderthals and the advocates of the twentieth century.

As a reduction plan, the President's bill sought three major changes. One was a reduction in individual income tax rates from the 20–91 percent range down to a 14–65 percent range. Although in fact probably no one enterprising enough to earn an income which would locate him in the 91 percent tax bracket actually paid that top percentage, still, the very existence of such rates was a subject of grievance among conservative Americans. More importantly, the rates led to much tax avoidance and the waste of a great deal of highly talented legal energy on tax finagling. Next, businessmen were offered a curtailment of corporate income tax rates, from 52 to 47 percent. As many noted, this change converted the Internal Revenue Service from senior to junior partnership in corporate profits. A third alteration was designed to do something especially pleasant for small businessmen. The corporate income tax applicable to the first $25,000 of profit was dropped from 30 to 22 percent. In addition, the administration

proposed some complex revisions in the tax treatment of capital gains, with an uncertain impact upon the size of federal tax receipts after the revisions. The rate reductions were to be spread over twenty-four months and to total $13.6 billion, $11 billion for individual taxpayers and $2.6 billion for corporate taxpayers.

Equally prominent and still more complicated was the second portion of the bill, a series of reforms aimed at increasing the equity of the tax system and producing $3.4 billion in additional revenue. At the 1963 level of the gross national product, the net reduction in taxes after the reforms were taken into the reckoning was expected, to be $10.2 billion. The reforms themselves were far from perfunctory. On the contrary they were the fruit of some of the best tax thinking of tax-law specialists, law-school teachers, and public officials. One of the reformers' major objectives was a reversal of the erosion of the tax base, which decades of chipping by particular interests had reduced alarmingly. A second aim was more nearly equitable treatment of taxpayers in similar circumstances, and a third was the closing of some of the loopholes which devoted lobbying had opened over the years. Even in this summary fashion, it should be clear that goals which threatened as many special interests as these were certain to start a large number of heated arguments.

One debate was over the proposed 5 percent ceiling on deductions for interest payments, medical expenses, and charitable contributions. The reform afflicted most severely middle- and upper-income families, especially the homeowners among their numbers who were equipped with heavy (and currently deductible) property taxes and mortgage interest payments. To the financially privileged, scarcely less irritating was the administration's desire to tax stock option profits at ordinary income tax rates instead of at the comforting 25 percent capital gains rate then applicable. Of all executive fringe benefits, stock options have been the most valuable. The reform thus threatened a major corporate recruiting device. Moving from outrage to outrage, the bill next sought to end the dividend credit and exclusion, an Eisenhower concession to stockholders. Almost boldest of all, there were even a gingerly attempt to control some of the grosser benefits of oil well ownership, a curb on the excessively generous depreciation treatment enjoyed by real estate, a tightening of the rule controlling holding companies, and with much the same objectives, many minor alterations of the tax code.

Taken together these provisions increased Treasury receipts by striking hard at the special privileges of the wealthy. In contrast a few of the remaining reforms would have cost the Treasury comparatively minor sums of money. Liberalized income-averaging arrangements, slightly more generous child-care allowances to working mothers, and marginally more favorable treatment of the elderly were justified both by the gains in equity and by the long history of effort by the experts to make them law. If that most conspicuous offender against tax justice, the oil company, got off lightly, the presence of a Texas Vice-President and potent Texas and California delegations in Congress made it astonishing that the administration had tried at all.

Most reasonably impartial students of American tax history considered the reforms well conceived and well drawn. If enacted they promised to move the tax code measurably nearer justice and consistency. In the main tax liberals were pleased by the President's program. Even though lower personal and corporate tax rates provided solace to the wealthy, the leaks in the tax sys-

tem were too numerous for anyone to take seriously the old schedule of personal income tax rates. What counted in the new measure was the closing of tax havens and the plugging of loopholes. Although there were tax radicals who evaluated the Administration program as excessively timid, the consensus of the moderates was that this was the fairest tax bill proposed by a President in a generation.

However, there now remained the task of persuading Congress to enact the bill without damaging alterations. Even a masterful President has his troubles piloting a tax bill through Congress; this combined political and economic exercise twangs far too many sensitive financial nerves. As President Kennedy analyzed the 1963 alignment of political forces, it appeared to him that the best way to secure tax reduction was to enlist the energies of those who preferred reform to reduction. Similarly, the way to get tax reform was to persuade the supporters of tax reduction to fight for the whole package.

Nevertheless, it was clear to the President's Council of Economic Advisers and to the President himself that the imperative of the hour was tax reduction. The priorities were set by consideration of the economic outlook. In January 1963 the United States was well into its third year of continuous business expansion. By past precedents the boom would not last very much longer. If Walter Heller's tax brake doctrine was valid, the boom's existence was even now being shortened by excessive tax collections. Hence it might be critically important that Congress approve tax reduction rapidly.

On the question of timing, the President himself was specific and exigent. As the President saw it, the first principle of congressional action was prompt enactment of the "entire tax re-

vision program" in the shape of a "single comprehensive bill." In the customary soaring language of legislative proposals, the administration's preamble to the bill promised an enlarged national income, faster economic growth, reduced unemployment, improvement in the balance of payments, higher living standards, and enlarged business investment. The aspirations were unremarkable. What was to prove astonishing was the substantial accuracy with which the administration predicted the results of its favorite program.

Accompanying the rhetoric were some down-to-earth calculations. If the estimates of the 1963 *Economic Report of the President* were accepted as reasonable, the gap between full employment and the 1963 levels of employment and output would be greatly narrowed. If the existing plant and equipment were really capable of turning out $30 to $40 billion worth more goods than in 1963, if the combined value of the multiplier and the accelerator was truly put at 3, and if the net tax cut finally approximated the administration's $10 billion, then the total impact of quick congressional action might very well be a $30 billion expansion of the gross national product, possibly just enough to gather up the existing economic slack and push the economy very close to full employment. Thus ran the Keynesian reasoning of the Council of Economic Advisers.

Congress did not yield readily even to logic so persuasive. It was February 1964, nearly three months after its great champion's assassination, before the tax bill ultimately became law. Intricate battles remained to be waged, and President Kennedy's early hope of welding tax trimmers and tax reformers into one huge coalition soon became a casualty of the fray. In the end the reforms were almost completely jettisoned by the President who had proposed them, a concession which enraged veteran tax reformers like Illinois' Senator Paul Douglas. In a full-dress, embittered Senate address delivered in August 1963, Douglas reproached President Kennedy for promising "a comprehensive tax reform program" in 1961, postponing it in 1962, finally presenting it in 1963, and then abandoning reform hastily "in the interest of quick enactment of a tax cut." Yet in the course of his speech, Senator Douglas himself identified the fear of recession as the strongest pressure upon the administration.

The primacy of antirecession action was accepted even by some of the liberal groups who had been most devoted to equitable reform. Although the National Planning Association and the Committee for Economic Development, two moderate groups, both favored the original reform-plus-reduction package, the American Federation of Labor–Congress of Industrial Organizations, more fearful of unemployment than eager to see the tax code rewritten, preferred a quick tax slash in 1963 and a postponement of reform until the following year. Among business supporters of tax change, enthusiasm for the closing of tax loopholes was understandably restrained. The administration's highly prized Business Committee for Tax Reduction, whose co-chairman was Henry Ford II, sincerely favored tax reduction and equally fervently opposed the decrease of tax privileges high in cash value to the Committee's own constituency.

In the end, possibly unavoidably, the man who did the most to kill the reform was the President himself. The President had never really concealed his own views. In his December 1962 Economic Club speech, again in the tax message to Congress, and still more candidly in a February 1963 address to a Washington meeting of the American Bankers Forum, President Kennedy emphasized both his interest in tax reform and the higher priority he attached to tax reduction. To attentive hearers it was evident that the President was willing, however reluctantly, to accept from Congress tax reduction by itself, if this was the best he could get. It is possible that he might have secured rather more tax reform if he had not revealed his own heart so openly.

This is conjecture. The outcome was always uncertain, and the practitioners of coalition politics move in a tricky milieu. When the affluent start brooding about their loss of privilege rather than potential reductions in tax rates, when the poor begin to reflect upon the large percentage of the benefits flowing to the business community, and when each special interest commences to place its own claims above a shared concern for continued prosperity, then the most carefully constructed alliance begins to disintegrate. Each group concentrates upon what it *doesn't* like; nobody speaks for what he admires.

In this instance the prospect of complete frustration was the greater because the public at large displayed amazing apathy and even hostility toward tax reduction. Walter Heller was not the only one astonished at the strength of the Puritan ethic in a free-spending, high-borrowing nation. Apparently there were large numbers of Americans who were more interested in balancing the federal budget, reducing the public debt, and curtailing federal spending than in improving their own financial condition. A Harris poll released on September 1, 1963, revealed that 63 percent of the population did indeed welcome a prompt tax reduction, but 36 percent virtuously preferred to see the budget balanced first (in direct negation of the expansionary principle underlying the administration program), and another 23 percent were uncertain about the whole issue. This was one occasion at least when a good many people were fully prepared to dislike Santa Claus.

To make matters worse, the congressional spokesmen for ancient ideas were in positions of great power. Senator Harry F. Byrd, chairman of the tax-writing Finance Committee, was an unequivocal budget balancer, deeply committed to the belief that private activity was good and federal spending was wasteful. Although Congressman Mills was far more temperate and in the event far more flexible in his opinions, he too was a long distance from an outright Keynesian position. On taxes he adopted the conservative position that "The function of taxation is to raise revenue. . . . I do not go along with economists who think of taxation primarily as an instrument for manipulating the economy." If Mr. Mills had acted in the light of this statement, the administration bill would have perished in the House Ways and Means Committee.

The President did still more to soothe his balky Congress. Himself a belated convert to the deficit gospel, Mr. Kennedy responded to the political pressures upon him by placing increasing emphasis on the restraint of federal expenditure. Again and again he came close to promising a ceiling on all government programs except defense and space. For social welfare proposals, "fiscal prudence" and "economic necessity" became the guiding criteria.

In pursuit of this tactic, as Congress continued its apparently interminable deliberations, the President sent a highly conciliatory letter to Chairman Mills on August 19, 1963. In it he sacrificed all but the barest essentials of fiscal stimulus in language which implicitly conceded a good deal to the economic myths which he had so recently been engaged in publicly dispelling. He started with a declaration of budgetary piety: "Our long-range goal remains a balanced budget in a balanced, full-employment economy." Even though tax reduction was now essential in order to enlarge national income, it "must . . . be accompanied by the exercise of an even tighter rein on Federal expenditures, limiting outlays only to those expenditures which meet strict criteria of national need." The President promised that "as the tax cut becomes fully effective and the economy climbs toward full employment, a substantial part of the increased tax revenues will be applied toward a reduction in the transitional deficits which accompany the initial cut in tax rates." Mr. Kennedy wound up with a promise that if Congress did enact the tax program, his next budget would plan a smaller deficit than the $9.2 billion estimated at the time for the fiscal year 1964.

The President's careful conciliation of contrary opinion, the diminishing support for tax reform, and the increasing pressure for congressional decision all began to shape the final accommodation between the opposing tax camps and between the chief executive and Congress. The tax reforms were almost completely deserted. The exemptions, privileges, and loopholes soothing to executives, homeowners, oil prospectors, real estate operators, organizers of charities, foundations, and universities were preserved. Even the expense account route to workaday affluence was left practically untouched. As for the tax reductions themselves, they gave all taxpayers something, but the large dollar gains made by the middle- and upper-income groups were no longer offset in part by diminished tax privileges.

Possibly not in intention but certainly in effect, the Tax Act of 1964 was a consistent exten-

sion of the policies of an administration which had somehow acquired the reputation of being antibusiness, just conceivably because a vivacious President adjudged most businessmen dull conversationalists. As politics is played in the United States, it is questionable whether a Republican administration, traditionally allied to business interests and accordingly eager to conciliate other groups, could have ventured to do as much for business as the Kennedy administration's combination of investment tax credit, liberalized depreciation, lowered corporate tax rates, and diminished progression in personal income taxes. To achieve his détente with conservatives, the President had gone even farther by promising to control federal spending and limit his requests for new social welfare programs. This was the price he had to pay for the acceptance of modern fiscal policy by those who clung to an older faith.

The act which became law was very different from the bill which President Kennedy had sent to Congress. What is a fair judgment on the new law? Passed in a year of economic expansion and existing budget deficit, amounting to the largest dollar tax reduction in American history, was it really, as *Business Week* proclaimed, "an historic event in U. S. public policy"? Were the periodical's editors accurate in labeling the act "the triumph of an idea"? Was "Keynes himself . . . the intellectual godfather of the tax cut"?

Whatever the reservations of tax reformers and the regrets of partisans of public spending, it is difficult not to answer yes to all three queries. Even though in shape the new program favored established interests, a new principle of economic policy had indeed won through, a rare event in human affairs. The effects of the victory will be felt for a long time, but the continued expan-

sion of the economy during 1964 and 1965, the steady downward drift of unemployment, and the gratifying increase of sales and profits gave immediate support to the claims of the new public finance and justified the slash in excise taxes enacted in June 1965. It is as certain as such things can be that never again will an American government profess helplessness in the face of unemployment, recession, and lagging economic growth. Rational fiscal policy expressed in the use of taxes as stabilizing agents and the acceptance of deficits without guilt may be a belated achievement but not the less treasurable because it comes a generation after the birth of the doctrine which justifies the public action.

In the calm which has followed a new national consensus, it is possible to see at last that Keynesian economics is not conservative, liberal, or radical. The techniques of economic stimulation and stabilization are simply neutral administrative tools capable of distributing national income either more or less equitably, improving the relative bargaining position of either unions or employers, and increasing or decreasing the importance of the public sector of the economy. Keynes's personal history and the early affiliation of liberals and radicals with Keynesian doctrine have obscured this vital point. In the United States, the fact is that two Presidents and two Congresses have chosen to stimulate the country's economy not by expanding public activity but by encouraging more private activity. Indeed, every tax reduction diminishes the federal government's relative share of the gross national product and correspondingly increases the relative importance of the private economy. Each tax cut contains the implicit proposition that dollars released to private discretion achieve benefits more valuable than could be attained by public expenditures of the same amount. Quite probably expressing a national preference, President Kennedy and President Johnson have placed a large bet on the capacity of business to produce the right goods in the right quantities and to distribute them to the right people.

The 1964 presidential campaign disguised this as it did other issues. Promoting neither himself nor public enlightenment, Mr. Goldwater ran a straightforward pre-Keynesian campaign. In it he advocated, *inter alia,* less federal spending, further tax reduction, and budgets balanced in all save extraordinary circumstances, of which recession was not one. He opposed labor "monopolies" and attacked the public use of fiscal policy as a stabilizing tool. It was all too consistent with a Senate voting record which featured opposition to the Reciprocal Trade Agreements Act, the Kennedy Trade Expansion Act, agricultural price supports, social security protection, medicare, minimum wage legislation, and all the other "interferences" in free markets which the enemies of liberty (Republican as well as Democratic) had forced upon the country. Under the circumstances President Johnson had no political reason to advance a detailed economic program or to discuss the genuine issues which now confront him and his constituents.

The major economic question which faces Americans in the Keynesian era is no longer a matter of whether modern fiscal policy should or should not be employed. For the reasonable, this is an issue finally resolved. It has been superseded by a much harder set of choices dependent on social valuations more complex than the simple preference of prosperity to depression, growth to stagnation, and progress to retrogression.

These are the choices which were foreshadowed by the controversy in the Kennedy administration over the best way to stimulate the American economy. When a President and a Congress acknowledge the need for fiscal stimulus, *how* should this stimulus be supplied? The practical choice, the major social valuation, and the continuing political argument focus upon the two routes to economic expansion which are open, the twentieth-century liberal route and the twentieth-century conservative alternative.

The modern economic conservative is no longer a budget balancer; he is perfectly willing to recognize deficiencies in aggregate demand as they present themselves. He may well accept the current diagnosis that the economic malaise of the 1950s and early 1960s was the consequence of insufficient private investment and a tax structure which withdrew the fruits of economic expansion too quickly and too copiously from the pockets of consumers and entrepreneurs. Defining the problem in this fashion, the conservative expansionist is prone to pin his hopes on a refashioning of the federal tax system and periodical infusions of fiscal stimulus in the shape of additional tax reductions. He is likely to be wary of large expenditures on social welfare and still suspicious of the enlargement of federal influence. Nevertheless, more and more he esteems the federal government as a partner in business prosperity.

As many of the preceding portions of this volume suggest, the thrust of two Democratic Presidents' legislative programs and administrative actions has been at the least consistent with the expectations of modern economic conservatives. The familiar roster of liberalized depreciation, investment tax credit, reduced corporate income tax rates, mod-

erated personal tax progression, and excise tax alteration all have amounted to direct or indirect attempts to stimulate business confidence, enlarge private investment, and emphasize the significance of private economic production. The Kennedy and Johnson appointments to the federal regulatory agencies and the Cabinet, and the decision to vest control of the communications satellite in private corporate hands, are additional acts of solicitude for business feelings and preferences. It is accurate rather than invidious to term the faith of modern businessmen commercial Keynesianism, and it is only sensible to welcome the perception by intelligent businessmen that private activity can be aided by a government sympathetic both to business and to high employment. Commercial Keynesianism is a giant step beyond older policies preferred by the business community.

Nevertheless, the opposing contemporary position also has its just claims. The liberal expansionist stance owes a debt to the Galbraith of *The Affluent Society,* the Harrington of *The Other America,* and the unemployment analyses of Charles Killingsworth. Liberal expansionists unite in denying that commercial Keynesianism is capable of meeting adequately the economic challenges of the next decade. By itself expansionary policy will not prepare the nation for a changing labor market.

One of the major concerns of liberal expansionists is the slow growth of manufacturing employment and output. Computers and servomechanisms are eliminating unskilled, semiskilled, and even skilled positions. Education requirements for steady employment are rising too sharply to allow much hope for many of today's unemployed. The uncertainties and dangers of the new market for human skill and energy are such that even advocates of tax reduction perceive that their favored device is less than the whole answer to unemployment. Testifying on poverty in 1964, Walter Heller phrased the position eloquently: "Open exits mean little to those who cannot move—to the millions who are caught in the web of poverty through illiteracy, lack of skills, racial discrimination, broken homes, and ill health—conditions which are hardly touched by prosperity and growth." On this front the alarmists insist upon the imminence of a transformation of production and employment larger in scale and more devastating in impact than the Industrial Revolution of the eighteenth century. Such is the diagnosis advanced by the signers of the Manifesto of the Ad Hoc Committee on the Triple Revolution, among them Michael Harrington and Gunnar Myrdal. But even the more cautious structural analysis of Charles Killingsworth implies the need for a good deal more than the simple stimulation of aggregate demand by tax reduction.

Clearly the persistence of poverty, the presence of structural unemployment, and the looming menace of automation all demand specific programs of public intervention. So also does the fact, in the Galbraithian view, that Americans allocate far too many resources to private activity and far too few to public purposes. What concerns Galbraithians is the number of places in the United States like Perry County, Kentucky, whose teachers start at a salary of $74.42 a week; Washington, D. C., whose Ludlow Elementary School contains one washbasin for its 260 students and whose General Hospital compels indigent patients to wait even in emergencies three to six hours before they can see a doctor; and even rich New York City, whose decades

of experiment with public housing have not eliminated the slums of Harlem. Liberal expansionists are convinced that the nation's schools, houses, hospitals, and social services will never be so high in quality as its automobiles, cosmetics, and detergents until large amounts of resources are shifted from low-priority private uses to high-priority public uses. The practical import of the judgment is that in a time of prosperity as in a time of recession, the role of the federal government should increase, not decrease.

Therefore, whether they emphasize poverty, structural unemployment, or the starvation of the public services, liberal expansionists favor public spending over tax reduction. It is exactly at this point in the practical politics of fiscal policy that they part company from conservative expansionists. Since each time taxes are reduced it is harder to achieve larger federal appropriations, liberal expansionists must in logic be the opponents of tax cuts and the friends of larger expenditures on urban redevelopment, regional rehabilitation, vocational education, manpower retraining, public recreation, aid to education, and low-cost, federally assisted housing. Liberal expansionists dislike tax reduction because they perceive it as the inevitable completion of the superior policies which assist the unemployed young, the victims of segregated education, the technologically displaced, and the miserably housed.

The art of democratic politics often lies in blurring the issues, not sharpening the definitions as intellectuals are fond of doing. It would be naive to expect a successful President to define his program in clear-cut ideological terms. Moreover, final judgments upon functioning political leaders are risky. As this is

written, Lyndon Johnson has been President in his own right only a year and a half. The ultimate shape of his own program preferences and accomplishments will depend on many factors, a number of them outside any President's control. The urgencies of foreign affairs, the necessities of the defense establishment, the temper of Congress, and the behavior of the economy are among the important variables which will influence presidential economic policy. Any present assessment must be provisional, the more so because 1965's Great Society legislation contains sufficiently varied emphases to permit of a number of different sequels during the next three or possibly seven years of President Johnson's administration. All the same it is useful to examine Mr. Johnson's unusually varied program up to now in the framework of liberal and conservative expansionism.

To begin with, the President's policies are often continuations of Kennedy, Truman, or even Roosevelt initiatives. The lines of development between the Kennedy and the Johnson years are particularly numerous. Originated by President Kennedy, the tax cut was enthusiastically embraced by President Johnson. The preliminary plans for the War on Poverty had already been laid by the Kennedy staff before President Johnson adopted the War on Poverty as the initial identifiable program of his own new administration. President Kennedy had urged Congress to enact medicare and aid to education. Assisted by a huge Democratic majority, President Johnson pressed the measures through Congress. The wage-price guidelines which appeared first in *The Economic Reports* of the Heller Council of Economic Advisers have been reiterated by the Council headed by Gardner Ackley.

It is style rather than legislative substance which separates the two Democratic Presidents. That Mr. Johnson has won business confidence seems to be the joint consequence of the demonstrated success of fiscal policy and Mr. Kennedy's apparent "hostility" and Mr. Johnson's evident sympathy to businessmen and their problems. The tragicomedy of President Kennedy's relations to the business community has already been told. In the months which preceded the assassination, there were signs that the President and business were moving toward reconciliation. Still, it is doubtful whether even proper courtesy between businessmen and their President could have been achieved. Rapport seemed a distant hope. A recollection of Theodore Sorensen's may exemplify the feelings on both sides. Mr. Sorensen cites the President as commenting caustically to him after addressing the Business Council that this was the only audience which did not stand when the President of the United States entered the room.

Birthplace, experience, and temperament have combined in President Johnson to produce a different set of feelings. Like any other successful Texas politician, Mr. Johnson, first as Congressman and then as Senator, had to reach an accommodation with the major economic interests of his region. Although Lyndon Johnson entered Congress as a New Dealer, the personal protégé of Franklin Roosevelt, and voted consistently for New Deal measures, he sought also to protect the tax advantages of his state's oil interests. Moreover, in his own private affairs, he entered into partnership with his wife in one of the period's more speculative industries —television. The texture of Mr. Johnson's personal experience equips him to understand concretely, directly, and intimately the financial and tax difficulties of ordinary businessmen. His experience also gives him insight into the way businessmen regard the regulatory agencies and the federal bureaucracy. His past activities have developed in him a taste for business company and business conversation. The presidency is a great symbolic office, and these small details of its present occupant's career can have large consequences.

One of them indeed has been the unexampled extent of business approbation of Mr. Johnson. It has been a long time since so conservative an organ as the *Monthly News Letter* of New York's First National City Bank could say publicly the kind of thing it said of this Democratic President's 1965 congressional program, that "These reports and messages indicate a marked evolution toward a more pronounced pro-business attitude, combined with an increasing stress on free enterprise and market competition in the allocation of resources."

The body of messages and reports which the writers of the encomium were commending were portions of the Great Society program. They offer an excellent opportunity to examine the quality of the expansionary program of this activist President. The chance is the better because the 1965 Congress was more nearly under the complete control of the chief executive than any has been since 1933. President Johnson made full use of his fortunate situation to press through Congress an unusually varied list of measures, covering topics ranging from highway beautification to immigration reform. Even though this legislative program is not the President's final word, it is an impressive first chapter.

Let us consider its elements. The documents which sound the major legislative themes are the budget message and *The Economic Report of the President*. The latter began with an account of the successes of the past twelve months. Nineteen sixty-four had been a year of expansion in which employment had risen by a million and a half, the gross national product had increased from $584 billion to $622 billion, corporate profits had continued a four-year ascent, and personal income per capita (after taxes) had touched $2,288 per year, up 17.5 percent in just four years. Any administration would have pointed proudly to another characteristic of its stewardship—the price stability which had accompanied economic expansion.

In allocating the credit, *The Economic Report* tactfully began with the "businessmen, workers, investors, farmers and consumers" whose investing, spending, and planting decisions had combined to stimulate economic growth. Then came the last partner, "Government policies which have sustained a steady, but non-inflationary growth of markets." The President stated his belief "that 1964 will go down in our economic and political history as the 'year of the tax cut.'"

From the attractive economic record President Johnson drew a semi-Keynesian lesson, that "Purposeful expenditure, stimulative tax reduction, and economy in government operations are the three weapons which, if used effectively, can relieve our society of the costs and consequences of waste." How the President intended to use the first two weapons rapidly emerged in his concrete legislative proposals.

The "stimulative tax reductions" included the remainder of the reductions already mandated under the 1964 tax measure— some $3 billion in personal tax benefits and another $1 billion in corporate tax remissions. The new tax item substantially reduced some excise taxes and eliminated a good many others. In combination these tax changes were a continuation of the fiscal stimulus initiated in 1964 by the passage of the Tax Reduction Act.

The "purposeful expenditure" list was an interesting agglomeration. It included enlargements of old programs like Social Security and the War on Poverty as well as initial financing for some new programs. The latter were a varied lot—aid to education, the rehabilitation of Appalachia, the construction of regional medical centers, rent subsidies, and medical assistance to the aged. Although so many programs were new (as objects of legislation if not of repeated proposal), requests for increased spending amounted to only a modest total. In fact, as a fiscal exercise, what unified this program of tax reduction and welfare extension was a constraint —the President's promise that both tax benefits and welfare spending would be financed out of the normal growth of an expanding economy. Both types of benefits depended upon the capacity of a growing economy to create a fiscal dividend each year to be distributed to its citizens.

Emphatically, the architects of this legislative design did not intend to reallocate the community's resources in the direction of greater public influence. During his first two budgets, President Johnson's insistence on not exceeding the $100 billion expenditure mark attested to the importance which he attached to keeping government activity within limits. It appears likely that the President would have recommended still greater fiscal stimulus in each of the budgets if he had not been restrained by his concern for the size of federal spending. That concern was itself related to the President's wish to retain within the bound-

aries of his political consensus the business support which he had won. In the end the implicit check on the size of social welfare expenditure delimited the amount of intervention that the business community was willing to accept.

The President's choices between tax reduction and larger spending continued to emphasize the former. Even after 1964's major tax surgery, the President offered new benefits in 1965 and intimations of future reductions in personal income levies. Only the escalation of the Vietnam war transformed administrative discussions and created the possibility of tax increases. As a result, even though the 1965 congressional record was startlingly enlightened by comparison with earlier congressional performances it remained true that the combined increases in old social programs and initial appropriations for new ones amounted to less than the reductions in personal income taxes, corporate imposts, and excises.

From the standpoint of the liberal expansionist, this was bad enough, but the distribution of the tax benefits and even the new public spending raised still livelier apprehensions for him. Like 1964's tax harvest, much of 1965's improvements would be realized by prosperous corporations and wealthy individuals. Reduced corporate income tax rates generated additional dividends and capital gains which flowed for the most part to upper-income investors. The same group would enjoy a very large percentage of the gains from additional reductions in personal income taxes. Some portion of reductions in excise taxes would be retained as extra profits by corporations which were already turning in highly satisfactory earnings records.

The design of the expenditure programs also raised a number

of questions about who precisely benefits from welfare policies besides the direct recipients of assistance. The interests of specific business groups sometimes appear to influence the shape of programs as much as the needs of the ostensible beneficiaries. Thus, the major innovation of the 1965 omnibus housing measure, the rent subsidy plan, undoubtedly enables a number of families, ineligible under other programs, to escape the slums and move into a decent environment. At best rent subsidies modestly promote housing integration. However, local governments have long known that under such programs financial benefits accrue to landlords and builders, helping them maintain the existing structure of building costs and apartment rentals. This is another way of saying that the rent subsidies tend to support the existing customs of an industry usually considered backward in both its technology and its social practices.

The Appalachian program raises somewhat similar issues. No reader of Harry Caudill's affecting *Night Comes to the Cumberlands* will question that most of Appalachia's inhabitants live in abject misery, nor that public help is unqualifiedly desirable in a region that has manifestly lost a grip on its own troubles. All the same, it is hard not to pause and wonder why the most expensive of the components of the administration program is a major road-building effort. Certainty on its merits is not easy, for in the long run, new roads in the appropriate places may indeed open the region to the tourist trade, promote the internal mobility of labor, and encourage industrialists to establish new plants. However, what appears all too likely in the short run of the next few years is that the road contractors will reap the major gains. There will be little immediate increase in local employment because of the highway construction. By now roadbuilding has become so skilled a trade and uses so much expensive equipment that much of the labor force employed on the new Appalachian highways will be imported from other more prosperous regions.

Not even the poverty program is totally exempt from the same reservation, that it contains an excessively generous tendency to distribute some portion of the available largess to the unneedy. The ample scale on which local poverty officials are paid has already aroused a quantity of sour humor about the identity of the program's major beneficiaries. This point may be comparatively minor administratively though it is surely significant psychologically. However, it can reasonably be argued that high salaries attract abler and more inventive human types into social welfare specialties than the social service bureaucrats who now dominate the field.

A more serious question about the goals and strategies of the War on Poverty concerns the participation of major corporations like Litton Industries, Philco, and International Telephone & Telegraph in poverty ventures which they define as commercial opportunities. These and other firms have signed up as operators of new job camps for unemployed youths. Although there is no reason to quarrel with the sincerity of either portion of a Litton executive's remark that "We got into the poverty war for two reasons, one the opportunity to serve the community, the other the business opportunity," serious issues are tied up in business sponsorship of training programs. Will the training become a variety of publicly subsidized preparation for semiskilled jobs with little future in the sponsoring corporations? Will a firm's concept of

training necessarily or even usually coincide with the interests of either the trainees or the community? Will the commercial limitations of even the best-intentioned business ventures really lead to the social transformations which in its more visionary moments the poverty program promises? Once more it is difficult to wonder whether the administration program, intentionally or unintentionally, does not offer as many benefits to the successful as prospects for the poor, the rejected, and the hopeless.

Under the circumstances it is not astonishing that many businessmen have extended substantial support to the administration's housing, poverty, and regional development plans. Thus far, at any rate, the total outlays required are small enough to be financed from that portion of the growth of federal tax receipts not pledged to tax reduction. The programs are so constructed as to favor existing agencies and interests. To their credit, a generation of more sophisticated business leaders have come to see that active fiscal policy and limited social welfare improvements are themselves conducive to business prosperity. Perhaps still more to their credit, many businessmen have come to identify themselves sufficiently with their employees to recognize a common interest in higher wages and steady employment.

When all this is said, the administration's program can be realistically appraised only within the context of a consensus whose limits are defined by the business community, not by trade union leaders or liberal intellectuals. In some areas these limits are narrow. In 1965, the repeal of Section 14(b) of the Taft-Hartley Act, the section enabling the individual states to outlaw union shop agreements, was put at the top of the AFL–

CIO's legislative agenda. Congress, which cheerfully passed a variety of Great Society proposals, stopped abruptly at the presidential request for the deletion of Section 14(b), and repeated its action at the start of 1966's congressional session. A similar reluctance to raise minimum wages and extend coverage to migratory farm workers and other unsheltered groups attests to the reluctance of influential portions of the business community to shift the existing balance between labor and industry.

Possibly the best illustration of all brings us back to the continuing shortage of low-income housing. This is a huge problem. As President Johnson sketched its dimensions, "In the remainder of the century . . . urban populations will double, city land will double and we will have to build in our cities as much as all that we have built since the first colonist arrived on these shores." As the President went on to observe, the cities are already overcrowded, the nation contains "over nine million homes, most of them in cities, which are run down or deteriorating," and "many of our central cities are in need of major surgery to overcome decay." The concluding sentence of Mr. Johnson's diagnosis—"The old, the poor, the discriminated against are increasingly concentrated in central city ghettos"—is both accurate and eloquent enough to command the agreement of most students of city affairs, not to mention the unfortunate city residents themselves.

Just here appears most glaringly the gap between the accurate description of a large problem and the means which the limits of business-defined consensus permit to be used. Although the 1965 Housing Act contains many commendable features, including the rent subsidy innovation, it fails at two crucial points. The amounts allocated to the rent subsidy program are very small, as are the benefits that the big cities, the accepted focus of the problem, can anticipate in 1965, 1966, and 1967. New York City, for example, can expect no more than 3500 units of low-income housing each year. Indeed, Mrs. Hortense Gabel, in 1965 the City's rent control administrator, observed that the federal government planned to spend less on all housing programs in New York City than it did four years earlier in 1961.

No one denies that improving housing and eliminating slums are enormously complex matters, made more difficult by the accumulation of past failures and the existence of contemporary prejudices. Nevertheless, successful advancement requires the creation of a huge, expensive, and coordinated program of urban renewal and public housing —and a willingness to upset comfortable commercial, union, and political practices. In the past the failures of urban renewal measures have flowed partly from the perversion of the program into a series of subsidies to luxury builders, real estate speculators, and business promoters; partly from municipal decisions to set the quite legitimate expansion needs of great universities like Chicago and Columbia ahead of the equally legitimate (and much more acute) housing requirements of displaced residents; and partly, perhaps mainly, from the circumstance that adequate quantities of public housing—attractively designed, socially mixed, and suitably located—were never supplied. In New York the consequence has been that at the end of a generation-long boom in private construction, there is still no decent place where most Negroes and Puerto Ricans can live. Though unenviable, this is a record readily matched by Chicago, Philadelphia, Los Angeles, Saint Louis, and Detroit.

Thus, in relation to need, the administration program is minute, far below Senator Robert A. Taft's goals for a smaller population and a poorer nation two decades ago. Yet where consensus is the objective, existing practices must be respected, and benefits are likely to accrue according to the relative weight of the different groups joined together in mutual accommodation. The real if very limited benefits to the poorly housed which present programs offer are provided in ways which please the construction industry, assist middle-income families also, elevate banking profits, enlarge city real estate tax rolls, and unfortunately leave in their present plight the mass of wretchedly sheltered urban slumdwellers. This judgment is less a moral statement than a summary of the fact that in this important sphere, established practices and social objectives are in conflict.

Even medicare, the triumph of an aspiration thirty years old, has its conservative, prudential aspects. A complex piece of legislation, this is the first extension of major significance to social security since the passage of the Social Security Act in 1935. Benefits to the elderly are enlarged, and existing child health and aid to dependent children programs are expanded. But the basic innovations are in the medical provisions. Henceforth social security pensioners are automatically entitled to payment of the expenses of hospitalization, post-hospital care, nursing home treatment, and home health visits. Moreover, a voluntary supplementary plan pays the bulk of medical and surgical costs incurred in clinics, homes, and medical offices.

In 1967, the program's first full year of operation, the entire medicare package will cost about $6 billion—$2.2 billion for the basic health care plan, an additional $1 billion for the supplementary plan, $2.3 billion for increased social security benefits to the elderly, and the remaining $500 million for the liberalization of existing public assistance programs. Particularly by comparison with recent social welfare spending, the scale of the new measure is generous. More welcome yet are the relief from anxiety and the gain in human dignity finally accorded the old. That this program has taken so long in coming detracts nothing from its very substantial merits.

However, this legislation also contains certain checks on benefits and on their extension to other age groups. Throughout, financing is exceedingly conservative. A case in point is the voluntary program. The premiums set are $3 per month per covered individual, adjustable upward as medical costs rise. Rise they will. If the precedent of the postwar history of Blue Cross premiums holds true, the elderly must anticipate rapid increases in these initially modest premium payments. Worse still, other portions of the program will be financed overwhelmingly by increases in payroll taxes, which are now scheduled to rise to 5.5 percent *each* for employer and employee in the next fifteen years. This bite will be the more ferocious because soon the first $6600 of earned income will be assessed instead of the $4800 now taxed.

Reliance upon payroll taxes has unfortunate consequences. Fiscally, these taxes are as much a drag on economic expansion as any other impost. From the standpoint of social fairness, they are inequitable, regressive imposts which will remove smaller percentages of total income from those who will earn over $6600 each year than from those who will earn less than that sum or derive their income from property. This rise in payroll taxes, coupled with recent decreases in personal and corporate income tax rates and progressions, involves a shift toward greater inequality of income distribution after taxes. Finally, the reinforcement of the precedent that social security benefits are to be financed only out of social security payroll taxes renders it exceedingly difficult to extend the benefits of medical protection to other age groups. Further increases in payroll levies may well arouse the opposition of ordinary wage earners on whom these deductions are an irksome present burden.

What can be achieved by the consensus of the major interest groups in the United States is very substantial. The flood of legislation in 1965 verified the possibility of moderate improvement within the fiscal limits set by business predominance in the administration coalition. In short, conservative expansionism is really capable of making American society tolerable for most Americans. Nevertheless, its limitations are such, its powerful tendencies to favor the prosperous are so dominant, and its suspicion of the public sector is still so strong that it will take a more vigorous path of government action, the road of liberal intervention, to convert even an enlightened commercial community into a Great Society, to move from Keynesian fiscal policy to the Keynesian vision of a rational community.

CHESTER L. COOPER
The Lost Crusade

No one man, not even the President of the United States, can fully understand all the variables that go into policy decisions as large and critical as those made in 1968 that decelerated but did not end the Vietnam war. Generations of historians will study the actions of thousands of men and institutions to construct a picture of events that will do justice to all the influences behind each decision and will place these momentous happenings in their proper perspective. For these are among the events affecting the life of an entire generation which merit such study.

The accounts of participants in the process of decision making are always among the first sources available for an understanding of policy. None is to be accepted as the perfect truth, but each must be weighed according to the inherent plausibility of its account and the author's access to inside knowledge. On this basis, Chester L. Cooper's The Lost Crusade is, at least for now, one of the more valuable narratives. Cooper served on the United States delegation at the 1954 Geneva Conference and at the 1961–1962 Geneva Conference on Laos, on the White House staff concerned with Asian affairs from 1964 to 1966, and on Averill Harriman's staff thereafter while he searched for an opening to negotiate with North Vietnam and the NLF. Cooper's attention to the intricacies of diplomatic maneuver is both illuminating of the course of events and revealing of the kind of thinking that went into American foreign policy formation. Perhaps the rather remote interest in public opinion and other such intangibles that this account demonstrates offers a basic comment on what went wrong even in the minds of those most committed to extricating the nation from the quagmire of Southeast Asia.

The section of Cooper's account included here discusses the events of 1968. On September 29, 1967, President Lyndon Johnson in a speech at San Antonio, Texas, offered a halt in the bombing of North Vietnam if Hanoi would agree not to "take advantage of the bombing cessation" and "promptly" to enter "productive discussions." This somewhat ambiguous "San Antonio Formula" set the stage for the diplomatic maneuvering—and the military response of the "Tet" offensive —that dominated both foreign policy and domestic politics in 1968.

The New Year [1968] began with two developments that were to have crucial influence on prospects for negotiations. On January first, midpoint in the brief holiday bombing pause, Radio Hanoi broadcast an important speech by Foreign Minister Trinh (made several days earlier at a reception for visiting Mongolian dignitaries). Trinh said that "after the United States had ended unconditionally the bombing and all other acts of war against the DRV, the DRV *will* hold talks with the United States on questions of concern." With the change of "could" to "will," Hanoi had launched a major new diplomatic initiative.

Trinh's speech was examined carefully by State Department experts in the Vietnamese language to make sure that the change of tense was not simply a mistranslation. But when it was established that Hanoi had actually changed its formulation, another gnawing question arose: How long would it take Hanoi to start talks after the bombing ceased? Even if talks were to take place within a few days, Washington officials were haunted by the fear of being trapped into a bombing cessation in exchange for endless, fruitless, and frustrating discussions like the Panmunjom talks in Korea. But even the most hard-nosed now acknowledged that Hanoi had gone a long way toward the President's "San Antonio Formula." Despite some difference in rhetoric, the American and North Vietnamese public positions were now very close. Nonetheless, the bombing of North Vietnam once more resumed on January 2.

On January 25 a major step was taken to narrow the gap even more between the North Vietnamese position and our own. Secretary of Defense-designate Clark Clifford appeared before the Senate Armed Services Committee to clarify the President's "San Antonio Formula."[1] Asked whether a cessation of North Vietnamese military activities would be expected to follow a cessation of bombing, Clifford replied that he did not "expect them to stop their military activities. I would expect that they would start negotiations promptly and not take advantage of the pause. . . ." Pressed on what he meant by "taking advantage," Clifford responded that "military activity will continue in South Vietnam, I assume, until there is a ceasefire. . . . I assume that they will continue to transport the normal amount of goods, munitions, and men to South Vietnam. I assume that we will continue to maintain our forces and support our forces during that period. . . . In the language of the President . . . he would insist that they not take advantage of the suspension of the bombing." But, Clifford admitted, "there is no way to keep them from taking advantage. If they state that they are going to refrain from taking advantage and then refuse to do so, then they have not met their agreement and the conditions for negotiations have failed."

In essence what Clifford was saying, reportedly without the President's advance knowledge and approval, was that if we suspended bombing, we did not expect Hanoi to stop the flow of men and material into South Vietnam but did expect that the flow would not go beyond "normal" current levels.[2] The President was reported to have been puzzled with this interpretation and it was several days before the State Department announced that Clifford's testimony represented the official Administration view. On the same day that Clifford was appearing on Capitol Hill, Secretary Rusk asked an audience in New York, "Do they really expect us to stop half the war while the other half of the war goes on?"

If Hanoi had any interest in negotiations, it was hard as of late January to explain why the North Vietnamese did not pick up Clifford's offer. Perhaps they felt we were about to cave in and that one more body-blow,

[1] Robert McNamara had announced his resignation on November 29, 1967. Clifford was appointed as McNamara's successor on January 19, 1968, and confirmed by the Senate on January 30. McNamara had become increasingly unhappy with the course of American policy in Vietnam. Early in 1967 he had revealed his doubts about the effectiveness and wisdom of the bombing. By summer his views had become widely known. In late August he told the Senate Preparedness Subcommittee that he opposed extending the scale and nature of bombing targets and doubted that any level of bombing, short of direct strikes on population centers, would affect Hanoi's will to continue the war. The issue, he emphasized, would be decided in South Vietnam. A few days later the Subcommittee, which was Johnson's principal source of support in the Senate, claimed that McNamara had "shackled" the bombing campaign. The President then felt it necessary to deny that there was a "deep division" within the Administration on the bombing question. Johnson must have been relieved to find a graceful way of replacing McNamara.

[2] One of the problems with the San Antonio Formula, especially as elaborated by Clifford, was that our information on the level of infiltration of men and materials into South Vietnam at any particular time was sketchy and unreliable. There was a lag of many weeks, sometimes months, before reliable data became available. We were able to observe major movements of men and supplies down the main roads of North Vietnam, but the daily flow of people slipping down the jungle-canopied Laos trails was almost impossible to observe. It was now evident, however, that the Administration was ready to take the calculated risk that gross violations could be detected.

Cholon section burning, Saigon, Vietnam. *(Philip Jones Griffiths, Magnum)*

either at home or in Vietnam, would put us on the ropes. As it turned out, both body-blows were on their way.

Clifford's statement came shortly before the Vietnamese New Year. There was some optimism that, with the Tet cease-fire in South Vietnam and the bombing halt in the North, and with the Trinh and Clifford statements on the record, the time was ripe for a diplomatic breakthrough. The optimistic reports from Vietnam with respect to the military and pacification programs led many to believe that negotiations might now be more acceptable to Hanoi and the Viet Cong than a continuation of the war. General Westmoreland had described 1967 as "The Year of the Offensive," and even the most cynical observers agreed that the North Vietnamese and the Viet Cong

had suffered tremendous casualties during that year. The North Vietnamese may well have lost a whole generation of young fighting men in 1967. As for the Viet Cong, green, young recruits with little or no training were being sent into battles. B-52 raids within South Vietnam had pounded away at those Viet Cong base areas that allied ground forces found difficult to penetrate. It was reasonable to believe in early January that Trinh's change of tense reflected a recognition in Hanoi that the odds were heavily weighted against a Communist military victory, rather than a change of heart with respect to a political settlement. Many hard-liners, both military and civilian, argued that negotiations should be stalled off as long as possible while the Allied forces continued to improve our military

position and political leverage. Thus Washington was in an optimistic mood—the hawks because they sensed military successes in sight at last, and the doves because they saw few remaining differences standing in the way of early American–North Vietnamese talks.

Some of the bloom was removed in mid-January. Mai Van Bo, Hanoi's man in Paris, told the press that the United States could expect no reciprocity for a bombing halt. And when the President said in his State of the Union message that he was "exploring the meaning" of Trinh's proposal but warned that Hanoi "must not take advantage" of a bombing cessation, the North Vietnamese quickly responded that the San Antonio Formula was a "habitual trick" and was accompanied by "insolent conditions." The mood was to change

even more dramatically in the course of a few days.

On January 30, in the midst of the Vietnamese New Year ceasefire, the Communists unleashed a tremendous onslaught on virtually every city and major town in South Vietnam. Saigon and Hue, the modern and ancient capital cities, were especially hard hit. Although Communist forces were finally driven out, large parts of Hue, including some of its historic monuments, were destroyed. The attack on Saigon was accompanied by a suicide raid against the American Embassy itself. According to General Westmoreland, "Even though by mid-January we were certain that a major offensive action was planned by the enemy at *Tet,* we did not surmise the true nature or the scope of the countrywide attack. . . . It did not occur to us that the enemy

would undertake suicidal attacks in the face of our power. But he did just that. . . . Over a long period of time . . . enemy troops in civilian dress . . . slipped into the cities, particularly Hue and Saigon. . . . The Vietnamese National Police were ineffective in stopping or detecting the magnitude of the enemy's effort. The minds of the Vietnamese in Saigon and other cities were preoccupied with the approaching *Tet* holiday. . . ." Although 1000 Americans, 2100 South Vietnamese, and 32,000 Communists were reportedly killed during the first two weeks of the Tet offensive, the most significant casualties were American prestige abroad and self-confidence at home.

It took several days for Washington to come to grips with what had actually happened in Vietnam—and with the effects

this sharp turn of events had in the United States itself. One thing came out loud and clear: despite ambitious pacification programs and optimistic claims of progress, the Communists still seemed to have sufficient control over the Vietnamese countryside to come and go virtually at will. It was tragically apparent that the efforts over the past two or three years to strengthen the rural areas against Communist assault or infiltration had been in vain. Even the cities, which up to now were regarded as under firm government control, were vulnerable. In the first few days of February it looked as if the non-Communist position and American policy in Vietnam were both in jeopardy.

While the Tet offensive had traumatic effects in both Saigon and Washington, it subsequently turned out that it was not the complete and unmitigated disaster it first appeared to be. The Communists had demonstrated their ability to move against virtually every part of South Vietnam if they were ready to make a determined effort, but it was never clear just what the enemy's ultimate objective was in this Wagnerian onslaught. In some of the cities and towns it is doubtful they planned to do more than demonstrate their strength and then withdraw; at least this seemed to be their tactic in most of the provincial capitals. In Hue they probably counted on being joined by the chronically restive Buddhists and students, who on so many other occasions had shown antipathy for the government in Saigon, but neither group rose up to assist the invading troops.

In Saigon too the Communist goals were not very clear. Captured prisoners said they had ex-

(Donald McCullin, Magnum)

pected the population to rise up against the government and cheer the invaders. Many of them supposed that the city would fall in short order. Some regular Viet Cong units were planning "victory parades." On January 31 a National Liberation Front broadcast stated that the objective of the general offensive was to topple the "Thieu-Ky puppet regime" and restore "national independence, peace, sovereignty, democracy and happiness to the people. . . ." Several days later NLF representatives in Moscow and Algiers echoed the broadcast, saying that their purpose was the destruction of the Saigon Government.

Communist agents and infiltrators found hospitality in parts of Saigon, and large sections of the city were damaged or destoyed by "friendly" artillery and air attacks. Nonetheless, government efforts against the Viet Cong did not have to be diverted to cope with popular uprisings.

In part based on its assumption that the Communists had failed to attain their maximum objectives, and in part because of its natural inclination to counter the sense of despair following the Tet offensive, the Administration announced that the Communists had met with a substantial defeat in February. Some spokesmen even claimed that the Tet offensive turned out to be an American and South Vietnamese victory. President Johnson declared that the Viet Cong suffered "a complete military failure," and added that "when all the facts are known, they will not achieve a psychological victory."[3] Sometime later Ambassador Bunker declared in an interview that the allies were

[3] In his televised reminiscences on February 6, 1970, Johnson described the Tet offensive as being "a disaster, a debacle, and a serious military loss" for the Communists. "I don't think that ever got communicated to the American people."

stronger after the offensive than before.

To be sure, the Communists suffered tremendous casualties and were eventually ejected from the major cities, but most Americans hardly equated this with a military victory for the men in the white hats. The hardest thing to swallow in Washington, Kansas, and California was that just a few short days before, reports from Vietnam were so bullish that an unqualified defeat of the Communist forces seemed within reach during 1968. Now the situation was once more in a shambles.

General Wheeler went to Vietnam on February 23 to make a personal investigation. He met with the President within hours after his return. The General was grim and the President even more so. Wheeler told the President that more troops were needed. The 500,000 American troops already deployed were insufficient to assist South Vietnam in protecting its population centers and still ward off fresh North Vietnamese attacks against key outposts along the DMZ and the Laos infiltration routes. Although the substance of Wheeler's report was closely guarded, it soon became public knowledge that Westmoreland and Wheeler were thinking of requesting very substantial additional forces. In response to a Washington query as to what might be needed in Vietnam, the military indicated that an early deployment of 30,000 troops was required, and that a total of 200,000 would be needed to buttress our forces in Vietnam and to replenish the strategic reserve. According to some who were present, the President was visibly shaken. He had doled out additional forces for Vietnam bit by bit over the past three years, but the military had been given what they said they needed. And their requests had been granted pretty much on the strength of their own cognizance. But with a half-million troops already in Vietnam, and with no military victory in prospect despite the optimism of a week or so before, the President seemed now, for the first time, to doubt that we were on the right military track.

After a few days of agonized reconsideration, it was announced that 10,500 troops would be airlifted to Vietnam, that there was no intent to raise the total beyond the 525,000 troops already authorized, and that a complete review of our military policy in Vietnam would be undertaken before any decision would be made on new deployments. The atmosphere of urgency and foreboding that accompanied both the official statement and the departure of the additional forces did nothing to reassure an anxious American public. The televised departure of the military airlift evoked a feeling that an emergency relief force was on its way to relieve a besieged garrison.

The President had selected Clifford to succeed McNamara not only because of his obvious talents, but because he was one of Johnson's most trusted advisers. Unlike the increasing number of vacillators and "nervous Nellies" in the Administration, he could be counted on for strong and steady advice on Vietnam. Johnson knew that with Clifford he would have someone close by who, together with his other stalwarts, Secretary of State Rusk, Special Assistant Rostow, and Chairman of the Joint Chiefs of Staff General Wheeler, would support him in his determination to see the Vietnam war through to a victorious end. Clifford and Abe Fortas regarded the long bombing pause of January 1966 as Johnson's biggest mistake. And accurate or not, it was common gossip that whenever the President rejected suggestions for cutting back the bombing, more

often than not it was after these two personal friends had dropped by the White House for an evening chat and a nightcap. For some of us the Clifford-Fortas relationship with the President was a source of frustration and despair. We had no idea how much or how little they read or heard about the situation in Vietnam. But while the in-house hard-liners could at least be written or talked to, there seemed to be no way of reaching these insiders. Clifford himself puts the point well: ". . . it was quickly apparent to me [after he took over the position of Secretary of Defense] how little one knows if he has been on the periphery of a problem and not truly in it."

Clifford's first task as Secretary of Defense was to chair the high-level review of Vietnam policy. A portent of the depth of the review was the presence of the Secretary of the Treasury. His participation reflected the Administration's concern over the impact of the war on the country's international and domestic economic position. Secretary Fowler emphasized that an increase of 200,000 American troops for Vietnam would mean tax increases, federal price and wage controls, and credit restrictions. According to one participant, Fowler's most telling argument against the troop increase was his warning of a devaluation of the dollar that might result.

Aside from the economic effects, the additional manpower requests would involve calling up the reserves, increasing the draft, lengthening the period of service, and sending Vietnam veterans back for second and third tours. Clifford pressed the military on whether the additional troops would make the difference between victory and stalemate. The Joint Chiefs of Staff were unable to assure him that it would. At the end of a week of intense deliberation the

group recommended, apparently with Clifford and a few others dragging their feet, that the military should be given a small initial increment, and then described how the remainder of the additional 200,000 troops requested could be delivered. The study was given to the President on March 5. One of those who participated during that long and arduous week described the product of their work as a "delaying action" rather than a series of recommendations. If that was the intent of those who drafted the paper for the President, they succeeded. Johnson had nagging and agonizing doubts to resolve and he was in no mood to make a quick decision.

During subsequent days Clifford, reinforced by worried and skeptical members of his own staff and some officials in the Department of State, became convinced that regardless of how

(Donald McCullin, Magnum)

many additional troops were sent to Vietnam the prospects for a military victory were dim within a tolerable period of time. But no matter how gradually the new increments were dispatched, the effects on the domestic, political, and economic situation would be grave. Daniel Davidson, a bright and outspoken member of Ambassador Harriman's staff, commenting on the review group's recommendation told his boss that "200 thousand or even 400 thousand" additional troops would probably not improve the military situation by the end of 1968.

The battle over troop augmentation ebbed and flowed for many days. It was fueled by leaks in *The New York Times* and *The Washington Post* on March 10 that the Administration was giving serious consideration to the possibility of deploying as many as 200,000 more troops. Rusk found it necessary on the following day to assure Congress that it would be consulted if, in fact, the Administration felt it necessary to send additional men to Vietnam. By the latter part of March it was clear that the proponents of a minimum military augmentation had carried the day. In the event, it was agreed to ask General Thieu to announce that he did not need additional American troops and that South Vietnam would substantially increase its own forces. An increase of 13,500 American support troops was agreed upon.

But the force augmentation question was only one of several momentous issues that were under microscopic scrutiny. There was the broader and more fundamental question of whether the Administration should move forward on a war or peace track. In a series of dramatic confrontations over a period of ten tense days the issue was ultimately decided by the only man who could turn American policy around—Lyndon Johnson. On

March 31 he placed the country, for the first time since we became involved in Vietnam, squarely and unequivocally on the peace track. He also announced that he would not run for re-election.

In retrospect the President's speech of March 31 seems to follow logically from the lessons of his Administration's involvement in Vietnam, from the Tet offensive, and from the burden of the arguments put forward by Clifford and subsequently by a convocation of "Wise Men" (including such formidable advisers as Dean Acheson, General Ridgway, and McGeorge Bundy). But other events, not unrelated to the issue of war or peace, may also have played an important role. By the turn of the year Americans had begun to transform insistent, but inchoate and loosely organized yearnings for an end to the Vietnam war into something much more tangible and significant—a movement that caused politicians and statesmen alike to prick up their ears. The enthusiasm for Senator Eugene McCarthy among moderates and radicals in the various peace movements provided a political outlet for those who wanted to get out of Vietnam—by negotiations if possible, but to get out anyway. His strong showing in the New Hampshire primary on March 12 was regarded by many professional politicians as a fluke, but it became harder for them to dismiss the Senator as an amateur politician surrounded by amateur strategists. The fact that an immediate settlement and withdrawal of American troops from Vietnam was his only campaign issue was not lost on the Administration.

The President may have assumed that he could ignore Eugene McCarthy (after all, many McCarthy supporters were not old enough to vote), but Robert Kennedy was another matter. Kennedy had announced his

candidacy on March 16, and while his campaign would clearly involve a broad range of issues, an early settlement of the Vietnam war was high on his list. Indeed there was a story afloat that Kennedy had agreed not to run if Johnson appointed a "Blue Ribbon" group to examine alternatives to the current Vietnam policy. Johnson's review group was probably not quite what Kennedy had in mind, either in terms of the cast of characters or the range of alternatives it was considering. So Kennedy, whose inside sources were good enough to know this (even if Johnson would not tell him), entered the race. The possibility of a tough primary fight began to loom. And if the Kennedy and McCarthy camps joined forces, as it was rumored they might, the Democratic party's renomination of Lyndon Johnson would not be quite the shoo-in it had appeared to be just a few short weeks before.

Other considerations may also have influenced the President's decision to take this new initiative and to return to private life. On February 28 Governor Romney had withdrawn from the Republican primary race leaving the field wide open for Richard Nixon—a much stronger candidate. And on March 16 the public opinion polls showed Johnson's popularity at its lowest point during the entire period of his presidency.

Johnson had said that he had long been seriously considering returning to the Ranch. But even his closest advisers admit they were staggered when they heard the last few words of his March 31 speech.

The President's announcement that he would not run again was a surprise dessert at an elaborate banquet of pronouncements. As the first step to de-escalate the conflict, he announced that aerial and naval bombardment of North Vietnam would not take place except "in the area north of the demilitarized zone where the continuing enemy buildup directly threatens Allied forward positions and where the movements of their troops and supplies are clearly related to that threat." The area exempted from the bombing would cover "almost 90 percent of North Vietnam's population and most of its territory." To clinch the point that he had opted for the peace track, he declared that "the United States is ready to send its representatives to any forum, at any time" and designated Ambassador Averell Harriman as his "personal representative for such talks." (Ambassador Llewellyn Thompson was also designated but was soon replaced by Cyrus Vance.) The next move was up to Hanoi.

Many of the State Department's senior officers, including those with the longest experience in dealing with the Communists, had serious doubts that Hanoi would accept a partial bombing halt in exchange for an agreement to start negotiations. Ambassador Harriman himself was initially skeptical that the North Vietnamese would respond favorably to anything but a complete cessation. Up until the last moment he urged the President to commit himself to stopping the bombing altogether once Hanoi sat down to talk. There were others (including myself) who felt that the President's revelation of his future personal plans would induce Hanoi to stall until after the political conventions. This seemed all the more compelling because of McCarthy's and Kennedy's growing strength.[4]

The doubters were wrong. On

[4] Many months later in Paris, Hanoi's "North American expert" told Daniel Davidson, a member of the American delegation, that the North Vietnamese leaders never took McCarthy seriously and had not expected Kennedy to be nominated.

April 3 Hanoi offered to meet. The North Vietnamese statement was carefully worded to milk the last drop of propaganda from the President's proposal and from their own reply: North Vietnamese representatives were ready to sit down with American representatives "with a view to determining with the American side the unconditional cessation of the U.S. bombing raids and all other acts of war against the

Democratic Republic of Vietnam so that talks may start."

There then followed a full month of volleying on the question of the meeting site. The President's reply to Hanoi had stated that he would be willing to send representatives "to any forum, at any time" to get negotiations started. This, together with his earlier statements that the United States would "go anywhere, anytime" to achieve

(Philip Jones Griffiths, Magnum)

(Philip Jones Griffiths, Magnum)

peace, put the Administration in an awkward position when Washington turned down various suggestions from Hanoi as to a meeting place. General Westmoreland's statement on April 7, a few days after the Hanoi-Washington exchange, that "the spirit of the offensive is now prevalent throughout Vietnam with advantage being taken of the enemy's weakened military position . . . militarily we have never been in a better relative position. . . ." fed speculation that Washington's dickering over a meeting place was a stalling action. The Administration in general, and Vice-President Humphrey in particular, began to feel on the defensive.

The location of the conference was not as inconsequential a matter as it might have appeared. Although it was contemplated that the first confrontation with Hanoi's representatives would deal merely with "arrangements," there was genuine concern that

this preliminary session would spill over into substantive discussions and that the American delegation would be locked into a site that would be inadequate or awkward. Despite earlier flamboyant expressions of willingness to go "anywhere," the United States had a few minimum, fundamental requirements that would have to be met for any conference other than a most preliminary and superficial one. There was no point, for example, in embarking on a long series of meetings in a country where facilities were insufficient to handle the necessary volume of communications. Not unnaturally, too, we preferred that the conference be held in a country where we had a diplomatic Mission. Finally, the site should be one the Saigon Government would accept. On all these counts, the original North Vietnamese suggestion of Cambodia, with whom we had no diplomatic relations and who recog-

nized the Viet Cong but not the South Vietnamese, was impractical. Still another requirement was that the meetings be held in a country where we could be reasonably confident that personal and official quarters would not be monitored and our people would not be under constant surveillance. This seemed to exclude most Communist capitals. On May 3 it was finally agreed that the representatives of Hanoi and Washington would gather in Paris on May 10.

The American delegation was small and high-powered, able, patient, and imaginative. In addition to Harriman and Vance, there was a gruff, knowledgeable, anti-hero from the State Department, Philip Habib; an ex-newspaperman who came to Walt Rostow's staff by way of the State Department, William Jorden; Harriman's bright Special Assistant, Daniel Davidson; and the highly respected General Andrew Goodpaster (who soon left the delegation to command the NATO forces). There was some early speculation that Cyrus Vance had initially been sent to Paris as the personal eyes and ears of the President, but whether or not this was true, there was little doubt about the mission of the member of Rostow's staff who was assigned to the delegation.

President Thieu gave the negotiators a grim sendoff. On the eve of their meeting he warned Hanoi (and presumably Washington as well) that "we will never cede an inch of land to the northern Communists, we will never set up a coalition government with the NFLSV [National Liberation Front of South Vietnam], and we will never recognize the NFLSV as a political entity equal to us, with which we must negotiate on an equal footing." But Thieu was not the only one in South Vietnam warily watching the Paris negotiations. At the end of April the "Alliance of National Democratic and Peace Forces," which had been organized during the Tet offensive, had met near Saigon and issued a manifesto stating that the Alliance "is prepared to enter into discussions with the U.S. Government." It also noted that the NLF "cannot be absent from the settlement of any problem in South Vietnam." The Alliance was a child, or at least an adopted child, of the NLF and Hanoi and consisted of a mix of obvious, if undistinguished South Vietnam front groups and leftists. The move evoked memories of the Laos Conference of 1961–1962 when the Communists successfully pressed for a coalition government built around a neutralist group. Although what emerged in Laos was a disappointment for the Communists, it would appear that they were preparing to try the tactic again in Vietnam. The problem in South Vietnam, of course, was the

paucity of card-carrying neutralists—the society was polarized into Communists and anti-Communists. Those in between had fled the country or were remaining very quiet. The creation of the Alliance was a transparent attempt to develop an instant "third force" around which non-Communists, it was hoped, would rally. It turned out to be a frail creature. Although Hanoi, the NLF, and even Peking and Moscow gave the Alliance a propaganda boost during the spring and early summer, it suffered from chronic undernourishment.

Washington, meanwhile, was under considerable pressure to get substantive discussions under way as soon as possible. Now at long last Americans and North Vietnamese were talking, or at least shouting, but the American public was becoming impatient. There were some who even harbored the hope that a settlement could be reached before the November election.

Humphrey found himself in a very uncomfortable spot. It was difficult to carve out a position on Vietnam that would maintain whatever lukewarm support he still had from President Johnson on the one hand, and compete with McCarthy and Kennedy on the other. If substantial progress could be made in Paris in the course of the next few months, however, he would be in an excellent position to capture the nomination and win the election.

But days folded into weeks and weeks into months without any visible movement in Paris. The sessions there had more the characteristics of a "happening" than a negotiation. The central point at issue was a complete bombing cessation and the terms on which it would be made. After much bickering on the question of whether bombing should be limited to the area south of the 20th or the 19th parallel, the decision was made to cut back to the 19th parallel.

The bombing cut-back to the 19th parallel permitted the heavily populated areas of North Vietnam to return to some semblance of normal life, but heavy raids continued in the southern part of the country and were interfering with Hanoi's efforts to supply its forces in South Vietnam. During the late spring the Pentagon was privately admitting that the concentration of our bombing south of the 19th parallel and in Laos was producing more effective results in terms of inhibiting infiltration into South Vietnam than did the full-scale bombing of a few months before—a contention that McNamara had strongly maintained. To those who had argued a year before that a bombing cut-back would result in fewer American losses, better military payoff, and possibly even political progress, this belated admission provided some bitter satisfaction.

By late June the American negotiators developed a formula designed to get around the "no advantage" versus "no conditions" impasse. The Americans would stop bombing, and Hanoi would then agree to restore and observe the demilitarized character of the buffer zone along the 17th parallel under the supervision of the International Control Commission. In a sense this was a variant of the old Phase A–Phase B approach. In addition the Americans would inform the North Vietnamese that the bombing cessation would be maintained on the "assumption" that the Communists would not launch indiscriminate attacks on the urban areas of South Vietnam. It would also be "assumed" that substantive talks which would include Saigon Government representatives would quickly follow.

The Americans in Paris were encouraged to believe that Hanoi would agree to such a proposal. The North Vietnamese had with-

(Rene Burri, Magnum)

drawn some regular units north across the DMZ and seemed ready to scale down the fighting in the South. But American forces, under a strategy of "maximum pressure," continued to hold the initiative and to maintain an offensive posture. The North Vietnamese have since charged that they demonstrated their good faith during this period but that we did not follow suit. There are some, particularly Ambassador Harriman, who feel that we could have made more, even definitive, progress in Paris by the end of the summer of 1968 if we had completely stopped the bombing of North Vietnam and had de-escalated our ground-force activity in South Vietnam toward the end of the previous year when the Communists seemed to be cutting back.

The new variant of Phase A–Phase B was presented to Hanoi's representatives in a secret private meeting early in July. By late in the month there was no response and indeed no hint from the North Vietnamese that a reply would be forthcoming. The lull in Viet Cong and North Vietnamese military activity had been continuing for several weeks, but there was evidence that an attack on Saigon was being planned. Although it was thought that such an attack might be timed to coincide with a meeting between Johnson and Thieu in Honolulu on July 20, the meeting took place without incident.

The North Vietnamese may have been waiting for the results of the Honolulu tête-à-tête before responding to the American proposal. That meeting must have given them food for thought. The Conference Communique affirmed that the Saigon Government "should be a full participant playing a leading role" in negotiations. In short, Honolulu did much to buttress Thieu's stature (he later confided that "he had gotten more out of Johnson than he had dared hope for," and that the Communique "was too good to be true"), but it did little to stimulate progress in Paris.

By the end of July Harriman and Vance felt it was time for them to launch an initiative of their own. I was then in Paris. A message was sent to Washington assessing the progress that had been made thus far. Harriman and Vance noted that Hanoi had not responded to the bombing cessation proposal, and they suggested the North Vietnamese might be stalling until after the political conventions. The chilling thought was ventured that Hanoi might try to delay its reply until after the election and possibly until after a change of Administration in January. Thus, Harriman and Vance said, it was conceivable that months could pass in Paris without visible progress. They expressed concern about the political climate in the United States under such circumstances. The disillusionment and the weakening of American resolve that would accompany drawn-out and inconclusive negotiations in Paris might force a new Administration to move toward a precipitate withdrawal from Vietnam. It was suggested that a new tack be taken in Paris immediately: instead of waiting indefinitely for a reply from Hanoi to the new Phase A–Phase B proposal, the United States should return to the essence of the San Antonio Formula. The current Communist military lull in Vietnam could plausibly be interpreted as a signal from Hanoi that it had gone far toward meeting American requirements.[5] Washington could stop the bombing of North Vietnam altogether, providing Hanoi was informed of certain "assumptions" the United States would make with respect to Communist military actions. It

[5] In particular, it was felt that Hanoi could be said to meet the conditions the President had publicly announced. At a News Conference on February 2, 1967, the following exchange had taken place:

"Q. Mr. President, we have said in the past that we would be willing to suspend the bombing of North Vietnam in exchange for some suitable step by the other side. Are you prepared at all to tell us what kind of other steps the other side should take for this suspension of the bombing?

"The President. *Just almost any step.*" [Italics mine]

was also suggested that Vance return to Washington to explain the proposed new initiative.

Washington's reaction, which came within hours, was sharp and negative. The President not only disapproved of a complete bombing halt at this time, but he was annoyed by references to the political conventions and to a change in the Administration. Any implication that Humphrey needed a major switch in Vietnam policy if he were going to win the Democratic nomination and the presidency directly touched exposed nerves at the White House. The fact that *The New York Times* also was currently pressing for a bombing halt was the final straw. Johnson was apparently convinced that there was a Humphrey-Paris-*New York Times*-Clifford conspiracy. Paris was to continue on its present track and to wait for a reply from the Hanoi delegation. Vance should not return to Washington to explain the new proposal.

Further evidence of the White House mood was provided in a presidential press conference on July 31 when Johnson told reporters that 30,000 North Vietnamese had moved into South Vietnam during the month, the highest infiltration rate to date. He noted that the North Vietnamese were preparing for a massive attack, consequently he could not order a bombing cessation. A bombing halt at this time, he implied, would lead "to the loss of heavy American and Allied casualties [sic]" and warned that he might have to move ahead with "additional military measures." It was a fighting, if somewhat exaggerated statement. Most intelligence analysts would have placed the infiltration during July at a lower figure than 30,000. And most nonmilitary analysts did not believe there was a direct relationship between the cessation of bombing of North Vietnam and the number of American casualties in South Vietnam.

Before leaving for Paris in mid-July, I had been visited by one of Humphrey's campaign aides. He told me the Vice-President had prepared a major speech on Vietnam which he hoped to deliver prior to the meeting of the Democratic Platform Committee. The speech proposed a complete cessation of bombing to be followed immediately by serious discussions of a political settlement. Humphrey was caught between a desire not to prejudice the talks in Paris and a need to establish himself as a candidate with views on Vietnam distinguishable from those of President Johnson. But since he was getting little information regarding the negotiations, and since the slightest departure from the President's Vietnam line would diminish his White House support (which was hardly robust at is was), he was painted into a corner. My visitor was anxious to get assurances from Paris that if Humphrey publicly advocated a

(Philip Jones Griffiths, Magnum)

(Philip Jones Griffiths, Magnum)

complete bombing cessation the negotiators would not cut the ground from under him. Would I ascertain whether Harriman and Vance felt Humphrey's proposal would prejudice or complicate the current talks?

When I returned to Washington, the Paris proposal had been rejected by the President, but reconsideration had been given to the idea of Vance's return. He was to come back for a short "private" visit during which he would brief presidential candidate Nixon on developments in Paris. Vance felt there was still some slight hope that he could convince the President of the desirability of stopping the bombing. The prospect of getting Johnson to turn around on this issue was remote, especially after his July 31 speech, but Humphrey's public advocacy of a bombing cessation would be the kiss of death. Humphrey agreed that the points he would score among the liberal Democrats were not worth prejudicing whatever chance there was for serious

negotiations. In an impressive act of statesmanship, he shelved his speech.

On August 19, a few days before the Democratic Convention, Johnson removed whatever maneuvering room Humphrey had left. In a speech to the Veterans of Foreign Wars, he said the United States would not halt the bombing "until it has reason to believe that the other side intends seriously to join with us in de-escalating the war and moving seriously toward peace." Since the Communists did not intend to "move seriously" until we had stopped all bombing, progress in Paris seemed destined for further delays.

Throughout the late summer many officials within the Administration continued to urge the White House to stop the bombing. If the hard-pressed Humphrey was going to win the election, the stalemate in Paris had to be broken. Clark Clifford was one of the strongest advocates of this course, much to Johnson's annoyance. In mid-

September the President struck Clifford's name from the distribution list for "sensitive" telegrams relating to negotiations.

In addition to bargaining over the terms of a bombing cessation, the Paris negotiators confronted the critical issue of the composition and the modalities of the "serious talks" if and when they got under way. The matter of NLF participation had had a long and murky history in terms of American policy discussions. In the early '60s Washington had taken the position that the NLF could not participate in negotiations as an independent party because it was a "creature of Hanoi." As time went on, however, this position softened. In July 1965 President Johnson, it will be remembered, had noted that "The Viet Cong would have no difficulty in being represented [at a conference] and having their views presented if Hanoi for a moment decides that she wants to cease aggression, and I would not think that would be an insurmountable problem at all. I think that could be worked out." And two years later Arthur Goldberg indicated that the Administration was prepared to agree to participation by the NLF in peace talks.

The Saigon Government had long maintained that it would not talk to the NLF in any forum that implied its recognition as an equal. As we have seen, Thieu reinforced this position on the eve of the Paris meeting. The NLF and Hanoi, for their part, had long insisted that the Saigon Government was a puppet of the United States and therefore had no right to sit at a negotiations table.

Various detours around this impasse had been brooded about in Washington. In 1967 there was some discussion of using a formula by which the "four belligerents" (i.e., Hanoi, the NLF, the United States, and the GVN) would be called to a negotiating table by some outside group such as the Geneva Co-Chairmen or the UN. The State Department legal staff, however, had objected on technical grounds to the use of the word "belligerent," and the idea was dropped. In due course a new approach was worked out, and this was the one the American negotiators proposed in mid-July at a private meeting. The idea was simply to refer to "two sides," leaving it to each "side" to work out its own composition. Thus if the Hanoi delegation wished to regard the NLF as a separate body it could do so, and the United States could do the same with the GVN. On the other hand, the United States need not recognize the NLF as being an independent group but only as a member of "the other side"; the Communists could interpret the composition of our "side" any way they wished. Thus was fashioned the "Our Side–Your Side" creature —a new entrant in the international conference parade of horribles.

By October it seemed that the two road blocks to "serious talks" were close to being removed. With the Soviet Ambassador in Paris applying fuel or lubrication whenever the process stalled, the American and North Vietnamese representatives pressed toward agreement on the terms of a bombing cessation and the modalities of the "Our Side–Your Side" solution to Saigon and NLF participation.

It was at about this point that McGeorge Bundy at De Pauw University advocated a bombing cessation and a troop reduction. As he had done at the council of "Wise Men" held in late March, Bundy acknowledged that a negotiated settlement was the only prudent course. "There is no prospect of military victory against North Vietnam by any level of U.S. military force which is acceptable or desirable." Although there was a flurry of speculation that Bundy was a chosen instrument for signaling a major change in the Administration's course, this was not the case. The President had seen an advance copy of the De Pauw speech but had made no comment. In any case there was a sense of movement, real or imagined, and attention

(Burk Uzzle, Magnum)

was focused on Paris where some dramatic new development was expected. The hopeful were soon to be rewarded.

On October 31 Johnson announced that "all air, naval, and artillery bombardment of North Vietnam" would stop as of 8 A.M., Washington time, on November 1. The Americans and North Vietnamese had evidently reached agreement in Paris on the "assumptions" and "Our Side–Your Side." At last the negotiators could get down to business. But could they? Within hours of the President's statement there were ominous noises out of Saigon. President Thieu pronounced that "the American Government has unilaterally decided to stop the bombing on the whole territory of North Vietnam." And from a member of the South Vietnamese Government came the candid remark: "We were informed last night, but we didn't go along with it. We are very unhappy." Presidential candidate Nixon was reportedly also unhappy; the timing of the bombing halt, just a few days before the election, seemed more than merely a coincidence.

Clark Clifford and other Defense Department officials were once more given access to information on the negotiations. After he became abreast of what had been going on in Paris over the previous five weeks, Clifford told the President that he was convinced the Saigon Government had discounted a Democratic victory in the elections. They were obviously stalling off their participation in the Paris talks until the Republicans, from whom they expected a tougher approach, took over.

On November 1 Hanoi's delegation issued a communique announcing that "a meeting including the representatives of the Democratic Republic of Vietnam, the South Vietnam National Liberation Front, the United States and the Republic of Vietnam will be held in Paris not earlier than November 6, 1968." But on the following day the Saigon Government announced that it would not attend the November 6 session; its conditions were not fulfilled. Either the Administration had goofed, or the South Vietnamese Government had double-crossed the Administration. In any case, whatever advantage Humphrey would be able to gain from the bombing cessation now looked very thin.

Some State Department experts feel that Thieu and Ky never really understood the "Our Side–Your Side" formula when Embassy representatives had explained it to them many weeks before. There are others who claim that the South Vietnamese did understand it but reneged at the last minute. According to this view, some overeager and possibly self-appointed emissaries from the Republican party had urged the South Vietnamese to stall going to Paris until after the election and a predicted Republican victory. The argument reportedly made to Saigon was that the South Vietnamese Government would get a better deal after the Republicans came into office. Behind this high-minded stint of foreign policy making was an underlying suspicion among some Republicans that Humphrey's chances would be significantly improved if it appeared that the negotiations were to get down to business on November 6. Clifford's hunch with respect to Republican maneuvering seemed to be right.

In any event, the South Vietnamese held to their position, the first session of the talks was postponed, and Humphrey lost the election. Relations between Washington and Saigon were more strained during November than they had been since December 1964 when the South Vietnamese military junta purged the government and dissolved the civilian High National Council. Thieu proposed on November 8 that the composition of the conference consist of two delegations: the non-Communist delegation would be headed by South Vietnam, and would include the United States. This suggestion did nothing to soothe Washington's ire. The American negotiators were beside themselves. After all the months of stewing and steaming, of clandestine meetings and spotlighted plenary sessions, of substantive proposals and verbal manipulations, Harriman and Vance felt they were now on the one-yard line. It seemed inconceivable that Thieu and Ky could block them. With a considerable assist from Clifford they argued that substantive talks should start as soon as possible after November 6, with or without representatives of the Saigon Government. Clifford told the press on November 12 that "we should make every reasonable effort to demonstrate to Saigon why it should come in and join the talks. At the same time, if they choose not to, I believe the President has the constitutional responsibility of proceeding with the talks." Later that day, when asked whether Clifford was speaking for the President, White House Press Secretary George Christian said Mr. Clifford "was expressing his views as he sees things." However, according to *The New York Times,* it was understood the White House had cleared Clifford's remarks. In any case, the President refused to permit the American delegation to meet alone with the representatives of Hanoi and the NLF, hoping somehow that Saigon could be brought around.

A few days later the South Vietnamese grudgingly agreed to attend. But now yet another major issue had to be addressed: how would the "sides" be seated? And so was born (or rather reborn, because in the bizarre world of International Conferences the seating question was not an uncommon one) the shape-of-the-table caper. If it had been left to the American and North Vietnamese delegations, agreement would have been reached on an oval table early in the game. The Saigon group had much more arcane tastes in interior decoration. Somehow the furniture too had to evoke the political mystique that the NLF representatives did not really exist as separate entities from the Hanoi delegation.

American diplomats in Washington and Saigon were irritated and chagrined. The Vietnamese Ambassador to Washington, Bui Diem, confided to a friend that the South Vietnamese were amazed during this period that the United States could be so tough. It was the first time in a long time that Washington exerted the kind of leverage that its relative strength and national interests warranted. On November 27, after precious weeks had been lost haggling about the shape of a table and similar momentous questions, the Saigon Government agreed that its conditions for participating had been met "in their essential aspects."

With a change in Administration on the horizon, the starch was removed from the Johnson team. Indeed it was not until January 16, a few days before the new President took office, that official word came out of Paris that the procedural matters had been settled. "Under the terms of the agreement, representatives of the United States, South Vietnam, North Vietnam and the National Liberation Front, or Vietcong, will sit at a circular table without nameplates, flags or markings. Two rectangular tables, measuring about 3 feet by 4½ feet, will be placed 18 inches from the circular table at opposite sides."

Substantive talks were, at long last, to start. And with that Ambassador Averell Harriman returned to Washington and private life. A new American team headed by Henry Cabot Lodge took over in Paris. It would be his task to rid the Nixon Administration of the Vietnam albatross, hopefully with dignity and honor —a not inconsiderable responsibility, especially for a man who a few years before maintained that the war would not end with a negotiated settlement but by the Communists simply "fading away." Lodge's tenure in Paris lasted less than a year, during which time the Communists neither negotiated nor faded away.

J. WILLIAM FULBRIGHT
The Arrogance of Power

J. William Fulbright, Democratic Senator for Arkansas and Chairman of the Foreign Relations Committee, places our intervention in Vietnam—and his own opposition to it—in a long historical perspective. Fulbright sees us as determined to set the impress of our curious "welfare imperialism" on the world. Like other empires before us, we have come to confuse power and virtue—convinced that because we are rich, prosperous, and successful, we have a right, and even an obligation, to meddle in the lives of other nations to raise them to our "standards." Misplaced good intentions have driven us to a situation in which we can do little but destroy native cultures and torment the small nations we originally tried to help.

It is somewhat startling to find that a man who has devoted most of his life to the conduct of foreign affairs condemns "an excessive preoccupation with foreign relations," or to see this long-time champion of internationalism call for a more limited American role in the concerns of other nations. The position that Fulbright and others have assumed is a measure of the extent to which events of the sixties, especially our involvement in Vietnam, have eroded older ways of viewing the world and forced men to rethink attitudes and aims about which they were once sure.

America is the most fortunate of nations—fortunate in her rich territory, fortunate in having had a century of relative peace in which to develop that territory, fortunate in her diverse and talented population, fortunate in the institutions devised by the founding fathers and in the wisdom of those who have adapted those institutions to a changing world.

For the most part America has made good use of her blessings, especially in her internal life but also in her foreign relations. Having done so much and succeeded so well, America is now at that historical point at which a great nation is in danger of losing its perspective on what exactly is within the realm of its power and what is beyond it. Other great nations, reaching this critical juncture, have aspired to too much, and by overextension of effort have declined and then fallen.

The causes of the malady are not entirely clear but its recurrence is one of the uniformities of history: power tends to confuse itself with virtue and a great nation is peculiarly susceptible to the idea that its power is a sign of God's favor, conferring upon it a special responsibility for other nations—to make them richer and happier and wiser, to remake them, that is, in its own shining image. Power confuses itself with virtue and tends also to take itself for omnipotence. Once imbued with the idea of a mission, a great nation easily assumes that it has the means as well as the duty to do God's work. The Lord, after all, surely would not choose you as His agent and then deny you the sword with which to work His will. German soldiers in the First World War wore belt buckles imprinted with the words *"Gott mit uns."* It was approximately under this kind of infatuation—an exaggerated sense of power and an imaginary sense of mission—that the Athenians attacked Syracuse, and Napoleon and then Hitler invaded Russia. In plain words, they overextended their commitments and they came to grief.

I do not think for a moment that America, with her deeply rooted democratic traditions, is likely to embark upon a campaign to dominate the world in the manner of a Hitler or Napoleon. What I do fear is that she may be drifting into commitments which, though generous and benevolent in intent, are so far-reaching as to exceed even America's great capacities. At the same time, it is my hope—and I emphasize it because it underlies all of the criticisms and proposals to be made in these pages —that America will escape those fatal temptations of power which have ruined other great nations and will instead confine herself to doing only that good in the world which she *can* do, both by direct effort and by the force of her own example.

The stakes are high indeed: they include not only America's continued greatness but nothing less than the survival of the human race in an era when, for the first time in history, a living generation has the power of veto over the survival of the next.

THE POWER DRIVE OF NATIONS

When the abstractions and subtleties of political science have been exhausted, there remain the most basic unanswered questions about war and peace and why nations contest the issues they contest and why they even care about them. As Aldous Huxley has written:

There may be arguments about the best way of raising wheat in a cold climate or of re-afforesting a denuded mountain. But such arguments never lead to organized slaughter. Organized slaughter is the result of arguments about such questions as the following: Which is the best nation? The best religion? The best political theory? The best form of government? Why are other people so stupid and wicked? Why can't they see how good and intelligent *we* are? Why do they resist our beneficent efforts to bring them under our control and make them like ourselves?[1]

Many of the wars fought by man—I am tempted to say most —have been fought over such abstractions. The more I puzzle over the great wars of history, the more I am inclined to the view that the causes attributed to them—territory, markets, resources, the defense or perpetuation of great principles—were not the root causes at all but rather explanations or excuses for certain unfathomable drives of human nature. For lack of a clear and precise understanding of exactly what these motives are, I refer to them as the "arrogance of power"—as a psychological need that nations seem to have in order to prove that they are bigger, better, or stronger than other nations. Implicit in this drive is the assumption, even on the part of normally peaceful nations, that force is the ultimate

[1] Aldous Huxley, "The Politics of Ecology" (Santa Barbara: Center for the Study of Democratic Institutions, 1963), p. 6.

proof of superiority—that when a nation shows that it has the stronger army, it is also proving that it has better people, better institutions, better principles, and, in general, a better civilization.

Evidence for my proposition is found in the remarkable discrepancy between the apparent and hidden causes of some modern wars and the discrepancy between their causes and ultimate consequences.

The precipitating cause of the Franco-Prussian War of 1870, for example, was a dispute over the succession to the Spanish throne, and the ostensible "underlying" cause was French resistance to the unification of Germany. The war was followed by the completion of German unification—which probably could have been achieved without war—but it was also followed by the loss of Alsace-Lorraine, the humiliation of France, and the emergence of Germany as the greatest power in Europe, which could not have been achieved without war. The peace treaty, incidentally, said nothing about the Spanish throne, which everyone apparently had forgotten. One wonders to what extent the Germans were motivated simply by the desire to cut those haughty Frenchmen down to size and have a good excuse to build another monument in Berlin.

The United States went to war in 1898 for the stated purpose of liberating Cuba from Spanish tyranny, but after winning the war—a war which Spain had been willing to pay a high price to avoid—the United States brought the liberated Cubans under an American protectorate and incidentally annexed the Philippines, because, according to President McKinley, the Lord told him it was America's duty "to educate the Filipinos, and uplift and civilize and Christianize them, and by God's grace do the very best we could by them, as our fellowmen for whom Christ also died."[2]

Isn't it interesting that the voice was the voice of the Lord but the words were those of Theodore Roosevelt, Henry Cabot Lodge, and Admiral Mahan, those "imperialists of 1898" who wanted America to have an empire just because a big powerful country like the United States *ought* to have an empire? The spirit of the times was expressed by Albert Beveridge, soon thereafter to be elected to the United States Senate, who proclaimed Americans to be "a conquering race": "We must obey our blood and occupy new markets and if necessary new lands," he said, because "In the Almighty's infinite plan . . . debased civilizations and decaying races" must disappear "before the higher civilization of the nobler and more virile types of man."[3]

In 1914 all Europe went to war, ostensibly because the heir to the Austrian throne had been assassinated at Sarajevo, but really because that murder became the symbolic focus of the incredibly delicate sensibilities of the great nations of Europe. The events of the summer of 1914 were a melodrama of abnormal psychology: Austria had to humiliate Serbia in order not to be humiliated herself but Austria's effort at recovering self-esteem was profoundly humiliating to Russia; Russia was allied to France, who had been feeling generally humiliated since 1871, and Austria in turn was allied to Germany, whose pride required that she support Austria no matter how insanely Austria behaved and who may in any case have felt that it would be fun to give the German Army another swing

down the Champs-Élysées. For these ennobling reasons the world was plunged into a war which took tens of millions of lives, precipitated the Russian Revolution, and set in motion the events that led to another world war, a war which took tens of millions more lives and precipitated the worldwide revolutions of our time, revolutions whose consequences are beyond the foresight of any of us now alive.

The causes and consequences of war may have more to do with pathology than with politics, more to do with irrational pressures of pride and pain than with rational calculations of advantage and profit. There is a Washington story, perhaps apocryphal, that the military intellectuals in the Pentagon conducted an experiment in which they fed data derived from the events of the summer of 1914 into a computer and that, after weighing and digesting the evidence, the machine assured its users that there was no danger of war. What this "proves," if anything, is that computers are more rational than men; it also suggests that if there is a root cause of human conflict and of the power drive of nations, it lies not in economic aspirations, historical forces, or the workings of the balance of power, but in the ordinary hopes and fears of the human mind.

It has been said that buried in every woman's secret soul is a drum majorette; it might also be said that in all of our souls there is a bit of the missionary. We all like telling people what to do, which is perfectly all right except that most people do not like being told what to do. I have given my wife some splendid suggestions on household management but she has been so consistently ungrateful for my advice that I have stopped offering it. The phenomenon is explained by the Canadian psychiatrist and former Director-General of the

World Health Organization, Brock Chisholm, who writes:

. . . Man's method of dealing with difficulties in the past has always been to tell everyone else how they should behave. We've all been doing that for centuries.

It should be clear by now that this no longer does any good. Everybody has by now been told by everybody else how he should behave. . . . The criticism is not effective; it never has been, and it never is going to be. . . .[4]

Ineffective though it has been, the giving—and enforcement—of all this unsolicited advice has at least until recently been compatible with the survival of the human race. Man is now, however, for the first time, in a situation in which the survival of his species is in jeopardy. Other forms of life have been endangered and many destroyed by changes in their natural environment; man is menaced by a change of environment which he himself has wrought by the invention of nuclear weapons and ballistic missiles. Our power to kill has become universal, creating a radically new situation which, if we are to survive, requires us to adopt some radically new attitudes about the giving and enforcement of advice and in general about human and international relations.

The enormity of the danger of extinction of our species is dulled by the frequency with which it is stated, as if a familiar threat of catastrophe were no threat at all. We seem to feel somehow that because the hydrogen bomb has not killed us yet, it is never going to kill us. This is a dangerous assumption because it encourages the retention of traditional attitudes about world politics when our responsibility, in Dr. Chisholm's words, is nothing less than to "re-examine all of the attitudes of our ancestors

[2] Quoted in Samuel Flagg Bemis, *A Diplomatic History of the United States* (New York: Holt, 1955), p. 472.
[3] Quoted in Barbara Tuchman, *The Proud Tower* (New York: Macmillan, 1966), p. 153.

[4] Brock Chisholm, *Prescription of Survival* (New York: Columbia University Press, 1957), p. 54.

and to select from those attitudes things which we, on our own authority in these present circumstances, with our knowledge, recognize as still valid in this new kind of world. . . ."[5]

The attitude above all others which I feel sure is no longer valid is the arrogance of power, the tendency of great nations to equate power with virtue and major responsibilities with a universal mission. The dilemmas involved are pre-eminently American dilemmas, not because America has weaknesses that others do not have but because America is powerful as no nation has ever been before, and the discrepancy between her power and the power of others appears to be increasing. One may hope that America, with her vast resources and democratic traditions, with her diverse and creative population, will find the wisdom to match her power; but one can hardly be confident because the wisdom required is greater wisdom than any great nation has ever shown before. It must be rooted, as Dr. Chisholm says, in the re-examination of "all of the attitudes of our ancestors."

It is a tall order. Perhaps one can begin to fill it by an attempt to assess the attitudes of Americans toward other peoples and some of the effects of America's power on small countries whom she has tried to help.

INNOCENTS ABROAD

There are signs of the arrogance of power in the way Americans act when they go to foreign countries. Foreigners frequently comment on the contrast between the behavior of Americans at home and abroad: in our own country, they say, we are hospitable and considerate, but as soon as we get outside our own bor-

ders something seems to get into us and wherever we are we become noisy and demanding and we strut around as if we owned the place. The British used to say during the war that the trouble with the Yanks was that they were "overpaid, oversexed, and over here." During a recent vacation in Mexico, I noticed in a small-town airport two groups of students on holiday, one group Japanese, the other American. The Japanese were neatly dressed and were talking and laughing in a manner that neither annoyed anybody nor particularly called attention to themselves. The Americans, on the other hand, were disporting themselves in a conspicuous and offensive manner, stamping around the waiting room in sloppy clothes, drinking beer, and shouting to each other as if no one else were there.

This kind of scene, unfortunately, has become familiar in many parts of the world. I do not wish to exaggerate its significance, but I have the feeling that just as there was once something special about being a Roman or a Spaniard or an Englishman, there is now something about the consciousness of being an American abroad, something about the consciousness of belonging to the biggest, richest country in the world, that encourages people who are perfectly well behaved at home to become boorish when they are in somebody else's country and to treat the local citizens as if they were not really there.

One reason Americans abroad may act as though they "own the place" is that in many places they very nearly do: American companies may dominate large segments of a country's economy; American products are advertised on billboards and displayed in shop windows; American hotels and snack bars are available to protect American tourists from foreign influence; American soldiers may be stationed in the country, and even if they are not,

the population are probably well aware that their very survival depends on the wisdom with which America uses her immense military power.

I think that when any American goes abroad, he carries an unconscious knowledge of all this power with him and it affects his behavior, just as it once affected the behavior of Greeks and Romans, of Spaniards, Germans, and Englishmen, in the brief high noons of their respective ascendancies. It was the arrogance of their power that led nineteenth-century Englishmen to suppose that if they shouted at a foreigner loud enough in English he was bound to understand, or that now leads Americans to behave like Mark Twain's "innocents abroad," who reported on their travels in Europe that

The people of those foreign countries are very, very ignorant. They looked curiously at the costumes we had brought from the wilds of America. They observed that we talked loudly at table sometimes. . . . In Paris they just simply opened their eyes and stared when we spoke to them in French! We never did succeed in making these idiots understand their own language.[6]

THE FATAL IMPACT

Reflecting on his voyages to Polynesia in the late eighteenth century, Captain Cook later wrote that "It would have been better for these people never to have known us." In a book on European explorations of the South Pacific, Alan Moorehead relates how the Tahitians and the Australian aborigines were corrupted by the white man's diseases, alcohol, firearms, laws, and concepts of morality, by what Moorehead calls "the long downslide into Western civilization." The first missionaries to Tahiti, says Moorehead, were "determined to recreate the island in

[5] Chisholm, *Prescription of Survival*, p. 9.

[6] Mark Twain, *The Innocents Abroad* (New York: The Thistle Press, 1962), p. 494.

the image of lower-middle-class Protestant England. . . . They kept hammering away at the Tahitian way of life until it crumbled before them, and within two decades they had achieved precisely what they set out to do."[7] It is said that the first missionaries to Hawaii went for the purpose of explaining to the Polynesians that it was sinful to work on Sunday, only to discover that in those bountiful islands nobody worked on any day.

Even when acting with the best of intentions, Americans, like other Western peoples who have carried their civilizations abroad, have had something of the same "fatal impact" on smaller nations that European explorers had on the Tahitians and the native Australians. We have not harmed people because we wished to; on the contrary, more often than not we have wanted to help people and, in some very important respects, we have helped them. Americans have brought medicine and education, manufactures and modern techniques to many places in the world; but they have also brought themselves and the condescending attitudes of a people whose very success breeds disdain for other cultures. Bringing power without understanding, Americans as well as Europeans have had a devastating effect in less advanced areas of the world; without knowing they were doing it, they have shattered traditional societies, disrupted fragile economies and undermined peoples' self-confidence by the invidious example of their own power and efficiency. They have done this in many instances simply by being big and strong, by giving good advice, by intruding on people who have not wanted them but could not resist them.

The missionary instinct seems to run deep in human nature,

[7] Alan Moorehead, *The Fatal Impact* (New York: Harper & Row, 1966), pp. 61, 80–81.

and the bigger and stronger and richer we are, the more we feel suited to the missionary task, the more indeed we consider it our duty. Dr. Chisholm relates the story of an eminent cleric who had been proselyting the Eskimos and said: "You know, for years we couldn't do anything with those Eskimos at all; they didn't have any sin. We had to teach them sin for years before we could do anything with them."[8] I am reminded of the three Boy Scouts who reported to their scoutmaster that as their good deed for the day they had helped an old lady to cross the street.

"That's fine," said the scoutmaster, "but why did it take three of you?"

"Well," they explained, "she didn't want to go."

The good deed above all others that Americans feel qualified to perform is the teaching of democracy. Let us consider the results of some American good deeds in various parts of the world.

Over the years since President Monroe proclaimed his doctrine, Latin Americans have had the advantages of United States tutelage in fiscal responsibility, in collective security, and in the techniques of democracy. If they have fallen short in any of these fields, the thought presents itself that the fault may lie as much with the teacher as with the pupils.

When President Theodore Roosevelt announced his "corollary" to the Monroe Doctrine in 1905, he solemnly declared that he regarded the future interventions thus sanctioned as a "burden" and a "responsibility" and an obligation to "international equity." Not once, so far as I know, has the United States regarded itself as intervening in a Latin American country for selfish or unworthy motives—a view not necessarily shared, however,

[8] Chisholm, *Prescription of Survival*, pp. 55–56.

by the beneficiaries. Whatever reassurance the purity of our motives may give must be shaken a little by the thought that probably no country in human history has ever intervened in another except for motives it regarded as excellent.

For all our noble intentions, the countries which have had most of the tutelage in democracy by United States Marines have not been particularly democratic. These include Haiti, which is under a brutal and superstitious dictatorship; the Dominican Republic, which languished under the brutal Trujillo dictatorship for thirty years and whose second elected government since the overthrow of Trujillo is threatened, like the first, by the power of a military oligarchy; and of course Cuba, which, as no one needs to be reminded, has replaced its traditional right-wing dictatorships with a communist dictatorship.

Maybe, in the light of this extraordinary record of accomplishment, it is time for us to reconsider our teaching methods. Maybe we are not really cut out for the job of spreading the gospel of democracy. Maybe it would profit us to concentrate on our own democracy instead of trying to inflict our particular version of it on all those ungrateful Latin Americans who stubbornly oppose their North American benefactors instead of the "real" enemies whom we have so graciously chosen for them. And maybe—just maybe— if we left our neighbors to make their own judgments and their own mistakes, and confined our assistance to matters of economics and technology instead of philosophy, maybe then they would begin to find the democracy and the dignity that have largely eluded them, and we in turn might begin to find the love and gratitude that we seem to crave.

Korea is another example. We

went to war in 1950 to defend South Korea against the Russian-inspired aggression of North Korea. I think that American intervention was justified and necessary: we were defending a country that clearly wanted to be defended, whose army was willing to fight and fought well, and whose government, though dictatorial, was patriotic and commanded the support of the people. Throughout the war, however, the United States emphasized as one of its war aims the survival of the Republic of Korea as a "free society," something which it was not then and is not now. We lost 33,629 American lives in that war and have since spent $5.61 billion on direct military and economic aid and a great deal more on indirect aid to South Korea. The country, nonetheless, remained until recently in a condition of virtual economic stagnation and political instability. Only now is economic progress being made, but the truly surprising fact is that having fought a war for three years to defend the freedom of South Korea, most Americans quickly lost interest in the state of the ward for whom they had sacrificed so much. It is doubtful that more than a handful of Americans now know or care whether South Korea is a "free society."

We are now engaged in a war to "defend freedom" in South Vietnam. Unlike the Republic of Korea, South Vietnam has an army which fights without notable success and a weak, dictatorial government which does not command the loyalty of the South Vietnamese people. The official war aims of the United States government, as I understand them, are to defeat what is regarded as North Vietnamese aggression, to demonstrate the futility of what the communists call "wars of national liberation," and to create conditions under which the South Vietnam-

ese people will be able freely to determine their own future.

I have not the slightest doubt of the sincerity of the President and the Vice-President and the Secretaries of State and Defense in propounding these aims. What I do doubt, and doubt very much, is the ability of the United States to achieve these aims by the means being used. I do not question the power of our weapons and the efficiency of our logistics; I cannot say these things delight me as they seem to delight some of our officials, but they are certainly impressive. What I do question is the ability of the United States or any other Western nation to go into a small, alien, undeveloped Asian nation and create stability where there is chaos, the will to fight where there is defeatism, democracy where there is no tradition of it, and honest government where corruption is almost a way of life.

In the spring of 1966 demonstrators in Saigon burned American jeeps, tried to assault American soldiers, and marched through the streets shouting "Down with American imperialists," while a Buddhist leader made a speech equating the United States with the communists as a threat to South Vietnamese independence. Most Americans are understandably shocked and angered to encounter expressions of hostility from people who would long since have been under the rule of the Viet Cong but for the sacrifice of American lives and money. Why, we may ask, are they so shockingly ungrateful? Surely they must know that their very right to parade and protest and demonstrate depends on the Americans who are defending them.

The answer, I think, is that "fatal impact" of the rich and strong on the poor and weak. Dependent on it though the Vietnamese are, American strength

is a reproach to their weakness, American wealth a mockery of their poverty, American success a reminder of their failures. What they resent is the disruptive effect of our strong culture upon their fragile one, an effect which we can no more avoid having than a man can help being bigger than a child. What they fear, I think rightly, is that traditional Vietnamese society cannot survive the American economic and cultural impact.

The evidence of that "fatal impact" is seen in the daily life of Saigon. A *New York Times* correspondent reported—and his information matches that of other observers on the scene—that many Vietnamese find it necessary to put their wives or daughters to work as bar girls or to peddle them to American soldiers as mistresses; that it is not unusual to hear a report that a Vietnamese soldier has committed suicide out of shame because his wife has been working as a bar girl; that Vietnamese have trouble getting taxicabs because drivers will not stop for them, preferring to pick up American soldiers who will pay outrageous fares without complaint; that as a result of the American influx bar girls, prostitutes, pimps, bar owners, and taxi drivers have risen to the higher levels of the economic pyramid; that middle-class Vietnamese families have difficulty renting homes because Americans have driven the rents beyond their reach, and some Vietnamese families have actually been evicted from houses and apartments by landlords who prefer to rent to the affluent Americans; that Vietnamese civil servants, junior army officers, and enlisted men are unable to support their families because of the inflation generated by American spending and the purchasing power of the GIs. One Vietnamese explained to the *New York Times* reporter that "Any time legions of prosperous white men descend on a rudimentary Asian society, you are bound to have trouble." Another said: "We Vietnamese are somewhat xenophobic. We don't like foreigners, any kind of foreigners, so that you shouldn't be surprised that we don't like you."[9]

Sincere though it is, the American effort to build the foundations of freedom in South Vietnam is thus having an effect quite different from the one intended. "All this struggling and striving to make the world better is a great mistake," said George Bernard Shaw, "not because it isn't a good thing to improve the world if you know how to do it, but because striving and struggling is the worst way you could set about doing anything."[10]

One wonders how much the American commitment to Vietnamese freedom is also a commitment to American pride—the two seem to have become part of the same package. When we talk about the freedom of South Vietnam, we may be thinking about how disagreeable it would be to accept a solution short of victory; we may be thinking about how our pride would be injured if we settled for less than we set out to achieve; we may be thinking about our reputation as a great power, fearing that a compromise settlement would shame us before the world, marking us as a second-rate people with flagging courage and determination.

Such fears are as nonsensical as their opposite, the presumption of a universal mission. They are simply unworthy of the richest, most powerful, most productive, and best educated people in the world. One can understand an uncompromising attitude on the part of such countries as China or France: both have been struck low in this century and a

certain amount of arrogance may be helpful to them in recovering their pride. It is much less comprehensible on the part of the United States—a nation whose modern history has been an almost uninterrupted chronicle of success, a nation which by now should be so sure of its own power as to be capable of magnanimity, a nation which by now should be able to act on the proposition that, as George Kennan said, "there is more respect to be won in the opinion of the world by a resolute and courageous liquidation of unsound positions than in the most stubborn pursuit of extravagant or uncompromising objectives."[11]

The cause of our difficulties in Southeast Asia is not a deficiency of power but an excess of the wrong kind of power, which results in a feeling of impotence when it fails to achieve its desired ends. We are still acting like Boy Scouts dragging reluctant old ladies across streets they do not want to cross. We are trying to remake Vietnamese society, a task which certainly cannot be accomplished by force and which probably cannot be accomplished by any means available to outsiders. The objective may be desirable, but it is not feasible. As Shaw said: "Religion is a great force—the only real motive force in the world; but what you fellows don't understand is that you must get at a man through his own religion and not through yours."[12]

With the best intentions in the world the United States has involved itself deeply in the affairs of developing nations in Asia and Latin America, practicing what

has been called a kind of "welfare imperialism." Our honest purpose is the advancement of development and democracy, to which end it has been thought necessary to destroy ancient and unproductive modes of life. In this latter function we have been successful, perhaps more successful than we know. Bringing skills and knowledge, money and resources in amounts hitherto unknown in traditional societies, the Americans have overcome indigenous groups and interests and become the dominant force in a number of countries. Far from being bumbling, wasteful, and incompetent, as critics have charged, American government officials, technicians, and economists have been strikingly successful in breaking down the barriers to change in ancient but fragile cultures.

Here, however, our success ends. Traditional rulers, institutions, and ways of life have crumbled under the fatal impact of American wealth and power but they have not been replaced by new institutions and new ways of life, nor has their breakdown ushered in an era of democracy and development. It has rather ushered in an era of disorder and demoralization because in the course of destroying old ways of doing things, we have also destroyed the self-confidence and self-reliance without which no society can build indigenous institutions. Inspiring as we have such great awe of our efficiency and wealth, we have reduced some of the intended beneficiaries of our generosity to a condition of dependency and self-denigration. We have done this for the most part inadvertently: with every good intention we have intruded on fragile societies, and our intrusion, though successful in uprooting traditional ways of life, has been strikingly unsuccessful in implanting the democracy and advancing the development which are the honest

[9] Neil Sheehan, "Anti-Americanism Grows in Vietnam," *The New York Times,* April 24, 1966, p. 3.

[10] George Bernard Shaw, *Cashel Byron's Profession* (1886), Chapter 5.

[11] George F. Kennan, "Supplemental Foreign Assistance Fiscal Year 1966—Vietnam," *Hearings Before the Committee on Foreign Relations,* United States Senate, 89th Congress, 2nd Session on S. 2793, Part I (Washington: U.S. Government Printing Office, 1966), p. 335.

[12] George Bernard Shaw, *Getting Married* (1911).

aims of our "welfare imperialism."

AMERICAN EMPIRE OR AMERICAN EXAMPLE?

Despite its dangerous and unproductive consequences, the idea of being responsible for the whole world seems to be flattering to Americans and I am afraid that it is turning our heads, just as the sense of universal responsibility turned the heads of ancient Romans and nineteenth-century British.

In 1965 Henry Fairlie, a British political writer for *The Spectator* and *The Daily Telegraph*, wrote what he called "A Cheer for American Imperialism."[13] An empire, he said, "has no justification except its own existence." It must never contract; it "wastes treasure and life"; its commitments "are without rhyme or reason." Nonetheless, according to Fairlie, the "American empire" is uniquely benevolent, devoted as it is to individual liberty and the rule of law, and having performed such services as getting the author released from a Yugoslav jail simply by his threatening to involve the American Consul, a service which he describes as "sublime."

What romantic nonsense this is. And what dangerous nonsense in the age of nuclear weapons. The idea of an "American empire" might be dismissed as the arrant imagining of a British Gunga Din except that it surely strikes a responsive chord in at least a corner of the usually sensible and humane American mind. It calls to mind the slogans of the past about the shot being fired at Concord being heard 'round the world, about "manifest destiny" and "making the world safe for democracy," and the demand for "unconditional surrender" in World War II. It calls to mind President McKinley

[13] *The New York Times Magazine,* July 11, 1965.

taking counsel with the Supreme Being about his duty to the benighted Filipinos.

The "Blessings-of-Civilization Trust," as Mark Twain called it, may have been a "Daisy" in its day, uplifting for the soul and good for business besides, but its day is past. It is past because the great majority of the human race is demanding dignity and independence, not the honor of a supine role in an American empire. It is past because whatever claim America may make for the universal domain of her ideas and values is balanced by the communist counterclaim, armed like our own with nuclear weapons. And, most of all, it is past because it never should have begun, because we are not God's chosen saviour of mankind but only one of mankind's more successful and fortunate branches, endowed by our Creator with about the same capacity for good and evil, no more or less, than the rest of humanity.

An excessive preoccupation with foreign relations over a long period of time is more than a manifestation of arrogance; it is a drain on the power that gave rise to it, because it diverts a nation from the sources of its strength, which are in its domestic life. A nation immersed in foreign affairs is expending its capital, human as well as material; sooner or later that capital must be renewed by some diversion of creative energies from foreign to domestic pursuits. I would doubt that any nation has achieved a durable greatness by conducting a "strong" foreign policy, but many have been ruined by expending their energies in foreign adventures while allowing their domestic bases to deteriorate. The United States emerged as a world power in the twentieth century, not because of what it had done in foreign relations but because it had spent the nineteenth century developing the North American conti-

nent; by contrast, the Austrian and Turkish empires collapsed in the twentieth century in large part because they had so long neglected their internal development and organization.

If America has a service to perform in the world—and I believe she has—it is in large part the service of her own example. In our excessive involvement in the affairs of other countries we are not only living off our assets and denying our own people the proper enjoyment of their resources, we are also denying the world the example of a free society enjoying its freedom to the fullest. This is regrettable indeed for a nation that aspires to teach democracy to other nations, because, as Edmund Burke said, "Example is the school of mankind, and they will learn at no other."[14]

The missionary instinct in foreign affairs may, in a curious way, reflect a deficiency rather than an excess of national self-confidence. In America's case the evidence of a lack of self-confidence is our apparent need for constant proof and reassurance, our nagging desire for popularity, our bitterness and confusion when foreigners fail to appreciate our generosity and good intentions. Lacking an appreciation of the dimensions of our own power, we fail to understand our enormous and disruptive impact on the world; we fail to understand that no matter how good our intentions—and they are, in most cases, decent enough—other nations are alarmed by the very existence of such great power, which, whatever its benevolence, cannot help but remind them of their own helplessness before it.

Those who lack self-assurance are also likely to lack magnanimity, because the one is the condition of the other. Only a nation at peace with itself, with its

[14] Edmund Burke, "On a Regicide Peace" (1796).

transgressions as well as its achievements, is capable of a generous understanding of others. Only when we Americans can acknowledge our own past aggressive behavior—in such instances, for example, as the Indian wars and the wars against Mexico and Spain—will we acquire some perspective on the aggressive behavior of others; only when we can understand the human implications of the chasm between American affluence and the poverty of most of the rest of mankind will we be able to understand why the American "way of life" which is so dear to us has few lessons and limited appeal to the poverty-stricken majority of the human race.

It is a curiosity of human nature that lack of self-assurance seems to breed an exaggerated sense of power and mission. When a nation is very powerful but lacking in self-confidence, it is likely to behave in a manner dangerous to itself and to others. Feeling the need to prove what is obvious to everyone else, it begins to confuse great power with unlimited power and great responsibility with total responsibility: it can admit of no error; it must win every argument, no matter how trivial. For lack of an appreciation of how truly powerful it is, the nation begins to lose wisdom and perspective and, with them, the strength and understanding it takes to be magnanimous to smaller and weaker nations.

Gradually but unmistakably America is showing signs of that arrogance of power which has afflicted, weakened, and in some cases destroyed great nations in the past. In so doing we are not living up to our capacity and promise as a civilized example for the world. The measure of our falling short is the measure of the patriot's duty of dissent.

SEYMOUR HERSH
The Day at My Lai 4

All wars are brutal and atrocious. Yet the events at My Lai 4 on March 16, 1968, have a special quality that not only conveys a particular horror, but also seems to capture much that is peculiar to the Vietnamese war. "We'd be out on a mission," Hersh quotes one participant, "and all of a sudden a dozen kids would come selling Cokes and sandwiches. I mean we were *out on a mission.* [Captain Ernest L.] Medina would come and chase them away, kick them in the ass, throw them out of there." Where was the war front? Who was the enemy? What was anyone doing where he was? What kind of war was this? Joseph Heller in the widely read novel *Catch-22* recognized absurdities of World War II many years after he had been a part of it. In Vietnam the very foot soldiers saw in bitterness and frustration the absurdity of what they had to do—and learned that absurdity need not equate with humor. On the contrary, meaninglessness leads just as easily to the ultimate in horror and brutality.

Telford Taylor, the United States prosecutor at the Nuremberg war crimes trials after World War II and a leading authority on the laws of war, has raised questions of whether it is possible to limit guilt for events like My Lai 4. The extent to which such acts come out of the sickness or confusion or misjudgment or moral turpitude of particular men, and the extent to which they are the direct outcome of official policy, both political and military, is the question that lies as a shadow across the still unresolved investigations and trials growing out of this grisly event.

Nobody saw it all. Some, like Roy Wood, didn't even know the extent of the massacre until the next day. Others, like Charles Sledge, who served that day as Calley's radioman, saw more than they want to remember.

But they all remember the fear that morning as they climbed onto helicopters at LZ Dotti for the assault on Pinkville. They all remember the sure knowledge that they would meet face-to-face for the first time with the enemy.

Calley and his platoon were the first to board the large black Army assault helicopters. They were heavily armed, each man carrying twice the normal load of rifle and machine-gun ammunition. Leading the way was Calley, who had slung an extra belt of M16 rifle bullets over his shoulder. There were nine helicopters in the first lift-off, enough for the first platoon—about twenty-five men—and Captain Medina and his small headquarters unit of three radiomen, some liaison officers and a medic. It was sunny and already hot when the first helicopter started its noisy flight to My Lai 4. The time was 7:22 A.M.; it was logged by a tape recorder at brigade headquarters. A brief artillery barrage had already begun; the My Lai 4 area was being "prepped" in anticipation of that day's search-and-destroy mission. A few heavily armed helicopters were firing thousands of small-caliber bullets into the area by the time Calley and his men landed in a soggy rice paddy 150 meters west of the hamlet. It was harvest season; the green fields were thick with growth.

The first platoon's mission was to secure the landing zone and make sure no enemy troops were left to fire at the second wave of helicopters—by then already airborne from LZ Dotti. As the flight of helicopters hovered over the landing area, the door gunners began spraying protective fire to keep the enemy—if he were there—busy. One of the helicopter's pilots had reported that the LZ was "hot," that is, Viet Cong were waiting below. The first platoon came out firing. But after a moment some men noticed that there was no return fire. "I didn't hear any bullets going past me," recalled Charles Hall, a machine gunner that day. "If you want to consider an area hot, you got to be fired on."

The platoon quickly formed a perimeter and secured the landing zone. Sergeant Cowen spotted an old man. Sledge was a few yards to Cowen's right: "We came to a well and there was a VC. We thought it was a VC. He was standing and waving his arms. Cowen fell back and said, 'Shoot the so-and-so.' I fired once, and then my [rifle] magazine fell out." Paul Meadlo noted that "the gook was standing up shaking and waving his arms and

then he was shot." Allen Boyce saw it a little differently: "Some guy was in a rice field, doing something to a rice plant. He looked up and he got it. That was the most confused operation I ever went on. Just everyone was screwed up."

By this time those Viet Cong who were in the area had slipped away. Some local supporters of the guerrillas also left, but they did not go too far. They watched as Charlie Company went through My Lai 4.

After about twenty minutes the second flight of helicopters landed, and the fifty men of the second and third platoons jumped off. Gary Garfolo heard the helicopter blades make sharp crackling sounds as they changed pitch for the landing. "It was a 'pop, pop, pop' sound like a rifle. Lots of us never even heard a hot LZ before. We knew we were going into a hot place. This got their adrenalin going." The men were quickly assembled. Calley's first platoon and Lieutenant Stephen Brooks' second platoon would lead the sweep into the hamlet—Calley to the south, and Brooks to the north. The third platoon, headed by Lieutenant Jeffrey La Crosse, would be held in reserve and move in on the heels of the other men. Captain Medina and his headquarters unit would move with the third platoon and then set up a command post (CP) inside to monitor the operation and stay in touch with other units. Charlie Company was not alone in its assault; the other two companies of Task Force Barker set up blocking positions to the north and south. They were there to prevent the expected Viet Cong troops from fleeing.

The My Lai 4 assault was the biggest thing going in the Americal Division that day. To get enough airlift, Task Force Barker had to borrow helicopters from other units throughout the divi-

sion. The air lanes above the action were carefully allotted to high-ranking officers for observation. Barker monitored the battle from the 1000-foot level. Major General Samuel Koster, commanding general of the division, was allotted the air space at 2000 feet. His helicopter was permanently stationed outside his door at division headquarters twenty-one miles to the north, waiting to fly him to the scene of any action within minutes. Oran K. Henderson, commander of the 11th Brigade, was given the top spot—at 2500 feet. All of the helicopters were to circle counterclockwise over the battle area. Flying low, beneath the 1000-foot level, would be the gunships, heavily armed helicopters whose mission was to shoot down any Viet Cong soldiers attempting to escape.

Brigade headquarters, sure that there would be a major battle, sent along two men from the Army's 31st Public Information Detachment to record the event for history. Jay Roberts of Arlington, Virginia, a reporter, and photographer Ronald L. Haeberle of Cleveland, Ohio, arrived with the second wave of helicopters and immediately attached themselves to the third platoon, which was bringing up the rear.

The hamlet itself had a population of about 700 people, living either in flimsy thatch-covered huts—"hootches," as the GIs called them—or in solidly made red-brick homes, many with small porches in front. There was an east-west footpath just south of the main cluster of homes; a few yards further south was a loose surface road that marked a hamlet boundary. A deep drainage ditch and then a rice paddy marked the eastern boundary. To the south of My Lai 4 was a large center, or plaza area—clearly the main spot for mass meetings. The foliage was dense: there were high bamboo trees, hedges and plant life everywhere. Medina couldn't see thirty feet into the hamlet from the landing zone.

The first and second platoons lined up carefully to begin the hundred-meter advance into My Lai 4. Walking in line is an important military concept; if one group of men gets too far in front, it could be hit by bullets from behind—those fired by colleagues. Yet even this went wrong. Ron Grzesik was in charge of a small first-platoon fire team of riflemen and a machine gunner; he took his job seriously. His unit was supposed to be on the right flank, protecting Calley and his men. But Grzesik's group ended up on Calley's left.

As Brooks' second platoon cautiously approached the hamlet, a few Vietnamese began running across a field several hundred meters on the left. They may have been Viet Cong, or they may have been civilians fleeing the artillery shelling or the bombardment from the helicopter gunships. Vernado Simpson, Jr., of Jackson, Mississippi, saw a man he identified as a Viet Cong soldier running with what seemed to be a weapon. A woman and a small child were running with him. Simpson fired . . . again and again. He killed the woman and the baby. The man got away. Reporter Roberts saw a squad of GIs jump off a helicopter and begin firing at a group of people running on a nearby road. One was a woman with her children. Then he saw them "shoot two guys who popped up from a rice field. They looked like military-age men . . . when certain guys pop up from rice fields, you shoot them." This was the young reporter's most dan-

Lt. William L. Calley, Jr., while he waited for military jury to decide his fate, March 31, 1971.   *(UPI)*

gerous assignment. He had never been in combat before. "You're scared to death out there. We just wanted to go home."

The first two platoons of Charlie Company, still unfired upon, entered the hamlet. Behind them, still in the rice paddy, were the third platoon and Captain Medina's command post. Calley and some of his men walked into the plaza area in the southern part of the hamlet. None of the people was running away; they knew that U. S. soldiers would assume that anyone running was a Viet Cong and would shoot to kill. There was no immediate sense of panic. The time was about 8 A.M. Grzesik and his fire team were a few meters north of Calley; they couldn't see each other because of the dense vegetation. Grzesik and his men began their usual job of pulling people from their homes, interrogating them, and searching for Viet Cong. The villagers were gathered up, and Grzesik sent Meadlo, who was in his unit, to take them to Calley for further questioning. Grzesik didn't see Meadlo again for more than an hour.

Some of Calley's men thought it was breakfast time as they walked in; a few families were gathered in front of their homes cooking rice over a small fire. Without a direct order, the first platoon also began rounding up the villagers. There still was no sniper fire, no sign of a large enemy unit. Sledge remembered thinking that "if there were VC around, they had plenty of time to leave before we came in. We didn't tiptoe in there."

The killings began without warning. Harry Stanley told the C.I.D. that one young member of Calley's platoon took a civilian into custody and then "pushed the man up to where we were standing and then stabbed the man in the back with his bayonet . . . The man fell to the ground and was gasping for breath." The GI then "killed

him with another bayonet thrust or by shooting him with a rifle . . . There was so many people killed that day it is hard for me to recall exactly how some of the people died." The youth next "turned to where some soldiers were holding another forty- or fifty-year-old man in custody." He "picked this man up and threw him down a well. Then [he] pulled the pin from an M26 grenade and threw it in after the man." Moments later Stanley saw "some old women and some little children—fifteen or twenty of them—in a group around a temple where some incense was burning. They were kneeling and crying and praying, and various soldiers . . . walked by and executed these women and children by shooting them in the head with their rifles. The soldiers killed all fifteen or twenty of them . . ."

There were few physical protests from the people; about eighty of them were taken quietly from their homes and herded together in the plaza area. A few hollered out, "No VC. No VC." But that was hardly unexpected. Calley left Meadlo, Boyce and a few others with the responsibility of guarding the group. "You know what I want you to do with them," he told Meadlo. Ten minutes later—about 8:15 A.M.—he returned and asked, "Haven't you got rid of them yet? I want them dead." Radioman Sledge, who was trailing Calley, heard the officer tell Meadlo to "waste them." Meadlo followed orders: "We stood about ten to fifteen feet away from them and then he [Calley] started shooting them. Then he told me to start shooting them. I started to shoot them. So we went ahead and killed them. I used more than a whole clip—used four or five clips." There are seventeen M16 bullets in each clip. Boyce slipped away, to the northern side of the hamlet, glad he hadn't been asked

to shoot. Women were huddled against their children, vainly trying to save them. Some continued to chant, "No VC." Others simply said, "No. No. No."

Do Chuc is a gnarled forty-eight-year-old Vietnamese peasant whose two daughters and an aunt were killed by the GIs in My Lai 4 that day. He and his family were eating breakfast when the GIs entered the hamlet and ordered them out of their homes. Together with other villagers, they were marched a few hundred meters into the plaza, where they were told to squat. "Still we had no reason to be afraid," Chuc recalled. "Everyone was calm." He watched as the GIs set up a machine gun. The calm ended. The people began crying and begging. One monk showed his identification papers to a soldier, but the American simply said, "Sorry." Then the shooting started. Chuc was wounded in the leg, but he was covered by dead bodies and thus spared. After waiting an hour, he fled the hamlet.

Nguyen Bat, a Viet Cong hamlet chief who later defected, said that many of the villagers who were eating breakfast outdoors when the GIs marched in greeted them without fear. They were gathered together and shot. Other villagers who were breakfasting indoors were killed inside their homes.

The few Viet Cong who had stayed near the hamlet were safely hidden. Nguyen Ngo, a former deputy commander of a Viet Cong guerrilla platoon operating in the My Lai area, ran to his hiding place 300 meters away when the GIs came in shooting, but he could see that "they shot everything in sight." His mother and sister hid in ditches and survived because bodies fell on top of them. Pham Lai, a former hamlet security guard, climbed into a bunker with a bamboo top and heard but did not see the shootings. His wife, hidden under a body, survived the massacre.

By this time, there was shooting everywhere. Dennis I. Conti, a GI from Providence, Rhode Island, later explained to C.I.D. investigators what he thought had happened: "We were all psyched up, and as a result, when we got there the shooting started, almost as a chain reaction. The majority of us had expected to meet VC combat troops, but this did not turn out to be so. First we saw a few men running . . . and the next thing I knew we were shooting at everything. Everybody was just firing. After they got in the village, I guess you could say that the men were out of control."

Brooks and his men in the second platoon to the north had begun to systematically ransack the hamlet and slaughter the people, kill the livestock and destroy the crops. Men poured rifle and machine-gun fire into huts without knowing—or seemingly caring—who was inside.

Roy Wood, one of Calley's men who was working next to Brooks' platoon, stormed into a hut, saw an elderly man hiding inside along with his wife and two young daughters: "I hit him with my rifle and pushed him out." A GI from Brooks' platoon, standing by with an M79 grenade launcher, asked to borrow his gun. Wood refused, and the soldier asked another platoon mate. He got the weapon, said, "Don't let none of them live," and shot the Vietnamese in the head. "These mothers are crazy," Wood remembered thinking. "Stand right in front of us and blow a man's brain out." Later he vomited when he saw more of the dead residents of My Lai 4.

The second platoon went into My Lai 4 with guns blazing. Gary Crossley said that some GIs, after seeing nothing but women and children in the hamlet, hesitated: "We phoned Medina and told him what the circumstances were, and he said just keep going. It wasn't anything we wanted to do. You can only kill so many women and children. The fact was that you can't go through and wipe out all of South Vietnam."

Once the first two platoons had disappeared into the hamlet, Medina ordered the third platoon to start moving. He and his men followed. Gary Garfolo was caught up in the confusion: "I could hear heavy shooting all the time. Medina was running back and forth everywhere. This wasn't no organized deal." So Garfolo did what most GIs did when they could get away with it. "I took off on my own." He ran south; others joined him. Terrified villagers, many carrying personal belongings in wicker baskets, were running everywhere to avoid the carnage. In most cases it didn't help. The helicopter gunships circling above cut them down, or else an unfortunate group ran into the third platoon. Charles West sighted and shot six Vietnamese, some with baskets, on the edge of My Lai 4: "These people were running into us, away from us, running every which way. It's hard to distinguish a mama-san from a papa-san when everybody has on black pajamas."

West and his men may have thought that these Vietnamese were Viet Cong. Later they knew better. West's first impression upon reaching My Lai 4: "There were no people in the first part . . . I seen bodies everywhere. I knew that everyone was being killed." His group quickly joined in.

Medina—as any combat officer would do during his unit's first major engagement—decided to move his CP from the rice paddy. John Paul, one of Medina's radiomen, figured that the time was about 8:15 A.M. West remembered that "Medina was right behind us" as his platoon moved inside the hamlet. There are serious contradictions about what happened next. Medina later said that he did not enter the hamlet proper until well after 10 A.M. and did not see anyone kill a civilian. John Paul didn't think that Medina ever entered the hamlet. But Herbert Carter told the C.I.D. that Medina did some of the shooting of civilians as he moved into My Lai 4.

Carter testified that soon after the third platoon moved in, a woman was sighted. Somebody knocked her down, and then, Carter said, "Medina shot her with his M16 rifle. I was fifty or sixty feet away and saw this. There was no reason to shoot this girl." The men continued on, making sure no one was escaping. "We came to where the soldiers had collected fifteen or more Vietnamese men, women and children in a group. Medina said, 'Kill every one. Leave no one standing.'" A machine gunner began firing into the group. Moments later one of Medina's radio operators slowly "passed among them and finished them off." Medina did not personally shoot any of them, according to Carter, but moments later the captain "stopped a seventeen- or eighteen-year-old man with a water buffalo. Medina told the boy to make a run for it," Carter told the C.I.D. "He tried to get him to run but the boy wouldn't run, so Medina shot him with his M16 rifle and killed him . . . I was seventy-five or eighty meters away at the time and I saw it plainly." At this point in Carter's interrogation, the investigator warned him that he was making very serious charges against his commanding officer. "What I'm telling is the truth," Carter replied, "and I'll face Medina in court and swear to it."

If Carter was correct, Medina walked first into the north side of

My Lai 4, then moved south with the CP to the hamlet plaza and arrived there at about the time Paul Meadlo and Lieutenant Calley were executing the first group of villagers. Meadlo still wonders why Medina didn't stop the shooting, "if it was wrong." Medina and Calley "passed each other quite a few times that morning, but didn't say anything. I don't know if the CO gave the order to kill or not, but he was right there when it happened . . . Medina just kept marching around."

Roberts and Haeberle also moved in just behind the third platoon. Haeberle watched a group of ten to fifteen GIs methodically pump bullets into a cow until it keeled over. A woman then poked her head out from behind some brush; she may have been hiding in a bunker. The GIs turned their fire from the cow to the woman. "They just kept shooting at her. You could see the bones flying in the air chip by chip." No one had attempted to question her; GIs inside the hamlet also were asking no questions. Before moving on, the photographer took a picture of the dead woman. Haeberle took many more pictures that day; he saw about thirty GIs kill at least a hundred Vietnamese civilians.

When the two correspondents entered My Lai 4, they saw dead animals, dead people, burning huts and houses. A few GIs were going through victims' clothing, looking for piasters. Another GI was chasing a duck with a knife; others stood around watching a GI slaughter a cow with a bayonet.

Haeberle noticed a man and two small children walking toward a group of GIs: "They just kept walking toward us . . . you could hear the little girl saying, 'No, no . . .' All of a sudden the GIs opened up and cut them down." Later he watched a machine gunner suddenly open fire on a group of civilians—women, children and babies—who had been collected in a big circle: "They were trying to run. I don't know how many got out." He saw a GI with an M16 rifle fire at two young boys walking along a road. The older of the two—about seven or eight years old—fell over the first to protect him. The GI kept on firing until both were dead.

As Haeberle and Roberts walked further into the hamlet, Medina came up to them. Eighty-five Viet Cong had been killed in action thus far, the captain told them, and twenty suspects had been captured. Roberts carefully jotted down the captain's statistics in his notepad.

The company's other Vietnamese interpreter, Sergeant Duong Minh, saw Medina for the first time about then. Minh had arrived on a later helicopter assault, along with Lieutenant Dennis H. Johnson, Charlie Company's intelligence officer. When he saw the bodies of civilians, he asked Medina what happened. Medina, obviously angry at Minh for asking the question, stalked away.

Now it was nearly nine o'clock and all of Charlie Company was in My Lai 4. Most families were being shot inside their homes, or just outside the doorways. Those who had tried to flee were crammed by GIs into the many bunkers built throughout the hamlet for protection—once the bunkers became filled, hand grenades were lobbed in. Everything became a target. Gary Garfolo borrowed someone's M79 grenade launcher and fired it point-blank at a water buffalo: "I hit that sucker right in the head; went down like a shot. You don't get to shoot water buffalo with an M79 every day." Others fired the weapon into the bunkers full of people.

Jay Roberts insisted that he saw Medina in My Lai 4 most of the morning: "He was directing the operations in the village. He was in the village the whole time I was—from nine o'clock to eleven o'clock."

Carter recalled that some GIs were shouting and yelling during the massacre: "The boys enjoyed it. When someone laughs and jokes about what they're doing, they have to be enjoying it." A GI said, "Hey, I got me another one." Another said, "Chalk up one for me." Even Captain Medina was having a good time, Carter thought: "You can tell when someone enjoys their work." Few members of Charlie Company protested that day. For the most part, those who didn't like what was going on kept their thoughts to themselves.

Herbert Carter also remembered seeing Medina inside the hamlet well after the third platoon began its advance: "I saw all those dead people laying there. Medina came right behind me." At one point in the morning one of the members of Medina's CP joined in the shooting. "A woman came out of a hut with a baby in her arms and she was crying," Carter told the C.I.D. "She was crying because her little boy had been in front of their hut and . . . someone had killed the child by shooting it." When the mother came into view, one of Medina's men "shot her with an M16 and she fell. When she fell, she dropped the baby." The GI next "opened up on the baby with his M16." The infant was also killed. Carter also saw an officer grab a woman by the hair and shoot her with a .45-caliber pistol: "He held her by the hair for a minute and then let go and she fell to the ground. Some enlisted man standing there said, 'Well, she'll be in the big rice paddy in the sky.' "

In the midst of the carnage, Michael Bernhardt got his first good look at My Lai 4. Bernhardt had been delayed when Medina asked him to check out a suspicious wood box at the landing zone. After discovering that it wasn't a booby trap, Bernhardt hurried to catch up with his mates in the third platoon. He went into the hamlet, where he saw Charlie Company "doing strange things. One: they were setting fire to the hootches and huts and waiting for people to come out and then shooting them. Two: they were going into the hootches and shooting them up. Three: they were gathering people in groups and shooting them. The whole thing was so deliberate. It was point-blank murder and I was standing there watching it. It's kind of made me wonder if I could trust people any more."

Grzesik and his men, meanwhile, had been slowly working their way through the hamlet. The young GI was having problems controlling his men; he was anxious to move on to the rice paddy in the east. About three quarters of the way through, he suddenly saw Meadlo again. The time was now after nine. Meadlo was crouched, head in his hands sobbing like a bewildered child. "I sat down and asked him what happened." Grzesik felt responsible; after all, he was supposed to be a team leader. Meadlo told him Calley had made him shoot people. "I tried to calm him down," Grzesik said, but the fire-team leader couldn't stay long. His men still hadn't completed their sweep of My Lai 4.

Those Vietnamese who were not killed on the spot were being shepherded by the first platoon to a large drainage ditch at the eastern end of the hamlet. After Grzesik left, Meadlo and a few others gathered seven or eight villagers in one hut and were preparing to toss in a hand grenade when an order came to take them to the ditch. There he found Calley, along with a dozen other first platoon members, and perhaps seventy-five Vietnamese,

mostly women, old men and children.

Not far away, invisible in the brush and trees, the second and third platoons were continuing their search-and-destroy operations in the northern half of My Lai 4. Ron Grzesik and his fire team had completed a swing through the hamlet and were getting ready to turn around and walk back to see what was going on. And just south of the plaza, Michael Bernhardt had attached himself to Medina and his command post. Shots were still being fired, the helicopters were still whirring overhead, and the enemy was still nowhere in sight.

One of the helicopters was piloted by Chief Warrant Officer Hugh C. Thompson of Decatur, Georgia. For him, the mission had begun routinely enough. He and his two-man crew, in a small observation helicopter from the 123rd Aviation Battalion, had arrived at the area around 9 A.M. and immediately reported what appeared to be a Viet Cong soldier armed with a weapon and heading south. Although his mission was simply reconnaissance, Thompson directed his men to fire at and attempt to kill the Viet Cong as he wheeled the helicopter after him. They missed. Thompson flew back to My Lai 4, and it was then, as he told the Army Inspector General's office in June 1969, that he began seeing wounded and dead Vietnamese civilians all over the hamlet, with no sign of an enemy force.

The pilot thought that the best thing he could do would be to mark the location of wounded civilians with smoke so that the GIs on the ground could move over and begin treating some of them. "The first one that I marked was a girl that was wounded," Thompson testified, "and they came over and walked up to her, put their weapon on automatic and let her have it." The man who did the shooting

was a captain, Thompson said. Later he identified the officer as Ernest Medina.

Flying with Thompson that day was Lawrence M. Colburn, of Mount Vernon, Washington, who remembered that the girl was about twenty years old and was lying on the edge of a dyke outside the hamlet with part of her body in a rice paddy. "She had been wounded in the stomach, I think, or the chest," Colburn told the Inspector General (IG). "This captain was coming down the dyke and he had men behind him. They were sweeping through and we were hovering a matter of feet away from them. I could see this clearly, and he emptied a clip into her."

Medina and his men immediately began moving south toward the Viet Cong sighted by Thompson. En route they saw the young girl in the rice paddy who had been marked by the smoke. Bernhardt had a ground view of what happened next: "He [Medina] was just going alone . . . he shot the woman. She seemed to be busy picking rice, but rice was out of season. What she really was doing was trying to pretend that she was picking rice. She was a hundred meters away with a basket . . . if she had a hand grenade, she would have to have a better arm than me to get us . . . Medina lifted the rifle to his shoulder, looked down the barrel and pulled the trigger. I saw the woman drop. He just took a potshot . . . he wasn't a bad shot. Then he walked up. He got up real close, about three or six feet, and shot at her a couple times and finished her off. She was a real clean corpse . . . she wasn't all over the place, and I could see her clothing move when the bullets hit . . . I could see her twitch, but I couldn't see any holes . . . he didn't shoot her in the head." A second later, Bernhardt remembered, the captain "gave me a look, a dumb shit-eating grin."

By now it was past 9:30 A.M. and the men of Charlie Company had been at work for more than two hours. A few of them flung off their helmets, stripped off their heavy gear, flopped down and took a smoke break.

II

Hugh Thompson's nightmare had only begun with the shooting of the girl. He flew north back over the hamlet and saw a small boy bleeding along a trench. Again he marked the spot so that the GIs below could provide some medical aid. Instead, he saw a lieutenant casually walk up and empty a clip into the child. He saw yet another wounded young-ster; again he marked it, and this time it was a sergeant who came up and fired his M16 at the child.

Larry Colburn, who was just eighteen years old at the time, noticed that "the infantrymen were killing everything in the vil-lage. The people didn't really know what was happening. Some of them began walking out of there and the GIs just started going up to them and shooting them all in the back of the head." He added, "We saw this one woman hiding there. She was alive and squatting; she looked up when we flew over. We dropped a smoke marker. When we came back she was in the same position—only she was dead. The back of her head was blown off. It had to be point-blank."

Thompson was furious. He tried unsuccessfully to radio the troops on the ground to find out what was going on. He then re-ported the wild firings and un-necessary shootings to brigade headquarters. All the command helicopters flying overhead had multi-channel radios and could monitor most conversations. Lieu-tenant Colonel Barker apparently intercepted the message and called down to Medina at the CP just

south of the plaza. John Kinch of the mortar platoon heard Medina answer that he "had a body count of 310." The captain added, "I don't know what they're doing. The first platoon's in the lead. I am trying to stop it." A moment later, Kinch said, Medina called Calley and ordered, "That's enough for today."

Harry Stanley was standing a few feet away from Calley near some huts at the drainage ditch when the call came from Medina. He had a different recollection: "Medina called Calley and said, 'What the fuck is going on?' Cal-ley said he got some VC, or some people that needed to be checked out." At this point Medina cau-tioned Calley to tell his men to save their ammunition because the operation still had a few more days to run.

It is not clear how soon or to whom Medina's order was given, but Stanley told the C.I.D. what Calley did next: "There was an old lady in a bed and I believe there was a priest in white pray-ing over her . . . Calley told me to ask about the VC and NVA and where the weapons were." The priest denied being a VC or NVA." Charles Sledge watched with horror as Calley pulled the old man outside: "He said a few more words to the monk. It looked like the monk was pleading for his life. Lieutenant Calley then took his rifle and pushed the monk into a rice paddy and shot him point-blank."

Calley then turned his atten-tion back to the crowd of Viet-namese and issued an order: "Push all those people in the ditch." Three or four GIs com-plied. Calley struck a woman with a rifle as he pushed her down. Stanley remembered that some of the civilians "kept try-ing to get out. Some made it to the top . . ." Calley began the shooting and ordered Meadlo to join in. Meadlo told about it later: "So we pushed our seven to eight people in with the big

bunch of them. And so I began shooting them all. So did Mitch-ell, Calley . . . I guess I shot maybe twenty-five or twenty peo-ple in the ditch . . . men, women and children. And babies." Some of the GIs switched from auto-matic fire to single-shot to con-serve ammunition. Herbert Carter watched the mothers "grabbing their kids and the kids grabbing their mothers. I didn't know what to do."

Calley then turned again to Meadlo and said, "Meadlo, we've got another job to do." Meadlo didn't want any more jobs. He began to argue with Calley. Sledge watched Meadlo once more start to sob. Calley turned next to Robert Maples and said, "Maples, load your machine gun and shoot these people." Maples replied, as he told the C.I.D., "I'm not going to do that." He remembered that "the people fir-ing into the ditch kept reloading magazines into their rifles and kept firing into the ditch and then killed or at least shot every-one in the ditch." William C. Lloyd of Tampa, Florida, told the C.I.D. that some grenades were also thrown into the ditch. Den-nis Conti noticed that "a lot of women had thrown themselves on top of the children to protect them, and the children were alive at first. Then the children who were old enough to walk got up and Calley began to shoot the children."

One further incident stood out in many GIs' minds: seconds after the shooting stopped, a bloodied but unhurt two-year-old boy miraculously crawled out of the ditch, crying. He began run-ning toward the hamlet. Some-one hollered, "There's a kid." There was a long pause. Then Calley ran back, grabbed the child, threw him back in the ditch and shot him.

Moments later Thompson, still in his helicopter, flew by. He told the IG what happened next: "I kept flying around and across a ditch . . . and it . . . had a bunch of bodies in it and I don't know how they got in the ditch. But I saw some of them were still alive." Captain Brian W. Livingston was piloting a large helicopter gunship a few hundred feet above. He had been monitoring Thompson's agonized complaints and went down to take a look for himself. He told a military hearing: "There were bodies lying in the trenches . . . I remember that we remarked at the time about the old Biblical story of Jesus turning water into wine. The trench had a grey color to it, with the red blood of the individuals lying in it."

By now Thompson was almost frantic. He landed his small helicopter near the ditch, and asked a soldier there if he could help the people out: "He said the only way he could help them was to help them out of their misery." Thompson took off again and noticed a group of mostly women and children huddled together in a bunker near the drainage ditch. He landed a second time. "I don't know," he explained, "maybe it was just my belief, but I hadn't been shot at the whole time I had been there and the gunships following hadn't . . ." He then saw Calley and the first platoon, the same group that had shot and wounded civilians he had earlier marked with smoke. "I asked him if he could get the women and kids out of there before they tore it [the bunker] up, and he said the only way he could get them out was to use hand grenades. 'You just hold your men right here,'" the angry Thompson told the equally angry Calley, "'and I will get the women and kids out.'"

Before climbing out of his aircraft, Thompson ordered Colburn and his crew chief to stay alert. "He' told us that if any of the Americans opened up on the Vietnamese, we should open up on the Americans," Colburn said. Thompson walked back to the ship and called in two helicopter gunships to rescue the civilians. While waiting for them to land, Colburn said, "he stood between our troops and the bunker. He was shielding the people with his body. He just wanted to get those people out of there." Colburn wasn't sure whether he would have followed orders if the GIs had opened fire at the bunker: "I wasn't pointing my guns right at them, but more or less toward the ground. But I was looking their way." He remembered that most of the soldiers were gathered alongside a nearby dyke "just watching. Some were lying down; some of them were sitting up, and some were standing." The helicopters landed, with Thompson still standing between the GIs and the Vietnamese, and quickly rescued nine persons—two old men, two women and five children. One of the children later died en route to the hospital. Calley did nothing to stop Thompson, but later stormed up to Sledge, his radioman, and complained that the pilot "doesn't like the way I'm running the show, but I'm the boss."

Gregory Olsen, who had watched the encounter from his machine-gun position a few dozen meters away, said that "the next thing I knew Mitchell was just shooting into the ditch." At this point Grzesik and his fire team came strolling into the area; they had gone completely through the hamlet, had a break, and were now returning. It was about ten o'clock. Grzesik saw bodies all over the northeastern quarter of My Lai 4. He glanced at the ditch. Suddenly Mitchell yelled, "Grzesik, come here." He walked over. Calley then ordered him to the ditch and "finish off the people." Grzesik had seen the helicopter carrying some wounded Vietnamese take off from the area a moment earlier; much later he concluded that Calley—furious with Thompson's intervention—wanted to make sure there were no more survivors in the ditch. Calley told Grzesik to gather his team to do the job. "I really believe he expected me to do it," Grzesik said later, with some amazement. Calley asked him again, and Grzesik again refused. The lieutenant then angrily ordered him to take his team and help burn the hootches. Grzesik headed for the hamlet plaza.

Thompson continued to fly over the ditch and noticed that some of the children's bodies had no heads. He landed a third time after his crew chief told him that he had seen some movement in the mass of bodies and blood below. The crew chief and Colburn began walking toward the ditch. "Nobody said anything," Colburn said. "We just got out." They found a young child still alive. No GIs were in the immediate area, but Colburn was carrying a rifle. The crew chief climbed into the ditch. "He was knee-deep in people and blood," Colburn recalled. The child was quiet, buried under many bodies. "He was still holding onto his mother. But she was dead." The boy, clinging desperately, was pried loose. He still did not cry. Thompson later told the IG, "I don't think this child was even wounded at all, just down there among all the other bodies, and he was terrified." Thompson and his men flew the baby to safety.

In other parts of My Lai 4, GIs were taking a break, or loafing. Others were systematically burning those remaining houses and huts and destroying food. Some villagers—still alive—were able to leave their hiding places and walk away. Charles West recalled that one member of his squad who simply wasn't able to slaughter a group of children asked for and received permission from an officer to let them go. West's third platoon went ahead, nonetheless, with the killing. They gathered a group of about ten women and children.

who huddled together in fear a few feet from the plaza, where dozens of villagers already had been slain. West and the squad had finished their mission in the north and west of the hamlet, and were looking for new targets. They drifted south toward the CP. Jay Roberts and Ron Haeberle, who had spent the past hour watching the slaughter in other parts of the hamlet, stood by—pencil and cameras at the ready. A few men now singled out a slender Vietnamese girl of about fifteen. They tore her from the group and started to pull at her blouse. They attempted to fondle her breasts. The old women and children were screaming and crying. One GI yelled, "Let's see what she's made of." Another said "VC Boom, Boom," meaning she was a Viet Cong whore. Jay Roberts thought that the girl was good-looking. An old lady began fighting with fanatical fury, trying to protect the girl. Roberts said, "She was fighting off two or three guys at once. She was fantastic. Usually they're pretty passive . . . They hadn't even gotten that chick's blouse off when Haeberle came along." One of the GIs finally smacked the old woman with his rifle butt; another booted her in the rear.

Grzesik and his fire team watched the fight develop as they walked down from the ditch to the hamlet center. Grzesik was surprised: "I thought the village was cleared . . . I didn't know there were that many people left." He knew trouble was brewing, and his main thought was to keep his team out of it. He helped break up the fight. Some of the children were desperately hanging onto the old lady as she struggled. Grzesik was worried about the cameraman. He may have yelled, "Hey, there's a photographer." He remembered thinking, "Here's a guy standing there with a camera that you've never seen before." Then somebody said, "What do we do with

them?" The answer was, "Waste them." Suddenly there was a burst of automatic fire from many guns. Only a small child survived. Somebody then carefully shot him, too. A photograph of the woman and child, with the young Vietnamese girl tucking in her blouse, was later published in *Life* magazine. Roberts tried to explain later: "It's just that they didn't know what they were supposed to do; killing them seemed like a good idea, so they did it. The old lady who fought so hard was probably a VC." He thought a moment and added, "Maybe it was just her daughter."

West was annoyed at the photographer: "I thought it was wrong for him to stand up and take pictures of this thing. Even though we had to do it, I thought, we didn't have to take pictures of it." Later he complained personally to Haeberle about it.

By now it was nearly 10:30 A.M. and most of the company began drifting aimlessly toward the plaza and the command post a few yards to the south. Their work was largely over; a good part of the hamlet was in flames. The villagers "were laying around like ants," William Wyatt remembered. "It was just like somebody had poisoned the water and everybody took a drink and started falling out."

Herb Carter and Harry Stanley had shed their gear and were taking a short break at the CP. Near them was a young Vietnamese boy, crying, with a bullet wound in his stomach. Stanley watched one of Captain Medina's three radio operators walk along a trail toward them; he was without his radio gear. As Stanley told the C.I.D., the radio operator went up to Carter and said, "Let me see your pistol." Carter gave it to him. The radio operator "then stepped within two feet of the boy and shot him in the neck with a pistol. Blood

gushed from the child's neck. He then tried to walk off, but he could only take two or three steps. Then he fell onto the ground. He lay there and took four or five deep breaths and then he stopped breathing." The radio operator turned to Stanley and said, "Did you see how I shot that son of a bitch?" Stanley told him, "I don't see how anyone could just kill a kid." Carter got his pistol back; he told Stanley, "I can't take this no more . . ." Moments later Stanley heard a gun go off and Carter yell. "I went to Carter and saw he had shot himself in the foot. I think Carter shot himself on purpose."

Other children were also last-minute targets. After the scene with the women and children, West noticed a small boy, about seven years old, staring dazedly beside a footpath. He had been shot in the leg. "He was just standing there staring; I don't think he was crying. Somebody asked, 'What do we do with him?'" At this point West had remembered there had been an order from Captain Medina to stop the shooting. "I just shrugged my shoulders," West recalled, "and said, 'I don't know,' and just kept walking." Seconds later he heard some shots, turned around and saw the boy no longer standing on the trail.

Haeberle and Roberts were walking together on the edge of the hamlet when they also noticed the wounded child with the vacant stare. In seconds, Roberts said, "Haeberle, envisioning the war-torn-wounded-waif picture of the year, got within five feet of the kid for a close-up. He was focusing when some guy, just walking along, leveled his rifle, fired three times and walked away." Haeberle saw the shooting through the lens of his camera. "He looked up in shock," Roberts added. "He just turned around and stared. I think that was the thing that stayed in our mind. It was so close, so real, we just saw some kid blown away."

By then a helicopter, called in by Medina, had landed near the command post to fly out the wounded Carter. Sergeant Duong Minh, the interpreter who had angered Medina with his questions about the dead civilians, was also put aboard.

One of Haeberle's photographs shows the company medic, Nicholas Capezza of Queens, New York, bandaging Carter, with Medina and a radio operator, Rodger Murray of Waukegan, Illinois, in the background near a partially destroyed red-brick house. Medina was on the radio. William Wyatt remembered the scene; that was the first time he'd seen Medina that morning. Roy Wood also saw him then for the first time. Others recalled, however, that the captain had left his CP south of the plaza many times during the late morning to tour the northern and western sections urging the men to stop the shooting and get on with the job of burning down the buildings. Some GIs from the second platoon, under Lieutenant Brooks, found three men still alive. Gary Crossley heard the GIs ask Brooks, "What do we do now?" The lieutenant relayed the question by radio to Medina. "Don't kill them," the captain said. "There's been too much of that already." Gary Garfolo remembered that Medina seemed frantic at times, literally dashing about the hamlet. "He was telling everybody, 'Let's start getting out—let's move out of here.' "

Roberts also thought that Medina "was all over." He and Haeberle had crossed from the south to the north side of the hamlet to look around, and saw the captain there. "Then Carter shot himself and Medina went back," Roberts said. At some point earlier in the morning, Roberts had watched some GIs interrogate an old man. He didn't know anything, and somebody asked the captain what to do with him. Medina "indicated he didn't care," Roberts said, "that the guy wasn't of any use to him, and walked away." The GIs shot the man. Sergeant Mitchell may have witnessed the same scene. He saw both Calley and Medina interrogating an old man; Mitchell thought he was a monk. "Four or five of us weren't far away. We were watching. The old monk mumbled something and Medina walked off. I looked away for a second, and when I looked back the old man had been shot and Calley was standing over him."

Richard Pendleton remembered Medina himself shooting a civilian that day. Pendleton was standing about fifty feet away from the captain sometime that morning—Pendleton isn't sure exactly when. Pendleton hadn't seen the captain earlier and he wondered what Medina thought about what was going on. "Medina was standing there with the rest of the CP. It was right there in the open. I was watching." There was a small Vietnamese child, "the only one alive among a lot of dead people." He said he watched Medina carefully aim his M16 rifle at the child. "He shot him in the head, and he went down."

Pendleton may have been mistaken. There was a child shot near the command post that day, after Carter shot himself. Charles Gruver of Tulsa, Oklahoma, remembered vividly how it happened: he saw a small boy, about three or four years old, standing by a trail with a wound in his arm. "He just stood there with big eyes staring like he didn't believe what was happening. Then the captain's RTO [radio operator] put a burst of 16 [M16 rifle fire] into him." Ronald Grzesik also saw it. He was just watching the child when he heard a rifle shot; he looked back and saw that the radio operator was still in braced firing position. But Medina, Grzesik recalled, "was around the corner" in the command post at the time. Roberts also witnessed the shooting; he thought the toddler was searching through the pile of dead bodies for his mother or father, or a sister. He was wearing only a shirt. The impact of the M16 flung the small body backward onto the pile.

After that incident Grzesik said he went up to John Paul, one of Medina's radiomen, and told him what had been going on inside My Lai 4. Paul promptly asked him to tell the captain. Grzesik declined, thinking that Medina "was going to find out anyway if he walked up a few feet."

There were some small acts of mercy. A GI placed a blanket over the body of a mutilated child. An elderly woman was spared when some GIs hollered at a soldier just as he was about to shoot her. Grzesik remembered watching a GI seem to wrestle with his conscience while holding a bayonet over a wounded old man. "He wants to stab somebody with a bayonet," Grzesik thought. The GI hesitated . . . and finally passed on, leaving the old man to die.

Some GIs, however, didn't hesitate to use their bayonets. Nineteen-year-old Nguyen Thi Ngoc Tuyet watched a baby trying to open her slain mother's blouse to nurse. A soldier shot the infant while it was struggling with the blouse, and then slashed at it with his bayonet. Tuyet also said she saw another baby hacked to death by GIs wielding their bayonets.

Le Tong, a twenty-eight-year-old rice farmer, reported seeing one woman raped after GIs killed her children. Nguyen Khoa, a thirty-seven-year-old peasant, told of a thirteen-year-old girl who was raped before being killed. GIs then attacked Khoa's wife, tearing off her clothes. Before they could rape her, however, Khoa said, their six-year-old son, riddled with bullets, fell and saturated her with blood. The GIs left her alone.

There were "degrees" of murder that day. Some were conducted out of sympathy. Michael Terry, the Mormon who was a squad leader in the third platoon, had ordered his men to take their lunch break by the bloody ditch in the rear of the hamlet. He noticed that there were no men in the ditch, only women and children. He had watched Calley and the others shoot into that ditch. Calley seemed just like a kid, Terry thought. He also remembered thinking it was "just like a Nazi-type thing." When one soldier couldn't fire any more and threw down his weapon, "Calley picked it up." Later, during lunch, Terry and his men saw that some of the victims were still breathing. "They were pretty badly shot up. They weren't going to get any medical help, and so we shot them. Shot maybe five of them."

James Bergthold saw an old man who had been shot in both legs: "He was going to die anyway, so I figured I might as well kill him." He took his .45-caliber pistol (as a machine-gun ammunition carrier, he was entitled to one), carefully placed the barrel against the upper part of the old man's forehead and blew off the top of his head. Carter had watched the scene and remembered thinking that Bergthold had done the old man a favor. "If me and you were together and you got wounded bad," Carter later told an interviewer, "and I couldn't get you to a doctor, I'd shoot you, too."

Most of the shooting was over by the time Medina called a break for lunch, shortly after eleven o'clock. By then Roberts and Haeberle had grabbed a helicopter and cleared out of the area, their story for the day far bigger than they wanted. Calley, Mitchell, Sledge, Grzesik and a few others went back to the command post west of My Lai 4 to take lunch with Captain Medina and the rest of his headquarters' crew. Grzesik recalled that at that point he'd thought there couldn't be a survivor left in the hamlet. But two little girls showed up, about ten and eleven years old. John Paul said they came in from one of the paddies, where they apparently had waited out the siege. "We sat them down with us [at the command post]," Paul recounted, "and gave them some cookies and crackers to eat." When a C.I.D. interrogator later asked Charles Sledge how many civilians he thought had survived, he answered, "Only two small children who had lunch with us."

In the early afternoon the men of Charlie Company mopped up to make sure all the houses and goods in My Lai 4 were destroyed. Medina ordered the underground tunnels in the hamlet blown up; most of them already had been blocked. Within another hour My Lai 4 was no more: its redbrick buildings demolished by explosives, its huts burned to the ground, its people dead or dying.

Michael Bernhardt later summarized the day: "We met no resistance and I only saw three captured weapons. We had no casualties. It was just like any other Vietnamese village—old papa-sans, women and kids. As a matter of fact, I don't remember seeing one military-age male in the entire place, dead or alive. The only prisoner I saw was in his fifties."

The platoons pulled out shortly after noon, rendezvousing in the rice paddies east of My Lai 4. Lieutenant Brooks' platoon had about eighty-five villagers in tow; it kept those of military age with them and told the rest to begin moving south. Following orders, Medina then marched the GIs northeast through the nearly deserted hamlets of My Lai 5 and My Lai 6, ransacking and burning as they went. In one of the hamlets, Medina ordered the residents gathered, and then told Sergeant Phu, the regular company interpreter, to tell them, as Phu later recalled, that "they were to go away or something will happen to them—just like what happened at My Lai 4."

By nightfall the Viet Cong were back in My Lai 4, helping the survivors bury the dead. It took five days. Most of the funeral speeches were made by the Communist guerrillas. Nguyen Bat was not a Communist at the time of the massacre, but the incident changed his mind. "After the shooting," he said, "all the villagers became Communists."

When Army investigators reached the barren area in November 1969, in connection with the My Lai probe in the United States, they found mass graves at three sites, as well as a ditch full of bodies. It was estimated that between 450 and 500 people—most of them women, children, and old men—had been slain and buried there.

NORMAN MAILER
The Siege of Chicago

What the missile crisis of 1962 was in foreign policy—the point beyond which one could not go—the Democratic Convention of 1968 was in domestic politics. All the hopes and frustrations of a great and terrible decade merged and were symbolized in the confrontation between Yippies and police, hawks and doves, youth and age, Chicago's Mayor Daley and the press. Liberals who had accomplished what seemed miracles of social legislation found themselves denounced by radicals; men who prided themselves on their modernity discovered that they were hopelessly square; flower children suddenly learned what their politics were; and, most of all, the deeply confused debate over Vietnam assumed cultural terms as it fused with seemingly disconnected issues of long hair or one's choice of stimulants and depressants. And at a more fundamental level was the question of what people in their secret hearts felt about country and flag and the whole meaning of the nation's history. We had arrived as a people at a special moment—Chicago, 1968—and the nation felt—correctly as it turned out—that nothing would ever be quite the same again.

The sixties was an age in which the anxieties of the world were too much with us, when politics to a remarkable extent infected feelings and aspirations. The life of politics and the life of myth had, as Mailer predicted early in the decade, been brought together and—as Henry Fairlie had assured us had to be the case—politics had been found wanting. Americans were less familiar than people of other nations with a world in which history impinged so directly on sensibility. This new experience had produced its archetypical literary form in a vast outpouring of cultural journalism; writers like Mailer composed histories that were part novels, and novels that were part history, to delineate not just the shape of events, but how these events had changed them as people. This personal sense of history's changing not only the participant but even the spectator represented a new form of mass awareness in American life. In the past, Americans had thought of themselves as products of nature, arising from the fertile soil of the frontier; in the sixties they were learning that history was something that happened to them, not just to other people.

Reprinted by permission of The World Publishing Company from *Miami & The Siege of Chicago* by Norman Mailer. Copyright © 1968 by Norman Mailer.

[On nominating day at the Democratic National Convention of 1968] the debate on the Vietnam peace plank took place. Indeed, it was also the evening when the Massacre of Michigan Avenue occurred, an extraordinary event: a massacre, equal on balance to some of the old Indian raids, yet no one was killed. Of course, a great many people were hurt. And several hundred delegates started to march back from the stockyards, early Thursday morning after the nomination, carrying lit candles in protest. It was obviously one of the more active days in the history of any convention.

Worn out by his portentous Southern sense of things to come, Lester Maddox, the fourth candidate, Governor of Georgia, even resigned his candidacy Wednesday morning. We quote from Walter Rugaber of the *New York Times:*

His wife, Virginia, sat beside him weeping softly as Mr. Maddox ended his 11-day fling with a last news conference in the brightly lit Grand Ballroom of the Conrad Hilton Hotel.

He talked about misinformed socialist and power-mad politicians. He assailed the Democrats as the party of "looting, burning, killing and draft-card burning. What's more," he said, "I denounce them all."

Then he caught a plane back to Atlanta. Who would declare that the chanting in Grant Park through the long hours of Tuesday night and the semi-obscene shouts—Dump the Hump!—had done nothing to accelerate his decision?

Originally, the debate on the Vietnam plank had been scheduled for Tuesday night, but the convention went on past mid-

Gathering in Grant Park, Chicago, 1968. *(Rick Winsor, Woodfin Camp, Inc.)*

night, so the hawks attempted to have it early in the morning. It was their hope to begin at 1 A.M. New York time, and thus obtain the pleasure of denying the doves a large television audience. But the doves raised a post-midnight demonstration on the floor which became progressively more obstreperous until Mayor Daley made the mistake of rising to remonstrate with the gallery warning that they would be cleared out of their seats if they did not quiet down. "Let's act like ladies and gentlemen, and let people be heard," said Daley to the convention and to millions on television, looking for all the world like the best b.o. ever to come out of *Guys and Dolls.* But it was obvious the greater share of the noise came from behind Daley on the floor, from the rear where McCarthy and McGovern delegates from New York, California, South Dakota, Massachusetts, Wisconsin and Oregon were placed far from the podium. At any rate, the Administration forces lost their play. It was one thing for them to cut off a discussion—that was simply accomplished. One had only to give a signal, then make a quick motion which could as quickly be recognized by the Chairman who would whip in a lightning move for a voice-vote. "The ayes . . . the nays . . . The ayes have it," he would say, and rap his gavel, walk off the podium, close the session. But here, after midnight, the hawks were not trying to cut off a discussion, rather they wished to begin one; the doves had nothing to lose by a noisy non-stop protest. Moves for silence, whacks of the gavel by Carl Albert looking poisonous for being ignored, loud music of the band to drown out the rear delegation. Nothing worked. The television cameras were focused on the doves who were protesting the lateness of the hour. The hawks could insist on their

move, but they would look like the worst of the cattle gang on television. So a signal was passed to Daley by an Administration spokesman who drew his finger across his throat, an unmistakable sign to cut off conversation for the night. Daley, looking like he had just been stuffed with a catfish, stood up, got the floor, made a move to adjourn. Immediately recognized by Carl Albert. The little Chairman was now sufficiently excited to start to say Mayor Daley of the Great State of Chicago. He recovered quickly, however, quick enough to rap his gavel, and declare that the Chair accepted the motion, snapping it through with a slick haste, as if it had been his idea all along! The debate was postponed until Wednesday afternoon.

The debate, however, proved anti-climactic. There had been hopes that McCarthy would speak, idle dreams he might make a great speech; but it was rumored that the Senator, weighing the imponderable protocol of these profoundly established convention manners, had decided he would not enter debate unless Lyndon Johnson came to the Amphitheatre for his birthday party. Johnson, however, was not in the hall; he was still in Texas where he would remain (on the advice of his best wise men since they could not guarantee the character of his reception in the Amphitheatre, nor the nature of the stimulation it might give the streets). Therefore, McCarthy, respecting the balance, was not present either.

The hawks had first proposed fifteen minutes for the debate, than thirty. An hour was the maximum obtainable by the doves. On the greatest national issue any convention had faced since the second world war, debate would provide an hour of speech for each side. Moreover, the sides would make alternate speeches. Thus, no massive presentation of argument nor avalanche of emotion would ever result . . .

Meanwhile, a mass meeting was taking place about the bandshell in Grant Park, perhaps a quarter of a mile east of Michigan Avenue and the Conrad Hilton. The meeting was under the auspices of the Mobilization, and a crowd of ten or fifteen thousand appeared. The Mayor had granted a permit to assemble, but had refused to allow a march. Since the Mobilization had announced that it would attempt, no matter how, the march to the Amphitheatre that was the first purpose of their visit to Chicago, the police were out in force to surround the meeting.

An episode occurred during the speeches. Three demonstrators climbed a flag pole to cut down the American flag and put up a rebel flag. A squad of police charged to beat them up, but got into trouble themselves, for when they threw tear gas, the demonstrators lobbed the canisters back, and the police, choking on their own gas, had to fight their way clear through a barrage of rocks. Then came a much larger force of police charging the area, overturning benches, busting up members of the audience, then heading for Rennie Davis at the bullhorn. He was one of the coordinators of the Mobilization, his face was known, he had been fingered and fingered again by plainclothesmen. Now urging the crowd to sit down and be calm, he was attacked from behind by the police, his head laid open in a three-inch cut, and he was unconscious for a period. Furious at the attack, Tom Hayden, who had been in disguise these last two days to avoid any more arrests for himself, spoke to the crowd, said he was leaving to perform certain special tasks, and suggested that others break up into small groups and go out into the streets of the Loop "to do what they have to do." A few left with him; the majority remained. While it was a People's Army and therefore utterly unorganized by uniform or unity, it had a variety of special troops and regular troops; everything from a few qualified Kamikaze who were ready to charge police lines in a Japanese snake dance and dare on the consequence, some vicious beatings, to various kinds of small saboteurs, rock-throwers, gauntlet-runners—some of the speediest of the kids were adept at taunting cops while keeping barely out of range of their clubs—not altogether alien to running the bulls at Pamplona. Many of those who remained, however, were still nominally pacifists, protesters, Gandhians—they believed in non-violence, in the mystical

The New Politics. *(Constantine Manos, Magnum)*

Mayor Richard J. Daley of Chicago congratulates Hubert Humphrey on his nomination. *(Wide World Photos)*

interposition of their body to the attack, as if the violence of the enemy might be drained by the spiritual act of passive resistance over the years, over the thousands, tens of thousands, hundreds of thousands of beatings over the years. So Allen Ginsberg was speaking now to them.

The police looking through the plexiglass face shields they had flipped down from their helmets were then obliged to watch the poet with his bald head, soft eyes magnified by horn-rimmed eyeglasses, and massive dark beard, utter his words in a croaking speech. He had been gassed Monday night and Tuesday night, and had gone to the beach at dawn to read Hindu Tantras to some of the Yippies, the combination of the chants and the gassings had all but burned out his voice, his beautiful speaking voice, one of the most powerful and hypnotic instruments of the Western world, was down to the scrapings of the throat now, raw as flesh after a curettage.

"The best strategy for you," said Ginsberg, "in cases of hysteria, overexcitement or fear, is still to chant 'OM' together. It helps to quell flutterings of butterflies in the belly. Join me now as I try to lead you."

The crowd chanted with Ginsberg. They were of a generation which would try every idea, every drug, every action—it was even possible a few of them had made out with freaky kicks on tear gas these last few days—so they would chant OM. There were Hindu fanatics in the crowd, children who loved India and scorned everything in the West; there were cynics who thought the best thing to be said for a country which allowed its excess population to die by the millions in famine-ridden fields was that it would not be ready soon to try to dominate the rest of the world. There were also militants who were ready to march. And the police there to prevent them, busy now in communication with other detachments of police, by way of radios whose aerials were attached to their helmets, thereby giving them the look of giant insects.

A confused hour began. Lincoln Park was irregular in shape with curving foot walks; but Grant Park was indeed not so much a park as a set of belts of greenery cut into files by major parallel avenues between Michigan Avenue and Lake Michigan half a mile away. Since there were also cross streets cutting the belts of green perpendicularly, a variety of bridges and pedestrian overpasses gave egress to the city. The park was in this sense an alternation of lawn with superhighways. So the police were able to pen the crowd. But not completely. There were too many bridges, too many choices, in effect, for the police to anticipate. To this confusion was added the fact that every confrontation of demonstrators with police, now buttressed by the National Guard, attracted hundreds of newsmen, and hence began a set of attempted negotiations between spokesmen for the demonstrators and troops; the demonstrators finally tried to force a bridge and get back to the city. Repelled by tear gas, they went to other bridges, still other bridges, finally found a bridge lightly guarded, broke through a passage and were loose in the city at six-thirty in the evening. They milled about in the Loop for a few minutes, only to encounter the mules and three wagons of the Poor People's Campaign. City officials, afraid of provoking the Negroes on the South Side, had given a permit to the Reverend Abernathy, and he was going to march the mules and wagons down Michigan Avenue and over to the convention. An impromptu march of the demonstrators formed behind the wagons immediately on encountering them and ranks of marchers, sixty, eighty, a hundred in line across the width of Michigan Avenue began to move forward in the gray early twilight of 7 P.M.; Michigan Avenue was now suddenly jammed with people in the march, perhaps so many as four or five thousand people, including onlookers on the sidewalk who jumped in. The streets of the Loop were also reeking with tear gas—the wind had blown some of the gas over Michigan Avenue from the drops on the bridges, some gas still was penetrated into the clothing of the marchers. In broken ranks, half a march, half a happy mob, eyes red from gas, faces excited by the tension of the afternoon, and the excitement of the escape from Grant Park, now pushing down Michigan Avenue toward the Hilton Hotel with dreams of a march on to the Amphitheatre four miles beyond, and in the full pleasure of being led by the wagons of the Poor People's March, the demonstrators shouted to everyone on the sidewalk, "Join us, join us, join us," and the sidewalk kept disgorging more people ready to march.

But at Balbo Avenue, just before Michigan Avenue reached the Hilton, the marchers were halted by the police. It was a long halt. Perhaps thirty minutes. Time for people who had been walking on the sidewalk to join the march, proceed for a few steps, halt with the others, wait, get bored, and leave. It was time for someone in command of the hundreds of police in the neighborhood to communicate with his headquarters, explain the problem, time for the dilemma to be relayed, alternatives examined, and orders conceivably sent back to attack and disperse the crowd. If so, a trap was first set. The mules were allowed to cross Balbo Avenue, then were separated by a line of police from the marchers, who now, several thousand compressed in this one place, filled the intersection of Michigan Avenue and Balbo. There, dammed by police on three sides, and cut off from the wagons of the Poor People's March, there, right beneath the windows of the Hilton which looked down on Grant Park and Michigan Avenue, the stationary march was abruptly attacked. The police attacked with tear gas, with Mace, and with clubs, they attacked like a chain saw cutting into wood, the teeth of the saw the edge of their clubs, they attacked like a scythe through grass, lines of twenty and thirty policemen striking out in an arc, their clubs beating,

Julian Bond at Chicago, 1968.
(*Charles Harbutt, Magnum*)

National Guardsman at the Hilton in Chicago, 1968. *(Fred McDarrah)*

demonstrators fleeing. Seen from overhead, from the nineteenth floor, it was like a wind blowing dust, or the edge of waves riding foam on the shore.

The police cut through the crowd one way, then cut through them another. They chased people into the park, ran them down, beat them up; they cut through the intersection at Michigan and Balbo like a razor cutting a channel through a head of hair, and then drove columns of new police into the channel who in turn pushed out, clubs flailing, on each side, to cut new channels, and new ones again. As demonstrators ran, they re-formed in new groups only to be chased by the police again. The action went on for ten minutes, fifteen minutes, with the absolute ferocity of a tropical storm, and watching it from a window on the nineteenth floor, there was something of the detachment of studying a storm at evening through a glass, the light was a lovely gray-blue, the police had uniforms of sky-blue, even the ferocity had an abstract elemental play of forces of nature at battle with other forces, as if sheets of tropical rain were driving across the street in patterns, in curving patterns which curved upon each other again. Police cars rolled up, prisoners were beaten, shoved into wagons, driven away. The rain of police, maddened by the uncoiling of their own storm, pushed against their own barricades of tourists pressed on the street against the Hilton Hotel, then pressed them so hard—but here is a quotation from J. Anthony Lukas in *The New York Times:*

Even elderly bystanders were caught in the police onslaught. At one point, the police turned on several dozen persons standing quietly behind police barriers in front of the Conrad Hilton Hotel watching the demonstrators across the street.

For no reason that could be immediately determined, the blue-helmeted policemen charged the barriers, crushing the spectators against the windows of the Haymarket Inn, a restaurant in the hotel. Finally the window gave way, sending screaming middle-aged women and children backward through the broken shards of glass.

The police then ran into the restaurant and beat some of the victims who had fallen through the windows and arrested them.

Now another quote from Steve Lerner in *The Village Voice:*

When the charge came, there was a stampede toward the sidelines. People piled into each other, humped over each other's bodies like coupling dogs. To fall down in the crush was just as terrifying as facing the police. Suddenly I realized my feet weren't touching the ground as the crowd pushed up onto the sidewalk. I was grabbing at the army jacket of the boy in front of me; the girl behind me had a stranglehold on my neck and was screaming incoherently in my ear.

Now, a longer quotation from Jack Newfield in *The Village Voice.* (The accounts in *The Voice* of September 5 were superior to any others encountered that week.)

At the southwest entrance to the Hilton, a skinny, long-haired kid of about seventeen skidded down on the sidewalk, and four overweight cops leaped on him, chopping strokes on his head. His hair flew from the force of the blows. A dozen small rivulets of blood began to cascade down the kid's temple and onto the sidewalk. He was not crying or screaming, but crawling in a stupor toward the gutter. When he saw a photographer take a picture, he made a V sign with his fingers.

A doctor in a white uniform and Red Cross arm band began to run toward the kid, but two other cops caught him from behind and knocked him down. One of them jammed his knee into the doctor's throat and began clubbing his rib cage. The doctor squirmed away, but the cops followed him, swinging hard, sometimes missing.

A few feet away a phalanx of

Gassed at Chicago, 1968.   *(Roger Malloch, Magnum)*

Mob Scene—Chicago, 1968.   *(Charles Harbutt, Magnum)*

police charged into a group of women, reporters, and young McCarthy activists standing idly against the window of the Hilton Hotel's Haymarket Inn. The terrified people began to go down under the unexpected police charge when the plate glass window shattered, and the people tumbled backward through the glass. The police then climbed through the broken window and began to beat people, some of whom had been drinking quietly in the hotel bar.

At the side entrance of the Hilton Hotel four cops were chasing one frightened kid of about seventeen. Suddenly, Fred Dutton, a former aide to Robert Kennedy, moved out from under the marquee and interposed his body between the kid and the police.

"He's my guest in this hotel," Dutton told the cops.

The police started to club the kid.

Dutton screamed for the first cop's name and badge number. The cop grabbed Dutton and began to arrest him, until a Washington *Post* reporter identified Dutton as a former RFK aide.

Demonstrators, reporters, McCarthy workers, doctors, all began to stagger into the Hilton lobby, blood streaming from face and head wounds. The lobby smelled from tear gas, and stink bombs dropped by the Yippies. A few people began to direct the wounded to a makeshift hospital on the fifteenth floor, the McCarthy staff headquarters.

Fred Dutton was screaming at the police, and at the journalists to report all the "sadism and brutality." Richard Goodwin, the ashen nub of a cigar sticking out of his fatigued face, mumbled, "This is just the beginning. There'll be four years of this."

The defiant kids began a slow orderly retreat back up Michigan Avenue. They did not run. They did not panic. They did not fight back. As they fell back they helped pick up fallen comrades who were beaten or gassed. Suddenly, a plainclothesman dressed as a soldier moved out of the shadows and knocked one kid down with an overhand punch. The kid squatted on the pavement of Michigan Avenue, trying to cover his face, while the Chicago plainclothesman punched him with savage accuracy. Thud, thud, thud. Blotches of blood spread over the kid's face. Two photographers moved in. Several police formed a closed circle around the beating to prevent pictures. One of the policemen then squirted Chemical Mace at the photographers, who dispersed. The plainclothesman melted into the line of police.

Let us escape to the street. The reporter, watching in safety from the nineteenth floor, could understand now how Mussolini's son-in-law had once been able to find the bombs he dropped from his airplane beautiful as they burst, yes, children, and youths, and middle-aged men and women were being pounded and clubbed and gassed and beaten, hunted and driven, sent scattering in all directions by teams of policemen who had exploded out of their restraints like the bursting of a boil, and nonetheless he felt a sense of calm and beauty, void even of the desire to be down there, as if in years to come there would be beatings enough, some chosen, some from nowhere, but it was as if the war had finally begun, and this was

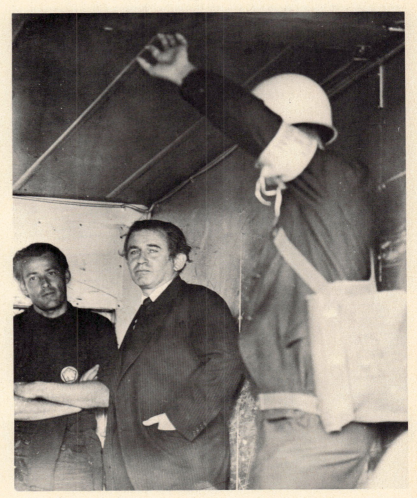

Norman Mailer at the March on the Pentagon. *(Tom McCarthy)*

therefore a great and solemn moment, as if indeed even the gods of history had come together from each side to choose the very front of the Hilton Hotel before the television cameras of the world and the eyes of the campaign workers and the delegates' wives, yes, there before the eyes of half the principals at the convention was this drama played, as if the military spine of a great liberal party had finally separated itself from the skin, as if, no metaphor large enough to suffice, the Democratic party had here broken in two before the eyes of a nation like Melville's whale charging right out of the sea.

A great stillness rose up from the street through all the small noise of clubbing and cries, small sirens, sigh of loaded arrest vans as off they pulled, shouts of police as they wheeled in larger circles, the intersection clearing further, then further, a stillness rose through the steel and stone of the hotel, congregating in the shocked centers of every room where delegates and wives and Press and campaign workers innocent until now of the intimate working of social force, looked down now into the murderous paradigm of Vietnam there beneath them at this huge intersection of this great city. Look—a boy was running through the park, and a cop was chasing. There he caught him on the back of the neck with his club! There! The cop is return-

ing to his own! And the boy stumbling to his feet is helped off the ground by a girl who has come running up.

Yes, it could only have happened in a meeting of the Gods, that history for once should take place not on some back street, or some inaccessible grand room, not in some laboratory indistinguishable from others, or in the sly undiscoverable hypocrisies of a committee of experts, but rather on the center of the stage, as if each side had said, "Here we will have our battle. Here we will win."

The demonstrators were afterward delighted to have been manhandled before the public eye, delighted to have pushed and prodded, antagonized and provoked the cops over these days with rocks and bottles and cries of "Pig" to the point where police had charged in a blind rage and made a stage at the one place in the city (besides the Amphitheatre) where audience, actors, and cameras could all convene, yes, the rebels thought they had had a great victory, and perhaps they did; but the reporter wondered, even as he saw it, if the police in that half hour of waiting had not had time to receive instructions from the power of the city, perhaps the power of the land, and the power had decided, "No, do not let them march another ten blocks and there disperse them on some quiet street, no, let it happen before all the land, let everybody

see that their dissent will soon be equal to their own blood; let them realize that the power is implacable, and will beat and crush and imprison and yet kill before it will ever relinquish the power. So let them see before their own eys what it will cost to continue to mock us, defy us, and resist. There are more millions behind us than behind them, more millions who wish to weed out, poison, gas, and obliterate every flower whose power they do not comprehend than heroes for their side who will view our brute determination and still be ready to resist. There are more cowards alive than the brave. Otherwise we would not be where we are," said the Prince of Greed.

Who knew. One could thank the city of Chicago where drama was still a property of the open stage. It was quiet now, there was nothing to stare down on but the mules, and the police guarding them. The mules had not moved through the entire fray. Isolated from the battle, they had stood there in harness waiting to be told to go on. Only once in a while did they turn their heads. Their role as actors in the Poor People's March was to wait and to serve. Finally they moved on. The night had come. It was dark. The intersection was now empty. Shoes, ladies' handbags, and pieces of clothing lay on the street outside the hotel. . . .

PART II
American Society

Introduction

American society throughout the twentieth century had been progressively fragmenting into discrete subcultures. Much of this process remained hidden by the overall conformity to the Anglo-American values that had dominated American society since the nineteenth century. Commentators talked about "assimilation" and "the melting pot" to describe how the multifarious groups making up American society all struggled toward a uniform language and ethos. During the 1960s, critics fully realized that the melting pot had in fact not coalesced Americans into a single mold, that instead the plurality of groups was consolidating into relatively separate subcultures vying for dominance in the society—or at least for their own places and identities within it. That this was the case among black Americans became increasingly apparent as the decade advanced. But it also seemed true generally of the poor—who were said to belong to a "culture of poverty"; of students—who turned into a separate "youth culture"; and even of "middle America"—which people now thought of as a style of life rather than as a least common denominator of the society.

However true or false these characterizations were—and certainly they contained as many inaccuracies as the old melting pot idea had—people not only believed them, but acted upon them, gearing their lives to their identity as blacks, Chicanos, students, women, hard hats, or intelligentsia. The search for community that dominated imaginations across the social spectrum, and the desperate grasping for something that would "bring us all together," such as a common concern about the quality of the environment, flowed directly from the fragmentation that Americans felt so strongly, especially later in the decade.

MICHAEL HARRINGTON
The Other America

Michael Harrington's *The Other America* is a classic in the
tradition of journalism often called "muckraking": reportage on
the abuses and outrages of society with a view toward spurring
the national conscience to reform them. Starting in the later
1950s and increasing in the next decade, this stream of
journalism has merged with the social sciences to produce
what might be called sociological muckraking, a combination
of social science theory, statistics, and conventional journalism.
No book in this genre has had a greater impact than Harrington's,
which helped Americans to recognize the poverty in their midst
and to move to eradicate it.

Harrington points out how unusual it is in world history for a
nation to have poverty whose existence is not obvious. The
poor in modern America are invisible—shut away in rural
poverty or tucked away beside express highways, dressed in
cheap versions of middle-class clothing, removed as objects
of middle-class sympathies by a culture of poverty and a
mistaken belief that existing social welfare programs are
adequate. And the poor are politically insignificant and
unrepresented. The "other Americans" whom Harrington
brought to the nation's attention have declined in number
significantly in the course of the decade—some benefiting from
the array of Great Society programs, many more profiting
from the economic boom that began about when Harrington's
book was published and that continued for over six years. Now,
in the seventies, the nation still has enough poor to constitute
a scandal, and signs abound that the public has tired of hearing
about them. The main legacy of books like Harrington's may
well be that poverty can no longer be wished into invisibility.

The millions who are poor in
the United States tend to become
increasingly invisible. Here is a
great mass of people, yet it takes
an effort of the intellect and will
even to see them.

I discovered this personally in
a curious way. After I wrote my
first article on poverty in America, I had all the statistics down
on paper. I had proved to my satisfaction that there were around
50,000,000 poor in the country.
Yet, I realized I did not believe
my own figures. The poor existed
in the Government reports; they
were percentages and numbers in
long, close columns, but they

Reprinted with permission of The Macmillan Company from *The Other America,*
by Michael Harrington. © by Michael Harrington, 1962.

were not part of my experience. I could prove that the other America existed, but I had never been there.

My response was not accidental. It was typical of what is happening to an entire society, and it reflects profound social changes in this nation. The other America, the America of poverty, is hidden today in a way that it never was before. Its millions are socially invisible to the rest of us. No wonder that so many misinterpreted Galbraith's title and assumed that "the affluent society" meant that everyone had a decent standard of life. The misinterpretation was true as far as the actual day-to-day lives of two-thirds of the nation were concerned. Thus, one must begin a description of the other America by understanding why we do not see it.

There are perennial reasons that make the other America an invisible land.

Poverty is often off the beaten track. It always has been. The ordinary tourist never left the main highway, and today he rides interstate turnpikes. He does not go into the valleys of Pennsylvania where the towns look like movie sets of Wales in the thirties. He does not see the company houses in rows, the rutted roads (the poor always have bad roads whether they live in the city, in towns or on farms), and everything is black and dirty. And even if he were to pass through such a place by accident, the tourist would not meet the unemployed men in the bar or the women coming home from a runaway sweatshop.

Then, too, beauty and myths are perennial masks of poverty.

Day Care Center for migrant workers' children. (Marcia Keegan)

The traveler comes to the Appalachians in the lovely season. He sees the hills, the streams, the foliage—but not the poor. Or perhaps he looks at a run-down mountain house and, remembering Rousseau rather than seeing with his eyes, decides that "those people" are truly fortunate to be living the way they are and that they are lucky to be exempt from the strains and tensions of the middle class. The only problem is that "those people," the quaint inhabitants of those hills, are undereducated, underprivileged, lack medical care, and are in the process of being forced from the land into a life in the cities, where they are misfits.

These are normal and obvious causes of the invisibility of the poor. They operated a generation ago; they will be functioning a generation hence. It is more important to understand that the very development of American society is creating a new kind of blindness about poverty. The poor are increasingly slipping out of the very experience and consciousness of the nation.

If the middle class never did like ugliness and poverty, it was at least aware of them. "Across the tracks" was not a very long way to go. There were forays into the slums at Christmas time; there were charitable organizations that brought contact with the poor. Occasionally, almost everyone passed through the Negro ghetto or the blocks of tenements, if only to get downtown to work or to entertainment.

Now the American city has been transformed. The poor still inhabit the miserable housing in the central area, but they are increasingly isolated from contact with, or sight of, anybody else. Middle-class women coming in from Suburbia on a rare trip may catch the merest glimpse of the other America on the way to an evening at the theater, but their children are segregated in sub-

urban schools. The business or professional man may drive along the fringes of the slums in a car or bus, but it is not an important experience to him. The failures, the unskilled, the disabled, the aged, and the minorities are right there, across the tracks, where they have always been. But hardly anyone else is.

In short, the very development of the American city has removed poverty from the living, emotional experience of millions upon millions of middle-class Americans. Living out in the suburbs, it is easy to assume that ours is, indeed, an affluent society.

This new segregation of poverty is compounded by a well-meaning ignorance. A good many concerned and sympathetic Americans are aware that there is much discussion of urban renewal. Suddenly, driving through the city, they notice that a familiar slum has been torn down and that there are towering, modern buildings where once there had been tenements or hovels. There is a warm feeling of satisfaction, of pride in the way things are working out: the poor, it is obvious, are being taken care of.

The irony in this . . . is that the truth is nearly the exact opposite to the impression. The total impact of the various housing programs in postwar America has been to squeeze more and more people into existing slums. More often than not, the modern apartment in a towering building rents at $40 a room or more. For, during the past decade and a half, there has been more subsidization of middle- and upper-income housing than there has been of housing for the poor.

Clothes make the poor invisible too: America has the best-dressed poverty the world has ever known. For a variety of reasons, the benefits of mass production have been spread much more evenly in this area than in many others. It is much easier in the United States to be decently dressed than it is to be decently housed, fed, or doctored. Even people with terribly depressed incomes can look prosperous.

This is an extremely important factor in defining our emotional and existential ignorance of poverty. In Detroit the existence of social classes became much more difficult to discern the day the companies put lockers in the plants. From that moment on, one did not see men in work clothes on the way to the factory, but citizens in slacks and white shirts. This process has been magnified with the poor throughout the country. There are tens of thousands of Americans in the big cities who are wearing shoes, perhaps even a stylishly cut suit or dress, and yet are hungry. It is not a matter of planning, though it almost seems as if the affluent society had given out costumes to the poor so that they would not offend the rest of society with the sight of rags.

Then, many of the poor are the wrong age to be seen. A good number of them (over 8,000,-000) are sixty-five years of age or better; an even larger number are under eighteen. The aged members of the other America are often sick, and they cannot move. Another group of them live out their lives in loneliness and frustration: they sit in rented rooms, or else they stay close to a house in a neighborhood that has completely changed from the old days. Indeed, one of the worst aspects of poverty among the aged is that these people are out of sight and out of mind, and alone.

The young are somewhat more visible, yet they too stay close to their neighborhoods. Sometimes they advertise their poverty through a lurid tabloid story about a gang killing. But generally they do not disturb the quiet streets of the middle class.

And finally, the poor are politically invisible. It is one of the cruelest ironies of social life in advanced countries that the dispossessed at the bottom of society are unable to speak for themselves. The people of the other America do not, by far and large, belong to unions, to fraternal organizations, or to political parties. They are without lobbies of their own; they put forward no legislative program. As a group, they are atomized. They have no face; they have no voice.

Thus, there is not even a cynical political motive for caring about the poor, as in the old days. Because the slums are no longer centers of powerful political organizations, the politicians need not really care about their inhabitants. The slums are no longer visible to the middle class, so much of the idealistic urge to fight for those who need help is gone. Only the social agencies have a really direct involvement with the other America, and they are without any great political power.

To the extent that the poor have a spokesman in American life, that role is played by the labor movement. The unions have their own particular idealism, an ideology of concern. More than that, they realize that the existence of a reservoir of cheap, unorganized labor is a menace to wages and working conditions throughout the entire economy. Thus, many union legislative proposals—to extend the coverage of minimum wage and social security, to organize migrant farm laborers—articulate the needs of the poor.

That the poor are invisible is one of the most important things about them. They are not simply neglected and forgotten as in the old rhetoric of reform; what is much worse, they are not seen. . . .

Forty to 50,000,000 people are becoming increasingly invisible. This is a shocking fact. But there is a second basic irony of poverty that is equally important: if one is to make the mistake of being born poor, he should choose a time when the majority of the people are miserable too.

J. K. Galbraith develops this idea in *The Affluent Society*, and in doing so defines the "new-

(Marcia Keegan)

Backyard on lower East Side of New York. *(Shelly Rusten)*

ness'' of the kind of poverty in contemporary America. The old poverty, Galbraith notes, was general. It was the condition of life of an entire society, or at least of that huge majority who were without special skills or the luck of birth. When the entire economy advanced, a good many of these people gained higher standards of living. Unlike the poor today, the majority poor of a generation ago were an immediate (if cynical) concern of political leaders. The old slums of the immigrants had the votes; they provided the basis for labor oganizations; their very numbers could be a powerful force in political conflict. At the same time the new technology required higher skills, more education, and stimulated an upward movement for millions.

Perhaps the most dramatic case of the power of the majority poor took place in the 1930s.

The Congress of Industrial Organizations literally organized millions in a matter of years. A labor movement that had been declining and confined to a thin stratum of the highly skilled suddenly embraced masses of men and women in basic industry. At the same time this acted as a pressure upon the Government, and the New Deal codified some of the social gains in laws like the Wagner Act. The result was not a basic transformation of the American system, but it did transform the lives of an entire section of the population.

In the thirties one of the reasons for these advances was that misery was general. There was no need then to write books about unemployment and poverty. That was the decisive social experience of the entire society, and the apple sellers even invaded Wall Street. There was political sympathy from middle-

class reformers; there were an élan and spirit that grew out of a deep crisis.

Some of those who advanced in the thirties did so because they had unique and individual personal talents. But for the great mass, it was a question of being at the right point in the economy at the right time in history, and utilizing that position for common struggle. Some of those who failed did so because they did not have the will to take advantage of new opportunities. But for the most part the poor who were left behind had been at the wrong place in the economy at the wrong moment in history.

These were the people in the unorganizable jobs, in the South, in the minority groups, in the fly-by-night factories that were low on capital and high on labor. When some of them did break into the economic mainstream—

when, for instance, the CIO opened up the way for some Negroes to find good industrial jobs—they proved to be as resourceful as anyone else. As a group, the other Americans who stayed behind were not originally composed primarily of individual failures. Rather, they were victims of an impersonal process that selected some for progress and discriminated against others.

Out of the thirties came the welfare state. Its creation has been stimulated by mass impoverishment and misery, yet it helped the poor least of all. Laws like unemployment compensation, the Wagner Act, the various farm programs, all these were designed for the middle third in the cities, for the organized workers, and for the upper third in the country, for the big market farmers. If a man works in an extremely low-paying job, he may not even be covered by social security or other welfare programs. If he receives unemployment compensation, the payment is scaled down according to his low earnings.

One of the major laws that was designed to cover everyone, rich and poor, was social security. But even here the other Americans suffered discrimination. Over the years social security payments have not even provided a subsistence level of life. The middle third have been able to supplement the Federal pension through private plans negotiated by unions, through joining medical insurance schemes like Blue Cross, and so on. The poor have not been able to do so. They lead a bitter life, and then have to pay for that fact in old age.

Indeed, the paradox that the welfare state benefits those least who need help most is but a single instance of a persistent irony in the other America. Even when the money finally trickles down, even when a school is built in a poor neighborhood, for

instance, the poor are still deprived. Their entire environment, their life, their values, do not prepare them to take advantage of the new opportunity. The parents are anxious for the children to go to work; the pupils are pent up, waiting for the moment when their education has complied with the law.

Today's poor, in short, missed the political and social gains of the thirties. They are, as Galbraith rightly points out, the first minority poor in history, the first poor not to be seen, the first poor whom the politicians could leave alone.

The first step toward the new poverty was taken when millions of people proved immune to progress. When that happened, the failure was not individual and personal, but a social product. But once the historic accident takes place, it begins to become a personal fate.

The new poor of the other America saw the rest of society move ahead. They went on living in depressed areas, and often they tended to become depressed human beings. In some of the West Virginia towns, for instance, an entire community will become shabby and defeated. The young and the adventurous go to the city, leaving behind those who cannot move and those who lack the will to do so. The entire area becomes permeated with failure, and that is one more reason the big corporations shy away.

Indeed, one of the most important things about the new poverty is that it cannot be defined in simple, statistical terms. Throughout this book a crucial term is used: aspiration. If a group has internal vitality, a will —if it has aspiration—it may live in dilapidated housing, it may eat an inadequate diet, and it may suffer poverty, but it is not impoverished. So it was in those ethnic slums of the immigrants that played such a dra-

matic role in the unfolding of the American dream. The people found themselves in slums, but they were not slum dwellers.

But the new poverty is constructed so as to destroy aspiration; it is a system designed to be impervious to hope. The other America does not contain the adventurous seeking a new life and land. It is populated by the failures, by those driven from the land and bewildered by the city, by old people suddenly confronted with the torments of loneliness and poverty, and by minorities facing a wall of prejudice. . . .

Finally, one might summarize the newness of contemporary poverty by saying: These are the people who are immune to progress. But then the facts are even more cruel. The other Americans are the victims of the very inventions and machines that have provided a higher living standard for the rest of the society. They are upside-down in the economy, and for them greater productivity often means worse jobs: agricultural advance becomes hunger.

In the optimistic theory, technology is an undisguised blessing. A general increase in productivity, the argument goes, generates a higher standard of living for the whole people. And indeed, this has been true for the middle and upper thirds of American society, the people who made such striking gains in the last two decades. It tends to overstate the automatic character of the process, to omit the role of human struggle. (The CIO was organized by men in conflict, not by economic trends.) Yet it states a certain truth—for those who are lucky enough to participate in it.

But the poor, if they were given to theory, might argue the exact opposite. They might say: Progress is misery.

As the society became more technological, more skilled, those who learn to work the machines, who get the expanding education, move up. Those who miss out at the very start find themselves at a new disadvantage. A generation ago in American life, the majority of the working people did not have high-school educations. But at that time industry was organized on a lower level of skill and competence. And there was a sort of continuum in the shop: the youth who left school at sixteen could begin as a laborer, and gradually pick up skill as he went along.

Today the situation is quite different. The good jobs require much more academic preparation, much more skill from the very outset. Those who lack a high-school education tend to be condemned to the economic underworld—to low-paying service industries, to backward factories, to sweeping and janitorial duties. If the fathers and mothers of the contemporary poor were penalized a generation ago for their lack of schooling, their children will suffer all the more. The very rise in productivity that created more money and better working conditions for the rest of the society can be a menace to the poor.

But then this technological revolution might have an even more disastrous consequence: it could increase the ranks of the poor as well as intensify the disabilities of poverty. At this point it is too early to make any final judgment, yet there are obvious danger signals. There are millions of Americans who live just the other side of poverty. When a recession comes, they are pushed onto the relief rolls. (Welfare payments in New York respond almost immediately to any economic decline.) If automation continues to inflict more and more penalties on the unskilled and the semiskilled, it could have the impact of permanently increasing the population of the other America.

Even more explosive is the possibility that people who participated in the gains of the thirties and the forties will be pulled back down into poverty. Today the mass-production industries where unionization made such a difference are contracting. Jobs are being destroyed. In the process, workers who had achieved a certain level of wages, who had won working conditions in the shop, are suddenly confronted with impoverishment. This is particularly true for anyone over forty years of age and for members of minority groups. Once their job is abolished, their chances of ever getting similar work are very slim.

It is too early to say whether or not this phenomenon is temporary, or whether it represents a massive retrogression that will swell the numbers of the poor. To a large extent, the answer to this question will be determined by the political response of the United States in the sixties. If serious and massive action is not undertaken, it may be necessary for statisticians to add some old-fashioned, pre-welfare-state poverty to the misery of the other America.

Poverty in the 1960s is invisible and it is new, and both these factors make it more tenacious. It is more isolated and politically powerless than ever before. It is laced with ironies, not the least of which is that many of the poor view progress upside-down, as a menace and a threat to their lives. . . .

II

Beauty can be a mask for ugliness. That is what happens in the Appalachians.

Driving through this area, particularly in the spring or the fall, one perceives the loveliness, the openness, the high hills, streams, and lush growth. Indeed, the people themselves are captivated by their mountain life. They cling to their patches of land and their way of living. Many of them refuse to act "reasonably"; they stay even though misery is their lot.

It is not just the physical beauty that blinds the city man to the reality of these hills. The people are mountain folk. They are of old American stock, many of them Anglo-Saxon, and old traditions still survive among them. Seeing in them a romantic image of mountain life as independent, self-reliant, and athletic, a tourist could pass through these valleys and observe only quaintness. But not quite: for suddenly the mountain vista will reveal slashed, scarred hills and dirty little towns living under the shadow of decaying mining buildings.

The irony is deep, for everything that turns the landscape into an idyl for the urban traveler conspires to hold the people down. They suffer terribly at the hands of beauty.

Though the steep slopes and the narrow valleys are a charming sight, they are also the basis of a highly unproductive agriculture. The very geography is an anachronism in a technological society. Even if the farmers had the money, machines would not make much difference. As it is, the people literally scratch their half-livings from the difficult soil.

The seasons are vivid here. The tourist perceives this in the brilliance of spring, the bracing air of fall, the lush charm of summer. The tourist will not, of course, come here in the winter. Yet the intensity of the weather also means a short growing season. The land is resistant, and even unapproachable for great portions of the year.

But, the traveler may say, granted that there is a low level of income, isn't it still true that these folk have escaped the anxiety and the rigors of industrialism? Perhaps this myth once held a real truth. Now it is becoming more false every day. Increasingly, these are a beaten people, sunk in their poverty and deprived of hope. In this, they are like the slum dwellers of the city.

During the decade of the fifties, 1,500,000 people left the Appalachians. They were the young, the more adventurous, those who sought a new life. As a result of their exile, they made colonies of poverty in the city. One newspaper in Cincinnati talked of "our 50,000 refugees." Those who were left behind tended to be the older people, the less imaginative, the defeated. A whole area, in the words of a Maryland State study, became suffused with a "mood of apathy and despair."

This, for example, is how one reporter saw the independent yeomanry, the family farmers, and the laid-off industrial workers in the Appalachians: "Whole counties are precariously held together by a flour-and-dried-milk paste of surplus foods. The school lunch program provides many children with their only decent meals. Relief has become a way of life for a once proud and aggressively independent mountain people. The men who are no longer needed in the mines and the farmers who cannot compete with the mechanized agriculture of the Midwest have themselves become surplus commodities in the mountains."

Perhaps the most dramatic statistical statement of the plight of these men and women occurred in a study produced in Kentucky: that, as the sixties begin, 85 percent of the youth in this area would have to leave or else accept a life of grinding poverty. And a place without the young is a place without hope, without future.

Indeed, it is difficult to find any basis for optimism in this area. And yet, the various states of the Appalachians have come up with a program to offer some basic relief for the incredible plight of these people. Still, the very candor of their analysis defeats much of their purpose. One study, for instance, estimated that the Appalachians would need slightly more than one million new jobs if the area were to begin catching up with the rest of America. As of now, the vicious circle is at work making such a development unlikely: the mountains are beautiful and quaint and economically backward; the youth are leaving; and because of this poverty modern industry hesitates to come in and agriculture becomes even more marginal.

The roads are bad. Less than half of the population has had more than one or two years of high school. There is no human backlog of ready skills. The industrial incentive is for the low-paying, manpower-exploiting sharp operator. In the Appalachians this has meant the coming of textiles and apparels plants. (This is the classic association of low-paying industry with low-paying agriculture.)

Some things could be done. The roads could be improved and brought up to the standards required by modern industry— but only with Federal grants. Education and the cultural life of the area could be improved. There could be regional planning. (Significantly, the Kennedy Task Force on depressed areas recommended only one regional planning commission specifically and by name: for the Appalachians.) The whole structure of backwardness and decay, including bad public facilities, lack of water control, and the struggle with soil erosion, could be dealt with.

But such a program would be truly massive. It would require a basic commitment from the Federal Government. As the sixties began, the nation cheered a Depressed-Areas law which provided that the bulk of the funds should be spent in the South. Yet even its proponents admitted that the money for bringing in industry was minimal, and the allocation for retraining and education almost miniscule. It seems likely that the Appalachians will continue going down, that its lovely mountains and hills will house a culture of poverty and despair, and that it will become a reservation for the old, the apathetic, and the misfits.

For the city traveler driving through the mountains, the beauty will persist. So too, probably, will the myth about the sturdy, happy, and uncomplicated mountain folk. But behind all this charm, nestled on the steep hills and in the plunging valleys, lies an incredible social ugliness. . . .

III

One of the most distinctive things about most American cities is that it is not easy to distinguish social class on the streets. Clothes are cheap and increasingly standardized. The old "proletarian" dress—the cloth hat, the work clothes—either disappeared or else was locked up at the shop.

But when you enter Stockton, California, a center of migrant labor, this generalization fails. The field hands are obvious. All wear broad-brimmed hats; all are tanned, sometimes to a mahogany color; and all are in levis and work clothes. The middle class, the shopkeepers, and practically everybody else, are familiar Americans from any place.

Black poverty, Charlotte, North Carolina. *(David Cupp)*

city dwellers. The migrants around Stockton are heavily "Anglo" (both white and not Mexican), yet it is almost as if one were looking at two different races. The field hands wear their calling like a skin.

Stockton is a town of about 90,000 permanent residents. At high tide of the migrant invasion, there are more pickers than regular inhabitants. Almost a hundred thousand of them are in the area. They sleep where they can, some in the open. They eat where they can (and sometimes when they can).

California agriculture is the richest in the nation, and its agricultural suffering is perhaps the most spectacular. People work ten-, eleven-, and twelve-hour days in temperatures over one hundred degrees. Sometimes there is no drinking water; sometimes big common barrels of it are used. Women and children work on ladders and with hazardous machinery. (The Industrial Welfare Commission was told in 1961 that 500 children are maimed each year.) Babies are brought to the fields and are placed in "cradles" of wood boxes.

In the Stockton area about a third of the migrants are "Anglos," another third, Mexican-American. Around 15 per cent are Filipinos, and the rest are Negroes. (On the East Coast the migrants are much more heavily Negro.) And everywhere, threatening the American workers, are the Braceros, the imported Mexican laborers.

I drove past the fields with an organizer from the Agricultural Workers Organizing Committee of the AFL-CIO. He had grown up in this area and had known the fields as a child. As we passed each farm, he told me who was working there. Whenever he saw a group of Braceros, his voice became sharp.

"They are poor people," he said. "That is why they come

here, and work for so little. The growers get them cheap, and they know that the union can't organize them. So that keeps the rates down for the American workers. We don't want to hurt these poor people; they are like us. But it is no way to help them to hurt us. Let the Government work out some kind of a deal with Mexico for aid, or something like that. But let the American farm workers have a decent living without having to hate other poor people."

In Stockton, as in most of the migrant centers in the area, the workers "shape up" at three o'clock in the morning. There is a milling mass of human beings down by skid row, and they are there to sell themselves in the market place. The various hiring men chant out piece-work prices or hourly rates. In some of these places in California, there is a regular exchange with a voice rasping over the public-address system, announcing the going rate for a hundred-weight or a basket of fruit.

Once the worker is taken on, he is driven to the field where he will work. The trucks are packed; safety regulations are often non-existent; and there is no pay for the time spent en route. South from Stockton, along the Riviera coast near Santa Barbara, I remember seeing a most incredible contrast: the lush line of beach, coastal mountains, and rich homes, and, passing by, a truckload of stolid-faced Mexican-Americans coming back from work.

The statistics of migrant wages are low enough—they will be described shortly—yet they conceal some of the misery of this life. The pay is often according to piece rates. The good fruit picker might even make a good sum on one of his better days. But behind him are women and children who may be toiling for $0.50 an hour or less, who receive for ten hours in the hot,

broiling sun less than $5.00. In 1960 and 1961, union pressure around Stockton drove the rates up somewhat, but the gain was relative. The workers are low paid, and in competition with themselves on piece rates.

These indignities are not, of course, confined to the fields. In Stockton many of the Anglos live in cheap skid-row hotels (which is better than being out in the open, but still miserable enough). They eat at the Missions. When a flood of Braceros come in and there is a layoff, it is common for men to go without food for two or three days.

Far to the South, in the Imperial Valley of California, the living is, if anything, more terrible than in Stockton. A friend of mine wrote me of some of the people there. One family he described lives in a shack and sleeps on flattened pasteboard boxes on the floor. There is no heat, and since the man of the house has been driven out of the fields by Braceros there is often no food. The mother is breast-feeding her infant—and her four-year-old as well, since that is the only way he will eat. (In this detail there is an eerie echo of the occasion in *The Grapes of Wrath* when the young girl breastfeeds a starving Okie man. That scene was set almost thirty years ago.)

Or there is the fruit tramp in southern California who was hired to pick tangerines. He works in a gang that includes Braceros, but the pickings were slim in his section of the grove. His job kept him on a ladder all day. He and his wife are charged $18 a week for a one-room shack, with the sink stopped up, and a community stand-in-line privy. The store from which he and the other workers buy their food is owned by the grower.

And yet, incredibly enough, one occasionally encounters a pride of métier, a spirit of loving the land, among some of the

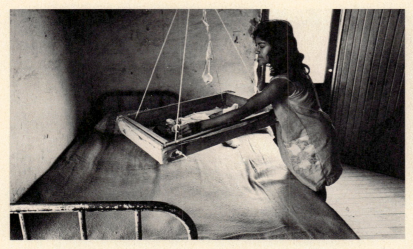

(Marcia Keegan)

migrants. I talked to one of the Filipino workers in Stockton, and he told me of his community which had been there for some years. The Filipinos work together in crews, and have developed speed and efficiency. As a result, they make much more money than the rest of the workers. They are, to be sure, a minority group and suffer discrimination. (The Filipino field hand and I ate in a cheap Chinese restaurant in Stockton; there is a sort of alliance between the minorities.) But, as so often happens at the bottom of society, they look down upon the other workers, and think of them as careless and irresponsible.

Or there was an Anglo worker who lived the year round in Stockton. I asked him why he stayed there, and he said: "It just gets in your blood. I been quitting for twelve years now."

Still, the impression of the California migrants is not one of romance and élan. It is, rather, a sight of near medieval poverty in the midst, of lush abundance....

IV

Every Negro ghetto in America is different.

In Atlanta on a soft evening, everyone sits out on the porches of the rooming houses and on the stoops. There is an excited, persistent hum of voices. In Los Angeles, the Negro slum sprawls like everything else. The only obvious thing about it is that the streets, like the streets of the poor everywhere, are badly paved. It takes a little while to learn that the innocent, individual houses are often as rotten inside as any tenement. In Chicago, on the South Side, there is the unmistakable feeling of the great metropolitan ghetto: high buildings, honky tonks, and on the fringes, a sense of tension in

(Editorial Photocolor Archives)

one of the most explosive racial situations in the country.

Harlem is different. It is not the solidest or the best organized Negro community (in Chicago, Negro political representation came a full decade before that in New York). It is not the most depressed, even in the New York area. That honor belongs to Bedford-Stuyvesant. But Harlem is the Negro capital, much as New York is an unofficial American capital. It is big, teeming, and brassy. It is where Marcus Garvey established the center of his Empire in Exile, where Joe Louis was cheered after he knocked out Max Schmeling, and where Fidel Castro stayed.

Yet Harlem is essentially the same as any other Negro ghetto. It exists in the midst of a city where liberal rhetoric is required for election to practically every public office. There is no legal segregation; there are a Fair Employment Practices Law, a State Commission Against Discrimination, a municipal Open Occupancy Law. And yet the white man is still way ahead, and in this Harlem is like any community of Negroes in the United States.

To live in Harlem is to be a

(Neal Slavin)

Negro; to be a Negro is to participate in a culture of poverty and fear that goes far deeper than any law for or against discrimination. In this sense Harlem could well be a warning: that after the racist statutes are all struck down, after legal equality has been achieved in the schools and in the courts, there remains the profound institutionalized and abiding wrong that white America has worked on the Negro for so long.

Harlem has a discriminatory economy, a discriminatory psychology, a discriminatory society. Like the young Negroes of *The Cool World,* it watches all the wonderful movies about America with a certain bitter cynicism.

If the population density in some of Harlem's worst blocks obtained in the rest of New York City, the entire population of the United States could fit into three of New York's boroughs.—CIVIL RIGHTS COMMISSION, 1959

Negro poverty is unique in every way. It grows out of a long American history, and it expresses itself in a subculture that is built up on an interlocking base of economic and racial injustice. It is a fact imposed from without, from white America.

And yet, there is the uniqueness of Negro poverty as an impression, as a walk through the streets of the ghetto will reveal. Here one sees the faces and attitudes behind the statistics: the fear, the food, the religion, the politics of Negro poverty. Looking at this surface of Negro life first, one gains a human perspective on the grim economic figures and occupational data that lie behind it.

Still, a few statistics are necessary for even the most impressionistic description of Harlem, and these can be dealt with briefly. In the mid-fifties (the last point when figures were available), there were almost 1,000,-000 Negroes in New York. In this group, 50 percent of the families had incomes under $4,000 a year (as compared with 20 per-

cent of the white families). On Home Relief and Aid to Dependent Children, Negroes formed the majority—and they were 40 percent of all the people who received public assistance. Negro unemployment in the city was somewhat more than double that of the whites, and wages were around half of what white workers got. This affected every other aspect of life: in 1959 the infant mortality rate in central Harlem was 45.3 per thousand (the white district with the lowest rate had 15.4 per thousand).

The statistics could be piled on and on, but the point is obvious: Harlem, as well as every other Negro ghetto, is a center of poverty, of manual work, of sickness, and of every typical disability which America's underdeveloped areas suffer. It is on this very real and material base that the ghetto builds its unique culture.

There is, on the very surface of Harlem life, the imminence of the Man.

The Man is white. He has

many guises: as policeman, as judge, as rent collector—as authority made tangible. He is to be feared and hated, for the law is especially swift and hard upon the crimes and vices that grow within these crowded, littered streets. Ultimately, he becomes anyone with a white skin. ("Ofay," the old Negro slang term for a white, is foe in pig Latin.) Because of this, Harlem is a place that is suspicious for all outsiders from the world of white America. It is stunted and sick, and the bread of its poverty has the taste of hatred and fear.

When I was doing research for this book in Harlem, I was walking around with a notebook. I stopped on Lenox Avenue to take down some prices in the window of a barbecue joint. When I looked up, everyone was watching me. I knew what they thought, and turned to the two men nearest me and said, "I'm not a cop." When I walked over and started to tell them that I was a writer, one accepted the story. The other listened for a moment, and then said, "I still think he's from the police." Then they were gone.

Part of the reason for this attitude is that there is more obvious crime in Harlem. The numbers game remains a community pastime; streetwalking still flourishes on 125th Street; and marijuana is easy to get. These things are not, of course, "natural" to the Negro. They are the by-products of a ghetto which has little money, much unemployment, and a life to be lived in the streets. Because of them, and because the white man is so ready to believe crime in the Negro, fear is basic to the ghetto. It gives Negro poverty a quality of psychological depth and torment that is unique among all the impoverished people in the United States.

So it is that Malcolm X, Harlem's Muslim leader, can boast that he can assemble a couple of hundred followers within a few minutes after any act of racial violence (or of alleged racial violence). Harlem, for all its brashness, for all the ubiquitous rhythms of rock 'n' roll, is afraid. And for good reason. The white has been the Man, and in many cases he still is.

Another aspect of this fear is the way the Negro in Harlem is a second-class citizen in his own neighborhood. Walking down 125th Street, one of the most obvious, surface impressions is that Harlem's economy is white. Practically all the stores are presided over by white men, and this has been true for years. (The situation is not nearly so extreme in other Negro ghettos, for instance in Chicago.) During the riot in the forties, the rage of the people was directed against these shops—so much so that a legendary Chinese is alleged to have put up a sign, "Me Colored Too." When the proprietor (or salesman, rent agent, or other contact) is Jewish as well as white, this has been a source of Harlem anti-Semitism. The most recent variations on this theme are played by Muslim orators who relate it to a pro-Arab, anti-Israel political line.

This aspect of the Negro ghetto is also unique. In the Puerto Rican section, which borders on Harlem, the situation is quite different. Almost as soon as the Puerto Ricans arrive, Spanish-speaking shops dot the avenue. And this was true even before the big migration of Puerto Ricans in the postwar period. Writing of Harlem in 1940, Claude McKay traced the pattern all the way back to the twenties, when the Puerto Ricans were only a fringe of Harlem.

Why is this so? The sociologist Nathan Glazer has suggested that the Negro suffers from being in, but not of, American society. There are no traditions of the "old country" that bind Harlem as a ghetto. This is the home of America's internal aliens. The people participate in the consumption cult of the white world —the Negro is an "exaggerated American" Mydral said, and Harlem is Hollywood carried to its logical conclusion the poet Thomas Merton wrote—yet the Negroes are poor. They do not huddle together around a language and a common memory from overseas, saving, planning, waiting for the breakthrough, isolated from the lures of easy life in the magazines and on television.

That is part of it. Another part is that Harlem is quite literally the center of a migration (as every ghetto is). In 1950 almost two-thirds of the nonwhite Americans moved (as compared to a rate of 13 percent for the entire nation). The Negro in Harlem, as Ralph Ellison has written of him, is often "shot up from the South into the busy city like wild jacks-in-the box broken loose from our springs—so sudden that our gait becomes like that of deep-sea divers suffering from the bends."

A white welfare worker tells of the children when they first begin school. They show off their books; they are interested and friendly. But then, in a few years, they learn. Their schools are crowded; the instruction is inferior; and the neighborhood is omnipresent and more powerful than the classroom.

These are only some of the factors, but they all point in the same direction: Harlem is not only afraid; more than that, Harlem does not even own itself; the Negro is not master even when he has retreated into the ghetto far from white eyes. The Man is still with him.

If all the discriminatory laws in the United States were immediately repealed, race would still remain as one of the most pressing moral and political problems in the nation. Negroes and other minorities are not simply the victims of a series of iniquitous statutes. The American economy, the American society, the American unconscious are all racist. If all the laws were framed to provide equal opportunity , a majority of the Negroes would not be able to take full advantage of the change. There would still be a vast, silent, and automatic system directed against men and women of color.

To belong to a racial minority is to be poor, but poor in a special way. The fear, the lack of self-confidence, the haunting, these have been described. But they, in turn, are the expressions of the most institutionalized poverty in the United States, the most vicious of the vicious circles. In a sense, the Negro is classically the "other" American, degraded and frustrated at every turn and not just because of laws.

There are sympathetic and concerned people who do not understand how deeply America has integrated racism into its structure. Given time, they argue, the Negroes will rise in the society like the Irish, the Jews, the Italians, and all the rest. But this notion misses two decisive facts: that the Negro is colored, and no other group in the United States has ever faced such a problem, and that the Negro of today is an internal migrant who will face racism wherever he goes, who cannot leave his oppression behind as if it were a czar or a potato famine. To be equal, the Negro requires something much more profound than a way "into" the society; he needs a transformation of some of the basic institutions of the society.

The Negro is poor because he is black; that is obvious enough. But, perhaps more importantly, the Negro is black because he is poor. The laws against color can be removed, but that will leave the poverty that is the historic and institutionalized consequence of color. As long as this is the case, being born a Negro will continue to be the most profound disability that the United States imposes upon a citizen.

Perhaps the quickest way to point up the racism of the American economy is to recall a strange case of jubilation.

Late in 1960 the Department of Labor issued a study, "The Economic Situation of Negroes in the United States." It noted that in 1939, nonwhite workers earned, on the average, 41 percent as much as whites, and that by 1958 their wages had climbed to 58 percent of that of whites. Not a little elation greeted this announcement. Some of the editorialists cited these statistics as indicating that slow and steady progress was being made. (At this rate, the Negro would reach parity with the white some time well after the year 2000.)

To begin with, the figures were somewhat more optimistic than the reality. Part of the Negro gain reflected the shift of rural Negroes to cities and Southern Negroes to the North. In both cases, the people involved increased their incomes by going into a more prosperous section of the country. But within each area their relative position remained the same: at the bottom. Then, the statistics take a depression year (1939) as a base for comparison, and contrast it to a year of recession (1958) . This tended to exaggerate the advance because Negroes in 1939 were particularly victimized.

Another important aspect of the problem was obscured by the sweeping comparisons most editorialists made between the 1939 and 1958 figures. Even the Department of Labor statistics themselves indicate that the major gain was made during World War II (the increase from 1939 to 1947 was from 41.4 percent to 54.3 of the white wage). In the postwar period the rate of advance slowed to a walk. Moreover, most of the optimism was based upon figures for Negro men. When the women are included, and when one takes a median family income from the Current Population Reports, Negroes rose from 51 percent of white family income in 1947 to 57 percent in 1952—and then declined back to the 1947 level by 1959.

But even without these qualifications, the fact is stark enough: the United States found cause for celebration in the announcement that Negro workers had reached 58 percent of the wage level of their white co-workers. This situation is deeply

imbedded in the very structure of American society.

Negroes in the United States are concentrated in the worst, dirtiest, lowest-paying jobs. A third continue to live in the rural South, most of them merely subsisting within a culture of poverty and a society of open terror. A third live in Southern cities and a third in Northern cities, and these have bettered their lot compared to the sharecroppers. But they are still the last hired and the first fired, and they are particularly vulnerable to recessions.

Thus, according to the Department of Labor in 1960, 4 percent of Negro employees were "professional, technical and kindred workers" (compared to 11.3 percent for the whites); 2.7 percent were "managers, officials and proprietors" (the white figure is 14.6 percent). In short, at the top of the economic structure there were 6.7 percent of the Negroes—and 25.9 percent of the whites. And this, in itself, represented considerable *gains* over the past two decades.

Going down the occupational scale, Negroes are primarily grouped in the bottom jobs. In 1960, 20 percent of the whites had high-skill industrial jobs, while the Negro share of this classification was 9 percent. Semiskilled mass production workers and laborers constituted around 48 percent of the Negro male population (and 25.3 percent of the white males). Negro women are the victims of a double discrimination. According to a New York State study, Negro female income as a percentage of white actually declined between 1949 and 1954 (and, in 1960, over a third of Negro women were still employed as domestics).

In part, this miserable structure of the Negro work force is an inheritance of the past. It reflects what happens to a people who have been systematically oppressed and denied access to skill

and opportunity. If this completely defined the problem, there would be a basis for optimism. One could assume that the Negro would leave behind the mess of pottage bequeathed him by white America and move into a better future. But that is not the case. For the present position of the Negro in the economy has been institutionalized. Unless something basic is done, it will reproduce itself for years to come.

Take, as an example, the problem of automation. This has caused "structural" unemployment through the American work force, that is, the permanent destruction of jobs rather than cyclical layoffs. When this happens, the blow falls disproportionately upon the Negro. As the last significant group to enter the factory, the Negroes have low seniority (if they are lucky enough to be in union occupations), and they are laid off first. As one of the least skilled groups in the work force, they will have the hardest time getting another job. The "older" Negro (over forty) may well be condemned to job instability for the rest of his life.

All of this is immediate and automatic. It is done without the intervention of a single racist, yet it is a profound part of racism in the United States.

However, more is involved than the inevitable working of an impersonal system. The Negro lives in the other America of poverty for many reasons, and one of them is conscious racism reinforcing institutional patterns of the economy. In 1960, according to the report of Herbert Hill, Labor Secretary of the National Association for the Advancement of Colored People, Negroes made up only 1.69 percent of the total number of apprentices in the economy. The exact figure offered by Hill has been disputed; the shocking fact which he describes is agreed upon by everyone. This means that Negroes are denied

access precisely to those jobs that are not low-paying and vulnerable to recession.

The main cause of this problem is the attitude of management, which fundamentally determines hiring policy. But in the case of apprenticeship programs, the labor movement and the Federal and state agencies involved also bear part of the responsibility. In the AFL-CIO, it is the politically conservative unions from the building trades who are the real stumbling block; the mass-production unions of the CIO have some bad areas, but on the whole they pioneered in bringing Negroes into the plants and integrating local organizations.

With the companies, one of the real difficulties in dealing with this structure of racism is that it is invisible. Here is a huge social fact, yet no one will accept responsibility for it. When questioned as to why there are no Negroes in sales, or in the office, the personnel man will say that he himself has nothing against Negroes. The problem, he will claim, is with subordinates who would revolt if Negroes were brought into their department, and with superiors who impose the policy. This response is standard up and down the line. The subordinates and the superiors make the same assertion.

Indeed, one of the difficulties in fighting against racist practices in the American economy is the popularity of a liberal rhetoric. Practically no one, outside of convinced white supremacists in the South, will admit to discriminatory policies. So it is that the Northern Negro has, in one sense, a more personally frustrating situation than his Southern brother. In Dixie, Jim Crow is personified, an actual living person who speaks in the accents of open racism. In the rest of the country, everybody is against discrimination for the record, and Jim Crow is a vast impersonal system that keeps the Negro down.

JAMES BALDWIN
The Fire Next Time

The 1960s abounded with apocalyptic prophecies. From the
time of the missile crisis, and even before, a sense of
threatening catastrophe permeated American public discourse.
James Baldwin's *The Fire Next Time*—the very title refers to
the end of the world—suggests why this millenarian mentality
reached so wide a public. Baldwin envisioned the small but
rapidly growing Black Muslim sect as a harbinger of potential
violence, hatred, and racial warfare on a large scale that could
"precipitate chaos and ring down the curtain on the American
dream." He linked these trends in the black community in
America with the rising tide of black aspiration in the world
and the declining influence of European civilization. He saw the
fragility of the coalition between blacks and liberals in the civil
rights movement and glimpsed the disorder that would attend the
failure of its gallant efforts. And, like the prophets of old, he
called for a community of love between black and white, which,
he himself acknowledged, seemed impossible.

Prophets are not without honor—even in their own country.
Baldwin's message, with those of other writers and leaders,
reached tens of thousands, and men of good will of both races
performed deeds—at Birmingham and Selma as well as in
Harlem and in the Congress—that brought more progress in one
decade than had been achieved in the previous century,
destroying the edifice of legal segregation and improving the
lives of large numbers of black—and white—Americans.
Nevertheless, in spite of the vital advances of the era, Baldwin's
vision of a nation in chaos came true in large measure:
a people who genuinely gave a great deal but could not give
themselves learned the truth of the hard message that
Baldwin delivered.

During a recent Muslim rally, George Lincoln Rockwell, the chief of the American Nazi party, made a point of contributing about twenty dollars to the cause, and he and Malcolm X decided that, racially speaking, anyway, they were in complete agreement. The glorification of one race and the consequent debasement of another—or others —always has been and always will be a recipe for murder. There is no way around this. If one is permitted to treat any group of people with special disfavor because of their race or the color of their skin, there is no limit to what one will force them to endure, and, since the entire race has been mysteriously indicted, no reason not to attempt to destroy it root and branch. This is precisely what the Nazis attempted. Their only originality lay in the means they used. It is scarcely worthwhile to attempt remembering how many times the sun has looked down on the slaughter of the innocents. I am very much concerned that American Negroes achieve their freedom here in the United States. But I am also concerned for their dignity, for the health of their souls, and must oppose any attempt that Negroes may make to do to others what has been done to them. I think I know—we see it around us every day—the spiritual wasteland ·to which that road leads. It is so simple a fact and one that is so hard, apparently, to grasp: *Whoever debases others is debasing himself.* That is not a mystical statement but a most realistic one, which is proved by the eyes of any Alabama sheriff—and I would not like to see Negroes ever arrive at so wretched a condition.

Now, it is extremely unlikely that Negroes will ever rise to power in the United States, because they are only approximately a ninth of this nation. They are not in the position of the Africans, who are attempting to reclaim their land and break the colonial yoke and recover from the colonial experience. The Negro situation is dangerous in a different way, both for the Negro qua Negro and for the country of which he forms so troubled and troubling a part. The American Negro is a unique creation; he has no counterpart anywhere, and no predecessors. The Muslims react to this fact by referring to the Negro as "the so-called American Negro" and substituting for the names inherited from slavery the letter "X." It is a fact that every American Negro bears a name that originally belonged to the white man whose chattel he was. I am called Baldwin because I was either sold by my African tribe or kidnapped out of it into the hands of a white Christian named Baldwin, who forced me to kneel at the foot of the cross. I am, then, both visibly and legally the descendant of slaves in a white, Protestant country,

James Baldwin.
(Danny Lyon, Magnum)

and this is what it means to be an American Negro, this is who he is—a kidnapped pagan, who was sold like an animal and treated like one, who was once defined by the American Constitution as "three-fifths" of a man, and who, according to the Dred Scott decision, had no rights that a white man was bound to respect. And today, a hundred years after his technical emancipation, he remains—with the possible exception of the American Indian—the most despised creature in his country. Now, there is simply no possibility of a real change in the Negro's situation without the most radical and far-reaching changes in the American political and social structure. And it is clear that white Americans are not simply unwilling to effect these changes; they are, in the main, so slothful have they become, unable even to envision them. It must be added that the Negro himself no longer believes in the good faith of white Americans—if, indeed, he ever could have. What the Negro *has* discovered, and on an international level, is that power to intimidate which he has always had privately but hitherto could manipulate only privately—for private ends often, for limited ends always. And therefore when the country speaks of a "new" Negro, which it has been doing every hour on the hour for decades, it is not really referring to a change in the Negro, which, in any case, it is quite incapable of assessing, but only to a new difficulty in keeping him in his place, to the fact that it encounters him (again! again!) barring yet another door to its spiritual and social ease. This is probably, hard and odd as it may sound, the most important thing that one human being can do for another—it is certainly *one* of the most important things; hence the torment and necessity of love —and this is the enormous con-

tribution that the Negro has made to this otherwise shapeless and undiscovered country. Consequently, white Americans are in nothing more deluded than in supposing that Negroes could ever have imagined that white people would "give" them anything. It is rare indeed that people give. Most people guard and keep; they suppose that it is they themselves and what they identify with themselves that they are guarding and keeping, whereas what they are actually guarding and keeping is their system of reality and what they assume themselves to be. One can give nothing whatever without giving oneself—that is to say, risking oneself. If one cannot risk oneself, then one is simply incapable of giving. And, after all, one can give freedom only by setting someone free. This, in the case of the Negro, the American republic has never become sufficiently mature to do. White Americans have contented themselves with gestures that are now described as "tokenism." For hard example, white Americans congratulate themselves on the 1954 Supreme Court decision outlawing segregation in the schools; they suppose, in spite of the mountain of evidence that has since accumulated to the contrary, that this was proof of a change of heart —or, as they like to say, progress. Perhaps. It all depends on how one reads the word "progress." Most of the Negroes I know do not believe that this immense concession would ever have been made if it had not been for the competition of the Cold War, and the fact that Africa was clearly liberating herself and therefore had, for political reasons, to be wooed by the descendants of her former masters. Had it been a matter of love or justice, the 1954 decision would surely have occurred sooner; were it not for the realities of power in this

difficult era, it might very well not have occurred yet. This seems an extremely harsh way of stating the case—ungrateful, as it were—but the evidence that supports this way of stating it is not easily refuted. I myself do not think that it can be refuted at all. In any event, the sloppy and fatuous nature of American good will can never be relied upon to deal with hard problems. These have been dealt with, when they have been dealt with at all, out of necessity— and in political terms, anyway, necessity means concessions made in order to stay on top. I think this is a fact, which it serves no purpose to deny, *but, whether it is a fact or not, this is what the black population of the world, including black Americans, really believe.* The word "independence" in Africa and the word "integration" here are almost equally meaningless; that is, Europe has not yet left Africa, and black men here are not yet free. And both of these last statements are undeniable facts, related facts, containing the gravest implications for us all. The Negroes of this country may never be able to rise to power, but they are very well placed indeed to precipitate chaos and ring down the curtain on the American dream.

This has everything to do, of course, with the nature of that dream and with the fact that we Americans, of whatever color, do not dare examine it and are far from having made it a reality. There are too many things we do not wish to know about ourselves. People are not, for example, terribly anxious to be equal (equal, after all, to what and to whom?) but they love the idea of being superior. And this human truth has an especially grinding force here, where identity is almost impossible to achieve and people are perpetually attempting to find their feet on the shifting sands of status. (Consider the history of labor in a country in which, spiritually speaking, there are no workers, only candidates for the hand of the boss's daughter.) Furthermore, I have met only a very few people—and most of these were not Americans—who had any real desire to be free. Freedom is hard to bear. It can be objected that I am speaking of political freedom in spiritual terms, but the political institutions of any nation are always menaced and are ultimately controlled by the spiritual state of that nation. We are controlled here by our confusion, far more than we know, and the American dream has therefore become something much more closely resembling a nightmare, on the private, domestic, and international levels. Privately, we cannot stand our lives and dare not examine them; domestically, we take no responsibility for (and no pride in) what goes on in our country; and, internationally, for many millions of people, we are an unmitigated disaster. Whoever doubts this last statement has only to open his ears, his heart, his mind, to the testimony of—for example—any Cuban peasant or any Spanish poet, and ask himself what *he* would feel about us if *he* were the victim of our performance in pre-Castro Cuba or in Spain. We defend our curious role in Spain by referring to the Russian menace and the necessity of protecting the free world. It has not occurred to us that we have simply been mesmerized by Russia, and that the only real advantage Russia has in what we think of as a struggle between the East and West is the moral history of the Western world. Russia's secret weapon is the bewilderment and despair and hunger of millions of people of whose existence we are scarcely aware. The Russian Communists are not in the least concerned about these people. But our ignorance and

indecision have had the effect, if not of delivering them into Russian hands, of plunging them very deeply in the Russian shadow, for which effect—and it is hard to blame them—the most articulate among them, and the most oppressed as well, distrust us all the more. Our power and our fear of change help bind these people to their misery and bewilderment, and insofar as they find this state intolerable we are intolerably menaced. For if they find their state intolerable, but are too heavily oppressed to change it, they are simply pawns in the hands of larger powers, which, in such a context, are always unscrupulous, and when, eventually, they do change their situation—as in Cuba—we are menaced more than ever, by the vacuum that succeeds all violent upheavals. We should certainly know by now that it is one thing to overthrow a dictator or repel an invader and quite another thing really to achieve a revolution. Time and time again, the people discover that they have merely betrayed themselves into the hands of yet another Pharaoh, who, since he was necessary to put the broken country together, will not let them go. Perhaps, people being the conundrums that they are, and having so little desire to shoulder the burden of their lives, this is what will always happen. But at the bottom of my heart I do not believe this. I think that people can be better than that, and I know that people can be better than they are. We are capable of bearing a great burden, once we discover that the burden is reality and arrive where reality is. Anyway, the point here is that we are living in an age of revolution, whether we will or no, and that America is the only Western nation with both the power and, as I hope to suggest, the experience that may help to make these revolutions real and mini-

mize the human damage. Any attempt we make to oppose these outbursts of energy is tantamount to signing our death warrant.

Behind what we think of as the Russian menace lies what we do not wish to face, and what white Americans do not face when they regard a Negro: reality—the fact that life is tragic. Life is tragic simply because the earth turns and the sun inexorably rises and sets, and one day, for each of us, the sun will go down for the last, last time. Perhaps the whole root of our trouble, the human trouble, is that we will sacrifice all the beauty of our lives, will imprison ourselves in totems, taboos, crosses, blood sacrifices, steeples, mosques, races, armies, flags, nations, in order to deny the fact of death, which is the only fact we have. It seems to me that one ought to rejoice in the *fact* of death—ought to decide, indeed, to *earn* one's death by confronting with passion the conundrum of life. One is responsible to life: It is the small beacon in that terrifying darkness from which we come and to which we shall return. One must negotiate this passage as notably as possible, for the sake of those who are coming after us. But white Americans do not believe in death, and this is why the darkness of my skin so intimidates them. And this is also why the presence of the Negro in this country can bring about its destruction. It is the responsibility of free men to trust and to celebrate what is constant—birth, struggle, and death are constant, and so is love, though we may not always think so—and to apprehend the nature of change, to be able and willing to change. I speak of change not on the surface but in the depths—change in the sense of renewal. But renewal becomes impossible if one supposes things to be constant that are not—safety, for example, or money, or power. One clings then to chimeras, by which one can only be betrayed, and the entire hope—the entire possibility—of freedom disappears. And by destruction I mean precisely the abdication by Americans of any effort really to be free. The Negro can precipitate this abdication because white Americans have never, in all their long history, been able to look on him as a man like themselves. This point need not be labored; it is proved over and over again by the Negro's continuing position here, and his indescribable struggle to defeat the stratagems that white Americans have used, and use, to deny him his humanity. America could have used in other ways the energy that both groups have expended in this conflict. America, of all the Western nations, has been best placed to prove the uselessness and the obsolescence of the concept of color. But it has not dared to accept this opportunity, or even to conceive of it as an opportunity. White Americans have thought of it as their shame, and have envied those more civilized and elegant European nations that were untroubled by the presence of black men on their shores. This is because white Americans have supposed "Europe" and "civilization" to be synonyms—which they are not—and have been distrustful of other standards and other sources of vitality, especially those produced in America itself, and have attempted to behave in all matters as though what was east for Europe was also east for them. What it comes to is that if we, who can scarcely be considered a white nation, persist in thinking of ourselves as one, we condemn ourselves, with the truly white nations, to sterility and decay, whereas if we could accept ourselves *as we are*, we might bring new life to the West-

ern achievements, and transform them. The price of this transformation is the unconditional freedom of the Negro; it is not too much to say that he, who has been so long rejected, must now be embraced, and at no matter what psychic or social risk. He is *the* key figure in his country, and the American future is precisely as bright or as dark as his. And the Negro recognizes this, in a negative way. Hence the question: Do I really *want* to be integrated into a burning house?

White Americans find it as difficult as white people elsewhere do to divest themselves of the notion that they are in possession of some intrinsic value that black people need, or want. And this assumption—which, for example, makes the solution to the Negro problem depend on the speed with which Negroes accept and adopt white standards—is revealed in all kinds of striking ways, from Bobby Kennedy's assurance that a Negro can become President in forty years to the unfortunate tone of warm congratulation with which so many liberals address their Negro equals. It is the Negro, of course, who is presumed to have become equal—an achievement that not only proves the comforting fact that perseverance has no color but also overwhelmingly corroborates the white man's sense of his own value. Alas, this value can scarcely be corroborated in any other way; there is certainly little enough in the white man's public or private life that one should desire to imitate. White men, at the bottom of their hearts, know this. Therefore, a vast amount of the energy that goes into what we call the Negro problem is produced by the white man's profound desire not to be judged by those who are not white, not to be seen as he is, and at the same time a vast amount of the white anguish is rooted in the white man's

equally profound need to be seen as he is, to be released from the tyranny of his mirror. All of us know, whether or not we are able to admit it, that mirrors can only lie, that death by drowning is all that awaits one there. It is for this reason that love is so desperately sought and so cunningly avoided. Love takes off the masks that we fear we cannot live without and know we cannot live within. I use the word "love" here not merely in the personal sense but as a state of being, or a state of grace—not in the infantile American sense of being made happy but in the tough and universal sense of quest and daring and growth. And I submit, then, that the racial tensions that menace Americans today have little to do with real antipathy—on the contrary, indeed—and are involved only symbolically with color. These tensions are rooted in the very same depths as those from which love springs, or murder. The white man's unadmitted—and apparently, to him, unspeakable—private fears and longings are projected onto the Negro. The only way he can be released from the Negro's tyrannical power over him is to consent, in effect, to become black himself, to become a part of that suffering and dancing country that he now watches wistfully from the heights of his lonely power and, armed with spiritual traveller's checks, visits surreptitiously after dark. How can one respect, let alone adopt, the values of a people who do not, on any level whatever, live the way they say they do, or the way they say they should? I cannot accept the proposition that the four-hundred-year travail of the American Negro should result merely in his attainment of the present level of the American civilization. I am far from convinced that being released from the African witch doctor was worthwhile if I am now—in order to support the moral contradictions and the spiritual aridity of my life—expected to become dependent on the American psychiatrist. It is a bargain I refuse. The only thing white people have that black people need, or should want, is power —and no one holds power forever. White people cannot, in the generality, be taken as models of how to live. Rather, the white man is himself in sore need of new standards, which will release him from his confusion and place him once again in fruitful communion with the depths of his own being. And I repeat: The price of the liberation of the white people is the liberation of the blacks—the total liberation, in the cities, in the towns, before the law, and in the mind. Why, for example —especially knowing the family as I do—I should *want* to marry your sister is a great mystery to me. But your sister and I have every right to marry if we wish to, and no one has the right to stop us. If she cannot raise me to her level, perhaps I can raise her to mine.

In short, we, the black and the white, deeply need each other here if we are really to become a nation—if we are really, that is, to achieve our identity, our maturity, as men and women. To create one nation has proved to be a hideously difficult task; there is certainly no need now to create two, one black and one white. But white men with far more political power than that possessed by the Nation of Islam movement have been advocating exactly this, in effect, for generations. If this sentiment is honored when it falls from the lips of Senator Byrd, then there is no reason it should not be honored when it falls from the lips of Malcolm X. And any Congressional committee wishing to investigate the latter must also be willing to investigate the former. They are expressing exactly the same sentiments and represent exactly the same danger. There is absolutely no reason to suppose that white people are better equipped to frame the laws by which I am to be governed than I am. It is entirely unacceptable that I should have no voice in the political affairs of my own country, for I am not a ward of America; I am one of the first Americans to arrive on these shores.

This past, the Negro's past, of rope, fire, torture, castration, infanticide, rape; death and humiliation; fear by day and night, fear as deep as the marrow of the bone; doubt that he was worthy of life, since everyone around him denied it; sorrow for his women, for his kinfolk, for his children, who needed his protection, and whom he could not protect; rage, hatred, and murder, hatred for white men so deep that it is often turned against him and his own, and made all love, all trust, all joy impossible—this past, this endless struggle to achieve and reveal and confirm a human identity, human authority, yet contains, for all its horror, something very beautiful. I do not mean to be sentimental about suffering—enough is certainly as good as a feast—but people who cannot suffer can never grow up, can never discover who they are. That man who is forced each day to snatch his manhood, his identity, out of the fire of human cruelty that rages to destroy it knows, if he survives his effort, and even if he does not survive it, something about himself and human life that no school on earth—and, indeed, no church—can teach. He achieves his own authority, and that is unshakable. This is because, in order to save his life, he is forced to look beneath appearances, to take nothing for granted, to hear the meaning behind the words. If one is continually surviving the worst that life can bring, one eventually ceases to be controlled by a fear of what life can bring; whatever it brings must be borne. And at this level of experience one's bitterness begins to be palatable, and hatred becomes too heavy a sack to carry. The apprehension of life here so briefly and inadequately sketched has been the experience of generations of Negroes, and it helps to explain how they have endured and how they have been able to produce children of kindergarten age who can walk through mobs to get to school. It demands great force and great cunning continually to assault the mighty and indifferent fortress of white supremacy, as Negroes in this country have done so long. It demands great spiritual resilience not to hate the hater whose foot is on your neck, and an even greater miracle of perception and charity not to teach your child to hate. The Negro boys and girls who are facing mobs today come out of a long line of improbable aristocrats— the only genuine aristocrats this country has produced. I say "this country" because their frame of reference was totally American. They were hewing out of the mountain of white supremacy the stone of their individuality. I have great respect for that unsung army of black men and women who trudged down back lanes and entered back doors, saying "Yes, sir" and "No, Ma'am" in order to acquire a new roof for the schoolhouse, new books, a new chemistry lab, more beds for the dormitories, more dormitories. They did not like saying "Yes, sir" and "No, Ma'am," but the country was in no hurry to educate Negroes, these black men and women knew that the job had to be done, and they put their pride in their pockets in order to do it. It is very hard to believe that they were in any way inferior to the white men and women who opened those back doors. It is very hard to believe that those men and women, raising their children, eating their greens, crying their curses, weeping their tears, singing their songs, making their love, as the sun rose, as the sun set, were in any way inferior to the white men and women who crept over to share these splendors after the sun went down. But we must avoid the European error; we must not suppose that, because the situation, the ways, the perceptions of black people so radically differed from those of whites, they were racially superior. I am proud of these people not because of their color but because of their intelligence and their spiritual force and their beauty. The country should be proud of them, too, but, alas, not many people in this country even know of their existence. And the reason for this ignorance is that a knowledge of the role these people played—and play—in American life would reveal more about America to Americans than Americans wish to know.

The American Negro has the great advantage of having never believed that collection of myths to which white Americans cling: that their ancestors were all freedom-loving heroes, that they were born in the greatest country the world has ever seen, or that Americans are invincible in battle and wise in peace, that Americans have always dealt honorably with Mexicans and Indians and all other neighbors or inferiors, that American men are the world's most direct and virile, that American women are pure. Negroes know far more about white Americans than that; it can almost be said, in fact, that they know about white Americans what parents—or, anyway, mothers—know about their children, and that they very often regard Americans

that way. And perhaps this attitude, held in spite of what they knew and have endured, helps to explain why Negroes, on the whole, and until lately, have allowed themselves to feel so little hatred. The tendency has really been, insofar as this was possible, to dismiss white people as the slightly mad victims of their own brainwashing. One watched the lives they led. One could not be fooled about that; one watched the things they did and the excuses that they gave themselves, and if a white man was really in trouble, deep trouble, it was to the Negro's door that he came. And one felt that if one had had that white man's worldly advantages, one would never have become as bewildered and as joyless and as thoughtlessly cruel as he. The Negro came to the white man for a roof or for five dollars or for a letter to the judge; the white man came to the Negro for love. But he was not often able to give what he came seeking. The price was too high; he had too much to lose. And the Negro knew this, too. When one knows this about a man, it is impossible for one to hate him, but unless he becomes a man—becomes equal—it is also impossible for one to love him. Ultimately, one tends to avoid him, for the universal characteristic of children is to assume that they have a monopoly on trouble, and therefore a monopoly on *you*. (Ask any Negro what he knows about the white people with whom he works. And then ask the white people with whom he works what they know about *him*.)

How can the American Negro past be used? It is entirely possible that this dishonored past will rise up soon to smite all of us. There are some wars, for example (if anyone on the globe is still mad enough to go to war) that the American Negro will not support, however many of

his people may be coerced—and there is a limit to the number of people any government can put in prison, and a rigid limit indeed to the practicality of such a course. A bill is coming in that I fear America is not prepared to pay. "The problem of the twentieth century," wrote W. E. B. Du Bois around sixty years ago, "is the problem of the color line." A fearful and delicate problem, which compromises, when it does not corrupt, all the American efforts to build a better world—here, there, or anywhere. It is for this reason that everything white Americans think they believe in must now be reexamined. What one would not like to see again is the consolidation of peoples on the basis of their color. But as long as we in the West place on color the value that we do, we make it impossible for the great unwashed to consolidate themselves according to any other principle. Color is not a human or a personal reality; it is a political reality. But this is a distinction so extremely hard to make that the West has not been able to make it yet. And at the center of this dreadful storm, this vast confusion, stand the black people of this nation, who must now share the fate of a nation that has never accepted them, to which they were brought in chains. Well, if this is so, one has no choice but to do all in one's power to change that fate, and at no matter what risk—eviction, imprisonment, torture, death. For the sake of one's children, in order to minimize the bill that *they* must pay, one must be careful not to take refuge in any delusion—and the value placed on the color of the skin is always and everywhere and forever a delusion. I know that what I am asking is impossible. But in our time, as in every time, the impossible is the least that one can demand—and one is, after all, emboldened by the spectacle of human history in general, and American Negro history in particular, for it testifies to nothing less than the perpetual achievement of the impossible.

When I was very young, and was dealing with my buddies in those wine- and urine-stained hallways, something in me wondered, *What will happen to all that beauty?* For black people, though I am aware that some of us, black and white, do not know it yet, are very beautiful. And when I sat at Elijah's table and watched the baby, the women, and the men, and we talked about God's—or Allah's—vengeance, I wondered, when that vengeance was achieved, *What will happen to all that beauty then?* I could also see that the intransigence and ignorance of the white world might make that vengeance inevitable—a vengeance that does not really depend on, and cannot really be executed by, any person or organization, and that cannot be prevented by any police force or army: historical vengeance, a cosmic vengeance, based on the law that we recognize when we say, "Whatever goes up must come down." And here we are, at the center of the arc, trapped in the gaudiest, most valuable, and most improbable water wheel the world has ever seen.

Everything now, we must assume, is in our hands; we have no right to assume otherwise. If we—and now I mean the relatively conscious whites and the relatively conscious blacks, who must, like lovers, insist on, or create, the consciousness of the others—do not falter in our duty now, we may be able, handful that we are, to end the racial nightmare, and achieve our country, and change the history of the world. If we do not now dare everything, the fulfillment of that prophecy, re-created from the Bible in song by a slave, is upon us: *God gave Noah the rainbow sign, No more water, the fire next time!*

CLARK KERR
The Uses of the University

Clark Kerr, for many years Chancellor of the University of California, was forced out of that position in a cross fire between conservative regents and radical students. Previously, this first major casualty of the academic wars of the sixties provided ammunition for both sides in his Godkin lectures of 1963, published as *The Uses of the University*. Kerr carefully described the vast transformation that the universities had undergone since World War II. The "knowledge industry" had become the growth center of the economy; the college professor had risen to a position of importance in every phase of American life; the federal government had become the great patron of the universities; the older, undergraduate teaching function had suffered under the society's demand for the products of research. In fact, Kerr asserted, the changes were of a magnitude sufficient to warrant a new term for the great establishments of higher education, and he offered the neologism "multiversity" to describe the new and complicated institution that had emerged.

Kerr recognized that the process he was describing had adverse effects on the student body and he detected signs of an "incipient revolt" over poor teaching, too many rules, and the impersonality of computer-run universities. He proved a good prophet: the revolt broke out first at the apex of his own university system, the Berkeley campus of the University of California, less than two years after he delivered these lectures —which remain an excellent guide to the intricate byways of the modern academic world.

Two great impacts, beyond all other forces, have molded the modern American university system and made it distinctive. Both impacts have come from sources outside the universities. Both have come primarily from the federal government. Both have come in response to national needs.

The first was the land grant movement. Abraham Lincoln signed the Morrill Act in 1862. This act set the tone for the development of American universities, both public and private, for most of the ensuing hundred years. It was one of the most seminal pieces of legislation ever enacted.

The land grant movement came in response to the rapid industrial and agricultural development of the United States that attained such momentum in the middle of the last century. Universities were to assist this development through training that went beyond the creation of "gentlemen," and of teachers, preachers, lawyers, and doctors; through research related to the technical advance of farming and manufacturing; through service to many and ultimately to almost all of the economic and political segments of society. The land grant movement was also responsive to a growing democratic, even egalitarian and populist, trend in the nation. Pursuing this trend, higher education was to be open to all qualified young people from all walks of life. It was to serve less the perpetuation of an elite class and more the creation of a relatively classless society, with the doors of opportunity open to all through education.

This was a dramatic break with earlier American traditions in higher education. It created a new social force in world history. Nowhere before had universities been so closely linked with the daily life of so much of their societies. The university campus came to be one of the most heavily traveled crossroads in America—an intersection traversed by farmers, businessmen, politicians, students from almost every corner of almost every state. The cloister and the ivory tower were destroyed by being thrown open to all qualified comers.

Supporting the impact of the land grant movement was the effect on American universities of the model supplied by Germany. This German model gave academic respectability and content to the "land grant" idea; and Harvard, a private university with a long academic tradition, could travel much the same path of development as Cornell, a newly established land grant institution. German intellectualism and American populism were merged in the new university. Pure intellect and raw pragma-tism made an unlikely but successful alliance.

The second great impact on the universities began with federal support of scientific research during World War II. The wartime laboratories that were the forerunners of such continuing government-financed research centers as the Lincoln Laboratory at the Massachusetts Institute of Technology, the Argonne at Chicago, and the Lawrence Radiation Laboratory at California, opened a new age. The major universities were enlisted in national defense and in scientific and technological development as never before. (In World War I the universities had only been a source of raw recruits.)

Instead of Gilman, Eliot, and White, there were now such new pioneers as Conant, Compton, and Bush to guide this alliance of the federal government with the universities. Don K. Price notes that "in the hands of Vannevar Bush, James B. Conant, and Karl T. Compton the government contract became a new type of federalism." In addition to the industrial revolution there was now the scientific revolution to be served. In addition to the stimulus of Germany, there was Russia —for Russian scientific achievements both before and after Sputnik were an immense spur to the new departure. American universities have been changed almost as much by the federal research grant as by the land grant idea.

It is interesting that American universities, which pride themselves on their autonomy, should have taken their special character as much or more from the pressures of their environment as from their own inner desires; that institutions which identify themselves either as "private" or as "state" should have found their greatest stimulus in federal initiative; that universities which are part of a highly decentralized and varied system of higher edu-cation should, nevertheless, have responded with such fidelity and alacrity to national needs; that institutions which had their historical origins in the training of "gentlemen" should have committed themselves so fully to the service of brute technology.

The "federal grant" university has been emerging over the past twenty years, but until recently it has developed more by force of circumstances than by conscious design. The universities most affected have been making largely piecemeal adjustments to the new phenomena without any great effort at an over-all view of what has been happening to them. Perhaps this was just as well—the transition probably was smoother precisely because it was not subjected to critical analysis. The federal government and the leading universities entered into a common-law marriage unblessed by predetermined policies and self-surveys—but nonetheless they formed a very productive union.

All this, however, as was inevitable, is being changed. Harvard has now studied itself. So has Princeton. Brookings and Carnegie have studied us all; so have the Department of Health, Education, and Welfare; the President's Science Advisory Committee; the American Council on Education; and the American Assembly. The principal conclusion was predictable: the federal colossus had the power to influence the most ruggedly individual of universities. A paradox emerged: the better and the more individual the university, the greater its chances of succumbing to the federal embrace. Washington did not waste its money on the second-rate.

Soon there will be a national policy as well as nationwide activity, and I am at least a little concerned. All these studies have identified problems that we knew all along to exist. But now that we have publicly identified the problems, we shall be expected to deal with them; and in dealing with them we shall create new problems. Mostly, we shall have to strive for "balance" in a number of different ways. We shall have to "balance" the wishes of individual scholars with those of their institutions; New England with the South; the sciences with the humanities; research with teaching; graduate training with undergraduate education; merit with politics; the judgment of specialists with general formulae. And yet one of the more productive aspects of federal involvement to date has been its imbalance.

We are clearly entering the second phase of the "federal grant" development. The first I shall identify as the phase of "intuitive imbalance," and the new phase just emerging as one of "bureaucratic balance." It is a good time to examine where we have been and where we may be going. We are in the midst of a vast transformation of university life and none of us can be too sure where we really are going; but we can try to peer ahead.

As a basis for discussing the two phases of federal grant development, I shall briefly review the essential facts about federal involvement with universities in this country.

¶Federal interest in higher education dates from 1787. That year saw the beginning of endowment of public institutions of higher education with public lands, following the example of the Northwest Ordinance of 1785, which provided land to support public schools at the lower levels. However, this interest was not made effective until the Morrill Land Grant Act of 1862. Then the Second Morrill Act in 1890 supplemented the original land grants with federal grants of funds to support college instruction in specified subjects; these grants still continue, and, in fact, have recently been expanded.

Federal interest in higher education was further made effective by the Hatch Act in 1887, establishing the Agricultural Experiment Stations, and by the Smith-Lever Act in 1914, creating the Agricultural Extension Service. During World War I, the ROTC program was established. During the Great Depression, universities were involved in the programs of the Work Projects Administration and National Youth Administration. During World War II, universities participated heavily in the Engineering, Science and Management War Training Program inaugurated in 1940. In that same year, the National Defense Research Committee (later the Office of Scientific Research and Development) was established, and leading universities became engaged in the various programs of war research which it set up.

After World War II and again after the Korean conflict, the "GI Bill" and the corresponding bill for Korean veterans sent a seismic shock through academic life.

Despite this long history of federal interest, however, it is evident that with the exception of the comparatively restricted areas of agriculture and military training, there was no continuing federal involvement with higher education until World War II.

¶Currently, federal support has become a major factor in the total performance of many universities, and the sums involved are substantial. Higher education in 1960 received about $1.5 billion from the federal government—a hundredfold increase in twenty years. About one third of this $1.5 billion was for university-affiliated research centers; about one third for project research within universities; and about one third for other things, such as residence hall loans, scholarships, and teaching programs. This last third was expended at colleges as well as universities, but the first two thirds almost

exclusively at universities, and at relatively few of them.

The $1 billion for research, though only 10 percent of total federal support for research and development, accounted for 75 percent of all university expenditures on research and 15 percent of total university budgets. Clearly the shape and nature of university research are profoundly affected by federal monies.

¶Federal research funds to universities flow primarily from six agencies. In 1961 the percentage distribution was as follows:

Department of Health, Education, and Welfare	39
(37 percent was from National Institutes of Health alone)	
Department of Defense	32
National Science Foundation	11
Atomic Energy Commission	8
Department of Agriculture	6
National Aeronautics and Space Administration	3
Other agencies	1

(These figures do not include funds for university-operated government research centers.)

This federal support has been almost exclusively identified with three great and somewhat interrelated national concerns: defense (40 percent of the total in 1961, including support by the Department of Defense and the Atomic Energy Commission); scientific and technological progress (20 percent—National Science Foundation, Department of Agriculture, and NASA); and health (37 percent—through the National Institutes of Health). Federal support has not been directed explicitly toward strengthening universities generally, or one or more universities specifically, in any over-all fashion—as might be said of the University Grants Committee in Great Britain.

¶Federal research expenditures have been largely restricted to the physical and biomedical sciences, and engineering, with only about 3 percent for the social sciences and hardly any support for the humanities.

¶Among the totality of university functions, federal support has been heavily concentrated on research and on graduate and postdoctoral training in fields of national interest.

¶The preferred approach of the federal government to the use of university facilities for research has been (a) the specialized research center—by 1963 there were fourteen major ones, and (b) the research project. Projects have been supported for relatively short terms and specific purposes; and support has been awarded, usually on the advice of qualified experts, on the basis of prospective performance.

¶Federal research expenditures have been heavily focused on a relatively few institutions. If both project research and large research centers are included, six universities received 57 percent of the funds in a recent fiscal year, and twenty universities received 79 percent. If project research alone is considered, the figures are 28 and 54 percent. As a percentage of total university expenditures for all purposes among the leading twenty recipients, federal funds have amounted to 20 to 50 percent when project research alone is counted and from 20 to over 80 percent when the research centers are added. These twenty universities are only about one tenth of all universities in the United States. They constitute the primary federal grant universities.

¶Recently there has been some spreading out of federal interest from the physical and biomedical to the social sciences; from graduate to undergraduate training; from a selective few to an expanded number of universities.

PHASE ONE: INTUITIVE IMBALANCE

For about twenty years now, Congress has been deciding in which general areas the partnership between the federal government and the universities should be developed. The areas chosen have been defense, scientific and technological progress, and health. Decisions have not been based on thorough study of national priorities. They have been made pragmatically, in response to the felt needs of the nation and of the people in accord with the possibilities of the times, and also, to an extent, in response to the urgings of very powerful lobbies. The atom was split, and could be used for war and peace. The

Students at Columbia University, April 1968.   (Charles Gatewood)

"cold war" followed World War II and necessitated further defense work. Health became a matter of great national concern. Possibilities for space exploration developed. Congress reacted quickly to each of these realities.

Once Congress initiated a program, federal administrative officers turned to those universities best able to give immediate and effective assistance on the individual programs; or rather they turned to those scientists in the best position to respond quickly and efficiently—and those scientists were principally located in a limited number of institutions. These actions were not undertaken on the basis of any general review of institutional capacity or potential capacity, but on quick and ready apprehension of possibilities and response to them. The test was who could most effectively do the job at hand. The process was more intuitive than studied.

For about twenty years, universities have been accepting the research centers and projects as proposed by faculty members and government agencies, making such day-to-day adjustments as were needed and possible. In consequence, these universities have been profoundly affected. The whole process has been one of starting new endeavors, and this has changed the pre-existing "balance" in several ways. Some real and some not so real issues have arisen for the universities.

1. Federal control and federal influence. Federal control as a substantive issue is, as Sidney Hook has said, a "red herring." With a few exceptions—the generally necessary exception of secrecy in certain types of work and the unnecessary exception of the disclaimer affidavit required by the National Defense Education Act—there has been no control in any deleterious sense. By way of contrast, state control of state universities has been a real problem. The federal government has customarily put scientifically trained persons in charge of science programs and they have operated fully within academic traditions.

The real problem is not one of federal control but of federal influence. A federal agency offers a project. A university need not accept—but, as a practical matter, it usually does. One of the quickest ways to lose a faculty member is by refusing to accept the grant he has just negotiated with his counterpart in Washington. Out of this reality have followed many of the consequences of federal aid for the universities; and they have been substantial. That they are subtle, slowly cumulative and gentlemanly, makes them all the more potent.

2. University control and the agency as alma mater. A university's control over its own destiny has been substantially reduced. University funds from tuition and fees, gifts and endowments, and state sources go through the usual budget-making procedures and their assignment is subject to review in accordance with internal policy. Federal research funds, however, are usually negotiated by the individual scholar with the particular agency, and so by-pass the usual review process. Thus 20 to 50 to 80 percent of a university's expenditures may be handled outside the normal channels. These funds in turn commit some of the university's own funds; they influence the assignment of space; they determine the distribution of time between teaching and research; to a large extent they establish the areas in which the university grows the fastest. Almost imperceptibly, a university is changed.

The authority of the department chairman, the dean, the president are thereby reduced; so also is the role of faculty government. This may have its advantages. Scholars seem to prefer dealing with their professional counterparts in Washington rather than with their colleagues and administrators at home. Also the university's internal process of distributing funds would be generally less selective and less flexible than the federal research project approach. Within a university, the tendency is to give each faculty member about the same opportunity and once having given it to keep giving it thereafter; but the project method allows more attention to exceptional merit and has the advantage that all projects may end some time. Additionally, federal agencies are more responsive to particular national needs than the universities would be, given the same amount of money to spend according to their own priority system.

There are, however, clearly detrimental effects. Some faculty members come to use the pressure of their agency contacts against their university. They may try to force the establishment of a new administrative unit or the assignment of land for their own special building, in defiance of general university policy or priorities. These pressures, of course, should be withstood; they speak well neither of the professor nor of the agency. Also, some faculty members tend to shift their identification and loyalty from their universiy to the agency in Washington. Their concern with the general welfare of the university is eroded and they become tenants rather than owners, taking their grants with them as they change their institutional lodgings. The university, as Allen Wallis, president of the University of Rochester, has remarked, becomes to an extent a "hotel." The agency becomes the new alma mater. The research entrepreneur becomes a euphoric schizophrenic.

It has been said that, in the face of federal aid, university presidents have "abdicated" their responsibilities for the general conduct of their institutions. I would put it differently—they have let some things go by that they would have liked to do differently; but this is often what they do anyway. There are, however, especially acute problems when the agency insists on the tie-in sale (if we do this for you, then you must do that for us) or when it requires frequent and detailed progress reports. Then the university really is less than a free agent. It all becomes a kind of "putting-out" system with the agency taking the place of the merchant-capitalist of old. Sweat shops have developed out of such a system in earlier times and in other industries.

3. *"Scientists Affluent, Humanists Militant."* Federal research support has added a new dimension to the eternal class struggles within a university. To student versus faculty, assistant versus tenure professors, and faculty versus administrators has been added a new hierarchical point of tension—that between humanists and scientists. The scientists, by and large, in the federal grant universities, get promoted faster, get more space, get more income through summer employment and consulting, have more secretaries and assistants, have greater access to travel funds and expense accounts, and accumulate a greater sense of status within and outside the academic community. Some humanists obviously resent all this and consider it quite unfair, even though their own situation has improved, relative to what it used to be.

However, there is still another side to the story. The scientist who gets a series of projects going can become caught in his own apparatus. Graduate students and staff members become dependent upon him. He is committed to project deadlines and periodic contract negotia-

tions. He is enmeshed in a web of obligations and it is very hard to break out. As a result, he often works hard at things he would rather not do—more often than need be true of the humanist.

There is some current tendency for the brightest of graduate students to prefer the sciences to the social sciences and the humanities, and this will have an impact on comparative faculty quality as between fields of study in the years to come. How much of this has been caused by federal aid and how much by the current liveliness of the different fields is not at all clear. My own impression is that the brightest graduate students flock to the areas with the brightest new ideas, regardless of federal aid.

All this is said to have destroyed the "balance" among fields and it is generally concluded that something should be done about it. The balance among fields, however, has never been a static thing. If it were, philosophy, theology, and the classics would still be the dominant areas of study, as they have not been for a long time. Assuming that the balance of 1942, say, was appropriate for 1942, this does not mean it would have been appropriate for 1962. It is not enough to say that the old "balance" has been destroyed. The real question is what should be the proper balance today? It is clear that the flowering of the Renaissance should have affected the "balance" in the sixteenth century. It would seem likely that the splitting of the atom and the deciphering of the genetic code should in their turn affect the balance of the twentieth century. We should expect the most money and the brightest students and the greatest prestige to follow the most exciting new ideas. By and large they have done so, and this is one way of defining the nature of balance. (Eco-

nomics was exciting in the 1930s; sociology was more exciting in the 1950s.)

The real question, it seems to me, is not one of balance in any historical or monetary sense, but rather what is most appropriate to each field in each period. "All fields are equal, only some are more equal than others." There should be no effort to do the same things in the same amounts for each field. Each should receive support in accordance with its current potentialities, and potentialities vary. There are no timeless priorities.

The academic community has lived with inequities before. Agriculture in the land grant institutions has had eleven-month appointments, low teaching loads, and heavy research subsidies for decades. Law and medicine have reflected within the academic world some of the power and affluence of their professions in the outside world. These are stated as matters of fact, not as ideal situations.

Generally, I think, it is remarkable and commendable that so high a degree of internal equity has thus far been preserved within the academic world in the face of quite chaotic pressures impinging upon it.

4. *The inevitability of concentration.* The project approach almost automatically led to concentration of federal research effort in a relatively few universities. The universities best equipped to undertake the research were also those with the faculty and facilities to provide for the training of Ph.D.s. It is no coincidence that the six universities with a little more than 25 percent of project funds graduated about 25 percent of the Ph.D.s; and a similar situation prevails for the top twenty universities. If "only the best will do," this concentration of effort is inevitable. A different result would have been quite surprising.

This concentration of effort has undoubtedly strengthened the facilities and improved the quality of faculties of universities already in the front rank. It has probably widened the gap between those of the first and those of the second and third ranks. It may, in fact, have actually injured universities of the second and third ranks and some colleges by turning their potential faculty members into research personnel in the front-rank universities. The good are better; the poor may well be worse. And it has greatly accentuated the differences between colleges and universities.

5. *Teaching the graduates versus teaching the undergraduates.* The much-advertised conflict between teaching and research puts the problem the wrong way. The teaching of graduate students is so closely tied to research that if research is improved, graduate instruction is almost bound to be improved also. And the almost universal experience seems to be that federal research support has improved graduate instruction. There have been better facilities, more research assistantships and fellowships, more research projects in which students can work directly with faculty members— all resulting from federal funds. At the graduate level, there has been a clear gain, and fortunately so, because graduate enrollments at the federal grant universities have been increasing rapidly.

At the undergraduate level, however, the "subtle discounting of the teaching process" has been aided and abetted. Harold Orlans, who conducted the excellent Brookings study of federal aid to universities, concludes that federal research aid "has accelerated the long-standing depreciation of undergraduate education at large universities." This is my own observation, with one exception—that a very few private institutions with long traditions

of very high-quality undergraduate instruction have been able to maintain their standards; and this is to their great credit.

The reasons for the general deterioration of undergraduate teaching are several. Teaching loads and student contact hours have been reduced. Faculty members are more frequently on leave or temporarily away from the campus; some are never more than temporarily on campus. More of the instruction falls to teachers who are not members of the regular faculty. The best graduate students prefer fellowships and research assistantships to teaching assistantships. Postdoctoral fellows who might fill the gap usually do not teach. Average class size has been increasing.

There seems to be a "point of no return" after which research, consulting, graduate instruction become so absorbing that faculty efforts can no longer be concentrated on undergraduate instruction as they once were. This process has been going on for a long time; federal research funds have intensified it. As a consequence, undergraduate education in the large university is more likely to be acceptable than outstanding; educational policy from the undergraduate point of view is largely neglected. How to escape the cruel paradox that a superior faculty results in an inferior concern for undergraduate teaching is one of our more pressing problems.

6. *The faculty and the un-faculty.* University scholars traditionally have both taught and conducted research. But now some scholars are added to the staff in exclusively research capacities—and increasingly with titles suggesting professorial status. They have no teaching responsibilities and are not as yet fully accepted members of the academic community. They usually are not members of the Academic Senate

and they usually are not given tenure—both traditional marks of faculty status. In many institutions, however, they may use the name of the university in getting projects under their own direction.

In a far less anomalous position is the faculty member who works on a federally sponsored project during the summer months and part-time during the regular year, and receives much of his pay from the project rather than from the university. But to what extent is he really a university employee and what security of employment does he really have? Obviously, it is no longer so clear as it once was just who is the faculty.

There has been an almost frantic remaking of the rules—new titles created, new relationships established, new classes of citizenship formulated and only partially assimilated. The Harvard catalogue now lists more than 5000 "Officers of Instruction and Administration," many of whom are not faculty in the traditional sense. The "faculty" in our universities becomes an ever-changing group as the definitions change. If there can still be said to be a "faculty" at all, it is most certainly a different composite than before. Much of the teaching, much of the research are done by the "un-faculty."

7. *University "aid" to the federal government.* Federal aid has been of great benefit to the universities. It has not, however, been without its costs in money and effort. Overhead allowances vary greatly from agency to agency but seldom cover all the indirect as well as the direct costs of sponsored research. Also, matching grants for construction may force a university to upset its own priority system in order to get federal funds. This, of course, is the intent.

Additionally, federal funds have placed great new administrative burdens on the universities—on faculty members, on department chairmen, on deans, on presidents. New classes of administrators have been created —the contracting officer and the research project manager. Administration becomes a much larger aspect of the total university enterprise. Julius A. Stratton has observed, "There is a basic incompatibility between the true spirit of a university and those elements of management which tend to creep into the organization of projects, the planning of programs, and the utilization of costly facilities."

8. *On the borders of temptation.* Immense sums of money have been poured into the universities by the federal government, and universities are highly atomistic entities. The university has the responsibility for but usually not the actual control of these funds. Some abuses have inevitably developed. Funds have been diverted at times from one use to another—and the other a use not intended by the federal agency. Some faculty members make informal alliances—if you consult on my project, then I should consult on yours—and total income has been pyramided through this exchange of consultancies to occasionally astounding levels. When these same faculty members sit on the federal panels that make the grants, the whole process becomes quite involved, to say the least. Excessive amounts of expensive equipment have at times been purchased, and equipment salesmen chase grants around. Some universities promise not only a base salary but substantial supplemental personal income and allowances from federal grants as a recruiting device in a wilder and wilder upward spiral.

There have been some scandals. There will be more. The federal agencies will exercise increasingly specific controls and the universities dependent on this new standard of living will accept these controls. The universities themselves will have to exercise more stringent controls by centralizing authority, particularly through the audit process. In a few situations, self-restraint has not been enough restraint; as one result, greater external restraint will be imposed in most situations.

With all its problems, however, federal research aid to universities has helped greatly in meeting national needs. It has greatly assisted the universities themselves. The nation is stronger. The leading universities are stronger. As Nathan Pusey reported the unanimous views of the presidents of universities participating in the Carnegie study, federal aid, over all, has been a "good thing." In their turn, the federal grant universities have adapted to their new role quite quickly and effectively.

Professor Don Price has made reference to the following limerick:

There was a young lady from Kent
Who said that she knew what
   it meant
   When men took her to dine,
   Gave her cocktails and wine;
She knew what it meant—but
   she went.

I am not so sure that the universities and their presidents always knew what it meant; but one thing is certain—they went.

PHASE TWO: BUREAUCRATIC BALANCE

The general policy of federal agencies in allocating research grants to universities for the last two decades has been one of "seeking excellence wherever it is," one of accepting the established pattern and following it. The new approach is to take more of an over-all view; to change the pattern to a degree. Balance is the new virtue; imbalance the old sin.

The charge, made by Logan Wilson among others, has been that "There is no federal program—merely programs." The response—in the proposed "National Education Improvement Act of 1963," for example—is to provide: "A comprehensive program of Federal aid to meet selected and urgent needs of American education on all levels from elementary school through graduate education; to promote educational quality, expand opportunity for education, and to increase the capacity of our educational institutions; to provide for the Nation's needs in skilled manpower, national growth, and national security."

The new balance calls for developing a larger number of outstanding centers of graduate instruction and research. The Seaborg report suggested an expansion from the present fifteen or twenty centers to thirty or forty over a fifteen-year period. The National Education Improvement Act envisages expansion from twenty to seventy. This demand for geographical dispersion of centers of strength follows, in part, the new realization of the role of a university as a factor influencing the location of industry. The Roswell L. Gilpatric report for the Department of Defense explained the concentration of defense contracts in California and Massachusetts by the concentration of research and development projects in these two states, which in turn was attributed to the availability of university centers of substantial strength. An educational and political effort of considerable dimensions now seeks to reorder the current pattern of distribution in the name of balance.

Under the National Defense Education Act of 1958, preference is already given to assisting *new* graduate programs in selected subject matter areas. Teaching is being emphasized along with research. Summer re-

New York City police at Columbia University, April 1968. *(Catherine Ursillo)*

fresher courses for teachers of science, improvement of science textbooks, and language laboratories are programs already well established. The National Science Foundation has a large effort under way to improve and renovate equipment for undergraduate teaching in the physical sciences. Undergraduates, as well as graduate students, are being assisted by loans and scholarships. The social sciences are receiving increasing sums of money. More funds are being granted to colleges as well as to universities, and to universities of all ranks. In particular, "institutional grants," to supplement project grants, are being given by the National Science Foundation and the National Institutes of Health. And NASA, among others, makes "training" grants to institutions instead of awarding fellowships to students who may then go

wherever they wish. Thus, efforts to achieve greater "balance" are already well under way.

The approach to a university "as an institution" is of particular interest. If additional universities are to be selected to become centers of strength in research and graduate instruction, then it will be necessary for the federal government to be concerned with the "general health of the institution." This will be a notable departure from historical practice, except in agriculture. The Land Grant Association, in commenting on recent recommendations by the President's Science Advisory Committee for dispersion through assistance to institutions as such, said: "The recommendations represent a return to the principles of government-institution relations laid down in the basic land grant legislation, in which the responsi-

bility for internal administration, fiscal management, and proper direction is vested with university officers rather than with agency staffs." It should be noted that *every* state has at least one land grant institution receiving federal support on a formula basis. The parallel with agriculture is not entirely apt, however, since agriculture by its very nature is locally and regionally oriented, but national defense and space exploration are not.

If we are to move toward federal orientation to the "total function of the university," then the University Grants Committee in Great Britain is the outstanding precedent, and one that has received some support in the United States. However, there are only about thirty universities in Great Britain and it is clear what is and what is not a university. Additionally, the University Grants Committee has come to exercise more influence over the establishment of new programs, the cost and size and even the appearance of new buildings, the equalization of faculty salaries among institutions, and the determination of admission policies than would currently be acceptable if it came from the federal government in this country.

Some hard choices must be faced. The decentralized project approach of the last two decades has much to recommend it. It is selective on merit, flexible in accordance with quality of performance, and responsive to national goals. The universities and their scholars retain substantial freedom. But such dominant reliance on the project approach is no longer likely. In fact, the project is already less the chosen instrument than it once was. Productive anarchy is no longer such a politically viable solution.

It is said that support to institutions as such will "give a university the necessary autonomy," and will permit dispersion of effort and better balance in several directions. It is not clear, however, how the particular institutions will be chosen, or, once chosen, how support might subsequently be withdrawn if performance should prove inadequate. It is difficult to assess the merit of a total institution as complex as a modern university. One alternative is to rely on a formula, as in the case of agriculture in the land grant institutions. Another is to be guided by political influence; and this is increasingly happening.

It is reported that Congress already senses its loss of control to the professional personnel in the various agencies and would like to regain it. "Congress knows it has forfeited much power over science to the Executive and it does not like it." The Harvard self-study report notes the danger of political interference and "log-rolling" inherent in block grants. Inter-university competition would be taken from the quasi-academic arena of the agency committee to the legislative halls.

Additionally, the selection of designated "centers of strength" assumes a single source of designation—a single over-all federal agency or committee. A single agency means a single source of control, as against the current pluralistic situation of several agencies and several sources of influence, with opportunity to pick and choose among them. A single source of control would turn an influential relationship into a really "perilous partnership." Finally, will funds necessarily be better spent for the national interest under institutional control than through the agencies, where decisions are freer from internal rigidities and egalitarian tendencies?

In the battle over institutional versus project support, Congressmen are more likely to prefer the institutional approach than are the professionals in the agencies; the presidents of universities than the researchers within the universities; the less well-established universities than the well-established ones; the humanists than the scientists—generally, those who have less under the project system than those who have more.

It is almost obligatory in educational circles these days to support "excellence" and "balance." They are the two magic words. Yet "excellence" and "balance" sometimes pull in different directions. It is also quite necessary to favor "institutional integrity" and to be against "federal control." Yet the institutional grants that aid what we are supposed to favor (integrity) may also aid what we are supposed to be against (control). Turning "integrity" over to the university president may also turn "control" over to the federal government.

How can we really best secure "aristocracy of achievement arising out of democracy of opportunity?"

SOME SUGGESTIONS

The nation does face some grave problems in the field of education. Vastly increased numbers of students are pouring into our schools. Many qualitative deficiencies exist. State and local subdivisions are caught with relatively fixed tax structures, and private endowments and gifts have their limits also. Federal support is the most obvious way out. But federal expenditures themselves are not unlimited, and there are some realistic barriers to certain types of federal involvement.

The first consideration is that the federal government need not and cannot do everything. It seems to me that the educational system of America, good as it generally is, is in the most trouble—and thus in the greatest need of federal help—at the bottom and at the top.

At the bottom is the problem of "drop-outs" from school and "drop-outs" of the unskilled from the employed labor force. Through occupational training and retraining, through counseling, guidance, and relocation, these "drop-outs" should be assisted to acquire skills valuable in a dynamic economy where skill levels are rising at perhaps the fastest rate in history. Full employment is the necessary complement to make such training effective.

At the top, the nation needs more research activity in a number of fields and more personnel of high skill—particularly engineers, scientists, mathematicians, teachers, and medical doctors. A recent Bureau of Labor Statistics survey shows that from now to 1970 the expected supply of engineers and scientists will fill only three quarters of the demand. This leaves a very large gap. The prospect is particularly critical for engineers.

Fortunately the levels where federal aid is most necessary are levels where it is most politically feasible. My suggestions will be limited to higher education, and to the university level in particular.

1. Federal research centers, whenever possible, should be located near and identified with a university. A university, with its libraries, colleagues to talk to, and graduate students to train, provides a uniquely favorable environment for such centers. In turn, such centers provide additional research opportunities for the university's faculty members and graduate students. Instead of establishing a research center in isolation and then, perhaps, having to build a new university at the same site, it seems to me best to put the center near some university—even if it doesn't happen to be our own.

2. The project system should be continued in essentially its present form as the major means of supporting the research and graduate instruction programs of universities as well as accomplishing the specific research purposes of the federal government. If project funds double or triple during the decade of the sixties, as now seems likely, it will be possible and necessary to extend more of them beyond the twenty institutions that constitute the primary group of federal grant universities at the present time. Orlans has identified about ten universities, mostly "public" ones, which already deserve considerably more project support on the basis of their existing Ph.D. programs. Other universities will soon be moving into this group in the natural course of events. The project system follows established lines of contact through disciplines and avoids the problems of establishing a new reliance on institutional lines of contact.

The project system has resulted in a "highly successful working relationship between the government's need for long- and short-term research and the academic scientist's abilities and interests."

To the extent that institutional grants are given, they should follow the project grants. Charles V. Kidd has suggested that 25 percent might be given as free funds to institutions, as against 75 percent in project funds. Twenty-five percent appears to be an adequate figure. These institutional grants could best be used by the universities for new projects, small projects, support of young faculty members unknown in Washington, and of fields neglected in direct federal grants—all on a very flexible basis. Thus the universities' rather different evaluation of "merit" could supplement the standards for merit of the federal agencies. I would hope that the institutional grants would be assigned automatically by the agencies as some percentage of the project grants which are themselves assigned on merit. If "quality must come first," this is the best way to assure it.

Alvin M. Weinberg has recently made the interesting suggestion that the panel system of reviewing research proposals could be improved as an instrument for making scientific judgments by including on the panels representatives of related fields, as well as representatives of the field in question. "I should think that advice from panels so constituted," he says, "would be tempered by concern for larger issues; in particular the support of a proposed research project would be viewed from the larger perspective of the relevance of that research to the rest of science." The greater impartiality of the panels would also be assured.

Contract and grant overhead should cover reasonable indirect as well as all direct costs.

Federal project funds are increasingly being used to bid salaries and allowances up and to bid teaching assignments down. How much further such competition can go without raising grave policy problems for the federal agencies is problematical. The market is sufficiently active without this added inflationary stimulus; and the universities are sufficiently in trouble with internal inequities and reduction of teaching time.

There is currently arising a three-sided competitive struggle for research and development work, involving industry, the universities should be preferred for basic research and for such other research as is readily related to graduate instruction.

It is being suggested, and also being implemented, that federal grants and contracts be channeled increasingly into liberal arts colleges to assist faculty research and the training of outstanding undergraduate students. This process can easily subvert the colleges from their primary obligation and start them on the way to becoming quite different types of institutions. With a project-by-project approach this is almost bound to happen. Would it not be well for the governing bodies of such colleges to examine the implications of this changed role before the process of project-by-project transformation of the nature of the institution is begun? If they accept the role they should accept it by a conscious policy decision.

3. To aid the teaching function of universities during the "deficit years" of greatly swollen enrollments just ahead, federal agencies should permit, even encourage, postdoctoral fellows and research professors to teach one-quarter or even one-third time at no cost to the institution. The present system increases the size of the "un-faculty" and widens the gap between the researcher

and the student. Also, the further creation of research career professorships might well be examined. Are they really necessary from a research point of view and is it really desirable to preclude their occupants from normal participation in the full range of academic life?

The universities themselves should see to it that teaching assistantships are fully competitive with research assistantships and fellowships.

4. Federal agencies should provide space and equipment for their postdoctoral fellows and research career professors and for all contracts and most grants without the requirement of matching funds. It is very difficult to obtain space and equipment for these purposes from either endowments or state support, and also not entirely appropriate.

5. A National Foundation for Higher Education might well be created on the model of the National Science Foundation. It could serve as a focal point for the interests of higher education and make grants outside the province of the National Science Foundation. Such a foundation would need to explore carefully the areas where support would be most productive, and also the appropriate forms of support, as did the National Science Foundation with such skill and judgment in its fields of interest. Areas for possible early consideration, as examples, are the creative arts, international studies, and environmental planning. Each is at a stage of considerable activity; each carries a high degree of national interest. Additionally, a Foundation for Higher Education might well undertake the support of great regional library resources with union catalogues made available to other university and college libraries in the region.

6. A number of other federal programs now in effect to aid higher education have generally worked well and should be continued.

The established program of the Federal Housing Authority in making loans for residence halls, student unions, and parking structures should be continued and expanded, as should the several programs under the National Defense Education Act. These programs are all widely dispersed in their efforts, and affect nearly all universities and many colleges.

Graduate fellowship programs should be expanded as there are capable graduate students to fill them. The availability of money does not by itself create a supply of competent candidates. At least half of the graduate fellowships should be transferable on a national basis, and not more than half tied to particular institutions. The practice of the Rockefeller Foundation and Woodrow Wilson Foundation of making an institutional grant to cover part of the institutional expenses for each scholar might well be more widely emulated.

The great need for curriculum reform in many fields, caused by the changing content and structure of knowledge growing out of research, should be recognized by federal agencies. They should support the efforts of universities to re-examine and improve the teaching in these areas. Some support is being given, particularly by the National Science Foundation in the physical sciences, but unfortunately some recent developments run counter to this trend. For example, the National Institutes of Health now cannot support any such efforts in the biological sciences—an area where they are greatly needed.

Foreign service projects conducted by universities for the federal government appear to be most fruitful if there is a major institutional assignment for a substantial period of time. *Ad hoc* projects accomplish little for the foreign country or for the contracting university.

7. Medical and dental doctors are in short supply and will be in shorter supply. Fellowships and facilities for their training deserve high federal priority.

8. A Council of Advisers on Education, as suggested by the American Assembly in 1960, would provide an opportunity for an over-all view of the educational system and the educational needs of the nation as no single agency can do. This would be something like the President's Council of Economic Advisers, but in the educational field. Education may well need a better-coordinated voice than it has had, as McGeorge Bundy has so eloquently argued, but the federal government also may need a more coordinated ear.

This council might assist in the preparation of a manpower budget covering the supply of, and demand for, the skills that depend on formal education. Indeed, beyond this the nation might benefit from an over-all manpower budget, supplementing its other budgets, for it would focus attention on human resources and on the importance of developing them.

The partnership of the federal government with higher education and particularly with the federal grant universities over the last two decades has been enormously productive in enlarging the pool of scientific ideas and skills. Now we are entering a new phase of widening and deepening relationships. This new phase can carry the American commitment to education to new heights of endeavor. It can also preserve the traditional freedom of higher education from excessive control. It can enlarge the horizons of equality of opportunity. It can maintain and even increase the margin for excellence. The challenge is to make certain it does all these things.

STUDENTS FOR A DEMOCRATIC SOCIETY
The Port Huron Statement

The first manifestation of student activism came at the end of the 1950s among socialist groups at a few campuses. Then the sit-ins in 1960 galvanized students into civil rights activities, and the Berlin crisis of 1961 stimulated a short-lived student peace movement. But the first group to advance with any success beyond a single issue was the Students for a Democratic Society (SDS), which in the course of the decade came closer than any other organization to being at the center of the largely anarchistic and leaderless student Left. Two activists at the University of Michigan, Al Haber and Tom Hayden, coordinated groups at numerous campuses and organized a national meeting. This convention, held at a United Auto Workers center in Port Huron, Michigan, approved a manifesto drafted by Hayden, "The Port Huron Statement," which became the first intellectual landmark of the student Left.

This document, which launched SDS, no longer appears terribly radical. It advocates cooperation with liberals and seeks to renovate existing institutions. It is written in the language of social science, is tentative in its assertions, and resolutely unromantic in its rhetoric. Yet the main notes are there: the insistence on an end to international tension, the rejection of anticommunism as an ideology, the antagonism to bureaucracy, the desire to overcome alienation and helplessness, to achieve community and a true politics, the search for a student identity and a place of power in modern life. In its quiet way, it fulfilled the claims of its opening paragraphs by providing an "agenda for a generation."

INTRODUCTION: AGENDA FOR A GENERATION

We are people of this generation, bred in at least modest comfort, looking uncomfortably to the world we inherit.

When we were kids the United States was the wealthiest and strongest country in the world; the only one with the atom bomb, the least scarred by modern war, an initiator of the United Nations that we thought would distribute Western influence throughout the world. Freedom and equality for each individual, government of, by, and for the people—these American values we found good, principles by which we could live as men. Many of us began maturing in complacency.

As we grew, however, our comfort was penetrated by events too troubling to dismiss. First, the permeating and victimizing fact of human degradation, symbolized by the Southern struggle against racial bigotry, compelled most of us from silence to activism. Second, the enclosing fact of the Cold War, symbolized by the presence of the Bomb, brought awareness that we ourselves, and our friends, and millions of abstract "others" we knew more directly because of our common peril, might die at any time. We might deliberately ignore, or avoid, or fail to feel all other human problems, but not these two, for these were too immediate and crushing in their impact, too challenging in the demand that we as individuals take the responsibility for encounter and resolution.

While these and other problems either directly oppressed us or rankled our consciences and became our own subjective concerns, we began to see complicated and disturbing paradoxes in our surrounding America. The declaration "all men are created equal . . ." rang hollow before the facts of Negro life in the South and the big cities of the North. The proclaimed peaceful intentions of the United States contradicted its economic and military investments in the Cold War status quo.

We witnessed, and continue to witness, other paradoxes. With nuclear energy whole cities can easily be powered, yet the dominant nation-states seem more likely to unleash destruction greater than that incurred in all wars of human history. Although our own technology is destroying old and creating new forms of social organization, men still tolerate meaningless work and idleness. While two-thirds of mankind suffers undernourishment, our own upper classes revel amidst superfluous abundance. Although world population is expected to double in forty years, the nations still tolerate anarchy as a major principle of international conduct and uncontrolled exploitation governs the sapping of the earth's physical resources. Although mankind desperately needs revolutionary leadership, America rests in national stalemate, its goals ambiguous and tradition-bound instead of informed and clear, its democratic system apathetic and manipulated rather than "of, by, and for the people."

Not only did tarnish appear on our image of American virtue, not only did disillusion occur when the hypocrisy of American ideals was discovered, but we began to sense that what we had originally seen as the American Golden Age was actually the decline of an era. The worldwide outbreak of revolution against colonialism and imperialism, the entrenchment of totalitarian states, the menace of war, overpopulation, international disorder, supertechnology—these trends were testing the tenacity of our own commitment to democracy and freedom and our abilities to visualize their application to a world in upheaval.

Our work is guided by the sense that we may be the last generation in the experiment with living. But we are a minority—the vast majority of our people regard the temporary equilibriums of our society and world as eternally functional parts. In this is perhaps the outstanding paradox: we ourselves are imbued with urgency, yet the message of our society is that there is no viable alternative to the present. Beneath the reassuring tones of the politicians, beneath the common opinion that America will "muddle through," beneath the stagnation of those who have closed their minds to the future, is the pervading feeling that there simply are no alternatives, that our times have witnessed the exhaustion not only of Utopias, but of any new departures as well. Feeling the press of complexity upon the emptiness of life, people are fearful of the thought that at any moment things might be thrust out of control. They fear change itself, since change might smash whatever invisible framework seems to hold back chaos from them now. For most Americans, all crusades are suspect, threatening.

The fact that each individual sees apathy in his fellows perpetuates the common reluctance to organize for change. The dominant institutions are complex enough to blunt the minds of their potential critics, and entrenched enough to swiftly dissipate or entirely repel the energies of protest and reform, thus limiting human expectancies. Then, too, we are a materially improved society, and by our own improvements we seem to have weakened the case for further change.

Some would have us believe that Americans feel contentment amidst prosperity—but might it not better be called a glaze above deeply felt anxieties about their role in the new world? And if these anxieties produce a developed indifference to human affairs, do they not as well produce a yearning to believe there *is* an alternative to present, that something *can* be done to change circumstances in the school, the workplaces, the bureaucracies, the government? It is to this latter yearning, at once the spark and engine of change, that we direct our present appeal. The search for truly democratic alternatives to the present, and a commitment to social experimentation with them, is a worthy and fulfilling human enterprise, one which moves us and, we hope, others today. On such a basis do we offer this document of our convictions and analysis: as an effort in understanding and changing the conditions of humanity in the late twentieth century, an effort rooted in the ancient, still unfulfilled conception of man attaining determining influence over his circumstances of life.

VALUES

Making values explicit—an initial task in establishing alternatives—is an activity that has been devalued and corrupted. The conventional moral terms of the age, the politician moralities—

"free world," "people's democracies"—reflect realities poorly, if at all, and seem to function more as ruling myths than as descriptive principles. But neither has our experience in the universities brought us moral enlightenment. Our professors and administrators sacrifice controversy to public relations; their curriculums change more slowly than the living events of the world; their skills and silence are purchased by investors in the arms race; passion is called unscholastic. The questions we might want raised—what is really important? can we live in a different and better way? if we wanted to change society, how would we do it?—are not thought to be questions of a "fruitful, empirical nature," and thus are brushed aside.

Unlike youth in other countries we are used to moral leadership being exercised and moral dimensions being clarified by our elders. But today, for us, not even the liberal and socialist preachments of the past seem adequate to the forms of the present. Consider the old slogans: Capitalism Cannot Reform Itself, United Front Against Fascism, General Strike, All Out on May Day. Or, more recently, No Cooperation with Commies and Fellow Travelers, Ideologies are Exhausted, Bipartisanship, No Utopias. These are incomplete, and there are few new prophets. It has been said that our liberal and socialist predecessors were plagued by vision without program, while our own generation is plagued by program without vision. All around us there is astute grasp of method, technique—the committee, the *ad hoc* group, the lobbyist, the hard and soft sell, the make, the projected image—but, if pressed critically, such expertise is incompetent to explain its implicit ideals. It is highly fashionable to identify oneself by old categories, or by naming a respected political figure, or by explaining "how we would vote" on various issues.

Theoretic chaos has replaced the idealistic thinking of old— and, unable to reconstitute theoretic order, men have condemned idealism itself. Doubt has replaced hopefulness—and men act out a defeatism that is labeled realistic. The decline of utopia and hope is in fact one of the defining features of social life today. The reasons are various: the dreams of the older left were perverted by Stalinism and never recreated; the congressional stalemate makes men narrow their view of the possible; the specialization of human activity leaves little room for sweeping thought; the horrors of the twentieth century, symbolized in the gas ovens and concentration camps and atom bombs, have blasted hopefulness. To be idealistic is to be considered apocalyptic, deluded. To have no serious aspirations, on the contrary, is to be "toughminded."

In suggesting social goals and values, therefore, we are aware of entering a sphere of some disrepute. Perhaps matured by the past, we have no sure formulas, no closed theories—but that does not mean values are beyond discussion and tentative determination. A first task of any social movement is to convince people that the search for orienting theories and the creation of human values is complex but worthwhile. We are aware that to avoid platitudes we must analyze the concrete conditions of social order. But to direct such an analysis we must use the guideposts of basic principles. Our own social values involve conceptions of human beings, human relationships, and social systems.

We regard *men* as infinitely precious and possessed of unfulfilled capacities for reason, freedom, and love. In affirming these principles we are aware of countering perhaps the dominant conceptions of man in the twentieth century; that he is a thing to be manipulated, and that he is inherently incapable of directing his own affairs. We oppose the depersonalization that reduces human beings to the status of things—if anything, the brutalities of the twentieth century teach that means and ends are intimately related, that vague appeals to "posterity" cannot justify the mutilations of the present. We oppose, too, the doctrine of human incompetence because it rests essentially on the modern fact that men have been "competently" manipulated into incompetence—we see little reason why men cannot meet with increasing skill the complexities and responsibilities of their situation, if society is organized not for minority, but for majority, participation in decision-making.

Men have unrealized potential for self-cultivation, self-direction, self-understanding, and creativity. It is this potential that we regard as crucial and to which we appeal, not to the human potentiality for violence, unreason, and submission to authority. The goal of man and society should be human independence: a concern not with image of popularity but with finding a meaning in life that is personally authentic; a quality of mind not compulsively driven by a sense of powerlessness, nor one which unthinkingly adopts status values, nor one which represses all threats to its habits, but one which has full, spontaneous access to present and past experiences, one which easily unites the fragmented parts of personal history, one which openly faces problems which are troubling and unresolved; one with an intuitive awareness of possibilities, an active sense of curiosity, an ability and willingness to learn.

This kind of independence does not mean egotistic individualism—the object is not to have one's way so much as it is to have a way that is one's own.

Nor do we deify man—we merely have faith in his potential.

Human relationships should involve fraternity and honesty. Human interdependence is contemporary fact; human brotherhood must be willed, however, as a condition of future survival and as the most appropriate form of social relations. Personal links between man and man are needed, especially to go beyond the partial and fragmentary bonds of function that bind men only as worker to worker, employer to employee, teacher to student, American to Russian.

Loneliness, estrangement, isolation describe the vast distance between man and man today. These dominant tendencies cannot be overcome by better personnel management, nor by improved gadgets, but only when a love of man overcomes the idolatrous worship of things by man. As the individualism we affirm is not egoism, the selflessness we affirm is not self-elimination. On the contrary, we believe in generosity of a kind that imprints one's unique individual qualities in the relation to other men, and to all human activity. Further, to dislike isolation is not to favor the abolition of privacy; the latter differs from isolation in that it occurs or is abolished according to individual will.

We would replace power rooted in possession, privilege, or circumstance by power and uniqueness rooted in love, reflectiveness, reason, and creativity. As a *social system* we seek the establishment of a democracy of individual participation, governed by two central aims: that the individual share in those social decisions determining the quality and direction of his life; that society be organized to encourage independence in men and provide the media for their common participation.

In a participatory democracy, the political life would be based in several root principles:

that decision-making of basic social consequence be carried on by public groupings;

that politics be seen positively, as the art of collectively creating an acceptable pattern of social relations;

that politics has the function of bringing people out of isolation and into community, thus being a necessary, though not sufficient, means of finding meaning in personal life;

that the political order should serve to clarify problems in a way instrumental to their solution; it should provide outlets for the expression of personal grievance and aspiration; opposing views should be organized so as to illuminate choices and facilitate the attainment of goals; channels should be commonly available to relate men to knowledge and to power so that private problems—from bad recreation facilities to personal alienation—are formulated as general issues.

The economic sphere would have as its basis the principles:

that work should involve incentives worthier than money or survival. It should be educative, not stultifying; creative, not mechanical; self-directed, not manipulated, encouraging independence, a respect for others, a sense of dignity and a willingness to accept social responsibility, since it is this experience that has crucial influence on habits, perceptions and individual ethics;

that the economic experience is so personally decisive that the individual must share in its full determination;

that the economy itself is of such social importance that its major resources and means of production should be open to democratic participation and subject to democratic social regulation.

Like the political and economic ones, major social institutions—cultural, educational, rehabilitative, and others—should be generally organized with the well-being and dignity of man as the essential measure of success.

In social change or interchange, we find violence to be abhorrent because it requires generally the transformation of the target, be it a human being or a community of people, into a depersonalized object of hate. It is imperative that the means of violence be abolished and the institutions—local, national, international—that encourage nonviolence as a condition of conflict be developed.

These are our central values, in skeletal form. It remains vital to understand their denial or attainment in the context of the modern world.

THE STUDENTS

In the last few years, thousands of American students demonstrated that they at least felt the urgency of the times. They moved actively and directly against racial injustices, the threat of war, violations of individual rights of conscience and, less frequently, against economic manipulation. They succeeded in restoring a small measure of controversy to the campuses after the stillness of the McCarthy period. They succeeded, too, in gaining some concessions from the people and institutions they opposed, especially in the fight against racial bigotry.

The significance of these scattered movements lies not in their success or failure in gaining objectives—at least not yet. Nor does the significance lie in the intellectual "competence" or "maturity" of the students involved—as some pedantic elders allege. The significance is in the fact the students are breaking the crust of apathy and overcoming the inner alienation that remain the defining characteristics of American college life.

If student movements for change are still rarities on the campus scene, what is commonplace there? The real campus, the familiar campus, is a place of private people, engaged in their notorious "inner emigration." It is a place of commitment to business-as-usual, getting ahead, playing it cool. It is a place of mass affirmation of the Twist, but mass reluctance toward the controversial public stance. Rules are accepted as "inevitable," bureaucracy as "just circumstances," irrelevance as "scholarship," selflessness as "martyrdom," politics as "just another way to make people, and an unprofitable one, too."

Almost no students value activity as citizens. Passive in public, they are hardly more idealistic in arranging their private lives: Gallup concludes they will settle for "low success, and won't risk high failure." There is not much willingness to take risks (not even in business), no setting of dangerous goals, no real conception of personal identity except one manufactured in the image of others, no real urge for personal fulfillment except to be almost as successful as the very successful people. Attention is being paid to social status (the quality of shirt collars, meeting people, getting wives or husbands, making solid contacts for later on); much, too, is paid to academic status (grades, honors, the med school rat race). But neglected generally is real intellectual status, the personal cultivation of the mind.

"Students don't even give a damn about the apathy," one has said. Apathy toward apathy begets a privately constructed universe, a place of systematic study schedules, two nights each week for beer, a girl or two, and early marriage; a framework infused with personality, warmth, and under control, no matter how unsatisfying otherwise.

Under these conditions university life loses all relevance to some. Four hundred thousand of our classmates leave college every year.

But apathy is not simply an attitude; it is a product of social institutions, and of the structure and organization of higher education itself. The extracurricular life is ordered according to *in loco parentis* theory, which ratifies the administration as the moral guardian of the young.

The accompanying "let's pretend" theory of student extracurricular affairs validates student government as a training center for those who want to spend their lives in political pretense, and discourages initiative from the more articulate, honest, and sensitive students. The bounds and style of controversy are delimited before controversy begins. The university "prepares" the student for "citizenship" through perpetual rehearsals and, usually, through emasculation of what creative spirit there is in the individual.

The academic life contains reinforcing counterparts to the way in which extracurricular life is organized. The academic world is founded on a teacher-student relation analogous to the parent-child relation which characterizes *in loco parentis*. Further, academia includes a radical separation of the student from the material of study. That which is studied, the social reality, is "objectified" to sterility, dividing the student from life—just as he is restrained in active involvement by the deans controlling student government. The specialization of function and knowledge, admittedly necessary to our complex technological and social structure, has produced an exaggerated compartmentalization of study and understanding. This has contributed to an overly parochial view, by faculty, of the role of its research and scholarship, to a discontinuous and truncated understanding, by students, of the surrounding social order; and to a loss of personal attachment, by nearly all, to the worth of study as a humanistic enterprise.

There is, finally, the cumbersome academic bureaucracy extending throughout the academic as well as the extracurricular structures, contributing to the sense of outer complexity and inner powerlessness that transforms the honest searching of many students to a ratification of convention and, worse, to a numbness to present and future catastrophes. The size and financing systems of the university enhance the permanent trusteeship of the administrative bureaucracy, their power leading to a shift within the university toward the value standards of business and the administrative mentality. Huge foundations and other private financial interests shape the under-financed colleges and universities, not only making them more commercial, but less disposed to diagnose society critically, less open to dissent. Many social and physical scientists, neglecting the liberating heritage of higher learning, develop "human relations" or "morale - producing" techniques for the corporate economy, while others exercise their intellectual skills to accelerate the arms race. . . .

There are no convincing apologies for the contemporary malaise. While the world tumbles toward the final war, while men in other nations are trying desperately to alter events, while the very future qua future is uncertain—America is without community impulse, without the inner momentum necessary for an age when societies cannot successfully perpetuate themselves by their military weapons, when democracy must be viable because of the quality of life, not its quantity of rockets.

The apathy here is, first, *subjective*—the felt powerlessness of ordinary people, the resignation before the enormity of events. But subjective apathy is encouraged by the *objective* American situation—the actual structural separation of people from power, from relevant knowledge, from pinnacles of decision-making. Just as the university influences the student way of life, so do major social institutions create the circumstances in which the isolated citizen will try hopelessly to understand his world and himself.

The very isolation of the individual—from power and community and ability to aspire—means the rise of a democracy without publics. With the great mass of people structurally remote and psychologically hesitant with respect to democratic institutions, those institutions themselves attenuate and become, in the fashion of the vicious circle, progressively less accessible to those few who aspire to serious participation in social affairs. The vital democratic connection between community and leadership, between the mass and the several elites, has been so wrenched and perverted that disastrous policies go unchallenged time and again.

POLITICS WITHOUT PUBLICS

The American political system is not the democratic model of which its glorifiers speak. In actuality it frustrates democracy by confusing the individual citizen, paralyzing policy discussion, and consolidating the irresponsible power of military and business interests.

A crucial feature of the political apparatus in America is that greater differences are harbored within each major party than the differences existing between them. Instead of two parties presenting distinctive and significant differences of approach, what dominates the system is a natural interlocking of Democrats from Southern states with the more conservative elements of the Republican party. This arrangement of forces is blessed by the seniority system of Congress which guarantees Congressional committee domination by conservatives—ten of seventeen committees in the Senate and thirteen of twenty-one in the House of Representatives are chaired currently by Dixiecrats.

The party overlap, however, is not the only structural antagonist of democracy in politics. First, the localized nature of the party system does not encourage discussion of national and international issues: thus problems are not raised by and for people, and political representatives usually are unfettered from any responsibilities to the general public except those regarding parochial matters. Second, whole constituencies are divested of the full political power they might have: many Negroes in the South are prevented from voting, migrant workers are disenfranchised by various residence requirements, some urban and suburban dwellers are victimized by gerrymandering, and poor people are too often without the power to obain political representation. Third, the focus of political attention is significantly distorted by the enormous lobby force, composed predominantly of business interests, spending hundreds of millions each year in an attempt to conform facts about productivity, agriculture, defense, and social services, to the wants of private economic groupings.

What emerges from the party contradiction and insulation of privately held power is the organized political stalemate: calcification dominates flexibility as the principle of parliamentary organization, frustration is the expectancy of legislators intending liberal reform, and Congress becomes less and less central to national decision-making, especially in the area of foreign policy. In this context, confusion and blurring is built into the formulation of issues, long-range priorities are not discussed in the rational manner needed for policy-making, the politics of personality and "image" become a more important mechanism than the construction of issues in a way that affords each voter a challenging and real option. The American voter is buffeted from all directions by pseudo-problems, by the structurally initiated sense that nothing political is subject to human mastery. Worried by his mundane problems which never get solved, but constrained by the common belief that politics is an agonizingly slow accommodation of views, he quits all pretense of bothering.

A most alarming fact is that few, if any, politicians are calling for changes in these conditions. Only a handful even are calling on the President to "live up to" platform pledges; no one is demanding structural changes, such as the shuttling of Southern Democrats out of the Democratic Party. Rather than protesting the state of politics, most politicians are reinforcing and aggravating that state. While in practice they rig public opinion to suit their own interests, in word and ritual they enshrine "the sovereign public" and call for more and more letters. Their speeches and campaign actions are banal, based on a degrading conception of what people want to hear. They respond not to dialogue, but to pressure: and knowing this, the ordinary citizen sees even greater inclination to shun the political sphere. The politician is usually a trumpeter to "citizenship" and "service to the nation," but since he is unwilling to seriously rearrange power relationships, his trumpetings only increase apathy by creating no outlets. Much of the time the call to "service" is justified not in idealistic terms, but in the crasser terms of "defending the free world from Communism"—thus making future idealistic impulses harder to justify in anything but Cold War terms.

In such a setting of status quo politics, where most if not all government activity is rationalized in Cold War anti-Communist terms, it is somewhat natural that discontented, super-patriotic groups would emerge through political channels and explain their ultra-conservatism as the best means of Victory over Communism. They have become a politically influential force within the Republican party, at a national level through Senator Goldwater, and at a local level through their important social and economic roles. Their political views are defined generally as the opposite of the supposed views of Communists: complete individual freedom in the economic sphere, non-participation by the government in the machinery of production. But actually "anti-Communism" becomes an umbrella by which to protest liberalism, internationalism, welfareism, the active civil rights and labor movements. It is to the disgrace of the United States that such a movement should become a prominent kind of public participation in the modern world—but, ironically, it is somewhat to the interests of the United States that such a movement should be a public constituency pointed toward realignment of the political parties, demanding a conservative Republican party in the South and an exclusion of the "leftist" elements of the national GOP. . . .

HARVEY G. COX
The "New Breed" in American Churches
Sources of Social Activism in American Religion

The "New Breed" of American churchmen, like the students to whom Hayden appealed in the "Port Huron Statement," were members of the buoyant and hopeful liberal coalition that flourished in the early and middle sixties. Consciences touched by the black struggle for civil rights went on to fight for the eradication of poverty, the improvement of cities, and the achievement of peace. The young churchmen—liberal rabbis, post-Vatican II nuns and priests, and Protestant ministers of nearly every denomination (who marched with Martin Luther King, Jr., organized community councils in the ghettos, and picketed draft boards and the Pentagon)—have wrought an enormous change in the American image of the cleric, polarizing churches, bringing not peace, but a sword.

Harvey Cox, a distinguished and highly controversial theologian, has been in the forefront of churchmen who have argued the churches' responsibility to adapt to a secular and urban world. He analyzes not only the social origins of the "new breed" in the organizational changes through which churches have moved in the past generation; he also shows that social activism has been a major theme in the history of American religion. The belief in the holiness of the poor and the search for a "blessed community" have led Americans periodically throughout their history in a quest for the realization of the Kingdom of God on earth. The activists of the sixties, Cox argues, are a part of this "honorable religious history."

Five years ago the colorless Hudson River city of Newburgh, New York, flashed briefly into national attention when its city manager proclaimed a "get-tough" policy with what he called "welfare chiselers." State and national welfare officials took a dim view of his program, however, and it was quickly terminated. The town dropped once again into obscurity. But this year, Newburgh was back in the news. On May 2, 1966, *The New York Times* carried a story with the headline: "CLERICS UNITE IN ATTACK ON NEWBURGH'S COLOR LINE." There followed an account of a rent strike in the city's Negro ghetto, a protest organized and supported by a group of the town's white and Negro clergy. Despite the opposition of most of the white population, the clergy said they would continue the strike until repairs were made to the dilapidated tenements in question. If their stated reason for being involved in this action ("The church must

Reprinted by permission from *Daedalus,* Journal of the American Academy of Arts and Sciences, Boston, Mass., vol. 96 (Winter 1967).

witness to the poor, and this includes the Negro") persuaded only a minority of white churchmen to support this action, this minority was still a conscious and articulate one.

Newburgh is not an unusual city. It has simply been fated, twice in five years, to become a stage for a larger drama. Five years ago its welfare crisis disclosed a national uneasiness with welfare policies. Today the battle raging there between socially militant churchmen and such custodians of the *status quo* as banks and real-estate institutions is part of a nationwide phenomenon: the emergence of a "New Breed" of socially activist clergy.

Churches today are facing an unprecedented institutional and theological crisis in their mission to the city. Most of their social services have been taken over by the municipal, state, and federal governments, or by secular agencies. This partial loss of function has precipitated a wrenching reappraisal of urban church strategy in America. It has also provided the occasion for the New Breed of church leaders to seize the initiative and to move the churches away from a social-service view of urban problems toward a political one.

The New Breed has brought to the fore a style of theology and a political vision that have lain dormant for some years although they have deep sources in the Christian tradition and in the American religious experience. In Buffalo, Philadelphia, Kansas City, Chicago, Oakland, and dozens of other cities, the New Breed can be found organizing welfare unions, tenants' councils, rent strikes, and school boycotts. Wherever they are at work, they have evoked opposition, both inside and outside the churches. The resulting tensions have made church politics livelier and more interesting today than they have been for decades.

In this paper I wish to examine certain of these tensions in church politics, describe the New Breed of activist churchmen, and indicate some of the theological and sociological factors operative in the situation.

I

Although the present battle within the churches has profound theological significance, it is not debated in overtly theological terms. Rather, the debate turns on questions of church strategy and policy. The best example of this is the discussion now going on inside the churches over what they should do about poverty.

The poverty question comes up in many ways: Should the church remain largely as one of the "helping agencies" and thereby continue its traditional social-service view of poverty? Should it cast its lot with non-governmental organizers, such as Saul Alinsky, investing money, staff, and prestige in building political power for the poor? These, not the Virgin Birth or the inerrancy of Scripture, are the issues church leaders discuss most ferociously today.

Protestant church historian Martin Marty describes the two sides this way: One side says that the Christian church should be involved in the struggle of today's poor in the city and on the farm—at the side of the delinquent, the racially oppressed, the politically exploited. The other side says the church should love these people, but should not become involved in the politics of their problems. As the new strategic-theological altercation unfolds, it becomes clear that the

Antiwar clergy, October 1967.
(John Goodwin)

dispute involves three principal parties. Each has a strategy, and a theology to back it. One group simply wants the church to "stay out of politics." It includes people who hold that religion should focus on a world beyond this one, on an inner or "spiritual" life separated from political conflict—the traditional pietists. It includes others who, though they believe the church should concern itself with justice, feel that it should not squander its efforts in the shifting sand of city politics, but should concentrate on larger, more universal quests.

Another group consists of the churchgoing Bourbons. They want the church to act as the custodian of property rights and the traditions of the *ancien régime*. These people regard religion as the sacred cement that binds a society to its past. They are not against the church becoming involved in controversial issues, so long as it always upholds the conservative side. This group is small but wealthy and disproportionately influential. It is linked with conservative business interests and with such reactionary religious publications as *Christian Economics*. Though it usually maintains an aura of respectability, on its right wing it shades into fanatical Birchite groups and Billy Joe Hargis' "Christian Anti-Communist Crusade."

The third group, also small but growing quickly in size and influence, is the New Breed, those laymen and clergy who are bent on moving the church toward a more direct role in supporting and inducing social change.

No one knows just how large the New Breed is. Certainly it includes a sizable minority of the ministers graduated from the main interdenominational seminaries and some of the denominational ones in the past ten years; it also includes some educated laymen who have been influenced in the years since World War II by college pastors and professors of religion.

Still, the main symbol of the New Breed is the socially activist clergyman. An indication of the weight of the New Breed's impact can be seen in the radical metamorphosis the public image of the American clergyman has undergone in the past few years. A decade ago, he was often depicted in cartoons and stories as a pompous bore, a disagreeable zealot, or a genial incompetent. Although these images still persist in certain areas, the average man is now just as likely to think of nuns, priests, and ministers leading protest marches, standing in picket lines, or organizing debates on Viet-Nam. This change in the stereotype of the churchman has affected the minister's self-image. It separates the New Breed from the Old. Among the clergy, the clear demarcation is between those who participate directly in the political or social struggle and those who do not.

The New Breed fights its battles mainly in the city. Although there are examples of church social activism in rural areas, the major theater of operations for the New Breed remains the American city. True, ministers and priests played a major role in the dramatic strike of the Delano, California, grape workers this year. Also, the Mississippi Delta Ministry sponsored by the National Council of Churches is perhaps the most controversial program operating under church auspices anywhere in the country. Yet the priests and ministers involved in these activities often come from urban backgrounds and hold many of the values and beliefs of the much larger group of New Breed churchmen now at work in the cities.[1]

Spokesmen for the New Breed have in the past decade moved

[1] See Leon Howell, "The Delta Ministry," *Christianity and Crisis,* 26, no. 14 (Aug. 8, 1966), 189–192.

Father Daniel Berrigan, Washington, D.C., January 1967. *(John Goodwin)*

into key positions in churches, seminaries, and city-mission structures. This group has accepted the "political" rather than the social-service definition of the crisis of urban poverty. Its leaders sharply criticize the traditional programs of churches and mission societies. They advocate the utilization of church resources to help mobilize the poor in various types of community organizations. They speak unapologetically of the struggle for power in the city and the churches' responsibility to enter into the struggle on the side of the exploited and powerless.[2] In Rochester, Buffalo, Chicago, and other cities they have used church funds to support Saul Alinsky or other organizers in setting up energetic programs for organizing the poor. Negro ministers who hold positions of leadership in the civil rights movement are a crucial component in the New Breed. They have helped churches form coalitions with civil rights groups,

[2] For example, see the February 1965 issue of *Social Action,* published by the Council for Christian Social Action of the United Church of Christ. The entire issue is devoted to "Strategy for Community Change."

neighborhood action organizations, and political reform movements.

Some people believe that this surprising new role the churches are playing in the cities has already begun to have an important effect. Saul Alinsky said in a recent interview that the churches in the 1960s have assumed the role played by the labor unions in the 1930s. "The unions are now the haves—they're part of the *status quo*," says Alinsky. "The Christian churches are now taking the leadership in social change." Alinsky has worked with priests and ministers to organize the poor in the ghettos and gray areas of a dozen American cities. He has had years of experience, but he recently conceded that he has never seen the equal of the "pure flame of passion for justice you find in these young ministers today." Although he admits that large sections of the church remain inert or reactionary, he still contends that the church is often less compromised than most other large urban institutions and that, in any case, it has a gospel that "constantly forces it to think about siding with the poor," even when such a posture militates against its own institutional interests.

Since Alinsky's work exposes him mainly to the militant minority within the churches, his evaluation is undoubtedly biased. He may underestimate the strength of those elements in the church today that are more sclerotic than any fossilized labor union and far removed from the hope and hates of the urban poor. But he has spotted an important trend. There is a new mood in the churches, and it is gaining ground quickly.[3]

The debate unleashed by the New Breed is far-reaching. It simmers just below the surface at the national meetings of denominations, church agencies, and church organizations. It often breaks out into open opposition as it often did against Eugene Carson Blake. Blake is now Secretary-General of the World Council of Churches; until May, 1966, he was Stated Clerk of the United Presbyterian Church. One of the first top church officials to be arrested in a civil rights demonstration, Blake is a hero of the New Breed. In an article on the task the church currently has before it, Blake said:

The Church must identify itself much more radically with the interests of the poor, the "losers," the outcasts and the alienated. . . . The mark of the presence of the awaited Messiah is still related to the poor having the Gospel preached to them and the captives being released.[4]

The debate also erupts frequently in city councils of churches. In Rochester, New York, the Council of Churches voted in 1964 to raise $100,000 to support a militant community organization among poor Negroes. The local radio station WHAM threatened to cancel the Council's weekly religious program. When the churches persisted in their plans for the community organization, they were shut off the air; the case is now before the FCC. The Council's executive insists that even though the church's radio voice has been silenced, the church is preaching the gospel by its identification with Rochester's dispossessed.

This argument rages in city after city and church after church. Although the fight seems at first to be about tactical considerations, it actually has profound

theological overtones. It raises the most basic questions about the mission of the church, the nature of its faith, and the central problem of where men encounter God in an urban secular world.

II

Why has a movement of militant, politically conscious churchmen emerged in American cities in the past decade? There are both sociological and theological reasons; the phenomenon cannot be understood without exploring both dimensions.

Sociologically, the emergence of the New Breed can be accounted for by the change in the distribution of power among ethnic and religious groups that has taken place, especially in the older cities of America, in recent years. A Catholic mayor and city council, who usually have close ties with the Irish, Polish, and Italian poor, have in some measure replaced the Protestant oligarchies in the city power structure. Of course, there are still many poor Catholics, but the noisy "new poor" in American cities are often Negroes and Appalachian whites, and mostly Protestants.

The sociological and political basis for the new role churches are playing in urban politics may be the common antagonism for City Hall shared by displaced middle-class white Protestants and by disinherited white and Negro poor. The coalition these groups form is sometimes strengthened by other partners: reform-minded Jews of the type who swallowed ethnic sentiment and voted against Beame and for Lindsay in New York, and "new" Catholics who are heartened by Vatican II and whose Catholicism is a matter of conviction rather than a badge of ethnic identification.

Admittedly this alliance of disparate groups is a recent one;

[3] For a good account of the debate in the churches over Alinsky, see Stephen C. Rose, "Saul Alinsky and His Critics," *Christianity and Crisis*, 24, no. 13 (July 20, 1964).

[4] Eugene Carson Blake, "The Church in the Next Decade," *Christianity and Crisis*, 26, no. 2 (Feb. 21, 1966), 17.

Pete Seeger at the National Cathedral. *(John Goodwin)*

and the connections between the parties, tenuous. Middle-class Protestants and Jews tend to have a League-of-Women-Voters mentality. On the whole, they are devoted to civic improvement, interested in constitutional reform, but suspicious of noisy, conflict-inducing community organization and of sharply partisan politics. Poor whites cooperate uneasily with the Negroes. Catholics are upset when they are accused of "betraying their kind." But however flimsy this coalition may sometimes appear, it is the expression of important social and political realities. If the coalition combines the vigor of the New Breed in the church and the energy of today's Negroes, we may be witnessing the appearance of a formidable new ingredient in the mixed stew of American urban politics. If so, it is a force that politicians will ignore to their peril.

The bureaucratization of religious organizations is the second factor contributing to the entrance of church groups into the political arena as forces to be considered. Although this may sound unlikely to some church members and even to some religious activists, there can be little real doubt that it is true. As Max Weber said, the rationalization of religions produces a group of religious specialists; these specialists then refine, restate, and clarify the beliefs and practices of the religion, often in ways that laymen disapprove. At the upper levels of governmental and private bureaucracies one sees today the development of a group of people who are in command of information and technical competence and can exert influence and leadership that goes considerably beyond the views of the people they are supposed to represent. Such professional initiators of policy populate the research staffs of many elected officials and of numerous public and quasi-public agencies. They often staff the foundations and the command posts of large voluntary associations. They can also be found on the staffs of church organizations, and this raises an important question about the relations between lay and professional members in religious groups. It is especially important for many Protestant groups where all authority ostensibly flows from laity to designated officials. Despite explicit doctrines of congregational autonomy and grassroots authority, something like a "managerial revolution" has taken place in the church. Many church leaders form and lead rather than merely reflect and represent the opinions of their constituencies.[5]

The coming of the managerial revolution to Protestantism means that the wrangle between the New Breed and its opponents is in no sense a battle for the freedom of laymen against a dominating clergy. It is often the reverse. Activist ministers must frequently contend with the socially conservative laymen who sit on the boards and committees that rule the churches. This is particularly important to point out in view of the vocal demands among Catholic laymen today for a wider responsibility in the governance of their church. Protestantism in America, at least in its main-line denominations, is far from being completely lay controlled, but it is often where lay control is most powerful that the social-service mentality and opposition to social action has been most vociferous. Correspondingly, where the managerial revolution has freed ministers and church executives from subservience to laymen, there is *more* of a tendency toward social involvement. Studies have shown that ministers who do not serve a local parish, and hence are somewhat more insulated from direct lay control, are much more likely to demonstrate and become involved in direct action than are pastors of local churches.[6] Of the hundreds of clergymen who flew to Selma, a disproportionate number were denominational and interdenominational staff people, college and university chaplains, and minis-

ters of mission churches not directly dependent on a congregation for their financial support. The same could be said for involvement in urban political issues. Ministers not directly answerable to lay constituencies are joined in New Breed activities by pastors, including Negroes, whose congregations approve their involvement. Ministers of conservative congregations in suburbs or downtown are less likely to lean toward New Breed activism. Likewise priests who belong to religious orders are more likely to take unpopular stands than are the secular priests who serve parish congregations.

Thus, the emergence of the New Breed can be understood in part from a strictly sociological perspective. It expresses a new constellation of political groupings in the American city. It springs from the bureaucratically secured freedom of church executives who have been liberated by tenure and specialization from immediate answerability to lay sentiment. But such explanations always leave much unsaid. One study shows that ministers who belong to denominations that have taken stronger stands on civil rights tend to become more deeply involved in this struggle than ministers whose national church bodies have issued weaker statements. In other words, there are religious and theological variables at work. Unless we specifically examine what Gerhard Lenski calls "the religious factor,"[7] our picture remains incomplete. Without a "religious factor," for example, it would be hard to explain why the behavior of certain Catholics conflicts markedly with ethnic and class expectations, or why church leaders urge courses of action that may threaten their class and institutional interests.

III

Two elements in the belief systems of the churches have a direct bearing on the emergence of the New Breed. One is the "holiness of the poor," the special status assigned to the poor in Christian theology. The other is the idea of the "blessed community," the high value put on equality and personal participation in the congregation and in the society as well, especially in religious groups deriving from the English Reformation. The Negro freedom movement, particularly as it is embodied in such charismatic leaders as Martin Luther King, has often served as the vehicle through which churchmen have moved toward activism on a wider range of issues. But King's persuasiveness lies in part in his ability to appeal to values that are deeply enmeshed in the American religious tradition. The Negro becomes the present embodiment of "the poor," while "integration" points to the vision of a holy community. All this is made explicit on such ritualistic occasions as the 1963 March on Washington where the ritual culminated in King's "I Have a Dream" sermon.

It is also essential to notice that the two elements, the holy outcast *and* the blessed community, must go together. Without the vision of restored community, the holiness ascribed to the poor would fall far short of politics and result in a mere perpetuation of charity and service activities. But the two together, mediated to American theology from the classical theological tradition by the emphasis on the Kingdom of God and the Social Gospel, produce a powerful ideological stimulus without which the New Breed remains incomprehensible.

Let us look first at the place of the poor in Christian theology. Saul Alinsky is correct in saying that whatever their degree of

[5] Paul Harrison, *Authority and Power in the Free Church Tradition* (Princeton, N.J., 1959).

[6] See some of the recent work of sociologist Jeffrey K. Hadden, especially "A Study of the Protestant Ministry of America," *Journal for the Scientific Study of Religion*, 5, no. 1 (1965), 10–23.

[7] Gerhard Lenski, *The Religious Factor* (Garden City, N.Y., 1961).

Martin Luther King, Jr., Riverside Church, New York City, 1967. *(John Goodwin)*

institutional compromise, the churches have an inconvenient gospel that constantly reminds them that they should be the protagonists of the poor. This tradition has deep roots. Although the ancient Jews saw prosperity as a sign of divine favor, they also believed that God would severely judge those in power who abused the poor. This is evident, for example, in Nathan's parable to King David (II Samuel 12:1–6) and in the preaching of such eighth-century prophets as Amos, Isaiah, and Micah. The Mosaic legislation and particularly the Priestly Code make the poor—especially widows, orphans, and sojourners—objects of special solicitude (see Leviticus 5 and 19). Among the Israelites, the poor had the privilege of gleaning and the right to the produce of the land during the sabbatical year.

From the outset, the outcast has occupied a special place in Christian theology. In Jesus' teaching it is the poor who inherit the Kingdom; his recorded utterances fairly seethe with invective against the rich. Whether these sayings are really his or whether they reflect the ethos of the early church is not important for our purpose. In either case, the poor, the disenfranchised, and the underprivileged were believed to be holy; they were thought to be in some way especially favored of God.

Most early Christian congregations were made up of poor people, as Paul discloses in the opening section of his first letter to the Christians at Corinth. Passages critical of the rich may reveal, therefore, an element of *ressentiment*. Still, these ideas were fixed in canon and liturgy and have periodically exerted an important influence on the church. This is obvious when one thinks of the continuous impact that one single text, "Sell all you have and give to the poor," has had throughout church history. It was a crucial determinant in the birth of the monastic movement and the Franciscan order among others. This case and countless others demonstrate the importance of value and belief to social change.[8]

With the rise, after Constantine, of the Medieval Catholic Church and the resulting alteration in the class composition of Christianity, there was a corresponding retreat from the mystique of the poor. Although the monastic movement tried to emphasize its religious importance, poverty was eventually defined, along with celibacy and obedience, as one of the "counsels of perfection" required of the dedicated religious elite within the church but not of the vast majority of believers. The poor, both clerical and lay, were viewed as those whose presence in the society provided the needed occasion to give alms and exercise the virtue of charity. In a subtle way, the virtue seen by early Christians in the poor themselves was now transferred to those who gave to the poor.

With the coming of the Protestant Reformation and the rise of capitalism, the idea that the poor were especially dear to God temporarily lost favor. Moral strictures on the poor became common. Their failure to flourish was interpreted as evidence of the displeasure and wrath of

God. Still, the value of comparison for poor people was never wholly lost, and England passed its first real poor-relief act in 1601, emphasizing work relief for able-bodied men and apprenticeships for children. But the suspicion that pauperism came mainly from sloth rather than from the inability to find a job caused relief payments to be kept lower than the wages paid to the poorest workers. In many European countries, the churches retained control of poor relief until the nineteenth century.

Throughout Western history, contempt for the poor as morally inferior people was constantly challenged by the belief in their holiness. The idea that the indigent were bearers of special virtue and religious significance was always kept alive. Roman Catholic orders stressed the value of poverty. Heretical groups such as the Waldensians, founded in 1179 by Peter Waldo as "The Poor Men of Lyons," tried to call the whole church back to apostolic poverty. Moravians and Methodists spread their doctrines at first mainly among the poor. Among modern Roman Catholics, writers such as Dorothy Day and her followers of *The Catholic Worker* kept the idea of God's presence among the poor alive in a church that was often debased and cheapened by American success standards. It is noteworthy that Michael Harrington, whose eloquent book on poverty *The Other America*[9] made such a mark on the American conscience, began his writing career with *The Catholic Worker*.

But this traditional emphasis on the holiness of the poor in Christian theology could not by itself have produced the New Breed. A tradition of *concern*

for the poor could just as easily lead the churches today into the social-service rather than the political attitude toward poverty. The other operative theological and ethical tradition is the equalitarian vision of the blessed community in which everyone participates without distinction. Although this image recurs many times in the Bible, it is perhaps best seen in Jesus' parable of workers in the vineyard, each of whom receives the same pay although they have worked different lengths of time. This parable illustrates the radically equalitarian eschatology of Christianity, in contrast, for example, to the ancient Egyptian belief that royalty would still reign and slaves still serve in the next life. When the principle of radical equality before God and equal participation in the community is applied to the present society, and not just to the church or to the world to come, it has explosive consequences for secular polity. This belief in "participatory democracy," along with a devotion to the poor and dispossessed, supplies in one way or another the theological fuel for today's New Breed.

Where did this conviction originate? The rankless equality of participants was a central feature of the earliest Christian congregations. The Apostle Paul speaks of equality between slave and free, Greek and barbarian, and men and women. With the development of a hierarchically ordered church and the assumption by Christian priests of the *privilegien* once accorded the priests of the imperial cultus, the principle of radical equality was, however, eclipsed. Again, as in the case of poverty, it was emphasized if not always practiced by the religious orders. Some historians contend that the practice of full electoral democracy began in the West in the Benedictine monasteries.

With the Reformation, the re-

---

[8] See J. A. Sanders, "The Banquet of the Dispossessed," *The Union Seminary Quarterly*, 10, no. 4 (May, 1965), 335.

[9] Michael Harrington, *The Other America* (New York, 1962). [See article beginning on p. 135 of this book. —ED.]

ligious equality of all was again strongly emphasized. Although the left-wing Reformers wanted to extend the idea to the entire society, Luther insisted that to confuse equality before God and equality among men was a serious error. It was in seventeenth-century England that the value of "participatory democracy" was most successfully lifted from the religious congregation alone and applied to society as a whole. In Cromwell's army "even cobblers and tinkers" were exhorted to reflect upon political problems. Thus the ideal of a society where everyone participates in politics, where no one is excluded in principle from decision-making in the commonwealth, entered the Anglo-Saxon tradition. It is still operative today and is unquestionably one of the beliefs motivating the New Breed of churchmen.

Not only were all men called by God to political participation, according to the Puritans, but it was possible to establish certain elements of God's Kingdom here on earth. The Calvinism of the English Puritans, as Michael Walzer has shown in *The Revolution of the Saints,* "appropriated worldly means and usages: magistracy, legislation, warfare. The struggle for a new human community, replacing the lost Eden, was made a matter of concrete political activity."[10]

This impulse toward the reconstruction of the political community along lines that would insure a greater realization of ethical and religious values continues to operate in our society today. When combined with a theologically grounded compassion for the poor, it produces a potent motivational factor. But it required a view of the possibilities of the outcast and his potential for political participation that had not been present

during the medieval period. Puritanism supplied this missing link. As Walzer goes on to say, the Puritan program required "a recognition that all subjects were knowledgeable and active citizens, rather than naïve political children, that government was not a household, the state not an extended family, and the king not a loving father."[11]

This same set of beliefs about man, when applied to the American scene today, results in a rejection of the social-service definition of poverty and an endorsement of the political definition. It provides the often unspoken assumption by means of which the young turks can argue that "poverty" is not merely the lack of money and of services by some people, but the failure of the political community as a whole.

IV

With the coming of the New Breed, the American churches have begun to reclaim a central element of their past. H. Richard Niebuhr has argued that the ideal of establishing the Kingdom of God on earth is the most persistent and pervasive theme in the history of American theology.[12] It brought many of the first settlers to a foreboding new continent. It helped inspire the founding fathers of the republic. It came to fervent expression in the nineteenth century in the Social Gospel Movement under Washington Gladden and Walter Rauschenbusch. In turn, the Social Gospel greatly influenced the social thinking of the Federal Council of Churches in its famous "social creed of the churches" of 1908. With the coming of World War I, the Social Gospel Movement, for

which pacifism was a central tenet, began to lose momentum. Later it was displaced theologically by the so-called neo-orthodox movement. Reinhold Niebuhr, with whom neo-orthodoxy is usually associated in this country, perpetuated many of the elements of the Social Gospel, though he was often critical of what he took to be its naïveté about power.[13]

The present renewed interest in political action for the poor among New Breed churchmen is not just a "return to the Social Gospel." It is more than that. It is a reclamation of the main stream of theology in America, a stream that was only temporarily diverted by the European existentialist theologies after World War I. Those who see in the New Breed a mere outburst of secular activism reveal a lack of familiarity with the history of religion in America. The Kingdom of God, which in the neo-orthodox period had become an "impossible possibility," has become once again something for which to work.

Still, there are differences between the current crop of socially militant churchmen and their spiritual forebears. The views of the New Breed tend to be more provisional. They do not believe that one push will bring in the Kingdom. They tend less to identify particular utopian schemes, such as socialism or pacifism, with the gospel. They are more appreciative of secular allies and see the church more as a supporter and strengthener of movements already under way than as a vanguard. They rely less on preaching and are more willing to lead the institutional church directly into the struggle for power for the poor. The New Breed has learned its lessons from Reinhold Niebuhr and combined them with the

---

[10] Michael Walzer, *The Revolution of the Saints* (Cambridge, Mass., 1965), p. 28.

[11] Walzer, *The Revolution of the Saints,* p. 33.

[12] H. Richard Niebuhr, *The Kingdom of God in America* (New York, 1959).

[13] See Robert T. Handy (ed.), *The Social Gospel in America 1870–1920* (New York, 1966).

Service at Christian Foundation. *(Thomas Hoepker, Woodfin Camp, Inc.)*

spirit of the Social Gospel. It has renewed the quest for the Kingdom of God on earth, but it has done so with a deeper realization of the intransigence of evil and a more realistic idea of power and how it functions.

This, then, is the theological perspective of the New Breed. It underlies its claim that the social-service agencies, including those operated by the church, do little to remove poverty. According to the New Breed, these agencies merely reduce the guilt of the non-poor by fostering the illusion that "something is being done." And this illusion leaves little strength or inclination to make the structural changes necessary to close the gap be-

tween the culture of poverty and the majority. So strong is the New Breed's contempt for the Lady-Bountiful attitude toward the poor that certain church agencies have advised their local congregations *against* any cooperation with the government's War on Poverty unless the programs guarantee power and participation for the poor. The April 1966 *Newsletter* of the Division of Church Strategy and Development of The United Presbyterian Church in the U.S.A. warns its readers about the War on Poverty:

There are serious dangers in the way current community action programs are being structured. Lines of control are being drawn tightly

to a central bureaucracy. Vital dynamic elements in the city are in danger of being smothered by the kinds of control of the local citizens which are built into the operations of the city poverty operation. Full endorsement seems inappropriate.[14]

Here the traditional Christian interest in the poor and their welfare has been informed by a social eschatology, a dedication to the restoration of full participation in the commonwealth. This hope for the realization of the blessed community, though expressing itself in secular political form, is, as we have seen, authentically religious in origin.

[14] See "Strategy for the Response of Religious Institutions to the War on Poverty," page 6.

The New Breed of activist churchmen stands in the succession of Roger Williams and William Penn, both of whom sought to establish a colony of heaven on earthly soil. They witness to their faith in a style that would have been familiar to their forefathers among the Free-Soilers, Abolitionists, Feminists, and Social Gospelers. This tradition, which was partially eclipsed by a generation of church theologians heavily influenced by Europe, represents the reappearance of an authentically American religious stream. The New Breed may appear "secularized" to some, but they have an honorable religious history behind them.

What will happen to the New Breed? They will probably not succeed completely, either in their efforts to win control of the church from the Old Guard or in their attempt to abolish poverty, war, and injustice in our society. They may even grow old and complacent. But at the moment, these young activists are trying with some real success to lead the American churches away from their nostalgic dream of the rural past and into the peril and promise of an urban future. In doing so they may restore to visibility a religious tradition at least as old as the American experience itself. Even if they do not fully succeed, they are writing a fascinating chapter in the history of not only the American church, but of the republic as well.

Summary of the Report of the National Advisory Commission on Civil Disorders, 1968

The President's Commission on Civil Disorders was appointed by Lyndon Johnson to investigate rioting in black ghettos. Its report, issued in March 1968, generated heated controversy, especially for its imputation that "white racism is essentially responsible for the explosive mixture which has been accumulating in our cities since the end of World War II." This conclusion, somewhat extravagant in its language, was widely misunderstood. It did not refer primarily to personal behavior and psychological attitudes (although these were factors) but to institutional patterns in which whites had power, some control over their own lives, and material goods, while blacks did not. White people, having power in the society, determined the social and economic patterns that created black ghettos. In the list of the causes of rioting, "disrespectful white attitudes" came far down on the scale, while institutional factors such as police practices, employment, and housing ranked as the most intense irritants. Nor were the Commission's recommendations of the we-must-love-our-brothers variety: they were for concrete policy changes to improve life in the ghettos and to provide for their eventual dispersion.

The Report's descriptions make grim reading. The record of enactment of its recommendations is no less grim, and the condition of life in the ghettos has deteriorated rather than improved since the Commission made its report. In this, it parallels the fate of similar reports after major riots—in 1919, in 1935, in 1943, and in 1965. All, in the words of Kenneth Clark, produced "the same analysis, the same recommendations, and the same inaction."

INTRODUCTION

The summer of 1967 again brought racial disorders to American cities, and with them shock, fear and bewilderment to the nation.

The worst came during a two-week period in July, first in Newark and then in Detroit. Each set off a chain reaction in neighboring communities.

On July 28, 1967, the President of the United States established this Commission and directed us to answer three basic questions:

What happened?

Why did it happen?

What can be done to prevent it from happening again?

To respond to these questions, we have undertaken a broad range of studies and investigations. We have visited the riot cities; we have heard many witnesses; we have sought the counsel of experts across the country.

This is our basic conclusion: Our nation is moving toward two societies, one black, one white—separate and unequal.

Reaction to last summer's disorders has quickened the movement and deepened the division. Discrimination and segregation have long permeated much of American life; they now threaten the future of every American.

This deepening racial division is not inevitable. The movement apart can be reversed. Choice is still possible. Our principal task is to define that choice and to press for a national resolution.

To pursue our present course will involve the continuing polarization of the American community and, ultimately, the destruction of basic democratic values.

The alternative is not blind repression or capitulation to lawlessness. It is the realization of common opportunities for all within a single society.

This alternative will require a commitment to national action—compassionate, massive and sustained, backed by the resources of the most powerful and the richest nation on this earth. From every American it will require new attitudes, new understanding, and, above all, new will.

The vital needs of the nation must be met; hard choices must be made, and, if necessary, new taxes enacted.

Violence cannot build a better society. Disruption and disorder nourish repression, not justice. They strike at the freedom of every citizen. The community cannot—it will not—tolerate coercion and mob rule.

Violence and destruction must be ended—in the streets of the ghetto and in the lives of people.

Segregation and poverty have created in the racial ghetto a destructive environment totally unknown to most white Americans.

What white Americans have never fully understood—but what the Negro can never forget—is that white society is deeply implicated in the ghetto. White institutions created it, white institutions maintain it, and white society condones it.

It is time now to turn with all the purpose at our command to the major unfinished business of this nation. It is time to adopt strategies for action that will produce quick and visible progress. It is time to make good the promises of American democracy to all citizens—urban and rural, white and black, Spanish-surname, American Indian, and every minority group.

Our recommendations embrace three basic principles:

To mount programs on a scale equal to the dimension of the problems;

To aim these programs for high impact in the immediate future in order to close the gap between promise and performance;

To undertake new initiatives and experiments that can change the system of failure and frustration that now dominates the ghetto and weakens our society.

These programs will require unprecedented levels of funding and performance, but they neither probe deeper nor demand more than the problems which called them forth. There can be no higher priority for national action and no higher claim on the nation's conscience.

We issue this Report now, four months before the date called for by the President. Much remains that can be learned. Continued study is essential.

As Commissioners we have worked together with a sense of the greatest urgency and have sought to compose whatever differences exist among us. Some differences remain. But the gravity of the problem and the pressing need for action are too clear to allow further delay in the issuance of this Report.

PART 1—WHAT HAPPENED?

Chapter 1—Profiles of Disorder

The report contains profiles of a selection of the disorders that took place during the summer of 1967. These profiles are designed to indicate how the disorders happened, who participated in them, and how local officials, police forces, and the National Guard responded. Illustrative excerpts follow:

NEWARK

... It was decided to attempt to channel the energies of the people into a nonviolent protest. While Lofton promised the crowd that a full investigation would be made of the Smith incident, the other Negro leaders began urging those on the scene to form a line of march toward the city hall.

Some persons joined the line of march. Other milled about in the narrow street. From the dark grounds of the housing project came a barrage of rocks. Some of them fell among the crowd. Others hit persons in the line of march. Many smashed the windows of the police station. The rock throwing, it was believed, was the work of youngsters; approximately 2500 children lived in the housing project.

Almost at the same time, an old car was set afire in a parking lot. The line of march began to disintegrate. The police, their heads protected by World War I-type helmets, sallied forth to disperse the crowd. A fire engine, arriving on the scene, was pelted with rocks. As police drove people away from the station, they scattered in all directions.

A few minutes later a nearby liquor store was broken into. Some persons, seeing a caravan of cabs appear at city hall to protest Smith's arrest, interpreted this as evidence that the disturbance had been organized, and generated rumors to that effect.

However, only a few stores were looted. Within a short period of time, the disorder appeared to have run its course....

... On Saturday, July 15 [Director of Police Dominick] Spina received a report of snipers in a housing project. When he arrived he saw approximately 100 National Guardsmen and police officers crouching behind vehicles, hiding in corners and lying on the ground around the edge of the courtyard.

Since everything appeared quiet and it was broad daylight, Spina walked directly down the middle of the street. Nothing happened. As he came to the last building of the complex, he heard a shot. All around him the troopers jumped, believing themselves to be under sniper fire. A moment later a young Guardsman ran from behind a building.

The Director of Police went over and asked him if he had fired the shot. The soldier said yes, he had fired to scare a man away from a window; that his orders were to keep everyone away from windows.

Spina said he told the soldier: "Do you know what you just did? You have now created a state of hysteria. Every Guardsman up and down this street and every state policeman and every city policeman that is present thinks that somebody just fired a shot and that it is probably a sniper."

A short time later more "gunshots" were heard. Investigating, Spina came upon a Puerto Rican sitting on a wall. In reply to a question as to whether he knew "where the firing is coming from?" the man said:

"That's no firing. That's fireworks. If you look up to the fourth floor, you will see the people who are throwing down these cherry bombs."

By this time four truckloads of National Guardsmen had arrived and troopers and policemen were again crouched everywhere looking for a sniper. The Director of Police remained at the scene for three hours, and the only shot fired was the one by the Guardsmen.

Nevertheless, at six o'clock that evening two columns of National Guardsmen and state troopers were directing mass fire at the Hayes Housing Project in response to what they believed were snipers....

DETROIT

...A spirit of carefree nihilism was taking hold. To riot and destroy appeared more and more to become ends in themselves. Late Sunday afternoon it appeared to one observer that the young people were "dancing amidst the flames."

A Negro plainclothes officer was standing at an intersection when a man threw a Molotov cocktail into a business establishment at the corner. In the heat of the afternoon, fanned by the 20 to 25 m.p.h. winds of both Sunday and Monday, the fire reached the home next door within minutes. As residents uselessly sprayed the flames with garden hoses, the fire jumped from roof to roof of adjacent two- and three-story buildings. Within the hour the entire block was in flames. The ninth house in the burning row belonged to the arsonist who had thrown the Molotov cocktail....

...Employed as a private guard, 55-year-old Julius L. Dorsey, a Negro, was standing in front of a market when accosted by two Negro men and a woman. They demanded he permit them to loot the market. He ignored their demands. They began to berate him. He asked a neighbor to call the police. As the argument grew more heated, Dorsey fired three shots from his pistol into the air.

The police radio reported: "Looters, they have rifles." A patrol car driven by a police officer and carrying three National Guardsmen arrived. As the looters fled, the law enforcement personnel opened fire. When the firing ceased, one person lay dead.

He was Julius L. Dorsey....

...As the riot alternately waxed and waned, one area of the ghetto remained insulated. On the northeast side the residents of the some 150 square blocks inhabited by 21,000 persons had, in 1966, banded together in the Positive Neighborhood Action Committee (PNAC). With professional help from the Institute of Urban Dynamics, they had organized block clubs and made plans for the improvement of the neighborhood....

When the riot broke out, the residents, through the block clubs, were able to organize quickly. Youngsters, agreeing to stay in the neighborhood, participated in detouring traffic. While many persons reportedly sympathized with the idea of a rebellion against the "system," only two small fires were set —one in an empty building....

...According to Lt. Gen. Throckmorton and Col. Bolling, the city, at this time, was saturated with fear. The National Guardsmen were afraid, the residents were afraid, and the police were afraid. Numerous persons, the majority of them Negroes, were being injured by gunshots of undetermined origin. The general and his staff felt that the major task of the troops was to reduce the fear and restore an air of normalcy.

In order to accomplish this, every effort was made to establish contact and rapport between the troops and the residents. The soldiers—20 percent of whom were Negro—began helping to clean up the streets, collect garbage, and trace persons who had disappeared in the confusion. Residents in the neighborhoods responded with soup and sandwiches for the troops. In areas where the National Guard tried to establish rapport with the citizens, there was a smaller response.

NEW BRUNSWICK

...A short time later, elements of the crowd—an older and rougher one than the night before —appeared in front of the police station. The participants wanted to see the mayor.

Mayor [Patricia] Sheehan went out onto the steps of the station. Using a bullhorn, she talked to the people and asked that she be given an opportunity to correct conditions. The crowd was boisterous. Some persons challenged the mayor. But, finally, the opinion, "She's new! Give her a chance!" prevailed.

A demand was issued by people in the crowd that all persons arrested the previous night be released. Told that this already had been done, the people were suspicious. They asked to be allowed to inspect the jail cells.

It was agreed to permit representatives of the people to look in the cells to satisfy themselves that everyone had been released.

The crowd dispersed. The New Brunswick riot had failed to materialize.

Chapter 2—Patterns of Disorder

The "typical" riot did not take place. The disorders of 1967 were unusual, irregular, complex and unpredictable social processes. Like most human events, they did not unfold in an orderly sequence. However, an analysis of our survey information leads to some conclusions about the riot process.

In general:

The civil disorders of 1967 involved Negroes acting against local symbols of white American society, authority and property in Negro neighborhoods—rather than against white persons.

Of 164 disorders reported during the first nine months of 1967, eight (5 per cent) were major in terms of violence and damage; 33 (20 percent) were serious but not major; 123 (75 percent) were minor and undoubtedly would not have received national attention as "riots" had the nation not been sensitized by the more serious outbreaks.

In the 75 disorders studied by a Senate subcommittee, 83 deaths were reported. Eighty-two percent of the deaths and more than half the injuries occurred in Newark and Detroit. About 10 percent of the dead and 38 percent of the injured were public employees, primarily law officers and firemen. The overwhelming majority of the persons killed or injured in all the disorders were Negro civilians.

Initial damage estimates were greatly exaggerated. In Detroit, newspaper damage estimates at first ranged from $200 million to $500 million; the highest recent estimate is $45 million. In Newark, early estimates ranged from $15 to $25 million. A month later damage was estimated at $10.2 million, over 80 percent in inventory losses.

In the 24 disorders in 23 cities which we surveyed:

The final incident before the outbreak of disorder, and the initial violence itself, generally took place in the evening or at night at a place in which it was normal for many people to be on the streets.

Violence usually occurred almost immediately following the occurrence of the final precipitating incident, and then escalated rapidly. With but few exceptions, violence subsided during the day, and flared rapidly again at night. The night-day cycles continued through the early period of the major disorders.

Disorder generally began with rock and bottle throwing and window breaking. Once store windows were broken, looting usually followed.

Disorder did not erupt as a result of a single "triggering" or "precipitating" incident. Instead, it was generated out of an increasingly disturbed social atmosphere, in which typically a series of tension-heightening incidents over a period of weeks or months became linked in the minds of many in the Negro community with a reservoir of underlying grievances. At some point in the mounting tension, a further incident—in itself often routine or trivial—became the breaking point and the tension spilled over into violence.

"Prior" incidents, which increased tensions and ultimately led to violence, were police actions in almost half the cases; police actions were "final" incidents before the outbreak in 12 of the 24 surveyed disorders.

No particular control tactic was successful in every situation. The varied effectiveness of control techniques emphasizes the need for advance training, planning, adequate intelligence systems, and knowledge of the ghetto community.

Negotiations between Negroes—including your militants as well as older Negro leaders—and white officials concerning "terms of peace" occurred during virtually all the disorders surveyed. In many cases, these negotiations involved discussion of underlying grievances as well as the handling of the disorder by control authorities.

The typical rioter was a teenager or young adult, a lifelong resident of the city in which he rioted, a high school dropout; he was, nevertheless, somewhat better educated than his nonrioting Negro neighbor, and was usually underemployed or employed in a menial job. He was proud of his race, extremely hostile to both whites and middle-class Negroes, and, although informed about politics, highly distrustful of the political system.

A Detroit survey revealed that approximately 11 percent of the total residents of two riot areas admitted participation in the rioting, 20 to 25 percent identified themselves as "bystanders," over 16 percent identified themselves as "counter-rioters" who urged rioters to "cool it," and the remaining 48 to 53 percent said they were at home or elsewhere and did not participate. In a survey of Negro males between the ages of 15 and 35 residing in the disturbance area in Newark, about 45 percent identified themselves as rioters, and about 55 percent as "noninvolved."

Most rioters were young Negro males. Nearly 53 percent of arrestees were between 15 and 24 years of age; nearly 81 percent between 15 and 35.

In Detroit and Newark about 74 percent of the rioters were brought up in the North. In contrast, of the noninvolved, 36 percent in Detroit and 52 percent in Newark were brought up in the North.

What the rioters appeared to be seeking was fuller participation in the social order and the material benefits enjoyed by the majority of American citizens. Rather than rejecting the American system, they were anxious to obtain a place for themselves in it.

Numerous Negro counter-rioters walked the streets urging rioters to "cool it." The typical counter-rioter was better educated and had higher income than either the rioter or the noninvolved.

The proportion of Negroes in local government was substantially smaller than the Negro proportion of population. Only three of the 20 cities studied had more than one Negro legislator; none had ever had a Negro mayor or city manager. In only four cities did Negroes hold other important policy-making positions or serve as heads of municipal departments.

Although almost all cities had some sort of formal grievance mechanism for handling citizen complaints, this typically was regarded by Negroes as ineffective and was generally ignored.

Although specific grievances varied from city to city, at least 12 deeply held grievances can be identified and ranked into three levels of relative intensity:

First Level of Intensity
1. Police practices
2. Unemployment and underemployment
3. Inadequate housing

Second Level of Intensity
4. Inadequate education
5. Poor recreation facilities and programs
6. Ineffectiveness of the political structure and grievance mechanisms

Third Level of Intensity
7. Disrespectful white attitudes
8. Discriminatory administration of justice
9. Inadequacy of federal programs
10. Inadequacy of municipal services
11. Discriminatory consumer and credit practices
12. Inadequate welfare programs

The results of a three-city survey of various federal programs—manpower, education, housing, welfare and community action—indicate that, despite substantial expenditures, the number of persons assisted constituted only a fraction of those in need.

The background of disorder is often as complex and difficult to analyze as the disorder itself. But we find that certain general conclusions can be drawn:

Social and economic conditions in the riot cities constituted a clear pattern of severe disadvantage for Negroes compared with whites, whether the Negroes lived in the area where the riot took place or outside it. Negroes had completed fewer years of education and fewer had attended high school. Negroes were twice as likely to be unemployed and three times as likely to be in unskilled and service jobs.

Negroes averaged 70 percent of the income earned by whites and were more than twice as likely to be living in poverty. Although housing cost Negroes relatively more, they had worse housing—three times as likely to be overcrowded and substandard. When compared to white suburbs, the relative disadvantage is even more pronounced.

A study of the aftermath of disorder leads to disturbing conclusions. We find that, despite the institution of some post-riot programs:

Little basic change in the conditions underlying the outbreak of disorder has taken place. Actions to ameliorate Negro grievances have been limited and sporadic; with but few exceptions, they have not significantly reduced tensions.

In several cities, the principal official response has been to train and equip the police with more sophisticated weapons.

In several cities, increasing polarization is evident, with continuing breakdown of inter-racial communication, and growth of white segregationist or black separatist groups.

Chapter 3—Organized Activity

The President directed the Commission to investigate "to what extent, if any, there has been planning or organization in any of the riots."

To carry out this part of the President's charge, the Commission established a special investigative staff supplementing the field teams that made the general examination of the riots in 23 cities. The unit examined data collected by federal agencies and congressional committees, including thousands of documents supplied by the Federal Bureau of Investigation, gathered and evaluated information from local and state law enforcement agencies and officials, and conducted its own field investigation in selected cities.

On the basis of all the information collected, the Commission concludes that:

The urban disorders of the summer of 1967 were not caused by, nor were they the consequence of, any organized plan or "conspiracy."

Specifically, the Commission has found no evidence that all or any of the disorders or the incidents that led to them were planned or directed by any organization or group, international, national or local.

Militant organizations, local and national, and individual agitators, who repeatedly forecast and called for violence, were active in the spring and summer of 1967. We believe that they sought to encourage violence, and that they helped to create an atmosphere that contributed to the outbreak of disorder.

We recognize that the continuation of disorders and the polarization of the races would provide fertile ground for organized exploitation in the future.

Investigations of organized activity are continuing at all levels of government, including committees of Congress. These investigations relate not only to the disorders of 1967 but also to the actions of groups and individuals, particularly in schools and colleges, during this last fall and winter. The Commission has cooperated in these investigations. They should continue.

PART II—WHY DID IT HAPPEN?
Chapter 4—The Basic Causes

In addressing the question "Why did it happen?" we shift our focus from the local to the national scene, from the particular events of the summer of 1967 to the factors within the society at large that created a mood of violence among many urban Negroes.

These factors are complex and interacting; they vary significantly in their effect from city to city and from year to year; and the consequences of one disorder, generating new grievances and new demands, become the causes of the next. Thus was created the "thicket of tension, conflicting evidence and extreme opinions" cited by the President.

Despite these complexities, certain fundamental matters are clear. Of these, the most fundamental is the racial attitude and behavior of white Americans toward black Americans.

Race prejudice has shaped our history decisively; it now threatens to affect our future.

White racism is essentially responsible for the explosive mixture which has been accumulating in our cities since the end of World War II. Among the ingredients of this mixture are:

Pervasive discrimination and segregation in employment, education and housing, which have resulted in the continuing exclusion of great numbers of Negroes from the benefits of economic progress.

Black in-migration and white exodus, which have produced the massive and growing concentrations of impoverished Negroes in our major cities, creating a growing crisis of deteriorating facilities and services and unmet human needs.

The black ghettos where segregation and poverty converge on the young to destroy opportunity and enforce failure. Crime, drug addiction, dependency on welfare, and bitterness and resentment against society in general and white society in particular are the result.

At the same time, most whites and some Negroes outside the ghetto have prospered to a degree unparalled in the history of civilization. Through television and other media, this affluence has been flaunted before the eyes of the Negro poor and the jobless ghetto youth.

Yet these facts alone cannot be said to have caused the disorders. Recently, other powerful ingredients have begun to catalyze the mixture:

Frustrated hopes are the residue of the unfulfilled expectations aroused by the great judicial and legislative victories of the Civil Rights Movement and the dramatic struggle for equal rights in the South.

A climate that tends toward approval and encouragement of violence as a form of protest has been created by white terrorism directed against nonviolent protest; by the open defiance of law and federal authority by state and local officials resisting desegregation; and by some protest groups engaging in civil disobedience who turn their backs on nonviolence, go beyond the constitutionally protected rights of petition and free assembly, and resort to violence to attempt to compel alteration of laws and policies with which they disagree.

The frustrations of powerlessness have led some Negroes to the conviction that there is no effective alternative to violence as a means of achieving redress of grievances, and of "moving the system." These frustrations are reflected in alienation and hostility toward the institutions of law and government and the white society which controls them, and in the reach toward racial consciousness and solidarity reflected in the slogan "Black Power."

A new mood has sprung up among Negroes, particularly among the young, in which self-esteem and enhanced racial pride are replacing apathy and submission to "the system."

The police are not merely a "spark" factor. To some Negroes police have come to symbolize white power, white racism and white repression. And the fact is that many police do reflect and express these white attitudes. The atmosphere of hostility and cynicism is reinforced by a widespread belief among Negroes in the existence of police brutality and in a "double standard" of justice and protection—one for Negroes and one for whites. . . .

To this point, we have attempted to identify the prime components of the "explosive mixture." In the chapters that follow we seek to analyze them in the perspective of history. Their meaning, however, is clear:

In the summer of 1967, we have seen in our cities a chain reaction of racial violence. If we are heedless, none of us shall escape the consequences.

Chapter 5—Rejection and Protest: An Historical Sketch

The causes of recent racial disorders are embedded in a tangle of issues and circumstances—social, economic, political and psychological—which arise out of the historic pattern of Negro-white relations in America.

In this chapter we trace the pattern, identify the recurrent themes of Negro protest and, most importantly, provide a perspective on the protest activities of the present era.

We describe the Negro's experience in America and the development of slavery as an institution. We show his persistent striving for equality in the face of rigidly maintained social, economic and educational barriers, and repeated mob violence. We portray the ebb and flow of the doctrinal tides—accommodation, separatism, and self-help—and their relationship to the current theme of Black Power. We conclude:

The Black Power advocates of today consciously feel that they are the most militant group in the Negro protest movement. Yet they have retreated from a direct confrontation with American society on the issue of integration and, by preaching separatism, unconsciously function as an accommodation to white racism. Much of their economic program, as well as their interest in Negro history, self-help, racial solidarity and separation, is reminiscent of Booker T. Washington. The rhetoric is different, but the ideas are remarkably similar.

Chapter 6—The Formation of the Racial Ghettos[1]

Throughout the 20th century the Negro population of the United States has been moving steadily from rural areas to urban and from South to North and West. In 1910, 91 percent of the nation's 9.8 million Negroes lived in the South and only 27 percent of American Negroes lived in cities of 2500 persons or more. Between 1910 and 1966 the total Negro population more than doubled, reaching 21.5 million, and the number living in metropolitan areas rose more than five-fold (from 2.6 million to 14.8 million). The number outside the South rose eleven-fold (from 880,000 to 9.7 million).

Negro migration from the South has resulted from the expectation of thousands of new and highly paid jobs for unskilled workers in the North and the shift to mechanized farming in the South. However, the Negro migration is small when compared to earlier waves of European immigrants. Even between 1960 and 1966, there were 1.8 million immigrants from abroad compared to the 613,000 Negroes who arrived in the North and West from the South.

As a result of the growing number of Negroes in urban areas, natural increase has replaced migration as the primary source of Negro population increase in the cities. Nevertheless, Negro migration from the South will continue unless economic conditions there change dramatically.

Basic data concerning Negro urbanization trends indicate that:

Almost all Negro population growth (98 percent from 1950 to

[1] The term "ghetto" as used in this report refers to an area within a city characterized by poverty and acute social disorganization, and inhabited by members of a racial or ethnic group under conditions of involuntary segregation.

1966) is occurring within metropolitan areas, primarily within central cities.[2]

The vast majority of white population growth (78 percent from 1960 to 1966) is occurring in suburban portions of metropolitan areas. Since 1960, white central-city population has declined by 1.3 million.

As a result, central cities are becoming more heavily Negro while the suburban fringes around them remain almost entirely white.

The twelve largest cities now contain over two-thirds of the Negro population outside the South, and one-third of the Negro total in the United States.

Within the cities, Negroes have been excluded from white residential areas through discriminatory practices. Just as significant is the withdrawal of white families from, or their refusal to enter, neighborhoods where Negroes are moving or already residing. About 20 percent of the urban population of the United States changes residence every year. The refusal of whites to move into "changing" areas when vacancies occur means that most vacancies eventually are occupied by Negroes.

The result, according to a recent study, is that in 1960 the average segregation index for 207 of the largest United States cities was 86.2. In other words, to create an unsegregated population distribution, an average of over 86 percent of all Negroes would have to change their place of residence within the city.

Chapter 7—Unemployment, Family Structure, and Social Disorganization

Although there have been gains in Negro income nationally, and a decline in the number of Negroes below the "poverty level,"

[2] A "central city" is the largest city of a standard metropolitan statistical area, that is, a metropolitan area containing at least one city of 50,000 or more inhabitants.

the condition of Negroes in the central city remains in a state of crisis. Between 2 and 2.5 million Negroes—16 to 20 percent of the total Negro population of all central cities—live in squalor and deprivation in ghetto neighborhoods.

Employment is a key problem. It not only controls the present for the Negro American but, in a most profound way, it is creating the future as well. Yet, despite continuing economic growth and declining national unemployment rates, the unemployment rate for Negroes in 1967 was more than double that for whites.

Equally important is the undesirable nature of many jobs open to Negroes and other minorities. Negro men are more than three times as likely as white men to be in low-paying, unskilled or service jobs. This concentration of male Negro employment at the lowest end of the occupational scale is the single most important cause of poverty among Negroes.

In one study of low-income neighborhoods, the "subemployment rate," including both unemployment and underemployment, was about 33 percent, or 8.8 times greater than the overall unemployment rate for all United States workers.

Employment problems, aggravated by the constant arrival of new unemployed migrants, many of them from depressed rural areas, create persistent poverty in the ghetto. In 1966, about 11.9 percent of the nation's whites and 40.6 percent of its nonwhites were below the "poverty level" defined by the Social Security Administration (currently $3335 per year for an urban family of four). Over 40 percent of the nonwhites below the poverty level live in the central cities.

Employment problems have drastic social impact in the ghetto. Men who are chronically unemployed or employed in the lowest status jobs are often unable or unwilling to remain with their families. The handicap imposed on children growing up without fathers in an atmosphere of poverty and deprivation is increased as mothers are forced to work to provide support.

The culture of poverty that results from unemployment and family breakup generates a system of ruthless, exploitative relationships within the ghetto. Prostitution, dope addiction, and crime create an environmental "jungle" characterized by personal insecurity and tension. Children growing up under such conditions are likely participants in civil disorder.

Chapter 8—Conditions of Life in the Racial Ghetto

A striking difference in environment from that of white, middle-class Americans profoundly influences the lives of residents of the ghetto.

Crime rates, consistently higher than in other areas, create a pronounced sense of insecurity. For example, in one city, one low-income Negro district had 35 times as many serious crimes against persons as a high-income white district. Unless drastic steps are taken, the crime problems in poverty areas are likely to continue to multiply as the growing youth and rapid urbanization of the population outstrip police resources.

Poor health and sanitation conditions in the ghetto result in higher mortality rates, a higher incidence of major diseases, and lower availability and utilization of medical services. The infant mortality rate for nonwhite babies under the age of one month is 58 percent higher than for whites; for one to 12 months it is almost three times as high. The level of sanitation in the ghetto is far below that in high-income areas. Garbage collection is often inadequate. Of an estimated 14,000 cases of rat bite in the United States in 1965, most were in ghetto neighborhoods.

Ghetto residents believe they are "exploited" by local merchants; and evidence substantiates some of these beliefs. A study conducted in one city by the Federal Trade Commission showed that distinctly higher prices were charged for goods sold in ghetto stores than in other areas.

Lack of knowledge regarding credit purchasing creates special pitfalls for the disadvantaged. In many states garnishment practices compound these difficulties by allowing creditors to deprive individuals of their wages without hearing or trial.

Chapter 9—Comparing the Immigrant and Negro Experience

In this chapter, we address ourselves to a fundamental question that many white Americans are asking: why have so many Negroes, unlike the European immigrants, been unable to escape from the ghetto and from poverty. We believe the following factors play a part:

The Maturing Economy: When the European immigrants arrived, they gained an economic foothold by providing the unskilled labor needed by industry. Unlike the immigrant, the Negro migrant found little opportunity in the city. The economy, by then matured, had little use for the unskilled labor he had to offer.

The Disability of Race: The structure of discrimination has stringently narrowed opportunities for the Negro and restricted his prospects. European immigrants suffered from discrimination, but never so pervasively.

Entry into the Political System: The immigrants usually settled in rapidly growing cities with powerful and expanding political machines, which traded economic advantages for political support. Ward-level grievance machinery, as well as personal representation, enabled the immigrant to make his voice heard and his power felt.

By the time the Negro arrived, these political machines were no longer so powerful or so well equipped to provide jobs or other favors, and in many cases were unwilling to share their influence with Negroes.

Cultural Factors: Coming from societies with a low standard of living and at a time when job aspirations were low, the immigrants sensed little deprivation in being forced to take the less desirable and poorer-paying jobs. Their vision of the future—one that led to a life outside of the ghetto—provided the incentive necessary to endure the present.

Although Negro men worked as hard as the immigrants, they were unable to support their families. The entrepreneurial opportunities had vanished. As a result of slavery and long periods of unemployment, the Negro family structure had become matriarchal; the males played a secondary and marginal family role—one which offered little compensation for their hard and unrewarding labor. Above all, segregation denied Negroes access to good jobs and the opportunity to leave the ghetto. For them, the future seemed to lead only to a dead end.

Today, whites tend to exaggerate how well and quickly they escaped from poverty. The fact is that immigrants who came from rural backgrounds, as many Negroes do, are only now, after three generations, finally beginning to move into the middle class.

By contrast, Negroes began concentrating in the city less than two generations ago, and under much less favorable conditions. Although some Negroes have escaped poverty, few have been able to escape the urban ghetto.

PART III—WHAT CAN BE DONE?

Chapter 10—The Community Response

Our investigation of the 1967 riot cities establishes that virtually every major episode of violence was foreshadowed by an accumulation of unresolved grievances and by widespread dissatisfaction among Negroes with the unwillingness or inability of local government to respond.

Overcoming these conditions is essential for community support of law enforcement and civil order. City governments need new and more vital channels of communication to the residents of the ghetto; they need to improve their capacity to respond effectively to community needs before they become community grievances; and they need to provide opportunity for meaningful involvement of ghetto residents in shaping policies and programs which affect the community.

The Commission recommends that local governments:

Develop Neighborhood Action Task Forces as joint community-government efforts through which more effective communication can be achieved, and the delivery of city services to ghetto residents improved.

Establish comprehensive grievance-response mechanisms in order to bring all public agencies under public scrutiny.

Bring the institutions of local government closer to the people they serve by establishing neighborhood outlets for local, state and federal administrative and public service agencies.

Expand opportunities for ghetto residents to participate in the formulation of public policy and the implementation of programs affecting them through improved political representation, creation of institutional channels for community action, expansion of legal services, and legislative hearings on ghetto problems.

In this effort, city governments will require state and federal support. The Commission recommends:

State and federal assistance for mayors and city councils to sup-

port the research, consultants, staff and other resources needed to respond effectively to federal program initiatives.

State cooperation in providing municipalities with the jurisdictional tools needed to deal with their problems; a fuller measure of financial aid to urban areas; and the focusing of the interests of suburban communities on the physical, social and cultural environment of the central city.

Chapter 11—Police and the Community

The abrasive relationship between the police and the minority communities has been a major—and explosive—source of grievance, tension and disorder. The blame must be shared by the total society.

The police are faced with demands for increased protection and service in the ghetto. Yet the aggressive patrol practices thought necessary to meet these demands themselves create tension and hostility. The resulting grievances have been further aggravated by the lack of effective mechanisms for handling complaints against the police. Special programs for bettering police-community relations have been instituted, but these alone are not enough. Police administrators, with the guidance of public officials, and the support of the entire community, must take vigorous action to improve law enforcement and to decrease the potential for disorder.

The Commission recommends that city government and police authorities:

Review police operations in the ghetto to ensure proper conduct by police officers, and eliminate abrasive practices.

Provide more adequate police protection to ghetto residents to eliminate their high sense of insecurity, and the belief of many Negro citizens in the existence of a dual standard of law enforcement.

Establish fair and effective mechanisms for the redress of grievances against the police, and other municipal employees.

Develop and adopt guidelines to assist officers in making critical decisions in areas where police conduct can create tension.

Develop and use innovative programs to ensure widespread community support for law enforcement.

Recruit more Negroes into the regular police force, and review promotion policies to ensure fair promotion for Negro officers.

Establish a "Community Service Officer" program to attract ghetto youths between the ages of 17 and 21 to police work. These junior officers would perform duties in ghetto neighborhoods, but would not have full police authority. The federal government should provide support equal to 90 percent of the costs of employing CSOs on the basis of one for every ten regular officers.

Chapter 12—Control of Disorder

Preserving civil peace is the first responsibility of government. Unless the rule of law prevails, our society will lack not only order but also the environment essential to social and economic progress.

The maintenance of civil order cannot be left to the police alone. The police need guidance, as well as support, from mayors and other public officials. It is the responsibility of public officials to determine proper police policies, support adequate police standards for personnel and performance, and participate in planning for the control of disorders.

To maintain control of incidents which could lead to disorders, the Commission recommends that local officials:

Assign seasoned, well-trained policemen and supervisory officers to patrol ghetto areas, and to respond to disturbances.

Develop plans which will quickly

muster maximum police manpower and highly qualified senior commanders at the outbreak of disorders.

Provide special training in the prevention of disorders, and prepare police for riot control and for operation in units, with adequate command and control and field communication for proper discipline and effectiveness.

Develop guidelines governing the use of control equipment and provide alternatives to the use of lethal weapons. Federal support for research in this area is needed.

Establish an intelligence system to provide police and other public officials with reliable information that may help to prevent the outbreak of a disorder and to institute effective control measures in the event a riot erupts.

Develop continuing contacts with ghetto residents to make use of the forces for order which exist within the community.

Establish machinery for neutralizing rumors, and enabling Negro leaders and residents to obtain the facts. Create special rumor details to collect, evaluate, and dispel rumors that may lead to a civil disorder.

The Commission believes there is a grave danger that some communities may resort to the indiscriminate and excessive use of force. The harmful effects of overreaction are incalculable. The Commission condemns moves to equip police departments with mass destruction weapons, such as automatic rifles, machine guns and tanks. Weapons which are designed to destroy, not to control, have no place in densely populated urban communities.

The Commission recognizes the sound principle of local authority and responsibility in law enforcement, but recommends that the federal government share in the financing of programs for improvement of police forces, both in their normal law enforcement activities as well as in their response to civil disorders.

To assist government authorities in planning their response to civil disorder, this report contains a Supplement on Control of Disorder. It deals with specific problems encountered during riot-control operations, and includes:

Assessment of the present capabilities of police, National Guard and Army forces to control major riots, and recommendations for improvement;

Recommended means by which the control operations of those forces may be coordinated with the response of other agencies, such as fire departments, and with the community at large;

Recommendations for review and revision of federal, state and local laws needed to provide the framework for control efforts and for the call-up and interrelated action of public safety forces.

Chapter 13—The Administration of Justice under Emergency Conditions

In many of the cities which experienced disorders last summer, there were recurring breakdowns in the mechanisms for processing, prosecuting and protecting arrested persons. These resulted mainly from long-standing structural deficiencies in criminal court systems, and from the failure of communities to anticipate and plan for the emergency demands of civil disorders.

In part, because of this, there were few successful prosecutions for serious crimes committed during the riots. In those cities where mass arrests occurred many arrestees were deprived of basic legal rights.

The Commission recommends that the cities and states:

Undertake reform of the lower courts so as to improve the quality of justice rendered under normal conditions.

Plan comprehensive measures by which the criminal justice system may be supplemented during civil disorders so that its deliberative functions are protected, and the quality of justice is maintained.

Such emergency plans require broad community participation and dedicated leadership by the bench and bar. They should include:

Laws sufficient to deter and punish riot conduct.

Additional judges, bail and probation officers, and clerical staff.

Arrangements for volunteer lawyers to help prosecutors and to represent riot defendants at every stage of proceedings.

Policies to ensure proper and individual bail, arraignment, pre-trial, trial and sentencing proceedings.

Procedures for processing arrested persons, such as summons and release, and release on personal recognizance, which permit separation of minor offenders from those dangerous to the community, in order that serious offenders may be detained and prosecuted effectively.

Adequate emergency processing and detention facilities.

Chapter 14—Damages: Repair and Compensation

The Commission recommends that the federal government:

Amend the Federal Disaster Act —which now applies only to natural disasters—to permit federal emergency food and medical assistance to cities during major civil disorders, and provide long-term economic assistance afterwards.

With the cooperation of the states, create incentives for the private insurance industry to provide more adequate property-insurance coverage in inner-city areas.

The Commission endorses the report of the National Advisory Panel on Insurance in Riot-Affected Areas: "Meeting the Insurance Crisis of Our Cities."

Chapter 15—The News Media and the Disorders

In his charge to the Commission, the President asked: "What effect do the mass media have on the riots?"

The Commission determined that the answer to the President's question did not lie solely in the performance of the press and broadcasters in reporting the riots. Our analysis had to consider also the overall treatment by the media of the Negro ghettos, community relations, racial attitudes, and poverty—day by day and month by month, year in and year out.

A wide range of interviews with government officials, law enforcement authorities, media personnel and other citizens, including ghetto residents, as well as a quantitative analysis of riot coverage and a special conference with industry representatives, leads us to conclude that:

Despite instances of sensationalism, inaccuracy and distortion, newspapers, radio and television tried on the whole to give a balanced, factual account of the 1967 disorders.

Elements of the news media failed to portray accurately the scale and character of the violence that occurred last summer. The overall effect was, we believe, an exaggeration of both mood and event.

Important segments of the media failed to report adequately on the causes and consequences of civil disorders and on the underlying problems of race relations. They have not communicated to the majority of their audience—which is white—a sense of the degradation, misery and hopelessness of life in the ghetto.

These failings must be corrected, and the improvement must come from within the industry. Freedom of the press is not the issue. Any effort to impose governmental restrictions would be inconsistent with fundamental constitutional precepts.

We have seen evidence that the news media are becoming aware of and concerned about their performance in this field. As that concern grows, coverage will improve. But much more must be done, and it must be done soon.

The Commission recommends that the media:

Expand coverage of the Negro community and of race problems through permanent assignment of reporters familiar with urban and racial affairs, and through establishment of more and better links with the Negro community.

Integrate Negroes and Negro activities into all aspects of coverage and content, including newspaper articles and television programming. The news media must publish newspapers and produce programs that recognize the existence and activities of Negroes as a group within the community and as a part of the larger community.

Recruit more Negroes into journalism and broadcasting and promote those who are qualified to positions of significant responsibility. Recruitment should begin in high schools and continue through college; where necessary, aid for training should be provided.

Improve coordination with police in reporting riot news through advance planning, and cooperate with the police in the designation of police information officers, establishment of information centers, and development of mutually acceptable guidelines for riot reporting and the conduct of media personnel.

Accelerate efforts to ensure accurate responsible reporting of riot and racial news, through adoption by all news gathering organizations of stringent internal staff guidelines.

Cooperate in the establishment of a privately organized and funded Institute of Urban Communications to train and educate journalists in urban affairs, recruit and train more Negro journalists, develop methods for improving police-press relations, review coverage of riots and racial issues, and support research in the urban field.

Chapter 16—The Future of the Cities

By 1985, the Negro population in central cities is expected to increase by 72 percent to approximately 20.8 million. Coupled with the continued exodus of white families to the suburbs, this growth will produce majority Negro populations in many of the nation's largest cities.

The future of these cities, and of their burgeoning Negro populations, is grim. Most new employment opportunities are being created in suburbs and outlying areas. This trend will continue unless important changes in public policy are made.

In prospect, therefore, is further deterioration of already inadequate municipal tax bases in the face of increasing demands for public services, and continuing unemployment and poverty among the urban Negro population:

Three choices are open to the nation:

We can maintain present policies, continuing both the proportion of the nation's resources now allocated to programs for the unemployed and the disadvantaged, and the inadequate and failing effort to achieve an integrated society.

We can adopt a policy of "enrichment" aimed at improving dramatically the quality of ghetto life while abandoning integration as a goal.

We can pursue integration by combining the ghetto "enrichment" with policies which will encourage Negro movement out of central city areas.

The first choice, continuance of present policies, has ominous consequences for our society. The share of the nation's resources now allocated to programs for the disadvantaged is insufficient to arrest the deterioration of life in central city ghettos. Under such conditions, a rising proportion of Negroes may come to see in the deprivation and segregation they experience, a justification for violent protest, or for extending support to now isolated extremists who advocate civil disruption. Large-scale and continuing violence could result, followed by white retaliation, and, ultimately, the separation of the two communities in a garrison state.

Even if violence does not occur, the consequences are unacceptable. Development of a racially integrated society, extraordinarily difficult today, will be virtually impossible when the present black ghetto population of 12.5 million has grown to almost 21 million.

To continue present policies is to make permanent the division of our country into two societies; one, largely Negro and poor, located in the central cities; the other, predominantly white and affluent, located in the suburbs and in outlying areas.

The second choice, ghetto enrichment coupled with abandonment of integration, is also unacceptable. It is another way of choosing a permanently divided country. Moreover, equality cannot be achieved under conditions of nearly complete separation. In a country where the economy, and particularly the resources of employment, are predominantly white, a policy of separation can only relegate Negroes to a permanently inferior economic status.

We believe that the only possible choice for America is the third—a policy which combines ghetto enrichment with programs designed to encourage integration of substantial numbers of Negroes into the society outside the ghetto.

Enrichment must be an important adjunct to integration, for no matter how ambitious or energetic the program, few Negroes now living in central cities can be quickly integrated. In the meantime, large-scale improvements in the quality of ghetto life is essential.

But this can be no more than an interim strategy. Programs must be developed which will permit substantial Negro movement out of the ghettos. The primary goal must be a single society, in which every citizen will be free to live and work according to his capabilities and desires, not his color.

Chapter 17—Recommendations for National Action

INTRODUCTION

No American—white or black—can escape the consequences of the continuing social and economic decay of our major cities.

Only a commitment to national action on an unprecedented scale can shape a future compatible with the historic ideals of American society.

The great productivity of our economy, and a federal revenue system which is highly responsive to economic growth, can provide the resources.

The major need is to generate new will—the will to tax ourselves to the extent necessary to meet the vital needs of the nation.

We have set forth goals and proposed strategies to reach those goals. We discuss and recommend programs not to commit each of us to specific parts of such programs but to illustrate the type and dimension of action needed.

The major goal is the creation of a true union—a single society and a single American identity. Toward that goal, we propose the following objectives for national action:

Opening up opportunities to those who are restricted by racial segregation and discrimination, and eliminating all barriers to their choice of jobs, education and housing.

Removing the frustration of powerlessness among the disadvantaged by providing the means for them to deal with the problems that affect their own lives and by increasing the capacity of our public and private institutions to respond to these problems.

Increasing communication across racial lines to destroy stereotypes, to halt polarization, end distrust and hostility, and create common ground for efforts toward public order and social justice.

We propose these aims to fulfill our pledge of equality and to meet the fundamental needs of a democratic and civilized society—domestic peace and social justice.

EMPLOYMENT

Pervasive unemployment and underemployment are the most persistent and serious grievances in minority areas. They are inextricably linked to the problem of civil disorder.

Despite growing federal expenditures for manpower development and training programs, and sustained general economic prosperity and increasing demands for skilled workers, about two million—white and non-white—are permanently unemployed. About ten million are underemployed, of whom 6.5 million work full time for wages below the poverty line.

The 500,000 "hard-core" unemployed in the central cities who lack a basic education and are unable to hold a steady job are made up in large part of Negro males between the ages of 18 and 25. In the riot cities which we surveyed, Negroes were three times as likely as whites to hold unskilled jobs, which are often part time, seasonal, low-paying and "dead end."

Negro males between the ages of 15 and 25 predominated among the rioters. More than 20 percent of the rioters were unemployed, and many who were employed held intermittent, low status, unskilled jobs which they regarded as below their education and ability.

The Commission recommends that the federal government:

Undertake joint efforts with cities and states to consolidate existing manpower programs to avoid fragmentation and duplication.

Take immediate action to create 2,000,000 new jobs over the next three years—one million in the public sector and one million in the private sector—to absorb the hard-core unemployed and materially reduce the level of underemployment for all workers, black and white. We propose 250,000 public sector and 300,000 private sector jobs in the first year.

Provide on-the-job training by both public and private employers with reimbursement to private employers for the extra costs of training the hard-core unemployed, by contract or by tax credits.

Provide tax and other incentives to investment in rural as well as urban poverty areas in order to offer to the rural poor an alternative to migration to urban centers.

Take new and vigorous action to remove artificial barriers to employment and promotion, including not only racial discrimination but, in certain cases, arrest records or lack of a high school diploma. Strengthen those agencies such as the Equal Employment Opportunity Commission, charged with eliminating discriminatory practices, and provide full support for Title VI of the 1964 Civil Rights Act allowing federal grant-in-aid funds to be withheld from activities which discriminate on grounds of color or race.

The Commission commends the recent public commitment of the National Council of the Building and Construction Trades Unions, AFL-CIO, to encourage and recruit Negro membership in apprenticeship programs. This commitment should be intensified and implemented.

EDUCATION

Education in a democratic society must equip children to develop their potential and to participate fully in American life. For the community at large, the schools have discharged this responsibility well. But for many minorities, and particularly for the children of the ghetto, the schools have failed to provide the educational experience which could overcome the effects of discrimination and deprivation.

This failure is one of the persistent sources of grievance and resentment within the Negro community. The hostility of Negro parents and students toward the school system is generating increasing conflict and causing disruption within many city school districts. But the most dramatic evidence of the relationship between educational practices and civil disorders lies in the high incidence of riot participation by ghetto youth who have not completed high school.

The bleak record of public education for ghetto children is growing worse. In the critical skills—verbal and reading ability—Negro students are falling further behind whites with each year of school completed. The high unemployment and underemployment rate for Negro youth is evidence, in part, of the growing educational crisis.

We support integration as the priority education strategy; it is essential to the future of American society. In this last summer's disorders we have seen the consequences of racial isolation at all levels, and of attitudes toward race, on both sides, produced by three centuries of myth, ignorance and bias. It is indispensable that opportunities for interaction between the races be expanded.

We recognize that the growing dominance of pupils from disadvantaged minorities in city school populations will not soon be reversed. No matter how great the effort toward desegregation, many children of the ghetto will not, within their school careers, attend integrated schools.

If existing disadvantages are not to be perpetuated, we must drastically improve the quality of ghetto education. Equality of results with all-white schools must be the goal.

To implement these strategies, the Commission recommends:

Sharply increased efforts to eliminate de facto segregation in our schools through substantial federal aid to school systems seeking to desegregate either within the system or in cooperation with neighboring school systems.

Elimination of racial discrimination in Northern as well as Southern schools by vigorous application of Title VI of the Civil Rights Act of 1964.

Extension of quality early childhood education to every disadvantaged child in the country.

Efforts to improve dramatically schools serving disadvantaged children through substantial federal funding of year-round compensatory education programs, improved teaching, and expanded experimentation and research.

Elimination of illiteracy through greater federal support for adult basic education.

Enlarged opportunities for parent and community participation in the public schools.

Reoriented vocational education emphasizing work-experience training and the involvement of business and industry.

Expanded opportunities for higher education through increased federal assistance to disadvantaged students.

Revision of state aid formulas to assure more per student aid to districts having a high proportion of disadvantaged school-age children.

THE WELFARE SYSTEM

Our present system of public welfare is designed to save money instead of people, and tragically ends up doing neither. This system has two critical deficiencies:

First, it excludes large numbers of persons who are in great need, and who, if provided a decent level of support, might be able to become more productive and self-sufficient. No federal funds are available for millions of men and women who are needy but neither aged, handicapped nor the parents of minor children.

Second, for those included, the system provides assistance well below the minimum necessary for a decent level of existence, and imposes restrictions that encourage continued dependency on welfare and undermine self-respect.

A welter of statutory requirements and administrative practices and regulations operate to remind recipients that they are considered untrustworthy, promiscuous and lazy. Residence requirements prevent assistance to people in need who are newly arrived in the state. Regular searches of recipients' homes violate privacy. Inadequate social services compound the problems.

The Commission recommends that the federal government, acting with state and local governments where necessary, reform the existing welfare system to:

Establish uniform national standards of assistance at least as high as the annual "poverty level" of income, now set by the Social Security Administration at $3,335 per year for an urban family of four.

Require that all states receiving federal welfare contributions participate in the Aid to Families with Dependent Children—Unemployed Parents program (AFDC-UP) that permits assistance to families with both father and mother in the home, thus aiding the family while it is still intact.

Bear a substantially greater portion of all welfare costs—at least 90 percent of total payments.

Increase incentives for seeking employment and job training, but remove restrictions recently enacted by the Congress that would compel mothers of young children to work.

Provide more adequate social services through neighborhood centers and family-planning programs.

Remove the freeze by the 1967 welfare amendments on the percentage of children in a state that can be covered by federal assistance. Eliminate residence requirements.

As a long-range goal, the Commission recommends that the federal government seek to develop a national system of income supplementation based strictly on need with two broad and basic purposes:

To provide, for those who can work or who do work, any necessary supplements in such a way as to develop incentives for fuller employment;

To provide, for those who cannot work and for mothers who decide to remain with their children, a minimum standard of decent living, and to aid in the saving of children from the prison of poverty that has held their parents.

A broad system of supplementation would involve substantially greater federal expenditures than anything now contemplated. The cost will range widely depending on the standard of need accepted as the "basic allowance" to individuals and families, and on the rate at which additional income above this level is taxed. Yet if the deepening cycle of poverty and dependence on welfare can be broken, if the children of the poor can be given the opportunity to scale the wall that now separates them from the rest of society, the return on this investment will be great indeed.

HOUSING

After more than three decades of fragmented and grossly underfunded federal housing programs, nearly six million substandard housing units remain occupied in the United States.

The housing problem is particularly acute in the minority ghettos. Nearly two-thirds of all non-white families living in the central cities today live in neighborhoods marked with substan-

dard housing and general urban blight. Two major factors are responsible.

First: Many ghetto residents simply cannot pay the rent necessary to support decent housing. In Detroit, for example, over 40 percent of the non-white occupied units in 1960 required rent of over 35 percent of the tenants' income.

Second: Discrimination prevents access to many non-slum areas, particularly the suburbs, where good housing exists. In addition, by creating a "back pressure" in the racial ghettos, it makes it possible for landlords to break up apartments for denser occupancy, and keeps prices and rents of deteriorated ghetto housing higher than they would be in a truly free market.

To date, federal programs have been able to do comparatively little to provide housing for the disadvantaged. In the 31-year history of subsidized federal housing, only about 800,000 units have been constructed, with recent production averaging about 50,000 units a year. By comparison, over a period only three years longer, FHA insurance guarantees have made possible the construction of over ten million middle- and upper-income units.

Two points are fundamental to the Commission's recommendations:

First: Federal housing programs must be given a new thrust aimed at overcoming the prevailing patterns of racial segregation. If this is not done, those programs will continue to concentrate the most impoverished and dependent segments of the population into the central-city ghettos where there is already a critical gap between the needs of the population and the public resources to deal with them.

Second: The private sector must be brought into the production and financing of low and moderate rental housing to supply the capabilities and capital necessary to meet the housing needs of the nation:

The Commission recommends that the federal government:

Enact a comprehensive and enforecable federal open housing law to cover the sale or rental of all housing, including single family homes.

Reorient federal housing programs to place more low- and moderate-income housing outside of ghetto areas.

Bring within the reach of low- and moderate-income families within the next five years six million new and existing units of decent housing, beginning with 60,000 units in the next year.

To reach this goal we recommend:

Expansion and modification of the rent supplement program to permit use of suplements for existing housing, thus greatly increasing the reach of the program.

Expansion and modification of the below-market interest rate program to enlarge the interest subsidy to all sponsors and provide interest-free loans to nonprofit sponsors to cover pre-construction costs, and permit sale of projects to nonprofit corporations, cooperatives, or condominiums.

Creation of an ownership supplement program similar to present rent supplements, to make home ownership possible for low-income families.

Federal writedown of interest rates on loans to private builders constructing moderate-rent housing.

Expansion of the public housing program, with emphasis on small units on scattered sites, and leasing and "turnkey" programs.

Expansion of the Model Cities program.

Expansion and reorientation of the urban renewal program to give priority to projects directly assisting low-income households to obtain adequate housing.

CONCLUSION

One of the first witnesses to be invited to appear before this Commission was Dr. Kenneth B. Clark, a distinguished and perceptive scholar. Referring to the reports of earlier riot commissions, he said:

I read that report . . . of the 1919 riot in Chicago, and it is as if I were reading the report of the investigating committee on the Harlem riot of '35, the report of the investigating committee on the Harlem riot of '43, the report of the McCone Commission on the Watts riot.

I must again in candor say to you members of this Commission —it is a kind of Alice in Wonderland—with the same moving picture re-shown over and over again, the same analysis, the same recommendations, and the same inaction.

These words come to our minds as we conclude this Report.

We have provided an honest beginning. We have learned much. But we have uncovered no startling truths, no unique insights, no simple solutions. The destruction and the bitterness of racial disorder, the harsh polemics of black revolt and white repression have been seen and heard before in this country.

It is time now to end the destruction and the violence, not only in the streets of the ghetto but in the lives of people.

HUGH DAVIS GRAHAM
TED ROBERT GURR

Conclusion: A Report to the National Commission on the Causes and Prevention of Violence

The violence of the 1960s profoundly upset dominant views of the American past. What scholars in the fifties had been arguing did not exist in the American past became unmistakably evident in the sixties: ideological conflict, civil disorder, and problems of national loyalty. Upon investigation, we now realize that assassinations, rioting, lynching, vigilantes, and intergroup violence have been commonplace in our history. As the Conclusion of the Report to the National Commission on the Causes and Prevention of Violence makes clear, we still do not know just what causes such violence, and we certainly are a long way from the ability to prevent its recurrence.

Hugh Davis Graham and Ted Robert Gurr, in the summary of the Report, point out that many of the same factors that scholars once claimed kept the nation orderly might in fact be productive of disorder. Our melting pot culture has at times created violence, especially when the melting did not occur or took place too slowly. The frontier, although it relieved social pressure in some places, encouraged lawlessness in others, as our endlessly repeated Western legends tell us. Our revolutionary ideology not only gave us equipment to meet change, but also planted the suggestion that in some circumstances violence was legitimate. Our stress on consensus in politics has sometimes meant that conflict could not be expressed through regular political channels but has had to find outlets in violence. Clearly, in order to understand the violence and conflict of the sixties, we will have to bring to our entire national past a fresh understanding of its violence.

I. THE COMMONALITY OF COLLECTIVE VIOLENCE IN THE WESTERN TRADITION

Future historians may marvel at the ostensible "rediscovery" of violence that has both fascinated and bemused contemporary observers. That the recent resurgence of collective nonmilitary violence in Western society is widely regarded as anomalous probably reflects both a cultural and a contemporary bias. We have tended to assume, perhaps unconsciously, that such violence was an uncivilized practice of more primitive societies that the civilized and affluent West had largely outgrown. Our historians have themselves been guilty of contributing to this popular illusion; while they have retained their fascination for military exploits, they have tended either to ignore the persistence of domestic turmoil except when it reached revolutionary proportions, or to minimize its significance by viewing it from the perspective of established authority. When viewed from the top down, violence was understandably regarded as an abnormal and undesirable breach of the public order.

On the contrary, Tilly concludes, "collective violence is normal."

Historically, collective violence has flowed regularly out of the central, political processes of western countries. Men seeking to seize, hold, or realign the levers of power have continually engaged in collective violence as part of their struggles. The oppressed have struck in the name of justice, the privileged in the name of order, those in between in the name of fear.

In Tilly's analysis, collective violence in the European experience was fundamentally transformed but not foredoomed by the processes of industrialization and urbanization. The old "primitive" forms of violence in feudal Europe—such as communal feuds and religious persecutions—were characterized by small scale, local scope, communal group participation, and inexplicit and unpolitical objectives. The subsequent evolution of the nation-state prompted such "reactionary" disturbances as food riots, Luddite destruction, tax revolts, and anticonscription rebellions. Although industrialization and urbanization muted such disorders by disrupting their cohesive communal base, the metropolitan society these forces forged gave rise to "modern" forms of protest—such as demonstrations and strikes—which involved relatively large and specialized associations with relatively well-defined and "forward-looking" objectives and which were explicitly organized for political or economic action.

Tilly's model suggests that modern collective protest, owing to its broader associational base, is more likely to occur on a large scale. But modern protest is less likely to become violent because the associational form gives the group a surer control over its own actions, and thus permits shows of force without concomitant damage or bloodshed. Moreover, the historic shift from communal to associational bases for collective protest brought into being a number of modern non-violent mechanisms for the regulation of conflicts: the strike, the demonstration, the parliament, and the political campaign. Collective violence, then, historically belongs to political life, and changes in its form tell us that something important is happening to the political system itself.

What is happening to the political system in contemporary America? Preliminary to such an inquiry is the historical task of surveying the patterns of group violence that have accompanied the development of the United States. Brown has traced an overview of American collective violence, and his organizational categories of "negative" and "positive" violence in some ways parallel Tilly's analytical distinctions between reactionary disturbances, which center on rights once enjoyed but now threatened, and modern disturbances, which center on rights not yet enjoyed but now within reach. It might be more appropriate in this conclusion to discuss the American historical legacy of violence in relation to the contemporary relevance of the various categories Brown employed. Brown catalogued as "negative" forms of American violence that associated with feuds, lynching, political assassination, free-lance multiple murder, crime, ethnic and racial prejudice, and urban rioting. "Positive" forms were associated with the American Rev-

olution and Civil War, agrarian uprisings, labor protests, vigilantism, Indian wars, and police violence.

Perhaps the historically violent episode that is least relevant to our contemporary concerns is the family feud. The famous and colorful clan feuding seems to have been triggered by the Civil War in border areas where loyalties were sharply divided and where the large extended family of the 19th century provided both a focus for intense loyalties and a ready instrument of aggression. But this tradition has waned with the fading of the circumstances that conditioned its birth. It is arguable, however, that the brutalizing traditions associated with the Indian wars have left their callous imprint on our national character long after the estimated 850,000 American Indians had been ruthlessly reduced by 1950 to 400,000. Similarly, the violence associated with the American Revolution, the Civil War, and Reconstruction has surely reinforced the ancient notion that the ends justify the means, and clearly the defeat of the Confederacy and the failure of Reconstruction has convinced generations of white Southerners that Negro political participation and Federal efforts at reform are irrevocably linked with corruption and subversion.

Whether the long association with violence of agrarian uprisings and the labor movement has permanently faded with changing modern circumstances is fervently to be hoped, but by no means certain. Employer acceptance of unions during and after the New Deal suggests that that long and bloody conflict is largely behind us. But the stubborn persistence of rural poverty constitutes a latent invitation to a resurgence of latter-day populism.

Two other sordid American traditions that have largely waned but that recently have shown some signs of revival are vigilantism and lynching. Although vigilantism is associated in the popular mind with such frontier and rural practices as antirustler and antihorsethief popular "justice" in areas largely devoid of regular enforcement agencies, the largest local American vigilance committee was organized in San Francisco in 1856. If vigilantism is defined more broadly to include regional and even national movements as well as local organizations, then America's preeminent vigilante movement has been the Ku Klux Klan—or rather, the Ku Klux Klans, for there have essentially been three of them. The original Klan arose in the South in response to radical Reconstruction, and through terror and intimidation was instrumental in the "redemption" of the Southern state governments by white conservatives. The second Klan, by far the largest, was resurrected in Atlanta in 1915 and boomed nationally in the 1920s. Strong in the Midwest and Far West as well as the South, and making inroads even in the cities, the Klan of the 1920s—despite its traditional racist and xenophobic rhetoric—focused its chastisement less upon Negroes, Catholics, and Jews than upon local white Protestants who were adjudged guilty of violating small-town America's Victorian moral code. The third Klan represented a proliferation of competing Klans in the South in response to the civil rights movement of the 1950s. Generally lacking the prestige and organizational strength of the earlier Klans, these groups engaged in a period of unrestrained terrorism in the rural and smalltown Black Belt South in the 1950s and early 1960s, but have belatedly been brought under greater control.

Lynching, vigilantism's supreme instrument of terror and summary "justice," has been widely practiced in America certainly since the Revolutionary era, when miscreant Tories were tarred and feathered, and worse. Although lynching is popularly associated with racial mob murder, this pattern is a relatively recent one, for prior to the late 19th century, white Americans perforce lynched one another—Negro slaves being far too valuable to squander at the stake. But lynching became predominantly racial from 1882 to 1903, when 1985 Negroes were murdered in the tragic but successful effort of those years to forge a rigid system of biracial caste, most brutal and explicit in the South but generally reflective of national attitudes. Once the point—that this was a white man's country—was made, lynching gradually declined. Its recent resurgence in response to the civil rights movement is notorious, but it nowhere approximates its scale at the turn of the century.

The contemporary relevance of political assassination and freelance multiple murder needs no documentation to a nation that has so recently witnessed the murders of John and Robert Kennedy, Dr. Martin Luther King, and, on television, Lee Harvey Oswald—in addition to the chilling mass slaughtering sprees of Charles Whitman in Austin, Texas, and Richard Speck in Chicago. Historically, political assassination has become a recurrent feature of the political system only in the South during (the first) Reconstruction and in New Mexico Territory. Although four American Presidents have been assassinated since 1865, prominent politicians and civil servants occupying the myriad lesser levels of government have been largely immune. Whether the current spate of public murder is an endemic symptom of a new social malaise is a crucial question that history cannot yet answer, other than to observe that precedents in our past are minimal.

Similarly, historical precedents are few regarding massive student and antiwar protests. American students have historically succumbed to the annual spring throes of the panty-raid syndrome, but the current wave of campus confrontations is essentially an unprecedented phenomenon—as is the massive and prolonged opposition to the war in Vietnam. As Professor Brooks has observed, "unfortunately the past does not have much to tell us; we will have to make our own history along uncharted and frightening ways."

But the past has much to tell us about the rioting and crime that have gripped our cities. Urban mobs are as old as the city itself. Colonial seaports frequently were rocked for days by roving mobs—groups of unruly and often drunken men whose energies were shrewdly put to political purpose as Liberty Boys in the American Revolution. Indeed, our two principal instruments of physical control evolved directly in response to 19th-century urban turmoil. The professional city police system replaced the inadequate constabulary and watch-and-ward in response to the rioting of the 1840s and 1850s, largely in the Northeast. Similarly, the national guard was organized in order to control the labor violence—or more appropriately, the antilabor violence—of the 1880s and 1890s.

Probably all nations are given to a kind of historical amnesia or selective recollection that masks unpleasant traumas of the past. Certainly Americans since the Puritans have historically regarded themselves as a latter-day "Chosen People" sent on a holy errand to the wilderness, there to create a New Jerusalem. One beneficent side effect of our current turmoil may be to force a harder and more candid look at our past and at our behavior in comparison with other peoples and nations.

II. CONTEMPORARY AMERICAN VIOLENCE IN HISTORICAL PERSPECTIVE

Our current eruption of violence must appear paradoxical to a generation of Americans who witnessed the successful emergence from depression to unparalleled affluence of a nation they regarded as the world's moral leader in defense of freedom. Only a decade ago America's historians were celebrating the emergence of a unique society, sustained by a burgeoning prosperity and solidly grounded on a broad political consensus. We were told—and the implications were reassuring—that our uniqueness was derived from at least half a dozen historical sources which, mutually reinforcing one another, had joined to propel us toward a manifestly benevolent destiny. We were a nation of immigrants, culturally enriched by the variety of mankind. Sons of the frontier, our national character had grown to reflect the democratic individualism and pragmatic ingenuity that had conquered the wilderness. Our new nation was born in anticolonial revolution and in its crucible was forged a democratic republic of unparalleled vitality and longevity. Lacking a feudal past, our political spectrum was so truncated about the consensual liberal center that, unlike Europe, divisive radicalism of the left or right had found no sizable constituency. Finally, we had both created and survived the great transformation from agrarian frontier to industrial metropolis, to become the richest nation of all time.

It was a justly proud legacy, one which seemed to make sense in the relatively tranquil 1950s. But with the 1960s came shock and frustration. It was a decade against itself: the students of affluence were marching in the streets; middle-class matrons were besieging the Pentagon; and Negro Americans were re-sponding to victories in civil rights and to their collectively unprecedented prosperity with a paradoxical venting of outrage. In a fundamental sense, history —the ancient human encounter with poverty, defeat and guilt as well as with affluence, victory, and innocence—had finally caught up with America. Or at least it had caught up with white America.

Historical analysis of our national experience and character would suggest that the seeds of our contemporary discontent were to a large extent deeply embedded in those same ostensibly benevolent forces which contributed to our uniqueness. First, we are a nation of immigrants, but one in which the original dominant immigrant group, the so-called Anglo-Saxons, effectively preempted the crucial levers of economic and political power in government, commerce, and the professions. This elite group has tenaciously resisted the upward strivings of successive "ethnic" immigrant waves. The resultant competitive hierarchy of immigrants has always been highly conducive to violence, but this violence has taken different forms. The Anglo-Americans have used their access to the levers of power to maintain their dominance, using legal force surrounded by an aura of legitimacy for such ends as economic exploitation; the restriction of immigration by a national-origin quota system which clearly branded later immigrants as culturally undesirable; the confinement of the original Indian immigrants largely to barren reservations; and the restriction of blacks to a degraded caste. But the system was also conducive to violence among the latter groups themselves—when, for instance, Irish-Americans rioted against Afro-American "scabs." Given America's unprecedented ethnic pluralism, simply being born American con-ferred no automatic and equal citizenship in the eyes of the larger society. In the face of such reservations, ethnic minorities had constantly to affirm their Americanism through a kind of patriotic ritual which intensified the ethnic competition for status. As a fragment culture based on bourgeois-liberal values, as Hartz has observed, yet one populated by an unprecedented variety of immigrant stock, America's tightened consensus on what properly constituted "Americanism" prompted status rivalries among the ethnic minorities which, when combined with economic rivalries, invited severe and abiding conflict.

Most distinctive among the immigrant minorities was the Negro. The eternal exception in American history, Afro-Americans were among the first to arrive and the last to emerge. To them, America meant slavery, and manumission meant elevation to the caste of black pariah. Comer has seen in the psychological legacy of slavery and caste a physically crippling Negro dependency and even self-hatred which is largely immune to mere economic advance. The contemporary black awareness of this tenacious legacy of racial shame is abundantly reflected in the radical rhetoric of black power and "Black-is-Beautiful," and goes far toward resolving the paradox of black rebellion against a backdrop of general—albeit uneven, as Davies suggests— economic improvement. Meier and Rudwick have charted the transformation of racial violence from white pogrom to black aggression—or, in the analysis of Janowitz, from "communal" to "commodity" rioting. While emphasizing that the transformation has led to violent black assault less against white persons than against white property, and while Janowitz speculates that the summer of 1968 may have been yet another turning point, we are reminded that history, even very recent history, is an imperfect guide to the future.

The second major formative historical experience was America's uniquely prolonged encounter with the frontier. While the frontier experience indubitably strengthened the mettle of the American character, it witnessed the brutal and brutalizing ousting of the Indians and the forceful incorporation of Mexican and other original inhabitants, as Frantz [Fanon] has so graphically portrayed. Further, it concomitantly created an environment in which, owing to the paucity of law enforcement agencies, a tradition of vigilante "justice" was legitimized. The longevity of the Ku Klux Klan and the vitality both of contemporary urban rioting and of the stiffening resistance to it owe much to this tradition. As Brown has observed, vigilantism has persisted as a socially malleable instrument long after the disappearance of the frontier environment that gave it birth, and it has proved quite congenial to an urban setting.

Similarly, the revolutionary doctrine that our Declaration of Independence proudly proclaims stands as a tempting model of legitimate violence to be emulated by contemporary groups such as militant Negroes and radical students who confront a system of both public and private government that they regard as contemptuous of their consent. Entranced by the resurgence of revolution in the underdeveloped world and of international university unrest, radical students and blacks naturally seize upon our historically sacrosanct doctrine of the inherent right of revolution and self-determination to justify their rebellion. That their analogies are fatefully problematical in no way dilutes the majesty of our own proud Declaration.

The fourth historic legacy, our consensual political philosophy of Lockean-Jeffersonian liberalism, was premised upon a pervasive fear of governmental power and has reinforced the tendency to define freedom negatively as freedom *from*. As a consequence, conservatives have been able paradoxically to invoke the doctrines of Jefferson in resistance to legislative reforms, and the Sumnerian imperative that "stateways cannot change folkways" has historically enjoyed a wide and not altogether unjustified allegiance in the public eye (witness the debacle of the first Reconstruction, and the dilemma of our contemporary second attempt). Its implicit corollary has been that forceful, and, if necessary, violent local and state resistance to unpopular federal stateways is a legitimate response; both Calhoun and Wallace could confidently repair to a strict construction of the same document invoked by Lincoln and the Warren Court.

A fifth historic source both of our modern society and our current plight is our industrial revolution and the great internal migration from the countryside to the city. Yet the process occurred with such astonishing rapidity that it produced widespread socioeconomic dislocation in an environment in which the internal controls of the American social structure were loose and the external controls were weak. Urban historian Richard Wade has observed that—

The cities inherited no system of police control adequate to the numbers or to the rapid increase of the urban centers. The modern police force is the creation of the 20th century; the establishment of genuinely professional systems is historically a very recent thing. Throughout the 18th and 19th century, the force was small, untrained, poorly paid, and part of the political system. In case of any sizeable disorder, it was hopelessly inadequate; and rioters sometimes routed the constabulary in the first confrontation.

Organized labor's protracted and bloody battles for recognition and power occurred during these years of minimal control and maximal social upheaval. The violence of workers' confrontations with their employers, Taft and Ross concluded, was partly the result of a lack of consensus on the legitimacy of workers' protests, partly the result of the lack of means of social control. Workers used force to press their grievances, employers organized violent resistance, and repeatedly state or federal toops had to be summoned to restore order.

The final distinctive characteristic—in many ways perhaps our most distinctive—has been our unmatched prosperity; we have been, in the words of David Potter, most characteristically a "people of plenty." Ranked celestially with life and liberty in the sacrosanct Lockean trilogy, property has generated a quest and prompted a devotion in the American character that has matched our devotion to equality and, in a fundamental sense, has transformed it from the radical leveling of the European democratic tradition into a typically American insistence upon equality of opportunity. In an acquisitive society of individuals with unequal talents and groups with unequal advantages, this had resulted in an unequal distribution of the rapid accumulation of abundance that, especially since World World II, has promised widespread participation in the affluent society to a degree unprecedented in history. Central to the notion of "revolutions of rising expectations," and to Davies' J-curve hypothesis as well, is the assumption that unproved economic rewards can coincide with and often obscure a degree of relative deprivation that generates frustration and can prompt men toward violent protest despite measurable gains.

Our historical evolution, then, has given our national character a dual nature: we strive, paradoxically, for both liberty and equality, which can be and often in practice are quite contradictory goals. This is not to suggest that American society is grounded in a fatal contradiction. For all the conflict inherent in a simultaneous quest for liberty and equality, American history is replete with dramatic instances of the successful adjustment of "the system" to the demands of disparate protesting groups. An historical appraisal of these genuine achievements should give pause to contemporary Cassandras who bemoan in self-flagellation how hopelessly wretched we all are. These radically disillusioned social critics can find abundant evil in our historical legacy: centuries of Negro slavery, the cultural deracination and near extinction of the Indians, our initiation of atomic destruction—ad infinitum. Much as the contemporary literary Jeremiahs have, in Lynn's view, libeled the American character by extrapolating violence from its literary context, these social critics in their over-compensations have distorted the American experience in much the same fashion, although in an opposite direction, as have the more familiar superpatriotic celebrants of American virtuosity. While a careful and honest historical appraisal should remind us that violence has been far more intrinsic to our past than we should like to think—Brooks reminds us, for example, that the New York Draft Riot of 1863 vastly exceeded the destruction of Watts—our assessment of the origins and dimensions of contemporary American violence must embrace the experience of other societies.

III. COMPARISONS OF PROTEST AND VIOLENCE

Whether the United States is now a "violent society" can be answered not in the abstract but only by comparison, either with the American past or with other nations. The historical evidence, above, suggests that we are somewhat more violent toward one another in this decade than we have been in most others, but probably less violent in total magnitude of civil strife than in the latter 19th century, when the turmoil of Reconstruction was followed by massive racial and labor violence. Even so, contemporary comparison with other nations, acts of collective violence by private citizens in the United States in the last 20 years have been extraordinarily numerous, and this is true also of peaceful demonstrations. In numbers of political assassinations, riots, politically relevant armed group attacks, and demonstrations the United States since 1948 has been among the half-dozen most tumultuous nations in the world. When such events are evaluated in terms of their relative severity, however, the rank of the United States is somewhat lower. The Feierabends and Nesvold have used ranking scales to weigh the severity and numbers of such events during the years 1948 to 1965, rating peaceful demonstrations as having the least serious impact, civil wars the most serious impact on political systems. In a comparison that gives greatest weight to the frequency of violent events, the United States ranks 14th among 84 nations. In another comparison, based mainly on the severity of all manifestations of political instability, violent or not, the United States stands below the midpoint, 46th among 84 nations. In other words, the United States up to 1965 had much political violence by comparison with other nations but relative stability of its political institutions in spite of it. Paradoxically, we have been a turbulent people but a relatively stable republic.

Some more detailed comparisons are provided by a study of the characteristics of civil strife in 114 nations and colonies in the 1960s. The information on "civil strife" includes all reported acts of collective violence involving 100 or more people; organized private attacks on political targets, whatever the number of participants; and antigovernment demonstrations involving 100 or more people. Three general kinds of civil strife are distinguished: (1) *Turmoil* is relatively spontaneous, partially organized or unorganized strife with substantial popular participation and limited objectives. (2) *Conspiracy* is intensively organized strife with limited participation but with terroristic or revolutionary objectives. (3) *Internal war* is intensively organized strife with widespread participation, always accompanied by extensive and intensive violence and usually directed at the overthrow of political regimes.

The comparisons of the strife study are proportional to population rather than absolute, on grounds that a demonstration by 10,000 of Portugal's 9 million citizens, for example, is more consequential for that nation than a demonstration by the same number of the United States' 200 million citizens is for ours. About 11 out of every 1000 Americans took part in civil strife, almost all of it turmoil, between mid-1963 and mid-1968, compared with an average of 7 per thousand in 17 other Western democracies during the 1961–1965 period. Six of these 17 had higher rates of participation than the United States, including Belgium, France, and Italy. About 9500 reported casualties resulted from American strife, most of them the result of police action. This is a rate of 48 per million population, compared was an average of 12 per million in other Western nations, but American casualties are almost certain to be overreported by comparison with casualties elsewhere. Strife was also of longer duration in the United States than in all but a handful of countries in the world. In total magnitude of strife, taking these three factors into account, the United States ranks first among the 17 Western democracies.

Despite its frequency, civil strife in the United States has taken much less disruptive forms than in many non-Western and some Western countries. More than a million citizens participated in 370 reported civil-rights demonstrations and marches in the 5-year period; almost all of them were peacefully organized and conducted. Of 170 reported antiwar demonstrations, which involved a total of about 700,000 people, the participants initiated violence in about 20. The most extensive violence occurred in 239 recorded hostile outbreaks by Negroes, which resulted in more than 8000 casualties and 191 deaths. Yet the nation has experienced no internal wars since the Civil War and almost none of the chronic revolutionary conspiracy and terrorism that plague dozens of other nations. The most consequential conspiratorial violence has been white terrorism against blacks and civil-rights workers, which caused some 20 deaths between 1963 and 1968, and black terrorism against whites, mostly the police, which began in 1968.

Although about 220 Americans died in violent civil strife in the 5 years before mid-1968, the rate of 1.1 per million population was infinitesimal compared with the average of all nations of 238 deaths per million, and less than the European average of 2.4 million. These differences reflect the comparative evidence that, from a worldwide perspective, Americans have seldom organized for violence. Most demonstrators and rioters are protesting, not rebelling. If there were many serious revolutionaries in the United

States, or effective revolutionary organizations, levels of violence would be much higher than they have been.

These comparisons afford little comfort when the tumult of the United States is contrasted with the relative domestic tranquillity of developed democratic nations like Sweden, Great Britain, and Australia, or with the comparable current tranquillity of nations as diverse as Yugoslavia, Turkey, Jamaica, or Malaysia. In total magnitude of strife, the United States ranks 24th among the 114 larger nations and colonies of the world. In magnitude of turmoil alone, it ranks sixth.

Though greater in magnitude, civil strife in the United States is about the same in kind as strife in other Western nations. The antigovernment demonstration and riot, violent clashes of political or ethnic groups, and student protests are pervasive forms of conflict in modern democracies. Some such public protest has occurred in every Western nation in the past decade. People in non-Western countries also resort to these limited forms of public protest, but they are much more likely to organize serious conspiratorial and revolutionary movements as well. Strife in the United States and other European countries is quite likely to mobilize members of both the working class and middle classes, but rarely members of the political establishment such as military officers, civil servants, and disaffected political leaders, who so often organize conspiracies and internal wars in non-European nations. Strife also is likely to occur within or on the periphery of the normal political process in Western nations, rather than being organized by clandestine revolutionary movements or cells of plotters. If some overt strife is an inevitable accompaniment of organized social existence, as all our comparative evidence suggests it is, it seems socially pref-

erable that it take the form of open political protest, even violent protest, rather than concerted, intensively violent attempts to seize political power.

One evident characteristic of civil strife in the United States in recent years is the extent to which it is an outgrowth of ethnic tensions. Much of the civil protest and collective violence in the United States has been directly related to the nation's racial problems. Comparative studies show evidence of parallel though not identical situations in other developed, European, and democratic nations. The unsatisfied demands of regional, ethnic, and linguistic groups for greater rights and socioeconomic benefits are more common sources of civil strife in Western nations than in almost any other group of countries. These problems have persisted long after the resolution of fundamental questions about the nature of the state, the terms of political power and who should hold it, and economic development. It seems ironical that nations that have been missionaries of technology and political organization to the rest of the world apparently have failed to provide satisfactory conditions of life for all the groups within their midst.

IV. THE SOURCES OF VIOLENCE

Is man violent by nature or by circumstance? In the Hobbesian view, the inescapable legacy of human nature is a "life of man solitary, poor, nasty, brutish, and short." This ancient pessimistic view is given recent credence by the ethologists, whose study of animals in their natural habitats had led them to conclude that the aggressive drive in animals is innate, ranking with the instinctive trilogy of hunger, sex, and fear or flight. But most psychologists and social scientists do not regard aggression as fundamentally spontaneous or instinctive, nor does the weight of their evidence support such a view. Rather they regard most aggression, including violence, as sometimes an emotional response to socially induced frustrations, and sometimes a dispassionate, learned response evoked by specific situations. This assumption underlies almost all the studies in this volume: nature provides us only with the capacity for violence; it is social circumstance that determines whether and how we exercise that capacity.

Man's cultural diversity offers concrete evidence that this essentially optimistic view of human nature is justified. Man can through his intelligence so construct his cultural traditions and institutions as to minimize violence and encourage the realization of his humanistic goals. Cultural anthropologists have identified societies, such as four contiguous language groups in the remote Eastern Highlands of New Guinea, in which the rhythms of life were focused on a deadly and institutionally permanent game of rape and cannibalism. But they have also studied such gentle societies as those of the Arapesh of New Guinea, the Lepchas of Sikkim, and the pygmies of the Congo rain forest, cultures in which an appetite for aggression has been replaced by an "enormous gusto for concrete physical pleasures—eating, drinking, sex, and laughter." Revealingly, these gentle societies generally lack the cultural model of brave, aggressive masculinity, a pervasive model that seems so conducive to violence. Evidence that culture is a powerful if not omnipotent determinant of man's propensity for violence is the melancholy contemporary fact that Manhattan Island (population 1.7 million) has more murders per year than all of England and Wales (population 49 million). We need not resolve the interminable hen-and-egg debate over the primacy of nature versus nurture to conclude that man

has the cultural capacity to minimize his recourse to violence.

One general approach to the explanation of the nature and extent of collective violence, supported by considerable evidence in this report, begins with the assumption that men's frustration over some of the material and social circumstances of their lives is a necessary precondition of group protest and collective violence. The more intense and widespread frustration-induced discontent is among a people, the more intense and widespread collective violence is likely to be. Several general attitudinal and social conditions determine the extent and form of consequent violence. People are most strongly disposed to act violently on their discontent if they believe that violence is justifiable and likely of success; they are likely to take violent political action to the extent that they regard their government as illegitimate and responsible for their frustrations. The extent, intensity, and organization of civil strife is finally determined by characteristics of the social system: the degree and consistency of social control, and the extent to which institutions afford peaceful alternatives to violent protest.

If discontent is a root cause of violence within the political community, what kinds of conditions give rise to the widespread discontents that lead to collective violence? All societies generate some discontent because organized social life by its very nature frustrates all human beings, by inhibiting some of their natural impulses. Socialized inhibitions and outlets for such discontents are provided by every society, though their relative effectiveness is certainly an underlying factor in national differences in rates of aggressive crimes. Another fundamental factor may be the ecological one. Carstairs summarizes evidence that overcrowding of human populations

may lead to aggressiveness. On the other hand, Tilly shows that high rates of immigration to French cities in the 18th and 19th centuries were, if anything, associated with civil peace rather than rising disorder. Lane also finds that increasing urbanization in 19th-century Massachusetts was accompanied by a decline in violent crime rates. Neither culture stress nor population concentrations per se seem to be consequential causes of upsurges in collective violence, though they probably contribute to the "background noise" of violence common to almost all cultures. Probably the most important cause of major increases in group violence is the widespread frustration of socially derived expectations about the goods and conditions of life men believe theirs by right. These frustratable expectations relate not only to material well-being but to more intangible conditions such as security, status, freedom to manage one's own affairs, and satisfying personal relations with others. Men's rightful expectations have many sources, among them their past experience of gain or loss, ideologies of scarcity or abundance, and the condition of groups with which they identify. In any case, men feel satisfactions and frustrations with reference to what they think they ought to have, not according to some absolute standard.

New expectations and new frustrations are more likely to be generated in times of social change than social stasis. The quantitative comparisons of the Feierabends and Nesvold suggest, for example, that nations undergoing the most rapid socioeconomic change also are likely to experience the highest levels of collective violence. Large-scale socioeconomic change is ordinarily accompanied by changes in people's values, by institutional dislocations that affect people on top as much as people "on the way up," and even by the temporary breakdown of some social institutions. Rapid social change is thus likely to add to the discontents of many groups at the same time that it improves the conditions of some. In addition, it may contribute to the partial breakdown of systems of normative control, to the collapse of old institutions through which some groups were once able to satisfy their expectations, and to the creation of new organizations of the discontented. Under these conditions the motivational and institutional potential for collective violence is high.

Some specific patterns of social change are directly indicted as causes of collective violence. One is a pattern of rising expectations among people so situated that lack of opportunity or the obdurate resistance of others precludes their attainment of those expectations. American society is especially vulnerable to the frustration of disappointed expectations, for we have proclaimed ourselves the harbinger of a New Jerusalem and invited millions of destitute immigrants to our shores to partake of its fulfillment. "Progressive" demands by such groups that have felt themselves unjustifiably excluded from a fair share of the social, economic, and political privileges of the majority have repeatedly provided motivation and justification for group conflict in our past, as they have in the history of Western Europe. Demands of workers for economic recognition and political participation were pervasive and chronic sources of turmoil in the United States and Europe. The aspirations of the Irish, Italians, Slavs, and—far most consequentially—Negroes have also provided repeated occasion for violence in America. Demands for an end to discriminatory privilege have not been confined to minorities or ethnic strata either. The struggle for women's suffrage in the United States was not peaceful, and America has not heard the last of women's claims for effective socioeconomic equality with men. Although the current resurgence of protest by many groups testifies to the continued inequity in the distribution of rewards, it also reflects the self-sustaining nature of social adjustment in this most pluralistic of nations. The same process through which Americans have made successive accommodations to demands for equity encourages the regeneration of new demands.

Protective resistance to undesirable change has been a more common source of collective violence in America than "revolutions of rising expectations," however. For example, most ethnic and religious violence in American history has been retaliatory violence by groups farther up the socioeconomic ladder who felt threatened by the prospect of the "new immigrant" and the Negro getting both "too big" and "too close." As Taft and Ross have demonstrated, most labor violence in American history was not a deliberate tactic of working class organization but a result of forceful employer resistance to worker organization and demands. Companies repeatedly resorted to coercive and sometimes terroristic activities against union organizers and to violent strike-breaking tactics. The violence of employers often provided both model and impetus to counterviolence by workers, leading in many situations to an escalating spiral of violent conflict to the point of military intervention or mutual exhaustion.

Aggressive vigilantism has been a recurrent response of middle- and working-class Americans to perceived threats by outsiders or lesser classes to their status, security, and cultural integrity. The most widely known manifestations have been the frontier tradition of citizens' enforcement of the law and Ku Klux Klan efforts to maintain class lines and the moral code by taking their version of the law into their own hands. Brown has traced the emergence of such vigilante groups as the "Regulators" of pre-Revolutionary South Carolina and the Bald Knobbers of the Missouri Ozarks in the late 1800s. There are many other manifestations of aggressive vigilantism as well; no regions and few historical eras have been free of it, including the present. A contemporary one is the sporadic harassment of "hippie" and "peacenik" settlements in rural and smalltown America, and the neovigilante organizations of urban Americans, white and black, for "group defense" that often have aggressive overtones. There also is a vigilantism of a somewhat different sort, an aggressive and active suppression of deviancy within an otherwise-cohesive group. An historical example was the White Cap movement of the 1880s and 1890s, a spontaneous movement for the moral regulation of the poor whites and ne'er-do-wells of rural America. Such vigilantism also is apparent in the internecine strife of defensive black organizations, which have occasionally used violence to rid themselves of innovative "traitors" like Malcolm X.

Agrarian protests and uprisings have characterized both frontier and settled regions of the United States since before the Revolution. They have reflected both progressive and protective sentiments, including demands for land reform, defense against more powerful economic interests, and relief from onerous political restrictions. Among them have been Shays' Rebellion in Massachusetts, 1786–1787; Fries' Rebellion in eastern Pennsylvania, 1799; some of the activities of the Grangers, Greenbackers, and Farmers' Alliance after the Civil War; and the "Green Corn Rebellion" of Oklahoma farmers during World War I.

Antiwar protest in American history also has a predominantly protective quality. The nation's 19th-century wars, especially the Civil War, led often to violent resistance to military conscription and the economic impositions of war. The 20th century has seen the development of a strong, indigenous strain of pacifism in the United States. The goals of those who have promoted the cause of peace, during both the First World War and the Vietnam war, have been protective in this sense: they adhere to a set of humanitarian values that are embodied in the basic social contract of American life, and see that contract threatened by those who regard force as the solution to American and foreign problems. The evidence of American history and comparative studies suggests no exact relationship between the occurrence of war and domestic protest against it, however. In the United States it appears to be the pervasive sense that a particular war and its demands are unjust or illegitimate that leads to protest and, occasionally, to violent resistance.

Davies identifies a third general pattern of change that is frequently associated with the outbreak of rebellion and revolution: the occurrence of a short period of sharp relative decline in socioeconomic or political conditions after a prolonged period of improving conditions. A period of steady progress generates expectations that progress will continue. If it does not continue, a pervasive sense of frustration develops which, if focused on the government, is likely to lead to widespread political violence. It is not only economic reversal in this pattern that leads to violence. People whose dignity, career expectations, or political ambitions are so frustrated are as likely to rebel as those whose pocketbooks are being emptied.

This specific pattern is identified in Davies' studies of socio-economic and political changes affecting various groups before the outbreak of the French Revolution, the American Civil War, and the Nazi revolution. It may also be present in data on relative rates of white and Negro socioeconomic progress in the United States during the last several decades. From 1940 to 1952, nonwhite family income relative to educational attainment appears to have increased steadily and substantially in comparison with white income. In 1940 the average Negro with a high school education was likely to receive 55 percent of the earnings of a white worker with comparable education. This figure increased to 85 percent in 1952—but then declined to a low of 74 percent by 1962. These data call into question simplistic notions to the effect that unsatisfied expectations of black Americans increased to the point of violence simply because of "agitation," or because of unfulfilled promises. Rather it may have been real progress, judged by the firsthand experience of the 1940s and early 1950s, and probably also by reference to the rise of the black bourgeoisie, which generated expectations that were substantially frustrated by events of the late 1950s and early 1960s.

Discontent is only the initial condition of collective violence, which raises the question of the extent to which the actualization of violence is determined by popular attitudes and institutional patterns. A cross-national study by Gurr was designed to provide preliminary answers to this question, by relating differences among nations in economic and political discontent, apparent justifications for violence, and institutional strength to differences in magnitudes and forms of civil strife. The results are that more than a third of the differences among contemporary nations in magnitudes of strife are accounted for by differences in the extent and intensity of their citizens' discontent, even though measured imprecisely. Attitudes about politics and violence are almost as important. Nations whose political systems have low legitimacy are likely to have extensive strife; nations with a violent past—and, by implication, popular attitudes that support violence—are likely to have a violent present, and future. Institutional patterns can meliorate or magnify these dispositions to violence. If physical controls are weak, and especially if they are inconsistent in application, strife is likely to be high. Similarly the weakness of conventional institutions, and the availability of material and organizational support for rebellion, lead to high levels of strife, particularly in its most intensive and violent forms.

The experience of the United States is consistent with this general pattern. For all our rhetoric, we have never been a very law-abiding nation, and illegal violence has sometimes been abundantly rewarded. Hence there have developed broad normative sanctions for the expression or acting out of discontent, somewhat limited inhibitions, and—owing to Jeffersonian liberalism's legacy of fear of central public authority—very circumscribed physical controls. Public sympathy has often been with the law-breaker—sometimes with the nightrider who punished the transgressor of community mores, sometimes with the integrationists who refused to obey racial segregation laws. Lack of full respect for law and support for violence in one's own interest have both contributed to the justifications for private violence, justifications that in turn have helped make the United States historically and at present a tumultuous society.

On the other hand, the United States also has characteristics that in other countries appear to minimize intense revolutionary conspiracies and internal wars. Thus far in our history the American political system has maintained a relatively high degree of legitimacy in the eyes of most of its citizens. American political and economic institutions are generally strong. They are not pervasive enough to provide adequate opportunities for some regional and minority groups to satisfy their expectations, but sufficiently pervasive and egalitarian that the most ambitious and talented men—if not women—can pursue the "American dream" with some chance of success. These are conditions that minimize the prospects of revolutionary movements: a majoritarian consensus on the legitimacy of government, and provision of opportunity for men of talent who, if intensely alienated, might otherwise provide revolutionary cadres. But if such a system is open to the majority yet partly closed to a minority, or legitimate for the majority but illegitimate for a minority, the minority is likely to create chronic tumult even though it cannot organize effective revolutionary movements. . . .

VII. THE ADEQUACY OF PRESENT KNOWLEDGE

Do we know enough about the sources, processes, and consequences of collective violence, or about its forms and participants, its relations to social change, or its remedies and alternatives? The preceding conclusions may imply that we know a good deal. We do not. Many, perhaps most, of these conclusions are educated guesses or conjecture. This volume seems to be the first attempt to link the historical and comparative dimensions of research on the subject of group violence in America, and all we have proposed is a tentative, partial synthesis. To use an analogy, this volume is not an accurate atlas to well-mapped terrain; rather, it is equivalent to a 16th-century map of the New World, replete with sea serpents and expanses of terra incognita, its purported ranges and rivers based on reports of lone explorers.

Consider how new and little verified some of the information in this volume is. It includes the first general, empirically based commentary on the precise nature of violent protest over the long span of Western European history (by Charles Tilly). It includes the first comprehensive roster of American vigilante movements (by Richard Maxwell Brown) and the first general survey of American labor violence (by Philip Taft and Philip Ross). It reports, as an appendix, some results of the first attempt ever made to collect systematic data on the incidence and types of individual and collective political violence over a substantial period of American history (by Sheldon Levy). It reports the first crude effort to categorize and count the types, motives, and objectives of participants in collective violence in all nations, for the contemporary or any other era (by Ted Robert Gurr). It includes a pioneering analysis of defensive withdrawal, a common, nonviolent kind of group response to severe stress (by Bernard Siegal).

The conclusions offer other examples. We can speculate about, but do not know with any certainty, what the relative importance is among the historical forces that have contributed to our relatively high American levels of violence. We do not even know with any exactitude how high those levels were, or the details of their causation, variation, or resolution. We have speculated on the relative importance of discontent, attitudes about violence, and institutional patterns as causes of collective violence. These causal questions have been examined systematically in only a handful of comparative studies, and rarely at any depth in the historical dimension for the United States or any other society. Evidence hints that Americans are and have been more willing to take the law in their own hands, and to use violence, than citizens of many other Western societies. But no one has done the survey and depth interview studies necessary to test this speculation or to identify the circumstances under which violence is thought to be justified. Nor have popular attitudes toward violence in most historical eras been thoroughly studied, though they could be either on the basis of what people did or what they wrote. We have speculated on the efficacy of public force in maintaining order and the uses of private violence in effecting change. Relatively few cases can be cited in support of the conclusions because few cases have been studied in this light; those few may be exceptional rather than typical, and only the examination of many cases representing different types of societies and situations can test the adequacy of our conclusions.

There are other uncharted regions. Something is known about the phases through which riots and some revolutions develop and decay. Not much is known about the processes of linked series of events, like the chronic labor violence or vigilante movements of the American past. What accounts for their establishment as a mode of action, and for their persistence or decline? Why, for instance, did the Ku Klux Klan of the 1920s collapse and disappear so suddenly, whereas rightist citizen groups in Europe evolved toward fascist regimes? Which groups took their cues from others, and how did they learn of others? Vigilante violence was often successful, and persisted; labor violence was seldom successful yet it too persisted; protest by suffragettes was successful and it ended. What accounts for such differences, both in outcome and duration? There are educated guesses, but no conclusions based on examination of many movements. Nor do we know much of the long-range consequences of violence. The farther removed we are in time from a major rebellion, or civil war, the less we know about its economic and social consequences. For riots and local uprisings we often know nothing of their aftermaths even a year later. Did the frontier rebellions of America leave any destructive and abiding traces in the attitudes or institutions or politics of the regions where they occurred? What has happened in the black ghettos wracked by riots between 1965 through 1968? Who is analyzing the consequences of different kinds of student tactics in the campus protests and rebellions of the last 4 years?

Alternatives to violence are little studied. More precisely, the peaceful processes by which most social conflicts are resolved have been studied in great detail in many Western societies, but we know of very few studies that have compared groups under similar kinds of stress, or with similar kinds of demands, to determine the options open to them and the consequences of their choice of those alternatives. On this kind of knowledge a crucial policy issue depends: whether it is necessary for groups seeking reforms to resort to limited violence to dramatize their demands, despite the dangers of creating "backlash." Presumably the answers vary, depending on the society in which reforms are sought, the nature of the reforms, and the groups making and resisting them. And with regard to the backlash, does it necessarily occur, and if so among what people, when, and with what immediate and persisting consequences? What backlashes can be identified in American history, and in the histories of other Western societies? Backlashes almost certainly occur even when demands are made peacefully, but do they inhibit reform just as much as the backlash to violence? Then there are the critical questions about the resolution of violence. Probably foremost in the minds of most public and private officials who deal with public protest and violence is: What are the relative merits of concessions and coercion for maintaining an orderly and reasonably contented community? A case can be made for the desirability of either policy approach and any combination of them, by selective choice of examples. The careful study of comparable cases, historically and comparatively, needed for a judicious answer has scarcely been started.

One of our most optimistic conclusions is that we know enough to say what some of the important but unanswered questions about American violence are. The studies in this volume demonstrate that the procedures of historical and comparative research are adequate to the task of seeking further and more precise knowledge, though we lack enough men and women with the requisite training and skills, and adequate support, to do so in the near future. This report provides substantial insights into the causes and character of violence in America; we have yet to understand fully how civil peace is created and maintained in these circumstances. But at least we know that it is possible, for Americans and other people have done so before.

ELDRIDGE CLEAVER
The White Race and Its Heroes

Just as James Baldwin was the major interpreter of the civil rights movement, so Eldridge Cleaver has emerged as the prime articulator of the mood of black nationalism that has gripped many of the ghettos' young. Cleaver, an ex-convict come to political awareness through the Black Muslims, the writings of Malcolm X, and finally the Black Panther party, of which he is Minister of Information, is not a political leader of any large population of black Americans. But he expresses a sensibility that contributes to many of the shifts of black politics and cultural assertion, from black mayors to Afro hairdos. Where Baldwin expostulated to white Americans on the mutual needs of black and white, and championed integration, Cleaver feels the winds of history on his back from Africa and the rest of the Third World (he is now in exile in Algeria) and argues for black leadership in social revolution. He is neither a black racist nor an integrationist. Rather, he is content to return love for love and hatred for hatred without any special attempt to convert the racist whites.

Cleaver puts his faith in the young generation, black and white, which he believes is capable of affection across the color line. He believes that the generational revolution taking place in white America is leading young Americans to turn to the Third World and black America for their heroes, and that they will join militant blacks in revolution against the racist and capitalist world of their forebears. The mixture of romantic desperation in tactics and overall optimism in theory and imagination, combined with a real critical ability as an observer of the American scene (Ofay watching), has enabled Cleaver in fact to become a hero to many a radically minded young white American.

White people cannot, in the generality, be taken as models of how to live. Rather, the white man is himself in sore need of new standards, which will release him from his confusion and place him once again in fruitful communion with the depths of his own being.

James Baldwin
—The Fire Next Time

Right from the go, let me make one thing absolutely clear: I am not now, nor have I ever been, a white man. Nor, I hasten to add, am I now a Black Muslim— although I used to be. But I *am* an Ofay Watcher, a member of that unchartered, amorphous league which has members on all continents and the islands of the seas. Ofay Watchers Anonymous, we might be called, because we exist concealed in the shadows wherever colored people have known oppression by whites, by white enslavers, colonizers, imperialists, and neo-colonialists.

Did it irritate you, compatriot,

for me to string those epithets out like that? Tolerate me. My intention was not necessarily to sprinkle salt over anyone's wounds. I did it primarily to relieve a certain pressure on my brain. Do you cop that? If not, then we're in trouble, because we Ofay Watchers have a pronounced tendency to slip into that mood. If it is bothersome to you, it is quite a task for me because not too long ago it was my way of life to preach, as ardently as I could, that the white race is a race of devils, created by their maker to do evil, and make evil appear as good; that the white race is the natural, unchangeable enemy of the black man, who is the original man, owner, maker, cream of the planet Earth; that the white race was soon to be destroyed by Allah, and that the black man would then inherit the earth, which has always, in fact, been his.

I have, so to speak, washed my hands in the blood of the martyr, Malcolm X, whose retreat from the precipice of madness created new room for others to turn about in, and I am now caught up in that tiny space, attempting a maneuver of my own. Having renounced the teachings of Elijah Muhammad, I find that a rebirth does not follow automatically, of its own accord, that a void is left in one's vision, and this void seeks constantly to obliterate itself by pulling one back to one's former outlook. I have

tried a tentative compromise by adopting a select vocabulary, so that now when I see the whites of *their* eyes, instead of saying "devil" or "beast" I say "imperialist" or "colonialist," and everyone seems to be happier.

In silence, we have spent our years watching the ofays, trying to understand them, on the principle that you have a better chance coping with the known than with the unknown. Some of us have been, and some still are, interested in learning whether it is *ultimately* possible to live in the same territory with people who seem so disagreeable to live with; still others want to get as far away from ofays as possible. What we share in common is the desire to break the ofays' power over us.

At times of fundamental social change, such as the era in which we live, it is easy to be deceived by the onrush of events, beguiled by the craving for social stability into mistaking transitory phenomena for enduring reality. The strength and permanence of "white backlash" in America is just such an illusion. However much this rear-guard action might seem to grow in strength, the initiative, and the future, rest with those whites and blacks who have liberated themselves from the master/slave syndrome. And these are to be found mainly among the youth.

Over the past twelve years there has surfaced a political conflict between the generations that is deeper, even, than the struggle between the races. Its first dra-

Eldridge Cleaver at Columbia University, 1968. *(Richard Howard, Bethel)*

matic manifestation was within the ranks of the Negro people, when college students in the South, fed up with Uncle Tom's hat-in-hand approach to revolution, threw off the yoke of the NAACP. When these students initiated the first sit-ins, their spirit spread like a raging fire across the nation, and the technique of non-violent direct action, constantly refined and honed into a sharp cutting tool, swiftly matured. The older Negro "leaders," who are all die-hard advocates of this tactic, scolded the students for sitting-in. The students rained down contempt upon their hoary heads. In the pre-sit-in days, these conservative leaders had always succeeded in putting down insurgent elements among the Negro people. (A measure of

their power, prior to the students' rebellion, is shown by their success in isolating such great black men as the late W. E. B. DuBois and Paul Robeson, when these stalwarts, refusing to bite their tongues, lost favor with the U.S. government by their unstinting efforts to link up the Negro revolution with national liberation movements around the world.)

The "Negro leaders," and the whites who depended upon them to control their people, were outraged by the impudence of the students. Calling for a moratorium on student initiative, they were greeted instead by an encore of sit-ins, and retired to their ivory towers to contemplate the new phenomenon. Others, less prudent because held on a tighter leash by the whites, had

their careers brought to an abrupt end because they thought they could lead a black/white backlash against the students, only to find themselves in a kind of Bay of Pigs. Negro college presidents, who expelled students from all-Negro colleges in an attempt to quash the demonstrations, ended up losing their jobs; the victorious students would no longer allow them to preside over the campuses. The spontaneous protests on southern campuses over the repressive measures of their college administrations were an earnest of the Free Speech upheaval which years later was to shake the UC campus at Berkeley. In countless ways, the rebellion of the black students served as catalyst for the brewing revolt of the whites.

What has suddenly happened is that the white race has lost its heroes. Worse, its heroes have been revealed as villains and its greatest heroes as the arch-villains. The new generations of whites, appalled by the sanguine and despicable record carved over the face of the globe by their race in the last five hundred years, are rejecting the panoply of white heroes, whose heroism consisted in erecting the inglorious edifice of colonialism and imperialism; heroes whose careers rested on a system of foreign and domestic exploitation, rooted in the myth of white supremacy and the manifest destiny of the white race. The emerging shape of a new world order, and

Malcolm X addressing Harlem audience, 1962. *(UPI)*

the requisites for survival in such a world, are fostering in young whites a new outlook. They recoil in shame from the spectacle of cowboys and pioneers—their heroic forefathers whose exploits filled earlier generations with pride—galloping across a movie screen shooting down Indians like Coke bottles. Even Winston Churchill, who is looked upon by older whites as perhaps the greatest hero of the twentieth century—even he, because of the system of which he was a creature and which he served, is an arch-villain in the eyes of the young white rebels.

At the close of World War Two, national liberation movements in the colonized world picked up new momentum and audacity, seeking to cash in on the democratic promises made by the Allies during the war. The Atlantic Charter, signed by President Roosevelt and Prime Minister Churchill in 1941, affirming "the right of all people to choose the form of government under which they may live," established the principle, although it took years of postwar struggle to give this piece of rhetoric even the appearance of reality. And just as world revolution has prompted the oppressed to re-evaluate their self-image in terms of the changing conditions, to slough off the servile attitudes inculcated by long years of subordination, the same dynamics of change have prompted the white people of the world to re-evaluate their self-image as well, to disabuse themselves of the Master Race psychology developed over centuries of imperial hegemony.

It is among the white youth of the world that the greatest change is taking place. It is they who are experiencing the great psychic pain of waking into consciousness to find their inherited heroes turned by events into villains. Communication and understanding between the older and younger generations of whites has entered a crisis. The elders, who, in the tradition of privileged classes or races, genuinely do not understand the youth, trapped by old ways of thinking and blind to the future, have only just begun to be vexed—because the youth have only just begun to rebel. So thoroughgoing is the revolution in the psyches of white youth that the traditional tolerance which every older generation has found it necessary to display is quickly exhausted, leaving a gulf of fear, hostility, mutual misunderstanding, and contempt.

The rebellion of the oppressed peoples of the world, along with the Negro revolution in America, have opened the way to a new evaluation of history, a re-examination of the role played by the white race since the beginning of European expansion. The positive achievements are also there in the record, and future generations will applaud them. But there can be no applause now, not while the master still holds the whip in his hand! Not even the master's own children can find it possible to applaud him —he cannot even applaud himself! The negative rings too loudly. Slave-catchers, slaveowners, murderers, butchers, invaders, oppressors—the white heroes have acquired new names. The great white statesmen whom school children are taught to revere are revealed as the architects of systems of human exploitation and slavery. Religious leaders are exposed as condoners and justifiers of all these evil deeds. Schoolteachers and college professors are seen as a clique of brainwashers and whitewashers.

The white youth of today are coming to see, intuitively, that to escape the onus of the history their fathers made they must face and admit the moral truth concerning the works of their fathers. That such venerated figures as George Washington and Thomas Jefferson owned hundreds of black slaves, that all of the Presidents up to Lincoln presided over a slave state, and that every President since Lincoln connived politically and cynically with the issues affecting the human rights and general welfare of the broad masses of the American people—these facts weigh heavily upon the hearts of these young people.

The elders do not like to give these youngsters credit for being able to understand what is going on and what has gone on. When speaking of juvenile delinquency, or the rebellious attitude of today's youth, the elders employ a glib rhetoric. They speak of the "alienation of youth," the desire of the young to be independent, the problems of "the father image" and "the mother image" and their effect upon growing children who lack sound models upon which to pattern themselves. But they consider it bad form to connect the problems of the youth with the central event of our era—the national liberation movements abroad and the Negro revolution at home. The foundations of authority have been blasted to bits in America because the whole society has been indicted, tried, and convicted of injustice. To the youth, the elders are Ugly Americans; to the elders, the youth have gone mad.

The rebellion of the white youth has gone through four broadly discernible stages. First there was an initial recoiling away, a rejection of the conformity which America expected, and had always received, sooner or later, from its youth. The disaffected youth were refusing to participate in the system, having discovered that America, far from helping the underdog, was up to its ears in the mud trying to hold the dog down. Because of the publicity and self-advertisements of the more vocal rebels, this period has come to be known as the beatnik era, although not all of the youth affected by these changes thought of themselves as beatniks. The howl of the beatniks and their scathing, outraged denunciation of the system—characterized by Ginsberg as Moloch, a blood-thirsty Semitic deity to which the ancient tribes sacrificed their firstborn children—was a serious, irrevocable declaration of war. It is revealing that the elders looked upon the beatniks as mere obscene misfits who were too lazy to take baths and too stingy to buy a haircut. The elders had eyes but couldn't see, ears but couldn't hear—not even when the message came through as clearly as in this remarkable passage from Jack Kerouac's *On the Road:*

At lilac evening I walked with every muscle aching among the lights of 27th and Welton in the Denver colored section, wishing I were a Negro, feeling that the best the white world had offered was not enough ecstasy for me, not enough life, joy, kicks, darkness, music, not enough night. I wished I were a Denver Mexican, or even a poor overworked Jap, anything but what I so drearily was, a "white man" disillusioned. All my life I'd had white ambitions. . . . I passed the dark porches of Mexican and Negro homes; soft voices were there, occasionally the dusky knee of some mysterious sensuous gal; the dark faces of the men behind rose arbors. Little children sat like sages in ancient rocking chairs.

The second stage arrived when these young people, having decided emphatically that the world, and particularly the U.S.A., was unacceptable to them in its present form, began an active search for roles they could play in changing the society. If many of these young people were content to lay up in their cool beat pads, smoking pot and listening to jazz in a perpetual orgy of esoteric bliss, there were others, less crushed by the system, who recognized the need for positive action. Moloch could

not ask for anything more than to have its disaffected victims withdraw into safe, passive, apolitical little nonparticipatory islands, in an economy less and less able to provide jobs for the growing pool of unemployed. If all the unemployed had followed the lead of the beatniks, Moloch would gladly have legalized the use of euphoric drugs and marijuana, passed out free jazz albums and sleeping bags, to all those willing to sign affidavits promising to remain "beat." The non-beat disenchanted white youth were attracted magnetically to the Negro revolution, which had begun to take on a mass, insurrectionary tone. But they had difficulty understanding their relationship to the Negro, and what role "whites" could play in a "Negro revolution." For the time being they watched the Negro activists from afar.

The third stage, which is rapidly drawing to a close, emerged when white youth started joining Negro demonstrations in large numbers. The presence of whites among the demonstrators emboldened the Negro leaders and allowed them to use tactics they never would have been able to employ with all-black troops. The racist conscience of America is such that murder does not register as murder, really, unless the victim is white. And it was only when the newspapers and magazines started carrying pictures and stories of white demonstrators being beaten and maimed by mobs and police that the public began to protest. Negroes have become so used to this double standard that they, too, react differently to the death of a white. When white freedom riders were brutalized along with blacks, a sigh of relief went up from the black masses, because the blacks knew that white blood is the coin of freedom in a land where for four hundred years black blood has been shed unremarked and with impunity.

America has never truly been outraged by the murder of a black man, woman, or child. White politicians may, if Negroes are aroused by a particular murder, say with their lips what they know with their minds they should feel with their hearts—but don't.

It is a measure of what the Negro feels that when the two white and one black civil rights workers were murdered in Mississippi in 1964, the event was welcomed by Negroes on a level of understanding beyond and deeper than the grief they felt for the victims and their families. This welcoming of violence and death to whites can almost be heard—indeed it can be heard—in the inevitable words, oft repeated by Negroes, that those whites, and blacks, do not die in vain. So it was with Mrs. Viola Liuzzo. And much of the anger which Negroes felt toward Martin Luther King during the Battle of Selma stemmed from the fact that he denied history a great moment, never to be recaptured, when he turned tail on the Edmund Pettus Bridge and refused to all those whites behind him what they had traveled thousands of miles to receive. If the police had turned them back by force, all those nuns, priests, rabbis, preachers, and distinguished ladies and gentlemen old and young—as they had done the Negroes a week earlier—the violence and brutality of the system would have been ruthlessly exposed. Or if, seeing King determined to lead them on to Montgomery, the troopers had stepped aside to avoid precisely the confrontation that Washington would not have tolerated, it would have signaled the capitulation of the militant white South. As it turned out, the March on Montgomery was a show of somewhat dim luster, stage-managed by the Establishment. But by this time the young whites were already active participants in the Negro revolution.

In fact they had begun to transform it into something broader, with the potential of encompassing the whole of America in a radical reordering of society.

The fourth stage, now in its infancy, sees these white youth taking the initiative, using techniques learned in the Negro struggle to attack problems in the general society. The classic example of this new energy in action was the student battle on the UC campus at Berkeley, California—the Free Speech Movement. Leading the revolt were veterans of the civil rights movement, some of whom spent time on the firing line in the wilderness of Mississippi/Alabama. Flowing from the same momentum were student demonstrations against U.S. interference in the internal affairs of Vietnam, Cuba, the Dominican Republic, and the Congo and U.S. aid to apartheid in South Africa. The students even aroused the intellectual community to actions and positions unthinkable a few years ago: witness the teach-ins. But their revolt is deeper than single-issue protest. The characteristics of the white rebels which most alarm their elders—the long hair, the new dances, their love for Negro music, their use of marijuana, their mystical attitude toward sex—are all tools of their rebellion. They have turned these tools against the totalitarian fabric of American society—and they mean to change it.

From the beginning, America has been a schizophrenic nation. Its two conflicting images of itself were never reconciled, because never before has the survival of its most cherished myths made a reconciliation mandatory. Once before, during the bitter struggle between North and South climaxed by the Civil War, the two images of America came into conflict, although whites North and South scarcely understood it. The image of America held by its most alienated citizens was advanced neither by the North nor by the South; it was perhaps best expressed by Frederick Douglass, who was born into slavery in 1817, escaped to the North, and became the greatest leader-spokesman for the blacks of his era. In words that can still, years later, arouse an audience of black Americans, Frederick Douglass delivered, in 1852, a scorching indictment in his Fourth of July oration in Rochester:

What to the American slave is your Fourth of July? I answer: a day that reveals to him, more than all other days in the year, the gross injustice and cruelty to which he is the constant victim. To him your celebration is a sham; your boasted liberty, an unholy licence; your national greatness, swelling vanity; your sounds of rejoicing are empty and heartless; your denunciation of tyrants, brass-fronted impudence; your shouts of liberty and equality, hollow mockery; your prayers and hymns, your sermons and thanksgivings, with all your religious parade and solemnity, are, to him, more bombast, fraud, deception, impiety, and hypocrisy— a thin veil to cover up crimes which would disgrace a nation of savages. . . .

You boast of your love of liberty, your superior civilization, and your pure Christianity, while the whole political power of the nation (as embodied in the two great political parties) is solemnly pledged to support and perpetuate the enslavement of three millions of your countrymen. You hurl your anathemas at the crown-headed tyrants of Russia and Austria and pride yourselves on your democratic institutions, while you yourselves consent to be the mere *tools and bodyguards* of the tyrants of Virginia and Carolina.

You invite to your shores fugitives of oppression from abroad, honor them with banquets, greet them with ovations, cheer them, toast them, salute them, protect them, and pour out your money to them like water; but the fugitive from your own land you advertise, hunt, arrest, shoot, and kill. You glory in your refinement and your universal education; yet you maintain a system as barbarous and dreadful as ever stained the character of a nation—a system begun in avarice, supported in pride, and perpetuated in cruelty.

You shed tears over fallen Hungary, and make the sad story of her wrongs the theme of your poets, statesmen and orators, till your gallant sons are ready to fly to arms to vindicate her cause against the oppressor; but, in regard to the ten thousand wrongs of the American slave, you would enforce the strictest silence, and would hail him as an enemy of the nation who dares to make these wrongs the subject of public discourse!

This most alienated view of America was preached by the Abolitionists, and by Harriet Beecher Stowe in her *Uncle Tom's Cabin*. But such a view of America was too distasteful to receive wide attention, and serious debate about America's image and her reality was engaged in only on the fringes of society. Even when confronted with overwhelming evidence to the contrary, most white Americans have found it possible, after steadying their rattled nerves, to settle comfortably back into their vaunted belief that America is dedicated to the proposition that all men are created equal and endowed by their Creator with certain inalienable rights—life, liberty and the pursuit of happiness. With the Constitution for a rudder and the Declaration of Independence as its guiding star, the ship of state is sailing always toward a brighter vision of freedom and justice for all.

Because there is no common ground between these two contradictory images of America, they had to be kept apart. But the moment the blacks were let into the white world—let out of the voiceless and faceless cages of their ghettos, singing, walking, talking, dancing, writing, and orating *their* image of America and of Americans—the white

(George Gardner)

world was suddenly challenged to match its practice to its preachments. And this is why those whites who abandon the *white* image of America and adopt the *black* are greeted with such unmitigated hostility by their elders.

For all these years whites have been taught to believe in the myth they preached, while Negroes have had to face the bitter reality of what America practiced. But without the lies and distortions, white Americans would not have been able to do the things they have done. When whites are forced to look honestly upon the objective proof of their deeds, the cement of mendacity holding white society together swiftly disintegrates. On the other hand, the core of the black world's vision remains intact, and in fact begins to expand

and spread into the psychological territory vacated by the non-viable white lies, i.e., into the minds of young whites. It is remarkable how the system worked for so many years, how the majority of whites remained effectively unaware of any contradiction between their view of the world and that world itself. The mechanism by which this was rendered possible requires examination at this point.

Let us recall that the white man, in order to justify slavery and, later on, to justify segregation, elaborated a complex, all-pervasive myth which at one time classified the black man as a subhuman beast of burden. The myth was progressively modified, gradually elevating the blacks on the scale of evolution, following their slowly changing status, until the plateau of separate-but-equal

was reached at the close of the nineteenth century. During slavery, the black was seen as a mindless Supermasculine Menial. Forced to do the backbreaking work, he was conceived in terms of his ability to do such work—"field niggers," etc. The white man administered the plantation, doing all the thinking, exercising omnipotent power over the slaves. He had little difficulty dissociating himself from the black slaves, and he could not conceive of their positions being reversed or even reversible.

Blacks and whites being conceived as mutually exclusive types, those attributes imputed to the blacks could not also be imputed to the whites—at least not in equal degree—without blurring the line separating the races. These images were based upon the social function of the

(David Cupp)

These doctrines were foisted off as *the epitome of enlightened justice, the highest expression of morality.* Sanctified by religion, justified by philosophy and legalized by the Supreme Court, separate-but-equal was enforced by day by agencies of the law, and by the KKK & Co. under cover of night. Booker T. Washington, the Martin Luther King of his day, accepted separate-but-equal in the name of all Negroes. W. E. B. DuBois denounced it.

Separate-but-equal marked the last stage of the white man's flight into cultural neurosis, and the beginning of the black man's frantic striving to assert his humanity and equalize his position with the white. Blacks ventured into all fields of endeavor to which they could gain entrance. Their goal was to present in all fields a performance that would equal or surpass that of the whites. It was long axiomatic among blacks that a black had to be twice as competent as a white in any field in order to win grudging recognition from the whites. This produced a pathological motivation in the blacks to equal or surpass the whites, and a pathological motivation in the whites to maintain a distance from the blacks. This is the rack on which black and white Americans receive their delicious torture! At first there was the color bar, flatly denying the blacks entrance to certain spheres of activity. When this no longer worked, and blacks invaded sector after sector of American life and economy, the whites evolved other methods of keeping their distance. The illusion of the Negro's inferior nature had to be maintained.

One device evolved by the whites was to tab whatever the blacks did with the prefix "Negro." We had *Negro* literature, *Negro* athletes, *Negro* music, *Negro* doctors, *Negro* politicians, *Negro* workers. The malignant ingeniousness of this device is

two races, the work they performed. The ideal white man was one who knew how to use his head, who knew how to manage and control things and get things done. Those whites who were not in a position to perform these functions nevertheless aspired to them. The ideal black man was one who did exactly as he was told, and did it efficiently and cheerfully. "Slaves," said Frederick Douglass, "are generally expected to sing as well as to work." As the black man's posi-

tion and function became more varied, the images of white and black, having become stereotypes, lagged behind.

The separate-but-equal doctrine was promulgated by the Supreme Court in 1896. It had the same purpose domestically as the Open Door Policy toward China in the international arena: to stabilize a situation and subordinate a non-white population so that racist exploiters could manipulate those people according to their own selfish interests.

that although it accurately describes an objective biological fact—or, at least, a sociological fact in America—it concealed the paramount psychological fact: that to the white mind, prefixing anything with "Negro" automatically consigned it to an inferior category. A well-known example of the white necessity to deny due credit to blacks is in the realm of music. White musicians were famous for going to Harlem and other Negro cultural centers literally to steal the black man's music, carrying it back across the color line into the Great White World and passing off the watered-down loot as their own original creations. Blacks, meanwhile, were ridiculed as *Negro* musicians playing inferior coon music.

The Negro revolution at home and national liberation movements abroad have unceremoniously shattered the world of fantasy in which the whites have been living. It is painful that many do not yet see that their fantasy world has been rendered uninhabitable in the last half of the twentieth century. But it is away from this world that the white youth of today are turning. The "paper tiger" hero, James Bond, offering the whites a triumphant image of themselves, is saying what many whites want desperately to hear reaffirmed: *I am still the White Man, lord of the land, licensed to kill, and the world is still an empire at my feet.* James Bond feeds on that secret little anxiety, the psychological white backlash, felt in some degree by most whites alive. It is exasperating to see little brown men and little yellow men from the mysterious Orient, and the opaque black men of Africa (to say nothing of these impudent American Negroes!) who come to the UN to talk smart to us, who are scurrying all over *our* globe in their strange modes of dress—much as if they were new, unpleasant arrivals from

another planet. Many whites believe in their ulcers that it is only a matter of time before the Marines get the signal to round up these truants and put them back securely in their cages. But it is away from this fantasy world that the white youth of today are turning.

In the world revolution now under way, the initiative rests with people of color. That growing numbers of white youth are repudiating their heritage of blood and taking people of color as their heroes and models is a tribute not only to their insight but to the resilience of the human spirit. For today the heroes of the initiative are people not usually thought of as white: Fidel Castro, Che Guevara, Kwame Nkrumah, Mao Tse-tung, Gamal Abdel Nasser, Robert F. Williams, Malcolm X, Ben Bella, John Lewis, Martin Luther King, Jr., Robert Parris Moses, Ho Chi Minh, Stokeley Carmichael, W. E. B. DuBois, James Forman, Chou En-lai.

The white youth of today have begun to react to the fact that the "American Way of Life" is a fossil of history. What do they care if their old baldheaded and crew-cut elders don't dig their caveman mops? They couldn't care less about the old, stiffassed honkies who don't like their new dances: Frug, Monkey, Jerk, Swim, Watusi. All they know is that it feels good to swing to way-out body-rhythms instead of dragassing across the dance floor like zombies to the dead beat of mind-smothered Mickey Mouse music. Is it any wonder that the youth have lost all respect for their elders, for law and order, when for as long as they can remember all they've witnessed is a monumental bickering over the Negro's place in American society and the right of people around the world to be left alone by outside powers? They have witnessed the law, both domestic and international, being

spat upon by those who do not like its terms. Is it any wonder, then, that they feel justified, by sitting-in and freedom riding, in breaking laws made by lawless men? Old funny-styled, zipper-mouthed political night riders know nothing but to haul out an investigating committee *to look into the disturbance* to find the cause of the unrest among the youth. Look into a mirror? The cause is you, Mr. and Mrs. Yesterday, you with your forked tongues.

A young white today cannot help but recoil from the base deeds of his people. On every side, on every continent, he sees racial arrogance, savage brutality toward the conquered and subjugated people, genocide; he sees the human cargo of the slave trade; he sees the systematic extermination of American Indians; he sees the civilized nations of Europe fighting in imperial depravity over the lands of other people—and over possession of the very people themselves. There seems to be no end to the ghastly deeds of which his people are guilty. *GUILTY*. The slaughter of the Jews by the Germans, the dropping of atomic bombs on the Japanese people— these deeds weigh heavily upon the prostrate souls and tumultuous consciences of the white youth. The white heroes, their hands dripping with blood, are dead.

The young whites know that the colored people of the world, Afro-Americans included, do not seek revenge for their suffering. They seek the same things the white rebel wants: an end to war and exploitation. Black and white, the young rebels are free people, free in a way that Americans have never been before in the history of their country. And they are outraged.

There is in America today a generation of white youth that is truly worthy of a black man's respect, and this is a rare event in the foul annals of American history. From the beginning of the contact between blacks and whites, there has been very little reason for a black man to respect a white, with such exceptions as John Brown and others lesser known. But respect commands itself and it can neither be given nor withheld when it is due. If a man like Malcolm X could change and repudiate racism, if I myself and other former Muslims can change, if young whites can change, then there is hope for America. It was certainly strange to find myself, while steeped in the doctrine that all whites were devils by nature, commanded by the heart to applaud and acknowledge respect for these young whites—despite the fact that they are descendants of the masters and I the descendant of slave. The sins of the fathers are visited upon the heads of the children—but only if the children continue in the evil deeds of the fathers.

ALEXANDER M. BICKEL
The Warren Court

The Supreme Court under Chief Justice Earl Warren has been celebrated by numerous liberal commentators. The Court cut a wide swath through the stasis of the fifties with its decisions protecting the rights of citizens attacked for their political opinions and, most of all, with its major enactments granting civil rights to black Americans. In the sixties the Court seemed particularly in tune with the achievements of the liberal administrations of the era, picking apart the edifices of segregation, extending protection to poor defendants who could not afford the same bail and lawyers as middle-class people, protecting the public schools from religious incursions, and offering long-denied relief from inequities in the apportionment of political power.

Alexander Bickel's critical account of the Court's role, therefore, represents a turn in a new direction. His objections to the Court's dedication to an egalitarian society and to the central government's role in maintaining uniform standards reveal a shift in values among scholars and intellectuals that may be called "postliberal." Fears of inefficiency and inhumanity in a centrally administered state have led many liberals to turn against the characteristic devices of national legislation, powerful presidencies, and judicial decision in favor of decentralization and the protection of minority interests and local variations. This is but one sign among many that a cycle of liberalism that began in the New Deal reached its end sometime in the sixties.

. . . Professors in New England —and elsewhere, to be sure— parse the glories of the Warren Court, criticize its syllogisms, reduce its purported logic to absurd consequences, disprove its factual assertions, answer the unavoidable questions it managed to leave unasked, and most often conclude by regretting its failures of method, while either welcoming its results or professing detachment from them. Historians a generation or two hence, however—other professors in New England—may barely note, and care little about, method, logic, or intellectual coherence, and may assess results in hindsight—only results, and by their own future lights.

Past historians have so dealt with the Court, as do many— outside the profession, most—

Abridged from Chapters 2 and 4 in *The Supreme Court and the Idea of Progress* by Alexander M. Bickel. Copyright © 1970 by Alexander M. Bickel. Reprinted by permission of Harper & Row, Publishers, Inc.

contemporary observers,[1] and one sensed that this was what the Justices of the Warren Court expected, and that they were content to take their chances.[2] They relied on events for vindication more than on the method of reason for contemporary validation. They were thoroughly conscious of the condemnation that has been visited on certain of their predecessors, who exalted rights of property, but responded with insufficient vigor to other claims, and they admired the generally admired force and vision of John Marshall, who is forgiven for his attachment to the rights of property. Like Marshall, who

[1] See, *e.g.:* "Only history will know whether the Warren Court has struck the balance right. For myself, I am confident that historians will write that the trend of decisions during the 1950s and 1960s was in keeping with the mainstream of American history —a bit progressive but also moderate, a bit humane but not sentimental, a bit idealistic but seldom doctrinaire and in the long run essentially pragmatic—in short, in keeping with the true genius of our institutions." Archibald Cox, *The Warren Court* (1968), pp. 133–134.

[2] Strictly speaking, the Justices of the Warren Court, in addition to the Chief Justice, were: Hugo L. Black, Stanley F. Reed, Felix Frankfurter, William O. Douglas, Robert H. Jackson, Harold H. Burton, Tom C. Clark, Sherman Minton, John M. Harlan, William J. Brennan, Jr., Charles E. Whittaker, Potter Stewart, Byron R. White, Arthur J. Goldberg, Abe Fortas, and Thurgood Marshall. In my usage, the terms "Warren Court" and "Justices of the Warren Court" refer to the dominant majority that gave the Court its character. That majority consisted over the years of the Chief Justice and Justices Black, Douglas, Brennan, Goldberg, Fortas, and Marshall. Of course, the majority was no monolith. There were defections, if that is the right word, in one or another case—on Justice Black's part, with increasing frequency toward the end—and the majority would now and then draw to itself a member of the opposition, if that, again, is the right word, such as Justice Stewart or Justice White. And in *Brown* v. *Board of Education* and a number of other racial cases, the Court was unanimous.

had, of course, the advantage of a clean slate, they bet on the future, even if to do so they had to wield, on their slate, eraser as well as chalk.

The eraser was used selectively, however, if often. For what informed the enterprise was the idea of progress. There was, therefore, discontinuity—open or disguised—in specifics, but it was sustained by an aspiration to a transcendent consistency with a preferred past, a striving for fidelity to a true line of progress. And so the Warren Court, as Namier said we all do, "imagine[d] the past and remember[ed] the future." The cast of mind is perhaps nowhere more saliently, more ingenuously—or more succinctly—exhibited than in a decisive remark of Mr. Justice Douglas, speaking for the Warren Court in one of the reapportionment cases. Said Justice Douglas: "The conception of political equality from the Declaration of Independence to Lincoln's Gettysburg Address, to the Fifteenth, Seventeenth, and Nineteenth Amendments can mean only one thing—one person, one vote." The key word is *can*, and the sentence is further notable for its references to documents not commonly taken as having legal effect, and to the extralegal significance of provisions that do have strictly legal, but circumscribed, application.

The Justices of the Warren Court thus ventured to identify a goal. It was necessarily a grand one—if we had to give it a single name, that name, as Professor Kurland has suggested, would be the Egalitarian Society. And the Justices steered by this goal, as Marshall did by his vision of a nation, in the belief that progress, called history, would validate their course, and that another generation, remembering its own future, would imagine them favorably. Such a faith need not conflict with, but it overrides standards of analytical

warrantors of the validity of reason and scientific inquiry as judgment. . . .

A broadly conceived egalitarianism was the main theme in the music to which the Justices of the Warren Court marched. It was evident, of course, in the racial cases, in decisions leveling qualifications for voting, and in those decreeing equal apportionment on a one-man, one-vote basis. And the egalitarian melody was strong in procedural decisions, chiefly criminal, seeking to minimize the disadvantages to which the poor are subject. Two accompanying themes were the enlargement of the dominion of law and the centralization in national institutions of the lawgiving function.

The Warren Court was quick to impose the same norms on state and national governments alike. In dealing with the obscenity problem, for example, the Court would not heed Mr. Justice Harlan's plea that separate rules might be made applicable to the federal government and to state and local governments. Yet the dangers of national censorship are not the same as the dangers of local suppression. The federal government is apt to impose the standards of Dubuque on Greenwich Village, whereas Dubuque can impose them only on Dubuque. Again, in its decisions on criminal procedure — decisions concerning, for example, unreasonable searches and seizures— the Warren Court sought to enforce national uniformity in every detail, without regard, so to speak, to varieties of criminal experience.

In pursuit of the ideal of equality, the Warren Court all too often assimilated private behavior to government action; it not only forbade, of course, as had its predecessors, discrimination at the hands of the state, or of any unit of government, but was keen to detect the hand of the state in private discrimina-

The Warren Court, 1967. *(UPI)*

tions. In the Warren era, moreover, as to a degree also in the heyday of the old faith at the turn of the century and after, a general tendency was noticeable to circumscribe and displace private ordering, to legalize the society, to rationalize it in the sense of which the great industrial consolidators spoke of rationalizing the economy, to impose order on the market of norms, values, and institutions. There was evidence, particularly in the subordinate federal courts, of an imperfectly bridled managerial drive.

A certain habit of command, an impatience to take charge of unruly affairs and impose a solution that seems apt, comes as readily to judges as to other able men of good intentions who are in a position to work their will. It came readily enough to the judges of the early decades of this century, who intervened routinely in labor disputes, for example, and in controversies concerning rates and services between public utilities and various states and municipalities. Rebuking—as it rarely did—a somewhat overzealous judge in such a case in 1910, the Supreme Court quoted the remark of an English Vice-Chancellor: "I am not sitting here as a Committee of Public Safety, armed with arbitrary power to prevent what it is said will be a great injury not to Birmingham only but to the whole of England; that is not my function." But it is a function that judges are prone to assume, and to which they were increasingly encouraged by the reach the Warren Court gave to law, and by the expectations that were thus induced. . . .

The Warren Court's tendency to disenthrall itself from jurisdictional fetters is a function of this conception of law. The Court has not by any means taken on all that has been pressed on it. It had declined opportunities to pass on the constitutionality of the President's actions in Vietnam. It has not dispensed with the need for a lawsuit; it is still, unlike the President or the Congress, a passive body that must wait for a litigant to move it to action. But in such decisions as *Flast* v. *Cohen* and *South Carolina* v. *Katzenbach,* the Court has substantially loosened the definition of a lawsuit, it has opened the door wider to more litigants, and has indeed come near to making the lawsuit something of a formality, still an expensive one, but within the reach of just about all who can afford it, at just about any time of their choice.

In assuming the power, like a legislature, to set an arbitrary date for the coming into effect of its decisions, the Warren Court further enlarged its freedom to address an ever-widening range of the society's problems, and to pronounce applicable law. The Court assumed this power, as we have seen, with respect to a number of its decisions concerning criminal procedure, which it did not allow to be, as is unusual, wholly retroactive, but which it did not announce for solely prospective application either. To have announced them altogether prospectively would have run the risk of stemming the flow of litigation, the Court said, since "the incentive of counsel to advance contentions requiring a change in the law" might have been decreased. Without running this risk, then —a telling and characteristic precaution—the Court liberated itself from the restraint naturally imposed by the retroactivity of decisions, which can work out inequitably, or otherwise in alarming fashion, and hence gives pause.

Another of the principal themes of the Warren Court, related to the egalitarian, legalitarian, and centralizing themes, was majoritarianism. The Court found the essence of political democracy in the power of a majority to impose its wishes through an election, except, to be sure, as the sway of the majority is limited by law. This is the

meaning of the one-man, one-vote rule of the apportionment cases. It is the meaning also, in part, of the decisions enlarging the electorate and leveling qualifications for voting, as is shown by Justice Douglas' citation of the apportionment cases in *Harper* v. *Virginia Board of Elections,* the poll-tax decision.

The main statement of the Court's position came in *Reynolds* v. *Sims.* Chief Justice Warren's opinion for the Court spoke of individual equality. One man's vote ought not to be worth more than another's. But there was great emphasis also, in *Reynolds* v. *Sims* and in the rest of the apportionment cases, on a statistical showing that malapportionment enabled a minority of voters to control a legislature, or under the Georgia county-unit system, elect a governor. The Chief Justice proclaimed: "Legislators represent people, not trees or acres. Legislators are elected by voters, not farms or cities or economic interest. . . . Logically, in a society ostensibly grounded on representative government, it would seem reasonable that a majority of the people of a State could elect a majority of that State's legislators. To conclude differently, and to sanction minority control of state legislative bodies, would appear to deny majority rights in a way that far surpasses any possible denial of minority rights that might otherwise be thought to result. Since legislatures are responsible for enacting laws by which all citizens are to be governed, they should be bodies which are collectively responsive to the popular will." And the Chief Justice laid it down explicitly that "economic or other sorts of group interests" were not factors that could constitutionally be taken into account in apportioning a legislature. "Citizens, not history or economic interests, cast votes," he said. In Colorado, a substantial majority of the voters had

by referendum approved a departure from the one-man, one-vote standard. Even the majority itself, the Court held, cannot deprive itself of the right to rule as a majority.

Populist majoritarianism, not some complex checked and balanced Madisonian adjustment among countervailing groups and factions, leading to rule by minorities . . . —populist majoritarianism was the principle of the apportionment cases. . . .

Majoritarianism is heady stuff. It is, in truth, a tide, flowing with the swiftness of a slogan— whether popular sovereignty, as in the past, or one man, one vote, as in the Warren Court's formulation. The tide is apt to sweep over all institutions, seeking its level everywhere. Now that the Warren Court has released it again, it bids fair, for example, to engulf the Electoral College, even though on a less simplistic view of political arrangements, on a less obtrusively chaste view, that peculiar institution may be seen as performing a valuable function. The tide could well engulf the Court itself also.

Analytically, supreme judicial autonomy is not easily reconciled with any theory of political democracy, Madisonian or majoritarian. Judicial autonomy is sustained, not by a self-consistent theory, but by an ambivalent practical accommodation, and by a rhetorical tradition. The tradition, however, is Madisonian in tenor. It will be difficult to evolve a rhetoric of survival in a climate of uncompromising majoritarianism—as difficult for the judges as for the Electoral College. The Court fared rather ill with the Populists and other majoritarian political reformers of the Progressive Era. In times when Madisonian theory is in favor, it is at least rhetorically possible to defend the power of the judges by pointing to all manner of checks and balances, to the limited nature of all power, which signifies the intended inability of any group, including a majority, always to get everything it wants, and the intended ability of many groups, all of them minorities, to exercise vetoes; and by declaiming that our government is, after all, republican, not in the majoritarian sense democratic. It is not so easy to say all this when populist slogans are the order of the day, as the Warren Court's one-man, one-vote decisions have caused them to be. Thoroughgoing majoritarians, the Court may discover, are no more reliable a constituency for judges than revolutionaries, and the Court-induced reapportionment revolution may turn into an ironic triumph.

The Warren Court achieved a certain symmetry in its deployment of the majoritarian principle and of a concept of centralized and pervasive law; and it mistook this symmetry for theoretical consistency. (The symmetrical arrangement I speak of has at least the virtue of bypassing—even though, unfortunately, quite without disowning —the sophistry of arguments that the supremacy of the judges is consistent with democratic theory so long as the judges enhance the democratic process rather than restricting it, which is supposedly what they do in First Amendment and apportionment cases.)

The Warren Court's implicit model of a government at once majoritarian and judicial had it that when individuals and groups are unsuccessful in attaching themselves to the ruling majority in a given constituency, or in getting satisfaction from it, they may appeal to the larger majority in the national constituency. This recourse the Court encouraged by enlarging the power of Congress under the Fourteenth Amendment, as for example in *Katzenbach* v. *Morgan*. If no remedy is forthcoming even from the central majoritarian legisla-

ture, then the loser in the political process may appeal to the Court, which was consequently concerned to make itself more readily available than it had been in the past. As early as the argument of *Brown* v. *Board of Education,* the late Justice Robert H. Jackson, stating a fact rather than his own preference, remarked that the plaintiffs were in court because Congress would not act.

Unmistakably the Warren Court considered itself under a special duty to act when recourse to Congress had failed or was likely to fail; and not unnaturally, for in a polity arranged on the majoritarian principle, and hence inescapably on the assumption that an identifiable majority exists at all times on most issues, and is coherent and relatively stable, the political process cannot be assumed to be accessible to all groups. In the Madisonian model, and one might say in purposefully malapportioned legislatures, most identifiable groups and interests in the society have access, and are likely to be able to maneuver for enough bargaining power to achieve at least some portion of their objectives. No such presumption is sensible in a more strictly majoritarian system.

It can be said, therefore, that the Warren Court's imposition of majoritarianism as the operative principle of political organization, and its conception of its own function were congruent. They met in the premise that the majoritarian process must, and perhaps if it works correctly will, produce certain results, which are given *a priori*. When it does not at the level of one constituency, it should be tried again at the higher level of another one. And when it doesn't at all, the Court will supply the deficiency. Madisonian theory also posits the possible miscarriage of the majoritarian process in a not dissimilar sense, and also has recourse to enlargement of the constituency. But it guards

against miscarriages by diffusing and limiting power through the introduction of a series of nonmajoritarian devices, and enlarges the constituency to this end. What the Warren Court crucially omitted to explain was why its model, unlike the Madisonian one, allowed for only a single locus of power countervailing that of the majority—the Court itself—and by reliance on the majoritarian principle forbade all others the Court could reach.

I am attempting now to identify and orchestrate the Warren Court's major themes; I am not now dealing with fragments of the music in one or another case, and not—to pursue a figure of Professor Kurland—with techniques of piano playing.[3] My object is not to formulate and defend the grounds of my own approval or disapproval—intellectual, moral, esthetic—although I should say that in my view the Court's majoritarianism is ill-conceived, egalitarianism is a worthy ideal but not in all circumstances a self-evident virtue, and centralized, unmitigatedly legalitarian government bears the seed of tyranny. But this is an assertion of ultimates put forward for revelatory rather than forensic purposes. And it is a parenthesis. My endeavor is to see whether the Warren Court's themes, whatever their worth as ultimates, were in harmony with each other, and whether they harmonized with so much of the future as contemporary history allows us to glimpse.

---

[3] "It behooves any critics of the Court's performance to close on a note reminiscent of the wall plaque of frontier times: 'Don't shoot the piano player. He's doing his best.' It is still possible, however, to wish that he would stick to the piano and not try to be a one-man band. It is too much to ask that he take piano lessons." P. B. Kurland, "Foreword: 'Equal in Origin and Equal in Title to the Legislative Branches of the Government,'" 78 *Harvard Law Review*, 143, 176 (1964).

There are heard in the society dissonant themes; not voices of opposition or resistance to the Court's law, albeit there are those, but in increasing volume notes that amount to another tune. There is in being a reaction to the steady unification and nationalization of recent years, a movement toward a decentralization and a diversity of which the as yet unacknowledged prophet—due, I should suppose, for a revival—is Brandeis. "The great America for which we long," wrote Brandeis in 1920, "is unattainable unless that individuality of communities becomes far more highly developed and becomes a common American phenomenon. For a century our growth has come through national expansion and the increase of the functions of the Federal Government. The growth of the future—at least of the immediate future—must be in quality and spiritual value. And that can come only through the concentrated, intensified striving of smaller groups. The field of special effort shall now be the State, the city, the village—and each should be led to seek to excel in something peculiar to it. If ideals are developed locally—the national ones will come pretty near to taking care of themselves."

Diversity implies less rather than more law, and certainly less centralized, national law. A striving for diversity is not necessarily in express conflict with the goal of an egalitarian society, but it connotes a different order of priorities. In politics, even as the Warren Court's virtually irresistible slogan—one man, one vote—may still be mouthed on all sides, the cry is for a group participation which presupposes, whether it knows it or not, the Madisonian more than the majoritarian model, and for a process calculated to heed the expression not only of desires and preferences, but of intensities that no ballot can register. These are all indications that the society of the rather near future may be forming beyond the horizon on which the Warren Court's gaze was fixed, that it may be taking on shapes the Court did not perceive and its law cannot accommodate; that, in sum, the society may not be conforming to the Warren Court's vision. . . .

NAOMI WEISSTEIN

Psychology Constructs the Female; or The Fantasy Life of the Male Psychologist

(With Some Attention to the Fantasies of His Friends, the Male Biologist and the Male Anthropologist)

Women in the 1960s have been discovering that they too are a subculture or interest group, a majority that is treated like a minority. Discriminated against in employment as well as in the psychic rewards that society offers, they also bear a special relation to their oppressors that makes revolt unthinkable to most and difficult for those committed to it. The revival of a movement for women's rights came in the early sixties after Betty Friedan published her much-quoted *The Feminine Mystique* in 1963. This marked a turnabout from a long period—since the 1920s—in which the gains won by the earlier movement had been eroded by a trend of women turning back to home and family. The percentages of women in the professions and in higher business positions had declined steadily for over a generation just when women in other countries had gained increasing opportunities.

The women's rights movement was given a radical turn late in the decade, as women radicals—fed up with being the coffee-makers, secretaries, and bed partners of male radicals, but not their equals in the movement—initiated women's liberation. Naomi Weisstein's analysis of psychological theories about women has had wide circulation among Women's Lib groups and is a good example of the way that a new concern for the dignity of women demands a rethinking of every field of thought, extending not only to the social sciences but to the humanities as well. For the question of women's rights has gone past issues of voting and jobholding to the manners, styles, and images that influence the lives of modern women.

It is an implicit assumption that the area of psychology which concerns itself with personality has the onerous but necessary task of describing the limits of human possibility. Thus when we are about to consider the liberation of women, we naturally look to psychology to tell us what "true" liberation would mean: what would give women the freedom to fulfill their own intrinsic natures. Psychologists have set about describing the true natures of women with a certainty and a sense of their own infallibility rarely found in the secular world. Bruno Bettelheim, of the University of Chicago, tells us (1965) that "We must start with the realization

This is a revised and expanded version of "Kinder, Kuche, Kirche as Scientific Law: Psychology Constructs the Female," published by the New England Free Press, 791 Tremont Street, Boston, Massachusetts, 1968. Copyright, Naomi Weisstein, 1971.

Traditional women's role.
(Robert Capa, Magnum)

that, as much as women want to be good scientists or engineers, they want first and foremost to be womanly companions of men and to be mothers." Erik Erikson of Harvard University (1964), upon noting that young women often ask whether they can "have an identity before they know whom they will marry, and for whom they will make a home," explains somewhat elegiacally that "Much of a young woman's identity is already defined in her kind of attractiveness and in the selectivity of her search for the man (or men) by whom she wishes to be sought. . . ." Mature womanly fulfillment, for Erikson, rests on the fact that a woman's ". . . somatic design harbors an 'inner space' destined to bear the offspring of chosen men, and with it, a biological, psychological, and ethical commitment to take care of human infancy." Some psychiatrists even see the acceptance of woman's role by

women as a solution to societal problems. "Woman is nurturance. . . ," writes Joseph Rheingold (1964), a psychiatrist at Harvard Medical School. ". . . anatomy decrees the life of a woman . . . when women grow up without dread of their biological functions and without subversion by feminist doctrine, and therefore enter upon motherhood with a sense of fulfillment and altruistic sentiment, we shall attain the goal of a good life and a secure world in which we live it." (p. 714)

These views from men who are assumed to be experts reflect, in a surprisingly transparent way, the cultural consensus. They not only assert that a woman is defined by her ability to attract men, they see no alternative definitions. They think that the definition of a woman in terms of a man is the way it should be; and they back it up with psychosexual incantation and biological ritual curses. A woman has an identity if she is attractive enough to obtain a man, and thus, a home; for this will allow her to set about her life's task of "joyful altruism and nurturance."

Business certainly does not disagree. If views such as Bettelheim's and Erikson's do indeed have something to do with real liberation for women, then seldom in human history has so much money and effort been spent on helping a group of people realize their true potential. Clothing, cosmetics, home furnishings, are multi-million dollar businesses: if you don't like investing in firms that make weaponry and flaming gasoline, then there's a lot of cash in "inner space." Sheet and pillowcase manufacturers are concerned to fill this inner space:

Mother, for a while this morning, I thought I wasn't cut out for married life. Hank was late for work and forgot his apricot juice and walked out without kissing me, and when I was all alone I started crying. But then the postman came with the sheets and towels you sent, that look like big bandana handkerchiefs, and you know what I thought? That those big red and blue handkerchiefs are for girls like me to dry their tears on so they can get busy and do what a housewife has to do. Throw open the windows and start getting the house ready, and the dinner, maybe clean the silver and put new geraniums in the box. *Everything to be ready for him when he walks through that door.* (Fieldcrest 1966; emphasis added.)

Of course, it is not only the sheet and pillowcase manufacturers, the cosmetics industry, the home furnishings salesmen who profit from and make use of the cultural definitions of man and woman. The example above is blatantly and overtly pitched to a particular kind of sexist stereotype: the child nymph. But almost all aspects of the media are normative, that is, they have to do with the ways in which beautiful people, or just folks, or ordinary Americans, or extraordinary Americans should live their lives. They define the possible; and the possibilities are usually in terms of what is male and what is female. Men and women alike are waiting for Hank, the Silva Thins man, to walk back through that door.

It is interesting but limited exercise to show that psychologists and psychiatrists embrace these sexist norms of our culture, that they do not see beyond the most superficial and stultifying media conceptions of female nature, and that their ideas of female nature serve industry and commerce so well. Just because it's good for business doesn't mean it's wrong. What I will show is that it *is wrong;* that there isn't the tiniest shred of evidence that these fantasies of servitude and childish dependence have anything to do with

women's true potential; that the idea of the nature of human possibility which rests on the accidents of individual development or genitalia, on what is possible today because of what happened yesterday, on the fundamentalist myth of sex organ causality, has strangled and deflected psychology so that it is relatively useless in describing, explaining or predicting humans and their behavior. It then goes without saying that present psychology is less than worthless in contributing to a vision which could truly liberate—men as well as women.

The central argument of my article, then, is this. Psychology has nothing to say about what women are really like, what they need and what they want, essentially because psychology does not know. I want to stress that this failure is not limited to women; rather, the kind of psychology which has addressed itself to how people act and who they are has failed to understand, in the first place, why people act the way they do, and certainly failed to understand what might make them act differently.

The kind of psychology which has addressed itself to these questions divides into two professional areas: academic personality research, and clinical psychology and psychiatry. The basic reason for failure is the same in both these areas: the central assumption for most psychologists of human personality has been that human behavior rests on an individual and inner dynamic, perhaps fixed in infancy, perhaps fixed by genitalia, perhaps simply arranged in a rather immovable cognitive network. But this assumption is rapidly losing ground as personality psychologists fail again and again to get consistency in the assumed personalities of their subjects (Block, 1968). Meanwhile, the evidence is collecting that what

a person does, and who he believes himself to be, will in general be a function of what people around him expect him to be, and what the overall situation in which he is acting implies that he is. Compared to the influence of the social context within which a person lives, his or her history and "traits," as well as biological makeup, may simply be random variations, "noise" superimposed on the true signal which can predict behavior.

Some academic personality psychologists are at least looking at the counter evidence and questioning their theories; no such corrective is occurring in clinical psychology and psychiatry. Freudians and neo-Freudians, Adlerians and neo-Adlerians, classicists and swingers, clinicians and psychiatrists, simply refuse to look at the evidence against their theory and practice. And they support their theory and their practice with stuff so transparently biased as to have absolutely no standing as empirical evidence.

To summarize: the first reason for psychology's failure to understand what people are and how they act is that psychology has looked for inner traits when it should have been looking for social context; the second reason for psychology's failure is that the theoreticians of personality have generally been clinicians and psychiatrists, and they have never considered it necessary to have evidence in support of their theories.

THEORY WITHOUT EVIDENCE

Let us turn to this latter cause of failure: the acceptance by psychiatrists and clinical psychologists of theory without evidence. If we inspect the literature of personality, it is immediately obvious that the bulk of it is written by clinicians and psychiatrists, and that the major support for their theories is "years of intensive clinical experience." This is a tradition started by Freud. His "insights" occurred during the course of his work with his patients. Now there is nothing wrong with such an approach to theory *formulation;* a person is free to make up theories with any inspiration which works: divine revelation, intensive clinical practice, a random numbers table. But he is not free to claim any validity for his theory until it has been tested and confirmed. But theories are treated in no such tentative way in ordinary clinical practice. Consider Freud. What he thought constituted evidence violated the most minimal conditions of scientific rigor. In *The Sexual Enlightenment of Children* (1963), the classic document which is supposed to demonstrate empirically the existence of a castration complex and its connection to a phobia, Freud based his analysis not on the little boy who had the phobia, but on the reports of the father of the little boy, himself in therapy, and a devotee of Freudian theory. I really don't have to comment further on the contamination in this kind of evidence. It is remarkable that only recently has Freud's classic theory on the sexuality of women —the notion of the double orgasm—been actually tested physiologically and found just plain wrong. Now those who claim that fifty years of psychoanalytic experience constitute evidence enough of the essential truths of Freud's theory should ponder the robust health of the double orgasm. Did women, until Masters and Johnson (1966), believe they were having two different kinds of orgasm? Did their psychiatrists intimidate them into reporting something that was not true? If so, were there other things they reported that were also not true? Did psychiatrists ever learn anything different than their theories had led them to believe? If clinical experience

means anything at all, surely we should have been done with the double orgasm myth long before the Masters and Johnson studies.

But certainly, you may object, "years of intensive clinical experience" is the only reliable measure in a discipline which rests for its findings on insight, sensitivity, and intuition. The problem with insight, sensitivity, and intuition is that they can confirm for all time the biases that one started out with. People used to be absolutely convinced of their ability to tell which of their number were engaging in witchcraft. All it required was some sensitivity to the workings of the devil.

Years of intensive clinical experience is not the same thing as empirical evidence. The first thing an experimenter learns in any kind of experiment which involves humans is the concept of the "double blind." The term is taken from medical experiments, where one group is given a drug which is presumably supposed to change behavior in a certain way, and a control group is given a placebo. If the observers or the subjects know which group took which drug, the result invariably comes out on the positive side for the new drug. Only when it is not known which subject took which pill, is validity remotely approximated. In addition, with judgments of human behavior, it is so difficult to precisely tie down just what behavior is going on, let alone what behavior should be expected, that one must test again and again the reliability of judgments. How many judges, blind, will agree in their observations? Can they replicate their own judgments at some later time? When, in actual practice, these judgment criteria are tested for clinical judgments, then we find that the judges cannot judge reliably, nor can they judge consistently: they do no better than chance in identifying which of a

certain set of stories were written by men and which by women; which of a whole battery of clinical test results are the products of homosexuals and which are the products of heterosexuals (Hooker, 1957); and which of a battery of clinical test results *and* interviews (where questions are asked such as "Do you have delusions?"—Little and Schneidman, 1959) are products of psychotics, neurotics, psychosomatics, or normals. Lest this summary escape your notice, let me stress the implications of these findings. The ability of judges, chosen for their clinical expertise, to distinguish male heterosexuals from male homosexuals on the basis of three widely used clinical projective tests—the Rorschach, the TAT, and the MAP—was *no better than chance.* The reason this is such devastating news, of course, is that sexuality is supposed to be of fundamental importance in the deep dynamic of personality; if what is considered gross sexual deviance cannot be caught, then what are psychologists talking about when they, for example, claim that at the basis of paranoid psychosis is "latent homosexual panic"? They can't even identify what homosexual anything is, let alone "latent homosexual panic."[1] More frightening, expert clinicians cannot be consistent on what diagnostic category to assign to a person, again on the basis of both tests

[1] It should be noted that psychologists have been as quick to assert absolute truths about the nature of homosexuality as they have about the nature of women. The arguments presented in this article apply to the nature of homosexuality; psychologists know nothing about it; there is no more evidence for the "naturalness" of heterosexuality than for the "naturalness" of homosexuality. Psychology has functioned as a pseudoscientific buttress for our cultural sex-role notions, that is, as a buttress for patriarchal ideology and patriarchal social organization: women's liberation and gay liberation fight against a common victimization.

and interviews; a number of normals in the Little and Schneidman study were described as psychotic, in such categories as "schizophrenic with homosexual tendencies" or "schizoid character with depressive trends." But most disheartening, when the judges were asked to rejudge the test protocols some weeks later, their diagnoses of the same subjects on the basis of the same protocol differed markedly from their initial judgments. It is obvious that even simple descriptive conventions in clinical psychology cannot be consistently applied; that these descriptive conventions have any explanatory significance is therefore, of course, out of the question.

As a graduate student at Harvard some years ago, I was a member of a seminar which was asked to identify which of two piles of a clinical test, the TAT, had been written by males and which by females. Only four students out of twenty identified the piles correctly, and this was after one and a half months of intensively studying the differences between men and women. Since this result is below chance —that is, this result would occur by chance about four out of a thousand times—we may conclude that there is finally a consistency here; students are judging knowledgeably within the context of psychological teaching about the differences between men and women; the teachings themselves are simply erroneous.

You may argue that the theory may be scientifically "unsound" but at least it cures people. There is no evidence that it does. In 1952, Eysenck reported the results of what is called an "outcome of therapy" study of neurotics which showed that, of the patients who received psychoanalysis the improvement rate was 44 percent; of the patients who received psychotherapy the improvement rate was 64 percent; and of the patients who received no treatment at all the improvement rate was 72 percent. These findings have never been refuted; subsequently, later studies have confirmed the negative results of the Eysenck study (Barron and Leary, 1955; Bergin, 1963; Cartwright and Vogel, 1960; Truax, 1963; Powers and Witmer, 1951). How can clinicians and psychiatrists, then, in all good conscience, continue to practice? Largely by ignoring these results and being careful not to do outcome-of-therapy studies. The attitude is nicely summarized by Rotter (1960) (quoted in Astin, 1961): "Research studies in psychotherapy tend to be concerned with psychotherapeutic procedure and less with outcome . . . to some extent, it reflects an interest in the psychotherapy situation as a kind of personality laboratory." Some laboratory.

THE SOCIAL CONTEXT

Thus, since clinical experience and tools can be shown to be worse than useless when tested for consistency, efficacy, agreement, and reliability, we can safely conclude that theories of a clinical nature advanced about women are also worse than useless. I want to turn now to the second major point in my article, which is that, even when psychological theory is constructed so that it may be tested, and rigorous standards of evidence are used, it has become increasingly clear that in order to understand why people do what they do, and certainly in order to change what people do, psychologists must turn away from the theory of the causal nature of the inner dynamic and look to the social context within which individuals live.

Before examining the relevance of this approach for the question of women, let me first sketch the groundwork for this assertion.

In the first place, it is clear (Block, 1968) that personality tests never yield consistent predictions; a rigid authoritarian on one measure will be an unauthoritarian on the next. But the reason for this inconsistency is only now becoming clear, and it seems overwhelmingly to have much more to do with the social situation in which the subject finds himself than with the subject himself.

In a series of brilliant experiments, Rosenthal and his coworkers (Rosenthal and Jacobson, 1968; Rosenthal, 1966) have shown that if one group of experimenters has one hypothesis about what it expects to find, and another group of experimenters has the opposite hypothesis, both groups will obtain results in accord with their hypotheses. The results obtained are not due to mishandling of data by biased experimenters; rather, somehow, the bias of the experimenter creates a changed environment in which subjects actually act differently. For instance, in one experiment, subjects were to assign numbers to pictures of men's faces, with high numbers representing the subject's judgment that the man in the picture was a successful person, and low numbers representing the subject's judgment that the man in the picture was an unsuccessful person. One group of experimenters was told that the subjects tended to rate the faces high; another group of experimenters was told that the subjects tended to rate the faces low. Each group of experimenters was instructed to follow precisely the same procedure: they were required to read to subjects a set of instructions, and to *say nothing else*. For the 375 subjects run, the results showed clearly that those subjects who performed the task with experimenters who expected high ratings gave high ratings, and those subjects who performed the task with experimenters who expected

Women "liberate" Gallagher's Bar, New York City.   (Tim Boxer, Pictorial Parade)

low ratings gave low ratings. How did this happen? The experimenters all used the same words; it was something in their conduct which made one group of subjects do one thing, and another group of subjects do another thing.[2]

The concreteness of the changed conditions produced by expectation is a fact, a reality: even with animal subjects, in two separate studies (Rosenthal and Fode, 1960; Rosenthal and Lawson, 1961), those experimenters who were told that rats learning mazes had been especially bred for brightness obtained better learning from their rats than did experimenters believing their rats to have been bred for dullness. In a very recent study, Rosenthal and Jacobson (1968) extended their analysis to the natural classroom situation. Here, they tested a group of students and reported to the teachers that some among

[2] I am indebted to Jesse Lemisch for his valuable suggestions in the interpretation of these studies.

the students tested "showed great promise." Actually, the students so named had been selected on a random basis. Some time later, the experimenters retested the group of students: those students whose teachers had been told that they were "promising" showed real and dramatic increments in their IQ's as compared to the rest of the students. Something in the conduct of the teachers towards those whom the teachers believed to be the "bright" students made those students brighter.

Thus, even in carefully controlled experiments, and with no outward or conscious difference in behavior, the hypotheses we start with will influence enormously the behavior of another organism. These studies are extremely important when assessing the validity of psychological studies of women. Since it is beyond doubt that most of us start with notions as to the nature of men and women, the validity of a number of obser-

vations of sex differences is questionable, even when these observations have been made under carefully controlled conditions. Second, and more important, the Rosenthal experiments point quite clearly to the influence of social expectation. In some extremely important ways, people are what you expect them to be or at least they behave as you expect them to behave. Thus, if women, according to Bettelheim, want first and foremost to be good wives and mothers, it is extremely likely that this is what Bruno Bettelheim, and the rest of society, want them to be.

There is another series of brilliant social psychological experiments which point to the overwhelming effect of social context. These are the obedience experiments of Stanley Milgram (1965) in which subjects are asked to obey the orders of unknown experimenters, orders which carry with them the distinct possibility that the subject is killing somebody.

In Milgram's experiments, a subject is told that he is administering a learning experiment, and that he is to deal out shocks each time the other "subject" (in reality, a confederate of the experimenter) answers incorrectly. The equipment appears to provide graduated shocks ranging upwards from 15 volts through 450 volts; for each of four consecutive voltages there are verbal descriptions such as "mild shock," "danger, severe shock," and, finally, for the 435 and 450 volt switches, a red XXX marked over the switches. Each time the stooge answers incorrectly the subject is supposed to increase the voltage. As the voltage increases, the stooge begins to cry in pain; he demands that the experiment stop; finally, he refuses to answer at all. When he stops responding, the experimenter instructs the subject to continue increasing the voltage; for each shock administered the stooge shrieks in agony. Under these conditions, about 62.5 percent of the subjects administered shock that they believed to be possibly lethal.

No tested individual differences between subjects predicted how many would continue to obey, and which would break off the experiment. When forty psychiatrists predicted how many of a group of 100 subjects would go on to give the lethal shock, their predictions were orders of magnitude below the actual percentages; most expected only one-tenth of one percent of the subjects to obey to the end.

But even though *psychiatrists* have no idea how people will behave in this situation, and even though individual differences do not predict which subjects will obey and which will not, it is easy to predict when subjects will be obedient and when they will be defiant. All the experimenter has to do is change the social situation. In a variant of the experiment, Milgram had two

stooges present in addition to the "victim"; these worked along with the subject in administering electric shocks. When these two stooges refused to go on with the experiment, only ten percent of the subjects continued to the maximum voltage. This is critical for personality theory. It says that behavior is predicted from the social situation, not from the individual history.

Finally, an ingenious experiment by Schachter and Singer (1962) showed that subjects injected with adrenalin, which produces a state of physiological arousal in all but minor respects identical to that which occurs when subjects are extremely afraid, became euphoric when they were in a room with a stooge who was acting euphoric, and became extremely angry when they were placed in a room with a stooge who was acting extremely angry.

To summarize: If subjects under quite innocuous and non-coercive social conditions can be made to kill other subjects and under other types of social conditions will positively refuse to do so; if subjects can react to a state of physiological fear by becoming euphoric because there is somebody else around who is euphoric or angry because there is somebody else around who is angry; if students become intelligent because teachers expect them to be intelligent, and rats run mazes better because experimenters are told the rats are bright, then it is obvious that a study of human behavior requires, first and foremost, a study of the social contexts within which people move, the expectations as to how they will behave, and the authority which tells them who they are and what they are supposed to do.

BIOLOGICALLY BASED THEORIES

Biologists also have at times assumed they could describe the

limits of human potential from their observations of animal rather than human behavior. Here, as in psychology, there has been no end of theorizing about the sexes, again with a sense of absolute certainty. These theories fall into two major categories.

One biological theory of differences in nature argues that since females and males differ in their sex hormones, and sex hormones enter the brain (Hamburg and Lunde in Maccoby, 1966), there must be innate behavioral differences. But the only thing this argument tells us is that there are differences in physiological state. The problem is whether these differences are at all relevant to behavior.

Consider, for example, differences in testosterone levels. A man who calls himself Tiger[3] has recently argued (1970) that the greater quantities of testosterone found in human males as compared with human females (of a certain age group) determine innate differences in aggressiveness, competitiveness, dominance, ability to hunt, ability to hold public office, and so forth. But Tiger demonstrates in this argument the same manly and courageous refusal to be intimidated by evidence which we have already seen in our consideration of the clinical and psychiatric tradition. The evidence does not support his argument, and in some cases, directly contradicts it. Testosterone level co-varies neither with hunting ability, nor with dominance, nor with aggression, nor with competitiveness. As Storch has pointed out (1970), all normal male mammals in the reproductive age group produce much greater quantities of testosterone than females; yet many of these males are neither hunters nor are they aggressive. Among some

[3] Schwarz-Belkin (1914) claims that the name was originally *Mouse,* but this may be a reference to an earlier L. Tiger (putative).

hunting mammals, such as the large cats, it turns out that more hunting is done by the female than the male. And there exist primate species where the female is clearly more aggressive, competitive, and dominant than the male (Mitchell, 1969; and see below). Thus, for some species, being female, and therefore, having less testosterone than the male of that species means hunting more, or being more aggressive, or being more dominant. Nor does having *more* testosterone preclude behavior commonly thought of as "female": there exist primate species where females do not touch infants except to feed them; the males care for the infants (Mitchell, 1969; see fuller discussion below). So it is not clear what testosterone or any other sex-hormonal difference means for differences in nature of sex-role behavior.

In other words, one can observe identical sex-role behavior (e.g., "mothering") in males and females despite known differences in physiological state, i.e., sex hormones. What about the converse to this? That is, can one obtain differences in behavior given a single physiological state? The answer is overwhelmingly yes, not only as regards non-sex-specific hormones (as in the Schachter and Singer 1962 experiment cited above), but also as regards gender itself. Studies of hermaphrodites with the same diagnosis (the genetic, gonadal, hormonal sex, the internal reproductive organs, and the ambiguous appearances of the external genitalia were identical) have shown that one will consider oneself male or female depending simply on whether one was defined and raised as male or female (Money, 1970; Hampton and Hampton, 1961):

"There is no more convincing evidence of the power of social interaction on gender-identity differentiation than in the case of congenital hermaphrodites who

are of the same diagnosis and similar degree of hermaphroditism but are differently assigned and with a different postnatal medical and life history." (Money, 1970, p. 432.)

Thus, for example, if out of two individuals diagnosed as having the adrenogenital syndrome of female hermaphroditism, one is raised as a girl and one as a boy, each will act and identify her/himself accordingly. The one raised as a girl will consider herself a girl; the one raised as a boy will consider himself a boy; and each will conduct her/himself successfully in accord with that self-definition.

So, identical behavior occurs given different physiological states; and different behavior occurs given an identical physiological starting point. So it is not clear that differences in sex hormones are at all relevant to behavior.

There is a second category of theory based on biology, a reductionist theory. It goes like this. Sex-role behavior in some primate species is described, and it is concluded that this is the "natural" behavior for humans. Putting aside the not insignificant problem of observer bias (for instance, Harlow, 1962, of the University of Wisconsin, after observing differences between male and female rhesus monkeys, quotes Lawrence Sterne to the effect that women are silly and trivial, and concludes that "men and women have differed in the past and they will differ in the future"), there are a number of problems with this approach.

The most general and serious problem is that there are no grounds to assume that anything primates do is necessary, natural, or desirable in humans, for the simple reason that humans are not non-humans. For instance, it is found that male chimpanzees placed alone with infants will not "mother" them. Jumping from hard data to ideological

speculation researchers conclude from this information that *human* females are necessary for the safe growth of human infants. It would be as reasonable to conclude, following this logic, that it is quite useless to teach human infants to speak, since it has been tried with chimpanzees and it does not work.

One strategy that has been used is to extrapolate from primate behavior to "innate" human preference by noticing certain trends in primate behavior as one moves phylogenetically closer to humans. But there are great difficulties with this approach. When behaviors from lower primates are directly opposite to those of higher primates, or to those one expects of humans, they can be dismissed on evolutionary grounds—higher primates and/or humans grew out of that kid stuff. On the other hand, if the behavior of higher primates is counter to the behavior considered natural for humans, while the behavior of some lower primate is considered the natural one for humans, the higher primate behavior can be dismissed also, on the grounds that it has diverged from an older, prototypical pattern. So either way, one can select those behaviors one wants to prove as innate for humans. In addition, one does not know whether the sex-role behavior exhibited is dependent on the phylogenetic rank, or on the environmental conditions (both physical and social) under which different species live.

Is there then any value at all in primate observations as they relate to human females and males? There is a value but it is limited: its function can be no more than to show some extant examples of diverse sex-role behavior. It must be stressed, however, that this is an extremely limited function. The extant behavior does not begin to suggest all the possibilities, either for non-human primates or for humans. Bearing these caveats in mind, it is nonetheless interesting that if one inspects the limited set of existing non-human primate sex-role behaviors, one finds, in fact, a much larger range of sex-role behavior than is commonly believed to exist. "Biology" appears to limit very little; the fact that a female gives birth does not mean, even in non-humans, that she necessarily cares for the infant (in marmosets, for instance, the male carries the infant at all times except when the infant is feeding [Mitchell, 1969]); "natural" female and male behavior varies all the way from females who are much more aggressive and competitive than males (e.g., Tamarins, see Mitchell, 1969) and male "mothers" (e.g., Titi monkeys, night monkeys, and marmosets, see Mitchell, 1969)[4] to submissive and passive females and male antagonists (e.g., rhesus monkeys).

But even for the limited function that primate arguments serve, the evidence has been misused. Invariably, only those primates have been cited which exhibit exactly the kind of behavior that the proponents of the biological basis of human female behavior wish were true for humans. Thus, baboons and rhesus monkeys are generally cited: males in these groups exhibit some of the most irritable and aggressive behavior found in primates, and if one wishes to argue that females are naturally passive and submissive, these groups provide vivid examples. There are abundant counter examples, such as those mentioned above (Mitchell, 1969); in fact, in general, a counter example can be found for every sex-role behavior cited, including, as mentioned in the case of marmosets, male "mothers."

[4] All these are lower-order primates, which makes their behavior with reference to humans unnatural, or more natural; take your choice.

Marilyn Monroe. *(Elliott Erwitt, Magnum)*

Jane Fonda. *(Shelly Rusten)*

But the presence of counter examples has not stopped florid and overarching theories of the natural or biological basis of male privilege from proliferating. For instance, there have been a number of theories dealing with the innate incapacity in human males for monogamy. Here, as in most of this type of theorizing, baboons are a favorite example, probably because of their fantasy value: the family unit of the hamadryas baboon, for instance, consists of a highly constant pattern of one male and a number of females and their young. And again, the counter examples, such as the invariably monogamous gibbon, are ignored.

An extreme example of this maiming and selective truncation of the evidence in the service of a plea for the maintenance of male privilege is a recent book, *Men in Groups* (1969) by Tiger (see above and footnote 3). The central claim of this book is that females are incapable of honorable collective action because they are incapable of "bonding" as in "male bonding." What is "male bonding"? Its surface definition is simple: "... a particular relationship between two or more males such that they react differently to members of their bonding units as compared to individuals outside of it" (pp. 19-20). If one deletes the word male, the definition, on its face, would seem to include all organisms that have any kind of social organization. But this is not what Tiger means. For instance, Tiger asserts that females are incapable of bonding; and this alleged incapacity indicates to Tiger that females should be restricted from public life. Why is bonding an exclusively male behavior? Because, says Tiger, it is seen in male primates. All male primates? No, very few male primates. Tiger cites two examples where male bonding is seen: rhesus monkeys and baboons. Surprise, surprise. But not even all baboons: as mentioned above, the hamadryas social organization consists of one-male units; so does that of the Gelada baboon (Mitchell, 1969). And the great apes do not go in for male bonding much either. The "male bond" is hardly a serious contribution to scholarship; one reviewer for *Science* has observed that the book ". . . shows basically more resemblance to a partisan political tract than to a work of objective social science," with male bonding being ". . . some kind of behavioral phlogiston" (Fried, 1969, p. 884).

In short, primate arguments have generally misused the evidence; primate studies themselves have, in any case, only the very limited function of describing some possible sex-role behavior; and at present, primate observations have been sufficiently limited so that even the range of possible sex-role behavior for non-human primates is not known. This range is not known since there is only minimal observation of what happens to behavior if the physical or social environment is changed. In one study (Itani, 1963), different troops of Japanese macaques were observed. Here, there appeared to be cultural differences: males in 3 out of the 18 troops observed differed in their amount of aggressiveness and infant-carrying behavior. There could be no possibility of differential evolution here; the differences seemed largely transmitted by infant socialization. Thus, the very limited evidence points to some plasticity in the sex-role behavior of non-human primates; if we can figure out experiments which massively change the social organization of primate groups, it is possible that we might observe great changes in behavior. At present, however, we must conclude that, since given a constant physical environment non-human primates do not seem to change their social conditions very much by themselves, the "innateness" and fixedness of their behavior is simply not known. Thus, even if there were some way, which there isn't, to settle on the behavior of a particular primate species as being the "natural" way for humans, we would not know whether or not this were simply some function of the present social organization of that species. And finally, once again it must be stressed that even if non-human primate behavior turned out to be relatively fixed, this would say little about our behavior. More immediate and relevant evidence, i.e., the evidence from social psychology, points to the enormous plasticity in human behavior, not only from one culture to the next, but

from one experimental group to the next. One of the most salient features of human social organization is its variety; there are a number of cultures where there is at least a rough equality between men and women (Mead, 1949). In summary, primate arguments can tell us very little about our "innate" sex-role behavior; if they tell us anything at all, they tell us that there is no one biologically "natural" female or male behavior, and that sex-role behavior in non-human primates is much more varied than has previously been thought.

CONCLUSION

In brief, the uselessness of present psychology (and biology) with regard to women is simply a special case of the general conclusion: one must understand the social conditions under which women live if one is going to attempt to explain the behavior of women. And to understand the social conditions under which women live, one must be cognizant of the social expectations about women.

How are women characterized in our culture, and in psychology? They are inconsistent, emotionally unstable, lacking in a strong conscience or superego, weaker, "nurturant" rather than productive, "intuitive" rather than intelligent, and, if they are at all "normal," suited to the home and the family. In short, the list adds up to a typical minority group stereotype of inferiority (Hacker, 1951): if they know their place, which is in the home, they are really quite lovable, happy, childlike, loving creatures. In a review of the intellectual differences between little boys and little girls, Eleanor Maccoby (1966) has shown that there are no intellectual differences until about high school, or, if there are, girls are slightly ahead of boys. At high school, girls begin to do worse on a few

intellectual tasks, such as arithmetic reasoning, and beyond high school, the achievement of women now measured in terms of productivity and accomplishment drops off even more rapidly. There are a number of other, non-intellectual tests which show sex differences; I chose the intellectual differences since it is seen clearly that women start becoming inferior. It is no use to talk about women being different but equal; all of the tests I can think of have a "good" outcome and a "bad" outcome. Women usually end up at the "bad" outcome. In light of social expectations about women, what is surprising is not that women end up where society expects they will; what is surprising is that little girls don't get the message that they are supposed to be stupid until high school; and what is even more remarkable is that some women resist this message even after high school, college, and graduate school.

My article began with remarks on the task of the discovery of the limits of human potential. Psychologists must realize that it is they who are limiting discovery of human potential. They refuse to accept evidence, if they are clinical psychologists, or, if they are rigorous, they assume that people move in a context-free ether, with only their innate dispositions and their individual traits determining what they will do. Until psychologists begin to respect evidence, and until they begin looking at the social contexts within which people move, psychology will have nothing of substance to offer in this task of discovery. I don't know what immutable differences exist between men and women apart from differences in their genitals; perhaps there are some other unchangeable differences; probably there are a number of irrelevant differences. But it is clear that until social expectations for men and women are equal, until we provide equal respect for both men and women, our answers to this question will simply reflect our prejudices.

REFERENCES

Astin, A. W., "The Functional Autonomy of Psychotherapy." *American Psychologist*, 1961, *16*, 75–78.

Barron, F., and Leary, T., "Changes in Psychoneurotic Patients with and without Psychotherapy." *Journal of Consulting Psychology*, 1955, *19*, 239–245.

Bergin, A. E., "The Effects of Psychotherapy: Negative Results Revisited." *Journal of Consulting Psychology*, 1963, *10*, 244–250.

Bettelheim, B., "The Commitment Required of a Woman Entering a Scientific Profession in Present-Day American Society." *Woman and the Scientific Professions*, the MIT Symposium on American Women in Science and Engineering, 1965.

Block, J., "Some Reasons for the Apparent Inconsistency of Personality." *Psychological Bulletin*, 1968, *70*, 210–212.

Cartwright, R. D., and Vogel, J. L., "A Comparison of Changes in Psychoneurotic Patients during Matched Periods of Therapy and No-therapy." *Journal of Consulting Psychology*, 1960, *24*, 121–127.

Erikson, E., "Inner and Outer Space: Reflections on Womanhood." *Daedalus*, 1964, *93*, 582–606.

Eysenck, H. J., "The Effects of Psychotherapy: an Evaluation." *Journal of Consulting Psychology*, 1952, *16*, 319–324.

Fieldcrest—Advertisement in the *New Yorker*, 1965.

Fried, M. H., "Mankind Excluding Woman," review of Tiger's *Men in Groups*. *Science*, 1969, *165*, 883–884.

Freud, S., *The Sexual Enlightenment of Children*. Collier Books Edition, 1963.

Goldstein, A. P., and Dean, S. J., *The Investigation of Psychotherapy: Commentaries and Readings*. New York: John Wiley & Sons, 1966.

Hacker, H. M., "Women as a Minority Group." *Social Forces*, 1951, *30*, 60–69.

Hamburg, D. A., and Lunde, D. T., "Sex Hormones in the Development of Sex Differences in Human Behavior." In Maccoby (ed.), *The Development of Sex Differences*. Stanford University Press, 1966, 1–24.

Hampton, J. L., and Hampton, J. C., "The Ontogenesis of Sexual Behavior in Man." In W. C. Young (ed.), *Sex and Internal Secretions*, 1961, 1401–1432.

Harlow, H. F., "The Heterosexual Affectional System in Monkeys." *The American Psychologist*, 1962, *17*, 1–9.

Hooker, E., "Male Homosexuality in the Rorschach." *Journal of Projective Techniques*, 1957, *21*, 18–31.

Itani, J. "Paternal Care in the Wild Japanese Monkeys, *Macaca Fuscata*." In C. H. Southwick (ed.), *Primate Social Behavior*. Princeton: Van Nostrand, 1963.

Little, K. B., and Schneidman, E. S., "Congruences among Interpretations of Psychological and Anamnestic Data." *Psychological Monographs*, 1959, *73*, 1–42.

Maccoby, Eleanor E., "Sex Differences in Intellectual Functioning." In Maccoby (ed.), *The Development of Sex Differences*. Stanford University Press, 1966, 25–55.

Masters, W. H., and Johnson, V. E., *Human Sexual Response*. Boston: Little, Brown, 1966.

Mead, M., *Male and Female: A Study of the Sexes in a Changing World*. New York: William Morrow, 1949.

Milgram, S., "Some Conditions of Obedience and Disobedience to Authority." *Human Relations*, 1965a, *18*, 57–76.

Milgram, S., "Liberating Effects of Group Pressure." *Journal of Personality and Social Psychology*, 1965b, *1*, 127–134.

Mitchell, G. D., "Paternalistic Behavior in Primates." *Psychological Bulletin*, 1969, *71*, 339–417.

Money, J., "Sexual Dimorphism and Homosexual Gender Identity." *Psychological Bulletin*, 1970, *74*, 6, 425–440.

Powers, E., and Witmer, H., *An Experiment in the Prevention of Delinquency*. New York: Columbia University Press, 1951.

Rheingold, J., *The Fear of Being a Woman*. New York: Grune & Stratton, 1964.

Rosenthal, R., "On the Social Psychology of the Psychological Experiment: The Experimenter's Hypothesis as Unintended Determinant of Experimental Results." *American Scientist*, 1963, *51*, 268–283.

Rosenthal, R., *Experimenter Effects in Behavioral Research*. New York: Appleton-Century-Crofts, 1966.

Rosenthal, R., and Fode, K. L., "The Effect of Experimenter Bias on the Performance of the Albino Rat." Unpublished Manuscript, Harvard University, 1960.

Rosenthal, R., and Jacobson, L., *Pygmalion in the Classroom: Teacher Expectation and Pupil's Intellectual Development*. New York: Holt, Rinehart and Winston, 1968.

Rosenthal, R., and Lawson, R., "A Longitudinal Study of the Effects of Experimenter Bias on the Operant Learning of Laboratory Rats." Unpublished Manuscript, Harvard University, 1961.

Rotter, J. B., "Psychotherapy." *Annual Review of Psychology*, 1960, *11*, 381–414.

Schachter, S., and Singer, J. E., "Cognitive, Social and Physiological Determinants of Emotional State." *Psychological Review*, 1962, *69*, 379–399.

Schwarz-Belkin, M. "Les Fleurs de Mal." In *Festschrift for Gordon Piltdown*. New York: Ponzi Press, 1914.

Storch, M., "Reply to Tiger," 1970. Unpublished Manuscript.

Tiger, L., *Men in Groups*. New York: Random House, 1969.

Tiger, L., "Male Dominance? Yes. Alas. A Sexist Plot? No." *New York Times Magazine*, Section N, Oct. 25, 1970.

Truax, C. B., "Effective Ingredients in Psychotherapy: an Approach to Unraveling the Patient-therapist Interaction. *Journal of Counseling Psychology*, 1963, *10*, 256–263.

CHARLES E. SILBERMAN
Murder in the Schoolroom

The murder of which Charles Silberman speaks is the "killing of dreams and the mutilation of spirits" that he discovered in three years spent studying American education. Silberman found that whatever the lesson presented to students, they were really being taught docility and the acceptance of orders from above. They were learning to live in institutions geared to arbitrary rules and petty regulations. They were being trained to forget their own desires and needs in order to survive in a world in which they could expect to be powerless. In short, they were receiving massive doses of the worst aspects of American life while they were still helpless to defend themselves.

It is an old tradition in America to blame the ills of society on the schools, but Silberman does not fall into this easy theory. He recognizes that America has had the kinds of schools that its citizens wanted—that the society prefers discipline to inquiry and docility to enthusiasm for learning, and that it regiments teachers and administrators as thoroughly as it does students. That this regimentation has been less and less accepted in recent years can only be a good thing. Silberman's account of the repression students endure in the first twelve (or more) years of their education throws a glaring light on the background of their revolt against the far milder discipline of their next four (or more) years in higher education. The question today is whether discipline in the university will be tightened to match the situation in the grade and high schools, or whether those schools will be humanized so that they will produce students who can maintain their own self-discipline in college, indeed in all their living.

"The most deadly of all possible sins," Erik Erikson suggests, "is the mutilation of a child's spirit." It is not possible to spend any prolonged period visiting public schools without being appalled by the mutilation visible everywhere: mutilation of spontaneity, of joy in learning, of pleasure in creating, of sense of self. The public schools, those "killers of the dream," to appropriate a phrase of Lillian Smith's, are the kind of institution one cannot really dislike until one gets to know them well. Because adults take the schools so much for granted, they fail to appreciate what grim, joyless places most American schools are, how oppressive and petty are the rules by which they are governed, how intellectually sterile and aesthetically barren the atmosphere, what an appalling lack of civility obtains on the part of teachers and principals, what contempt they unconsciously display for children as children.

And it need not be! Public schools *can* be organized to facilitate joy in learning and aesthetic expression and to develop character—in the rural and urban slums no less than in the prosperous suburbs. This is no utopian hope; there are models now in existence that can be followed.

What makes the change possible, moreover, is that what is mostly wrong with the public schools is not due to venality, or indifference, or stupidity, but to mindlessness. To be sure, teaching has its share of sadists and clods, of insecure and angry men and women who hate their students for their openness, their exuberance, their color, or their affluence. But by and large, teachers, principals, and superintendents are decent, intelligent, and caring people who try to do their best, by their lights. If they make a botch of it, and an uncomfortably large number do, it is because it simply never occurs to more than a handful to ask *why* they are doing what they are doing—to think seriously or deeply about the purposes or consequences of education. This mindlessness—the failure or refusal to think seriously about educational purpose, the reluctance to question established practice—is not the monopoly of the public school; it is diffused remarkably evenly throughout the entire educational system, and indeed the entire society.

The solution must lie in infusing the various educating institutions with purpose; more important, with thought about purpose, and about the ways in which techniques, content, and organization fulfill or alter purpose. And given the tendency of institutions to confuse day-to-day routine with purpose, to transform the means into the end itself, the infusion cannot be a one-shot affair. The process of self-examination, of "self-renewal," to use John Gardner's useful term, must be continuous. We must find ways of stimulating educators—public school teachers, principals, and superintendents; college professors, deans, and presidents; radio, television, and film directors and producers; newspaper, magazine, and TV journalists and executives—to think about what they are doing and why they are doing it. And we must persuade the general public to do the same.

Students need to learn far more than the basic skills. Children who have just started school may still be in the labor force in the year 2030. For them, nothing could be more wildly impractical than an education designed to prepare them for specific vocations or professions or to facilitate their adjustment to the world as it is. To be practical, an education should prepare a man for work that doesn't yet exist and whose nature cannot even be imagined. This can be done only by teaching people how to learn, by giving them the kind of intellectual discipline that will enable them to apply man's accumulated wisdom to new problems as they arise, the kind of wisdom that will enable them to *recognize* new problems as they arise.

Education should prepare people not just to earn a living but to live a life: a creative, humane, and sensitive life. This means that the schools must provide a liberal, humanizing education. And the purpose of liberal education must be, and indeed always has been, to educate educators—to turn out men and women who are capable of educating their families, their friends, their communities, and most important, themselves.

Of what does the capacity to educate oneself consist? It means that one has both the desire and the capacity to learn for himself, to dig out what he needs to know. It means that one has the capacity to judge what is worth learning. It means, too, that one can think for himself, so that he is dependent on neither the opinions nor the facts of others, and that he uses that capacity to think about his own education, which means to think about his own nature and his place in the universe—about the meaning of life and of knowledge and of the relations between them. "To refuse the effort to understand," Wayne Booth, dean of the College of the University of Chicago, argues, "is to resign from the human race." You cannot distinguish an educated man, he continues, "by whether or not he believes in God, or in UFO's. But you can tell an educated man by the way he takes hold of the question of whether God exists, or whether UFO's are from Mars."

To be educated in this sense means also to know something of the experience of beauty, if not in the sense of creating it or discoursing about it, then at the very least, in the sense of being able to respond to it—to respond, that is to say, both to the beauty of nature and to the beauty of the art made by our fellowmen.

To be educated also means to understand something of how to make our intentions effective in the real world, of how to apply knowledge to the life one lives and the society in which one lives it. The aim of education, as Alfred North Whitehead has written, "is the acquisition of the art of the utilization of knowledge." Indeed, a "merely well-informed man is the most useless bore on God's earth."

In all of this, the schools fail utterly and dismally. They fail in another and equally important

A New York City high school. *(Leslie Bauman)*

way. Education is not only a preparation for later life; it is an aspect of life itself. The great bulk of the young now spend a minimum of twelve years in school; with kindergarten attendance, and now preschool programs, becoming more widespread, more and more of the young will have spent thirteen to fifteen years attending school by the time they have finished high school. The quality of that experience must be regarded as important in its own right.

The most important characteristic that nearly all schools share is a preoccupation with order and control. And one of the most important controls is the clock. Things happen because it is time for them to occur. This means that a major part of the teacher's role is to serve as traffic manager and timekeeper, either deciding on a schedule himself or making sure that a schedule others have made is adhered to.

Several things follow from this. Adherence to a timetable means that a great deal of time is wasted, the experiencing of delay being one of the inevitable outcomes of traffic management. No one who examines classroom life carefully can fail to be astounded by the proportion of the students' time that is taken up just in waiting. The time is rarely used productively. Hence in the elementary grades, an able student can be absent from school for as long as two to three weeks and, quite literally, catch up with all he has missed in a single morning.

Adherence to the schedule also means that lessons frequently end before the students have mastered the subject at hand. As Herbert Kohl points out, "the tightness with time that exists in the elementary school has nothing to do with the quantity that must be learned or the children's needs. It represents the teacher's fear of loss of control and is nothing but a weapon used to weaken the solidarity and opposition of the children that too many teachers unconsciously dread."

ITEM: An elite private school in the East, once a bastion of progressive education. A fifth-grade teacher is conducting a mathematics class, demonstrating a technique for quick multiplication and division by recognizing certain arithmetic patterns. A few students grasp the point instantly; a few ignore the teacher altogether; most struggle to grasp the concept. Just as they are beginning to catch on—mutterings of "I get it, I get it," "I think I see," "Oh, that's how it works" can be heard all over the classroom—the lesson ends. No bell has rung; bells would violate the school's genteel progressive atmosphere. But the time schedule on the board indicates that math ends and social studies begins at 10:40, and it is now 10:37; the teacher tells the children to put away the math worksheets and take out their social studies texts. Some of the children protest; they're intrigued with the patterns they are discovering, and another five or ten minutes would enable them to consolidate what

they have only begun to grasp. No matter; the timetable rules.

ITEM: All over the United States, that last week of November 1963, teachers reported the same complaint: "I can't get the children to concentrate on their work; all they want to do is talk about the assassination." The idea that the children might learn more from discussing President Kennedy's assassination—or that, like most adults, they were simply too obsessed with the horrible events to think about anything else— didn't occur to these teachers. It wasn't in that week's lesson plan.

It is all too easy, of course, for the outsider to criticize. Unless one has taught (as this writer and members of his staff have), or has studied classroom procedures close up, it is hard to imagine the extent of the demands made on a teacher's attention. Philip W. Jackson's studies of teacher-student interchange, for example, indicate that "the teacher typically changes the focus of his concern about 1000 times daily," with many shifts of interest lasting only a few seconds, most of them less than a minute.

There are occasions when it is wise to depart from the lesson plan—surely the assassinations of a President, a distinguished civil rights leader and Nobel Laureate, and a senator contending for the presidency are such occasions— but there are also times when the teacher may be well advised to resist the seduction of talking about the day's headlines.

The trouble, then, is not with the schedule or the lesson plan per se, but with the fact that teachers too often see them as ends in themselves, rather than as means to an end. Even when children are excited about something directly related to the curriculum, teachers ignore or suppress the interest if it is not on the agenda for that period.

ITEM: A scholar studying curriculum reform visits a classroom

using a new elementary science curriculum. Arriving a few minutes before the class was scheduled to begin, he sees a cluster of excited children examining a turtle with enormous fascination and intensity. "Now children, put away the turtle," the teacher insists. "We're going to have our science lesson." The lesson is on crabs.

The tyranny of the lesson plan in turn encourages an obsession with routine for the sake of routine. School is filled with countless examples of teachers and administrators confusing means with ends, thereby making it impossible to reach the ends for which the means were devised.

ITEM: A fourth-grader is discovered by his parents to have abandoned reading E. B. White and the Dr. Doolittle books in favor of Little Golden Books—at his teacher's request. The young teacher—a dear, sweet, loving human being— explains that students are required to submit a weekly book report on a 4 x 6 filing card. If the student were to read books as long as *Charlotte's Web* or *Dr. Doolittle*, he wouldn't be able to submit a weekly report, and his reports might be too long to fit on the file card. "I urged him to continue reading those books on his own," the teacher explains, "but not for school." The youngster does not continue, of course; he has learned all too well that the object of reading is not enjoyment, but to fill out file cards.

ITEM: A suburban community boasts of its new three-million-dollar elementary "school of the future," with classrooms all built around a central library core, which one piece of promotional literature describes as "the nerve center of all educational processes in the school." There is not even a full-time librarian, and children are permitted to use the library only during scheduled "library periods," when they practice taking books from the shelves and returning them. They are not permitted to *read* the books they take off the shelves, however; they are there to learn "library skills," and the librarian will not permit them to "waste time." Nor are children permitted to borrow books to read over Christmas or Easter vacation; the librarian wants her books "in order." If a parent protests vigorously enough, the librarian makes an exception—after warning the child that "you'd better take care of that book and bring it back on time."

ITEM: A junior high school in a West Coast city. The day after a student has thrown a book out of a classroom window, a distinguished professor of education doing research in the school reports, all the teachers received a memorandum from the principal: "Please keep all books away from students."

ITEM: With considerable fanfare, a New York City school district introduces what it calls "The Balanced Class Project" in a neighborhood containing a rich mixture of black, white, and Puerto Rican youngsters. The experiment, which involves heterogeneous grouping of children in classes, is designed to demonstrate the values of diversity. But instead of the English-speaking youngsters learning Spanish from their Puerto Rican classmates and teaching them English in turn, all children are taught French.

Administrators tend to be even guiltier of this kind of mindlessness and slavish adherence to routine for the sake of routine. It is, in a sense, built into their job description, and into the way in which they view their role. Most schools are organized and run to facilitate order; the principal or superintendent is considered, and considers himself, a manager whose job is to keep the organization running as efficiently as possible.

This preoccupation with efficiency, which is to say, with order and control, turns the teacher into a disciplinarian as well as a timekeeper and traffic manager. In the interests of efficiency, moreover, discipline is defined in simple but rigid terms: the absence of noise and of movement. "When we ask chil-

dren *not* to move, we should have excellent reasons for doing so," the English psychologist and educator, Susan Isaacs, of the University of London, argued in 1932. "It is stillness we have to justify, not movement." But no justification is offered or expected. Indeed, there is no more firmly rooted school tradition than the one that holds that children must sit still, at their desks, without conversing at all, both during periods of waiting, when they have nothing to do, and during activities that almost demand conversation. Yet even on an assembly line, there is conversation and interaction among workers, and there are coffee breaks and work pauses as well.

ITEM: A new suburban elementary school is being hailed in architectural circles for its "open design." The building has no corridors; the sixteen classrooms open instead onto "project areas" with worktables, sinks, et al., connected to a central library core. What the architects don't know, however, is that in most classrooms, the project areas go unused: if some children are in the project area and some are in the regular classroom, the teacher might not be able to see every child, and so some of them might be carrying on a conversation without detection.

ITEM: In lecturing the assembled students on the need for and virtue of absolute silence, an elementary school principal expostulates on the wonders of a school for the "deaf and dumb" he had recently visited. The silence was just wonderful, he tells the assembly; the children could all get their work done because of the total silence. The goal is explicit: to turn normal children into youngsters behaving as though they were missing two of their faculties.

ITEM: A high school in a New England city is very proud of its elaborately equipped language laboratory, with a new "Random Access Teaching Equipment" system touted as "tailored to the individual student's progress, as each position permits the instructor to

gauge the progress of all students on an individual basis." To make sure that its expensive equipment is used properly, the high school gives students careful instructions, among them the following:

■ No one is an individual in the laboratory. Do nothing and touch nothing until instructions are given by the teacher. Then listen carefully and follow directions exactly.
■ The equipment in the laboratory is not like ordinary tape recorders. The principles involved are quite different. Please do not ask unnecessary questions about its operation.
■ You will stand quietly behind the chair at your booth until the teacher asks you to sit. Then sit in as close to the desk as possible.

The instructions for the lab assistants are equally explicit. They include the following:

1. Keep watching the students all the time.
   a) By standing in the middle of the lab on window side you can see most of the lab.
   b) Walk along the rows to make sure all arms are folded; politely but firmly ask the students to do this.

ITEM: A first-grade classroom has the following sign prominently posted:

RULES FOR CLASSES 1–7
1. Keep your hands at your sides.
2. Raise your hand to speak.
3. Be polite and kind to all.
4. Fold hands when not working.

The sign does not indicate how a child can fold hands that are required to be at his side.

The obsession with silence and lack of movement is not limited to American schools, of course; it is a characteristic of schools everywhere.

ITEM: From *Socialist Competition in the Schools,* a Soviet manual for "school directors, supervisors, teachers, and Young Pioneer leaders" prepared by the Institute on the Theory and History of Pedagogy at the USSR's Academy of Pedagogical Sciences. The manual begins with instructions for the teacher standing before the class on the first day of school:

It is not difficult to see that a direct approach to the class with the command, "All sit straight" often doesn't bring the desired effect since a demand in this form does not reach the sensibilities of the pupils and does not activate them.

In order to "reach the sensibilities of the pupils" and "activate them" according to principles of socialist competition, the teacher should say, "Let's see which row can sit the straightest."

In the United States, training in sitting still begins in kindergarten, the function of which is, in large measure, to instill the behavior patterns the rest of the school demands.

ITEM: The report card which a well-to-do suburban school system uses for kindergarteners grades the five-year-olds on their "Readiness for First-Grade Work." Readiness involves some seventeen attributes, the first three of which read as follows:

1. Sits still and works at assigned task for 15 to 20 minutes.
2. Listens and follows directions.
3. Displays good work habits.

The fourth attribute is "Has intellectual curiosity."

Moreover, despite the fact that schoolchildren work in very close quarters, silence is demanded, and the pupils are required to ignore those around them.

ITEM: An art teacher, conducting a class for fourth-graders, orders all children to put their crayons away for the rest of the period. The offense: some children who had finished the pictures they were drawing were showing their pictures to their neighbors. (Crayons were being used because the principal had forbidden the use of paints, for fear that the paint might spill on the carpeting with which the floors in this brand-new school are covered.)

Silence is demanded even when students are moving from one class to another.

ITEM: A visitor asks a junior high school principal why his school's twelve-, thirteen-, and fourteen-year-old students are required to "line up" in each classroom before being permitted to leave for the next class. "Didn't you notice how narrow our halls are?" he replies. "Yes," the visitor answers. "But I also noticed that the youngsters abandon the single lines as soon as they leave the classroom." The principal thinks for a minute, then announces his solution: "I guess we'll have to get more marshals to patrol the halls."

ITEM: In that same school system, the principal of the elementary school serving the city's wealthiest neighborhood insists that all students carry their books in their left hand when going from room to room. Asked why, the principal looks surprised—apparently no one had ever asked that question before—and after some hesitation and fumbling, explains that the children need to have their right hand free to hold on to the banisters to avoid falling when going up or down stairs. And besides, he adds, if children were permitted to carry books in their right hand, they might bang them against, and thus damage, the steel coat lockers that line some of the halls. (The students are also required to walk only on the right side of the corridors and stairs.)

The ban on movement extends to the entire school. Thus, students in most schools cannot leave the classroom, or the library or the study hall, without permission, even to get a drink of water or to go to the toilet, and the length of time they can spend there is rigidly prescribed. In high schools and junior highs, the corridors are usually guarded by teachers and students on patrol duty, whose principal function is to check the credentials of any student walking through. In the typical high school, no student may walk down the corridor without a form, signed by a teacher, telling where he is coming from, where he is going, and the time, to the minute, during which the pass is valid. In many schools, the toilets are kept locked except during class breaks, so that a student not only must obtain a pass but must find the custodian and persuade him to unlock the needed facility. There are schools, of course, where some of these arrangements have a rational basis: where school authorities are legitimately concerned about the intrusion of outsiders, where traffic in heroin and other narcotics is brisk. But these regulations began long before schools had any drug problem; they have obtained for as long as anyone can recall. Even during periods when students do not have a class, they must be in a study hall or some other prescribed place. It is a rare school, for example, in which students are permitted to go to the library if they have a free period: the library is open to them only if they have an assigned "library period," or if they manage to wangle a pass for that purpose from the librarian or some other person in authority.

ITEM: From an article in the September 1969, *Today's Education*, one of a series "presenting the handling of a troublesome classroom incident by a teacher": "Last year the faculty of our high school adopted a plan to control excessive loitering in the halls. Each teacher received a hall pass for his room— a good-sized piece of wood, painted bright yellow, marked with the room number. No student was allowed to leave the room without the pass, and the pass was issued only for trips to the rest room or the nurse's office. . . . In a few minutes, a boy got the pass from me in order to go to the rest room. I would never have noticed that he hadn't returned within a reasonable period of time if another student hadn't asked for the pass." (The boy was delayed because he had to use a toilet at the opposite end of the building; workmen were making repairs on the one nearby.)

ITEM: Over an elementary school's PA system comes the principal's announcement: "Children are not using the lavatories correctly. No child may be out of his room for more than three minutes."

These petty rules and regulations are necessary not simply because of the importance schoolmen attach to control—they like to exercise control, it would seem, over what comes out of the bladder as well as the mouth —but also because schools, and school systems, operate on the assumption of distrust.

"The school board has no faith in the central administration, the central administration has no faith in the principals, the principals have no faith in the teachers, and the teachers have no faith in the students," Christopher Jencks observes. "In such a system it seems natural not to give the principal of a school control over his budget, not to give the teachers control over their syllabus, and not to give the students control over anything. Distrust is the order of the day."

ITEM (from an N.E.A. volume on *Discipline in the Classroom*): "May an old hand give a beginning teacher some tips about keeping classroom discipline? I have found these procedures helpful:

...Plan the lesson. Be ready to use the first minute of class time. If you get Johnny right away, he has no time to cook up interesting ideas that do not fit into the class situation. [Emphasis in original.]

The result, of course, is that the classroom becomes a battleground, with students and teachers devoting an inordinate amount of energy to the search for ways of outwitting one another.

ITEM (from *Discipline in the Classroom*):

"Avoid standing with your back to the class for any length of time. If you do, you may invite disorderly conduct. Learn to write on the board with only your right shoulder toward the board. Student attention tends to be focused on what you are writing if the words are not obscured by your body. Whenever possible, anything you need to put on the board should be written before class time...."

"Avoid emotion-charged topics. Discussing them may lead to an argument so explosive that fighting can result. Until a group has achieved enough maturity to keep itself under control, it is better to risk boredom than pandemonium."

But how can a group "achieve enough maturity to keep itself under control" if its members never have an opportunity to exercise control? Far from helping students to develop into mature, self-reliant, self-motivated individuals, schools seem to do everything they can to keep youngsters in a state of chronic, almost infantile, dependency. The pervasive atmosphere of distrust, together with rules covering the most minute aspects of existence, teaches students every day that they are not people of worth, and certainly not individuals capable of regulating their own behavior.

ITEM: A precocious sixth-grader has become attached to a particular pencil, now down to a small stub. His teacher orders him to use a larger pencil; the youngster politely informs her that so long as his work and his penmanship are satisfactory (he is receiving A's on all his work), what pencil he uses is a matter for him to decide. The teacher sends him to see the principal, who summons the boy's parents for a conference to discuss his "disobedience."

Even when schools set out to develop self-direction, they seem incapable of letting go the traces.

ITEM: A Southern high school has received a national award as its state's "Pacemaker school of the year" for its innovative climate in which the school "seeks to provide an atmosphere in which the student will be motivated toward self-direction." As the school's handbook adds, "Self-direction cannot be taught but must be experienced." Discipline is regarded "as a learning process by which the student is guided in the development of self-control and in the recognition of his responsibilities to himself and to the group." But the school's regulations include the following:

Students should move from one area to another within a four minute period following the module tone. There will be no movement through the halls, nor will any student be in the halls, except by written permission from a teacher, at any time other than during the four minutes following the module tone....

General propriety rules out boisterousness, excessively loud talking in the talking commons, failure to be seated while in the commons area (not more than four at a small table, eight at large tables), running in the building, throwing trash on the floor, and all other areas displaying lack of self-discipline.

More important, schools discourage students from developing the capacity to learn by and for themselves; they make it impossible for a youngster to take responsibility for his own education, for they are structured in such a way as to make students totally dependent upon the teachers. Whatever rhetoric they may subscribe to, most schools in practice define education as something teachers do to or for students, not something students do to and for themselves, with a teacher's assistance. "Seated at his desk, the teacher is in a position to do something," Jackson reports. *"It is the teacher's job to declare what that something shall be."* (Emphasis added.) "It is the teacher who decides who will speak and in what order," and it is the teacher who decides who will have access to the materials of learning. The result is to destroy students' curiosity, along with their ability—more serious, their desire—to think or act for themselves.

ITEM: A large suburban high school informs its juniors that they will be able, the following year, to pursue a course of independent study on a topic of their own choosing, under faculty guidance, in lieu of a conventional course. In a class of eight or nine hundred, half of whom will be going to college, and in a year in which "relevance" has become an almost universal student catchword and demand, only three students bother to apply. The school has done its job well!

At the heart of the schoolmen's inability to turn responsibility over to the students is the fact that the teacher-student relationship in its conventional form is, as Willard Waller states, "a form of institutionalized dominance and subordination. Teacher and pupil confront each other in the school with an original conflict of desires, and however much that conflict may be reduced in amount, or however much it may be hidden, it still remains. The teacher represents the adult group, ever the enemy of the spontaneous life of groups of children. The teacher represents the formal curriculum, and his interest is in imposing that curriculum upon the children in the form of tasks; pupils are much more interested in life in their own world than in the desiccated bits of adult life which teachers have to offer. The teacher represents the established social order in the school, and his interest is in maintaining that order, whereas pupils have only a negative interest in that feudal superstructure. Teacher and pupil confront each other with attitudes from which the underlying hostility can never be altogether removed." There is a kernel of truth in short, as well as an element of self-pity, in the young rebels' fondness for the metaphor of the "student as nigger."

A major source of the underlying hostility is the preoccupation with evaluation. Almost anything and everything the student does is likely to be evaluated, and the teacher, of course, is the chief source of evaluation. Evaluation per se is not the problem. It is an important and indeed intrinsic part of education, essential if teachers are to judge the effectiveness of their teaching, and if students are to judge what they know and what they are having trouble learning. The purpose should be diagnostic: to indicate where teachers and students have gone wrong, and how they might improve their performance. And since students will have to judge their own performance, they need experience in self-evaluation.

But schools rarely evaluate this way; they make clear that the purpose of evaluation is rating to produce grades that enable administrators to rate and sort children—to categorize them so rigidly that they can rarely escape. The assault on the student's self-esteem and sense of self is frequently overt, with teachers virtually demanding failure from some children.

ITEM: A fourth-grade math teacher writes a half-dozen problems on the board for the class to do. "I think I can pick at least four children who can't do them," she tells the class, and proceeds to call four youngsters to the board to demonstrate, for all to see, how correct the teacher's judgment is. Needless to say, the children fulfill the prophecy.

ITEM: An elementary school in a wealthy Northeastern suburb whose name is almost synonymous with concern for education. Three children are in a special class for children with perceptual problems. The teacher insists on talking with the visitor about the children in their presence, as though congenital deafness were part of their difficulty. "Now, watch, I'm giving them papers to see if they can spot the ovals, but you'll see that this one"—he nods in the direction of a little boy—"isn't going to be able to do it." A few seconds later, he says triumphantly, "See, I told you he couldn't. He never gets that one right. Now I'll put something on the overhead projector, and this one"—this time a nod toward a little girl—"won't stay with it for more than a line." Five seconds later, with evident disappointment: "Well, that's the first time she ever did *that*. But keep watching. By the next line, she'll have flubbed it." The child gets the next one right, too, and the teacher's disappointment mounts. "This *is* unusual, but just stick around . . ." Sure enough, the child goofs at line five. "See, I told you so!"

ITEM: An elementary school in the Southeast, widely publicized for its variety of innovations, has abolished letter grades. Instead, children receive one of three evaluations: "working below your ability"; "working to your ability"; or "working above your ability." It is hard to imagine anything better calculated to reduce a child's sense of self than this last grade.

The problem is compounded by the misuse of IQ and other standardized tests. "Although the validity and reliability of all standardized tests is far from perfect," David A. Goslin of the Russell Sage Foundation writes, "a precise numerical score frequently takes on a kind of absolute validity when it appears on a child's record card. Teachers and administrators alike, when confronted with a child's IQ score or his percentile rank on an achievement test like the Iowa Test of Basic Skills, often tend to disregard the considerable degree of imprecision that is inherent in such measures." The result, Goslin adds, "is that in a variety of ways we are tending to put individuals into cubby holes."

A corollary of teacher dominance is the teacher's role in doling out privileges, from which status flows. "In elementary classrooms, it is usually the teacher who assigns coveted duties, such as serving on the safety patrol, or running the movie projector, or clapping erasers, or handing out supplies," Jackson observes. "Although the delegation of these duties may not take up much of the teacher's time, it does help to give structure to the activities of the room and to fashion the quality of the total experience for many of the participants."

Still another by-product of teacher dominance, one that has profound consequences for children's attitudes toward learning, is the sharp but wholly artificial dichotomy between work and play which schools create and maintain. Young children make no such distinction. They learn through play, and until they have been taught to make the distinction ("Let's stop playing now, children; it's time to start our work"), they regard all activities in the same light. But the dichotomy grows out of the assumption that nothing can happen unless the teacher makes it happen.

ITEM: A kindergarten teacher calls to her class to gather round her to hear her read a story. Most come immediately; several do not, for they are totally absorbed in what they are doing: one is building a complicated tower with blocks, another is counting the number of steps on a ladder, a third is absorbed with a picture book. Sweetly but firmly, the teacher insists that they drop what they are doing: "It's time to hear a story." Reluctantly, the children come; they have learned that work is what someone else wants you to do.

Why are schools so bad? To read some of the more important and influential contemporary critics of education, men like Edgar Friedenberg, Paul Goodman, John Holt, Jonathan Kozol, one might think that the schools are staffed by sadists and clods who are drawn into teaching by the lure of upward mobility and the opportunity to take out their anger—Friedenberg prefers the sociological term, *ressentiment,* or "A kind of free-floating illtemper"—on the students. This impression is conveyed less by explicit statement than by nuance and tone—a kind of "aristocratic insouciance," as David Riesman calls it, which these writers affect, in turn reflecting the general snobbery of the educated upper middle class toward the white-collar, lower-middleclass world of teachers, social

workers, civil servants, and policemen.

This snobbery has become, in recent years, a nasty and sometimes spiteful form of bigotry on the part of many self-made intellectuals, who seem to feel the need to demonstrate their moral and cultural superiority to the lower middle class from which they escaped.

A number of critics of American education and culture, moreover, such as Edgar Friedenberg, a conscious elitist, Paul Goodman, Norman Mailer, and Leslie Fiedler seem to be particularly attracted by the virility and violence of lower-class life, which they tend to romanticize. They seem unable to show empathy for the problems of the lowermiddle-class teacher, whose passivity and fear of violence they deride as effeminate and whose humanity they seem, at times, almost to deny.

But teachers *are* human. To be sure, teaching, like the ministry, law, medicine, business, and government, has its share of angry, hostile, mean, and incompetent people. Most teachers, however, are decent, honest, well-intentioned people who do their best under the most trying circumstances. If they appear otherwise, it is because the institution in which they are engulfed demands it of them. In fact, transforming the school transforms teacher as well as student behavior. If placed in an atmosphere of freedom and trust, that is to say, if treated as professionals and as people of worth, teachers behave like the caring, concerned people they would like to be. They, no less than their students, are victimized by the way in which schools are presently organized and run.

Certainly nothing in the way most schools are built or run suggests respect for teachers as teachers, or as human beings. After visiting some 260 classrooms in 100 elementary schools

in 13 states, for example, John Goodlad, dean of the UCLA Graduate School of Education, concluded that the schools are "anything but the 'palaces' of an affluent society." On the contrary, he writes, they look "more like the artifacts of a society that did not really care about its schools, a society that expressed its disregard by creating schools less suited to human habitation than its prisons." Goodlad and his colleagues had hoped to conduct long interviews with the teachers they observed, for example, but found that hardly any schools had either quiet or attractive places in which to meet: they held their interviews on the run, therefore, unless they were able to meet the teachers for breakfast or dinner. Nor was Goodlad's experience atypical. Teachers rarely have offices of their own, and if there is a teachers' lounge, more often than not it is a shabbily furnished room designed to permit no more than a fast smoke.

The shabbiness of the teachers' physical environment is exceeded only by the churlishness of their social environment, a fact which educational critics and reformers tend to ignore, or to acknowledge only in passing. "Reform literature," as Dean Robert J. Schaeffer of Teachers College has written, "has failed to examine the total educational experience of teachers, and has narrowly concentrated upon preservice preparation to the neglect of the educative or the debilitating effects of the job itself." And the job *is* debilitating. In a section on "What Teaching Does to Teachers" in *The Sociology of Teaching,* Willard Waller talks about "that peculiar blight which affects the teacher mind, which creeps over it gradually, and possessing it bit by bit, devours its creative resources."

This "peculiar blight" is a product of a number of forces. There is the low regard in which teachers are held by the rest of the community, reflected not only in the salaries and physical plants teachers are provided, but in the unflattering stereotypes of teachers with which American literature and films and TV programs are filled. In a study of occupational prestige conducted by the National Opinion Research Center, teaching ranked thirty-fifth from the top, just below the building contractor and just above the railroad engineer. The status problem mainly affects male teachers, the great majority of whom teach in secondary schools. For women, teaching is a highly prestigious occupation; indeed, teaching is a low-status and low-paying occupation for men in large part because of the fact that it traditionally has been dominated by women, and so is regarded as a female occupation.

There is the atmosphere of meanness and distrust in which teachers work: they punch time clocks like clerks or factory workers and are rarely, if ever, consulted about the things that concern them most: the content of the curriculum, the selection of textbooks, and so forth. And there are the conditions of work themselves, in particular teaching loads and schedules that provide no time for reflection or for privacy, as well as the incredible array of clerical and mental tasks that occupy their nonteaching time—for example, patrolling the halls and cafeterias. "Whatever becomes of our method, the conditions stand fast—six hours, and thirty, fifty, or a hundred and fifty pupils," Ralph Waldo Emerson observed more than a century ago. "Something must be done and done speedily, and in this distress the wisest are tempted to adopt violent means, to proclaim martial law, corporal punishment, mechanical arrangements, bribes, spies, wrath, main strength and ignorance. . . . And the gentle teacher, who wishes to be a Providence to youth, is

grown a martinet, sore with suspicions . . . and his love of learning is lost in the routine of grammar and books of elements."

Despite the continuous contact with children, moreover, teaching is a lonely profession. Teachers rarely get a chance to discuss their problems or their successes with their colleagues, nor do they, as a rule, receive any kind of meaningful help from their supervisors, not even in the first years of teaching. "When we first started working in the schools," members of the Yale University Psycho-Educational Clinic report, "we were asked in several instances in the early weeks not to go into several classrooms *because* the teachers were new." (Emphasis in the original.)

If teachers are obsessed with silence and lack of movement, therefore, it is in large part because it is the chief means by which their competence is judged. A teacher will rarely, if ever, be called on the carpet or denied tenure because his or her students haven't learned anything: she most certainly will if her students are talking or moving about the classroom, or, even worse, found outside the room, and she may earn the censure of her colleagues as well. Nor will teachers receive suggestions from their supervisors as to how to improve their teaching methods and materials; they will receive suggestions for improving discipline. Thus, the vows of silence and stillness are often imposed on teachers who might prefer a more open, lively classroom.

ITEM (from *Up the Down Staircase*): "There was one heady moment when I was able to excite the class by an idea: I had put on the blackboard Browning's 'A man's reach should exceed his grasp, or what's a heaven for?' and we got involved in a spirited discussion of aspiration vs. reality. Is it wise, I asked, to aim higher than one's capacity? Does it not doom one to failure? No, no, some said, that's ambition and progress! No,

no, others cried, that's frustration and defeat! What about hope? What about despair?—You've got to be practical!—You've got to have a dream! They said this in their own words, you understand, startled into discovery. To the young, clichés seem freshly minted. Hitch your wagon to a star! Shoemaker, stick to your last! And when the dismissal bell rang, they paid me the highest compliment: they groaned! They crowded in the doorway, chirping like agitated sparrows, pecking at the seeds I had strewn—when who should appear but (the Administrative Assistant to the Principal).

"'What is the meaning of this noise?'

"'It's the sound of thinking, Mr. McHabe,' I said.

"In my letter box that afternoon was a note from him, with copies to my principal and chairman (and—who knows?—perhaps a sealed indictment dispatched to the Board?) which read:

I have observed that in your class the class entering your room is held up because the pupils exiting from your room are exiting in a disorganized fashion, blocking the doorway unnecessarily and *talking*. An orderly flow of traffic is the responsibility of the teacher whose class is exiting from the room.

"The cardinal sin, strange as it may seem in an institution of learning, is talking." (Emphasis in the original.)

ITEM (from real life): A sixth-grade science teacher in a highly regarded suburban school, learning that one of his pupils is the son of a local butcher, obtains the heart and lungs of a cow. Next day, elbow-deep in tissue and blood, he shows the class how the respiratory system operates. When he returns from lunch, he finds a note from the superintendent, who had looked in on the class that morning: "Teachers are not supposed to remove their jackets in class. If the jacket must be removed, the shirtsleeves certainly should not be rolled up."

ITEM: An inexperienced teacher in a slum school, struggling valiantly to do her best with a particularly difficult six-grade class—the youngsters had been labeled "difficult" by the school's "tracking" system—is visited by the system's supervisor of elementary education. The supervisor's only comment: one child was chewing gum in class.

If the schools are repressive, moreover, it is not the teachers' fault, or certainly not their fault alone. Nearly two thirds of the high school students' parents surveyed for *Life* by Louis Harris, for example, believe that "maintaining discipline is more important than student self-inquiry"; the comparable figure among teachers is only 27 percent. The United States, in short, has the kinds of schools its citizens have thus far demanded. The role of taskmaster is thrust upon teachers, some of whom accept it willingly, some reluctantly: all are affected by it. "The teacher-pupil relationship," Waller writes, "is a special form of dominance and subordination, a very unstable relationship and in quivering equilibrium. . . . It is an unfortunate role, that of Simon Legree, and has corrupted the best of men."

To survive in school, as in other "total institutions," the students, like the teachers, are forced to develop a variety of adaptive strategies and attitudes. And survival—getting through and compiling a good record or avoiding a bad record—does become the goal. It is inevitable that this be so, given the obsession with routine and given also the frequency with which students are evaluated, the arbitrariness and mysteriousness (at least to the students) of the criteria by which they are judged, and the importance attached to these evaluations by parents, teachers, colleges, graduate and professional schools, and prospective employers.

ITEM: A high school student talking: "School is just like roulette or something. You can't just ask: 'Well, what's the point of it?' . . . The point of it is to do it, to get through and get into college. But you have to figure the system or you can't win, because the odds are all on the house's side."

Unfortunately, survival has little to do with learning in the sense of cognitive development. "For children," as John Holt documents in some detail, "the central business of school is not learning, whatever this vague word means; it is getting those daily tasks done, or at least out of the way, with a minimum of effort and unpleasantness. Each task is an end in itself."

In any case, the student has no cognitive map to guide him through the labyrinth of knowledge he is asked to master. He is guided instead, Professor Mary Alice White of Teachers College suggests, by his map of school experience which is organized by the way in which school life itself is organized. Thus elementary school students almost invariably regard mathematics as the most important subject in the curriculum—not because of its structure or its elegance, but because math has the most homework, because the homework is corrected the most promptly, and because tests are given more frequently in math than in any other subject. The youngsters regard spelling as the next most important subject—because of the frequency of spelling tests. "To a pupil," Professor White explains, "the workload and evaluation demands obviously must reflect what the teacher thinks is important to learn."

It is not simply the students' ignorance of the purposes of what they are asked to learn that makes learning subordinate to survival. Almost from the first day, students learn that the game is not to acquire knowledge but to discover what answer the teacher wants, and in what form she wants it; there are few classroom scenes more familiar than that of the teacher brushing aside, or penalizing, correct answers that don't happen to be the ones she had in mind. "It is soon clear to students what types of responses are likely to be successful at playing the school game," a group of dissident Maryland students write in a biting critique of their country's schools. "And so, before long, a student's approach to questions and problems undergoes a basic change. It quickly becomes clear that approaching a question on a test by saying 'What is my own response to this question?' is risky indeed, and totally unwise if one covets the highest grade possible (and the school system teaches the student that he should). Rather, the real question is clear to any student who knows anything about how schools work: 'What is the answer the teacher wants me to give? What can I write that will please the teacher?' "

These tendencies are built into the way classrooms operate. Without realizing it, most teachers dominate the classroom, giving students no option except that of passivity. Exhaustive studies of classroom language by scholars in almost every part of the country and almost every kind of school reveal a pattern that is striking in its uniformity: teachers do almost all the talking, accounting, on average, for two thirds to three quarters of all classroom communication. There are differences, of course, from teacher to teacher, but the differences are surprisingly small. In the most child-centered classroom in a private school known for its child-centeredness, for example, Philip Jackson found that the teacher initiated 55.2 percent of the conversation; in the most teacher-dominated room, the ratio was 80.7 percent. Equally significant, analyses of the nature of student and teacher conversation indicate that the student's role is passive, being confined, for the most part, to responses to teacher questions or statements. In almost all the systems of "interaction analysis" which have been devised to analyze the different kinds of classroom communication—there are now several dozen—three quarters or so of the "talk" categories refer to teachers. Small wonder, then, that students seem unable to take responsibility for their learning.

The phenomenon is not limited to elementary and secondary schools. College students' academic relationship to faculty and administration is also one of subjection. In medical school, too, the goal is to get through. One of the ways of getting through is by cheating. Some of the forms of falsification involve little more than the petty dissembling common to adult social discourse, for example, feigning interest in what another is saying. Some involve outright cheating, copying on a test. In their classic studies of character education of forty years ago. H. Hartshorne and M. A. May discovered that children's tendency to cheat depended on the risk of detection and the effort required rather than on the intrinsic notions of morality; noncheaters were more cautious than the cheaters, but not more honest. These findings, which have been confirmed by a number of subsequent studies, reflect the primitive morality which the culture of the school cultivates.

Getting through school also involves learning how to suppress one's feelings and emotions and to subordinate one's own interests and desires to those of the teachers. Up to a point, this, too, is useful, a necessary aspect of learning to live in society. But schools tend to turn what could be a virtue into a fault by in effect excluding the child's interests altogether. The result, Peter Marin, a former high school principal suggests, is to create "a cultural schizophrenia, in which the student is forced to choose between his own rela-

tion to reality and the one demanded by the institution." Children frequently respond by learning to live in two worlds.

Some students, however, survive by withdrawing into apathy, whether feigned or real; in the constantly evaluative atmosphere of the school, one way to avoid the pain of failure is to persuade yourself that you do not care. But those who do care, and who do do well on tests, are not free from pain, either; they may bear the marks of caring for the rest of their lives, particularly if they go on to college and graduate or professional school. One of the first discoveries that Sigmund Freud made when he began studying the significance of dreams was the near universality, among people with advanced degrees, of what he called the "examination dream." In it, the dreamer imagines himself back at school and about to take an examination for which he is hopelessly unprepared and almost certain to fail. The dream, still common among university graduates, is marked by acute anxiety; the dreamer often awakens in a cold sweat.

The most important strategy for survival, however, is docility and conformity. The encouragement of docility may explain why girls tend to be more successful in school than boys: passivity and docility are more in keeping with the behavior the culture expects of girls outside school than the behavior it expects of boys. The phenomenon is cumulative and self-reinforcing: the behavior demanded in school is more feminine than masculine; girls adapt better; therefore school, and an interest in school affairs, tends to be defined as feminine, particularly among ethnic and social groups that place a high premium on masculinity. Perhaps as a result—or perhaps also because boys develop at a different rate than girls, a fact which the schools ignore—boys

tend to do less well in school than girls, and are vastly more susceptible to learning and emotional problems. For example, boys account for three quarters of all referrals to reading clinics; more than two thirds of the children who are left back in a grade for one or more years are boys; between three and four times as many boys as girls are stutterers.

Docility is not only encouraged; it frequently is demanded, for teachers and administrators seem unable to distinguish between authority and power. "The generalization that the schools have a despotic political structure," Waller writes, "seems to hold true for nearly all types of schools, and for all about equally, without very much difference in fact to correspond to radical differences in theory."

ITEM: The director of physical education for girls in a well-regarded suburban school system insists that a thirteen-year-old girl change into gym shorts and sit on the sidelines each time her class has gym despite the fact that the girl has been excused for medical reasons. "There is no reason you can't watch, or keep score, if the other girls are playing a game," the director tells the child, whose cancerous right leg has just been amputated at the hip, and who cannot yet be fitted with an artificial limb. Not until her mother carries the appeal to the superintendent of schools is the youngster spared this thrice-weekly humiliation.

ITEM (from the film *High School*, produced by Frederick Wiseman): A boy, being put on detention, protests his innocence, politely but insistently presenting his version of what happened. (The incident in question had involved another teacher.) The teacher giving the punishment responds each time by telling the boy how important it is to respect his elders, insisting that he should go on detention first, and then tell the teacher involved why he thought the punishment was unfair. "You have to prove you're a man and can take orders." The boy finally agrees to go to detention, "but under protest." The scene ends with the teacher smirking as the boy walks away.

Docility is demanded outside the classroom and the school as well as inside it; students learn pretty rapidly that their participation in civic affairs is not welcome, except for one ceremonial day a year when they are allowed to play at being superintendent of schools, principal, teacher, and so on, for the photographers from the local newspaper.

ITEM: A high school senior— eighth in a class of 779, active in a host of extracurricular activities (student marshals, General Organizations, Key Club, after-school tutoring program, president of the Debate Society, among others), and described on the school's record as "intelligent, highly motivated and mature," with "excellent leadership and academic potentials"—is barred from the school's chapter of the National Honor Society on the grounds of poor character. At an open meeting of school board candidates the preceding spring, he had politely asked a question which implied some criticism of the high school. In the opinion of eight of the Honor Society's fifteen faculty advisers, none of whom had been present at the meeting in question, and none of whom had ever met the boy in question, criticism of the high school is equivalent to disloyalty, and disloyalty constitutes bad character. The seven faculty advisers who do know the youngster fight for his admission but are overruled.

ITEM: Memorandum to teachers from the principal of a high school in a Washington, D.C., suburb: "If you see any copies of the *Washington Free Press* [NB: a local student "underground" newspaper] in the possession of a student, confiscate it immediately. Any questions from the student regarding this confiscation should be referred to the administration. If you see a student selling or distributing this paper, refer them [*sic*] to an administrator and they will be suspended."

ITEM: The principal of a Queens, New York, high school went further: every student *"seen reading or carrying—or even suspected of possessing—copies"* of a New York underground paper, was suspended. (Emphasis added.)

For students who plan to go to college, the threat of an unfavorable reference is a frequent means of keeping them in line.

ITEM (from the Montgomery County, Maryland, Student Alliance Report): "In the way of a few examples: one student who insisted that he would protest against the Vietnam War in front of the school was told by a vice-principal that if the student persisted the school official would see to it that he could not get into college. . . . Another high school student, a National Merit Scholarship Finalist, as it happened, was told by his counselor that he would get a bad recommendation for college because he was a 'nihilist.' He had been arguing with her over the values of the county school system."

Most students, however, are only too willing to comply. The tragedy is that the great majority do not rebel; they accept the stultifying rules, the lack of privacy, the authoritarianism, the abuse of power—indeed, virtually every aspect of school life— as The Way Things Are. "All weakness tends to corrupt, and impotence corrupts absolutely," Edgar Friedenberg sardonically observes. Hence students "accept the school as the way life is and close their minds against the anxiety of perceiving alternatives. Many students like high school; others loathe and fear it. But even these do not object to it on principle; the school effectively obstructs their learning of the principles on which objection might be based."

ITEM: A high school student talking: "The main thing is not to take it personal, to understand that it's just a system and it treats you the same way it treats everybody else, like an engine or a machine or something mechanical. Our names get fed into it—*we* get fed into it— when we're five years old, and if we catch on and watch our step, it spits us out when we're 17 or 18 . . ."

The sociologist Buford Rhea, who set out to study high school students' alienation, discovered that most students are not alienated and do not want power, because they feel they would not know what to do with it if they had it. They have remarkable faith in the high schools' paternalism, and so see no need to question what their teachers are doing or why. "It is the teacher's job to know what to tell the student to do, and it is therefore the teacher's responsibility to know *why* the student should do it," Rhea reports. (Emphasis his.) Indeed, academically ambitious students quite literally will themselves into believing in their teachers' ability. "Unable to withdraw or rebel (this route leads to failure), these ambitious students seem eager to detect, and perhaps even to fantasy, competence and concern among the staff."

As a result, schools are able to manipulate students into doing much of the dirty work of control under the guise of self-government. As Willard Waller pointed out nearly forty years ago, "Self-government is rarely real. Usually it is but a mask for the rule of the teacher oligarchy," or "in its most liberal form the rule of a student oligarchy carefully selected and supervised by the faculty."

To be sure, students are less pliable than they were even a few years ago. As already noted, dissent and protest are becoming widespread high school phenomena, and in his 1969 survey of high school students' attitudes, Louis Harris discovered a large reservoir of discontent with adult authority. Even so, the discontent was rather narrowly focused. Two thirds of the students Harris surveyed felt that they should have more say in making rules and in deciding on curriculum, but fewer than half felt they should have more say in determining discipline.

More important, while students want some role in making the rules, surprisingly few of them question either the rules themselves or the way they are enforced. A clear majority, for example, think the school regulations are "about right," including rules on dress, haircuts, and use of free time. Three times as many students think the rules are enforced too leniently than feel enforcement is too severe: the great majority (two thirds) think enforcement is about right. Students are equally satisfied with the curriculum: 50 percent of them think they "learn a lot" in high school, nearly two thirds think the grading system is fair (they voted over two to one against abolishing grades), and 81 percent rate their teachers as good to excellent. Belief in the beneficence of the paternalism to which they are subject exists, Buford Rhea suggests, "because there is a need for faith of this sort"; without it, students might find school intolerable. It is "the myth of institutional paternalism," in short, that keeps students from being alienated. Whether this is a virtue is something else again.

PAUL R. EHRLICH
Eco-catastrophe!

In this age of dire prophecies, the most awesome predictions have involved ecology. Walt Kelly's Pogo says, "We have me the enemy, and he is us!"; and ecologists agree. Man, by his power over nature and his lack of control of his own technology and his own reproduction, threatens us with a catastrophe possibly equal in magnitude to nuclear war. This realization has been slowly building since the 1950s when people began worrying about nuclear fallout. In 1962 Rachel Carson, in her book *Silent Spring,* warned of the dangers of DDT. Throughout the sixties small but influential groups such as the Sierra Club fought for conservation and enlisted some political support against the wholesale destruction of the environment. Then suddenly, toward the end of the decade, the nation awoke to the dangers it faced and the environment became a major popular concern, evoking warnings such as the widely circulated one that follows.

Some saw the ecology question as a unifying concern to replace the divisive arguments over the war in Vietnam, civil rights, and the youth culture that had rent the nation in 1968. Others realized that the question had a potential for stirring conflict at least equal to the issues it was crowding out—that it could become a hook on which to hang hostility to government, business, and all the major institutions of American life, which would hold long after Vietnam and the Chicago riot faded into history. In Ehrlich's scenario one sees a hostility toward both industry and politicians that could become the focus of an ecological crusade. Whatever its effect on the divisions in American life, few could doubt that concern over the environment would be a major issue of the seventies, deeply affecting the way Americans lived, worked, and voted.

I

The end of the ocean came late in the summer of 1979, and it came even more rapidly than the biologists had expected. There had been signs for more than a decade, commencing with the discovery in 1968 that DDT slows down photosynthesis in marine plant life. It was announced in a short paper in the technical journal *Science,* but to ecologists it smacked of doomsday. They knew that all life in the sea depends on photosyn-

Reprinted with the permission of Paul R. Ehrlich and the Editors of *Rampart*.

thesis, the chemical process by which green plants bind the sun's energy and make it available to living things. And they knew that DDT and similar chlorinated hydrocarbons had polluted the entire surface of the earth, including the sea.

But that was only the first of many signs. There had been the final gasp of the whaling industry in 1973, and the end of the Peruvian anchovy fishery in 1975. Indeed, a score of other fisheries had disappeared quietly from over-exploitation and various eco-catastrophes by 1977. The term "eco-catastrophe" was coined by a California ecologist in 1969 to describe the most spectacular of man's attacks on the systems which sustain his life. He drew his inspiration from the news which spread among naturalists that virtually all of the Golden State's seashore bird life was doomed because of chlorinated hydrocarbon interference with its reproduction. Eco-catastrophes in the sea became increasingly common in the early 1970s. Mysterious "blooms" of previously rare microorganisms began to appear in offshore waters. Red tides—killer outbreaks of a minute single-celled plant—returned to the Florida Gulf coast and were sometimes accompanied by tides of other exotic hues.

It was clear by 1975 that the entire ecology of the ocean was changing. A few types of phytoplankton were becoming resistant to chlorinated hydrocarbons and were gaining the upper hand. Changes in the phytoplankton community led inevitably to changes in the community of zooplankton, the tiny animals which eat the phytoplankton. These changes were passed on up the chains of life in the ocean to the herring, plaice, cod and tuna. As the diversity of life in the ocean diminished, its stability also decreased.

Other changes had taken place by 1975. Most ocean fishes that returned to fresh water to breed, like the salmon, had become extinct, their breeding streams so dammed up and polluted that their powerful homing instinct only resulted in suicide. Many fishes and shellfishes that bred in restricted areas along the coasts followed them as onshore pollution escalated.

By 1977 the annual yield of fish from the sea was down to 30 million metric tons, less than one half the per capita catch of a decade earlier. This helped malnutrition to escalate sharply in a world where an estimated 50 million people per year were already dying of starvation. The United Nations attempted to get all chlorinated hydrocarbon insecticides banned on a worldwide basis, but the move was defeated by the United States. This opposition was generated primarily by the American petrochemical industry, operating hand in glove with its subsidiary, the United States Department of Agriculture. Together they persuaded the government to oppose the UN move—which was not difficult since most Americans believed that Russia and China were more in need of fish products than was the United States. The United Nations also attempted to get fishing nations to adopt strict and enforced catch limits to preserve dwindling stocks. This move was blocked by Russia, who, with the most modern electronic equipment, was in the best position to glean what was left in the sea. It was, curiously, on the very day in 1977 when the Soviet Union announced its refusal that another ominous article appeared in *Science*. It announced that incident solar radiation had been so reduced by worldwide air pollution that serious effects on the world's vegetation could be expected.

II

Apparently it was a combination of ecosystem destabilization, sunlight reduction, and a rapid escalation in chlorinated hydrocarbon pollution from massive Thanodrin applications which triggered the ultimate catastrophe. Seventeen huge Soviet-financed Thanodrin plants were operating in underdeveloped countries by 1978. They had been part of a massive Russian "aid offensive" designed to fill the gap caused by the collapse of America's ballyhooed "Green Revolution."

It became apparent in the early '70s that the "Green Revolution" was more talk than substance. Distribution of high yield "miracle" grain seeds had caused temporary local spurts in agricultural production. Simultaneously, excellent weather had produced record harvests. The combination permitted bureaucrats, especially in the United States Department of Agriculture and the Agency for International Development (AID), to reverse their previous pessimism and indulge in an outburst of optimistic propaganda about staving off famine. They raved about the approaching transformation of agriculture in the underdeveloped countries (UDCs). The reason for the propaganda reversal was never made clear. Most historians agree that a combination of utter ignorance of ecology, a desire to justify past errors, and pressure from agro-industry (which was eager to sell pesticides, fertilizers, and

The Stream.   *(Charles Gatewood)*

farm machinery to the UDCs and agencies helping the UDCs) was behind the campaign. Whatever the motivation, the results were clear. Many concerned people, lacking the expertise to see through the Green Revolution drivel, relaxed. The population-food crisis was "solved."

But reality was not long in showing itself. Local famine persisted in northern India even after good weather brought an end to the ghastly Bihar famine of the mid-'60s. East Pakistan was next, followed by a resurgence of general famine in northern India. Other foci of famine rapidly developed in Indonesia, the Philippines, Malawi, the Congo, Egypt, Colombia, Ecuador, Honduras, the Dominican Republic, and Mexico.

Everywhere hard realities destroyed the illusion of the Green Revolution. Yields dropped as the progressive farmers who had first accepted the new seeds found that their higher yields brought lower prices—effective demand (hunger plus cash) was not sufficient in poor countries to keep prices up. Less progressive farmers, observing this, refused to make the extra effort required to cultivate the "miracle" grains. Transport systems proved inadequate to bring the necessary fertilizer to the fields where the new and extremely fertilizer-sensitive grains were being grown. The same systems were also inadequate to move produce to markets. Fertilizer plants were not built fast enough, and most of the underdeveloped countries could not scrape together funds to purchase supplies, even on concessional terms. Finally, the inevitable happened, and pests began to reduce yields in even the most carefully cultivated fields. Among the first were the famous "miracle rats" which invaded Philippine "miracle rice" fields early in 1969. They were quickly followed by many insects and viruses, thriving on the relatively pest-susceptible new grains, encouraged by the vast and dense plantings, and rapidly acquiring resistance to the chemicals used against them. As chaos spread until even the most obtuse agriculturists and economists realized that the Green Revolution had turned brown, the Russians stepped in.

In retrospect it seems incredible that the Russians, with the American mistakes known to them, could launch an even more incompetent program of aid to the underdeveloped world. Indeed, in the early 1970s there were cynics in the United States who claimed that outdoing the stupidity of American foreign aid would be physically impossible. Those critics were, however, obviously unaware that the Russians had been busily de-

Picnic on the grass. *(Eliot Hess)*

Earthmoving equipment. *(John Goodwin)*

The Suburbs. *(Eliot Hess)*

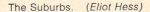

The Ocean. *(Eliot Hess)*

stroying their own environment for many years. The virtual disappearance of sturgeon from Russian rivers caused a great shortage of caviar by 1970. A standard joke among Russian scientists at that time was that they had created an artificial caviar which was indistinguishable from the real thing—except by taste. At any rate the Soviet Union, observing with interest the progressive deterioration of relations between the UDCs and the United States, came up with a solution. It had recently developed what it claimed was the ideal insecticide, a highly lethal chlorinated hydrocarbon complexed with a special agent for penetrating the external skeletal armor of insects. Announcing that the new pesticide, called Thanodrin, would truly produce a Green Revolution, the Soviets entered into negotiations with various UDCs for the construction of massive Thanodrin factories. The USSR would bear all the costs; all it wanted in return were certain trade and military concessions.

It is interesting now, with the perspective of years, to examine in some detail the reasons why the UDCs welcomed the Thanodrin plan with such open arms. Government officials in these countries ignored the protests of their own scientists that Thanodrin would not solve the problems which plagued them. The governments now knew that the basic cause of their problems was overpopulation, and that these problems had been exacerbated by the dullness, daydreaming, and cupidity endemic to all governments. They knew that only population control and limited development aimed primarily at agriculture could have spared them the horrors they now faced. They knew it, but they were not about to admit it. How much easier it was simply to accuse the Americans of failing to give them proper aid; how much simpler to accept the Russian panacea.

And then there was the general worsening of relations between the United States and the UDCs. Many things had contributed to this. The situation in America in the first half of the 1970s deserves our close scrutiny. Being more dependent on imports for raw materials than the Soviet Union, the United States had, in the early 1970s, adopted more and more heavy-handed policies in order to insure continuing supplies. Military adventures in Asia and Latin America had further lessened the international credibility of the United States as a great defender of freedom—an image which had begun to deteriorate rapidly during the pointless and fruitless Viet-Nam conflict. At home, acceptance of the carefully manufactured image lessened dramatically, as even the more romantic and chauvinistic citizens began to understand the role of the military and the industrial system in what John Kenneth Galbraith had aptly named "The New Industrial State."

At home in the USA the early '70s were traumatic times. Racial violence grew and the habitability of the cities diminished, as nothing substantial was done to ameliorate either racial inequities or urban blight. Welfare rolls grew as automation and general technological progress forced more and more people into the category of "unemployable." Simultaneously a taxpayers' revolt occurred. Although there was not enough money to build the schools, roads, water systems, sewage systems, jails, hospitals, urban transit lines, and all the other amenities needed to support a burgeoning population, Americans refused to tax themselves more heavily. Starting in Youngstown, Ohio, in 1969 and followed closely by Richmond,

California, community after community was forced to close its schools or curtail educational operations for lack of funds. Water supplies, already marginal in quality and quantity in many places by 1970, deteriorated quickly. Water rationing occurred in 1723 municipalities in the summer of 1974, and hepatitis and epidemic dysentery rates climbed about 500 percent between 1970–1974.

III

Air pollution continued to be the most obvious manifestation of environmental deterioration. It was, by 1972, quite literally in the eyes of all Americans. The year 1973 saw not only the New York and Los Angeles smog disasters, but also the publication of the Surgeon General's massive report on air pollution and health. The public had been partially prepared for the worst by the publicity given to the UN pollution conference held in 1972. Deaths in the late '60s caused by smog were well known to scientists, but the public had ignored them because they mostly involved the early demise of the old and sick rather than people dropping dead on the freeways. But suddenly our citizens were faced with nearly 200,000 corpses and massive documentation that they could be the next to die from respiratory disease. They were not ready for that scale of disaster. After all, the UN conference had not predicted that accumulated air pollution would make the planet uninhabitable until amost 1990. The population was terrorized as TV screens became filled with scenes of horror from the disaster areas. Especially vivid was NBC's coverage of hundreds of unattended people choking out their lives outside of New York's hospitals. Terms like nitrogen oxide, acute bron-

chitis and cardiac arrest began to have real meaning for most Americans.

The ultimate horror was the announcement that chlorinated hydrocarbons were now a major constituent of air pollution in all American cities. Autopsies of smog disaster victims revealed an average chlorinated hydrocarbon load in fatty tissue equivalent to 26 parts per million of DDT. In October 1973, the Department of Health, Education and Welfare announced studies which showed unequivocally that increasing death rates from hypertension, cirrhosis of the liver, liver cancer and a series of other diseases had resulted from the chlorinated hydrocarbon load. They estimated that Americans born since 1946 (when DDT usage began) now had a life expectancy of only 49 years, and predicted that if current patterns continued, this expectancy would reach 42 years by 1980, when it might level out. Plunging insurance stocks triggered a stock market panic. The president of . . ., a major producer, went on television to "publicly eat a teaspoonful of DDT" (it was really powdered milk) and announce that HEW had been infiltrated by Communists. Other giants of the petrochemical industry, attempting to dispute the indisputable evidence, launched a massive pressure campaign on Congress to force HEW to "get out of agriculture's business." They were aided by the agro-chemical journals, which had decades of experience in misleading the public about the benefits and dangers of pesticides. But by now the public realized that it had been duped. The Nobel Prize for medicine and physiology was given to Drs. J. L. Radomski and W. B. Deichmann, who in the late 1960s had pioneered in the documentation of the long-term lethal effects of chlorinated hy-

Pakistan disaster, 1970. *(Marilyn Silverstone, Magnum)*

drocarbons. A Presidential Commission with unimpeachable credentials directly accused the agro-chemical complex of "condemning many millions of Americans to an early death." The year 1973 was the year in which Americans finally came to understand the direct threat to their existence posed by environmental deterioration.

And 1973 was also the year in which most people finally comprehended the indirect threat. Even the president of Union Oil Company and several other industrialists publicly stated their concern over the reduction of bird populations which had resulted from pollution by DDT and other chlorinated hydrocarbons. Insect populations boomed because they were resistant to most pesticides and had been freed, by the incompetent use of those pesticides, from most of their natural enemies. Rodents swarmed over crops, multiplying rapidly in the absence of predatory birds. The effect of pests on the wheat crop was especially disastrous in the summer of 1973, since that was also the year of the great drought. Most of us can remember the shock which greeted the announcement by atmospheric physicians that the shift of the jet stream which had caused the drought was probably permanent. It signalled the birth of the Midwestern desert. Man's air-polluting activities had by then caused gross changes in climatic patterns. The news, of course, played hell with commodity and stock markets. Food prices skyrocketed, as savings were poured into hoarded canned goods. Official assurances that food supplies would remain ample fell on deaf ears, and even the government showed signs of nervousness when California migrant field workers went out on strike again in protest against the continued use of pesticides by growers. The strike burgeoned into farm burning and

riots. The workers, calling themselves "The Walking Dead," demanded immediate compensation for their shortened lives, and crash research programs to attempt to lengthen them.

It was in the same speech in which President Edward Kennedy, after much delay, finally declared a national emergency and called out the National Guard to harvest California's crops, that the first mention of population control was made. Kennedy pointed out that the United States would no longer be able to offer any food aid to other nations and was likely to suffer food shortages herself. He suggested that, in view of the manifest failure of the Green Revolution, the only hope of the UDCs lay in population control. His statement, you will recall, created an uproar in the underdeveloped countries. Newspaper editorials accused the United States of wishing to prevent small countries from becoming large nations and thus threatening American hegemony. Politicians asserted that President Kennedy was a "creature of the giant drug combine" that wished to shove its pills down every woman's throat.

Among Americans, religious opposition to population control was very slight. Industry in general also backed the idea. Increasing poverty in the UDCs was both destroying markets and threatening supplies of raw materials. The seriousness of the raw material situation had been brought home during the Congressional Hard Resources hearings in 1971. The exposure of the ignorance of the cornucopian economists had been quite a spectacle—a spectacle brought into virtually every American's home in living color. Few would forget the distinguished geologist from the University of California who suggested that economists be legally required to learn at least the most elementary

facts of geology. Fewer still would forget that an equally distinguished Harvard economist added that they might be required to learn some economics, too. The overall message was clear: America's resource situation was bad and bound to get worse. The hearings had led to a bill requiring the Departments of State, Interior, and Commerce to set up a joint resource procurement council with the express purpose of "insuring that proper consideration of American resource needs be an integral part of American foreign policy."

Suddenly the United States discovered that it had a national consensus: population control was the only possible salvation of the underdeveloped world. But that same consensus led to heated debate. How could the UDCs be persuaded to limit their populations, and should not the United States lead the way by limiting its own? Members of the intellectual community wanted America to set an example. They pointed out that the United States was in the midst of a new baby boom: her birth rate, well over 20 per thousand per year, and her growth rate of over one percent per annum were among the very highest of the developed countries. They detailed the deterioration of the American physical and psychic environments, the growing health threats, the impending food shortages, and the insufficiency of funds for desperately needed public works. They contended that the nation was clearly unable or unwilling to properly care for the people it already had. What possible reason could there be, they queried, for adding any more? Besides, who would listen to requests by the United States for population control when that nation did not control her own profligate reproduction?

Those who opposed population controls for the U.S. were equally vociferous. The military-industrial complex, with its all-too-human mixture of ignorance and avarice, still saw strength and prosperity in numbers. Baby food magnates, already worried by the growing nitrate pollution of their products, saw their market disappearing. Steel manufacturers saw a decrease in aggregate demand and slippage for that holy of holies, the Gross National Product. And military men saw, in the growing population-food-enviroment crisis, a serious threat to their carefully nurtured Cold War. In the end, of course, economic arguments held sway, and the "inalienable right of every American couple to determine the size of its family," a freedom invented for the occasion in the early '70s, was not compromised.

The population control bill, which was passed by Congress early in 1974, was quite a document, nevertheless. On the domestic front, it authorized an increase from 100 to 150 million dollars in funds for "family planning" activities. This was made possible by a general feeling in the country that the growing army on welfare needed family planning. But the gist of the bill was a series of measures designed to impress the need for population control on the UDCs. All American aid to countries with overpopulation problems was required by law to consist in part of population control assistance. In order to receive any assistance each nation was required not only to accept the population control aid, but also to match it according to a complex formula. "Overpopulation" itself was defined by a formula based on UN statistics, and the UDCs were required not only to accept aid, but also to show progress in reducing birth rates. Every five years the status of the aid program for each nation was to be re-evaluated.

The reaction to the announcement of this program dwarfed the response to President Kennedy's speech. A coalition of UDCs attempted to get the UN General Assembly to condemn the United States as a "genetic aggressor." Most damaging of all to the American cause was the famous "25 Indians and a dog" speech by Mr. Shankarnarayan, Indian Ambassador to the UN. Shankarnarayan pointed out that for several decades the United States, with less than six percent of the people of the world had consumed roughly 50 percent of the raw materials used every year. He described vividly America's contribution to worldwide environmental deterioration, and he scathingly denounced the miserly record of United States foreign aid as "unworthy of a fourth-rate power, let alone the most powerful nation on earth."

It was the climax of his speech, however, which most historians claim once and for all destroyed the image of the United States. Shankarnarayan informed the assembly that the average American family dog was fed more animal protein per week than the average Indian got in a month. "How do you justify taking fish from protein-starved Peruvians and feeding them to your animals?" he asked. "I contend," he concluded, "that the birth of an American baby is a greater disaster for the world than that of 25 Indian babies." When the applause had died away, Mr. Sorensen, the American representative, made a speech which said essentially that "other countries look after their own self-interest, too." When the vote came, the United States was condemned.

IV

This condemnation set the tone of U.S.-UDC relations at the time the Russian Thanodrin proposal was made. The proposal seemed to offer the masses in the UDCs an opportunity to save themselves and humiliate the United States at the same time; and in human affairs, as we all know, biological realities could never interfere with such an opportunity. The scientists were silenced, the politicians said yes, the Thanodrin plants were built, and the results were what any beginning ecology student could have predicted. At first Thanodrin seemed to offer excellent control of many pests. True, there was a rash of human fatalities from improper use of the lethal chemical, but as Russian technical advisers were prone to note, these were more than compensated for by increased yields. Thanodrin use skyrocketed throughout the underdeveloped world. The Mikoyan design group developed a dependable, cheap agricultural aircraft which the Soviets donated to the effort in large numbers. MIG sprayers became even more common in UDCs than MIG interceptors.

Then the troubles began. Insect strains with cuticles resistant to Thanodrin penetration began to appear. And as streams, rivers, fish culture ponds and on-shore waters became rich in Thanodrin, more fisheries began to disappear. Bird populations were decimated. The sequence of events was standard for broadcast use of a synthetic pesticide: great success at first, followed by removal of natural enemies and development of resistance by the pest. Populations of crop-eating insects in areas treated with Thanodrin made steady comebacks and soon became more abundant than ever. Yields plunged, while farmers in their desperation increased the Thanodrin dose and shortened the time between treatments. Death from Thanodrin poisoning became common. The first violent incident occurred in the Canete Valley of Peru, where farmers had suffered a similar chlorinated hydrocarbon disaster in the mid-'50s. A Russian adviser serving as an agricultural pilot was assaulted and killed by a mob of enraged farmers in January 1978. Trouble spread rapidly during 1978, especially after the word got out that two years earlier Russia herself had banned the use of Thanodrin at home because of its serious effects on ecological systems. Suddenly Russia, and not the United States, was the *bête noir* in the UDCs. "Thanodrin parties" became epidemic, with farmers, in their ignorance, dumping carloads of Thanodrin concentrate into the sea. Russian advisers fled, and four of the Thanodrin plants were leveled to the ground. Destruction of the plants in Rio and Calcutta led to hundreds of thousands of gallons of Thanodrin concentrate being dumped directly into the sea.

Mr. Shankarnarayan again rose to address the UN, but this time it was Mr. Potemkin, representative of the Soviet Union, who was on the hot seat. Mr. Potemkin heard his nation described as the greatest mass killer of all time as Shankarnarayan predicted at least 30 million deaths from crop failures due to overdependence on Thanodrin. Russia was accused of "chemical aggression," and the General Assembly, after a weak reply by Potemkin, passed a vote of censure.

It was in January 1979 that huge blooms of a previously unknown variety of diatom were reported off the coast of Peru. The blooms were accompanied by a massive die-off of sea life and of the pathetic remainder of the birds which had once feasted on the anchovies of the area. Almost immediately another huge bloom was reported in the Indian ocean, centering around the Seychelles, and then a third in the South Atlantic off the African coast. Both of these were accompanied by spectacular die-offs of marine animals. Even more ominous were growing reports of fish and bird kills at oceanic points where there were no spectacular blooms. Biologists were soon able to explain the phenomena: the diatom had evolved an enzyme which broke down Thanodrin; that enzyme also produced a breakdown product which interfered with the transmission of nerve impulses, and was therefore lethal to animals. Unfortunately, the biologists could suggest no way of repressing the poisonous diatom bloom in time. By September 1979 all important animal life in the sea was extinct. Large areas of coastline had to be evacuated, as windrows of dead fish created a monumental stench.

But stench was the least of man's problems. Japan and China were faced with almost instant starvation from a total loss of the seafood on which they were so dependent. Both blamed Russia for their situation and demanded immediate mass shipments of food. Russia had none to send. On October 13, Chinese armies attacked Russia on a broad front. . . .

V

A pretty grim scenario. Unfortunately, we're a long way into it already. Everything mentioned as happening before 1970 has actually occurred; much of the rest is based on projections of trends already appearing. Evidence that pesticides have long-term lethal effects on human beings has started to accumulate, and recently Robert Finch, Secretary of the Department of Health, Education and Welfare expressed his extreme apprehension about the pesticide situation. Simultaneously the petrochemical industry continues its unconscionable poison-peddling. For instance, Shell Chemical has been carrying on a high-pressure campaign to sell the insecticide Azodrin to farmers as a killer of cotton pests. They continue their program even though they know that Azodrin is not only ineffective, but often *increases* the pest density. They've covered themselves nicely in an advertisement which states, "Even if an overpowering migration [sic] develops, the flexibility of Azodrin lets you regain control fast. Just increase the dosage according to label recommendations." It's a great game—get people to apply the poison and kill the natural enemies of the pests. Then blame the increased pests on "migration" and sell even more pesticide!

Right now fisheries are being wiped out by overexploitation, made easy by modern electronic equipment. The companies producing the equipment know this. They even boast in advertising that only their equipment will keep fishermen in business until the final kill. Profits must obviously be maximized in the short run. Indeed, Western society is in the process of completing the rape and murder of the planet for economic gain. And, sadly, most of the rest of the world is eager for the opportunity to emulate our behavior. But the underdeveloped peoples will be denied that opportunity—the days of plunder are drawing inexorably to a close.

Most of the people who are going to die in the greatest cataclysm in the history of man have already been born. More than three and a half billion people already populate our moribund globe, and about half of them are hungry. Some 10 to 20 million will starve to death *this year*. In spite of this, the population of the earth will increase by 70 million souls in 1969. For mankind has artificially lowered the death rate of the human population, while in general birth rates have remained high. With the input side of the population system in high gear and the output side slowed down, our fragile planet has filled with people at an incredible rate. It took several million years for the population to reach a total of two billion people in 1930, while a *second two billion will have been added by 1975!* By that time some experts feel that food shortages will have escalated the present level of world hunger and starvation into famines of unbelievable proportions. Other experts, more optimistic, think the ultimate food-population collision will not occur until the decade of the 1980s. Of course more massive famine may be avoided if other events cause a prior rise in the human death rate.

Both worldwide plague and thermonuclear war are made more probable as population growth continues. These, along with famine, make up the trio of potential "death rate solutions" to the population problem—solutions in which the birth rate–death rate imbalance is redressed by a rise in the death rate rather than by a lowering of the birth rate. Make no mistake about it, *the imbalance will be redressed.* The shape of the population growth curve is one familiar to the biologist. It is the outbreak part of an outbreak-crash sequence. A population grows rapidly in the presence of abundant resources, finally runs out of food or some other necessity, and crashes to a low level or extinction. Man is not only running out of food, he is also destroying the life support systems of the Spaceship Earth. The situation was recently summarized very succinctly: "It is the top of the ninth inning. Man, always a threat at the plate, has been hitting Nature hard. It is important to remember, however, that NATURE BATS LAST."

PART III
American Culture

Introduction

The characteristic art form of the 1960s was the happening.
The characteristic literary form was journalism. To most of us
who lived through them, the sixties formed a collage of events.
It was enough to place events in an interesting pattern; to
understand or to find some overarching order in them was
beyond the age's ambition. Whether this means that the decade
understood itself more or less than other eras is a difficult
question. Certainly its journalism was the wonder of history:
its novelists turned journalists, its social scientists as well,
even its universities; and high-powered communications networks
sped every message or bore witness to every event. The sense of
time and of space suffered continual erosion, and prophets
arose instructing us on how to live in a limitless present—the
world as a global village with no past and no way to reason
about the future. Intellectuals, as a result, made mighty efforts
to regain ''relevance'' for their disciplines, and everyone
struggled franticly to remain up to date.

The sixties were particularly an age of fashion, of modishness,
of new beginnings. In some areas the era was highly creative.
This was especially true of its vivid popular culture. What jazz
was to the period from the 1920s into the 1950s, the source of
most of the vitality in popular entertainment, rock seemed
destined to be not only for the sixties, but for a long period
afterward. We had entered upon a new cycle of feeling and had
lived through its freshest period. It was an exciting age in which
to live, and future generations—who will be delighted by much
of it—will be amazed that so few people seemed to find
it enjoyable.

ALLEN GINSBERG
Howl
for
Carl Solomon

Unlike major events in politics, diplomacy, or war, those in the history of a culture are usually unheralded by trumpet and drum, protocol, or newsmen. The publication of a tiny paperback edition of *Howl and Other Poems* by an obscure San Francisco publisher in 1955 went scarcely noticed at the time, yet it now marks the advent of a new sensibility. Allen Ginsberg's brilliant poem described the netherworld of the "beat" generation, seeking redemption and community in drugs and sex, exotic religion, mystical inspiration, poetry and jazz, and rejecting the materialism and mass culture of American society in the 1950s. "Beat," and its condescending derivative "beatnik," rapidly became images for the mass media: the life-style parodied and commercialized, the literary output scorned by professional critics, the drug culture attacked by moralists and the police. Somewhere in California a hostess could rent a beatnik to add color to her parties.

Ginsberg has long survived the fad of the beatnik. His works are the major literary legacy of the "beat" generation and he remains an important poet. In addition, Ginsberg has proven startlingly relevant to young people in the 1960s who reject a world of materialism and power. Ginsberg's message was never tied to any particular politics. His program was always a crash course in the minimal adjustments necessary to psychic survival: and his celebration of the ancient values of community and of the sensual, impulsive, and immediate life have offered a constant and useful antidote to the materialism and technological values that young people have frequently found so oppressing.

I

  I saw the best minds of my generation destroyed by madness,
    starving hysterical naked,
  dragging themselves through the negro streets at dawn looking
    for an angry fix,
  angelheaded hipsters burning for the ancient heavenly connec-
    tion to the starry dynamo in the machinery of night,

who poverty and tatters and hollow-eyed and high sat up smoking in the supernatural darkness of cold-water flats floating across the tops of cities contemplating jazz,

who bared their brains to Heaven under the El and saw Mohammedan angels staggering on tenement roofs illuminated,

who passed through universities with radiant cool eyes hallucinating Arkansas and Blake-light tragedy among the scholars of war,

who were expelled from the academies for crazy & publishing obscene odes on the windows of the skull,

who cowered in unshaven rooms in underwear, burning their money in wastebaskets and listening to the Terror through the wall,

who got busted in their public beards returning through Laredo with a belt of marijuana for New York,

who ate fire in paint hotels or drank turpentine in Paradise Alley, death, or purgatoried their torsos night after night

with dreams, with drugs, with waking nightmares, alcohol and cock and endless balls,

incomparable blind streets of shuddering cloud and lightning in the mind leaping toward poles of Canada & Paterson, illuminating all the motionless world of Time between,

Peyote solidities of halls, backyard green tree cemetery dawns, wine drunkenness over the rooftops, storefront boroughs of teahead joyride neon blinking traffic light, sun and moon and tree vibrations in the roaring winter dusks of Brooklyn, ashcan rantings and kind king light of mind,

who chained themselves to subways for the endless ride from Battery to holy Bronx on benzedrine until the noise of wheels and children brought them down shuddering mouth-wracked and battered bleak of brain all drained of brilliance in the drear light of Zoo,

who sank all night in submarine light of Bickford's floated out and sat through the stale beer afternoon in desolate Fugazzi's, listening to the crack of doom on the hydrogen jukebox,

who talked continuously seventy hours from park to pad to bar to Bellevue to museum to the Brooklyn Bridge,

a lost battalion of platonic conversationalists jumping down the stoops off fire escapes off windowsills off Empire State out of the moon,

yacketayakking screaming vomiting whispering facts and memories and anecdotes and eyeball kicks and shocks of hospitals and jails and wars,

whole intellects disgorged in total recall for seven days and nights with brilliant eyes, meat for the Synagogue cast on the pavement,

who vanished into nowhere Zen New Jersey leaving a trail of ambiguous picture postcards of Atlantic City Hall,

suffering Eastern sweats and Tangerian bone-grindings and migraines of China under junk-withdrawal in Newark's bleak furnished room,

who wandered around and around at midnight in the railroad yard wondering where to go, and went, leaving no broken hearts,

who lit cigarettes in boxcars boxcars boxcars racketing through snow toward lonesome farms in grandfather night,

who studied Plotinus Poe St. John of the Cross telepathy and

bop kaballa because the cosmos instinctively vibrated at their
feet in Kansas,

who loned it through the streets of Idaho seeking visionary
indian angels who were visionary indian angels,

who thought they were only mad when Baltimore gleamed in
supernatural ecstasy,

who jumped in limousines with the Chinaman of Oklahoma on
the impulse of winter midnight streetlight smalltown rain,

who lounged hungry and lonesome through Houston seeking
jazz or sex or soup, and followed the brilliant Spaniard to
converse about America and Eternity, a hopeless task, and
so took ship to Africa,

who disappeared into the volcanoes of Mexico leaving behind
nothing but the shadow of dungarees and the lava and ash
of poetry scattered in fireplace Chicago,

who reappeared on the West Coast investigating the F.B.I. in
beards and shorts with big pacifist eyes sexy in their dark
skin passing out incomprehensible leaflets,

who burned cigarette holes in their arms protesting the narcotic
tobacco haze of Capitalism,

(George Gardner)

who distributed Supercommunist pamphlets in Union Square weeping and undressing while the sirens of Los Alamos wailed them down, and wailed down Wall, and the Staten Island ferry also wailed,

who broke down crying in white gymnasiums naked and trembling before the machinery of other skeletons,

who bit detectives in the neck and shrieked with delight in policecars for committing no crime but their own wild cooking pederasty and intoxication,

who howled on their knees in the subway and were dragged off the roof waving genitals and manuscripts,

who let themselves be . . . . . . in the . . . by saintly motorcyclists, and screamed with joy,

who blew and were blown by those human seraphim, the sailors, caresses of Atlantic and Caribbean love,

who balled in the morning in the evenings in rosegardens and the grass of public parks and cemeteries scattering their semen freely to whomever come who may,

who hiccupped endlessly trying to giggle but wound up with a sob behind a partition in a Turkish Bath when the blonde & naked angel came to pierce them with a sword,

who lost their loveboys to the three old shrews of fate the one eyed shrew of the heterosexual dollar the one eyed shrew that winks out of the womb and the one eyed shrew that does nothing but sit on her ass and snip the intellectual golden threads of the craftsman's loom,

who copulated ecstatic and insatiate with a bottle of beer a sweetheart a package of cigarettes a candle and fell off the bed, and continued along the floor and down the hall and ended fainting on the wall with a vision of ultimate c . . . and come eluding the last gyzym of consciousness,

who sweetened the snatches of a million girls trembling in the sunset, and were red eyed in the morning but prepared to sweeten the snatch of the sunrise, flashing buttocks under barns and naked in the lake,

who went out whoring through Colorado in myriad stolen night-cars, N.C., secret hero of these poems, cocksman and Adonis of Denver—joy to the memory of his innumerable lays of girls in empty lots & diner backyards, moviehouses, rickety rows on mountaintops in caves or with gaunt waitresses in familiar roadside lonely petticoat upliftings & especially secret gas-station solipsisms of johns, & hometown alleys too,

who faded out in vast sordid movies, were shifted in dreams, woke on a sudden Manhattan, and picked themselves up out of basements hungover with heartless Tokay and horrors of Third Avenue iron dreams & stumbled to unemployment offices,

who walked all night with their shoes full of blood on the snowbank docks waiting for a door in the East River to open to a room full of steamheat and opium,

who created great suicidal dramas on the apartment cliff-banks of the Hudson under the wartime blue floodlight of the moon & their heads shall be crowned with laurel in oblivion,

who ate the lamb stew of the imagination or digested the crab at the muddy bottom of the rivers of Bowery,

who wept at the romance of the streets with their pushcarts full of onions and bad music, who sat in boxes breathing in the darkness under the bridge, and rose up to build harpsichords in their lofts,

who coughed on the sixth floor of Harlem crowned with flame under the tubercular sky surrounded by orange crates of theology,

who scribbled all night rocking and rolling over lofty incantations which in the yellow morning where stanzas of gibberish,

who cooked rotten animals lung heart feet tail borsht & tortillas dreaming of the pure vegetable kingdom,

who plunged themselves under meat trucks looking for an egg,

who threw their watches off the roof to cast their ballot for Eternity outside of Time, & alarm clocks on their heads every day for the next decade,

who cut their wrists three times successively unsuccessfully, gave up and were forced to open antique stores where they thought were growing old and cried,

who were burned alive in their innocent flannel suits on Madison Avenue amid blasts of leaden verse & the tanked-up clatter of the iron regiments of fashion & the nitroglycerine shrieks of the fairies of advertising & the mustard gas of sinister intelligent editors, or were run down by the drunken taxicabs of Absolute Reality,

who jumped off the Brooklyn Bridge this actually happened and walked away unknown and forgotten into the ghostly daze of Chinatown soup alleyways & firetrucks, not even one free beer,

who sang out of their windows in despair, fell out of the subway window, jumped in the filthy Passaic, leaped on negroes, cried all over the street, danced on broken wineglasses barefoot smashed phonograph records of nostalgic European 1930's German jazz finished the whiskey and threw up groaning into the bloody toilet, moans in their ears and the blast of colossal steamwhistles,

who barreled down the highways of the past journeying to each other's hotrod-Golgotha jail-solitude watch or Birmingham jazz incarnation,

who drove crosscountry seventytwo hours to find out if I had a vision or you had a vision or he had a vision to find out Eternity,

who journeyed to Denver, who died in Denver, who came back to Denver & waited in vain, who watched over Denver & brooded & loned in Denver and finally went away to find out the Time, & now Denver is lonesome for her heroes,

who fell on their knees in hopeless cathedrals praying for each other's salvation and light and breasts, until the soul illuminated its hair for a second,

who crashed through their minds in jail waiting for impossible criminals with golden heads and the charm of reality in their hearts who sang sweet blues to Alcatraz,

who retired to Mexico to cultivate a habit, or Rocky Mount to tender Buddha or Tangiers to boys or Southern Pacific to the black locomotive or Harvard to Narcissus to Woodlawn to the daisychain or grave,

who demanded sanity trials accusing the radio of hypnotism & were left with their insanity & their hands & a hung jury,

who threw potato salad at CCNY lecturers on Dadaism and subsequently presented themselves on the granite steps of the madhouse with shaven heads and harlequin speech of suicide demanding instantaneous lobotomy,

and who were given instead the concrete void of insulin metrasol electricity hydrotherapy psychotherapy occupational therapy pingpong & amnesia,

who in humorless protest overturned only one symbolic pingpong table, resting briefly in catatonia,

returning years later truly bald except for a wig of blood, and tears and fingers, to the visible madman doom of the wards of the madtowns of the East,

Pilgrim State's Rockland's and Greystone's foetid halls, bickering with the echoes of the soul, rocking and rolling in the midnight solitude-bench dolmen-realms of love, dream of life a nightmare, bodies turned to stone as heavy as the moon,

with mother finally ******, and the last fantastic book flung out of the tenement window, and the last door closed at 4 AM and the last telephone slammed at the wall in reply and the last furnished room emptied down to the last piece of mental furniture, a yellow paper rose twisted on a wire hanger in the closet, and even that imaginary, nothing but a hopeful little bit of hallucination—

ah, Carl, while you are not safe I am not safe, and now you're really in the total animal soup of time—

and who therefore ran through the icy streets obsessed with a sudden flash of the alchemy of the use of the ellipse the catalog the meter & the vibrating plane,

who dreamt and made incarnate gaps in Time & Space through images juxtaposed, and trapped the archangel of the soul between 2 visual images and joined the elemental verbs and set the noun and dash of consciousness together jumping with sensation of Pater Omnipotens Aeterna Deus

to recreate the syntax and measure of poor human prose and stand before you speechless and intelligent and shaking with shame, rejected yet confessing out the soul to conform to the rhythm of thought in his naked and endless head,

the madman bum and angel beat in Time, unknown, yet putting down here what might be left to say in time come after death,

and rose reincarnate in the ghostly clothes of jazz in the goldhorn shadow of the band and blew the suffering of America's naked mind for love into an eli eli lamma lamma sabacthani saxophone cry that shivered the cities down to the last radio

with the absolute heart of the poem of life butchered out of their own bodies good to eat a thousand years.

II

What sphinx of cement and aluminum bashed upon their skulls and ate up their brains and imagination?

Moloch! Solitude! Filth! Ugliness! Ashcans and unobtainable dollars! Children screaming under the stairways! Boys sobbing in armies! Old men weeping in the parks!

Moloch! Moloch! Nightmare of Moloch! Moloch the loveless! Mental Moloch! Moloch the heavy judger of men!

Moloch the incomprehensible prison Moloch the crossbone soulless jailhouse and Congress of sorrows! Moloch whose buildings are judgement! Moloch the vast stone of war! Moloch the stunned governments!

Moloch whose mind is pure machinery! Moloch whose blood is running money! Moloch whose fingers are ten armies! Moloch whose breast is a cannibal dynamo! Moloch whose ear is a smoking tomb!

Moloch whose eyes are a thousand blind windows! Moloch whose skyscrapers stand in the long streets like endless Jehovahs! Moloch whose factories dream and croak in the fog! Moloch whose smokestacks and antennae crown the cities!

Moloch whose love is endless oil and stone! Moloch whose soul is electricity and banks! Moloch whose poverty is the specter of genius! Moloch whose fate is a cloud of sexless hydrogen! Moloch whose name is the Mind!

Moloch in whom I sit lonely! Moloch in whom I dream Angels! Crazy in Moloch! C . . . sucker in Moloch! Lacklove and manless in Moloch!

Moloch who entered my soul early! Moloch in whom I am a consciousness without a body! Moloch who frightened me out of my natural ecstasy! Moloch whom I abandon! Wake up in Moloch! Light streaming out of the sky!

Moloch! Moloch! Robot apartments! invisible suburbs! skeleton treasuries! blind capitals! demonic industries! spectral nations! invincible madhouses! granite cocks! monstrous bombs!

They broke-their backs lifting Moloch to Heaven! Pavements, trees, radios, tons! lifting the city to Heaven which exists and is everywhere about us!

Visions! omens! hallucinations! miracles! ecstasies! gone down the American river!

Dreams! adorations! illuminations! religions! the whole boatload of sensitive bullshit!

Breakthroughs! over the river! flips and crucifixions! gone down the flood! Highs! Epiphanies! Despairs! Ten years' animal screams and suicides! Minds! New loves! Mad generation! down on the rocks of Time!

Real holy laughter in the river! They saw it all! the wild eyes! the holy yells! They bade farewell! They jumped off the roof! to solitude! waving! carrying flowers! Down to the river! into the street!

III

Carl Solomon! I'm with you in Rockland
    where you're madder than I am
I'm with you in Rockland
    where you must feel very strange
I'm with you in Rockland
    where you imitate the shade of my mother
I'm with you in Rockland
    where you've murdered your twelve secretaries
I'm with you in Rockland
    where you laugh at this invisible humor
I'm with you in Rockland
    where we are great writers on the same dreadful typewriter
I'm with you in Rockland
    where your condition has become serious and is reported on
    the radio

I'm with you in Rockland
  where the faculties of the skull no longer admit the worms
  of the senses
I'm with you in Rockland
  where you drink the tea of the breasts of the spinsters of
  Utica
I'm with you in Rockland
  where you pun on the bodies of your nurses the harpies of
  the Bronx
I'm with you in Rockland
  where you scream in a straightjacket that you're losing the
  game of the actual pingpong of the abyss
I'm with you in Rockland
  where you bang on the catatonic piano the soul is innocent
  and immortal it should never die ungodly in an armed
  madhouse
I'm with you in Rockland
  where fifty more shocks will never return your soul to
  body again from its pilgrimage to a cross in the void
I'm with you in Rockland
  where you accuse your doctors of insanity and plot the
  Hebrew socialist revolution against the fascist national
  Golgotha
I'm with you in Rockland
  where you will split the heavens of Long Island and resurrect
  your living human Jesus from the superhuman tomb
I'm with you in Rockland
  where there are twentyfive-thousand mad comrades all
  together singing the final stanzas of the Internationale
I'm with you in Rockland
  where we hug and kiss the United States under our bedsheets
  the United States that coughs all night and won't let us sleep
I'm with you in Rockland
  where we wake up electrified out of the coma by our own
  souls' airplanes roaring over the roof they've come to drop
  angelic bombs the hospital illuminates itself imaginary walls
  collapse   O skinny legions run outside   O starry-spangled
  shock of mercy the eternal war is here   O victory forget
  your underwear we're free
I'm with you in Rockland
  in my dreams you walk dripping from a sea-journey on the
  highway across America in tears to the door of my cottage
  in the Western night

San Francisco   1955–56

TERRY SOUTHERN
The Magic Christian

The Magic Christian, published in 1963, remains an excellent introduction to an extravagant decade of American life. Begun as a parody on the materialism of the fifties and the early sixties, it ends as nothing less than a parable of America in the 1960s. Guy Grand's ship, the subject of the second excerpt, is America. Once simply the *Griffin,* it is now decked out in good but gaudy taste as the *S.S. Magic Christian.* The word "griffin" is the many guises of the American past: a mythical monster, half lion and half eagle; also, a Westerner new to the Orient; as well, a slang term for "mulatto." But past and dubious identities are brushed aside by the magic hand of Guy Grand, as prosperous Americans learn a high and racy style of consumption in the Kennedy era. The *Magic Christian* is a grand vessel where everyone is apparently rich and everything apparently well ordered. On one wall of each cabin is a television screen, which shows mysterious creatures locked in silent combat, representing foreign disturbances that can be viewed intimately but safely from behind a protective wall of glass. The passengers of the ship turn out to be a curious mixture of publicly displayed aristocrats and nouveaux riches and a hidden group of ruffians and outcasts—a liberal coalition one might say.

The cruise does not proceed uneventfully. The captain is attacked, as some passengers witness on television sets, and both the public order and the technology of the ship gradually break down. Wild and extreme emotions surface and incomprehensible but prophetic signs appear. Yet when anyone suggests that something must be wrong he is quickly sent to the ship's friendly doctor-psychiatrist, who chides him for asking for drugs and questions him about his "early childhood." Nevertheless, the passengers are fortunate: no one who matters gets hurt on the cruise, even though the ship never reaches its destination and the people are made somewhat uncomfortable by the collapse of smokestacks and the rampages of outcasts. And even in quieter times, when Guy no longer leads his passengers on glorious quests for higher standards of living and higher levels of excitement, people still search for telltale signs that the magic world of Guy Grand—in which some uniquely fortunate individual will be able to get 1000 cases of Grape-Ade for only one-naught-five—still exists.

Guy would arrive in faultless evening attire, attended by his poker-faced valet, who carried a special gourmet's chair and a large valise of additional equipment. The chair, heavily weighted at the bottom so it could not be easily overturned, was also fitted with a big waist strap which was firmly secured around Grand's middle as soon as he was seated. Then the valet would take from the valise a huge rubber bib and attach it to Guy while the latter surveyed the menu in avid conference with a bevy of hosts—the maître d', the senior waiter, the wine steward, and at least one member of the chef's staff.

Guy Grand was the last of the big spenders and, as such, a great favorite at these restaurants; due to his eccentric behavior during the meal, however, the management always took care to place him at a table as decentralized as possible—on the edge of the terrace, in a softly lit alcove, or, preferably, at a table entirely obscured by a canopy arrangement which many restaurants, after his first visit, saw fit to have on hand for Guy's return.

Following the lengthy discussion to determine the various courses, the waist strap was checked, and Guy would sit back in his chair, rubbing his hands together in sophisticated anticipation of the taste treats to come.

When the first course did arrive, an extraordinary spectacle would occur. At the food's very aroma, Grand, still sitting well back from the table, as in fanatical self-restraint, would begin to writhe ecstatically in his chair, eyes rolling, head lolling, saliva streaming over his ruddy jowls. Then he would suddenly stiffen, his face a mask of quivering urgency, before shouting: *"Au table!"* whereupon he would lurch forward, both arms cupped

out across the table, and wildly scoop the food, dishes and all, towards his open mouth. Following this fantastic clatter and commotion—which left him covered from the top of his head to his waist with food—the expressionless valet would lean forward and unfasten the chair strap, and Guy would bolt from the table and rush pell-mell towards the kitchen, covered and dripping with food, hair matted with it, one arm extended full length as in a congratulatory handshake, shouting at the top of his voice:

"MES COMPLIMENTS AU CHEF!"

Upon his return to the table, he would be strapped into the chair again, hosed-down by a little water pump from the valet's case, and dried with a big towel; then the performance would be repeated with each course.

Restaurants who used a special canopy to conceal Grand from the other diners did so at considerable risk, because at the moment of completing each course he would bolt for the kitchen so quickly that, unless the waiters were extremely alert and dexterous in pulling aside the canopy, he would bring the thing down on his head and, like a man in a collapsed tent, would flail about inside it, upsetting the table, and adding to the general disturbance, or worse, as sometimes did happen, he might regain his feet within the canopy and careen blindly through the plush restaurant, toppling diners everywhere, and spreading the disturbance—and, of course, if he ever reached the kitchen while still inside the canopy, it could be actually calamitous.

The open-mouthed astonishment of waiters, diners and others who were witness to these scenes was hardly lessened by the bits of bland dialogue they might overhear between the maître d', who was also in on the gag, and the valet.

"Chef's *Béarnaise* pleased him," the maître d' would remark soberly to the valet, "I could tell."

The valet would agree with a judicious nod, as he watched Grand storming through the restaurant. "He's awful keen tonight."

"In the *Béarnaise*," the maître d' would suddenly confide in an excited whisper, "the peppercorns were *bruised* merely by dropping them!" And the two men would exchange dark knowing glances at this revelation.

By the last course Grand would be utterly exhausted, and the exquisite dessert would invariably prove too much for his overtaxed senses. At the first taste of it, he would go into a final tantrum and then simply black out. He always had to be carried from the restaurant on a stretcher, leaving waiters and diners staring agape, while the maître d' stood respectfully by the door with several of his staff.

II

It was along towards the end though that Grand achieved, in terms of public outrage, his *succès d'estime,* as some chose to call it, when he put out to sea in his big ship, the *S.S. Magic Christian* . . . the ship sometimes later referred to as "The Terrible Trick Ship of Captain Klaus." Actually it was the old *Griffin,* a passenger liner which Grand bought and had reconditioned for fifty million.

A vessel of 30,000 tons, the *Christian* had formerly carried some eleven-hundred-odd passengers. Grand converted it into a one-class ship, outfitted to accommodate four hundred passengers, in a style and comfort perhaps unknown theretofore outside princely domains of the East. Each cabin on the *Christian* was a palace in miniature; the appointments were so lavish and so exquisitely detailed that they might better be imagined than described. All the cabins were of course above deck and outside, each with a twenty-foot picture window and French doors to a private patio commanding a magnificent expanse of sea and sky. There were fine deep rugs throughout each suite and period-furnishings of first account, private bars, chaise longues, log-burning fireplaces, king-sized beds (canopy optional), an adjoining library-den (with a set of the *Britannica* and the best in smart fiction), tape recorders, powder rooms, small Roman bath and steam cabinet. Walls were generally in a quiet tone of suede with certain paneling of teak and rosewood.

Ship's dining room was styled after Maxim's in Paris whose staff had been engaged to prepare the meals and to serve them with inconspicuous grace against a background of soft music provided by the Julliard String Quartette. The balance of ship's appointments were in harmoni-ous key—there was, for example, a veritable jewel box of a theatre, seating just four hundred, fashioned in replica of the one in the Monte Carlo Casino; and the versatile repertory group, Old Vic Players, were on stand-by for two shows a day.

Ship's doctor, aside from being an able physician, was also a top-flight mental specialist, so that Problem-Counseling was available to the passengers at all hours.

But perhaps the most carefully thought-out nicety of the *Christian* was its principal lounge, the Marine Room—a large room, deep below decks, its walls (that which was part of ship's hull) glassed so that the passengers sat looking out into the very heart of the sea. An ocean-floor effect was maintained by the regular release of deep-sea creatures from a waterline station near the bow, and through the use of powerful daylight kliegs there was afforded a breath-taking panorama—with giant octopi, huge rainbow-colored ray, serpents, great snowy angelfish, and fantastic schools of luminous tetra constantly gliding by or writhing in silent majestic combat a few feet from the relaxed passengers.

Though the *Magic Christian* received its share of prevoyage hullabaloo (*Life* magazine devoted an issue to photographs,

Scenes from *The Magic Christian* with Peter Sellers and Ringo Starr. *(Consolidated Poster Service)*

enthusiastically captioned), its only form of paid advertisement was a simple announcement of its sailing date, which appeared in *The Times* and in the *National Geographic*. The fare was not mentioned (though *Life* had said it was "about five thousand") and the announcement was set in small heavy type, boxed with a very black border. "For the Gracious Few . . ." it opened, and went on to state in a brief, restrained apology, that *not everyone* could be accepted, that applications for passage on the *Christian* were necessarily carefully screened, and that those who were refused should not take offense. "Our criteria," it closed, "may *not* be yours."

Ship's quarters were not shown until the applicant had been accepted, and then were shown by appointment.

The ship was christened by the Queen of England.

All of this had a certain appeal and the applications poured in. More than a few people, in fact, were *demanding* passage on the *Christian's* first voyage. Those just back from holiday were suddenly planning to go abroad again; scores rushed home simply to qualify and make the trip. For many, the maiden voyage of the *Magic Christian* became a must.

Meanwhile Guy Grand, well in the background, was personally screening the applications according to some obscure criteria of his own, and apparently he had himself a few laughs in this connection. In the case of one application, for example, from a venerable scioness of Roman society, he simply scrawled moronically across it in blunt pencil: "Are *you* kidding?!? *No* wops!" The woman was said to have had a nervous breakdown and did later file for a million on defamation. It cost Grand a pretty to clear it.

On the other hand, he accepted—or rather, engaged—as passengers, a group from a fairly sordid freak show, most of whom could not be left untended, along with a few gypsies, Broadway types and the like, of offensive appearance and doubtful character. These, however, were to be kept below decks for the first few days out, and, even so, numbered only about forty in all, so that a good nine-tenths of the passenger list, those on deck when the *Christian* set sail in such tasteful fanfare that Easter morn, were top-drawer gentry and no mistake.

Unique among features of the *Christian* was its video communication system from the bridge to other parts of the ship. Above the fireplace in each cabin was a small TV screen and this provided direct visual communication with the Captain at the wheel and with whatever other activity was going on there, giving as it did a view of almost the entire bridge. These sets could be switched *on* or *off*, but the first day they were left *on* before the passengers arrived, in order to spare anyone the embarrassment of not knowing what the new gimmick was. So that when passengers entered their cabins now they saw at once, there on the screen above the fireplace: the Captain at the wheel. Captain Klaus. And for this person, Guy Grand had engaged a professional actor, a distinguished silver-haired man whose every gesture inspired the deepest confidence. He wore a double row of service ribbons on his dark breast and deported himself in a manner both authoritative and pleasingly genial —as the passengers saw when he turned to face the screen, and this he did just as soon as they were all settled and under way.

He was filling his pipe when he turned to camera, but he paused from this to smile and touch his cap in easy salute.

"Cap'n Klaus," he said, introducing himself with warm informality, though certainly at no sacrifice to his considerable bearing. "Glad to have you aboard."

He casually picked up a pointer stick and indicated a chart on the nearby wall.

"Here's our course," he said, "nor' by nor'east, forty-seven degrees."

Then he went on to explain the mechanics and layout of the bridge, the weather and tide conditions at present, their prospects, and so on, using just enough technical jargon throughout all this to show that he knew what he was about. He said that the automatic-pilot would be used from time to time, but that he personally preferred handling the wheel himself, adding good-humoredly that in his opinion "a ship favored men to machines."

"It may be an old-fashioned notion," he said, with a wise twinkle, " . . . but to me, a ship is a woman."

At last he gave a final welcome-salute, saying again: "Glad to have you aboard," and turned back to his great wheel.

This contact with the bridge and the fatherly Captain seemed to give the passengers an added sense of participation and security; and, indeed, things couldn't have gone more smoothly for the first few hours.

It was in the very early morning that something untoward occurred, at about three A.M.—and of course almost everyone was asleep. They had watched their screens for a while: the Captain in the cozy bridge house, standing alone, pipe glowing, his strong eyes sweeping the black water ahead—then they had switched off their sets. There were a few people though who were still up and who had their sets on; and, of these few, there were perhaps three who happened to be watching the screen at a certain moment—when in the corner of the bridge house, near the door, there was a shadow, an odd movement . . . then suddenly the appearance of a sinister-looking person, who crept up behind the Captain, hit him on the head, and seized the wheel as the screen blacked out.

The people who had seen this were disturbed and, in fact, were soon rushing about, rousing others, wanting to go to the bridge and so on. And they did actually get up a party and went to the bridge—only to be met at the top of the ladder by the Captain himself, unruffled, glossing it over, blandly assuring them that nothing was wrong, nothing at all, just a minor occurrence. And, of course, back in the cabins, there he was on the screen again, Captain Klaus, steady at the helm.

Those three who had seen the outrage, being in such a hopeless minority, were thought to have been drunk or in some way out of their minds, and were gently referred to ship's doctor, the mental specialist, so the incident passed without too much notice.

And things went smoothly once more, until the next evening—in the exquisite gaming rooms just off the Marine Lounge, one of the roulette croupiers was seen, by several people, to be cheating . . . darting his eyes about in a furtive manner and then interfering with the bets, snatching them up and stuffing them in his pocket, that sort of thing.

It was such an unheard-of outrage that one old duke fainted dead away. The croupier was hustled out of the gaming room by Captain Klaus himself, who deplored the incident profusely and declared that the next dozen spins were on the house, losing bets to remain untouched for that time—gracious recompense, in the eyes of a sporting crowd, and applauded as such; still, the incident was not one easily forgotten.

Another curious thing occurred when some of the ladies went, individually, to visit the ship's doctor. For the most part they had simply dropped around to pick up a few aspirin, sea-sickness pills—or merely to have a reassuring chat with the amiable physician. Several of these ladies, however, were informed that they looked "rather queer" and that an examination might be in order.

"Better safe than sorry," the doctor said, and then, during the examination, he invariably seemed to discover what he termed "a latent abrasion"—on the waist, side, hip, or shoulder of the woman—and though the abrasion could not be seen, the doctor deemed it required a compress.

"Nothing serious," he explained, "still it's always wise to take precautions." And so saying he would apply a *huge compress* to the area, a sort of gigantic Band-Aid about a foot wide and several inches thick, with big adhesive flaps that went halfway around the body. The tremendous bulk of these compresses was a nuisance, causing as they did, great deforming bulges beneath the women's smart frocks. They were almost impossible to remove. One woman was seen running about with one on her head, like a big white hat.

First lifeboat drill was scheduled for the following morning. Shortly before it, Captain Klaus came on the screen and smilingly apologized for the inconvenience and gave a leisurely and pleasantly informative talk about the drill and its necessity.

"Better safe than sorry," he said in a genial close to his little talk.

When the drill signal sounded, they all got into life jackets—which were the latest thing and quite unlike standard passenger-ship equipment—and then, grumbling good-naturedly, they started for their boat stations; but an extraordinary thing happened: two minutes after they had put them on, the life jackets began inflating in a colossal way. Apparently the very act of donning the jacket set off some device which inflated it. The extraordinary thing was that each one blew up so big that it simply obscured the person wearing it, ballooning out about them, above their heads, below their feet, and to a diameter of perhaps twelve feet—so that if they were in an open space, such as their cabins, the lounge, or on deck, they simply rolled or lolled about on the floor, quite hidden from view, whereas if they were in a corridor, they were hopelessly stuck.

In any event, almost no one escaped the effects of the faulty life jacket; so it was—after they deflated—with a good deal of annoyance that they came back to the cabins, quite ready to hear Captain Klaus' explanation of what had gone amiss.

Unfortunately though, the foghorn, which had been put to practice during the drill, was now evidently jammed. At any rate, it continued steadily during the Captain's after-drill talk and completely shut out his voice, so that it was like looking at someone talk behind several layers of glass. The Captain himself didn't seem to realize that he wasn't coming through, and he went on talking for quite a while, punctuating his remarks with various little facial gestures to indicate a whole gamut of fairly intense feelings about whatever it was he was saying.

The business with the foghorn was more serious than at first imagined; it continued, blasting without let-up, for the rest of the voyage.

Quite incidental to what was happening during the drill, fifty crew members took advantage of the occasion to go around to the cabins, lounges, and dining rooms, and to substitute a thin length of balsa wood for one leg of every chair, table, and dresser on ship.

When the Captain finished his lengthy and voiceless discourse, he smiled, gave an easy salute and left the bridge house. It was about this time that all the furniture began to collapse—in half an hour's time there wasn't one standing stick of it aboard the *Christian*.

Strange and unnatural persons began to appear—in the drawing rooms, salons, at the pool. During the afternoon tea dance, a gigantic *bearded-woman,* stark naked, rushed wildly about over the floor, interfering with the couples, and had to be forcibly removed by ship's doctor.

The plumbing went bad, too; and finally one of the *Christian's* big stacks toppled—in such a way to give directly on to ship's dining room, sending oily smoke billowing through. And, in fact, from about this point on, the voyage was a veritable nightmare.

Large curious posters were to be seen in various parts of the ship:

SUPPORT MENTAL HEALTH

LET'S KEEP THE CLAP OUT OF CHAPPAQUIDDICK

as well as rude slogans, vaguely political, scrawled in huge misshapen letters across walls and decks alike:

DEATH TO RICH!

BLOW UP U.S.!

Due to the strain of untoward events, more than one passenger sought solace and reassurance from the problem-counselor, the ship's distinguished doctor.

"Doctor, what *in the name of God* is going on here!" the frenzied passenger would demand.

The doctor would answer with a quizzical smile, arching his brows, only mildly censorious. "Fair-weather sailor?" he would gently chide, ". . . hmm? Cross and irritable the moment things aren't going exactly to suit you?

Now just what seems to be the trouble?"

"'Trouble'!?!" exclaimed the outraged passenger. "Good Lord, Doctor, surely you don't think my complaint is an . . . an unreasonable one?"

The doctor would turn his gaze out to sea, thin fingers pressed beneath his chin in a delicate pyramid of contemplation, wistfully abstract for a moment before turning back to address the patient frankly.

"Deep-rooted and unreasonable fears," he would begin in a grand, rich voice, "are most often behind our anxieties . . ." and he would continue in this vein until the passenger fairly exploded with impatience.

"Great Scott, Doctor! I didn't come here for a lecture on *psychology*—I came to find out what *in the name of Heaven* is going on *aboard this ship!*"

In the face of these outbursts, however, the doctor almost invariably retained his calm, regarding the patient coolly, searchingly, making a few careful notes on his pad.

"Now, you say that 'the life jacket *overinflated,*' and that you were 'stuck in the corridor'—that was your expression, I believe, *'stuck in the corridor'*—and at that moment you felt a certain *malaise,* so to speak. Now, let me ask you *this* . . ." Or again, on other occasions, he might behave eccentrically, his head craned far to one side, regarding the patient out of the corners of his eyes, a sly, mad smile on his lips which moved in an inaudible whisper, almost a hiss.

Finally, the patient, at the end of his tether, would leap to his feet.

"Well, in the name of God, Doctor, the least you can do is let me have some *tranquilizers!*"

But the doctor, as it turned out, was not one given to prescribing drugs promiscuously.

"Escape into drugs?" he

would ask, wagging his head slowly. "Mask our fears in an artificial fog?" And there was always a trace of sadness in his smile, as he continued, "No, I'm afraid the trouble is *in ourselves,* you see." Then he would settle back expansively and speak with benign countenance. "Running away from problems is scarcely the solution to them. I *believe* you'll thank me in years to come." And at last he would lean forward in quiet confidence. "Do you mind if I ask you a few questions about your . . . your *early childhood?*"

When Captain Klaus next appeared on the screen, he looked as though he had been sleeping in two feet of water. Completely disheveled, his ribbons dangling in unsightly strands, his open coat flapping, his unknotted tie strung loosely around his collar, he seemed somewhat drunk as well. With a rude wave of his hand he dismissed bridge personnel and lurched toward the video screen, actually crashing into it, and remaining so close that his image was all distorted.

"We'll get the old tub through!" he was shouting at deafening volume, and at that moment he was attacked from behind by a ruffian type who was carrying a huge hypodermic and appeared to overpower the Captain and inject something into the top of his head, then to seize the wheel, wrenching it violently, before the screen went black.

Also, it was learned about this time that because of fantastic miscalculation on the part of the ship's-stores officer, the only food left aboard now was potatoes.

Thus did the *Christian* roar over the sea, through fair weather and foul.

Guy Grand was aboard, of course, as a passenger, complaining bitterly, and in fact kept leading assault parties in an effort to find out, as he put it, "What the devil's going on on the bridge!"

But they were always driven back by a number of odd-looking men with guns and knives near the ladder.

"Who the deuce are those chaps?" Grand would demand as he and the others beat a hasty retreat along the deck. "I don't like the looks of this!"

Occasionally the communications screen in each of the cabins would light up to reveal momentarily what was taking place on the bridge, and it was fairly incredible. The bridge house itself now was a swaying rubble heap and the Captain was seen intermittently, struggling with various assailants, and finally with what actually appeared to be a gorilla —the beast at last overpowering him and flinging him bodily out of the bridge house and, or so it seemed, into the sea itself, before seizing the wheel, which he seemed then to be trying to tear from its hub.

It was about this time that the ship, which, as it developed, had turned completely around in the middle of the ocean, came back into New York harbor under full steam, and with horns and whistles screaming, ploughed headlong into the big Forty-Seventh Street pier.

Fortunately no one was injured on the cruise; but, even so, it went far from easy with Grand—he had already sunk plenty into the project, and just how much it cost him to keep clear in the end, is practically anyone's guess.

III

The *S.S. Magic Christian* was Grand's last major project—at least it was the last to be brought into open account. After that he began to taper off. However, he did like "keeping in touch," as he expressed it, and, for one thing, he bought himself a grocery store in New York City. Quite small, it was more or less indistinguishable from the several others in the neighborhood, and Grand put up a little sign in the window.

*New Owner—New Policy
Big Get-Acquainted Sale*

Grand was behind the counter himself, wearing a sort of white smock—not too unlike his big Vanity lab smock—when the store opened that evening.

His first customer was a man who lived next door to the store. He bought a carton of Grape-Ade.

"That will be three cents," said Grand.

"*How much?*" asked the man, with a frown.

"Three cents."

"Three *cents?* For six Grape-Ade? Are you kidding?"

"It's our two-for-one Get-Acquainted on Grape-Ade," said Grand. "It's new policy."

"Boy, *I'll* say it's new," said the man. "And how! Three *cents?* Okay by me, brother!" He slapped three cents on the counter. "There it is!" he said and still seemed amazed when Grand pushed the carton towards him.

"Call again," said Grand.

"That's some policy all right," said the man, looking back over his shoulder as he started for the door. At the door, however, he paused.

"Listen," he said, "do you sell it . . . uh, you know, by the *case?*"

"Well, yes," said Grand, "you would get some further reduction if you bought it by the case—not too much, of course; we're working on a fairly small profit-margin during the sale, you see and—"

"Oh, I'll pay the two-for-one all right. Christ! I just wanted to know if I could *get* a case at that price."

"Certainly, would you like a case?"

"Well, as a matter of fact, I could *use* more than one case . . ."

"How many cases could you use?"

"Well, uh . . . how many . . . how many have you *got?*"

"Could you use a thousand?"

"A *thousand?!?* A thousand case of Grape-Ade?"

"Yes, I could give you . . . say, ten percent off on a thousand . . . and at twenty-four bottles to the case, twelve cents a case . . . would be one hundred and twenty dollars, minus ten percent, would be one hundred and eight . . . call it one-naught-five, shall we?"

"*No, no.* I couldn't use a thousand cases. Jesus! I meant, say, *ten* cases."

"That would be a dollar twenty."

"Right!" said the man. He slapped down a dollar twenty on the counter. "Boy, that's some policy you've got there!" he said.

"It's our Get-Acquainted policy," said Grand.

"It's some policy all right," said the man. "Have you got any other . . . *specials* on? You know, 'two-for-one,' that sort of thing?"

"Well, most of our items have been reduced for the Get-Acquainted."

The man hadn't noticed it before, but price tags were in evidence, and all prices had been sharply cut: milk, two cents a quart—butter, ten cents a pound—eggs, eleven cents a dozen—and so on.

The man looked wildly about him.

"How about cigarettes?"

"No, we decided we wouldn't carry cigarettes; since they've been linked, rather authoritatively, to cancer of the lung, we thought it wouldn't be exactly in the best of taste to sell them —being a *neighborhood* grocery, I mean to say."

"Uh-huh, well—listen, I'm just going home for a minute now to get a sack, or a . . . trunk, or maybe a truck . . . I'll be right back . . ."

Somehow the word spread through the neighborhood and in two hours the store was clean as a whistle.

The next day, a sign was on the empty store:

MOVED TO NEW LOCATION

And that evening, in another part of town, the same thing occurred—followed again by a quick change of location. The people who had experienced the phenomenon began to spend a good deal of their time each evening looking for the new location. And occasionally now, two such people meet—one who was at the big Get-Acquainted on West 4th Street, for example, and the other at the one on 139th—and so, presumably, they surmise not only that it wasn't a dream, but that it's still going on.

And some say it does, in fact, still go on—they say it accounts for the strange searching haste which can be seen in the faces, and especially the eyes, of people in the cities, every evening, just about the time now it starts really getting dark.

LESLIE FIEDLER
Hemingway in Ketchum

Ernest Hemingway died in Ketchum, Idaho, of a self-inflicted wound in 1961. More than any other single figure, Hemingway had defined the sensibility that since the 1920s critics had called "modern." Hemingway, as Fiedler says, invented "a major prose style viable in the whole western world." He caught the speech of men and women who had survived the collapse of European and American culture in World War I, who refused any longer to be romantic or idealistic in any public way, who dedicated themselves to the moment and to the fact. Yet a private and even laconic honor drove them to feats of stoical heroism, ironic but humorless, in which they risked all to achieve a curious delight or to complete a particular moment—in the bullring, on the hunt, on the seas, or in a war. They fought for no cause but their own integrity; they risked their lives for nothing beyond those lives, only to give them definition. Most of all, Hemingway described manhood in flat, minimal terms in and for the age when causes and ideals had proven invalid.

The point of Leslie Fiedler's disturbing account of his meeting with the aged and soon-to-die Hemingway is perhaps that the "modern" world that Hemingway symbolized had, by 1961, ceased to be modern. The Hemingway model of the cool hero (so close to the John Kennedy that Norman Mailer describes) had become the author's pose, his mask. Perhaps it was Fiedler's mask as well. The terms under which so many had learned to live fitted no longer, and the modern age that began in the 1920s had closed in caricature of itself. The sixties, with their renewed romanticism, their causes and public passions, would be a very different epoch, and one in which Hemingway obviously did not care to live.

But what a book they both agreed, would be the real story of Hemingway, not those he writes but the confessions of the real Ernest Hemingway . . .

—*The Autobiography of Alice B. Toklas*

"An Almost Imaginary Interview: Hemingway in Ketchum." *Partisan Review,* 29 (Summer 1962), pp. 395–405. Reprinted by permission of the author.

I am writing now the article which I have known for months I must someday write, not merely because he is dead but because there sits on the desk before me a telegram from a disturbed lady whom I can not quite remember or despise. "Your confiding reminiscences of Papa Hemingway," it reads, "reminiscent of Louella (Hearst)." The clichés of "Papa" and "Hearst" date but do not identify the sender; and the fact that she has wired her malice from Seattle only confuses me. Why Seattle? Surely the few cagey remarks I have made to a reporter about my experiences in Ketchum, Idaho, do not constitute "confiding reminiscences"— dictated as they were as much by a desire to conceal as to reveal, and concerned as they are with my own dismay rather than the details of Hemingway's life. How did they get to Seattle? And in what form?

I am aware, of course, of having told over the past six months in at least as many states the story of my inconclusive encounter with Hemingway last November. I have never been able to tell it until after the third drink or the fourth, and then always to those who, I was convinced, would understand that I was talking about a kind of terror which rather joined me to than separated me from a stranger whose voice I have known all my adult life—a stranger obviously flirting with despair, a stranger whose destruction I could not help feeling my own calamity, too. After all, I was only talking the way everyone talks all the time about American letters, the plight of the American writer. What could be more banal or harmless?

But I can tell from the poor conventional ironies of the telegram before me what I have come to suspect already from my need to say over and over precisely how it was in Ketchum: that what is at stake is an image by which we have all lived— surviving haters of Hearst, middlebrow adulators of *For Whom the Bell Tolls,* Jews who have managed somehow to feel closer to Jake Barnes than to Robert Cohn—the lady from Seattle and I. That image I must do my best to shatter, though on one level I cannot help wishing that it will survive my onslaught.

I do not want ever to see the newspaper article that cued the wire. I am willing to accept responsibility for whatever the press in its inaccuracy and confusion made of my own inaccuracy and confusion; but I want to accept it without having read it. If amends are to be made for pieties offended, they must be made by setting down the best version of what I am able to remember, by my writing this

For Whom the Bell Tolls with Gary Cooper.   *(Museum of Modern Art Film Stills Archive)*

piece which perhaps already is being misunderstood by those who have managed to get so far.

I went to see Hemingway just after Hallowe'en last year along with Seymour Betsky, a colleague from Montana State University, the university attended briefly by one of Hemingway's sons; and, much more importantly, the one from which Robert Jordan took off for the War in Spain in *For Whom the Bell Tolls*. From a place as much myth as fact, from Hemingway's mythical home (I am told that during his last trip to Spain he signed tourist autographs, "E. Hemingway, Red Lodge, Montana"), I set out across the three hundred miles to his last actual home near Sun Valley, a winter resort out of season. We were charged with persuading Hemingway to give a public lecture at our school, to make the kind of appearance he has resolutely refused to make, to permit—like a good American —a larger audience to look at him than would ever read him, even in *Life*. Actually, we felt ourselves, though we did not confess it aloud, neither professors nor promoters, but pilgrims— seeking the shrine of a God in whom we were not quite sure we believed.

I had long since put on record my only slightly begrudged acknowledgment of Hemingway's achievement: his invention of a major prose style viable in the whole western world, his contrivance of the kind of short story young writers are not yet done imitating, his evocation in *The Sun Also Rises* of a peculiar terror and a special way of coming to terms with it that must seem to the future the very hallmark of our age. But I had also registered my sense of his mindlessness, his sentimentality, his failure to develop or grow. And I could not help recalling as I hurtled half-asleep beside the driver through the lucid air of not-yet winter, up and down the slopes of such mountains as haunted Hemingway, a symposium in Naples just ten years before. I had been arguing in a tongue not my own against what I took to be the uncritical Italian veneration of Hemingway; and I was shouting my protest to one of those young writers from Rome or Palermo or Milan who write in translated Hemingwayese about hunting and *grappa* and getting laid—but who have no sense of the night-time religious anguish which makes Hemingway a more Catholic writer than most modern Italians. "Yes," I remembered saying, "yet—sometimes he puts down the closest thing to silence attainable in words, but often what he considers reticence is only the garrulousness of the inarticulate." This I hoped at least I was managing to say.

What really stirred in me on that long blue ride into dusk and the snowless valley (there was near dismay in the shops and cafés since the season was at hand and no snow had fallen) was an old resentment at those, chiefly but not exclusively Europeans, unable to understand that Hemingway was to be hated and loved not merely as a special American case, but more particularly as a Western writer, even as an imaginary Montanan. It seemed only fair that revolutions and illness and time bring him to Sun Valley to die, to the western slopes of America, rather than to Spain or Africa or Cuba; and it was scarcely ironical that his funeral be held in a tourists' haven, a place where the West sells itself to all comers.

Hemingway never wrote a book set in the mountain West, but he wrote none in which innocence and nobility, heroism and cowardice, devotion and passion (not love but *afición*) are not defined as they are in the TV Westerns which beguile a nation. The West he exploited is the West not of geography but of our dearest and most vulnerable dreams, not a locale but a fantasy, whose meanings do not change when it is called Spain or Africa or Cuba. As long as the hunting and fishing is good. And the women can be left behind. In Gary Cooper, all at which Hemingway merely hinted was made explicit; for Cooper was what Hemingway only longed to be, the West made flesh—his face, in its inarticulate blankness, a living equivalent of Hemingway's prose style.

It is not at all odd to find a dramatist and a favorite actor collaborating in the creation of character and image; what Tennessee Williams imagines, for instance, Marlon Brando is—or has obligingly become. But a similar collaboration between novelist and actor seems to me unparalleled in literary history —a little strange, though in this case inevitable. How aptly the paired deaths of Cooper and Hemingway, each greeted as a national calamity, climaxed and illuminated their relationship, their joint role in sustaining on upper cultural levels an image of our character and fate common enough in pulps, comic books and TV. That they did not manage to see each other before Cooper died seemed to the press (and to me) a more than minor disaster, mitigated perhaps by the fact that the one did not long survive the other. And like everyone else, I was moved by Hemingway's telegram offering Cooper odds of two to one that he would "beat him to the barn."

Death had presided over their association from the start, since their strongest link was Robert Jordan, invented by one, played by the other: the Westerner as fighter for Loyalist Spain, the anti-Fascist cowboy, the Montana innocent in a West turned oddly political and complex, a land ravaged not by the conflict of outlaw and sheriff but by the struggle between Communist and

Nazi. In such a West, what can the Western Hero do but—despite the example of his immortal prototypes—die? Unlike the War for the American West, the War in Spain was lost by Our Side; and finally only its dead seemed true heroes. Hemingway's vision in *For Whom the Bell Tolls* is something less than tragic; but his self-pity is perhaps more adequate than tragedy itself to an age unsure of who its heroes are or what it would like to do with them.

Only a comic view could have been truer to our times, and this Hemingway notoriously lacks. He never knew how funny the Westerner had come to seem in our world, whether played by Roy Rogers or Cooper or Hemingway himself—only how sad. Of all his male leads, Jake Barnes comes closest to being redeemed from self-pity by humor—the humor implicit in his comic wound. And consequently Jake could no more have been played by Cooper than could the Nick Adams of the earliest stories, or the old men of the last books. Never quite young, Cooper was not permitted to grow really old —only to betray his age and suffering through the non-committal Montana mask. He represents ideally the protagonists of Hemingway's middle novels, Lieutenant Henry and, of course, Jordan; but he will not do for anything in *To Have and To Have Not*, a depression book and, therefore, an ill-conceived sport sufficient unto Humphrey Bogart. The roles on either side of middle age, Hemingway was able to play himself, off the screen yet in the public eye: the beautiful young man of up to twenty-three with his two hundred and thirty-seven wounds, the old stud with his splendid beard and his guns chased in silver. We cannot even remember the face of his middle years (except as represented by Cooper), only the old-fashioned photographs of the youth who became the "Papa" of cover-stories in *Look* and *Life*: his own doomed father, his own remotest ancestor as well as ours.

At any rate, it was a pilgrimage we contemplated, my colleague and I, leaving Missoula some twenty-five years after the fictional departure of Robert Jordan. But it was also—hopefully —a raid: an expedition intended to bring Hemingway home to Montana, where he might perhaps succeed in saying what he had never been able to say to outlanders, speak the meanings of the place in which we had been born or had improbably chosen to live. It was, I suppose, *my* Western I hoped Hemingway would play out (becoming for me what Cooper had been for him); and there would have been something appropriately comic, after all, in casting the boy from Oak Park, Illinois, in a script composed by the boy from Newark, New Jersey, both of them on location in the Great West. But, of course, the first words we exchanged with Hemingway made it clear that if he had ever been able to speak in public, he was unable to do so now; that if he did, indeed, possess a secret, he was not about to reveal it from the platform. And how insolent, how absurd the quest seems in retrospect—excused only by a retrospective sense that what impelled us was a need to identify with an image we thought we despised. If it was not an act of love we intended, it was a more typical American effort magically to establish something worthy of love. *Here or Nowhere is America*. Surely the phrase rang someplace in the back of my head as we approached Ketchum; but Here turned out to be Nowhere and Hemingway in the middle of it.

At first, however, we were elated, for we were able to reach quickly the young doctor we had been told was Hemingway's friend and hunting companion; and we were as much delighted as embarrassed (everything seemed to be composing itself more like a poem than a mere event) by the fact that he was called, symbolically, Dr. Saviers. They hunted together during the afternoons, Dr. Saviers told us, though Hemingway could no longer crouch in a blind, only walk in search of birds, his last game. Hemingway worked mornings, but perhaps he would adjust his routine, find some time for us the next day before noon . . . after all, we had driven three hundred miles . . . and even though he never made public appearances, still . . .

We sat that night in a half-deserted bar, where the tourists had not yet come and the help waited on each other, making little ingroup jokes. No one noticed us nursing over our drinks the elation about which we scarcely dared speak. God knows what unworthy elements fed our joy: a desire for scraps of gossip or occasions for articles, a secret yearning to be disappointed, to find the world figure fatuous or comic or—No, surely there were motives less ignoble at its root: a genuine hope that emanating from greatness (the word came unbidden to our minds) there would be a *mana* we could share, a need somehow to verify the myth. We entered Hemingway's house through a back porch in character with the legend—limp ducks hanging from the rafters, a gun against the wall—the home of the hunter; but to step into the kitchen was to step out of the mythic world. There were the neatly wrapped trick-or-treat packages left over from the week before, loot unclaimed by kids; *The Reader's Digest*, the *TV Guide* open on tables; and beyond, the nondescript furniture of a furnished house, a random selection of meaningless books on the half-empty shelves.

And the Hemingway who greeted us, framed by the huge blank television screen that dominated the living room, was an old man with spectacles slipping down his nose. An old man at sixty-one. For an instant, I found myself thinking absurdly that this must be not the Hemingway we sought but his father, the ghost of that long-dead father—materialized at the age he would have been had he survived. Hemingway's handclasp I could scarcely feel; and I stood there baffled, a little ashamed of how I had braced myself involuntarily for a bone-crushing grip, how I must have yearned for some wordless preliminary test of strength. I had not known, I realized standing dumb before one even dumber, how completely I had been victimized by

Hemingway and wife, Martha Gelhorn, pheasant shooting.   *(Robert Capa, Magnum)*

the legend Hemingway had worn himself out imagining, writing, living.

Why should he not, after all, inhabit a bourgeois house, sit before TV with a drink in his hand, while his wife passed out Hallowe'en packages to children? Why the hell not? But he dwindled so abruptly, so touchingly from the great red and white head to his spindly legs, accentuated by tapered pants, legs that seemed scarcely able to hold him up. Fragile, I found myself thinking, breakable and broken—one time too often broken, broken beyond repair. And I remembered the wicked sentence reported by Gertrude Stein, "Ernest is very fragile, whenever he does anything sporting something breaks, his arm, his leg, or his head." The scar of one or more recent break was particularly evident on his forehead as he stood before us, inarticulately courteous: a scar just above the eyes that were the wrong color—not blue or gray as they should have been, not a hunter's eyes at all, but the eyes of a poet who dreamed of hunters, brown, soft, scared . . .

These, at least, I knew could not have changed. Whatever had recently travestied him, whatever illness had ravaged his flesh, relaxed his handclasp, could not have changed his eyes. These must have been the same always, must always have tried to confess the secret he had perhaps more hoped than feared would be guessed. "But Jake Barnes is in some sense then a self-portrait," I almost said aloud. "And that's why *The Sun Also Rises* seems your truest book, the book of fear and fact, not bravado and bullshit." I did not speak the words, of course, and anyhow he was saying in a hesitant voice, after having listened politely to our names, "Fiedler? Leslie Fiedler. Do you still believe that st— st— stuff about Huck Finn?"

He did not stammer precisely but hesitated over the first sounds of certain words as if unsure he could handle them, or perhaps only a little doubtful that they were the ones he really wanted. And when I had confessed that yes, I did, did still think that most American writers, not only Twain but Hemingway, too (naturally, we did not either of us mention his name in this context), could imagine an ennobling or redemptive love only between males in flight from women and civilization, Hemingway tried to respond with an appropriate quotation. "I don't believe what you say," he tried to repeat, "but I will defend to the death your right to say it." He could not quite negotiate this platitude, however, breaking down somewhere in the neighborhood of "defend." Then— silence.

I knew the motives of my own silence though I could only speculate about his. I had been cast, I could see, in the role of The Critic, hopelessly typed; and I would be obliged to play out for the rest of our conversation not the Western I had imagined, but quite another fantasy: the tragicomic encounter of the writer and the mistrusted professional reader upon whom his reputation and his survival depend. That Hemingway was aware at all of what I had written about him somehow disconcerted me. He was, I wanted to protest, a character in my *Love and Death in the American Novel*; and how could a character have read the book in which he lived? One does not imagine Hamlet reading the play that bears his name. But I was also, I soon gathered, a semi-fictional character—generically, to be sure, rather than particularly—a Hemingway character, an actor in his imaginary world. So that finding me before him made flesh, he felt obliged to play out with me a private drama, for which he would, alas,

never be able to frame quite appropriate sentences, an allegorical quarrel with posterity. At least, for an hour he could get the dialogue out of his haunted head.

He had read or glanced at, I could soon see, not only my essays but practically everything anyone had written on the modern novel in the United States. I fancied him flipping the pages, checking the indexes (or maybe he got it all out of book reviews in *Time*), searching out the most obscure references to himself, trying to find the final word that would allay his fears about how he stood; and discovering instead, imbedded in the praise that could never quite appease his anguish, qualifications, slights, downright condemnations. "T-tell Norman Mailer," he said at one point, "I never got his book. The mails in Cuba are— are— terrible." But who would have guessed that Hemingway had noticed the complaint in *Advertisements for Myself* about his never having acknowledged a presentation of *The Naked and the Dead*. And yet the comment was not out of character; for at another point he had said, really troubled, "These d-damn students. Call me up in the middle of the night to get something they can h-hang me with. So they can get a Ph.D." And most plaintively of all, "Sometimes when a man's in—when he can stand it least, they write just the things that—"

Between such observations, we would regard each other in the silence which seemed less painful than talk until Seymour Betsky would rescue us. I did not really want to be rescued, it seems to me now, finding silence the best, the only way of indicating that I knew what was racking the man I faced, knew his doubt and torment, his fear that he had done nothing of lasting worth, his conviction that he must die without adequate reas-

Resting in a hospital after African
plane crash. *(Robert Capa, Magnum)*

surance. It was not for Hemingway that I felt pity; I was not
capable of such condescension.
It was for myself, for all American writers. Who, *who*, I kept
thinking, would ever know in
these poor United States whether
or not he had made it, if Hemingway did not. I may even have
grown a little angry at his ob-
tuseness and uncertainty.

"A whole life-time of achievement," I wanted to shout at him,
"a whole life-time of praise, a
whole life-time of revelling in
both. What do you want?" But
I said nothing aloud, of course,
only went on to myself. "Okay,
so you've written those absurd
and trivial pieces on Spain and
published them in *Life*. Okay,
you've turned into the original
old dog returning to his vomit.
But your weaknesses have never
been a secret either from us, or,
we've hoped at least, from you.
We've had to come to terms with
those weaknesses as well as with
your even more disconcerting
strengths—to know where we
are and who, where we go from
here and who we'll be when we
get there. Don't we have the
right to expect the same from
you? Don't we have the right
to—" But all the while he kept

watching me warily, a little ac-
cusingly, like some youngster
waiting for the reviews of his
first book and trying desperately
not to talk about it to one he
suspects may be a reviewer.

And what could I have told
him, I ask myself now, that
might have helped, and what
right did I really have anyhow,
brought there by whim and
chance? What could anyone
have said to him that had not
already been repeated endlessly
and without avail by other critics
or by sodden adulators at bars?
The uncertainty that Hemingway
betrayed was a function surely
of the depression that was about
to destroy him; but, in a deeper
sense, that depression must have
been the product of the uncertainty—of a life-time of uncertainty behind the bluster and the
posturing, a life-time of terror
indissoluble in alcohol and action, a life-time of fearing the
leap out of the dark, never al-
layed no matter how many beasts
he brought down in bush or
boondocks.

It was only 9:30 A.M. but,
after a longer than customary
lapse in our talk, Hemingway
broke out a bottle of wine to
help ease us all. "Tavel—a fine

little wine from the Pyrenees,"
he said, without, apparently, any
defensive irony or even any sense
of the comic overtones of the
cliché. Silence and platitude.
Platitude and silence. This was
the pattern of what never became a conversation. And I felt,
not for the first time, how close
Hemingway's prose style at its
best was to both; how it lived
in the meager area of speech between inarticulateness and banal-
ity: a triumph wrung from the
slenderest literary means ever
employed to contrive a great
style—that great decadent style
in which a debased American
speech somehow survives itself.

"It's hard enough for me to
wr-write much less—talk," he
said twice I think, obviously
quoting a favorite platitude of
his own invention; and, only
once, but with equal satisfaction,
"I don't want to talk about literature or politics. Once I talked
about literature and I got—sick."
One could hear in his tone how
often he must, in similar circumstances, have used both; but he
meant the first of them at least.
The word "articulate" became
in his mouth an insult, an epi-
thet. Of Norman Mailer, for instance, he said between pauses,

quietly, "He's s-so— articu-late—" and there was only a little envy to mitigate the contempt. But he wanted to talk about literature really, or, more precisely, wanted to talk about authors, his colleagues and rivals. Yet his comments on them boiled down to two only: the first for writers over fifty, "Great guy, you should've known him!"; the second for those under that critical age, "That boy has talent!" Vance Bourjaily, I recall, seemed to him the "boy" with the most "talent." The one author he did not mention ever was himself, and I abided by the taboo he tacitly imposed, though, like him I fear, more out of cowardice than delicacy.

When I noticed in a particularly hard moment the *TV Guide* beside me open to the Saturday Night Fights, I welcomed the cue, tried to abandon Bourjaily in favor of Tiger Jones, though I really admire the style of the one not much more than that of the other. "Terrible what they make those boys do on television," Hemingway responded, like the joker next to you at the bar who baffles your last attempt at communication. And it didn't help a bit when Mrs. Hemingway entered to apologize in an attractive cracked voice for the state of the house. "If I had only known that someone was coming . . ." But why was everyone apologizing and to whom?

It was the *politeness* of the whole affair which seemed somehow the final affront to the legend. Hemingway was like a well-behaved small boy, a little unsure about the rules, but resolved to be courteous all the same. His very act of asking us to come and talk during his usual working hours and at a moment of evident distress was a gesture of genuine courtesy. And he fussed over the wine as if set on redeeming our difficult encounter

with a show of formality. At one point, he started to pour some Tavel into my glass before his own, then stopped himself, put a little into his glass, apologized for having troubled to remember protocol, apologized for apologizing—finally insisted on drinking to my next book, when I lifted my glass to his.

But what were we doing talking of next books when I could not stop the screaming inside of my head, "How will anyone ever know? How will I ever know unless the critics, foolish, biased, bored, tell me, tell us?" I could foresee the pain of reading the reviews of my first novel, just as I could feel Hemingway's pain reading the reviews of his later work. And I wanted to protest in the name of the pain itself that not separated but joined us: The critic is obliged only to the truth though he knows that truth is never completely in his grasp. Certainly he cannot afford to reckon with private anguish and despair in which he is forbidden to believe, like the novelist, inventing out of his friends and his own shame Lady Brett or Robert Cohn.

And I looked up into Hemingway's smile—the teeth yellowish and widely spaced, but bared in all the ceremonious innocence of a boy's grin. He was suddenly, beautifully, twelve years old. A tough, cocky, gentle boy still, but also a fragile, too-often-repaired old man, about (how could I help knowing it?) to die. It puzzled me a little to discover him, who had never been able to invent a tragic protagonist, so much a tragic figure himself— with meanings for all of us, meanings utterly different from those of his myth, meanings I would have to figure out later . . . Yet he seemed, too, as we had always suspected, one who had been *only* a boy and an old man, never what the rest of us for too

wearily long must endure being —all that lies between. I could not help recalling the passage where Gertrude Stein tells of Hemingway at twenty-three crying out that he was too young to be a father. And I could hear him now in my inner ear crying out that he was too young to be an old man. Too young to be an ancestor.

But he was not too young to be my ancestor, not too young for me to resent as one resents what is terribly there when he is born. I would not be able to say the expected things about him ever, I knew, not even after he was dead. And who would understand or believe me when I was ready to say what I could: that I loved him for his weakness without ceasing to despise him for his strength.

We had left Seymour Betsky's car in town, and as the four of us looked at each other now, more than ready to be done with our meeting, Hemingway and his wife offered to drive us back in to pick it up. He had to do some small chores, chiefly go to the bank. But it was a Saturday, as we had all forgotten; and Betsky and I stood for a moment after we had been dropped off watching Hemingway bang at the closed glass doors, rather feebly perhaps but with a rage he was obviously tickled to be able to feel. "Shit," he said finally to the dark interior and the empty street; and we headed for our car fast, fast, hoping to close the scene on the first authentic Hemingway line of the morning. But we did not move quite fast enough, had to hear over the slamming of our car door the voice of Mrs. Hemingway calling to her husband (he had started off in one direction, she in another), "Don't forget your vitamin tablets, daddy."

TOM BURKE
The New Homosexuality

From every corner comes evidence that American sexual mores have been changing rapidly. Certainly, standards of permissible display—both in the arts and in personal attire—altered considerably in the 1960s. Tom Burke's account of the ''new homosexuals'' presents one of the farthest extensions of this trend and touches on much that is typical of the culture of the age. Burke suggests that generational differences among homosexuals are in some ways even greater than differences between ''straights'' and ''gays.'' The main division, as one of Burke's subjects points out, seems to be between those who suffer from guilt feelings about their sexual activities and those who do not. But all the nation seems to have matured in tolerance for the various forms of sexual behavior. With some unfortunate exceptions, the sixties have witnessed an unprecedented toleration for the new style of young people and, generally, for a pluralism in regard to personal standards.

Equally typical of the 1960s is the political organization of homosexuals to protect their own rights and to communicate to the nation their sense of identity. ''Gay power'' is not anything one could have imagined in America ten years ago. Yet this emergence of a subculture into a political entity is quite common: among blacks, women, Indians, Chicanos, even groups like the intelligentsia and the hard hats. Cultural issues seem to have political meaning, especially when a group shifts from gratitude at being ''permitted'' to indulge in whatever it chooses to assertion of its right to live as its own values and integrity demand.

Pity: just when Middle America finally discovered the homosexual, he died. Countless stolid burghers, reconciled to the idea of such opulent phenomena as acid rock and the male pill, are finally prepared to empathize with (if not quite approve of) this thirty-fiveish semi-neuter whom they imagine to be the prototypical modern deviate: a curio-shop proprietor with an uncertain mouth, wet basset eyes, a Coppertone tan and a miniature Yorkshire, who lives in a white and silver Jean Harlow apartment, drinks pink gin, cooks *boeuf Bourguignon*, mourns Judy, makes timid liaisons on Forty-second Street, gets mugged by midnight cowboys, and masturbates while watching televised swimming meets. The public is now prepared to have a gingerly if patronizing romance with him, and, alas, the attachment is necrophilic: he has expired, with a whimper, to make way for the new homosexual of the Seventies, an unfettered, guiltless male child of the new morality in a Zapata moustache and an outlaw hat, who couldn't care less for Establishment approval, would as soon sleep with boys as girls, and thinks that "Over the Rainbow" is a place to fly on 200 micrograms of lysergic acid diethylamide.

That the public's information vis-à-vis the new deviate is now hopelessly outdated is not the public's fault. It cannot examine him on its own because, from a polite distance, he is indistinguishable from the heterosexual hippie. It cannot read about him, because novelists have not written about him, and journalists concentrate on the protest actions of a handful of homosexual radicals. Television may be aware of him, but it isn't telling. Which leaves movies and the stage, the principal purveyors of a homosexual image that is at least five years behind reality. The worst current offender is, of course, the play *The Boys in the Band* (anyone who doubts that the heartland has embraced deviation may ponder the fact that the play recently enjoyed a successful run at Caesar's Palace, Las Vegas). Its characters are touted as representative contemporary homosexuals, and will soon be perpetuated in a carbon-copy film version, when actually they are about as pertinent to our time as the snood. As most of the world now knows, *The Boys in the Band* concerns a gay birthday party given by a thirty-year-old boy with a penchant for elaborate duplex apartments, jet-set watering holes, vicuña sweaters, hair sprays and lunches at the Oak Room of the Plaza Hotel, none of which he can afford. His eight guests all reflect his stereotyped behavior in one way or another. They eat canapés, drink excessively, do a chorus-line dance called the Madison (popular on Fire Island in the Fifties), quote old movies, and imitate

Judy, Betty and Kate. They submit masochistically when asked to play a game in which their collective Guilt is revealed. When they leave, their chastened host weeps a bit ("If we could just not hate ourselves so much") and exits bravely, for midnight mass. Curtain. The audience files out, feeling educated. Except for George Cassard, who smiles with irony, shakes his head, and then yawns, luxuriously.

George Cassard, who looks somewhat like Jim Morrison, and believes that he looks more like Jim Morrison than he actually does, was twenty-three on August 6, 1969, and is therefore a Leo, though his moon is in Scorpio. On the wall of his rather Spartan Chelsea cold-water flat, he has drawn, with the meticulousness of an ancient mapmaker, his horoscope: the sun, moon and planets placed correctly in the twelve houses of the zodiac. "Scorpio is the sex sign," he will say, smiling enigmatically at his moon.

He is an art assistant in a staid advertising agency. He has his teeth cleaned every three months, rather than the usual six. He has read *Steppenwolf*. At home, on Long Island, he was a Boy Scout. He still collects coins. He flies kites. He is a homosexual. Through friends of friends and similar contacts, I have met a number of young men very much like him, and each has allowed me to accompany him to one of the parties he attends. The parties are nearly identical, except that George's happens to be a birthday celebration. Like the other boys, he has been told that I am a writer, but does not seem to care especially what I may write about him, or whether his name will be used. After the party, when I ask him if he would like me to make up a pseudonym for him, which, in fact, I have done, he seems mildly surprised.

"Why, man?"

"Well, your job, or your parents."

"My parents know about me. They're quite young, for parents. My dad is only forty-four. They're very hip. Very groovy, very beautiful. My mom smokes hash." He breaks off, making a curious small exhaling sound. "But she doesn't drop acid. They do worry about me dropping acid. I told them I only tripped twice, which isn't exactly true, and they know it. Anyway. What did you ask me? Oh, yeh, the job. Well, why should I pretend to be something I'm not? I mean, uh, pretend not to be something I am. They never asked me, but if they did, I wouldn't lie. How can you live a lie, man? That's not living. If they get uptight, up theirs. I don't want to work for somebody that bigoted. Print *their* name too, if you want."

He frowns and exhales again. I assume that he is reconsidering, but he says, "You're not going to put in my address, are you, or the phone or anything.

"No, why should I?"

"Good. I mean, I don't want a lot of freaks phoning. Like I was putting a balling ad in *Screw,* or something."

George Cassard has said to meet him on the corner of Christopher Street and Greenwich Avenue at ten o'clock. From there we are to proceed to the party. At this point, we have not met, only talked on the phone, and it occurs to me that we have not discussed a way of recognizing one another in the armies of young men who idle here on a clear evening. But, without hesitation, he comes to the store window where I wait, guided, perhaps, by some sixth sense afforded him by astrology, or Boy Scouting.

"Cool," he says. He does not offer his hand. "I was afraid you might be old, being a writer. Groovy. Everybody at this party will be pretty young, too." He tosses his long hair once, emphatically, as if inserting a "stop" in a telegram. It tosses minimally, because it is secured by a Cherokee beaded headband. His necklace is made of Navaho talismans. His white body-shirt looks beige, shaded by his resolutely tanned chest. A chain belt and tapestry-look bell-bottoms hang at his bony hips; a suede pouch hangs from the belt.

"You wanta smoke?" His voice seems to come from under the tanned chest. Without waiting for an answer, he produces from the pouch a joint wrapped in yellow Stella Sweet Banana Paper, lights it, and starts up Greenwich, motioning to me with his head. Follow the yellow brick road. He exhales, and a passing boy catches the scent. "Beautiful," the boy murmurs into the air, grinning straight ahead.

"Lay, lady lay—lay across my big brass bed," Dylan invites from within. The walls of the loft are black; slender lengths of plumbing, painted silver, angle up them and across the ceiling. Beneath dim hanging lamps made of Sinclair Oil cans, Fresca can clusters and antique vegetable graters, on Pakistani cushions and Moroccan mats, twelve young men and four girls, all of whom look rather like Jim Morrison, sit cross-legged or recline euphorically. Leon, the guest of honor—it is his twenty-first birthday—comes forward; he is small, and grins, gnome-like, welcoming us with an ill-defined acknowledging gesture. The guests look up at us, nodding; introductions are unnecessary, made extraneous by Dylan. Joel, Leon's lover, approaches slowly, as if the smoke in the air is mildly obstructive, and offers his pipe of hash, a glass of lime-colored, acid-laced Kool Aid, and the ice-cream log melting on the kitchen counter. From his suede pouch, George takes the birthday gift: a half ounce of Acapulco

Gold tied in a Baggie. Leon darts his small head to George's face; it is not so much a kiss as a pleased little aside, a tiny piece of affectionate choreography. Uxoriously, he hands the Baggie to Joel, who opens it and sniffs. Joel wears only a felt outlaw's hat and a sort of loincloth. His body is offhandedly muscular as if, not long ago, he played a mild sport regularly. His legs and torso are finger-painted in rudimentary art nouveau, and on his chest is lettered, "Happy Birthday, Little Leon," and "Love" and "Peace."

We drop to the floor to participate in a group endeavor: blowing soap bubbles, and the inflating of party balloons. Paper hats are passed. Stella Sweet Strawberry Red, Sweet Mint Green, and Pure Licorice Paper joints circulate with the tarnished brass hash pipe and the Benzedrex Inhaler, stuffed with a wad of cotton that has been dipped in liquid amyl nitrite. Your dope is my dope is our dope; we are a commune, no stimulant is individually owned. "I took a ride in your car-a-van" sings the Rotary Connection, and all heads nod, affirming the beat. One of the girls, a short, plump blonde with violet eyes and an oddly dissatisfied mouth, touches George's hair lovingly. He touches her hair lovingly. "Beautiful," he says. A dark boy kneels before George and deals out cards from a tarot deck. Someone bats an inflated balloon up over the circle of heads, and it hangs a moment in the air. Two more balloons, three, are launched and re-launched until a dozen of them bob across the circle like languid volleyballs.

The doorbell. Four more boys —no, men—tumble in, laughing above the music. That they are older, in their early thirties, is noticeable only if one bothers to take inventory, of furrows between eyebrows and slight hardenings, or softenings, of jawlines. They are costumed exactly as

the original company; moreover, they have learned to imitate the sunny, ingenuous style, the fluid, unquestioning way of moving. But they are more verbal, and more excitable. One turns the music up even louder, until it rattles the silver pipes. Another, laughing in the kitchen, playfully smears Joel's naked back with white frosting from the ice-cream log. Joel yells, pleasantly surprised, and retaliates with a handful of soupy ice cream, splashing it down his attacker's paisley shirt, spilling some onto Leon, who joyously grabs from the refrigerator a plate of cherry tomatoes. Everyone is suddenly in the kitchen, tossing handfuls of ice cream and tomatoes, smearing white bells with pink, streaking faces red, hurling gobs of lime-scented shaving cream from an aerosol can, soaking one another with sprays of Fresca and Kool Aid. The body shirts, bells and Navaho talismans fall to the floor as if they had unfastened themselves, until all the guests, the girls and all the boys, are tangled together on the cushions and Moroccan mats, less lewd than amused, at what can occur spontaneously in the course of another routine evening with the folks.

A few days later, I arrange to talk to one of the guests, Jim Pasieniti, who is twenty-four, lives in the east Eighties, and commutes every morning to graduate school in New Jersey. The uptown gay bar in which he asks me to meet him is nearly empty at cocktail hour, and it bears no resemblance to the ornate recherché homosexual habitats of *The Detective* or *The City and the Pillar*. A scruffy, well-worn room that smells of stale draft beer and billiard chalk, it could be a Bronx workingman's pub, except for the absence of American flags and girlie calendars. When Jim has ordered a Coke—he says that he almost never drinks—I ask him if he agrees with me about the party being representative.

"Yeh. Well, they don't all end like that," he says, laughing. "That happened partly because we were stoned, but dope wasn't the only reason. I mean, everybody knows that *straight* kids get into group sex these days. So do gay ones. It's very different with the older gay crowd, the guys in their forties. The orgies they have are calculated, planned things, and would never, never include women. Old fags are too inhibited for that. Don't get me wrong: younger homosexuals aren't group-groping twenty-four hours a day, but that sort of thing *is* much more prevalent. Why? Well, gay kids in their twenties don't have the hang-ups that old queens had when *they* were in *their* twenties, so they start making out much earlier, and get bored sooner with sex in pairs. So they start using poppers pretty young, and getting interested in group activities such as the baths, or in playing around in places like the Christopher Street docks, or even the subway johns, because those places are more dangerous—they're watched by the fuzz, naturally—and therefore more of a challenge. Also, those scenes are more virile, in an odd way; more masculine. They're kind of a young answer to the old guys who have to take you home very formally and mix you a Martini and made a big deal of doing the traditional sex number, alone, in private. Danger is groovy. It's always

He chews the ice from his Coke glass thoughtfully. "Uh, I don't mean by 'masculine' and 'virile' that kids are going in for the rough, sado-masochistic sex. I think there's less of that among young guys because they're more honest with themselves than the older crowd. That leather ritual satisfies the old queen's need to prove to himself that he's a man. The young kids just don't feel that need."

I ask Jim if he knows any homosexuals of the type depicted in *The Boys in the Band* and similar efforts. He shrugs and shakes his head.

"If those queens are still around, you don't see them. If you do, they're *really* older, like in their sixties. The summer I was eighteen—six years ago—I worked as a waiter in a gay bar. There were plenty of younger ones like that in those days. They would bring their poodles into the bar, and set drinks on the floor for the dogs to sip. Christ. There was something so lonely about them—the guys, not the dogs. They planned their whole schedules around these squeaky, high-strung little poodles that couldn't have cared less about them. Like old women with cats —something to give the days a pattern. One of them asked me up to his place for dinner. Christ, that apartment. It looked like the Castro showroom on Times Square, only not as masculine. Everything . . . *embellished*. You know: not a straight line in the whole apartment. I remember that The Beatles were still new then, but very big, and—you won't believe this—*he had never heard of The Beatles!* He had this old Ethel Merman record. And Judy Garland—everything of Judy Garland. She was interesting, but I mean, who wants to *listen* to that stuff? It's all external, while rock is, you know, internal. That theatrical music is kind of a denial of sex, while rock is *pure* sex."

He stretches, and cracks his knuckles loudly; the noise wakes the dozing bartender. "It struck me as weird, that a guy who really resented and feared women could relate only to these *female* singers—Ethel Merman and so on. Some of his buddies came up, and they drank a lot and kept arguing about how Ann Sheridan laughed. I mean, they seemed to cling to this trivia to avoid reality, which was, to them, the old

guilt bit. *That's* what has died: this homosexual feeling of being isolated from the straight world by guilt. The whole country has divided into two groups: those who care about what people do in bed, and those who don't. The guilty and the guiltless. The old queens are in the first category, the kids are in the second. That's why this camp business means nothing to them. I think camp was a way for queens to distract themselves from their guilt, and today, who needs it? I'm getting pretty heavy here, you want me to go on? Okay: there used to be this syndrome of drink, guilt and camp. Now, its dope, freedom and—well, rock, and soul, and the humor of the head. Beauty, and gentleness, and love in homosexual terms used to be essentially feminine. Now, they don't have a gender. Movies were camp, and queens could only identify with women. Today, gay kids identify with males—with Peter Fonda, or Dustin Hoffman. And they aren't interested in, you know, 'theatre,' or 'Broadway'—except of course *Hair*. And the whole matter of chicks. It used to be that fags couldn't relate to females that weren't mothers. Today homos think of chicks as chicks. They don't want mothers. Take the chicks at that party. About half the gay guys I know have had sex with chicks like them. . . ."

Through Jim, I find the girls of the party, not all of whom are quite so cooperative. One says she does not "approve of the press" and hangs up. Another says she can't talk, is "nonverbal" and "non-analytical" and hangs up. The third is the girl with the violet eyes. Her name, she asserts, is Arleth; well, it is not the name on her birth certificate, but she hasn't used *that* name for two years, since her eighteenth birthday. Last name? "Just Arleth." She is interested in talking, but vague about where and when; eventually, I trace her to a dance bar that is, if anything, multi-sexual. In the huge, dim, sea-green and silver room, boys dance with boys, and with girls, and various trio and quartet arrangements gyrate together. The music is almost tangible. Arleth sits at a small table, being nuzzled on the neck by a pale boy in Peter Fonda sunglasses. She stares, then remembers me, and motions to the vacant ice-cream-parlor chair.

"Uh, I'm slightly stoned. You wouldn't happen to have an upper, would you? Oh, well."

I ask my questions.

"Well, uh, for one thing, bis are groovier."

Bis?

"Bisexual. Some of these guys that *you* think of as *gay* are really *bi*. They lean more toward boys than girls, that's all. And they're beautiful. I mean, I know straight boys who are just *as* beautiful, but I think I prefer gays. On a superficial level, they are more fun. They laugh more, they are such groovy dancers, they know clothes. This one very *bi* boy goes with me sometimes when I buy clothes. He thinks of color combinations that I never would. And *he* certainly isn't a fairy. Last summer, he was a lifeguard. . . ."

A boy in a Western vest (he is otherwise topless) slides up to the table and asks Peter Fonda sunglasses to dance. The crowd absorbs them; Arleth glances after them benignly.

"I'm attracted to some of them, some not, the same as with straights. I have made it privately with three guys at that party. It wasn't a big thing, it just happened. It was a little different than with straights. Slower, tenderer. I don't think that any of the gay guys I know have any particular problem about balling girls. They just, uh, got used to guys when they were young, and some of them are too lazy to try something different than what

they're used to. Why does it have to be any heavier than that? Scientists and doctors *complicate* it so. Only squares make such a big deal of homosexuality. It's so unimportant. It's beautiful if it's your thing. It's not necessarily *my* thing. I mean, I tried it with a girl friend. We both decided we prefer a man. *Any* kind."

She gets up. Mama Cass is singing: "Sweet breezes seem to whisper 'I love you.' " Western vest holds sunglasses close, barely moving. Arleth taps him gently on the shoulder, cutting in.

What is hard to understand is how the writer of a serious play or movie about modern homosexuals could have missed all this. Even if he shuns parties and bars, he could hardly have avoided several other symptoms of the new homosexual life-style —its political maneuvers, for instance, as reported in detail by news media since at least the middle sixties. The Mattachine Society of New York, most famous of the homophile organizations, has been getting its name in print constantly since the demise of Robert Wagner (who tended not to answer when they phoned). John Lindsay had barely been sworn in before Dick Leitsch, the Mattachine's vociferous director, rose at one of the Mayor's town meetings to denounce the entrapment of homosexuals by police. Even as he spoke, a plainclothesman was entrapping an innocent but effete young man in the back room of Julius Bar, Greenwich Village. An Episcopal minister (who had stopped in the bar for a sandwich) witnessed this, and phoned another minister, who phoned the Mayor and almost everyone else of any importance with a listed number. The result was a meeting in a village café attended by an influential *heterosexual* group that included the Mayor, the police commissioner, the police commissioner's wife,

Allen Ginsberg, the Civil Liberties Union, and The Fugs. Entrapment ended the next morning.

Leitsch's next move, of course, got nationwide coverage. Attended by the press, he approached four Manhattan bars armed with a card stating his sexual persuasion and demanding service. Three places served him cheerfully; the fourth, Julius Bar, which had been serving non-card-carrying homosexuals for years, refused, and Leitsch instantly lodged a complaint with the Human Rights Commission.[1] Within two months, the State Liquor Authority lifted its traditional ban on homosexual bars, and, during the next two years, various state courts decided that "intra-sexual" dancing, touching and even kissing were not necessarily disorderly, as long as the various sexes refrained from touching one another upon "primary sex organs." (Police who disapproved of this new climate of tolerance insisted there was a fine line between primary and secondary sex organs, and that when homosexuals danced, they frequently touched one another upon the buttocks, a possibly criminal act, as to many deviates the buttocks are decidedly not secondary.)

As the new milieu was being legalized, it was also being boosted by myriad aberrations of the new heterosexual permissiveness: by unisex clothing, innocently born in the forties when the first bobby-soxer bought her first pair of boy's Levi's, finally labeled, sanctioned

[1] The Mattachine's highly publicized New York stand motivated similar actions in other places, but none were especially effective. In San Francisco, for example, Mattachine members who found the Society too conservative formed radical splinter groups, called SIR and, inevitably, The Pink Panthers, but their most aggressive move so far has been to protest the drafting of homosexuals, a rather frivolous ploy, since homosexuals are draft-exempt anyway.

and merchandised by Seventh Avenue; by the altered straight reaction to overt gay activity in "mixed" environments such as the locker rooms of public beaches (indignation gave way to amused indifference, then marked curiosity); by the public's sympathy for Walter Jenkins during his 1964 Y.M.C.A. men's-room debacle; by casual use of the terrible ten-letter word not only on television panel discussions but on prime-time network entertainments (culminating in the deviant gags now standard on every major variety program except *The King Family Presents*); by the spate of "major" gay films, especially *The Detective*; by the national burgeoning of such overt homosexual diversions as the exclusively gay pleasure boat which currently steams up the Ohio every clear weekend from the public landing at Cincinnati; by the evolution of homosexual ghetto streets from places of clandestine meeting to approximations of West Point's Flirtation Walk; and, indeed, by the sudden embracing of the film version of *The Boys in the Band* by key members of the New York power structure. Bergdorf Goodman, the Sherry-Netherland Hotel, Doubleday Bookstores, Julius Bar, the New York City Transit Authority and La Guardia Airport all consented to appear in the movie, and invitations to the somewhat fey party given to publicize it were sent out in the names of New York Society leader Mrs. William ("Chessy") Rayner, Mrs. Mortimer Hall (nee Diana Lynn, movie actress turned social doyenne in the manner of Merle Oberon), and Natalie Wood. Moreover, the party was reported at length on the "Food Fashions Family Furnishings" page of the New York *Times,* along with a symphony benefit and other less-dubious galas.

While such developments were reassuring the New Homosex-uality, the psychedelic life-style was giving it a form. Not that one subculture simply aped another; in point of fact the majority of contemporary homosexuals under forty are confirmed pot-heads and at least occasional acid-trippers. For those now in their early and mid-twenties, drugs were just another part of adolescence, like The Beatles and puberty. They smoked the same grass and dropped the same acid as their heterosexual peers, but drug-oriented behavior—autistic, passive, childlike, alienated—was especially gratifying to them, partly because it so annoyed *straight* adults. Their heterosexual fellow-heads, after all, though properly alienated, did maintain one important allegiance with The System: heterosexuality.

Homosexual senior citizens—anybody over twenty-nine—embrace psychedelia for an even simpler reason: the well-known homosexual compulsion to postpone old age by carefully imitating the young. The middle-aged deviate merely grows what is left of his hair very long, wears beads, body shirts, Western vests and peace emblems, studies the head's manner of movement and speech, and goes right on getting high on alcohol, because he considers drugs unsafe. But the typical thirtyish aspiring adolescent lays in supplies of pot, hash, etc., and makes quite a project of going on the wagon. First he smokes weekends, then week-nights. He already owns some denim bells, perhaps a string of beads, but now his building superintendent receives the stacks of collegiate chinos, the elbow-patched J. Press jackets and bleeding Madras shorts, as he buys whole new wardrobes in little shops with silver walls and Mick Jagger on the stereo. As the liquor dealer misses him, so does the barber: his hair grows until eyes in the office narrow, but even that, like the selling of mutual funds itself, suddenly seems so irrelevant, while the secretary's cerulean-blue cup of bright-colored pencils becomes so . . . immediate. His smiles are bemused, his laughter suddenly leprechaunish. He acquires a nickname. He buys new books; *Astrology, the Space-Age Science, The Little Prince,* the I Ching, Kierkegaard, and composes little private exercises in Kierkegaardian freedom—"I choose *not* to go in and sell mutual funds tomorrow, thereby recovering my freedom to *do* so." In the end, however, it is much more attractive to call in sick and stay home to read Kierkegaard, or to get up at noon, smoke, and then go shopping, for black paint for the dull white apartment walls, inexpensive strobes, prisms, colored plastic boxes, aluminum paper, incense, scented candles. Life takes on a delightfully transient quality, as meals become fanciful little picnics of Scooter Pies, Fresca and Tootsie Pops. Lists are made, new records purchased: Blood, Sweat & Tears, The Rotary Connection, the *2001* sound track, and *Hair,* the new deviate's only acceptable cast album.

He had frequented the handful of refined cocktail bars where the older contingent still gathers (places referred to even by their patrons as "wrinkle rooms"). Occasionally, he had stopped in the hangouts of the leather crowd, who tend to be the aged cocktail drinkers re-costumed in motorcycle jackets and chains. Now, he smokes at home, puts on surplus Navy bells, and visits a bastion of the New Homosexuality on Christopher Street. All replicas of Jim Pasieniti's uptown retreat, they have retained the ambience of the neighborhood gin mill because that is how their new clientele prefers them. The lighting is harsh, the floor, the walls and the blues on the jukebox dirty. Semi-heterosexual construction-worker types mix easily with the other patrons; the pool players take their games very seriously, swaggering around the billiard table, pausing to pose slue-foot. No one holds a cigarette as if he longed for a cigarette holder.

And one head knows another; conversation is standardized.

". . . Uh, what did you say? I'm a little stoned."

"Yeh, well, so am I."

Gentle laughter.

"Uh, I was going home and smoke some more. Want to come?"

He does. Heads, though unacquainted, know that they will find so much in common. The same esoteric frame of reference, the same rather elaborate, pleasantly inventive approach to sex. Straights—nonsmokers—simply wouldn't understand. And in the light of the strobe, minds expanded, age differences, if they did exist, suddenly count for so little.

Timothy Leary and other Brahmins of psychedelia assert that LSD cures homosexuality. According to homosexuals, what it actually cures is the notion that a cure for homosexuality ought to be sought at all. But acid does seem to produce in most homosexuals a new, if somewhat ill-defined and subordinate interest in the opposite sex. "In high school, I never noticed girls," says Paul, a manly twenty-one-year-old who migrated from an Oklahoma farm to Los Angeles two years ago, and leans now on his flower-painted Volkswagen outside a Hollywood gay bar. "I guess I was afraid of them. I was uptight about everything: very serious, very heavy. When I came out here I started smoking regularly, and tripping. During my second trip, I was walking along the Strip at night, and passing these pretty girls—and suddenly, I was *smiling* at them. Wow! Oh, wow. I wasn't trying to, it just happened. On acid. The same thing happened

to my two roommates. Now, there always seem to be some girls around when we go out. It's groovy. They don't seem to expect anything of us. Except it *is* a little like they are, uh, waiting for us to get around to them. . . ."

I give Paul my hotel phone number and a few days later he calls to take me to a party, in a run-down cottage in Laurel Canyon, hippie mecca. The walls of the house are faded cream stucco, the furnishings motel contemporary; otherwise, the atmosphere is reminiscent of Leon's birthday. Paul loses himself in a cluster of admirers, and I speak to a remarkable girl named Joy, who wears a silver Dynel wig and says she is on speed.

"Isn't this outasight? Everybody grooving together. What? Of course they're gay. Everybody is gay. I want to sleep with every gay boy in this room. They are beautiful and I am going to lay every one of them. They make me feel more like a woman than straight squares. I hate straight pigs who treat women like pieces of meat. Say, what are you pumping me for? Are you some kind of talk freak?"

After smoking a passed joint, Paul brings the oven rack from the stove in the kitchen, ties two strings to one side of it, winds the strings around his index fingers, places his fingers in his ears, and enlists someone to "play" the rack with a metal spoon. The effect, he says, is like hearing Tibetan chimes from a great distance. When I have tried the rack, he listens politely to more questions.

"Yeh, I know some older guys. Last year, I answered a roommate-wanted ad in the paper, and the guy turned out to be forty. The 'room' turned out to be a ten-room pad in Beverly Hills. It looked like a French whorehouse. I did live there for about four months, and he never mentioned my share of the rent. But

the idea of smoking grass freaked him. 'It's addictive,' he would scream. '*I* don't need that kind of escape,' he'd say, finishing a bottle of gin. He could have been sort of groovy if he'd have smoked. But he was such an old maid. He had this shelf full of books about homos where there was very little sex but a lot of crying and suffering and in the end one of the boys always killed himself. I could never figure out *why*. I brought home a copy of this groovy dirty book called *Song of the Loot*. . . ."

"Would that be *'Loon'*?"

"Yeh, *Loon*, which is all sex, and he started it and didn't like it because it didn't have enough suffering. Such a—lady, but at the same time, a drunk. Mostly he'd just pass out and go to sleep. Wow: drink is evil. I think there ought to be some kind of law against it, like there used to be."

He stops a minute, thinking, then says: "We were talking about acid before. There's something else about it. Uh . . . well, the kind of work I do is, I'm a hairdresser. When I first got out of beauty school, in L.A., I used to bleach my hair, and, uh, wear mascara and scream a lot, with the other kids."

He shakes his head at the memory; watching him now, it does seem hard to believe. "Well, acid changed that. The first trip —wow. It was the most important twelve hours of my life. I saw what I was. A fruit. And I was able to change. I just got more cool. It brought back my masculinity. The guys I live with are also hairdressers, but you'd never know it. They went through the same acid thing I did. Now one races a bike—uh, motorcycle—and the other races this old Corvette he bought. He even learned how to take a motor apart. This dike taught him. Cool?"

When I asked Paul about printing his name, he agrees

readily ("I can't hide or play games, that's what screws up straight people"), then bites his thumbnail and asks if I am going to write about drugs. "Oh. Well, then I gotta say no. I am not copping out. If I lived anywhere else, I wouldn't care. But the L.A. fuzz! Four of my friends got busted for possession, just last month."

Up and down Sunset Boulevard, or Wabash Avenue, or Christopher Street, this is the common reaction. If today's homosexual is secretive about anything, it is drug use, not homosexuality. Naturally, those who are eager to declare themselves in print are still a minority, but what is significant is the surprising number who will, and the much larger number who refuse to dissemble for family or friends. The mood of belligerence has apparently spread even to homosexuals who marry. Though they are older, determinedly conservative, and excessively concerned with appearances, even they no longer seem to pretend very elaborately, either before or after marriage. Lesbians, of course, have never had to be as covert as homosexual males, simply because the Establishment has always tended to regard them merely as harmless eccentrics. (This, too, may change: the Establishment does not attend meetings of the new militant women's liberation groups.)

If this is where homosexuality is, where is it going? Where will it be in three years? Ten? "Groovier," says Jim Pasieniti. "Maybe we'll reach the Hindu ideal—man and woman united." He smiles sardonically. "Once, the good old apple-pie idea was that men and women screwed conventionally in the popular position, or abstained and took cold showers. Separately. Okay, so now 'normal' people are finding out that fellatio and cunnilingus are just as 'normal' as

anything else. So doesn't it follow that the whole world is readjusting its concept of what is normal and what is perverted—and what is homo or heterosexual? Nobody *has* to be one thing or the other anymore. Even homos who are still afraid of sex with women—well, with all these nudes everywhere, how is anybody going to remain very freaked at the sight of anybody else's privates? I don't know— bisexual isn't really a valid word now, because its connotations are old-fashioned. And somebody better come up with the right word, because we're going to need it. Within ten years, we'll have the first group marriage. The communes already prophesy it, the population problem will push it along. By 1990, the old husband-and-wife unit will be nearly obsolete. First, there will be trio marriages—though the marriage ceremony will be obsolete, too—in which, say, two guys and a girl live together and all groove on each other with no specific sexual roles. After that, group living. Group grooving. It's coming."

What about "Gay Power"? Will it hasten group grooving, and the rest? "Well, you want to laugh at all that, the riots, the Gay Power meetings, and so on, but I don't know. If it gets organized, finds a leader, anything could happen."

Abruptly, he does laugh. "You know what the best bit of irony was? The riots started the night Judy Garland was buried."

It did almost seem that the New Homosexuality had picked the night to wreak havoc upon Manhattan, scorning the elder traditionalists who flew the flags on their Cherry Grove cottages at half-mast and sat home in decorous seclusion, mourning. Actually, the Village disturbance probably had nothing to do with either the death of an old homosexual idol, or the first night of

the full moon. But it was significant as the most dramatic indication to date of just how aggressively the New Homosexual may speed his own evolution.

And Christopher Street had looked so routine: the usual gaggles of teen-age boys, who, though accompanied by girls, are, one must admit, distinctly *tapette* (rather as Paul of Los Angeles described himself, preacid); skittish old ladies walking Scotties; mobs of tourists in shorts and peaked caps. No one seems particularly interested in the quiet arrival of police at the Stonewall Inn, the street's notorious all-male private dancing club.

When the bars of the old homosexuality were raided, patrons tended to leave the scene as rapidly as possible. The Stonewall's ejected customers, however, young and belligerent, gather on the sidewalk, complaining loudly. Passersby linger. "Pig cops!" a boy shouts, and the cry is taken up. An empty beer can strikes a patrol car, then another, then rains of cans, bottles and coins. The amazed police quickly lock themselves inside the club, as the mob charges, battering the doors with an uprooted parking meter. One boy throws lighter fluid inside the club, then a lighted match. Sirens scream as dozens of police materialize. By the time the sidewalks are cleared and the crowds dispersed, it is nearly dawn.

The next day, Saturday, the Village, all its sexes, can talk of nothing else. The police have told reporters that they closed the Stonewall only because it had refused to apply for a liquor license. This statement is widely doubted. The Mattachine Society, in a hastily mimeographed pamphlet, charges the SLA and the police with renewed homosexual harassment, and vows retribution. Rumors fly up and down Christopher—that the demonstration was instigated by the

SDS, the CLU, the Black Panthers, the White Panthers, the Pink Panthers, rival bars, and a homosexual police officer whose roommate went dancing at the Stonewall against the officer's wishes. On the club's battered facade, someone has scrawled, in chalk, "GAY POWER." The movement has a motto.

Disturbances continue for a week. Each evening by sundown the sidewalks overflow, with earnest liberal couples from uptown, with middle-aged homosexuals in from Fire Island, looking nervous and bewildered, with pugnacious pairs of young men, some holding hands, their eyes bright with new resolve. "Gay Power!" they shout, defying the swarms of Tactical Police. "Gay Power!" echo delighted neighborhood children, circling on bicycles. It is rumored that the now-ubiquitous "Equality for Homosexuals" stickers, printed by the Mattachine in snappy Day-Glo blue and fuchsia, have been attached surreptitiously by night to the patrol cars parked outside the Sixth Precinct, on Charles Street. The Stonewall, deferring to its new notoriety, strings a double strand of bright bulbs from its roof to the sign over its door. On Waverly Place, a crowd gathers to witness a sidewalk debate between a portly man in a white shirt and a boy in an acid-green tank top and long unkempt red hair tangled like a fright wig. The man seems to be trying to speak for his Village neighbors, heterosexual; he has been talking to everyone on the block, he is saying, and the straight residents sympathize with the oppressed homosexual, but the boy will not listen. "The hell you say!" he shouts. "You don't impress me. *You* are straight and *you* are my enemy! Don't give me that phony liberal bull. *You* made the laws! Nixon's silent army!"

The audience laughs. He leans close to his opponent, his face turning deep red. "Now *we* are gonna get *you*!"

The man looks ashen, quite frightened. Clearly, he would like to escape, but fears the boy's reaction.

"I was in Vietnam, man, how does that grab you? Huh? Huh? Two Congressional Medals! And, man, I'll screw your daughter. *But I'll screw your son first!*"

He does not appear at the town meeting called by the Mattachine after the July Fourth weekend, but he is there in spirit. It is to be an open forum, held in St. John's in the Village Episcopal Church, on Waverly, in a huge, low-ceilinged room, its floors gently scarred by countless chicken suppers. The air is heavy and unwelcoming, like that of a winter-clothes closet opened in summer. Rows of funeral-parlor chairs hold at least two hundred people, most of them male, and young. They fan themselves with Mattachine handbills, yawning; the proceedings have not begun auspiciously. A thin, motherly woman has stood before them, introduced herself as Mrs. Cervantes, the Mattachine's secretary, and said that Dick Leitsch will be late.

"Now I, personally, am not gay," she continues, smiling as if she addressed a garden club or cooking class, "but believe me, *your* cause is *my* cause."

"*What* cause?" an older man with yellow-grey curls whispers sideways. His friend, who holds a tiny, agitated terrier in his lap like a muff, shrugs, making a moue. The whites of his eyes are gin-red. What, they seem to be asking, are these children so concerned about? *We* are satisfied with things as they are. Our bars have always been raided. It is our cross. We go to other bars, and, like Judy, keep on smiling. What are *we* doing here? There must be an *All About Eve* re-

vival somewhere in town. *What* cause?

Dick Leitsch, in a staid brown suit, strides to the front. From a distance, he looks somewhat like a dependable, fortyish Cartier salesclerk. Mrs. Cervantes steps aside. With professional aplomb, he reopens the meeting. Police brutality and heterosexual indifference must be protested, he asserts; at the same time, the gay world must retain the favor of the Establishment, especially those who make and change the laws. Homosexual acceptance will come slowly, by educating the straight community, with grace and good humor and. . . .

A tense boy with leonine hair is suddenly on his feet. "We don't want acceptance, goddamn it! We want respect! Demand it! We're through hiding in dark bars behind Mafia doormen. We're going to go where straights go and do anything with each other they do and if they don't like it, well, *fuck them!* And if some of us enjoy a little group sex at the docks or in the subways we're going to have it without apologizing to anybody! Straights don't have to be ashamed of anything sexy they happen to feel like doing in public, and neither do we! We're through cringing and begging like a lot of nervous old nellies at Cherry Grove!"

The men with the terrier wince. So does Dick Leitsch.

"We're going to protest in front of St. Patrick's," another boy calls. "The Catholics have put us down long enough!"

"If every homosexual in New York boycotted Bloomingdale's, they'd be out of business in two weeks!"

"Well, now, *I* think," says Mrs. Cervantes, "that what we ought to have is a gay vigil, in a park. Carry candles, perhaps. A peaceful vigil. I think we should be firm, but just as amicable and sweet as. . . ."

"Sweet!" The new speaker resembles Billy the Kid. He is James Fouratt, New Left celebrity, seminarian *manqué,* the radical who burned the real money on the floor of the New York Stock Exchange as a war protest.

"Sweet! *Bullshit!* There's the stereotype homo again, man! Soft, weak, sensitive! Bullshit! That's the role society has been forcing these queens to play, and they just sit and accept it. We have got to radicalize, man! Why? Because as long as we accept getting fired from jobs because we are gay, or not being hired at all, or being treated like second-class citizens, we're going to remain neurotic and screwed up. No matter what you do in bed, if you're not a man out of it, you're going to be screwed up. Be proud of what you are, man! And if it takes riots or even guns to show them what we are, well, that's the only language that the pigs understand!"

Wild applause. The handbills fall to the floor.

Dick Leitsch tries to reply, but Fouratt shouts him down.

"All the oppressed have got to unite! The system keeps us all weak by keeping us separate. Do you realize that not one straight radical group showed up during all those nights of rioting? If it had been a black demonstration. they'd have been there. We've got to work together with *all* the New Left."

A dozen impassioned boys are on their feet, cheering. They are the new radicals who will rally in Washington Square, and lead a mass march down Sixth Avenue, halting astonished traffic, carrying the lavender "Gay Power" banner, chanting "Gay Power to Gay People," singing *We Shall Overcome* solemnly in Sheridan Square.

Again and again, Dick Leitsch tugs frantically at his clean white tie, shouting for the floor, scream- for order. He is firmly ignored.

WARREN HINCKLE
A Social History of the Hippies

To some observers, the hippies are a fad, creatures of the mass media and helpless victims of the violence and exploitation that surround their fragile communities. To others, they are a new departure, the ''greening of America,'' experimenting with the sensibilities and living-styles of the future. There is evidence for both views. Haight-Ashbury, the hippie mecca in 1967, was a shambles a year later, and the hippies themselves urged other youths not to follow them there. On the other hand, young workers on the Ford asembly lines now wear love beads and refuse overtime work if they have enough money for the week. College students have donned the hippie uniform and have turned from their studies to a cultivation of their sensibilities. Acid rock, the use of drugs, and the desire to experiment with new forms of community—all marks of the hippie style—have spread to an ever wider public among young people and sometimes to the not so young.

When Hinckle studied them in 1967, the hippies were still essentially pastoral. Their attraction was that they offered a way station in which young people could discover themselves in an interlude free from the pressures of life. But Hinckle recognized that there was an implicit politics in the hippie life style. A year later it was manifested by the Yippies at the Chicago Democratic convention. The quietism of Haight-Ashbury, with its large-scale rejection of values characteristic of the established society, also contained within it the potential for an active politics of rage, an emotional rejection of the institutions by which the nation is governed. After 1968, the hippies were no longer pastoral: they had entered the mainstream of American society.

An elderly school bus, painted like a fluorescent Easter egg in orange, chartreuse, cerise, white, green, blue and, yes, black, was parked outside the solitary mountain cabin, which made it an easy guess that Ken Kesey, the novelist turned psychedelic Hotspur, was inside. So, of course, was Neal Cassady, the Tristram Shandy of the Beat Generation, prototype hero of Jack Kerouac's *On The Road*, who had sworn off allegiance to Kerouac when the beat scene became menopausal and signed up as the driver of Kesey's fun and games bus, which is rumored to run on LSD. Except for these notorious luminaries, the Summit Meeting of the leaders of the new hippie subculture, convened in the lowlands of California's High Sierras during an early spring weekend last month, seemed a little like an Apalachin Mafia gathering without Joe Bananas.

Where was Allen Ginsberg, father goddam to two generations of the underground? In New York, reading his poetry to freshmen. And where was Timothy Leary, self-styled guru to tens or is it hundreds of thousands of turned-on people? Off some nowhere place like Stockton, to preach the gospel of Lysergic Acid Diethylamide to nice ladies in drip-dry dresses.

The absence of the elder statesmen of America's synthetic gypsy movement meant something. It meant that the leaders of the booming psychedelic bohemia in the seminal city of San Francisco were their own men—and strangely serious men, indeed, for hippies. Ginsberg and Leary may be Pied Pipers, but they are largely playing old tunes. The young men who make the new scene accept Ginsberg as a revered observer from the elder generation; Leary they abide as Elmer Gantry on their side, to be used for proselytizing squares only.

The mountain symposium had been called for the extraordinary purpose of discussing the political future of the hippies. Hippies are many things, but most prominently the bearded and beaded inhabitants of the Haight-Ashbury, a little psychedelic city-state edging Golden Gate Park.

There, in a daily street-fair atmosphere, upwards of 15,000 unbonded girls and boys interact in a tribal, love-seeking, free-swinging, acid-based type of society where, if you are a hippie and you have a dime, you can put it in a parking meter and lie down in the street for an hour's suntan (30 minutes for a nickel) and most drivers will be careful not to run you over.

Speaking, sometimes all at once, inside the Sierra cabin were many voices of conscience and vision of the Haight-Ashbury—belonging to men who, except for their Raggedy Andy hair, paisley shirts and pre-mod western levi jackets, sounded for all the world like Young Republicans.

They talked about reducing governmental controls, the sanctity of the individual, the need for equality among men. They talked, very seriously, about the kind of society they wanted to live in, and the fact that if they wanted an ideal world they would have to go out and make it for themselves, because nobody, least of all the government, was going to do it for them.

The utopian sentiments of these hippies were not to be put down lightly. Hippies have a

Scene from the musical *Hair*.

clear vision of the ideal community—a psychedelic community, to be sure—where everyone is turned on and beautiful and loving and happy and floating free. But it is a vision that, despite the Alice in Wonderland phraseology hippies usually breathlessly employ to describe it, necessarily embodies a radical political philosophy: communal life, drastic restriction of private property, rejection of violence, creativity before consumption, freedom before authority, de-emphasis of government and traditional forms of leadership.

Despite a disturbing tendency to quietism, all hippies *ipso facto* have a political posture—one of unremitting opposition to the Establishment which insists on branding them criminals because they take LSD and marijuana, and hating them, anyway, because they enjoy sleeping nine in a room and three to a bed, seem to have free sex and guiltless minds, and can raise healthy children in dirty clothes.

The hippie choice of weapons is to love the Establishment to death rather than protest it or blow it up (hippies possess a confounding disconcern about traditional political methods or issues). But they are decidedly and forever outside the Consensus on which this society places such a premium, and since the hippie scene is so much the scene of those people under 25 that *Time* magazine warns will soon constitute half our population, this is a significant political fact.

This is all very solemn talk about people who like to skip rope and wear bright colors, but after spending some time with these fun and fey individuals you realize that, in a very unexpected way, they are as serious about what they're doing as the John Birch Society or the Junior League. It is not improbable, after a few more mountain seminars by those purposeful young men wearing beads, that the Haight-Ashbury may spawn the first utopian collectivist community since Brook Farm.

That this society finds it so difficult to take such rascally looking types seriously is no doubt the indication of a deep-rooted hang-up. But to comprehend the psychosis of America in the computer age, you have to know what's with the hippies.

KEN KESEY—I

Games People Play, Merry Prankster Division

Let us go, then, on a trip.

You can't miss the Tripmaster: the thick-necked lad in the blue and white striped pants with the red belt and the golden eagle buckle, a watershed of wasted promise in his pale blue eyes, one front tooth capped in patriotic red, white and blue, his hair downy, flaxen, straddling the incredibly wide divide of his high forehead like two small toupees pasted on sideways. Ken Kesey, Heir Apparent Number One to the grand American tradition of blowing one's artistic talent to do some other thing, was sitting in a surprisingly comfortable chair inside the bus with the psychedelic crust, puffing absentmindedly on a harmonica.

The bus itself was ambulatory at about 50 miles an hour, jogging along a back road in sylvan Marin County, four loudspeakers turned all the way up, broadcasting both inside and outside Carl Orff's Carmina Burana and filled with two dozen people simultaneously smoking marijuana and looking for an open ice cream store. It was the Thursday before the Summit Meeting weekend and Kesey, along with some 15 members of the turned-on yes men and women who call him "Chief" and whom he calls the "Merry Pranksters" in return, was demonstrating a "game" to a delegation of visiting hippie firemen.

Crossing north over the Golden Gate Bridge from San Francisco to Marin County to pay Kesey a state visit were seven members of The Diggers, a radical organization even by Haight-Ashbury standards, which exists to give things away, free. The Diggers started out giving out free food, free clothes, free lodging and free legal advice, and hope eventually to create a totally free cooperative community. They had come to ask Kesey to get serious and attend the weekend meeting on the state of the nation of the hippies.

The dialogue had hardly begun, however, before Kesey loaded all comers into the bus and pushed off into the dark to search for a nocturnal ice cream store. The bus, which may be the closest modern man has yet come to aping the self-sufficiency of Captain Nemo's submarine, has its own power supply and is equipped with instruments for a full rock band, microphones, loudspeakers, spotlights and comfortable seats all around. The Pranksters are presently installing microphones every three feet on the bus walls so everybody can broadcast to everybody else all at once.

At the helm was the Intrepid Traveler, Ken Babbs, who is auxiliary chief of the Merry Pranksters when Kesey is out of town or incommunicado or in jail, all three of which he has recently been. Babbs, who is said to be the model for the heroes of both Kesey novels, *One Flew Over the Cuckoo's Nest* and *Sometimes A Great Notion*, picked up a microphone to address the guests in the rear of the bus, like the driver of a Grayline tour: "We are being followed by a police car. Will someone watch and tell me when he turns on his red light."

The law was not unexpected, of course, because any cop who sees Kesey's bus just about *has* to follow it, would probably end up with some form of profes-

Conversation piece. *(Ken Heyman)*

sional DT's if he didn't. It is part of the game: the cop was now playing on their terms, and Kesey and his Pranksters were delighted. In fact, a discernible wave of disappointment swept across the bus when the cop finally gave up chasing this particular UFO and turned onto another road.

The games he plays are very important to Kesey. In many ways his intellectual rebellion has come full circle; he has long ago rejected the structured nature of society—the foolscap rings of success, conformity and acceptance "normal" people must regularly jump through. To the liberated intellect, no doubt, these requirements constitute the most sordid type of game. But, once rejecting all the norms of society, the artist is free to create his own structures—and along with any new set of rules, however personal, there is necessarily, the shell of the tortoise, a new set of games. In Kesey's case, at least, the games are

usually fun. Running around the outside of an insane society, the healthiest thing you can do is laugh.

It helps to look at this sort of complicated if not confused intellectual proposition in bas relief, as if you were looking at the simple pictures on Wedgwood china. Stand Successful Author Ken Kesey off against, say, Successful Author Truman Capote. Capote, as long as his game is accepted by the system, is free to be as mad as he can. So he tosses the biggest, most vulgar ball in a long history of vulgar balls, and achieves the perfect idiot synthesis of the upper-middle and lower-royal classes. Kesey, who cares as much about the system as he does about the Eddie Cantor Memorial Forest, invents his own game. He purchases a pre-40's International Harvester school bus, paints it psychedelic, fills it with undistinguished though lovable individuals in varying stages of eccentricity, and drives bra-

zenly down the nation's highways, high on LSD, watching and waiting for the cops to blow their minds.

At the least, Kesey's posture has the advantage of being intellectually consistent with the point of view of his novels. In *One Flew Over the Cuckoo's Nest,* he uses the setting of an insane asylum as a metaphor for what he considers to be the basic insanity, or at least the fundamentally bizarre illogic, of American society. Since the world forces you into a game that is both mad and unfair, you are better off inventing your own game. Then, at least, you have a chance of winning. At least that's what Kesey thinks.

KEN KESEY—II

The Curry Is Very Hot; Merry Pranksters Are Having Pot

There wasn't much doing on late afternoon television, and the Merry Pranksters were a little restless. A few were turning on;

one Prankster amused himself squirting his friends with a yellow plastic watergun; another staggered into the living room, exhausted from peddling a bicycle in ever-diminishing circles in the middle of the street. They were all waiting, quite patiently, for dinner, which the Chief was whipping up himself. It was a curry, the recipe of no doubt cabalistic origin. Kesey evidently took his cooking seriously, because he stood guard by the pot for an hour and a half, stirring, concentrating on the little clock on the stove that didn't work.

There you have a slice of domestic life, February 1967, from the swish Marin County home of Attorney Brian Rohan. As might be surmised, Rohan is Kesey's attorney, and the novelist and his *aides de camp* had parked their bus outside for the duration. The duration might last a long time, because Kesey has dropped out of the hippie scene. Some say that he was pushed, because he fell, very hard, from favor among the hippies last year when he announced that he, Kesey, personally, was going to help reform the psychedelic scene. This sudden social conscience may have had something to do with beating a jail sentence on a compounded marijuana charge, but when Kesey obtained his freedom with instructions from the judge "to preach an anti-LSD warning to teenagers" it was a little too much for the Haight-Ashbury set. Kesey, after all, was the man who had turned on the Hell's Angels.

That was when the novelist was living in La Honda, a small community in the Skyline mountain range overgrown with trees and, after Kesey invited the Hell's Angels to several house parties, overgrown with sheriff's deputies. It was in this Sherwood Forest setting, after he had finished his second novel with LSD as his co-pilot, that Kesey inaugurated his band of Merry Pranksters (they have an official seal from the State of California incorporating them as "Intrepid Trips, Inc."), painted the school bus in glow sock colors, announced he would write no more ("Rather than write, I will ride buses, study the insides of jails, and see what goes on"), and set up funtime housekeeping on a full-time basis with the Pranksters, his wife and their three small children (one confounding thing about Kesey is the amorphous quality of the personal relationships in his entourage— the several attractive women don't seem, from the outside, to

Digger Free Store, New York City, 1967. *(Shelly Rusten)*

belong to any particular man; children are loved enough, but seem to be held in common).

When the Hell's Angels rumbled by, Kesey welcomed them with LSD. "We're in the same business. You break people's bones, I break people's heads," he told them. The Angels seem to like the whole acid thing, because today they are a fairly constant act in the Haight-Ashbury show, while Kesey has abdicated his role as Scoutmaster to fledgling acid heads and exiled himself across the Bay. This self-imposed Elba came about when Kesey sensed that the hippie community had soured on him. He had committed the one mortal sin in the hippie ethic: *telling* people what to do. "Get into a responsibility bag," he urged some 400 friends attending a private Halloween party. Kesey hasn't been seen much in the Haight-Ashbury since that night, and though the Diggers did succeed in getting him to attend the weekend discussion, it is doubtful they will succeed in getting the novelist involved in any serious effort to shape the Haight-Ashbury future. At 31, Ken Kesey is a hippie has-been.

KEN KESEY——III

The Acid Tests—from Unitarians to Watts

Kesey is now a self-sufficient but lonely figure—if you can be lonely with dozens of Merry Pranksters running around your house all day. If he ever gets maudlin, which is doubtful, he can look back fondly on his hippie memories, which are definitely in the wow! category, because Ken Kesey did for acid roughly what Johnny Appleseed did for trees, and probably more.

He did it through a unique and short-lived American institution called the Acid Test. A lot of things happened at an Acid Test, but the main thing was that, in the Haight-Ashbury vernacular, everyone in the audience got zonked out of their minds on LSD. LSD in Pepsi. LSD in coffee. LSD in cake. LSD in the community punch. Most people were generally surprised, because they didn't know they were getting any LSD until it was too late. Later, when word got around that this sort of mad thing was happening at Acid Tests, Kesey sometimes didn't give out LSD on purpose, just so people wouldn't know whether they did or did not have LSD. Another game.

The Acid Test began calmly enough. In the early versions Kesey merely gave a heart-to-heart psychedelic talk and handed LSD around like the Eucharist, which first happened at a Unitarian conference in Big Sur in August of 1965. He repeated this ritual several times, at private gatherings in his home in La Honda, on college campuses, and once at a Vietnam Day Committee rally at Berkeley. Then Kesey added the Grateful Dead, a pioneer San Francisco rock group, to his Acid Tests and, the cherry on the matzos, the light show atmospheric technique of projecting slides and wild colors on the walls during rock dances. This combination he called "trips." Trip is the word for an LSD experience, but in Kesey's lexicon it also meant kicks, which were achieved by rapidly changing the audience's sensory environment what seemed like approximately ten million times during an evening by manipulating bright colored lights, tape recorders, slide projectors, weird sound machines, and whatever else may be found in the electronic sink, while the participants danced under stroboscopic lights to a wild rock band or just played around on the floor.

It was a fulgurous, electronically orgiastic thing (the most advanced Tests had closed circuit television sets on the dance floor so you could see what you were doing), which made psychedelics very "fun" indeed, and the hippies came in droves. Almost every hippie in the Bay area went to at least one Acid Test, and it is not exceeding the bounds of reasonable speculation to say that Kesey may have turned on at least 10,000 people to LSD during the 24 presentations of the Acid Test. (During these Tests the Merry Pranksters painted everything including themselves in fluorescent tones, and bright colors became the permanent in-thing in psychedelic dress.)

Turning so many unsuspecting people on to LSD at once could be dangerous, as the Pranksters discovered on a 1965 psychedelic road show when they staged the ill-fated Watts Acid Test. Many of the leading citizens of Watts came to the show, which was all very fine except that whoever put the LSD in the free punch that was passed around put in too much by a factor of about four. This served to make for a very wild Acid Test, and one or two participants "freaked out" and had a very hard time of it for the next few days.

After the California legislature played Prohibition and outlawed LSD on October 6, 1966, Kesey wound up the Acid Test with what was billed as a huge "Trips Festival" in San Francisco. People who regularly turn on say the Trips Festival was a bore: it embodied all the Acid Test elements except acid and, happily for the coffers of Intrepid Trips, Inc., attracted a huge crowd of newspapermen, narcotics agents and other squares, but very few hippies. The Merry Pranksters slyly passed out plain sugar cubes for the benefit of the undercover agents.

Suddenly San Francisco, which for a grown-up city gets excited very easily, was talking about almost nothing but "trips" and

LSD. Hippies, like overnight, had become fashionable.

If you are inclined to give thanks for this sort of thing, they go to the bad boy wonder of Psychedelphia, disappearing there over the horizon in his wayward bus.

HISTORIAN
CHESTER ANDERSON—I

The Ghosts of Scenes Past, or How We Got Here from There

Like Frederick J. Turner and Arnold Toynbee, Chester Anderson has a theory of history. His theory is psychedelic, but that is perfectly natural since he is a veteran acid head. Anderson, a 35-year-old professional bohemian who looks 45, considers himself the unofficial historian of the psychedelic movement and has amassed enough footnotes to argue somewhat convincingly that the past 15 years of social change in the United States—all the underground movements, and a significant part of the cultural changes—have been intimately connected with drugs.

If he is going to press his argument all the way, he may have to punch it out with Marshall McLuhan, who no doubt would assert that such phenomena as hippie colonies are nothing but a return to "tribal" culture, an inevitable reaction to our electronic age. And any social historian worth his salt will put it that every society has found some way to allow the sons and daughters of its middle class to drop out and cut up (most hippies, by the way, are from middle-class stock, so what's the difference from, say, the Teddy Boys?). Maybe lots, maybe none. But there is no disputing the cultural and artistic flipflops this country has gone through in the last decade. The jazz musicians' vogue meant something. So did the Beat Generation. So, we suppose, did Pop Art, and Rock and Roll,

and so, of course, the hippies. If, in briefly tracing the derivation of the hippies from their seminal reasons in the intellectual uneasiness of the early 1950s, we chance to favor the testimony of Chester Anderson, it is only because he was there.

That was some bad year, 1953. There was a war on in Korea, a confusing, undefined war, the first big American war that wasn't the one to end all wars, because the aftermath of World War II had blown that phobia. And now the Bomb was with us, and with it the staccato series of disturbing headline events that stood for the Cold War; college was the only escape from the draft, but eggheads were becoming unpopular; Stevenson had lost the election and the Rosenbergs had been executed. It was all gloom, gloom, and dullsville, and if you were young and intellectual you were hard-pressed to find a hero or even a beautiful person. The only really alive, free thing, it seemed, was jazz—and the arrival of the long playing record had sparked a jazz renaissance, and with it the first drug heroes; most kids sympathized with Gene Krupa's marijuana busts, the agony of Lady Day's junk hangup was universal, and Charlie Parker had his own drugstore.

Lady Day's way wasn't the way of the new generation, Chester Anderson will be quick to tell you, because she was on "body" drugs. Whatever else body drugs—heroin, opium, barbiturates, alcohol, tranquilizers —may do, they eventually turn you off, and contemporary heads like to be turned on—i.e., senses intensified, stimulated rather than depressed. "Head" drugs, which do the latter, are both cheaper and easier to get than body drugs, and come in approximately 18 varieties in three different classifications—natural drugs like marijuana, hashish, peyote, morning glory seeds, Hawaiian wood rose

seeds, and certain types of Mexican mushrooms; artificial psychedelics like mescaline, LSD, psilocybin and psilocin, and whatever the ingredient is that makes Romilar cough syrup so popular with young heads; and synthetic stimulants which, used in large doses by heads are known as "speed"—dexedrine, benzedrine and methedrine.

But in the early 1950s there wasn't such a complete psychedelic medicine shelf to choose from, and the culturally disenchanted pioneers who began to settle new colonies in New York's Village and San Francisco's North Beach had to make do with pot. In a climate dominated by Dwight Eisenhower in the newspapers and Ed Sullivan on television, they also began to turn on to the pacifist, humanist philosophies of Asia—particuly Buddhism, most especially Zen—while Christianity as a workable concept became more meaningless, despite the exemplary efforts of such men as Brother Antoninus and Thomas Merton. American churchmen seemed to have neither the patience nor the fortitude to deal with people who were, well, unsettled. Folk music, which had been slowly dying, perked up a little, and there was a new interest in fresh tuned-in poetry. As the '50s approached middle age and McCarthy went on the rampage, the few signs of life in a stagnant society centered around the disoriented peace movement, the fledgling civil rights movement, the young political left, jazz and folk music, poetry and Zen. Most of these followers were, of course, taking pot, while the rest of the country remained on booze and sleeping pills.

(If, in memory of the 85th anniversary of Anthony Trollope's death; we may be permitted an aside to the reader, it would be to say that one of the things that is considered original, but is in fact not, about the hippies is the concept of "dropping out" of society. Without adopting the histrionics of Hogarth crusading against the masses drinking gin, it is true that alcohol is an opiate which serves to help tens of millions of busy businessmen and lethargic housewives to "drop out" of any essential involvement in life and remain political and artistic boors. But alcohol is legal so nobody cares. If pot and LSD were ever legalized, it would be a mortal blow to this bohemia. Hippies have a political posture essentially because of the enforced criminality of their daily dose, and if taking LSD meant no more in society than the commuter slugging down his seventh martini, the conspiratorial magic would go out of the movement.)

Meanwhile, in San Francisco, Allen Ginsberg remembers an evening in 1955 which could stand as well as any for the starting point of what was to become the most thorough repudiation of America's middlebrow culture since the expatriates walked out on the country in the 1930s. The vanguard of what was to be the Beat Generation had gathered at the 6 Galley on Fillmore Street for a poetry reading moderated by Kenneth Rexroth, a respectable leftish intellectual who was later to become the Public Defender of the Beats. Lawrence Ferlinghetti was in the audience, and so were Kerouac and his then sidekick, Neal Cassady, lis-

tening to Michael McClure, Phil Lamantia, Gary Snyder and Philip Whalen read their poetry. Ginsberg was there too, and delighted everyone with a section of the still unfinished "Howl," better known to Beats as the Declaration of Independence.

Two distinct strains in the underground movement of the '50s were represented at this salient gathering. One was a distinctly fascist trend, embodied in Kerouac, which can be recognized by a totalitarian insistence on action and nihilism, and usually accompanied by a Superman con-

cept. This strain runs, deeper and less silent, through the hippie scene today. It is into this fascist bag that you can put Kesey and his friends, the Hell's Angels, and, in a more subtle way, Dr. Timothy Leary.

The other, majority, side of the Beats was a cultural reaction to the existential brinkmanship forced on them by the Cold War, and a lively attack on the concurrent rhetoric of complacency and self-satisfaction that pervaded the literary establishment all the way from the Atlantic Monthly to Lionel Trilling. Led

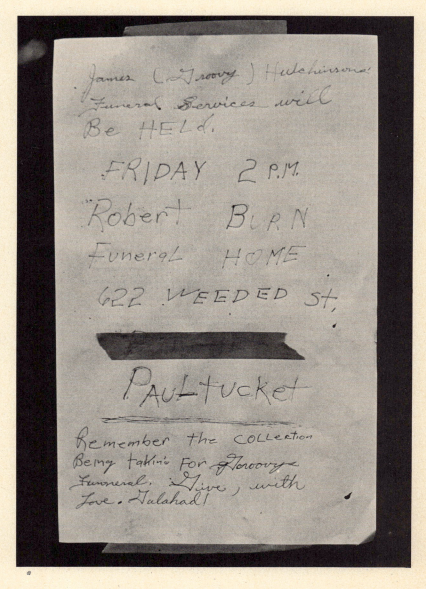

The murder of James (Groovy) Hutchinson and Linda Fitzpatrick in the East Village, 1967, destroyed the "Love" scene. *(Shelly Rusten)*

by men like Ginsberg and Ferlinghetti, the early Beats weighed America by its words and deeds, and found it pennyweight. They took upon themselves the role of conscience for the machine. They rejected all values and when, in attempting to carve a new creative force, they told America to "go fuck itself," America reacted, predictably, with an obscenity trial.

The early distant warnings of the drug-based culture that would dominate the Haight-Ashbury a decade later were there in the early days of North Beach. Marijuana was as popular as Coke at a Baptist wedding, and the available hallucinogens—peyote and mescaline—were part of the Beat rebellion. Gary Snyder, poet, mountain climber, formal Yamabushi Buddhist, and a highly respected leader of the hippie scene today, first experimented with peyote while living with the Indian tribe of the same name in 1948; Ginsberg first took it in New York in 1951; Lamantia, Kerouac and Cassady were turned on by Beat impresario Hymie D'Angolo at his Big Sur retreat in 1952. And Beat parties, whether they served peyote, marijuana or near beer, were rituals, community sacraments, setting the format for contemporary hippie rituals.

But the psychedelic community didn't really begin to flourish until late 1957 and 1958 in New York, and for that story we take you to Chester Anderson in the Village.

HISTORIAN
CHESTER ANDERSON—II

Was the Kingston Trio Really Red Guards?

On Thanksgiving Day, 1957, Chester Anderson was turned on to grass by a bongo-playing superhippie who went by the code name of Mr. Sulks. Grass, if you don't know and don't have an underground glossary handy, is translated marijuana, and from that day forward, Anderson, who once studied music at the University of Miami so he could write string quartets like Brahms, became a professional Turn-On and migrated with bohemia, east to west to east to west, from the Village to North Beach back to the Village to the Haight-Ashbury, where he can be found today—a prototype of the older psychedelic type who mixes with the drifting, turning on kids to form the central nervous system of any body of hippies.

The first psychedelic drug to reach the Village in any quantity was peyote, an obscure hallucinatory cactus bud used by Indians in religious ceremonies. Peyote was cheap and plentiful (it can still be ordered by mail from Laredo at $10 for 100 "buttons") and became highly touted—Havelock Ellis and Aldous Huxley recommended it. The only problem with peyote was that it tasted absolutely terrible, and, as peyote cults sprang up, peyote cookbooks came out with recipes for preparing the awful stuff in ways that would kill the taste. "Man," Chester recalls a head telling him at the time, "if I thought it'd get me high, I'd eat shit." As with most new head drugs, the taking of peyote was treated as a quasi-religious event. The first time Chester took it, he did so with great ritual before a statue of the Buddha.

Peyote was the thing in late 1957, and by the summer of 1958 mescaline, the first synthetic psychedelic, was widely distributed. The heads reacted like unwed mothers being handed birth control pills—they were no longer dependent on nature. Turn-ons could be *manufactured!*

According to Chester's files, LSD didn't arrive in any large, consumer-intended supply in the Village until the winter of 1961–1962, and not in the Bay Area until the summer of 1964, but by that time something unusual had happened to America's psychedelic gypsies: they had become formal enemies of the State. Massive harassment by the cops in San Francisco, by the coffeehouse license inspectors in New York, had led the heads and the young middle-class types who came in caravan proportions, to test the no-more-teachers, no-more-books way of bohemian life, to view the Establishment as the bad guy who would crush their individuality and spirituality in any way he could. This is the derivation of whatever political posture the hippies have today. It will be significant, of course, only if the Haight-Ashbury scene doesn't go the way of the Beat Generation—assimilated by a kick-hungry society. For the serious, literary Beats, it was all over but the shouting when the Co-existence Bagel Shop became a stop on sightseeing tours.

In 1962, the Village was pulsating with psychedelic evangelism. LSD was so cheap and so plentiful that it became a big thing among heads to turn on new people as fast as they could give LSD away.

Pot, also, was being used more widely than ever by middle-class adults, and spread from the urban bohemias to the hinterlands by small folk music circles that were to be found everywhere from Jacksonville, Florida, to Wausau, Wisconsin. At the same time, almost the entire Village was treating LSD like it was a selection on a free lunch counter, and a scruffy folknik called Bobby Dylan was beginning to play charitable guest sets in the Washington Square coffeehouses. "Things," Chester said, "were happening more rapidly than we knew."

What was happening, Mr. Jones, was that folk music, under the influence of early acid culture, was giving way to rock and roll. Rock spread the hippie way of life like a psychedelic plague,

and it metamorphosed in such rapid fashion from the popularity of folk music, that a very suspicious person might ask if seemingly safe groups like the Kingston Trio were not, in fact, the Red Guards of the hippie cultural revolution.

There was a rock and roll before, of course, but it was all bad seed. The likes of Frankie Avalon, Fabian and Elvis Presley sent good rock and roll musicians running to folk music. Then absolutely the world's greatest musical blitz fell and the Beatles landed, everywhere, all at once. The impact of their popular music was analogous to the Industrial Revolution on the 19th century. They brought music out of the juke box and into the street. The Beatles' ecstatic, alive, electric sound had a total sensory impact, and was inescapably participational. It was "psychedelic music." "The Beatles are a trip," Chester said. Whether the Beatles or Dylan or the Rolling Stones actually came to their style through psychedelic involvement (Kenneth Tynan says a recent Beatles song "Tomorrow Never Knows" is "the best musical evocation of LSD I've ever heard") is not as important as the fact that their songs reflect LSD values—love, life, getting along with other people, and that this type of involving, turn-on music galvanized the entire hippie underground into overt, brassy existence—particularly in San Francisco.

Drug song lyrics may, in fact, be the entire literary output of

Woodstock Festival, 1969.
(Ken Heyman)

Arthur Brown at the Fillmore East, 1968.   *(John Goodwin)*

the hippie generation. The hippies' general disregard for anything as static as a book is a fact over which Chester Anderson and Marshall McLuhan can shake hands. For acid heads are, in McLuhan's phrase, "post-literate." Hippies do not share our written, linear society—they like textures better than surfaces, prefer the electronic to the mechanical, like group, tribal activities. Theirs is an ecstatic, do-it-now culture, and rock and roll is their art form.

THE MERCHANT PRINCES—I
Dr. Leary—Pretender to the Hippie Throne

The suit was Brooks Brothers '59, and the paisley tie J. Press contemporary, but the bone-carved Egyptian mandala hanging around his neck, unless it was made in occupied Japan, had to be at least 2000 years old. Dr. Timothy Leary, B.A. University of Alabama, Ph.D. University of California, LSD Cuernavaca and 86'd Harvard College, was dressed up for a night on the town, but as his devotees say of this tireless proselytizer of the psychedelic cause, it was work, work, work. Tonight Leary was scouting somebody else's act, a Swami's at that, who was turning on the hippies at the Avalon Ballroom by leading them in an hour-long Hindu chant without stopping much for breath. The Avalon is one of the two great, drafty ballrooms where San Francisco hippies, hippie-hangers-on and young hippies-to-be congregate each weekend to participate in the psychedelic rock and light shows that are now as much a part of San Francisco as cable cars and a lot noisier.

This dance was a benefit for the new Swami, recently installed in a Haight-Ashbury storefront, with a fair passage sign from Allen Ginsberg whom he had bumped into in India. The hippies were turning out to see just what the Swami's *schtick* was, but Dr. Leary had a different purpose. He has a vested, professional interest in turning people on, and here was this Swami, trying to do it with just chant, like it was natural childbirth or something.

The word professional is not used lightly. There is a large group of professionals making it by servicing and stimulating the hippie world—in the spirit of the Haight-Ashbury we should refer to these men as merchant princes —and Timothy Leary is the pretender to the throne.

Dr. Leary claims to have launched the first indigenous religion in America. That may very well be, though as a religious leader he is Aimee Semple McPherson in drag. Dr. Leary, who identifies himself as a "prophet," recently played the Bay Area in his LSD road show, where he sold $4 seats to lots of squares but few hippies (Dr. Leary's pitch is to the straight world), showed a technicolor movie billed as simulating an LSD experience (it was big on close-

ups of enlarged blood vessels), burned incense, dressed like a holy man in white cotton pajamas, and told everybody to "turn on, tune in, and drop out."

In case you are inclined to make light of this philosophic advice you should not laugh out loud. Because Dr. Leary is serious about his work, he can not be dismissed as a cross between a white Father Divine and Nietzsche, no matter how tempting the analogy. He has made a substantial historical contribution to the psychedelic scene, although his arrest records may figure more prominently than his philosophy in future hippie histories.

Since, something like Eve, he first bit into the sacred psychedelic mushroom while lounging beside a swimming pool in Cuernavaca, he has been hounded by the consequences of his act. Since Dr. Leary discovered LSD; he has been booted out of Harvard for experimenting a little too widely with it among the undergraduate population, asked to leave several foreign countries for roughly the same reasons, and is now comfortably if temporarily ensconced in a turned-on billionaire friend's estate near Poughkeepsie, New York, while awaiting judicial determination of a 30-year prison sentence for transporting a half-ounce of marijuana across the Rio Grande without paying the Texas marijuana tax, which has not been enforced since the time of the Lone Ranger.

If he were asked to contribute to the "L" volume of the World Book Encyclopedia, Dr. Leary would no doubt sum up his work as "having turned on American culture," though his actual accomplishments are somewhat more prosaic. Together with Richard Alpert, who was to Dr. Leary what Bill Moyers was to President Johnson, Leary wrote an article in May 1962 in, surprise, The Bulletin of the Atomic

Scientists. The article warned that in the event of war, the Russians were likely to douse all our reservoirs with LSD in order to make people so complacent that they wouldn't particularly care about being invaded, and as a civil defense precaution we ought to do it ourselves first—you know, douse our own reservoirs —so that when the reds got *their* chance the country would know just what was coming off. It was back to the old drawing board after that article, but Alpert and Dr. Leary made their main contribution to the incredibly swift spread of LSD through the nation in 1964 by the simple act of publishing a formula for LSD, all that was needed by any enterprising housewife with a B-plus in high school chemistry and an inclination for black market activity. Dr. Leary's religious crusade has been a bust, convert-wise, and not so salutary financially, either, so he announced recently that he was dropping out, himself, to contemplate his navel under the influence. It would be easier to take Dr. Leary seriously if he could overcome his penchant for treating LSD as a patent snake-bite medicine.

An enlightening example of this panacea philosophy is found back among the truss ads in the September 1966 issue of *Playboy*. In the midst of a lengthy interview when, as happens in *Playboy*, the subject got around to sex, Dr. Leary was all answers. "An LSD session that does not involve an ultimate merging with a person of the opposite sex isn't really complete," he said, a facet of the drug he neglected to mention to the Methodist ladies he was attempting to turn on in Stockton, California. But this time, Dr. Leary was out to turn on the *Playboy* audience.

The following selection from the interview is reprinted in its entirety. Italics are *Playboy*'s.

PLAYBOY We've heard that some

women who ordinarily have difficulty achieving orgasm find themselves capable of multiple orgasms under LSD. Is that true?

LEARY In a carefully prepared, loving LSD session, a woman will inevitably have several hundred orgasms.

PLAYBOY Several *hundred*?

LEARY Yes. Several hundred.

After recovering from that intelligence, the *Playboy* interviewer, phrasing the question as diplomatically as possible, asked Dr. Leary if he got much, being such a handsome LSD turn-on figure. Dr. Leary allowed that women were always falling over him, but responded with the decorum of Pope Paul being translated from the Latin: "Any charismatic person who is conscious of his own mythic potency awakens this basic hunger in women and pays reverence to it at the level that is harmonious and appropriate at the time."

Dr. Leary also said that LSD is a "specific *cure* for homosexuality."

The final measurement of the tilt of Dr. Leary's windmill, his no doubt earnest claim to be the prophet of this generation, must be made by weighing such recorded conversations against his frequent and urgent pleas to young people to "drop out of politics, protest, petitions and pickets" and join his "new religion" where, as he said recently:

"You have to be out of your mind to pray."

Perhaps, and quite probably so.

THE MERCHANT PRINCES—II
Where Dun & Bradstreet Fears to Tread

Allen Ginsberg asked 10,000 people to turn towards the sea and chant with him. They all did just that, and then picked up the papers and miscellaneous droppings on the turf of Golden Gate Park's Polo Field and went contentedly home. This was the end of the first Human Be-In,

a gargantuan hippie happening held only for the joy of it in mid-January. The hippie tribes gathered under clear skies with rock bands, incense, chimes, flutes, feathers, candles, banners and drums. Even the Hell's Angels were on their good behavior—announcing that they would guard the sound truck against unspecified evil forces. It was all so successful that the organizers are talking about another be-in this summer to be held at the bottom of the Grand Canyon with maybe 200,000 hippies being-in.

The local papers didn't quite know how to treat this one, except for the *San Francisco Chronicle's* ace society editor Frances Moffat, who ran through the crowd picking out local socialites and taking notes on the fashions.

Mrs. Moffat's intense interest reflects the very in, very marketable character of San Francisco Hippiedom. Relatively high-priced mod clothing and trinket stores are as common in the Haight-Ashbury as pissoirs used to be in Paris. They are run by hippie merchants mostly for square customers, but that doesn't mean that the hippies themselves aren't brand name conscious. Professing a distaste for competitive society, hippies are, contradictorily, frantic consumers. Unlike the Beats, they do not disdain money. Indeed, when they have it, which with many is often, they use it to buy something pretty or pleasureful. You will find only the best hi-fi sets in hippie flats.

In this commercial sense, the hippies have not only accepted assimilation (the Beats fought it, and lost), they have swallowed it whole. The hippie culture is in many ways a prototype of the most ephemeral aspects of the larger American society; if the people looking in from the suburbs want change, clothes, fun, and some lightheadedness

from the new gypsies, the hippies are delivering—and some of them are becoming rich hippies because of it.

The biggest Robber Baron is dance promoter Bill Graham, a Jewish boy from New York who made it big in San Francisco by cornering the hippie bread and circuses concession. His weekend combination rock and roll dances and light shows at the cavernous, creaky old Fillmore Auditorium on the main street of San Francisco's Negro ghetto are jammed every night. Even Andy Warhol played the Fillmore. Although Graham is happy providing these weekend spiritual experiences, he's not trying to be a leader. "I don't want to make cadres, just money," he said. Graham's crosstown competitor is Chet Helms, a rimless-glasses variety hippie from Texas who has turned the pioneer, non-profit San Francisco rock group called The Family Dog, into a very profit-making enterprise at the Avalon Ballroom.

A side-product of the light show dances, and probably the only other permanent manifestation of hippie culture to date, is the revival in a gangbusters way of Art Nouveau poster art. Wes Wilson, who letters his posters in 18, 24 and 36 point Illegible . . . , originated the basic style in posters for the Fillmore dances. Graham found he could make as much money selling posters as dance tickets, so he is now in the poster business, too.

Haight Street, the Fifth Avenue of Hippiedom, is geographically parallel to Golden Gate Park but several blocks uphill, where rows of half vacant store fronts once indicated the gradual decline of a middle-class neighborhood. But all that changed, dramatically, during the past 18 months. Haight Street now looks like the Metropolitan Opera Company backstage on the opening night of Aida. The stores are all occupied, but with mercantile ventures that might give Dun & Bradstreet cause to wonder. Threaded among the older meat markets, discount furniture stores, laundromats and proletarian bars are a variety of leather goods shops, art galleries, mod clothing stores and boutiques specializing in psychedelic paraphernalia like beads, prisms and marijuana pipes, and of course there is the Psychedelic Shop itself.

The Psychedelic Shop is treated as a hippie landmark of sorts, but the Haight-Ashbury scene was percolating long before the Thelin brothers, Ron and Jay, stuffed a disconcertingly modern glass and steel store front full of amulets, psychedelic books, a large stock of the underground press and some effete gadgetry for acid heads. The hippie phenomena began to metamorphose from a personal to a social happening around the fall of 1965 after the kids at Berkeley turned on to LSD, Ken Kesey started holding Acid Tests, and The Family Dog staged its first dance.

Instrumental in spreading the word was the *Chronicle's* highly regarded jazz critic, Ralph J. Gleason. Gleason is read religiously by hippies. Besides explaining to his square readers what is happening, he is also the unofficial arbitrator of good taste in the Haight-Ashbury community. Gleason was quick to tell Ken Kesey, in print, when he was out of line, and did the same for Dr. Leary. Gleason's writing tuned in other members of the *Chronicle* staff, and the extensive, often headline publicity the newspaper gave to the hippie scene (Kesey's return from a self-imposed Mexican exile was treated with the seriousness of a reasonably large earthquake) helped escalate the Haight-Ashbury population explosion.

So there is plenty of business for the hippie merchants, but some of them, like the Thelin brothers, are beginning to wonder where it will all lead. At the prodding of The Diggers, the Thelins are considering making the store a non-profit cooperative that will help "the kids get high and stay high" at low cost. They may also take the same steps with The Oracle, the Haight-Ashbury monthly tabloid. The majority of the hip merchants, however, are very comfortable with the ascending publicity and sales, and have as little vision of what they are helping create than did Alexander Bell when he spilled acid on himself....

EMMETT GROGAN—I

Will the Real Frodo Baggins Please Stand Up?

Except for the obvious fact that he wasn't covered with fur, you would have said to yourself that for sure there was old Frodo Baggins, crossing Haight Street. Frodo Baggins is the hero of the English antiquarian J.R.R. Tolkien's classic trilogy, *Lord of the Rings,* absolutely the favorite book of every hippie, about a race of little people called Hobbits who live somewhere in prehistory in a place called Middle Earth. Hobbits are hedonistic, happy little fellows who love beauty and pretty colors. Hobbits have their own scene and resent intrusion, pass the time eating three or four meals a day and smoke burning leaves of herb in pipes of clay. You can see why hippies would like Hobbits.

The hustling, heroic-looking fellow with the mistaken identity was Emmett Grogan, kingpin of The Diggers and the closest thing the hippies in the Haight-Ashbury have to a real live hero. Grogan, 23, with blond, unruly hair and a fair, freckled Irish face, has the aquiline nose of a leader, but he would prefer to say that he "just presents alter-natives." He is in and out of jail 17 times a week, sometimes busted for smashing a cop in the nose (Grogan has a very intolerant attitude toward policemen), sometimes bailing out a friend, and sometimes, like Monopoly, just visiting. The alternatives he presents are rather disturbing to the hippie bourgeoisie, since he thinks they have no business charging hippies money for their daily needs and should have the decency to give things away free, like The Diggers do, or at least charge the squares and help out the hippies.

Grogan has a very clear view of what freedom means in society ("Why can't I stand on the corner and wait for nobody? Why can't everyone?") and an even clearer view of the social position of the hippie merchants ("They just want to expand their sales, they don't care what happens to people here; they're nothing but goddamn shopkeepers with beards.").

Everyone is a little afraid of Grogan in the Haight-Ashbury, including the cops. A one-man crusade for purity of purpose, he is the conscience of the hippie community. He is also a bit of a daredevil and a madman, and could easily pass for McMurphy, the roguish hero in Kesey's novel set in an insane asylum. There is a bit of J. P. Donleavy's *Ginger Man* in him, too.

A few weeks ago, out collecting supplies for The Diggers' daily free feed, Grogan went into a San Francisco wholesale butcher and asked for soup bones and meat scraps. "No free food here, we work for what we eat," said the head butcher, a tattooed Bulgar named Louie, who was in the icebox flanked by his seven assistant butchers. "You're a fascist pig and a coward," replied Grogan, whom Louie immediately smashed in the skull with the blunt side of a carving knife. That turned out to be a mistake, because the seven assistant butch-

On the bus. *(John Goodwin)*

ers didn't like Louie much, and all jumped him. While all those white coats were grunting and rolling in the sawdust, a bleeding Grogan crawled out with four cardboard boxes full of meat.

This was a typical day in Dogpatch for Grogan, who has had his share of knocks. A Brooklyn boy, he ran away from home at 15 and spent the next six years in Europe, working as a busboy in the Alps, and, later, studying film making in Italy under Antonioni. Grogan had naturally forgotten to register for the draft, so when he returned to the United States he was in the Army four days later. That didn't last long, however, because the first thing Grogan had to do was clean the barracks. His idea of cleaning barracks was to throw all the guns out the window, plus a few of the rusty beds, and artistically displeasing foot lockers. Then he began painting the remaining bed frames yellow. "I threw out everything that was not esthetically pleasing," he told the sergeant.

Two days later Grogan was in the psychiatric ward of Letterman Hospital in San Francisco where he stayed for six months before the authorities decided they couldn't quite afford to keep him. That was shortly after an Army doctor, learning of his film training, ordered Grogan to the photo lab for "work therapy." It was a "beautiful, tremendously equipped lab," Grogan recalls, and since it wasn't used very much, he took a picture of his own big blond face and proceeded to make 5000 prints. When the doctors caught up with

him, he had some 4700 nine by twelve glossies of Emmett Grogan neatly stacked on the floor, and all lab machines: driers, enlargers, developers were going like mad, and the water was running over on the floor. "What did you do *that* for?" a doctor screamed.

Grogan shrugged. "I'm crazy," he said.

He was released a little later, and acted for a while with the San Francisco Mime Troupe, the city's original and brilliant rad-

ical theatre ensemble. Then last fall, when the Negro riots broke out in San Francisco and the National Guard put a curfew on the Haight-Ashbury, the Diggers happened. "Everybody was trying to figure how to react to the curfew. The SDS came down and said ignore it, go to jail. The merchants put up chicken posters saying 'for your own safety, get off the street.' Somehow, none of those ideas seemed right. If you had something to do on the streets, you should do it and tell the cops to go screw off. If you didn't, you might as well be inside."

Something to do, to Grogan, was to eat if you were hungry, so at 8 P.M., at the curfew witching hour, he and an actor friend named Billy Landau set up a delicious free dinner in the park, right under the cops' noses, and the hippies came and ate and have been chowing down, free, every night since. The Haight-Ashbury has never quite been the same.

EMMET GROGAN—II

A Psychedelic "Grapes of Wrath"

Every Bohemian community has its inevitable coterie of visionaries who claim to know what it is all about. But The Diggers are, somehow, different. They are bent on creating a wholly co-operative subculture and, so far, they are not just hallucinating, they are doing it.

Free clothes (used) are there for whoever wants them. Free meals are served every day. Next, Grogan plans to open a smart mod clothing store on Haight Street and give the clothes away free, too (the hippie merchants accused him of "trying to undercut our prices"). He wants to start Digger farms where participants will raise their own produce. He wants to give away free acid, to eliminate junky stuff and end profiteering. He wants co-operative living to forestall inevitable rent exploitation when the Haight-Ashbury becomes chic.

Not since Brook Farm, not since the Catholic Workers, has any group in this dreadfully co-optive, consumer society been so serious about a utopian community.

If Grogan succeeds or fails in the Haight-Ashbury it will not be as important as the fact that he has tried. For he is, at least, providing the real possibility of what he calls "alternatives" in the down-the-rabbit-hole-culture of the hippies.

Grogan is very hung up on freedom. "Do your thing, be what you are, and nothing will ever bother you," he says. His heroes are the Mad Bomber of New York who blissfully blew up all kinds of things around Manhattan over 30 years because he just liked to blow things up, and poet Gary Snyder, whom he considers the "most important person in the Haight-Ashbury" because instead of sitting around sniffing incense and talking about it, he went off to Japan and became a Zen master. "He did it, man."

This is an interesting activist ethic, but it remains doubtful just what the hippies will do. Not that many, certainly, will join Grogan's utopia, because utopias, after all, have a size limit.

The New Left has been flirting with the hippies lately, even to the extent of singing "The Yellow Submarine" at a Berkeley protest rally, but it looks from here like a largely unrequited love.

The hip merchants will, of course, go on making money.

And the youngsters will continue to come to the Haight-Ashbury and do—what?

That was the question put to the hippie leaders at their Summit Meeting. They resolved their goals, but not the means, and the loud noise you heard from outside was probably Emmett Grogan pounding the table with his shoe.

The crisis of the happy hippie ethic is precisely this: it is all right to turn on, but it is not enough to drop out. Grogan sees the issue in the gap "between the radical political philosophy of Jerry Rubin and Mario Savio and psychedelic love philosophy." He, himself, is not interested in the war in Vietnam, but on the other hand he does not want to spend his days like Ferdinand sniffing pretty flowers.

This is why he is so furious at the hip merchants. "They created the myth of this utopia; now they aren't going to do anything about it." Grogan takes the evils of society very personally, and he gets very angry, almost physically sick, when a pregnant 15-year-old hippie's baby starves in her stomach, a disaster which is not untypical in the Haight-Ashbury, and which Grogan sees being repeated ten-fold this summer when upwards of 200,000 migrant teenagers and college kids come, as a psychedelic "Grapes of Wrath," to utopia in search of the heralded turn-on.

The danger in the hippie movement is more than overcrowded streets and possible hunger riots this summer. If more and more youngsters begin to share the hippie political posture of unrelenting quietism, the future of activist, serious politics is bound to be affected. The hippies have shown that it can be pleasant to drop out of the arduous task of attempting to steer a difficult, unrewarding society. But when that is done, you leave the driving to the Hell's Angels.

KENNETH KENISTON
Youth, Change and Violence

The youth culture has tempted journalists and scholars to make easy generalizations. Yet, as Kenneth Keniston points out, the culture is really a composite—of New Left, of hippies, of students. Moreover, within it are important generational differences, for in the speeded-up timetable of life in which we live, five years or less has become a generation—a group with its own experiences and cultural preferences. The discontinuity among groups within the youth culture has prevented the emergence of very many heroes and leaders: those a few years older, however brave and good, have their own thing. And the youth culture eschews sharply etched identities, holding lines of possibility open, refusing to close off the interesting experiences that life might offer.

Keniston had been studying young people, especially college students, long before they became a fashionable subject in the mass media. His analysis of the origins of this culture takes into account most of the factors that commentators have mentioned: the permissiveness of modern parents, the rapidity of change, the revolt against technology, and the unsettling effect of growing up in a world of exceptional violence. And his discussion of the problem of violence belongs in the large category of prophecies about the 1960s that have come true.

We often feel that today's youth are somehow "different." There is something about today's world that seems to give the young a special restlessness, an increased impatience with the "hypocrisies" of the past, and yet an open gentleness and a searching honesty more intense than that of youth in the past. Much of what we see in today's students and nonstudents is of course familiar: to be young is in one sense always the same. But it is also new and different, as each generation confronts its unique historical position and role.

Yet we find it hard to define the difference. Partly the difficulty derives from the elusive nature of youth itself. Still this generation seems even more elusive than most—and that, too, may be one of the differences. Partly the problem stems from the sheer variety and number of "youth" in a society where youth is often protracted into the mid-twenties. No one characterization can be adequate to the drop-outs and stay-ins, hawks and doves, up-tights and cools, radicals and conservatives, heads and seekers that constitute American youth. But although we understand that the young are as various as the old in our complex society, the sense that they are different persists.

In giving today's American youth this special quality and mood, two movements have

Reprinted by permission of Kenneth Keniston. From *American Scholar,* vol. 37 (Spring 1968), 227–245.

played a major role: the New Left and the hippies. Both groups are spontaneous creations of the young; both are in strong reaction to what Paul Goodman calls the Organized System; both seek alternatives to the institutions of middle-class life. Radicals and hippies are also different from each other in numerous ways, from psychodynamics to ideology. The hippie has dropped out of a society he considers irredeemable: his attention is riveted on interior change and the expansion of personal consciousness. The radical has not given up on this society: his efforts are aimed at changing and redeeming it. Furthermore, both "movements" together comprise but a few percent of their contemporaries. But, although neither hippies nor New Leftists are "representative" of their generation, together they are helping to give this generation its distinctive mood. By examining the style of these young men and women, we come closer to understanding what makes their generation "different."

THE STYLE OF POST-MODERN YOUTH

Today's youth is the first generation to grow up with "modern" parents; it is the first "post-modern" generation. This fact alone distinguishes it from previous generations and helps create a mood born out of modernity, affluence, rapid social change and violence. Despite the many pitfalls in the way of any effort

to delineate a post-modern style, the effort seems worth making. For not only in America but in other nations, new styles of dissent and unrest have begun to appear, suggesting the slow emergence of youthful style that is a reflection of and reaction to the history of the past two decades.[1]

In emphasizing "style" rather than ideology, program or characteristics, I mean to suggest that the communalities in post-modern youth groups are to be found in the *way* they approach the world, rather than in their actual behavior, ideologies or goals. Indeed, the focus on process rather than program is itself a prime

[1] In the effort to delineate this style, I have been helped and influenced by Robert J. Lifton's concept of Protean Man. For a summary of his views, see *Partisan Review,* Winter 1968.

characteristic of the post-modern style, reflecting a world where flux is more obvious than fixed purpose. Post-modern youth, at least in America, is very much in process, unfinished in its development, psychologically open to a historically unpredictable future. In such a world, where ideologies come and go, and where revolutionary change is the rule, a style, a *way* of doing things, is more possible to identify than any fixed goals or constancies of behavior.

Fluidity, Flux, Movement. Post-modern youth display a special personal and psychological openness, flexibility and unfinishedness. Although many of today's youth have achieved a sense of inner identity, the term "identity" suggests a fixity, stability and "closure" that many of them

Summer of Love, 1967.
(John Goodwin)

(George Gardner)

are not willing to accept: with these young men and women, it is not always possible to speak of the "normal resolution" of identity issues. Our earlier fear of the ominous psychiatric implications of "prolonged adolescence" must now be qualified by an awareness that in post-modern youth many adolescent concerns and qualities persist long past the time when (according to the standards in earlier eras) they should have ended. Increasingly, post-modern youth are tied to social and historical changes that have not occurred, and that may never occur. Thus, psychological "closure," shutting doors and burning bridges, becomes impossible. The concepts of the personal future and the "life work" are ever more hazily defined; the effort to change oneself, redefine oneself or reform oneself does not cease with the arrival of adulthood.

This fluidity and openness extends through all areas of life. Both hippie and New Left movements are nondogmatic, non-ideological, and to a large extent hostile to doctrine and formula. In the New Left, the focus is on "tactics"; amongst hippies, on simple direct acts of love and communication. In neither group does one find clear-cut long-range plans, life patterns laid out in advance. The vision of the personal and collective future is blurred and vague: later adulthood is left deliberately open. In neither group is psychological development considered complete; in both groups, identity, like history, is fluid and indeterminate. In one sense, of course, identity development takes place; but, in another sense, identity is always undergoing transformations that parallel the transformations of the historical world.

Generational Identification.

Post-modern youth views itself primarily as a part of a generation rather than an organization; they identify with their contemporaries as a group, rather than with elders; and they do not have clearly defined leaders and heroes. Their deepest collective identification is to their own group or "Movement"—a term that in its ambiguous meanings points not only to the fluidity and openness of post-modern youth, but to its physical mobility, and the absence of traditional patterns of leadership and emulation. Among young radicals, for example, the absence of heroes or older leaders is impressive: even those five years older are sometimes viewed with mild amusement or suspicion. And although post-modern youth is often widely read in the "literature" of the New Left or that of consciousness-expansion, no one person or set of people is central to their intellectual beliefs. Although they live together in groups, these groups are without clear leaders.

Identification with a generational movement, rather than a cross-generational organization or a nongenerational ideology, distinguishes post-modern youth from its parents and from the "previous" generation. In addition, it also creates "generational" distinctions involving five years and less. Within the New Left, clear lines are drawn between the "old New Left" (approximate age, thirty), the New Left (between twenty-two and twenty-eight) and the "new New Left" or "young kids" (under twenty-two). Generations, then, are separated by a very brief span; and the individual's own phase of youthful usefulness— for example, as an organizer—is limited to a relatively few years. Generations come and go quickly; whatever is to be accomplished must therefore be done soon.

Generational consciousness also entails a feeling of psychological disconnection from previous generations, their life situations and their ideologies. Among young radicals, there is a strong feeling that the older ideologies are exhausted or irrelevant, expressed in detached amusement at the doctrinaire disputes of the "old Left" and impatience with "old liberals." Among hippies, the irrelevance of the parental past is even greater: if there is any source of insight, it is the time-

less tradition of the East, not the values of the previous generation in American society. But in both groups, the central values are those created in the present by the "Movement" itself.

Personalism. Both groups are highly personalistic in their styles of relationship. Among hippies, personalism usually entails privatism, a withdrawal from efforts to be involved in or to change the wider social world; among young radicals, personalism is joined with efforts to change the

world. But despite this difference, both groups care most deeply about the creation of intimate, loving, open and trusting relationships between small groups of people. Writers who condemn the depersonalization of the modern world, who insist on "I-thou" relationships, or who expose the elements of anger, control and sadism in nonreciprocal relationships, find a ready audience in post-modern youth. The ultimate measure of man's life is the quality of his personal relation-

(George Gardner)

SDS member arguing a point at University of Denver. *(David Cupp)*

ships; the greatest sin is to be unable to relate to others in a direct, face-to-face, one-to-one relationship.

The obverse of personalism is the discomfort created by any nonpersonal, "objectified," professionalized and, above all, exploitative relationship. Manipulation, power relationships, superordination, control and domination are at violent odds with the I-thou mystique. Failure to treat others as fully human, inability to enter into personal relationships with them, is viewed with dismay in others and with guilt in oneself. Even with opponents the goal is to establish intimate confrontations in which the issues can be discussed openly. When opponents refuse to "meet with" young radicals, this produces anger and frequently demonstrations. The reaction of the Harvard Students for a Democratic Society when

Secretary McNamara did not meet with them to discuss American foreign policies is a case in point. Equally important, perhaps the most profound source of personal guilt among post-modern youth is the "hangups" that make intimacy and love difficult.

Nonasceticism. Post-modern youth is nonascetic, expressive and sexually free. The sexual openness of the hippie world has been much discussed and criticized in the mass media. One finds a similar sexual and expressive freedom among many young radicals, although it is less provocatively demonstrative. It is of continuing importance to these young men and women to overcome and move beyond inhibition and puritanism to a greater physical expressiveness, sexual freedom, capacity for intimacy, and ability to enjoy life.

In the era of the Pill, then,

responsible sexual expression becomes increasingly possible outside of marriage, at the same time that sexuality becomes less laden with guilt, fear and prohibition. As asceticism disappears, so does promiscuity: the personalism of post-modern youth requires that sexual expression must occur in the context of "meaningful" human relationships, of intimacy and mutuality. Marriage is increasingly seen as an institution for having children, but sexual relationships are viewed as the natural concomitant of close relationships between the sexes. What is important is not sexual activity itself, but the context in which it occurs. Sex is right and natural between people who are "good to each other," but sexual exploitation—failure to treat one's partner as a person—is strongly disapproved.

Inclusiveness. The search for

personal and organizational inclusiveness is still another characteristic of post-modern youth. These young men and women attempt to include both within their personalities and within their movements every opposite, every possibility and every person, no matter how apparently alien. Psychologically, inclusiveness involves an effort to be open to every aspect of one's feelings, impulses and fantasies, to synthesize and integrate rather than repress and dissociate, not to reject or exclude any part of one's personality or potential. Interpersonally, inclusiveness means a capacity for involvement with, identification with and collaboration with those who are superficially alien: the peasant in Vietnam, the poor in America, the nonwhite, the deprived and deformed. Indeed, so great is the pressure to include the alien, especially among hippies, that the apparently alien is often treated more favorably than the superficially similar: thus, the respect afforded to people and ideas that are distant and strange is sometimes not equally afforded those who are similar be they one's parents or their middle-class values. One way of explaining the reaction of post-modern youth to the war in Vietnam is via the concept of inclusiveness: these young men and women react to events in Southeast Asia much as if they occurred in Newton, Massachusetts, Evanston, Illinois, Harlem, or Berkeley, California: they make little distinction in their reactions to

their fellow Americans and those overseas.

One corollary of inclusiveness is intense internationalism. What matters to hippies or young radicals is not where a person comes from, but what kind of relationship is possible with him. The nationality of ideas matters little: Zen Buddhism, American pragmatism, French existentialism,

Indian mysticism or Yugoslav communism are accorded equal hearings. Interracialism is another corollary of inclusiveness: racial barriers are minimized or nonexistent, and the ultimate expressions of unity between the races, sexual relationships and marriage, are considered basically natural and normal, whatever the social problems they

New Culture. *(Thomas Hoepker, Woodfin Camp, Inc.)*

currently entail. In post-modern youth, then, identity and ideology are no longer parochial or national; increasingly, the reference group is the world, and the artificial subspeciation of the human species is broken down.

Antitechnologism. Post-modern youth has grave reservations about many of the technological aspects of the contemporary world. The depersonalization of life, commercialism, careerism and familism, the bureaucratization and complex organization of advanced nations—all seem intolerable to these young men and women, who seek to create new forms of association and action to oppose the technologism of our day Bigness, impersonality, stratification and hierarchy are rejected, as is any involvement with the furtherance of technological values. In reaction to these values, post-modern youth seeks simplicity, naturalness, personhood and even voluntary poverty.

But a revolt against technologism is only possible, of course, in a technological society; and to be effective, it must inevitably exploit technology to overcome technologism. Thus in post-modern youth, the fruits of technology—synthetic hallucinogens in the hippie subculture, modern technology of communication among young radicals—and the affluence made possible by technological society are a precondition for a post-modern style. The demonstrative poverty of the hippie would be meaningless in a society where poverty is routine; for the radical to work for subsistence wages as a matter of choice is to *have* a choice not available in most parts of the world. Furthermore, to "organize" against the pernicious aspects of the technological era requires high skill in the use of modern technologies of organization: the long-distance telephone, the use of the mass media, high-

New Liturgies. *(Thomas Hoepker, Woodfin Camp, Inc.)*

speed travel, the mimeograph machine and so on. In the end, then, it is not the material but the spiritual consequences of technology that post-modern youth opposes: indeed, in the developing nations, those who exhibit a post-modern style may be in the vanguard of movements toward modernization. What *is* adamantly rejected is the contamination of life with the values of technological organization and production. It seems probable that a comparable rejection of the psychological consequences of current technology, coupled

with the simultaneous ability to exploit that technology, characterizes all dissenting groups in all epochs.

Participation. Post-modern youth is committed to a search for new forms of groups, of organizations and of action where decision-making is collective, arguments are resolved by "talking them out," self-examination, interpersonal criticism and group decision-making are fused. The objective is to create new styles of life and new types of organization that humanize rather than dehumanize, that activate and strengthen the participants rather than undermining or weakening them. And the primary vehicle for such participations is the small, face-to-face primary group of peers.

The search for new participatory forms of organization and action can hardly be deemed successful as yet, especially in the New Left where effectiveness in the wider social and political scene remains to be demonstrated. There are inherent differences between the often taskless, face-to-face group that is the basic form of organization for both hippies and radicals and the task-oriented organization—differences that make it difficult to achieve social effectiveness based solely on small primary groups. But there may yet evolve from the hippie "tribes," small Digger communities and primary groups of the New Left, new forms of association in which self-criticism, awareness of group interaction, and the accomplishment of social and political goals go hand in hand. The effort to create groups in which individuals grow from their participation in the group extends far beyond the New Left and the hippie world; the same search is seen in the widespread enthusiasm for "sensitivity training" groups and even in the increasing use of groups as a therapeutic instrument. Nor is this solely an American search: one sees a similar focus, for example, in the Communist nations, with their emphasis on small groups that engage in the "struggle" of mutual criticism and self-criticism.

The search for effectiveness combined with participation has also led to the evolution of "new" styles of social and political action. The newness of such forms of political action as parades and demonstrations is open to some question; perhaps what is most new is the *style* in which old forms of social action

are carried out. The most consistent effort is to force one's opponent into a personal confrontation with one's own point of view. Sit-ins, freedom rides, insistence upon discussions, silent and nonviolent demonstrations—all have a prime objective to "get through to" the other side, to force reflection, to bear witness to one's own principles and to impress upon others the validity of these same principles. There is much that is old and familiar about this, although few of today's young radicals or hippies are ideologically committed to Gandhian views of nonviolence. Yet the underlying purpose of many of the emerging forms of social and political action, whether they be "human be-ins," "love-ins," peace marches or "teach-ins," has a new motive—hope that by expressing one's own principles, by "demonstrating" one's convictions, one can through sheer moral force win over one's opponents and lure them as well into participating with one's own values.

Antiacademicism. Among post-modern youth, one finds a virtually unanimous rejection of the "merely academic." This rejection is one manifestation of a wider insistence on the relevance, applicability and personal meaningfulness of knowledge. It would be wrong simply to label this trend "anti-intellectual," for many new radicals and not a few hippies are themselves highly intellectual people. What is demanded is that intelligence be engaged with the world, just as action should be informed by knowledge. In the New Left, at least amongst leaders, there is enormous respect for knowledge and information, and great impatience with those who act without understanding. Even amongst hippies, where the importance of knowledge and information is less stressed, it would be wrong simply to identify the rejection of the academic

world and its values with a total rejection of intellect, knowledge and wisdom.

To post-modern youth, then, most of what is taught in schools, colleges and universities is largely irrelevant to living life in the last third of the twentieth century. Many academics are seen as direct or accidental apologists for the Organized System in the United States. Much of what they teach is considered simply unconnected to the experience of post-modern youth. New ways of learning are sought: ways that combine action with reflection upon action, ways that fuse engagement in the world with understanding of it. In an era of rapid change, the accrued wisdom of the past is cast into question, and youth seeks not only new knowledge, but new ways of learning and knowing.

Nonviolence. Finally, post-modern youth of all persuasions meets on the ground of nonviolence. For hippies, the avoidance of and calming of violence is a central objective, symbolized by gifts of flowers to policemen and the slogan, "Make love, not war." And although nonviolence as a philosophical principle has lost most of its power in the New Left, nonviolence as a psychological orientation is a crucial—perhaps *the* crucial—issue. The nonviolence of post-modern youth should not be confused with pacifism: these are not necessarily young men and women who believe in turning the other cheek or who are systematically opposed to fighting for what they believe in. But the basic style of both radicals and hippies is profoundly opposed to warfare, destruction and exploitation of man by man, and to violence whether on an interpersonal or an international scale. Even among those who do not consider nonviolence a good in itself, a psychological inoculation against violence, even a fear of it, is a unifying theme.

The Bomb Factory, Greenwich Village, 1970. *(UPI)*

THE CREDIBILITY GAP:
PRINCIPLE AND PRACTICE

In creating the style of today's youth, the massive and violent social changes of the past two decades have played a central role. Such social changes are not only distantly perceived by those who are growing up, but are immediately interwoven into the texture of their daily lives as they develop. The social changes of the post-war era affect the young in a variety of ways: in particular, they contribute to a special sensitivity to the discrepancy between principle and practice. For during this era of rapid social change the values most deeply embedded in the parental generation and expressed in their behavior in time of crisis are frequently very different from the more "modern" principles,

ideals and values that this generation has professed and attempted to practice in bringing up its children. Filial perception of the discrepancy between practice and principle may help explain the very widespread sensitivity amongst post-modern youth to the "hypocrisy" of the previous generation.

The grandparents of today's twenty-year-olds were generally born at the end of the nineteenth century, and brought up during the pre-World War I years. Heirs of a Victorian tradition as yet unaffected by the value revolutions of the twentieth century, they reared their own children, the parents of today's youth, in families that emphasized respect, the control of impulse, obedience to authority, and the traditional "inner-directed" values of hard work, deferred gratification and self-restraint. Their children, born around the time of the First World War, were thus socialized in families that remained largely Victorian in outlook.

During their lifetimes, however, these parents (and in particular the most intelligent and advantaged among them) were exposed to a great variety of new values that often changed their nominal faiths. During their youths in the 1920s and 1930s, major changes in American behavior and American values took place. For example, the "emancipation of women" in the 1920s, marked by the achievement of suffrage for women, coincided with the last major change in actual sexual behavior in America: during this period, women began to become the equal part-

ners of men, who no longer sought premarital sexual experience solely with women of a lower class. More important, the 1920s and the 1930s were an era when older Victorian values were challenged, attacked and all but discredited, especially in educated middle-class families. Young men and women who went to college during this period (as did most of the parents of those who can be termed "post-modern" today) were influenced outside their families by a variety of "progressive," "liberal," and even psychoanalytic ideas that contrasted sharply with the values of their childhood families. Moreover, during the 1930s, many of the parents of today's upper middle-class youth were exposed to or involved with the ideals of the New Deal, and sometimes to more radical interpretations of man, society and history. Finally, in the 1940s and 1950s, when it came time to rear their own children, the parents of today's elite youth were strongly influenced by "permissive" views of child-rearing that again contrasted sharply with the techniques by which they themselves had been raised. Thus, many middle-class parents moved during their lifetime from the Victorian ethos in which they had been socialized to the less moralistic, more humanitarian, and more "expressive" values of their own adulthoods.

But major changes in values, when they occur in adult life, are likely to be far from complete. To have grown up in a family where unquestioning obedience to parents was expected, but to rear one's own children in an atmosphere of "democratic" permissiveness and self-determination—and never to revert to the practices of one's own childhood—requires a change of values more total and comprehensive than most adults can achieve. Furthermore, behavior that springs from values acquired

in adulthood often appears somewhat forced, artificial or insincere to the sensitive observer. Children, clearly the most sensitive observers of their own parents, are likely to sense a discrepancy between their parents' avowed and consciously-held values and their "basic instincts" with regard to child-rearing. Furthermore the parental tendency to "revert to form" is greatest in times of family crisis, which are of course the times that have the greatest effect upon children. No matter how "genuinely" parents held their "new" values, many of them inevitably found themselves falling back on the lessons of their own childhoods when the chips were down.

In a time of rapid social change, then, a special *credibility gap* is likely to open between the generations. Children are likely to perceive a considerable discrepancy between what their parents avow as their values and the actual assumptions from which parental behavior springs. In many middle-class teen-agers today, for example, the focal issue of adolescent rebellion against parents often seems to be just this discrepancy: the children arguing that their parents' endorsement of independence and self-determination for their children is "hypocritical" in that it does not correspond with the real behavior of the parents when their children actually seek independence. Similar perceptions of parental "hypocrisy" occur around racial matters: for example, there are many parents who in principle support racial and religious equality, but become violently upset when their children date someone from another race or religion. Around political activity similar issues arise. For example, many of the parents of today's youth espouse in principle the cause of political freedom, but are not involved themselves in politics and oppose their children's involvement lest they "jeopardize their record" or "ruin their later career."

Of course, no society ever fully lives up to its own professed ideals. In every society there is a gap between creedal values and actual practices, and in every society, the recognition of this gap constitutes a powerful motor for social change. But in most societies, especially when social change is slow and institutions are powerful and unchanging, there occurs what can be termed *institutionalization of hypocrisy*. Children and adolescents routinely learn when it is "reasonable" to expect that the values people profess will be implemented in their behavior, and when it is not reasonable. There develops an elaborate system of exegesis and commentary upon the society's creedal values, excluding certain people or situations from the full weight of these values, or "demonstrating" that apparent inconsistencies are not really inconsistencies at all. Thus, in almost all societies, a "sincere" man who "honestly" believes one set of values is frequently allowed to ignore them completely, for example, in the practice of his business, in his interpersonal relationships, in dealings with foreigners, in relationships to his children, and so on—all because these areas have been officially defined as exempt from the application of his creedal values.

In a time of rapid social change and value change, however, the institutionalization of hypocrisy seems to break down.

"New" values have been in existence for so brief a period that the exemptions to them have not yet been defined, the situations to be excluded have not yet been determined, and the universal gap between principle and practice appears in all of its nakedness. Thus, the mere fact of a discrepancy between creedal values and practice is not at all unusual. But what is special about the present situation of rapid value change is, first, that parents themselves tend to have two conflicting sets of values, one related to the experience of their early childhood, the other to the ideologies and principles acquired in adulthood; and second, that no stable institutions or rules for defining hypocrisy out of existence have yet been fully evolved. In such a situation, children see the Emperor's nakedness with unusual clarity, recognizing the value conflict within their parents and perceiving clearly the hypocritical gap between creed and behavior.

"Yip-In," New York, 1968.
(*Charles Gatewood*)

This argument suggests that the post-modern youth may not be confronted with an "objective" gap between parental preaching and practice any greater than that of most generations. But they are confronted with an unusual internal ambivalence within the parental generation over the values that parents successfully inculcated in their children, and they are "deprived" of a system of social interpretation that rationalizes the discrepancy between creed and deed. It seems likely, then, that today's youth may simply be able to perceive the universal gulf between principle and practice more clearly than previous generations have done.

This points to one of the central characteristics of post-modern youth: they insist on taking seriously a great variety of political, personal and social principles that "no one in his right mind" ever before thought of attempting to extend to such situations as dealings with strangers, relations between the races, or international politics. For example, peaceable openness has long been a creedal virtue in our society, but it has never been extended to foreigners, particularly with dark skins. Similarly, equality has long been preached, but the "American dilemma" has been resolved by a series of institutionalized hypocrisies that exempted Negroes from the application of this principle. Love has always been a central value in Christian society, but really to love one's enemies—to be generous to policemen, customers, criminals, servants and foreigners—has been considered folly.

These speculations on the credibility gap between the generations in a time of rapid change may help explain two crucial facts about post-modern youth: first, they frequently come from highly principled families with whose principles they continue to agree; second, that they have the outrageous temerity to insist that individuals and societies live by the values they preach. And these speculations may also explain the frequent feeling of those who have worked intensively with student radicals or hippies that, apart from the "impracticality" of some of their views, these sometimes seem to be the only clear-eyed and sane people in a society and a world where most of us are still systematically blind to the traditional gap between personal principle and practice, national creed and policy, a gap that we may no longer be able to afford.

(Ernest Baxter, Black Star)

VIOLENCE: SADISM
AND CATACLYSM

Those who are today in their early twenties were born near the end of World War II, the most violent and barbarous war in world history. The lasting imprint of that war can be summarized in the names of three towns: Auschwitz, Hiroshima and Nuremberg. *Auschwitz* points to the possibility of a "civilized" nation embarking on a systematized, well-organized and scientific plan of exterminating an entire people. *Hiroshima* demonstrated how "clean," easy and impersonal cataclysm could be to those who perpetrate it, and how demonic, sadistic and brutal to those who experience it. And *Nuremberg* summarizes the principle that men have an accountability above obedience to national policy, a responsibility to conscience more primary even than fidelity to national law. These three lessons are the matrix for the growth of post-modern youth.

The terror of violence that has hung over all men and women since the Second World War has especially shaped the outlooks of today's youth. In the first memories of a group of young radicals, for example, one finds the following recollections: a dim recall of the end of World War II; childhood terror of the atomic bomb; witnessing the aftermath of a violent riot in the United States; being frightened by a picture of a tank riding over rubble; being violently jealous at the birth of a younger brother; taking part in "gruesome" fights in the school yard. Such memories mean many things, but in them, violence-in-the-world finds echo and counterpart in the violence of inner feelings. The term "violence" suggests both of these possibilities: the *psychological* violence of sadism, exploitation and aggression, and the *historical* violence of war, cataclysm and holocaust. In the lives of most

of this generation, the threats of inner and outer violence are fused, each activating, exciting and potentiating the other. To summarize a complex thesis into a few words: *the issue of violence is to this generation what the issue of sex was to the Victorian world.*

Stated differently, what is most deeply repressed, rejected, feared, controlled and projected onto others by the post-modern generation is no longer their own sexuality. Sex, for most of this generation, is much freer, more open, less guilt- and anxiety-ridden. But violence, whether in one's self or in others, has assumed new prominence as the prime source of inner and outer terror. That this should be so in the modern world is readily understandable. Over all of us hangs the continual threat of a technological violence more meaningless, absurd, total and unpremeditated than any ever imagined before. Individual life always resonates with historical change; history is not merely the backdrop for development, but its ground. To be grounded in the history of the past two decades is to have stood upon, to have experienced both directly and vicariously, violent upheaval, violent worldwide revolution, and the unrelenting possibility of worldwide destruction. To have been alive and aware in America during the past decade has been to be exposed to the assassination of a President and the televised murder of his murderer, to the well-publicized slaughter of Americans by their fellow countrymen, and to the recent violence in our cities. To have been a middle-class child in the past two decades is to have watched daily the violence of television, both as it reports the bloodshed and turmoil of the American and non-American world, and as it skillfully elaborates and externalizes in repetitive dramas the poten-

tial for violence within each of us.

It therefore requires no assumption of an increase in biological aggression to account for the salience of the issue of violence for post-modern youth. The capacity for rage, spite and aggression is part of our endowment as human beings: it is a constant potential of human nature. But during the past two decades—indeed, starting before the Second World War—we have witnessed violence and imagined violence on a scale more frightening than ever before. Like the angry child who fears that his rage will itself destroy those around him, we have become vastly more sensitive to and fearful of our inner angers, for we live in a world where even the mildest irritation, multiplied a billionfold by modern technology, might destroy all civilization. The fact of violent upheaval and the possibility of cataclysm has been literally brought into our living rooms during the past twenty years: it has been interwoven with the development of a whole generation.

It should not surprise us, then, that the issue of violence is a focal concern for those of contemporary youth with the greatest historical consciousness. The hippie slogan "Make love, not war" expresses their sentiment, albeit in a form that the "realist" of previous generations might deem sentimental or romantic. Although few young radicals would agree with the wording of this statement, the underlying sentiment corresponds to their basic psychological orientation. For them, as for many others of their generation, the primary task is to develop new psychological, political and international controls on violence. Indeed, many of the dilemmas of today's young radicals seem related to their extraordinarily zealous efforts to avoid any action or relationship in which inner or outer violence might be evoked. Distaste for violence animates the profound revulsion many of today's youth feel toward the war in Southeast Asia, just as it underlies a similar revulsion against the exploitation or control of man by man. The same psychological nonviolence is related to young radicals' avoidance of traditional leadership lest it lead to domination, to their emphasis on person-to-person participation and "confrontation," and even to their unwillingness to "play the media" in an attempt to gain political effectiveness. Even the search for forms of mass political action that avoid physical violence—a preference severely tested and somewhat undermined by the events of recent months—points to a considerable distaste for the direct expression of aggression.

I do not mean to suggest that post-modern youth contains a disproportionate number of tight-lipped pacifists or rage-filled deniers of their own inner angers. On the contrary, among today's youth, exuberance, passionateness and zest are the rule rather than the exception. Nor are hippies and young radicals incapable of anger, rage and resentment—especially when their principles are violated. But for many of these young men and women, the experiences of early life and the experience of the postwar world are joined in a special sensitivity to the issue of violence, whether in themselves or in others. This confluence of psychological and historical forces helps explain the intensity of their search for new forms of social organization and political action that avoid manipulation, domination and control, just as it contributes to their widespread opposition to warfare of all kinds.

Yet the position of psychologically nonviolent youth in a violent world is difficult and paradoxical. On the one hand, he seeks to minimize violence, but on the other, his efforts often elicit violence from others. At the same time that he attempts to work to actualize his vision of a peaceful world, he must confront more directly and continually than do his peers the fact that the world is neither peaceful nor just. The frustration and discouragement of his work repetitively reawaken his anger, which must forever be rechanneled into peaceful paths. Since he continually confronts destructiveness and exploitation in the world, his own inevitable potential for destructiveness and exploitiveness inevitably arouses in him great guilt. The young men and women who make up the New Left in America, like other post-modern youth, have far less difficulty in living with their sexual natures than did their parents; but what they continue to find difficult to live with, what they still repress, avoid and counteract is their own potential for violence. It remains to be seen whether, in the movement toward "resistance" and disruption of today's young radicals, their psychological nonviolence will continue to be reflected in their actions.

In pointing to the psychological dimension of the issue of violence, I do not mean to attribute causal primacy either to the experiences of early life or to their residues in adulthood. My thesis is rather that for those of this generation with the greatest historical awareness, the psychological and historical possibilities of violence have come to potentiate each other. To repeat: witnessing the acting out of violence on a scale more gigantic than ever before, or imaginatively participating in the possibility of worldwide holocaust activates the fear of one's own violence; heightened awareness of one's inner potential for rage, anger or destructiveness increases sensitivity to the possibility of violence in the world.

This same process of historical potentiation of inner violence has occurred, I believe, throughout the modern world, and brings with it not only the intensified efforts to curb violence we see in this small segment of post-modern youth, but other more frightening possibilities. Post-modern youth, to an unusual degree, remain open to and aware of their own angers and aggressions, and this awareness creates in them a sufficient understanding of inner violence to enable them to control it in themselves and oppose it in others. Most men and women, young or old, possess less insight: their inner sadism is projected onto others whom they thereafter loathe or abjectly serve; or, more disastrously, historically-heightened inner violence is translated into outer aggression and murderousness, sanctioned by self-righteousness.

Thus, if the issue of violence plagues post-modern youth, it is not because these young men and women are more deeply rage-filled than most. On the contrary, it is because such young men and women have confronted this issue more squarely in themselves and in the world than have any but a handful of their fellows. If they have not yet found solutions, they have at least faced an issue so dangerous that most of us find it too painful even to acknowledge, and they have done so, most remarkably, without identifying with what they oppose. Their still-incomplete lives pose for us all the question on which our survival as individuals and as a world depends: Can we create formulations and forms to control historical and psychological violence before their fusion destroys us all?

Index